Peggy Talbot-Daniel.

Her book.

20th Feb. 1918.

To La Peffzé
on her birthday
from
Cotel.

EVERYMAN'S LIBRARY
EDITED BY ERNEST RHYS

POETRY AND
THE DRAMA

DANTE'S DIVINE COMEDY
WITH AN INTRODUCTION
AND NOTES BY EDMUND
G. GARDNER, M.A.

POETS ARE THE TRUMPETS WHICH SING TO BATTLE. POETS ARE THE UNACKNOWLEDGED LEGISLATORS OF THE WORLD. SHELLEY

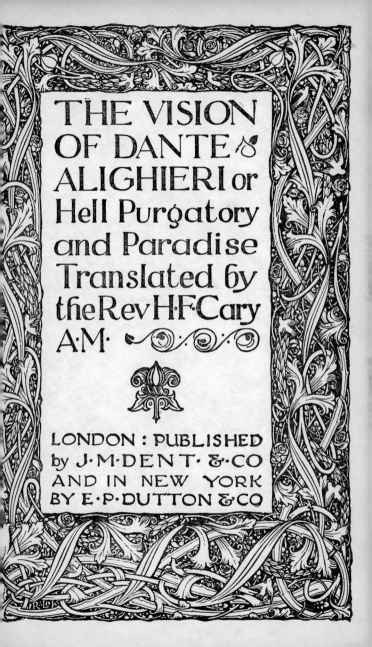

THE VISION OF DANTE ALIGHIERI or Hell Purgatory and Paradise Translated by the Rev H F Cary A·M·

LONDON : PUBLISHED by J·M·DENT·&·CO AND IN NEW YORK BY E·P·DUTTON &·CO

First Edition, March 1908
Reprinted, January 1909

INTRODUCTION

MEDIÆVAL literature may be said to begin with the *Vulgate* of St. Jerome (405) and the *City of God* of St. Augustine (426). It ends with the *Summa Theologica* of St. Thomas Aquinas (1265–1274) and the *Divina Commedia* of Dante Alighieri (1300–1321).

All the noblest thought and work of the ages that passed between the fall of the Roman Empire and the closing year of the thirteenth century, when Dante figures himself in allegorical fashion as having passed in ecstatic vision through the world beyond the grave, finds supreme artistic expression in his great poem. The intellectual subtleties of the schoolmen, the spiritual soarings of the mystics, the chivalrous worship of women that had been the gift of the troubadours of Provence to the sons of men, the philosophical devotion that the new poets of central Italy had reared upon it, the political dreams and theories of papal and imperial statesmen, builders of vast aerial fabrics of universal Roman Church and universal Roman Empire, have all shared in the making of it. Dante gives them fresh life; handling them with poetic passion, he endues them with unity of a new kind; these things, fused in his glowing imagination, become the harmonious accessories to his picture of man, his nature, his duties, his life, his destiny.

Dante was born at Florence in 1265, probably in the latter part of May, some eight months before the victory of Charles of Anjou over King Manfred at Benevento extinguished the power of the Empire in Italy and placed a French dynasty on the throne of Naples. His father, Alighiero di Bellincione Alighieri, came of an ancient but decadent and impoverished family, too unimportant to be officially ranked among the *grandi*, or magnates, who were excluded from the administration by the democratic rulers of the Republic. His mother, Monna Bella, died soon after his birth. In 1283, at the age of eighteen, he wrote the first of his poems that has been preserved to us: a sonnet in which he demands an explanation of a dream from " all the faithful of Love "; and, in consequence, found himself recognised as a poet by the chief Italian poet then living, Guido di Cavalcante Cavalcanti, who became the first of all his friends. Study and manly exercise filled up the next few years of Dante's life. He served in the Florentine cavalry, " fighting valiantly on horseback in the front rank," at the battle of Campaldino on June 11, 1289, when the Aretines and other Tuscan Ghibellines were defeated by the forces of the Guelf league, of which Florence was the head. In June, 1290, Beatrice, the woman of the poet's romantic love and poetical homage, died; and, within the next few years, probably between 1292 and 1294, Dante gathered together the lyrics that he had written in her honour and connected them with a prose narrative, thus composing the *Vita Nuova*, the book of his " New Life," which he dedicated to Guido Cavalcanti, " my friend to whom I am writing this."

The *Vita Nuova*, in its exquisite mingling of poetry and prose, shows us how, at the very outset, Dante learned to make of the love of woman a pathway from earth to Heaven. It sets forth a creed of love, as ideal as human nature can well sustain. The lover finds all his beatitude in the words that praise his lady, the splendour of whose soul has reached even to the throne of God. All evil thoughts perish when she passes by; she ennobles all upon whom she looks; she is the mirror of the Divine Beauty, " a thing come from Heaven to earth to make manifest a miracle." " He seeth perfectly all salvation who seeth my lady." When she passes out of the world : " the delight of her beauty, departing itself from our view, became great spiritual loveliness, that spreads through Heaven a light of love that salutes the Angels, and makes even their high and noble intellects wonder." The pilgrim spirit, passing in ecstatic contemplation through the spheres, guided up by the new intelligence that love has infused, is overwhelmed by the sight of her glory in Paradise, where she " gloriously gazeth upon the countenance of Him who is blessed for ever and ever."

In the years that immediately followed the death of Beatrice, Dante fell into what he afterwards came to regard as a morally unworthy life. He became involved, too, in the politics of his native city, was called to play a prominent part therein, in the turbulent time that passed from 1295 to 1301 ; and bore himself manfully, but (as a fragment preserved from one of his lost letters admits) with some lack of prudence. In 1300, the year of the jubilee of Pope

Boniface VIII., the year when the predominant Guelf party in Florence split into the two factions of Bianchi and Neri, "Whites" and "Blacks," he sat for two months among the chief magistrates of the Republic, in which capacity he was compelled to send his dearest friend, Guido Cavalcanti, into the banishment which proved his death-warrant. When, in November, 1301, through the machinations of Pope Boniface and the treachery of Charles of Valois, the Neri triumphed, Dante was one of their first victims. After a preliminary condemnation, dated January 27, 1302, he was sentenced (together with fifteen other Florentine citizens) to be burned to death, if he should at any time come into the power of the Commune of Florence.

Already Dante seemed to himself to have found the key to the whole political riddle of the universe in the meaning of Roman history. He had become convinced that the Roman Empire of old was divinely ordained for the civilisation of the world and the promulgation of law, and that the Empire of his own day (for he does not distinguish between the two) was a divine institution no less than the Church, with authority proceeding directly from God for the establishment of universal peace and the renovation of mankind. In a famous passage at the beginning of the second book of the *De Monarchia*, he tells us how the realisation that the Roman People obtained the monarchy of the world by right came to him as a complete revelation, throwing light over the whole dark forest of mediæval politics, showing him the part he had to play, the doctrine he was to teach. And (he may well have asked himself, later on), although the imperial eagle was now held in the hand of a German prince, might not the Empire again become Italian, Roman once more in deed as it still was in name?

With the "vision splendid" of that old ideal love, albeit dimmed in one who had become a votary of the world and the flesh, and with this newly apprehended, world-embracing political faith, Dante went forth to exile, with the Republic's sentence of death upon his head. For a brief while, he made common cause with his fellow-exiles, even with the enemies of his native land, striving to win his way back to Florence by force of arms. Then, probably in 1303, disgusted with his associates, he turns from them with contempt, to make a party for himself. He begins, but leaves unfinished, two prose works : the *De Vulgari Eloquentia* (*circa* 1304), "On Vernacular Eloquence," in which he expounds the metrical form of the Italian lyric, and attempts to establish an ideal Italian language for the expression of the national idea; the *Convivio* (1306–1308), or "Banquet," in which he sets himself to bring the fruits of philosophical reasoning down to the reach of the unlearned, in the form of a commentary on his own wonderful *Canzoni*, a series of philosophical, didactic, and amatory odes.

Then he is dragged back into the turmoil of politics. For it seems that the Imperial Redeemer is at hand, now that the new Emperor, Henry of Luxemburg, has crossed the Alps (1310), and is coming to the Eternal City that sat widowed and alone, crying day and night for her spouse. We may read in the poet's letters how his spirit exulted in Henry, as in the heavenly directed regenerator of Christendom, the new Lamb of God who was to take away the sins of the world. And at the beginning of the *De Monarchia*, the treatise on the great question of Church and State, Papacy and Empire, which Dante probably wrote at this time in anticipation of Henry's coming, we find that all his previous work now appeared to him as nothing, that he seemed to himself still open to the charge of the buried talent —with the mission still unachieved of "keeping vigil for the good of the world." But, in less than three years from his coming to Italy, the Emperor had died in disgrace and failure (1313), and Dante was still a homeless wanderer, under proscription and ban, with a new condemnation pronounced against him by the magistrates of the Republic.

The alternations of impassioned hope, bitter disillusion, temporary despair, during the Emperor's unfortunate enterprise, had wrought a complete revulsion of the poet's being. Spiritual experiences, too, had been his—of the kind known only to man himself and to the higher powers to whom he holds himself responsible. It is as one who has lost the world, and gained his own soul, that Dante now turned to the completion of his *Divina Commedia*, to combine the charge he believed laid upon him, of "keeping vigil for the good of the world," with the promise he had made at the end of the *Vita Nuova*, to say of Beatrice "what had never been said of any woman."

Gradually, during those long, weary years of exile, wandering in poverty from city to city throughout Italy, and perchance beyond its confines, showing against his will the wounds that fortune had dealt him, the poet's own life-story had become merged into that of all humanity. As from a celestial watch-tower of contemplation, he had seen the world a prey to anarchy and tyranny, abandoned to lust, pride, and avarice. He had watched the oppressors of the poor at their work; had seen the evil deeds of the kings, the priests abandoning the teaching of the Gospel to acquire wealth and temporal power, the moral corruption of high and low spreading like a black torrent over the land. And, in his cell of self-knowledge, he had traced a like process in his own heart; he had seen the fair promise of his " new life " fade away, and had found himself sunk in what he deemed a life of sin. His own conversion becomes but a symbol of that to which he would incite man in general. His return, in an agony of repentance, to the memory of Beatrice, the love of his youth, now become the type of Divine Philosophy, is symbolical of the renovation which he believes in store for the whole human race, if it will but hearken to his message.

The *Divina Commedia* was finished at Ravenna, shortly before Dante's death, which took place on September 14, 1321. The concluding cantos of the *Purgatorio* and the whole of the *Paradiso*, in particular, bear the imprint of those last years of Dante's life, when, secure in the friendship of Can Grande della Scala, the warrior lord of Verona, and under the protection of Guido Novello da Polenta, the pacific ruler of Ravenna, with friends and disciples gathering round him, the poet found a not uncongenial refuge in that ancient Romagnole city, amidst the monuments of Cæsars and the records in mosaic of primitive Christianity, where the church walls testified the glory of Justinian, and the music of the Pine Forest sounded in his ears.

The vision of the world beyond the grave was no new thing in mediæval literature; but it had never before been made the basis of a work of universal appeal and universal significance. Dante's true precursors are not the obscure dreamers of dreams : Tundal, Alberic of Monte Cassino, the Monk of Eynsham, and the like; who described imaginary journeys through Hell, Purgatory, and Paradise. His inspiration on this side was purely Virgilian, and derived from the sixth book of the *Æneid*. Rather is he the poetic heir of Augustine's confession and spiritual reading of history; of Boëthius' philosophical passion and attempted reconciliation of man's freedom with God's foreknowledge; of Bernard's reforming zeal and contemplative fervour; of Richard of St. Victor in his mystical mounting upward of the human soul to union with the Divine; of Thomas Aquinas, in his adopting the wisdom of Aristotle to give organic form to the truths of revelation. Only, as a poet, Dante transcends all these things; while, at the same time, he brings them down from the possession of the few, to be the common heritage of all who listen to his song.

The *Divina Commedia* is thus far more than a mere vision of the spirit world, however perfectly realised. In it Dante has condensed all the wisdom and devotion of his age, and summed up all the finest spirit of the ages that have gone before his own. He is the soul of mediæval Catholicism, painting his picture of the material universe in the form of an allegorical vision of the supernatural world. He is a man with a mission; fiercely, terribly in earnest, to reform the corruption of the Church, to give new life to the State, to heal the wounds of his country. The object of his poem is professedly to remove men from their state of misery, and to lead them to the state of felicity. " Not by the grace of riches, but by the grace of God," he writes to the Italian Cardinals, " I am what I am, and the zeal of His House hath eaten me up." A famous passage, at the opening of the third book of his *De Monarchia*, strikes the key-note of all his work. Taking confidence from the words of Daniel : " He shut the mouths of the lions, and they have not hurt me; for justice was found in me in His sight "; he declares that, since Truth appeals to him from her immutable throne, and the Philosopher bids him sacrifice friendship for her sake : " Putting on the breast-plate of faith, according to the admonition of Paul, in the heat of that coal which one of the Seraphims took from the celestial altar and laid upon the lips of Isaiah, I will enter upon the present contest, and by the arm of Him who delivered us from the powers of darkness in His blood, I will cast the wicked and the liar out of the lists in the sight of all the world."

For his poetical purpose, Dante goes back to the year of the papal jubilee, 1300, the year in which he had sat for two months in the chief magistracy of the Florentine Republic. He is in the position of a man who is now, at the end of his life, relating to the world a vision which was vouchsafed to him, nearly twenty years before, for seven days, beginning at sunrise on Good Friday, which, in 1300, fell upon April 8. Hence, everything that happened to him, or to his fellow-men, after April, 1300, is spoken of as future, by way of prophecy, beginning with the account, in the sixth canto of the *Inferno*, of the faction fight between the Bianchi and Neri in Florence on the May Day of that year.

Coming to himself in the dark forest of political anarchy and alienation from God, the forest into which he has, as it were in slumber, strayed, Dante, representative of the human race, is guided by Virgil (who stands for Human Philosophy and natural reason), through Hell and Purgatory, to the state of temporal felicity figured in the Earthly Paradise. There, in the state of innocence regained by the purgatorial pains, a further revelation is given him of the past, present, and future of the Church and the Empire; thence he is guided by Beatrice herself, the type of the Divine Philosophy that includes the sacred science of Theology (of which the ultimate end is the contemplation of primal truth in man's celestial native land), through the nine moving spheres, into the spaceless, timeless Empyrean Heaven of Heavens. There Beatrice resumes her throne in the white and gold Rose of Paradise, and Bernard, type of the loving contemplation in which the eternal life of the soul consists, commends the poet to the Blessed Virgin, through whose intercession he obtains a foretaste of the Beatific Vision of the Divine Essence.

But this is merely the framework, within which the society of thirteenth-century Italy is pictured. And, out of the Italy of his day, the poet grasps but the essentials of human nature—for man is avowedly the subject of the *Divina Commedia*. While, taken literally, the theme is the state of souls after death, the subject in the allegorical sense (Dante tells us in the letter dedicating the *Paradiso* to Can Grande) is " man as by good or ill deserts, in the exercise of the freedom of his will, he becomes liable to the justice that rewards or punishes."

Understood as Dante would have it, the *Inferno* is one of the most appalling things in literature. No doubt, the poet held some belief as to the torments of the damned in another life, more or less similar to what he has here depicted. But, at the same time, there is an allegorical significance throughout. Dante's Hell is the wickedness and corruption of the life that he saw around him, revealed in its proper aspect. "We still have judgment here!" That word of Shakespeare's is not without bearing upon Dante's conception of tragedy. In the *Inferno*, the poet may naturally seem more concerned with what he believes concerning the judgment hereafter; but, at the same time, he undoubtedly means the torments of his Hell to be taken, in part, as symbolical of the effects of sin in this life, when there is no repentance. Witte has admirably expressed this : " Hell itself is neither more nor less than the protraction of unrepented sin ; the symbolical interpretation of the sinful life." With one apparent exception, there is no personal vindictiveness in Dante's treatment of sinners. Nothing is further from the truth than the assertion that he condemned his own private enemies, or his political opponents, to eternal infamy. He is the man, to adopt his own phrase, to whom Truth appeals from her immutable throne. There are no friends or foes at the bar of that dread tribunal. The robes of earthly pomp and power, of hypocrisy and false semblance, are stripped off ; the whited sepulchres are forced to yield up their secrets. The torments of Dante's Hell are but the sins themselves, revealed in their essence, recognised by their results ; the poet shows how the souls of the condemned have made their choice in this life, and how they work out their own damnation. Dante, in his allegory, is investigating the full realities of vice ; in the light of reason, and under the guidance of human philosophy, he is anatomising sinner after sinner, laying bare the secret motives of remembered and forgotten tragedies ; he is striving to answer Lear's question : " Is there any cause in nature that makes these hard hearts?"

Apart from its allegory, the machinery of Dante's Hell is more or less that of mediæval tradition. It is otherwise with his Purgatory. There are few things in literature so wonderful, and in the highest sense original, as his conception of the mountain of Purgation, where, beneath the sun and stars, in the glory of sunrise and of sunset, man purges away the dross of the world, until he recovers his primal blessedness, his moral and intellectual liberty, in the Earthly Paradise. Throughout, in its pure spirituality, its radiant charity, its ineffable tenderness, the *Purgatorio* makes a direct and universal appeal to the heart and conscience. And, from the outset, the note of love is struck ; the poet sees " the fair planet, which gives us strength to love, making the whole east radiant." For love is the informing spirit, the compelling law of the rest of Dante's poem ; Love, not merely in our modern sense, which is practically restricted to the idealisation of one special passion, but in the sense in which it means the force that impels every creature, inanimate or animate, sensitive or rational, to obey the highest dictates of its true nature. *Ordina quest' amore, O tu che m'ami*, wrote the Franciscan, Jacopone da Todi, speaking in the person of Christ : " Set this love in order, O thou that lovest Me." The whole of the *Purgatorio* is based upon the necessity of thus setting love in order, of ordering love rightly.

Shelley has well told us that the *Paradiso* is the story of " how all things are transfigured except Love." Love is the guide, the rule, the interpretation of Dante's mysticism. He shows us in the *Purgatorio* how, in rational beings, love is the seed of every virtue and of every vice, because love's natural tendency to good is the material upon which free will works for bliss or for bane. In the *Paradiso*, he conceives of the whole motion of the universe as one cosmic dance of love, beginning in the Seraphim, that highest Angelic order which knows most and therefore loves most, and continued through all nature. And, at the consummation of his vision, the poet beholds, by penetrative intuition into the Divine Light, how it is that Love thus binds the universe into one, to make it resemble the Supreme Unity :—

> " Nel suo profondo vidi che s'interna,
>   legato con amore in un volume,
>   ciò che per l'universo si squaderna " :

" Within its depths I saw gathered up the scattered leaves of all the universe, bound by love into one volume."

In the relations between Dante and Beatrice, we have the secret of the poet's mysticism ; for, as Father Tyrrell has beautifully said, " If love be mysticism, then we have the key to all mysticism within ourselves." Love, set in order by the purifying ascent of Purgatory, grows more and more perfected in Paradise, from sphere to sphere, until the crowning vision in the Empyrean Heaven of Heavens ; where, with all desires set at rest, all wills made one with the Divine Will, the soul is absorbed in the Beatific Vision ; all its powers of spiritual vision actualised, all its capacity of knowing and of loving realised to the full, in the possession of absolute Truth and absolute Beauty in union with the Divine Essence.

EDMUND G. GARDNER.

1908.

Henry Francis Cary was born in 1772 and died in 1844. His translation of the *Inferno* was first issued in 1805 and 1806, together with the Italian text. In 1814, he published the complete *Divina Commedia* in English alone, at his own expense. The work earned the enthusiastic and generous admiration of Coleridge. A revised edition appeared in 1819, and another in 1844, the year of the translator's death. Of the merits of the work, Dr. Richard Garnett writes in the *Dictionary of National Biography:* "Notwithstanding the competition of more exact versions of no mean poetical power, it has remained the translation which, on Dante's name being mentioned, occurs first to the mind. Cary's standard is lower, and his achievement less remarkable, than that of many of his successors, but he, at least, has made Dante an Englishman, and they have left him half an Italian. He has, nevertheless, shown remarkable tact in avoiding the almost inevitable imitation of the Miltonic style, and, renouncing the attempt to clothe Dante with a stateliness which does not belong to him, has in a great measure preserved his transparent simplicity and intense vividness." In the present edition, a very few slight corrections in the text of the translation are indicated in italics. Cary's scholarly and learned notes being partly out of date, partly not suited to the purposes of a purely popular issue, it has been thought advisable to substitute an almost entirely new commentary, for which (together with the Chronological Table) the writer of this Introduction is responsible.[1] He wishes to acknowledge a very special debt to the editors of the complete works of Dante in the *Temple Classics*, to Dr. Paget Toynbee's invaluable *Dante Dictionary*, and to the first volume of Dr. Moore's *Studies in Dante*.

The following are the works of Henry Francis Cary (1772–1844) :—

Sonnets and Odes, 1788; Ode to General Kosciuszko, 1797; translation of the "Inferno," 1805; remainder of the "Commedia,"

---

[1] The references are to the *Temple Classics* and to the *Oxford Dante*. *Inf. = Inferno, Purg. = Purgatorio, Par. = Paradiso, V. N. = Vita Nuova, V. E. = De Vulgari Eloquentia, Mon. = De Monarchia, Conv. = Convivio, Epist. = Letters.* The *Temple Classics* translations of the Minor Works are usually quoted. In the case of the *Divina Commedia* itself, it has seemed better to avoid confusion by giving references to the cantos alone, as Cary's version does not always correspond, line for line, with the original text.

1814 ; new edition, 1819, and numerous re-issues, up to the present date ; translation of "The Birds," 1824 ; translation of "Pindar," 1832.

Cary's earliest publication, while still a schoolboy, was an ode to Lord Heathfield on his defence of Gibraltar. He was a regular contributor to the *Gentleman's Magazine* in his younger years, and in this periodical were published, after his death, his notices of the Italian Poets. In 1846 appeared "The Early French Poets ; a series of Notices and Translations," and "Lives of English Poets from Johnson to Kirke White," these having previously been published in the *London Magazine*.

Cary's further works were editions of Pope, Milton, Cowper, Thomson, and Young.

A Memoir of him by his son was published in 1847.

CHRONOLOGICAL TABLE

OF

THE CHIEF EVENTS IN DANTE'S LIFE

[1215. In consequence of the murder of Buondelmonte de' Buondelmonti, the Florentines become involved in the factions of Guelfs and Ghibellines. *Inf.* xxviii.; *Par.* xvi.

1249. With the aid of Frederick II., the Ghibellines expel the Guelfs from Florence. *Inf.* x.

1250. Death of the Emperor Frederick II. *Inf.* x.; *Conv.* iv. 3.

1251. The Guelfs return to Florence, and, shortly after, drive out the Ghibellines, changing the white lily on the standard of the Republic to red. *Par.* xvi.

1258. Further expulsion of Ghibelline nobles.

1260, September 4. The Florentine Guelfs are utterly defeated at the battle of Montaperti, by the Sienese and exiled Florentine Ghibellines, aided by the German troops of King Manfred. *Inf.* x. and xxxii. The Guelfs leave Florence, and a Ghibelline despotism is established.

1265. At the invitation of Clement IV., Charles of Anjou comes to Italy as the champion of the Church against the Ghibellines. *Purg.* vii. and xx.]

1265. Dante is born at Florence, between May 18 and June 17. *Par.* xxii.

1266 (February 26). Manfred is defeated and slain by Charles of Anjou at the battle of Benevento. *Purg.* iii. The Ghibellines are expelled from Florence, and the democratic Guelf predominance finally assured. *Inf.* x.

1268 (August). Conradin is defeated by Charles of Anjou at the battle of Tagliacozzo. *Inf.* xxviii. He is beheaded at Naples (October). *Purg.* xx.

1269 (June). Defeat of the Sienese Ghibellines under Provenzano Salvani at the battle of Colle in Valdelsa. *Purg.* xi. and xiii. Siena, hitherto the chief Ghibelline power in Tuscany, ultimately becomes Guelf.

1274 (May). Dante first meets Beatrice. *V. N.* § 2.

1278. Attempted reconciliation of Guelfs and Ghibellines in Florence.

1282. The "Sicilian Vespers." *Par.* viii.

1283. Dante writes his first extant sonnet. *V. N.* § 3.

1288. Overthrow of Count Ugolino at Pisa. *Inf.* xxxiii.

1289 (June 11). The battle of Campaldino. *Purg.* v.

1290 (June). Death of Beatrice. *V. N.* § 29; *Purg.* xxx.–xxxii. Between 1292 and 1294, Dante writes the *Vita Nuova*. Probably about 1296, he marries Gemma Donati.

1293. The democratic character of the Florentine government is secured by the Ordinances of Justice, whereby nobles and magnates are more strictly excluded from office, and subjected to severe penalties for offences against the people.

1294. Abdication of Pope Celestine V. and election of Boniface VIII. *Inf.* iii., xix., xxvii.

1295. Dante enters public life. On July 6, he speaks in the General Council of the Commune, in support of modifications in the Ordinances of Justice.

1300. The Jubilee proclaimed (*Purg.* ii.). A papal conspiracy against the liberties of Florence discovered in April. The Guelfs having split into Bianchi and Neri, "Whites" and "Blacks," led by Vieri de' Cerchi and Corso Donati respectively, the factions come to blood on May 1 (*Inf.* vi.). On May 7, Dante goes on an embassy to San Gimignano. From June 15 to August 15, he sits by election in the chief magistracy of the Republic, as one of the Priors. Together with his colleagues, he resists the interference of the papal legate, Cardinal Matteo d'Acquasparta (*Par.* xii.), and banishes the leaders of both factions, including Guido Cavalcanti. Guido contracts a fatal malady at Sarzana, and, returning to Florence after Dante's term of office is concluded, dies at the end of August (*Inf.* x.)

1301. The Bianchi hold the government of Florence, and, in May, expel the Neri from Pistoia (*Inf.* xxiv.). On June 19, Dante, speaking in the Council of the Hundred, opposes the grant of money to the King of Naples and of soldiers to the Pope. On November 1, Charles of Valois, as papal peacemaker, enters Florence, and causes a state of anarchy, in which the Bianchi are overthrown and the Neri return in triumph (*Purg.* xx., xxiv.; *Par.* xvii.). Dante is said to have been absent at Rome on an embassy to the Pope—but this is questioned.

1302. Dante, with four others, sentenced to fine and banishment (January 27). Together with fifteen others, he is sentenced to be burned to death (March 10). Cf. *V. E.* i. 6, *Inf.* xv., *Par.* xvii., and *Canzone* xx. The whole faction of the Bianchi is expelled from Florence (April 4). Dante at first shares their fortunes; but, between June 8, 1302, and June 18, 1303, he breaks away from them in disgust, and takes refuge with Bartolommeo della Scala at Verona. *Par.* xvii.

1303 (October). Death of Boniface VIII. *Purg.* xx.

1304. Dante probably goes to Bologna, where he writes, but leaves unfinished, the *De Vulgari Eloquentia.* Cf. *V. E.* i. 9, 15; ii. 12.

1305. By the election of Clement V., the Papacy is translated from Rome to Avignon. *Inf.* xix.; *Purg.* xxxii.

1306. Expulsion of the Florentine exiles from Bologna (March). Dante at Padua (August), and with the Malaspina in the Lunigiana (October). Cf. *Purg.* viii. Between 1306 and 1308, he writes, but leaves unfinished, the *Convivio.* About 1307 or 1308, he is said to have gone to Paris.

1308 (November). Henry of Luxemburg elected Emperor, as Henry VII.

1309. Dante probably writes the *De Monarchia.*

1310. Dante's Letter to the Princes and Peoples of Italy (*Epist.* v.). Henry arrives in Italy in September.

1311. Henry takes the iron crown at Milan (January), in which city Dante probably pays him homage. From the Casentino, Dante writes letters to " the most wicked Florentines within " (March 31, *Epist.* vi.), and to the Emperor himself (April 16, *Epist.* vii.). On September 2, by the " reform " of Baldo d'Aguglione, he is for ever excepted from amnesty and excluded from Florence.

1312. The Emperor crowned in Rome (June 29). He unsuccessfully besieges Florence (September 19 to October 31).

1313 (August 24). The Emperor dies at Buonconvento, near Siena. *Par.* xxx.

1314. Death of Clement V. (April 20). *Inf.* xix.; *Par.* xxx. Dante writes his Letter to the Italian Cardinals (*Epist.* viii.), urging them to restore the Papacy to Rome.

1315. Dante probably at Lucca, under the protection of Uguccione della Faggiuola. Cf. *Purg.* xxiv. On August 29, Uguccione defeats the united armies of Naples and Florence at the battle of Montecatini. On November 6, the Florentine government, through the vicar of King Robert, renews the sentence of death against Dante, as a Ghibelline and a rebel; his two sons, Pietro and Jacopo, are included in the condemnation.

1316. Dante, in his Letter to a Florentine friend, refuses to return to Florence on dishonourable conditions (*Epist.* ix.). Probably towards the close of this year, he goes to Can Grande della Scala at Verona. *Par.* xvii.; *Epist.* x. 1.

1317. Dante settles at Ravenna.

1318–1320. Dante writes his Letter to Can Grande, dedicating the *Paradiso* to him (*Epist.* x.). He enters into a correspondence with Giovanni del Virgilio (*Eclogues* I. and II.), refusing the laurel crown at Bologna. At the end of 1319, he perhaps visits Piacenza, Mantua, and Verona, and at the last-named city (January 20, 1320) delivers a discourse concerning the relative position of earth and water on the globe's surface (*Quæstio de Aqua et Terra*, of which the authenticity is disputed).

1321. In July, Dante undertakes an embassy from Guido da Polenta to Venice. He dies at Ravenna on September 14. The manuscript of the last thirteen cantos of the *Divina Commedia*, left unpublished at his death, is found by his son Jacopo, and forwarded to Can Grande della Scala.

1311. Henry takes the iron crown of Milan (Jan. 6), in which city Dante probably then meets ... Henry. The Cancelleria Henry writes letters to the states on ... "Florentine within" (Oxon. 5r, Epist. v), and to the Emperor himself (April 16, Epist. vii). On September 27 the "Florentines" are again excluded from the ever-excepted from amnesty and excluded from ... ...

1312. The Emperor crowned in Rome (June 29). The insurgents ... the Florentine Pro ... (September 10 to October 21).

1313. (August 24). The Emperor dies at Buonconvento near Siena. Thus exxo.

1314. Death of Clement V at Avignon for which Was said Dante writes his Letter to the Italian Cardinals (Epist. viii), urging them to return to Rome from Paris to to Rome.

1315. Dante probably ... Lucca under the protection of Uguccione della Faggiuola. On Aug. xxiv ... (Aug. ?) pardons defacto the united against ... Ghibel and Florence, on the basis of the Magnanini. On November 6 the Florentine government, through the vicar of King Robert ... the amnesty ... an amnesty ... Dante was ... unwilling and ... rebel. The two sons, Pietro and Jacopo are included in the condemnation.

1316. Dante, in his Letter to a Florentine friend, refuses to return to Florence on dishonourable conditions (Epist. ix). Probably towards the close of this year he goes to Can Grande della Scala at Verona (Par. xvii. 1) Par. xv. 1).

1317. Dante writing the Letter to Can Grande, dedicating the Paradiso to him (Epist. x). He enters into correspondence with Giovanni del Virgilio (Aec. i and ii.) ...

1318. ... to Ravenna, at the end of 1317, perhaps under Guido ... Polenta, and Ven ... and ... Florence then seems to have ... within a diminished ... any the relative position of earth and within ... the ... battle identification date of Comp. of y with the authenticity is a question.

1321. In July Dante undertakes an embassy from Guido da Polenta to Venice. He dies at Ravenna of "September 13. The anniversary of this last (thirteen cantos of the Paradiso being unpublished at his death) are found by his son Jacopo and returned to Can Grande della Scala.

CONTENTS

THE VISION OF DANTE

THE VISION OF DANTE

Hell

CANTO I

ARGUMENT

The writer, having lost his way in a gloomy forest, and being
  hindered by certain wild beasts from ascending a mountain,
  is met by Virgil, who promises to show him the punishments
  of Hell, and afterwards of Purgatory; and that he shall then
  be conducted by Beatrice into Paradise. He follows the
  Roman poet.

In the midway [1] of this our mortal life,
I found me [2] in a gloomy wood, astray
Gone from the path direct: and e'en to tell,
It were no easy task, how savage wild
That forest, how robust and rough its growth,
Which to remember only, my dismay
Renews, in bitterness not far from death.
Yet, to discourse of what there good befel,
All else will I relate discover'd there.

    How first I enter'd it I scarce can say,
Such sleepy dulness in that instant weigh'd
My senses down, when the true path I left;
But when a mountain's foot I reach'd, where closed
The valley that had pierced my heart with dread,
I look'd aloft, and saw his shoulders broad
Already vested with that planet's beam,
Who leads all wanderers safe through every way. [3]

[1] "The days of our years are threescore years and ten" (Psalm
xc. 10). In the *Convivio* (iv. 23), Dante compares human life to
an arch, of which the highest point, "in those of perfect nature,"
is in the thirty-fifth year. The poem opens at sunrise on Good
Friday in 1300, when the Poet was at the end of his thirty-fifth
year.

[2] *Mi ritrovai*, "I came to myself."

[3] The wood is "the wood of error," spiritual alienation from
God and political anarchy. The mountain is the "Holy Hill"
of the Psalmist, the mountain of the Lord, to which only the
innocent in hands and the clean of heart shall ascend. According
to Ptolemaic astronomy, the sun is a planet; its beams here
symbolise the Divine Light.

Then was a little respite to the fear,
That in my heart's recesses deep had lain
All of that night, so pitifully past:
And as a man, with difficult short breath,
Forespent with toiling, 'scaped from sea to shore,
Turns to the perilous wide waste, and stands
At gaze; e'en so my spirit, that yet fail'd,
Struggling with terror, turn'd to view the straits
That none hath past and lived. My weary frame
After short pause recomforted, again
I journey'd on over that lonely steep,
The hinder foot still firmer. Scarce the ascent
Began, when, lo! a panther, nimble, light,
And cover'd with a speckled skin, appear'd;
Nor, when it saw me, vanish'd; rather strove
To check my onward going; that oft-times,
With purpose to retrace my steps, I turn'd.

The hour was morning's prime, and on his way
Aloft the sun ascended with those stars,[1]
That with him rose when Love Divine first moved
Those its fair works: so that with joyous hope
All things conspired to fill me, the gay skin
Of that swift animal, the matin dawn,
And the sweet season. Soon that joy was chased,
And by new dread succeeded, when in view
A lion came, 'gainst me as it appear'd,
With his head held aloft and hunger-mad,
That e'en the air was fear-struck. A she-wolf
Was at his heels, who in her leanness seem'd
Full of all wants, and many a land hath made
Disconsolate ere now.[2] She with such fear
O'erwhelm'd me, at the sight of her appall'd,

1 The sun was in Aries, as, according to mediæval tradition, it was when God first created the world.

2 The panther (or leopard), lion, and she-wolf probably represent Lust, Pride, and Avarice. It was a commonplace of mediæval ethics that lust, pride, and avarice were the roots of all the sins of the world. The actual imagery of the three beasts was evidently suggested to Dante by the words of Jeremiah (v. 6): "A lion out of the forest shall slay them, and a wolf of the evenings shall spoil them, a leopard shall watch over their cities." It was first suggested at the beginning of the nineteenth century that the panther, lion, and she-wolf stood for Florence, France, and Rome (the Temporal Power of the Papacy) respectively. This interpretation found general acceptance, but it is now almost entirely discredited.

That of the height all hope I lost.   As one,
Who, with his gain elated, sees the time
When all unwares is gone, he inwardly
Mourns with heart-griping anguish; such was I,
Haunted by that fell beast, never at peace,
Who coming o'er against me, by degrees
Impell'd me where the sun in silence rests.

    While to the lower space with backward step
I fell, my ken discern'd the form of one
Whose voice seem'd faint through long disuse of
    speech.
When him in that great desert I espied,
" Have mercy on me," cried I out aloud,
" Spirit ! or living man ! whate'er thou be."

    He answer'd : " Now not man, man once I was,
And born of Lombard parents, Mantuans both
By country, when the power of Julius [1] yet
Was scarcely firm.   At Rome my life was past,
Beneath the mild Augustus, in the time
Of fabled deities and false.   A bard
Was I, and made Anchises' upright son
The subject of my song, who came from Troy,
When the flames prey'd on Ilium's haughty towers.[2]
But thou, say wherefore to such perils past
Return'st thou? wherefore not this pleasant mount
Ascendest, cause and source of all delight?"
" And art thou then that Virgil, that well-spring,
From which such copious floods of eloquence
Have issued?"   I with front abash'd replied.
" Glory and light of all the tuneful train !
May it avail me, that I long with zeal
Have sought thy volume, and with love immense
Have conn'd it o'er.   My master thou, and guide !
Thou he from whom alone I have derived
That style, which for its beauty into fame
Exalts me.   See the beast, from whom I fled.
O save me from her, thou illustrious sage !
For every vein and pulse throughout my frame
She hath made tremble."   He, soon as he saw
That I was weeping, answer'd, " Thou must needs

[1] Virgil was born at Mantua, B.C. 70.   He is here the type of Human Philosophy, which leads man from moral unworthiness and guides him to temporal felicity.
[2] In the *Æneid*.

Another way pursue, if thou wouldst 'scape
From out that savage wilderness. This beast,
At whom thou criest, her way will suffer none
To pass, and no less hindrance makes than death :
So bad and so accursed in her kind,
That never sated is her ravenous will,
Still after food more craving than before.
To many an animal in wedlock vile
She fastens, and shall yet to many more,
Until that Greyhound come, who shall destroy
Her with sharp pain. He will not life support
By earth nor its base metals, but by love,
Wisdom, and virtue ; and his land shall be
The land 'twixt either Feltro.[1] In his might
Shall safety to Italia's plains arise,
For whose fair realm, Camilla, virgin pure,
Nisus, Euryalus, and Turnus fell.[2]
He, with incessant chase, through every town
Shall worry, until he to Hell at length
Restore her, thence by envy first let loose.
I, for thy profit pondering, now devise
That thou mayst follow me ; and I, thy guide,
Will lead thee hence through an eternal space,

[1] This prophecy of the *Veltro*, or Greyhound, the coming Deliverer, is one of the insoluble problems of the *Divina Commedia*. The earliest commentators did not recognise any specific individual under this imagery, and took the word *feltro* not as the name of a place, *Feltro*, but as the material "felt," for which they suggested various far-fetched allegorical meanings. They supposed the prophecy to be derived from Virgil's fourth *Eclogue*, and to refer either to the second coming of Christ, or to the advent of some heroic personage, preferably an Emperor or a Pope, who should renovate the world and bring back the golden age. It was first suggested in 1477, more than 150 years after Dante's death, that Can Grande della Scala, whose birthplace, Verona, lies between Feltre in Venetia and Montefeltro in Romagna, is the person meant. " He shall not feed on earth nor pelf, but on wisdom and love and power ; and his birthplace shall be between Feltro and Feltro. Of that humble Italy he shall be the salvation." In any case, the Deliverer, be he Can Grande or another, is to accomplish the ideals of the Poet's *De Monarchia :* to restore the imperial power, make Roman law obeyed throughout Italy, extirpate avarice, establish universal peace, and reform the world. This prophecy is repeated in other forms at intervals throughout the poem (*Purg.* xx., xxxiii., *Par.* xxvii.), though it may be doubted whether Dante had always the same solution in his mind.

[2] Their deaths are described in the *Æneid*, ix. and xi.

Where thou shalt hear despairing shrieks, and see
Spirits of old tormented, who invoke
A second death;[1] and those next view, who dwell
Content in fire,[2] for that they hope to come,
Whene'er the time may be, among the blest,
Into whose regions if thou then desire
To ascend, a spirit worthier[3] than I
Must lead thee, in whose charge, when I depart,
Thou shalt be left: for that Almighty King,
Who reigns above, a rebel to His law
Adjudges me; and therefore hath decreed
That, to His city, none through me should come.
He in all parts hath sway; there rules, there holds
His citadel and throne.   O happy those,
Whom there He chuses!"   I to him in few:
" Bard! by that God, whom thou didst not adore,
I do beseech thee (that this ill and worse
I may escape) to lead me where thou said'st,
That I Saint Peter's gate[4] may view, and those
Who, as thou tell'st, are in such dismal plight."
    Onward he moved, I close his steps pursued.

CANTO II

ARGUMENT

After the invocation, which poets are used to prefix to their works,
    he shows, that, on a consideration of his own strength, he
    doubted whether it sufficed for the journey proposed to him,
    but that, being comforted by Virgil, he at last took courage,
    and followed him as his guide and master.

Now was the day departing, and the air,
Imbrown'd with shadows, from their toils released
All animals on earth; and I alone
Prepared myself the conflict to sustain,
Both of sad pity, and that perilous road,
Which my unerring memory shall retrace.

1 The souls in Hell. Cf. Rev. ix. 6.
2 In Purgatory.
3 Beatrice, type of Divine Philosophy; Virgil himself being con-
signed to the Limbo of the virtuous heathen, who " without hope
live in desire."
4 The gate of Purgatory. Cf. Purg. ix.

O Muses ! O high genius ! now vouchsafe
Your aid. O mind ![1] that all I saw hast kept
Safe in a written record, here thy worth
And eminent endowments come to proof.

I thus began : " Bard ! thou who art my guide,
Consider well, if virtue be in me
Sufficient, ere to this high enterprise
Thou trust me. Thou hast told that Silvius' sire,[2]
Yet clothed in corruptible flesh, among
The immortal tribes had entrance, and was there
Sensibly present. Yet if Heaven's great Lord,
Almighty foe to ill, such favour show'd
In contemplation of the high effect,
Both what and who from him should issue forth,
It seems in reason's judgment well deserved ;
Sith he of Rome and of Rome's empire wide,
In Heaven's empyreal height was chosen sire :
Both which, if truth be spoken, were ordain'd
And stablish'd for the holy place, where sits
Who to great Peter's sacred chair succeeds.
He from this journey, in thy song renown'd,
Learn'd things, that to his victory gave rise
And to the papal robe.[3] In after-times
The Chosen Vessel also travel'd there,[4]
To bring us back assurance in that faith
Which is the entrance to salvation's way.
But I, why should I there presume? or who
Permits it? not Æneas I, nor Paul.
Myself I deem not worthy, and none else
Will deem me. I, if on this voyage then
I venture, fear it will in folly end.
Thou, who art wise, better my meaning know'st,
Than I can speak." As one, who unresolves

[1] *O mente*, " O memory."

[2] The account of the descent of Æneas, the father of Silvius, to
the infernal regions in the sixth book of Virgil's *Æneid* was
probably the original source of Dante's inspiration for the *Divina
Commedia*.

[3] According to Dante's theory, the victory of Æneas in Italy
led to the foundation of Rome, which was divinely ordained as
the seat of Pope and Emperor alike.

[4] A mediæval legend, familiar in Dante's time, described the
descent of St. Paul into Hell. Others take this as simply referring
to the famous passage in the second epistle to the Corinthians
(2 Cor. xii. 2), and understand the " immortal tribes " (*immortale
secolo*) in a more general sense.

What he hath late resolved, and with new thoughts
Changes his purpose, from his first intent
Removed; e'en such was I on that dun coast,
Wasting in thought my enterprise, at first
So eagerly embraced. " If right thy words
I scan," replied that shade magnanimous,
" Thy soul is by vile fear assail'd, which oft
So overcasts a man, that he recoils
From noblest resolution, like a beast
At some false semblance in the twilight gloom.
That from this terror thou mayst free thyself,
I will instruct thee why I came, and what
I heard in that same instant, when for thee
Grief touch'd me first. I was among the tribe
Who rest suspended,[1] when a dame, so blest
And lovely I besought her to command,
Call'd me; her eyes were brighter than the star
Of day; and she, with gentle voice and soft,
Angelically tuned, her speech address'd :
' O courteous shade of Mantua ! thou whose fame
' Yet lives, and shall live long as nature lasts !
' A friend, not of my fortune but myself,[2]
' On the wide desert in his road has met
' Hindrance so great, that he through fear has turn'd.
' Now much I dread lest he past help have stray'd,
' And I be risen too late for his relief,
' From what in heaven of him I heard. Speed now,
' And by thy eloquent persuasive tongue,
' And by all means for his deliverance meet,
' Assist him. So to me will comfort spring.
' I, who now bid thee on this errand forth,
' Am Beatrice ;[3] from a place I come
' Revisited with joy. Love brought me thence,
' Who prompts my speech. When in my Master's sight
' I stand, thy praise to him I oft will tell.'
    " She then was silent, and I thus began :
' O Lady ! by whose influence alone
' Mankind excels whatever is contain'd

[1] In Limbo.

[2] *Amico mio e non della ventura* is better understood and translated : " My friend, and not the friend of fortune " (Carlyle).

[3] Beatrice, symbol of Divine Philosophy, but no less the real
woman who, even from her throne in Paradise, is caring for her
lover's salvation and watching over him. *Cf.* Christina Rossetti,
The Convent Threshold.

' Within that heaven which hath the smallest orb,
' So thy command delights me, that to obey,
' If it were done already, would seem late.
' No need hast thou farther to speak thy will:
' Yet tell the reason, why thou art not loth
' To leave that ample space, where to return
' Thou burnest, for this centre here beneath.'
   " She then : ' Since thou so deeply wouldst inquire,
' I will instruct thee briefly why no dread
' Hinders my entrance here. Those things alone
' Are to be fear'd whence evil may proceed ;
' None else, for none are terrible beside.
' I am so framed by God, thanks to his grace !
' That any sufferance of your misery
' Touches me not, nor flame of that fierce fire
' Assails me. In high Heaven a blessed Dame [1]
' Resides, who mourns with such effectual grief
' That hindrance, which I send thee to remove,
' That God's stern judgment to her will inclines.
' To Lucia [2] calling, her she thus bespake :
" Now doth thy faithful servant need thy aid,
" And I commend him to thee." At her word
' Sped Lucia, of all cruelty the foe,
' And coming to the place, where I abode
' Seated with Rachel, [3] her of ancient days,
' She thus address'd me : " Thou true praise of God !
" Beatrice ! why is not thy succour lent
" To him, who so much loved thee, as to leave
" For thy sake all the multitude admires ?
" Dost thou not hear how pitiful his wail,
" Nor mark the death, which in the torrent flood,
" Swoln mightier than a sea, him struggling holds ?"
' Ne'er among men did any with such speed
' Haste to their profit, flee from their annoy,
' As, when these words were spoken, I came here,
' Down from my blessed seat, trusting the force
' Of thy pure eloquence, which thee, and all
' Who well have mark'd it, into honour brings.'
   " When she had ended, her bright beaming eyes
Tearful she turn'd aside ; whereat I felt

[1] The Blessed Virgin Mary, symbol of Divine Mercy.
[2] Lucia or St. Lucy, the virgin martyr of Syracuse and Dante's patron saint, is here the symbol of Illuminating Grace.
[3] Rachel, type of Contemplation.

Redoubled zeal to serve thee.   As she will'd,
Thus am I come : I saved thee from the beast,
Who thy near way across the goodly mount
Prevented.   What is this comes o'er thee then?
Why, why dost thou hang back? why in thy breast
Harbour vile fear? why hast not courage there,
And noble daring; since three maids,[1] so blest,
Thy safety plan, e'en in the court of Heaven;
And so much certain good my words forebode?"
    As florets, by the frosty air of night
Bent down and closed, when day has blanch'd their
        leaves,
Rise all unfolded on their spiry stems;
So was my fainting vigour new restored,
And to my heart such kindly courage ran,
That I as one undaunted soon replied :
" O full of pity she, who undertook
My succour ! and thou kind, who didst perform
So soon her true behest ! With such desire
Thou hast disposed me to renew my voyage,
That my first purpose fully is resumed.
Lead on : one only will is in us both.
Thou art my guide, my master thou, and lord."
    So spake I; and when he had onward moved,
I enter'd on the deep and woody way.

CANTO III

ARGUMENT

Dante, following Virgil, comes to the gate of Hell; where, after
  having read the dreadful words that are written thereon, they
  both enter. Here, as he understands from Virgil, those were
  punished who had passt their time (for living it could not be
  called) in a state of apathy and indifference both to good and
  evil. Then pursuing their way, they arrive at the river
  Acheron; and there find the old ferryman Charon, who takes
  the spirits over to the opposite shore; which as soon as Dante
  reaches, he is seized with terror, and falls into a trance.

" THROUGH me you pass into the city of woe :
Through me you pass into eternal pain :
Through me among the people lost for aye.

[1] Mary, Lucia, and Beatrice. Cf. *Par.* xxxii.

Justice the founder of my fabric moved:
To rear me was the task of Power divine,
Supremest Wisdom, and primeval Love.[1]
Before me things create were none, save things
Eternal,[2] and eternal I endure.
All hope abandon, ye who enter here."

    Such characters, in colour dim, I mark'd
Over a portal's lofty arch inscribed.
Whereat I thus: " Master, these words import
Hard meaning."   He as one prepared replied:
" Here thou must all distrust behind thee leave;
Here be vile fear extinguish'd.   We are come
Where I have told thee we shall see the souls
To misery doom'd, who intellectual good
Have lost."   And when his hand he had stretch'd forth
To mine, with pleasant looks, whence I was cheer'd,
Into that secret place he led me on.

    Here sighs, with lamentations and loud moans,
Resounded through the air pierced by no star,
That e'en I wept at entering. Various tongues,
Horrible languages, outcries of woe,
Accents of anger, voices deep and hoarse,
With hands together smote that swell'd the sounds,
Made up a tumult, that for ever whirls
Round through that air with solid darkness stain'd,
Like to the sand that in the whirlwind flies.

    I then, with error[3] yet encompast, cried:
" O master! what is this I hear? what race
Are these, who seem so overcome with woe?"

    He thus to me: " This miserable fate
Suffer the wretched souls of those, who lived
Without or praise or blame, with that ill band
Of angels mix'd, who nor rebellious proved,
Nor yet were true to God, but for themselves
Were only.   From his bounds Heaven drove them forth,
Not to impair his lustre; nor the depth
Of Hell receives them, lest the accursed tribe
Should glory thence with exultation vain."

    I then: " Master! what doth aggrieve them thus,

---

1 Power, Wisdom, and Love are the special attributes of the
three Persons of the Blessed Trinity: the Father, Son, and Holy
Ghost, respectively.

2 Eternal things: primal matter, the Angels, and the Heavens.

3 The right reading is *orror* (horror), not *error*.

That they lament so loud?'' He straight replied :
'' That will I tell thee briefly. These of death
No hope may entertain : and their blind life
So meanly passes, that all other lots
They envy. Fame of them the world hath none,
Nor suffers ; Mercy and Justice scorn them both.
Speak not of them, but look, and pass them by.''

And I, who straightway look'd, beheld a flag,
Which whirling ran around so rapidly,
That it no pause obtain'd : and following came
Such a long train of spirits, I should ne'er
Have thought that death so many had despoil'd.

When some of these I recognised, I saw
And knew the shade of him, who to base fear
Yielding, abjured his high estate.[1] Forthwith
I understood, for certain, this the tribe
Of those ill spirits both to God displeasing
And to His foes. These wretches, who ne'er lived,
Went on in nakedness, and sorely stung
By wasps and hornets, which bedew'd their cheeks
With blood, that, mix'd with tears, dropp'd to their feet,
And by disgustful worms was gather'd there.

Then looking further onwards, I beheld
A throng upon the shore of a great stream :
Whereat I thus : '' Sir ! grant me now to know
Whom here we view, and whence impell'd they seem
So eager to pass o'er, as I discern
Through the blear light?'' He thus to me in few :
'' This shalt thou know, soon as our steps arrive
Beside the woeful tide of Acheron.''

Then with eyes downward cast, and fill'd with shame,
Fearing my words offensive to his ear,

---

[1] Although disputed from the fourteenth century down to the
present day, there seems no reasonable doubt that this personage,
colui che fece per viltate il gran rifiuto, '' he who made from
cowardice the great renunciation,'' is Pope Celestine V. The evidence of Jacopone da Todi, Fazio degli Uberti, and Petrarch seems
conclusive on this point. Pietro da Morrone, an old and saintly
hermit from the Abruzzi, was compelled by the Cardinals to accept
the papal dignity in 1294, and assumed the title of Celestine V.
Men looked to him as a possible reformer of the Church ; but five
months later, worn out and realising his utter helplessness, he
abdicated. Benedetto Gaetani, who had probably urged him to this
step, was elected to succeed him as Boniface VIII., and kept him
closely imprisoned till his death in 1296. He was canonised in
1313.

Till we had reach'd the river, I from speech
Abstain'd. And lo! toward us in a bark
Comes on an old man, hoary white with eld,
Crying, " Woe to you, wicked spirits ! hope not
Ever to see the sky again. I come
To take you to the other shore across,
Into eternal darkness, there to dwell
In fierce heat and in ice. And thou, who there
Standest, live spirit ! get thee hence, and leave
These who are dead." But soon as he beheld
I left them not, " By other way," said he,
" By other haven shalt thou come to shore,
Not by this passage; thee a nimbler boat
Must carry." Then to him thus spake my guide :
" Charon ! thyself torment not : so 'tis will'd,
Where will and power are one : ask thou no more."
    Straightway in silence fell the shaggy cheeks
Of him, the boatman o'er the livid lake,
Around whose eyes glared wheeling flames. Meanwhile
Those spirits, faint and naked, colour changed,
And gnash'd their teeth, soon as the cruel words
They heard. God and their parents they blasphemed,
The human kind, the place, the time, and seed,
That did engender them and give them birth.
    Then all together sorely wailing drew
To the curst strand, that every man must pass
Who fears not God. Charon, demoniac form,
With eyes of burning coal, collects them all,
Beckoning, and each, that lingers, with his oar
Strikes. As fall off the light autumnal leaves,
One still another following, till the bough
Strews all its honours on the earth beneath;
E'en in like manner Adam's evil brood
Cast themselves, one by one, down from the shore,
Each at a beck, as falcon at his call.
    Thus go they over through the umber'd wave;
And ever they on the opposing bank
Be landed, on this side another throng
Still gathers. " Son," thus spake the courteous guide,
" Those who die subject to the wrath of God
All here together come from every clime,
And to o'erpass the river are not loth :
For so Heaven's justice goads them on, that fear
Is turn'd into desire. Hence ne'er hath past

Good spirit. If of thee Charon complain,
Now mayst thou know the import of his words."
    This said, the gloomy region trembling shook
So terribly, that yet with clammy dews
Fear chills my brow. The sad earth gave a blast,
That, lightening, shot forth a vermilion flame,
Which all my senses conquer'd quite, and I
Down dropp'd, as one with sudden slumber seized.

CANTO IV

ARGUMENT

The Poet, being roused by a clap of thunder, and following his
    guide onwards, descends into Limbo, which is the first circle
    of Hell, where he finds the souls of those, who, although they
    have lived virtuously and have not to suffer for great sins,
    nevertheless, through lack of baptism, merit not the bliss of
    Paradise. Hence he is led on by Virgil to descend into the
    second circle.

BROKE the deep slumber in my brain a crash
Of heavy thunder, that I shook myself,
As one by main force roused. Risen upright,
My rested eyes I moved around, and search'd,
With fixed ken, to know what place it was
Wherein I stood. For certain, on the brink
I found me of the lamentable vale,
The dread abyss, that joins a thundrous sound
Of plaints innumerable. Dark and deep,
And thick with clouds o'erspread, mine eye in vain
Explored its bottom, nor could aught discern.
    " Now let us to the blind world there beneath
Descend;" the bard began, all pale of look :
" I go the first, and thou shalt follow next."
    Then I, his alter'd hue perceiving, thus :
" How may I speed, if thou yieldest to dread,
Who still art wont to comfort me in doubt?"
    He then : " The anguish of that race below
With pity stains my cheek, which thou for fear
Mistakest. Let us on. Our length of way
Urges to haste." Onward, this said, he moved ;
And entering led me with him, on the bounds
Of the first circle that surrounds the abyss.
    Here, as mine ear could note, no plaint was heard

Except of sighs, that made the eternal air
Tremble, not caused by tortures, but from grief
Felt by those multitudes, many and vast,
Of men, women, and infants. Then to me
The gentle guide : " Inquirest thou not what spirits
Are these which thou beholdest? Ere thou pass
Farther, I would thou know, that these of sin
Were blameless ; and if aught they merited,
It profits not, since baptism was not theirs,
The portal to thy faith.   If they before
The Gospel lived, they served not God aright ;
And among such am I.   For these defects,
And for no other evil, we are lost ;
Only so far afflicted, that we live
Desiring without hope." Sore grief assail'd
My heart at hearing this, for well I knew
Suspended in that Limbo many a soul
Of mighty worth.   " O tell me, sire revered !
Tell me, my master !" I began, through wish
Of full assurance in that holy faith
Which vanquishes all error ; " say, did e'er
Any, or through his own or other's merit,
Come forth from thence, who afterward was blest?"

    Piercing the secret purport of my speech,
He answer'd : " I was new to that estate,
When I beheld a puissant one [1] arrive
Amongst us, with victorious trophy crown'd.
He forth the shade of our first parent drew,
Abel his child, and Noah righteous man,
Of Moses lawgiver for faith approved,
Of patriarch Abraham, and David king,
Israel with his sire and with his sons,
Nor without Rachel whom so hard he won,
And others many more, whom He to bliss
Exalted. Before these, be thou assured,
No spirit of human kind was ever saved."

    We, while he spake, ceased not our onward road,
Still passing through the wood ; for so I name
Those spirits thick beset. We were not far
On this side from the summit, when I kenn'd

---

[1] The names of Christ and Mary are never uttered during
Dante's passage through Hell ; thus, here, the former is simply
un possente, " a puissant one," and the latter was referred to as
donna gentil nel ciel, " a noble lady in Heaven."

A flame, that o'er the darken'd hemisphere
Prevailing shined.[1]　Yet we a little space
Were distant, not so far but I in part
Discover'd that a tribe in honour high
That place possess'd.　" O thou, who every art
And science valuest ! who are these, that boast
Such honour, separate from all the rest?"

He answer'd : " The renown of their great names,
That echoes through your world above, acquires
Favour in Heaven, which holds them thus advanced."
Meantime a voice I heard : " Honour the bard
Sublime ![2] his shade returns, that left us late !"
No sooner ceased the sound, than I beheld
Four mighty spirits toward us bend their steps,
Of semblance neither sorrowful nor glad.

When thus my master kind began : " Mark him,
Who in his right hand bears that falchion keen,
The other three preceding, as their lord.
This is that Homer, of all bards supreme :
Flaccus the next, in satire's vein excelling ;
The third is Naso ; Lucan is the last.
Because they all that appellation own,
With which the voice singly accosted me,
Honouring they greet me thus, and well they judge."

So I beheld united the bright school
Of him the monarch of sublimest song,
That o'er the others like a eagle soars.[3]

When they together short discourse had held,
They turn'd to me, with salutation kind
Beckoning me ; at the which my master smiled :
Nor was this all ; but greater honour still
They gave me, for they made me of their tribe ;
And I was sixth amid so learn'd a band.

[1] The light of mere human wisdom and genius.
[2] Virgil himself.
[3] Dante could have known little of Homer save his name, and a few isolated quotations which he found in the Latin translations of Aristotle and elsewhere. Dr. Moore points out that *satiro*, which Dante here applies to Horace, means " moralist " rather than " in satire's vein excelling," and that " the writings of Dante give little evidence of familiarity with his works, at any rate beyond the limits of the *Ars Poetica*." Ovid, on the other hand, is Dante's main mythological authority, especially in the *Metamorphoses*, which was known as the *Ovidio Maggiore*, while the *Pharsalia* of Lucan was one of his chief poetical guides in his conception of Roman History.

Far as the luminous beacon on we pass'd,
Speaking of matters, then befitting well
To speak, now fitter left untold.   At foot
Of a magnificent castle we arrived,
Seven times with lofty walls begirt, and round
Defended by a pleasant stream. O'er this
As o'er dry land we pass'd. Next, through seven gates,
I with those sages enter'd, and we came
Into a mead with lively verdure fresh.[1]
There dwelt a race, who slow their eyes around
Majestically moved, and in their port
Bore eminent authority : they spake
Seldom, but all their words were tuneful sweet.

We to one side retired, into a place
Open and bright and lofty, whence each one
Stood manifest to view. Incontinent,
There on the green enamel of the plain
Were shown me the great spirits, by whose sight
I am exalted in my own esteem.

Electra there I saw accompanied
By many, among whom Hector I knew,
Anchises' pious son, and with hawk's eye
Cæsar all arm'd, and by Camilla there
Penthesilea. On the other side,
Old king Latinus seated by his child
Lavinia, and that Brutus I beheld
Who Tarquin chased, Lucretia, Cato's wife
Marcia, with Julia and Cornelia there ;
And sole apart retired, the Soldan fierce.[2]

[1] The Castle of Fame is surrounded by the seven walls of the
four moral and three intellectual virtues : prudence, justice, forti-
tude, and temperance ; wisdom, knowledge, and understanding.
It is defended by the " pleasant stream " of eloquence, and entered
by seven gates, which are probably the seven liberal arts of the
Trivium and Quadrivium, in the mediæval system of education :
Grammar, Logic, and Rhetoric ; Music, Arithmetic, Geometry, and
Astronomy.

[2] The Soldan, Saladin (d. 1193), stands apart as the supreme
representative of Mahometan nobility and magnificence. The others
are types of the noble men and women of the Trojan and Roman
race (the two being regarded by Dante as one), from Electra, the
mother of Dardanus who was the ancestor of the royal house of
Troy as also of Æneas, to Cæsar, his greatest descendant, and Julia,
Cæsar's daughter. Penthesilea, the Amazonian Queen, slain by
Achilles when fighting in defence of Troy, and Camilla, who aided
Turnus against Æneas, are regarded as, in some sort, martyrs for
the divinely ordained plan of the establishment of the Roman

Then when a little more I raised my brow,
I spied the master of the sapient throng,[1]
Seated amid the philosophic train.
Him all admire, all pay him reverence due.
There Socrates and Plato [2] both I mark'd
Nearest to him in rank, Democritus,
Who sets the world at chance, Diogenes,
With Heraclitus, and Empedocles,
And Anaxagoras, and Thales sage,
Zeno, and Dioscorides well read
In nature's secret lore. Orpheus I mark'd
And Linus, Tully and moral Seneca,
Euclid and Ptolemy, Hippocrates,
Galenus, Avicen, and him who made
That commentary vast, Averroes.[3]

Empire. Latinus, King of Latium, through his daughter Lavinia, the third wife of Æneas, is likewise the ancestor of the Roman People. Cf. *Mon.* ii. 3. Cornelia, daughter of Scipio Africanus and mother of the Gracchi, is mentioned again in the *Paradiso* (Canto xv.), as a type of noble womanhood.

[1] Aristotle (B.C. 384–322), the Philosopher by excellence, for Dante is the supreme exponent of scientific truth. Dr. Toynbee notes: " With the exception of the Bible, Aristotle's works are quoted by Dante more frequently than those of any other author." The Poet's boundless reverence for his authority is emphatically expressed in the *Convivio*, especially iii. 5 and iv. 6. He naturally knew him only in Latin translations.

[2] Of Plato (B.C. 428–348), Dante knew only the *Timæus*, in the Latin translation by Chalcidius.

[3] Democritus (*d.* B.C. 361) taught that the world was formed by the fortuitous coming together of atoms; Diogenes, the Cynic, died B.C. 323; Heraclitus (sixth century B.C.) originated the theory of the perpetual flux; Empedocles (fifth century B.C.) " taught that the universe exists by reason of the discord of the elements, and that if harmony were to take the place of this discord, a state of chaos would ensue " (Oelsner on *Inf.* xii. 42, 43); Anaxagoras (*d.* B.C. 428), the friend of Pericles and Euripides, " taught that a supreme intelligence was the cause of all things " (Toynbee); Thales of Miletus (seventh century B.C.), called the father of Greek philosophy, made water the first principle, as Heraclitus afterwards did fire; Zeno is not the Eleatic philosopher of that name, but Zeno of Cittium, the founder of Stoicism (circa 310 B.C.). Dioscorides was a Greek physician and author of a work on *Materia Medica*, especially in relation to botany, who lived about the middle of the first century of the Christian era. The mythological Greek poets, Orpheus and Linus, were probably regarded by Dante as historical personages no less than Cicero (*d.* B.C. 43) and Seneca (*d.* A.D. 65), whose writings so profoundly influenced the mediæval mind, or Euclid (circa 300 B.C.), the father of mathematical literature, and Claudius Ptolemæus (second cen-

Of all to speak at full were vain attempt;
For my wide theme so urges, that oft-times
My words fall short of what bechanced. In two
The six associates part.   Another way
My sage guide leads me, from that air serene,
Into a climate ever vex'd with storms :
And to a part I come, where no light shines.

CANTO V

ARGUMENT

Coming into the second circle of Hell, Dante at the entrance
beholds Minos the Infernal Judge, by whom he is admonished
to beware how he enters these regions. Here he witnesses
the punishment of carnal sinners, who are tost about cease-
lessly in the dark air by the most furious winds. Amongst
these, he meets with Francesca of Rimini, through pity at
whose sad tale he falls fainting to the ground.

FROM the first circle I descended thus
Down to the second, which, a lesser space
Embracing, so much more of grief contains,
Provoking bitter moans. There Minos stands,
Grinning with ghastly feature :[1] he, of all
Who enter, strict examining the crimes,
Gives sentence, and dismisses them beneath,
According as he foldeth him around :
For when before him comes the ill-fated soul,
It all confesses; and that judge severe
Of sins, considering what place in Hell
Suits the transgression, with his tail so oft
Himself encircles, as degrees beneath

tury A.D.), the chief founder of the Ptolemaic system of astronomy
which held sway until the advent of Copernicus in the sixteenth
century. Hippocrates (d. circa 377 B.C.) and Galen (d.
200 A.D.) are the two most famous physicians of antiquity. Avi-
cenna (d. 1037) and Averroës (d. circa 1200) were Arabian
physicians and commentators on Aristotle ; it was through a Latin
translation of the work of Averroës, who was known as the Com-
mentator by excellence, that the philosophy of Aristotle first gained
its supremacy in the Middle Ages.

1 Minos, mythological lawgiver of Crete, the judge of the
infernal regions in Virgil's *Æneid*, is here the symbol of the
sinner's own guilty conscience.

He dooms it to descend. Before him stand
Alway a numerous throng; and in his turn
Each one to judgment passing, speaks, and hears
His fate, thence downward to his dwelling hurl'd.

   " O thou! who to this residence of woe
Approachest!" when he saw me coming, cried
Minos, relinquishing his dread employ,
" Look how thou enter here; beware in whom
Thou place thy trust; let not the entrance broad
Deceive thee to thy harm." To him my guide:
" Wherefore exclaimest? Hinder not his way
By destiny appointed; so 'tis will'd,
Where will and power are one. Ask thou no more."

   Now 'gin the rueful wailings to be heard.
Now am I come where many a plaining voice
Smites on mine ear. Into a place I came
Where light was silent all. Bellowing there groan'd
A noise, as of a sea in tempest torn
By warring winds. The stormy blast of Hell
With restless fury drives the spirits on,
Whirl'd round and dash'd amain with sore annoy.
When they arrive before the ruinous sweep,
There shrieks are heard, there lamentations, moans,
And blasphemies 'gainst the good Power in Heaven.

   I understood, that to this torment sad
The carnal sinners are condemn'd, in whom
Reason by lust is sway'd. As in large troops
And multitudinous, when winter reigns,
The starlings on their wings are borne abroad;
So bears the tyrannous gust those evil souls.
On this side and on that, above, below,
It drives them: hope of rest to solace them
Is none, nor e'en of milder pang. As cranes,
Chanting their dolorous notes, traverse the sky,
Stretch'd out in long array; so I beheld
Spirits, who came loud wailing, hurried on
By their dire doom. Then I: " Instructor! who
Are these, by the black air so scourged?"—" The first
'Mong those, of whom thou question'st," he replied,
" O'er many tongues was empress. She in vice
Of luxury was so shameless, that she made
Liking be lawful by promulged decree,
To clear the blame she had herself incurr'd.
This is Semiramis, of whom 'tis writ,

That she succeeded Ninus her espoused ;[1]
And held the land, which now the Soldan rules.
The next in amorous fury slew herself,
And to Sicheus' ashes broke her faith :[2]
Then follows Cleopatra, lustful queen." [3]

   There mark'd I Helen,[4] for whose sake so long
The time was fraught with evil; there the great
Achilles, who with love fought to the end.[5]
Paris I saw, and Tristan [6] ; and beside,
A thousand more he show'd me, and by name
Pointed them out, whom love bereaved of life.

   When I had heard my sage instructor name
Those dames and knights of antique days, o'erpower'd
By pity, well-nigh in amaze my mind
Was lost; and I began : " Bard ! willingly
I would address those two together coming,
Which seem so light before the wind." He thus :
" Note thou, when nearer they to us approach.
Then by that love which carries them along,
Entreat; and they will come." Soon as the wind
Sway'd them towards us, I thus framed my speech :
" O wearied spirits ! come, and hold discourse
With us, if by none else restrain'd." As doves
By fond desire invited, on wide wings
And firm, to their sweet nest returning home,
Cleave the air, wafted by their will along ;
Thus issued, from that troop where Dido ranks,
They, through the ill air speeding : with such force

[1] Semiramis was the mythical Queen of Assyria or Babylonia,
which Dante apparently confuses with Babylon in Egypt.

[2] Dido, Queen of Carthage, broke faith with the memory of
Sychæus, her husband, for the sake of Æneas, and, when deserted
by the latter, killed herself.

[3] Cleopatra, the famous Queen of Egypt (d. B.C. 30), was the
mistress successively of Julius Cæsar and Marcus Antonius.

[4] Helen of Troy :

   " The face that launched a thousand ships,
      And burnt the topless towers of Ilium " (Marlowe).

[5] According to the later versions of the Trojan war, Achilles
met his death at the hands of Paris through his passion for
Polyxena, a daughter of Priam.

[6] Paris and Tristram, the famous lovers of the Homeric and
Arthurian legend respectively, profoundly impressed the romantic
imagination of the Middle Ages, and are frequently, as here,
coupled together. Mr. Swinburne, in his Prelude to Tristram of
Lyonesse, and again in Four Songs of Four Seasons, supposes
that Iseult is here united with her lover.

My cry prevail'd, by strong affection urged.[1]
  " O gracious creature and benign ! who go'st
Visiting, through this element obscure,
Us, who the world with bloody stain imbrued;
If, for a friend, the King of all, we own'd,
Our prayer to him should for thy peace arise,
Since thou hast pity on our evil plight.
Of whatsoe'er to hear or to discourse
It pleases thee, that will we hear, of that
Freely with thee discourse, while e'er the wind,
As now, is mute. The land,[2] that gave me birth,
Is situate on the coast, where Po descends
To rest in ocean with his sequent streams.

  " Love, that in gentle heart is quickly learnt,[3]
Entangled him by that fair form, from me
Ta'en in such cruel sort, as grieves me still :
Love, that denial takes from none beloved,
Caught me with pleasing him so passing well,
That, as thou seest, he yet deserts me not.
Love brought us to one death : Caïna [4] waits.
The soul, who spilt our life." Such were their words ;
At hearing which, downward I bent my looks,

[1] These two are Francesca da Rimini and Paolo Malatesta.
Francesca, daughter of Guido Vecchio da Polenta, was married
to Gianciotto Malatesta, one of the sons of Malatesta da Verrucchio,
lord of Rimini. Gianciotto was a brave and able soldier, but
apparently deformed, and Francesca fell in love with his younger
brother Paolo, known as " il Bello " from his handsome person,
who was himself a married man. The two were slain together by
the outraged husband, about the year 1285. According to one
version of the story, Francesca had been led to believe that Paolo,
who acted as his brother's proxy in the marriage, was her
intended husband. It is she alone who now speaks with Dante
for both.   [2] Ravenna.
  [3] Cary notes : " That the reader of the original may not be
misled as to the exact sense of the word *s'apprende*, which I have
rendered ' is learnt,' it may be right to apprise him that it signifies
' is caught,' and that it is a metaphor from a thing taking fire.
Thus it is used by Guido Guinicelli, whom, indeed, our Poet seems
here to have had in view :

      " Fuoco d'Amore in gentil cor s'apprende,
        Come vertute in pietra preziosa :

      ' The fire of love in gentle heart is caught,
        As virtue in the precious stone.' "

  [4] *Caïna* is the first division of the ninth circle of Hell, in which
the treacherous murderers of their kindred are punished. See
below, Canto xxxii. Gianciotto died in 1304, and was therefore
alive at the date of the vision.

And held them there so long, that the bard cried:
" What art thou pondering?" I in answer thus:
" Alas! by what sweet thoughts, what fond desire,
Must they at length to that ill pass have reach'd!"
    Then turning, I to them my speech address'd,
And thus began: " Francesca! your sad fate
Even to tears my grief and pity moves.
But tell me; in the time of your sweet sighs,
By what, and how Love granted, that ye knew
Your yet uncertain wishes?" She replied:
" No greater grief than to remember days
Of joy, when misery is at hand.   That kens
Thy learn'd instructor.[1]   Yet so eagerly
If thou art bent to know the primal root,
From whence our love gat being, I will do
As one, who weeps and tells his tale.   One day,
For our delight we read of Lancelot,
How him love thrall'd.   Alone we were, and no
Suspicion near us.   Oft-times by that reading
Our eyes were drawn together, and the hue
Fled from our alter'd cheek.   But at one point
Alone we fell.   When of that smile we read,
The wished smile, so rapturously kiss'd
By one so deep in love, then he, who ne'er
From me shall separate, at once my lips
All trembling kiss'd.   The book and writer both
Were love's purveyors.   In its leaves that day
We read no more." [2]   While thus one spirit spake,
The other wail'd so sorely, that heart-struck
I, through compassion fainting, seem'd not far
From death, and like a corse fell to the ground.

[1] The passage quoted is from Boëthius, *De Consolatione Philosophiæ;* but by " thy learned instructor," *il tuo dottore,* Francesca more probably means Virgil, who has had experience of this
sad truth in Limbo.

[2] *Galeotto fu il libro, e chi lo scrisse,* literally " A Gallehault
was the book, and he who wrote it." " Gallehault (not by any
means to be confounded with Galahad) was the knight who acted
as intermediary between Lancelot and Guenever, and who, having
brought them together, urged the Queen to give Lancelot the kiss
which was the beginning of their guilty love. From the part
played by Gallehault on this occasion, his name came to be used,
like that of ' Sir Pandarus of Troy,' as a synonym for a pandar.
Hence Francesca's meaning is that the book and its author played
the same part with Paolo and herself as they read the story
together, that Gallehault did with Lancelot and Guenever in the

CANTO VI

ARGUMENT

On his recovery, the Poet finds himself in the third circle, where
the gluttonous are punished. Their torment is to lie in the
mire, under a continual and heavy storm of hail, snow, and
discoloured water; Cerberus meanwhile barking over them
with his threefold throat, and rending them piecemeal. One
of these, who on earth was named Ciacco, foretells the divisions
with which Florence is about to be distracted. Dante proposes
a question to his guide, who solves it; and they proceed
towards the fourth circle.

My sense reviving, that erewhile had droop'd
With pity for the kindred shades, whence grief
O'ercame me wholly, straight around I see
New torments, new tormented souls, which way
Soe'er I move, or turn, or bend my sight.
In the third circle I arrive, of showers
Ceaseless, accursed, heavy and cold, unchanged
For ever, both in kind and in degree.
Large hail, discolour'd water, sleety flaw
Through the dun midnight air stream'd down amain :
Stank all the land whereon that tempest fell.

Cerberus, cruel monster, fierce and strange,
Through his wide threefold throat, barks as a dog
Over the multitude immersed beneath.
His eyes glare crimson, black his unctuous beard,
His belly large, and claw'd the hands, with which
He tears the spirits, flays them, and their limbs
Piecemeal disparts.[1]   Howling there spread, as curs,
Under the rainy deluge, with one side
The other screening, oft they roll them round,
A wretched, godless crew.   When that great worm
Descried us, savage Cerberus, he oped
His jaws, and the fangs show'd us ; not a limb

romance itself '' (Paget Toynbee). The passage from the old
French romance of *Lancelot du Lac*, in the form in which Dante
(and, therefore, Francesca and Paolo) read it, with an English
translation, will be found in Dr. Toynbee's *Dante Studies and
Researches*. *Cf.* below, *Paradiso*, Canto xvi. Similarly, the
immoral tendency of Boccaccio's *Decameron* gained for it the title
of *Principe Galeotto*, '' the prince of pandars.''

[1] Cerberus is a symbol of the effects of gluttony upon the soul ;
its votaries have subjected themselves to an eternally horrible
nightmare.

Of him but trembled. Then my guide, his palms
Expanding on the ground, thence fill'd with earth
Raised them, and cast it in his ravenous maw.
E'en as a dog, that yelling bays for food
His keeper, when the morsel comes, lets fall
His fury, bent alone with eager haste
To swallow it; so dropp'd the loathsome cheeks
Of demon Cerberus, who thundering stuns
The spirits, that they for deafness wish in vain.

   We, o'er the shades thrown prostrate by the brunt
Of the heavy tempest passing, set our feet
Upon their emptiness, that substance seem'd.

   They all along the earth extended lay,
Save one, that sudden raised himself to sit,
Soon as that way he saw us pass. " O thou !"
He cried, " who through the infernal shades art led,
Own, if again thou know'st me. Thou wast framed
Or ere my frame was broken." I replied :
" The anguish thou endurest perchance so takes
Thy form from my remembrance, that it seems
As if I saw thee never. But inform
Me who thou art, that in a place so sad
Art set, and in such torment, that although
Other be greater, none disgusteth more."
He thus in answer to my words rejoin'd :
" Thy city, heap'd with envy to the brim,
Aye, that the measure overflows its bounds,
Held me in brighter days. Ye citizens
Were wont to name me Ciacco.[1] For the sin
Of gluttony, damned vice, beneath this rain,
E'en as thou seest, I with fatigue am worn :
Nor I sole spirit in this woe : all these
Have by like crime incurr'd like punishment."

   No more he said, and I my speech resumed :
" Ciacco ! thy dire affliction grieves me much,
Even to tears. But tell me, if thou know'st,
What shall at length befall the citizens
Of the divided city ;[2] whether any

---

[1] A Florentine parasite, contemporary of Dante, otherwise known only by a story in Boccaccio, *Decameron*, ix. 8.

[2] Florence, which, at the date of the vision (1300), was divided by the factions of Bianchi and Neri, Whites and Blacks. From Boccaccio's story, it would seem that Ciacco sponged impartially upon the leaders of both parties.

Just one inhabit there : and tell the cause,
Whence jarring Discord hath assail'd it thus.''
    He then : '' After long striving they will come
To blood ; and the wild party from the woods
Will chase the other with much injury forth.
Then it behoves that this must fall, within
Three solar circles ; and the other rise
By borrow'd force of one, who under shore
Now rests.[1] It shall a long space hold aloft
Its forehead, keeping under heavy weight
The other opprest, indignant at the load,
And grieving sore. The just are two in number,[2]
But they neglected. Avarice, envy, pride,
Three fatal sparks, have set the hearts of all
On fire.'' Here ceased the lamentable sound ;
And I continued thus : '' Still would I learn
More from thee, further parley still entreat.
Of Farinata and Tegghiaio say,
They who so well deserved ; of Giacopo,
Arrigo, Mosca,[3] and the rest, who bent

[1] Ciacco utters this prophecy in the night between Good Friday
(April 8) and Holy Saturday (April 9), 1300. The factions '' came
to blood '' on May 1. In June, Dante being then one of the Priors
or chief magistrates of the Republic, the heads of both factions
were put under bounds. The leaders of the Bianchi, '' the wild
party from the woods,'' were recalled at the end of August (after
the expiration of Dante's two months of office), and shortly afterwards succeeded in driving the Neri into exile. These latter, however, with the aid of Charles of Valois and Pope Boniface VIII.
(it is uncertain which of the two is meant by '' one who under
shore now rests ''), returned in November, 1301, and at the beginning of April, 1302, drove out the whole of the rival faction,
burghers and nobles alike, from Florence. All this thus befell
'' within three solar circles,'' that is, within three years from the
professed date of the vision.

[2] It is quite uncertain who these two are. Some take them as
Dante himself and Guido Cavalcanti—which seems hardly probable,
as far as Guido is concerned, seeing that he was deeply implicated
in the factions. Others identify them with Barduccio and Giovanni
da Vispignano, two devout and charitable Florentine laymen who
died in 1331. Dante's son, Pietro Alighieri, takes the passage as
a merely symbolical reference to natural law and positive law.

[3] Of these once famous Florentines, now among the damned,
Farinata degli Uberti is in the sixth circle (Canto x.), Tegghiaio
Aldobrandi and Jacopo Rusticucci in the seventh (Canto xvi.), and
Mosca de' Lamberti in the eighth circle (Canto xxviii.). We hear
no more of Arrigo, and it is uncertain to what family he belonged ;
he is usually supposed to have been one of Mosca's accomplices in

Their minds on working good. Oh ! tell me where
They bide, and to their knowledge let me come.
For I am prest with keen desire to hear
If Heaven's sweet cup, or poisonous drug of Hell,
Be to their lip assign'd.'' He answer'd straight :
'' These are yet blacker spirits. Various crimes
Have sunk them deeper in the dark abyss.
If thou so far descendest, thou mayst see them.
But to the pleasant world, when thou return'st,
Of me make mention, I entreat thee, there.
No more I tell thee, answer thee no more.''

    This said, his fixed eyes he turn'd askance,
A little eyed me, then bent down his head,
And 'midst his blind companions with it fell.

    When thus my guide : '' No more his bed he leaves,
Ere the last angel-trumpet blow. The Power
Adverse to these shall then in glory come,
Each one forthwith to his sad tomb repair,
Resume his fleshly vesture and his form,
And hear the eternal doom re-echoing rend
The vault.'' So pass'd we through that mixture foul
Of spirits and rain, with tardy steps ; meanwhile
Touching, though slightly, on the life to come.
For thus I question'd : '' Shall these tortures, Sir !
When the great sentence passes, be increased,
Or mitigated, or as now severe ?''

    He then : '' Consult thy knowledge ; that decides,
That, as each thing to more perfection grows,
It feels more sensibly both good and pain.
Though ne'er to true perfection may arrive
This race accurst, yet nearer then, than now,
They shall approach it.'' Compassing that path,
Circuitous we journey'd ; and discourse,
Much more than I relate, between us pass'd :
Till at the point, whence the steps led below,
Arrived, there Plutus, the great foe, we found.

the murder of Buondelmonte, and therefore sharing his fate in
the eighth circle among the '' blacker spirits.''

CANTO VII

ARGUMENT

In the present Canto, Dante describes his descent into the fourth
circle, at the beginning of which he sees Plutus stationed.
Here one like doom awaits the prodigal and the avaricious;
which is, to meet in direful conflict, rolling great weights
against each other with mutual upbraidings. From hence
Virgil takes occasion to show how vain the goods that are
committed into the charge of Fortune; and this moves our author
to inquire what being that Fortune is, of whom he speaks:
which question being resolved, they go down into the fifth
circle, where they find the wrathful and gloomy tormented in
the Stygian lake. Having made a compass round great part
of this lake, they come at last to the base of a lofty tower.

" Ah me ! O Satan ! Satan !" loud exclaim'd
Plutus,[1] in accent hoarse of wild alarm :
And the kind sage, whom no event surprised,
To comfort me thus spake : " Let not thy fear
Harm thee, for power in him, be sure, is none
To hinder down this rock thy safe descent."
Then to that swoln lip turning, " Peace !" he cried,
" Curst wolf ! thy fury inward on thyself
Prey, and consume thee ! Through the dark profound,
Not without cause, he passes. So 'tis will'd
On high, there where the great Archangel pour'd
Heaven's vengeance on the first adulterer proud." [2]

    As sails, full spread and bellying with the wind,
Drop suddenly collapsed, if the mast split ;
So to the ground down dropp'd the cruel fiend.

    Thus we, descending to the fourth steep ledge,
Gain'd on the dismal shore, that all the woe
Hems in of all the universe. Ah me !
Almighty Justice ! in what store thou heap'st
New pains, new troubles, as I here beheld.
Wherefore doth fault of ours bring us to this ?
    E'en as a billow, on Charybdis rising,

---

[1] Dante probably identified Pluto, the ruler of the underworld,
with Plutus, the personification of riches in classical mythology.
The latter is " the great foe," because, according to St. Thomas
Aquinas, " the sin of avarice, whereby the appetite of man is
subjected even to exterior things, has in some sense a greater
deformity than other sins."

[2] More literally, " the proud adultery "—in the sense in which
" fornication " is frequently used in the Scriptures.

Against encounter'd billow dashing breaks;
Such is the dance this wretched race must lead,
Whom more than elsewhere numerous here I found.
From one side and the other, with loud voice,
Both roll'd on weights, by main force of their breasts,
Then smote together, and each one forthwith
Roll'd them back voluble, turning again;
Exclaiming these, " Why holdest thou so fast?"
Those answering, " And why castest thou away?"
So, still repeating their despiteful song,
They to the opposite point, on either hand,
Traversed the horrid circle; then arrived,
Both turn'd them round, and through the middle space
Conflicting met again. At sight whereof
I, stung with grief, thus spake : " O say, my guide !
What race is this? Were these, whose heads are shorn,
On our left hand, all separate to the Church?"
    He straight replied : " In their first life, these all
In mind were so distorted, that they made,
According to due measure, of their wealth
No use. This clearly from their words collect,
Which they howl forth, at each extremity
Arriving of the circle, where their crime
Contrary in kind disparts them. To the Church
Were separate those, that with no hairy cowls
Are crown'd, both Popes and Cardinals, o'er whom
Avarice dominion absolute maintains."
    I then : " 'Mid such as these some needs must be,
Whom I shall recognise, that with the blot
Of these foul sins were stain'd." He answering thus :
" Vain thought conceivest thou. That ignoble life,
Which made them vile before, now makes them dark
And to all knowledge indiscernible.
For ever they shall meet in this rude shock :
These from the tomb with clenched grasp shall rise,
Those with close-shaven locks. That ill they gave,
And ill they kept, hath of the beauteous world
Deprived, and set them at this strife, which needs
No labour'd phrase of mine to set it off.
Now mayst thou see, my son ! how brief, how vain,
The goods committed into Fortune's hands,
For which the human race keep such a coil !
Not all the gold that is beneath the moon,
Or ever hath been, of these toil-worn souls

Might purchase rest for one." I thus rejoin'd :
" My guide ! of thee this also would I learn ;
This Fortune, that thou speak'st of, what it is,
Whose talons grasp the blessings of the world."

    He thus : " O beings blind ! what ignorance
Besets you ! Now my judgment hear and mark.
He, whose transcendent wisdom passes all,
The heavens creating, gave them ruling powers
To guide them ; so that each part shines to each,
Their light in equal distribution pour'd.
By similar appointment he ordain'd,
Over the world's bright images to rule,
Superintendence of a guiding hand
And general minister,[1] which, at due time,
May change the empty vantages of life
From race to race, from one to other's blood,
Beyond prevention of man's wisest care :
Wherefore one nation rises into sway,
Another languishes, e'en as her will
Decrees, from us conceal'd, as in the grass
The serpent train. Against her nought avails
Your utmost wisdom. She with foresight plans,
Judges, and carries on her reign, as theirs
The other powers divine. Her changes know
None intermission : by necessity [2]
She is made swift, so frequent come who claim
Succession in her favours. This is she,
So execrated e'en by those whose debt
To her is rather praise : they wrongfully
With blame requite her, and with evil word ;
But she is blessed, and for that recks not :
Amidst the other primal beings glad,
Rolls on her sphere, and in her bliss exults.
Now on our way pass we, to heavier woe
Descending : for each star [3] is falling now,
That mounted at our entrance, and forbids
Too long our tarrying." We the circle cross'd
To the next steep, arriving at a well,

[1] " Even as the Intelligences were created by God to regulate
the Heavens, so a power was ordained by Him to guide the
destinies of man on earth ; and this power is Fortune " (Oelsner).

[2] This passage was regarded as tainted with heresy, in that it
seemed to deny to man the possession of free-will.

[3] That is, it is past midnight on Good Friday, and we are now
in the early hours of Holy Saturday (April 9).

That boiling pours itself down to a foss
Sluiced from its source.   Far murkier was the wave
Than sablest grain : and we in company
Of the inky waters, journeying by their side,
Enter'd, though by a different track, beneath.
Into a lake, the Stygian named, expands
The dismal stream, when it hath reach'd the foot
Of the grey wither'd cliffs. Intent I stood
To gaze, and in the marish sunk descried
A miry tribe, all naked, and with looks
Betokening rage. They with their hands alone
Struck not, but with the head, the breast, the feet,
Cutting each other piecemeal with their fangs.
   The good instructor spake : " Now seest thou, son !
The souls of those, whom anger overcame.
This, too, for certain know, that underneath
The water dwells a multitude, whose sighs
Into these bubbles make the surface heave,
As thine eye tells thee wheresoe'er it turn.
Fix'd in the slime, they say : ' Sad once were we,
' In the sweet air made gladsome by the sun,
' Carrying a foul and lazy mist within :
' Now in these murky settlings are we sad.'
Such dolorous strain they gurgle in their throats,
But word distinct can utter none." Our route
Thus compass'd we, a segment widely stretch'd
Between the dry embankment and the core
Of the loath'd pool, turning meanwhile our eyes
Downward on those who gulp'd its muddy lees ;
Nor stopp'd, till to a tower's low base we came.

CANTO VIII

ARGUMENT

A signal having been made from the tower, Phlegyas, the ferryman
   of the lake, speedily crosses it, and conveys Virgil and Dante
   to the other side. On their passage, they meet with Filippo
   Argenti, whose fury and torment are described. They then
   arrive at the city of Dis, the entrance whereto is denied, and
   the portals closed against them by many Demons.

My theme pursuing,[1] I relate, that ere
We reach'd the lofty turret's base, our eyes

[1] By the opening words of this canto, *io dico seguitando*, " my

Its height ascended, where we mark'd uphung
Two cressets,[1] and another saw from far
Return the signal, so remote, that scarce
The eye could catch its beam.   I, turning round
To the deep source of knowledge, thus inquired :
" Say what this means ; and what, that other light
In answer set : what agency doth this?"

    " There on the filthy waters," he replied,
" E'en now what next awaits us mayst thou see,
If the marsh-gender'd fog conceal it not."

    Never was arrow from the cord dismiss'd,
That ran its way so nimbly through the air,
As a small bark, that through the waves I spied
Toward us coming, under the sole sway
Of one that ferried it, who cried aloud :
" Art   thou   arrived,   fell   spirit?"—" Phlegyas,
    Phlegyas,[2]
This time thou criest in vain," my lord replied ;
" No longer shalt thou have us, but while o'er
The slimy pool we pass."   As one who hears
Of some great wrong he hath sustain'd, whereat
Inly he pines ; so Phlegyas inly pined
In his fierce ire.   My guide, descending, stepp'd

theme pursuing, I relate," there hangs a tale.   Boccaccio states
that, when Dante's exile fell upon him, he had already composed
the first seven cantos of the *Inferno ;* the manuscript, left behind
him in his house at Florence, was discovered (apparently some
years later), and forwarded to the Poet, who was then staying with
the Marquis Moroello Malaspina, at whose instigation he resumed
the work, and followed on with the words that open this canto :
" where the joining on of the interrupted work can be quite
clearly recognised."   This story seems invalidated by the prophecy
uttered by Ciacco, in Canto vi., which clearly refers to events that
happened after Dante's exile ; but, at the same time, it must be
noted that the seven previous cantos differ considerably in tone from
what is to follow, and seem even to indicate a different scheme
of the *Inferno* from what Dante ultimately adopted.   It appears
thus just possible that there may be some foundation for Boccaccio's
statement (which is almost universally rejected at the present day),
and that Dante may have rewritten these cantos so as to bring them
up to date.

[1] Beacon-lights.

[2] Phlegyas, to avenge his daughter Coronis who had been
ravished by Apollo, set fire to the god's temple at Delphi, for
which he was condemned to Tartarus.   The part he plays here
was evidently suggested to Dante by the *Æneid,* vi. 618–620,
where he is made to utter a fearful warning against scorning the
supernal powers.

Into the skiff, and bade me enter next,
Close at his side; nor, till my entrance, seem'd
The vessel freighted. Soon as both embark'd,
Cutting the waves, goes on the ancient prow,
More deeply than with others it is wont.

While we our course o'er the dead channel held,
One drench'd in mire before me came, and said:
" Who art thou, that thus comest ere thine hour?"
    I answer'd: " Though I come, I tarry not:
But who art thou, that art become so foul?"
    " One, as thou seest, who mourn:" he straight
        replied.
    To which I thus: " In mourning and in woe,
Curst spirit! tarry thou. I know thee well,
E'en thus in filth disguised."[1] Then stretch'd he
        forth
Hands to the bark; whereof my teacher sage
Aware, thrusting him back: " Away! down there
To the other dogs!" then, with his arms my neck
Encircling, kiss'd my cheek, and spake: " O soul,
Justly disdainful! blest was she in whom
Thou wast conceived. He in the world was one
For arrogance noted: to his memory
No virtue lends its lustre; even so
Here is his shadow furious. There above,
How many now hold themselves mighty kings,
Who here like swine shall wallow in the mire,
Leaving behind them horrible dispraise."
    I then: " Master! him fain would I behold
Whelm'd in these dregs, before we quit the lake."
    He thus: " Or ever to thy view the shore
Be offer'd, satisfied shall be that wish,
Which well deserves completion." Scarce his words
Were ended, when I saw the miry tribes
Set on him with such violence, that yet
For that render I thanks to God, and praise.
" To Filippo Argenti!" cried they all:
And on himself the moody Florentine

---

[1] This is Filippo Argenti, who figures together with Ciacco
in Boccaccio's *Decameron*, ix. 8. He was a Florentine noble,
notorious for his furious temper and overbearing conduct, and is
said to have been a personal enemy of Dante's—which latter fact,
however, is not needed to explain the Poet's detestation of this kind
of man.

Turn'd his avenging fangs. Him here we left,
Nor speak I of him more. But on mine ear
Sudden a sound of lamentation smote,
Whereat mine eye unbarr'd I sent abroad.

And thus the good instructor : " Now, my son,
Draws near the city, that of Dis is named,
With its grave denizens, a mighty throng."

I thus : " The minarets already, Sir !
There, certes, in the valley I descry,
Gleaming vermilion, as if they from fire
Had issued." He replied : " Eternal fire,
That inward burns, shows them with ruddy flame
Illumed ; as in this nether Hell thou seest."

We came within the fosses deep, that moat
This region comfortless. The walls appear'd
As they were framed of iron. We had made
Wide circuit, ere a place we reach'd, where loud
The mariner cried vehement : " Go forth :
The entrance is here." Upon the gates I spied
More than a thousand, who of old from Heaven
Were shower'd. With ireful gestures, " Who is
    this,"
They cried, " that, without death first felt, goes
    through
The regions of the dead ?" My sapient guide
Made sign that he for secret parley wish'd ;
Whereat their angry scorn abating, thus
They spake : " Come thou alone ; and let him go,
Who hath so hardily enter'd this realm.
Alone return he by his witless way ;
If well he know it, let him prove. For thee,
Here shalt thou tarry, who through clime so dark
Hast been his escort." Now bethink thee, reader !
What cheer was mine at sound of those curst words.
I did believe I never should return.

" O my loved guide ! who more than seven times
Security hast render'd me, and drawn
From peril deep, whereto I stood exposed,
Desert me not," I cried, " in this extreme.
And, if our onward going be denied,
Together trace we back our steps with speed."

My liege, who thither had conducted me,
Replied : " Fear not : for of our passage none
Hath power to disappoint us, by such high

                                                    c

Authority permitted.   But do thou
Expect me here; meanwhile, thy wearied spirit
Comfort, and feed with kindly hope, assured
I will not leave thee in this lower world."

This said, departs the sire benevolent
And quits me.   Hesitating I remain
At war, 'twixt will and will not, in my thoughts.

I could not hear what terms he offer'd them,
But they conferr'd not long, for all at once
Pellmell rush'd back within.   Closed were the gates,
By those our adversaries, on the breast
Of my liege lord: excluded, he return'd
To me with tardy steps.   Upon the ground
His eyes were bent, and from his brow erased
All confidence, while thus in sighs he spake:
" Who hath denied me these abodes of woe?"
Then thus to me: " That I am anger'd, think
No ground of terror: in this trial I
Shall vanquish, use what arts they may within
For hindrance.   This their insolence, not new,[1]
Erewhile at gate less secret they display'd,
Which still is without bolt; upon its arch
Thou saw'st the deadly scroll: and even now,
On this side of its entrance, down the steep,
Passing the circles, unescorted, comes
One whose strong might can open us this land."

CANTO IX

ARGUMENT

After some hindrances, and having seen the hellish furies and other
monsters, the Poet, by the help of an Angel, enters the city
of Dis, wherein he discovers that the heretics are punished
in tombs burning with intense fire : and he, together with
Virgil, passes onwards between the sepulchres and the walls
of the city.

THE hue, which coward dread on my pale cheeks
Imprinted when I saw my guide turn back,

[1] " Virgil assures our Poet that these evil spirits had formerly
shown the same insolence when our Saviour descended into Hell.
They attempted to prevent him from entering at the gate, over
which Dante had read the fatal inscription : ' That gate which,'
says the Roman poet, ' an Angel has just passed, by whose aid
we shall overcome this opposition, and gain admittance into the
city ' " (Cary).

Chased that from his which newly they had worn,
And inwardly restrain'd it. He, as one
Who listens, stood attentive: for his eye
Not far could lead him through the sable air,
And the thick-gathering cloud. " It yet behoves
We win this fight;" thus he began : " if not,
Such aid to us is offer'd.—Oh ! how long
Me seems it, ere the promised help arrive."
    I noted, how the sequel of his words
Cloked their beginning; for the last he spake
Agreed not with the first. But not the less
My fear was at his saying; sith I drew
To import worse, perchance, than that he held,
His mutilated speech. " Doth ever any
Into this rueful concave's extreme depth
Descend, out of the first degree, whose pain
Is deprivation merely of sweet hope?"
    Thus I inquiring. " Rarely," he replied,
" It chances, that among us any makes
This journey, which I wend. Erewhile, 'tis true,
Once came I here beneath, conjured by fell
Erichtho, sorceress, who compell'd the shades
Back to their bodies. No long space my flesh
Was naked of me, when within these walls
She made me enter, to draw forth a spirit
From out of Judas' circle.[1] Lowest place
Is that of all, obscurest, and removed
Farthest from Heaven's all-circling orb. The road
Full well I know : thou therefore rest secure.
That lake, the noisome stench exhaling, round
The city of grief encompasses, which now
We may not enter without rage." Yet more
He added : but I hold it not in mind,
For that mine eye toward the lofty tower
Had drawn me wholly, to its burning top;
Where, in an instant, I beheld uprisen
At once three hellish furies stain'd with blood :
In limb and motion feminine they seem'd;
Around them greenest hydras twisting roll'd

[1] Erichtho was a Thessalian sorceress mentioned by Lucan (*Phars.* vi. 507–826) as conjuring up a spirit for Sextus Pompeius. It is uncertain whether the story of her having compelled the soul of Virgil to fetch up a spirit from the lowest region of Hell (the *Giudecca*) is some mediæval legend that has not come down to us, or a mere invention of Dante's own.

Their volumes; adders and cerastes crept
Instead of hair, and their fierce temples bound.
    He, knowing well the miserable hags
Who tend the queen of endless woe, thus spake:
" Mark thou each dire Erynnis. To the left,
This is Megæra; on the right hand, she
Who wails, Alecto; and Tisiphone
I' th' midst." This said, in silence he remain'd.
Their breast they each one clawing tore; themselves
Smote with their palms, and such thrill clamour raised
That to the bard I clung, suspicion-bound.
" Hasten Medusa: so to adamant
Him shall we change;" all looking down exclaim'd:
" E'en when by Theseus' might assail'd, we took
No ill revenge." " Turn thyself round, and keep
Thy countenance hid; for if the Gorgon dire
Be shown, and thou shouldst view it, thy return
Upwards would be for ever lost." This said,
Himself, my gentle master, turn'd me round;
Nor trusted he my hands, but with his own
He also hid me.   Ye of intellect
Sound and entire, mark well the lore [1] conceal'd
Under close texture of the mystic strain.
    And now there came o'er the perturbed waves
Loud-crashing, terrible, a sound that made
Either shore tremble, as if of a wind
Impetuous, from conflicting vapours sprung,
That, 'gainst some forest driving all his might,
Plucks off the branches, beats them down, and hurls
Afar; then, onward passing, proudly sweeps
His whirlwind rage, while beasts and shepherds fly.

---

[1] The Erinyes or Furies are symbols of hopeless remorse, and
Medusa of the despair which renders repentance impossible.
According to Isidore of Seville, " The commission of a grievous
sin is death; but to despair is to go down into Hell." Human
Philosophy, personified in Virgil, can guard Dante from this, but
he can do no more without celestial aid.   " A critical point in the
journey has been reached, and for the first time we are brought
into contact with beings over whom the mere recital of God's
command has no power.   These are resolved to use any means to
hinder Dante's progress; that is, the advance of the soul towards
true penitence.   One of the most effectual means to this end is to
call up the recollection of past sins (the Furies), and cause the
soul to persist in sin by urging to despair of God's mercy, indicated here by the Gorgon, who turns men to stone "
(A. J. Butler).

Mine eyes he loosed, and spake : " And now direct
Thy visual nerve along that ancient foam,
There, thickest where the smoke ascends.'' As frogs,
Before their foe the serpent, through the wave
Ply swiftly all, till at the ground each one
Lies on a heap ; more than a thousand spirits
Destroy'd, so saw I fleeing before one
Who pass'd with unwet feet the Stygian sound.
He, from his face removing the gross air,
Oft his left hand forth stretch'd, and seem'd alone
By that annoyance wearied. I perceived
That he was sent from Heaven ; and to my guide
Turn'd me, who signal made, that I should stand
Quiet, and bend to him. Ah me ! how full
Of noble anger seem'd he. To the gate
He came, and with his wand touch'd it, whereat
Open without impediment it flew.[1]

" Outcasts of heaven ! O abject race, and scorn'd !''
Began he, on the horrid grunsel standing,
" Whence doth this wild excess of insolence
Lodge in you ? wherefore kick you 'gainst that will
Ne'er frustrate of its end, and which so oft
Hath laid on you enforcement of your pangs ?
What profits, at the Fates to butt the horn ?
Your Cerberus,[2] if ye remember, hence
Bears still, peel'd of their hair, his throat and maw.''

This said, he turn'd back o'er the filthy way,
And syllable to us spake none ; but wore
The semblance of a man by other care
Beset, and keenly prest, than thought of him
Who in his presence stands. Then we our steps
Toward that territory moved, secure
After the hallow'd words. We, unopposed,
There enter'd ; and, my mind eager to learn
What state a fortress like to that might hold,
I, soon as enter'd, throw mine eye around,
And see, on every part, wide-stretching space,
Replete with bitter pain and torment ill.

---

[1] This " messenger of God " is clearly an Angel. The theories
of old and new commentators that he is Mercury or Æneas may
be disregarded.

[2] " Cerberus is feigned to have been dragged by Hercules, bound
with a threefold chain, of which, says the Angel, he still bears
the marks " (Cary).

As where Rhone stagnates on the plains of Arles,
Or as at Pola, near Quarnaro's gulf,
That closes Italy and laves her bounds,
The place is all thick spread with sepulchres;[1]
So was it here, save what in horror here
Excell'd: for 'midst the graves were scatter'd flames,
Wherewith intensely all throughout they burn'd,
That iron for no craft there hotter needs.

Their lids all hung suspended; and beneath,
From them forth issued lamentable moans,
Such as the sad and tortured well might raise.

I thus: " Master! say who are these, interr'd
Within these vaults, of whom distinct we hear
The dolorous sighs." He answer thus return'd:
" The arch-heretics are here, accompanied
By every sect their followers; and much more,
Than thou believest, the tombs are freighted: like
With like is buried; and the monuments
Are different in degrees of heat." This said,
He to the right hand turning, on we pass'd
Betwixt the afflicted and the ramparts high.

CANTO X

ARGUMENT

Dante, having obtained permission from his guide, holds discourse
  with Farinata degli Uberti and Cavalcante Cavalcanti, who lie
  in their fiery tombs, that are yet open, and not to be closed up
  till after the last judgment. Farinata predicts the Poet's exile
  from Florence; and shows him that the condemned have knowledge of future things, but are ignorant of what is at present
  passing, unless it be revealed by some new comer from earth.

Now by a secret pathway we proceed,
Between the walls, that hem the region round,
And the tormented souls: my master first,
I close behind his steps. " Virtue supreme!"
I thus began: " who through these ample orbs
In circuit lead'st me, even as thou will'st;
Speak thou, and satisfy my wish. May those,

[1] At Arles in Provence, according to the Carlovingian legend,
were the tombs of Charlemagne's warriors who had fallen in
battle against the Saracens. Numbers of Slavonians were said to
have been brought down to the sea for burial at Pola in Istria.

Who lie within these sepulchres, be seen?
Already all the lids are raised, and none
O'er them keeps watch.''   He thus in answer spake:
'' They shall be closed all, what-time they here
From Josaphat [1] return'd shall come, and bring
Their bodies, which above they now have left.
The cemetery on this part obtain,
With Epicurus, all his followers,
Who with the body make the spirit die. [2]
Here therefore satisfaction shall be soon,
Both to the question ask'd, and to the wish
Which thou conceal'st in silence.''   I replied:
'' I keep not, guide beloved! from thee my heart
Secreted, but to shun vain length of words;
A lesson erewhile taught me by thyself.''

'' O Tuscan! thou, who through the city of fire
Alive art passing, so discreet of speech:
Here, please thee, stay awhile. Thy utterance
Declares the place of thy nativity
To be that noble land, with which perchance
I too severely dealt.'' Sudden that sound
Forth issued from a vault, whereat, in fear,
I somewhat closer to my leader's side
Approaching, he thus spake: '' What dost thou?
    Turn:
Lo! Farinata [3] there, who hath himself

[1] Cf. Joel iii. 2.

[2] The heretics of the thirteenth and fourteenth centuries, known
as the Catari and Paterini, were supposed to deny the resurrection
of the body, and even to question the immortality of the soul. This
was probably, to some extent, a misrepresentation of their enemies;
but there was undoubtedly much sheer materialism rampant,
especially among the adherents of the Emperor Frederick II. and
the Ghibellines in general, who opposed the Popes in the spiritual
field as well as in the political. We shall, however, find Dante
including Cavalcante de' Cavalcanti, who was a staunch Guelf,
in the number of these neo-Epicureans.

[3] Farinata degli Uberti, the head of the chief Florentine house
that adhered to the Ghibellines, was instrumental in bringing
about the annihilation of the Florentine Guelfs and their allies
at the battle of Montaperti, on September 4, 1260. At a council
held by the victorious Ghibellines at Empoli, it was proposed by
the Sienese and Pisan representatives that Florence should be
razed to the ground, and the city was only saved by the vigorous
opposition of Farinata himself. Nevertheless, after the final
triumph of the Guelfs in 1266, the Uberti were always and for
ever excluded from all amnesties, and doomed to perpetual banishment. Such was the hatred with which the whole family was

Uplifted: from his girdle upwards, all
Exposed, behold him.'' On his face was mine
Already fix'd: his breast and forehead there
Erecting, seem'd as in high scorn he held
E'en Hell.   Between the sepulchres, to him
My guide thrust me, with fearless hands and prompt;
This warning added: '' See thy words be clear.''

   He, soon as I there stood at the tomb's foot,
Eyed me a space; then in disdainful mood
Address'd me: '' Say what ancestors were thine.''

   I, willing to obey him, straight reveal'd
The whole, nor kept back aught: whence he, his brow
Somewhat uplifting, cried: '' Fiercely were they
Adverse to me, my party, and the blood
From whence I sprang: twice,[1] therefore, I abroad
Scatter'd them.'' '' Though driven out, yet they each time
From all parts,'' answer'd I, '' return'd; an art
Which yours have shown they are not skill'd to learn.''

   Then, peering forth from the unclosed jaw,
Rose from his side a shade,[2] high as the chin,
Leaning, methought, upon its knees upraised.
It look'd around, as eager to explore
If there were other with me; but perceiving
That fond imagination quench'd, with tears
Thus spake: '' If thou through this blind prison go'st,
Led by thy lofty genius and profound,
Where is my son? and wherefore not with thee?''

   I straight replied: '' Not of myself I come;
By him, who there expects me, through this clime
Conducted, whom perchance Guido thy son
Had in contempt.'' [3] Already had his words

regarded that, when Arnolfo di Cambio founded the great Palazzo
Vecchio, he was forbidden to build any part of the house of the
Republic on the spot where the dwellings of these '' rebels '' had
once stood.   Farinata died in 1264, or thereabouts.   His great-
grandson, Fazio degli Uberti, was one of the most important
Italian poets of the fourteenth century.
  [1] He refers to the expulsion of the Guelfs from Florence in
1249 and 1260.
  [2] Cavalcante de' Cavalcanti, the father of Dante's friend Guido.
Although a Guelf, he belonged to the Florentine sect of the neo-
Epicureans, and is said to have believed that the soul perished with
the body.
  [3] Guido Cavalcanti, whom Dante in the *Vita Nuova* calls '' the

And mode of punishment read me his name,
Whence I so fully answered. He at once
Exclaim'd, up starting, " How ! said'st thou, he *had* ?
No longer lives he ?   Strikes not on his eye
The blessed daylight ?" Then, of some delay
I made ere my reply, aware, down fell
Supine, nor after forth appear'd he more.

 Meanwhile the other, great of soul, near whom
I yet was station'd, changed not countenance stern,
Nor moved the neck, nor bent his ribbed side.
" And if," continuing the first discourse,
" They in this art," he cried, " small skill have shown ;
That doth torment me more e'en than this bed.
But not yet fifty times shall be relumed
Her aspect, who reigns here queen of this realm,[1]
Ere thou shalt know the full weight of that art.
So to the pleasant world mayst thou return,

---

first of my friends," was about ten years older than the Poet.
In his youth, he was married to Farinata's daughter Beatrice—
one of the political unions arranged with a view of reconciling
the Guelfs and Ghibellines in Florence. As a poet, he stands
second only to Dante among the Italians of the late thirteenth
century (contemporaneous, of course, with the *Vita Nuova* rather
than with the *Divina Commedia*) ; several of his best compositions
are translated by Rossetti in his *Early Italian Poets*. A singularly
attractive picture of his character is given us by his contemporaries, Dino Compagni and Giovanni Villani, while one of the
best stories of the *Decameron* (vi. 9) shows that he had the reputation of being a sceptic in religion. Personal hostility towards
Corso Donati led him to adhere to the Bianchi, and he was one
of the leaders of the faction who were exiled in June, 1300 (two
months after the assumed date of the vision), when Dante was
one of the Priors of the Republic. Put under bounds at Sarzana,
he contracted a fatal illness ; returning to Florence in the latter
part of August, after Dante's term of office had expired, he died
almost immediately, and was buried on August 29. There is a
whole literature on the meaning of Guido's alleged contempt for
Virgil. According to one interpretation, it means that he esteemed
philosophy more than poetry, or the vernacular more than Latin ;
according to another, he, being inclined to scepticism, rejected the
allegorical Virgil, the type of human philosophy leading to
repentance and to faith ; according to yet another view, he had
not grasped the conception of the divine ordination in the establishment of the Roman Empire, and its right to universal sway, which
Dante had first learned from the *Æneid*.

[1] Time in Hell is reckoned by the moon, since there " the
sun is silent." Fifty months shall not pass before Dante learns
by personal experience the difficulty of an exile winning his way
back to Florence.

As thou shalt tell me why, in all their laws,
Against my kin this people is so fell."
    " The slaughter and great havoc," I replied,
" That colour'd Arbia's flood with crimson stain—
To these impute, that in our hallow'd dome
Such orisons ascend." [1]   Sighing he shook
The head, then thus resumed : " In that affray
I stood not singly, nor without just cause,
Assuredly, should with the rest have stirr'd ;
But singly there I stood, when, by consent
Of all, Florence had to the ground been razed,
The one who openly forbade the deed."
    " So may thy lineage find at last repose,"
I thus adjured him, " as thou solve this knot,
Which now involves my mind. If right I hear,
Ye seem to view beforehand that which time
Leads with him, of the present uninform'd."
    " We view,[2] as one who hath an evil sight,"
He answer'd, " plainly, objects far remote ;
So much of his large splendour yet imparts
The Almighty Ruler : but when they approach,
Or actually exist, our intellect
Then wholly fails ; nor of your human state,
Except what others bring us, know we aught.
Hence therefore mayst thou understand, that all
Our knowledge in that instant shall expire,
When on futurity the portals close."
    Then conscious of my fault, and by remorse
Smitten, I added thus : " Now shalt thou say
To him there fallen, that his offspring still
Is to the living join'd ;[3] and bid him know,
That if from answer, silent, I abstain'd,

---

[1] The Arbia, a small river near the battlefield of Montaperti,
ran red with the blood of the slaughtered Guelfs. Farinata's share
in bringing about their overthrow outweighed all remembrance of
how he had saved their city from destruction. The " orisons "
probably refer to the fact that the decrees excluding the Uberti
for ever from amnesty, after the final triumph of the Guelfs in
1266, were signed in church.
[2] Cary aptly quotes Sir Thomas Browne's *Urn-Burial :* " The
departed spirits know things past and to come ; yet are ignorant of
things present. Agamemnon foretells what should happen unto
Ulysses ; yet ignorantly inquires what is become of his own son."
[3] That is, at the assumed date of the vision, April, 1300—which
Dante never forgets although he is actually writing many years
later.

'Twas that my thought was occupied, intent
Upon that error, which thy help hath solved."
    But now my master summoning me back
I heard, and with more eager haste besought
The spirit to inform me, who with him
Partook his lot. He answer thus return'd:
" More than a thousand with me here are laid.
Within is Frederick,[1] second of that name,
And the Lord Cardinal;[2] and of the rest
I speak not." He, this said, from sight withdrew.
But I my steps toward the ancient bard
Reverting, ruminated on the words
Betokening me such ill. Onward he moved,
And thus, in going, question'd: " Whence the amaze
That holds thy senses wrapt?" I satisfied
The inquiry, and the sage enjoin'd me straight:
" Let thy safe memory store what thou hast heard
To thee importing harm; and note thou this,"
With his raised finger bidding me take heed,
" When thou shalt stand before her gracious beam,[3]
Whose bright eye all surveys, she of thy life
The future tenour will to thee unfold."
    Forthwith he to the left hand turn'd his feet:
We left the wall, and towards the middle space
Went by a path that to a valley strikes,
Which e'en thus high exhaled its noisome steam.

CANTO XI

ARGUMENT

Dante arrives at the verge of a rocky precipice which encloses the
    seventh circle, where he sees the sepulchre of Anastasius the
    Heretic; behind the lid of which pausing a little, to make
    himself capable by degrees of enduring the fetid smell that

---

[1] The Emperor Frederick II., " the wonder of the world "
(1194–1250). His reputation as a sensualist and an unbeliever was
probably well deserved; but Dante elsewhere (V. E. i. 12) describes
him as an " illustrious hero," extolling the " nobility and
righteousness " of his character.

[2] Cardinal Ottaviano degli Ubaldini, who died in 1273, was
known to his contemporaries as " the Cardinal " by excellence.
There was a legend that he had said: " If there is a soul, I have
lost mine a thousand times for the Ghibellines."

[3] Beatrice. Cf. Par. xvii.

steamed upward from the abyss, he is instructed by Virgil
concerning the manner in which the three following circles are
disposed, and what description of sinners is punished in each.
He then inquires the reason why the carnal, the gluttonous,
the avaricious and prodigal, the wrathful and gloomy, suffer
not their punishments within the city of Dis. He next asks
how the crime of usury is an offence against God; and at
length the two Poets go towards the place from whence a
passage leads down to the seventh circle.

UPON the utmost verge of a high bank,
By craggy rocks environ'd round, we came,
Where woes beneath, more cruel yet, were stow'd:
And here, to shun the horrible excess
Of fetid exhalation upward cast
From the profound abyss, behind the lid
Of a great monument we stood retired,
Whereon this scroll I mark'd: "I have in charge
Pope Anastasius,[1] whom Photinus drew
From the right path."—" Ere our descent, behoves
We make delay, that somewhat first the sense,
To the dire breath accustom'd, afterward
Regard it not." My master thus; to whom
Answering I spake: "Some compensation find,
That the time pass not wholly lost." He then:
"Lo! how my thoughts e'en to thy wishes tend.
My son! within these rocks," he thus began,[2]

[1] Pope Anastasius II. (496–498) was supposed by mediæval
writers to have been led by Photinus, a deacon of Thessalonica,
into adopting the heresy of Acacius, who denied the divine birth
of Christ. The legend may, perhaps, have originated in some
confusion between the Pope and his contemporary, the Emperor,
of the same name—but, in any case, the misunderstanding is not
due to Dante.

[2] The rest of this canto is an explanation of the moral topo-
graphy, or ethical system, of the Poet's Hell. Dante combines
the dictum of Cicero (De Officiis, i. 13) that injury is done by
violence or by fraud, with Aristotle's threefold division of things
to be morally shunned (Nicomachean Ethics, vii. 1) into incontinence, malice, and brutishness or bestiality. He equates the
Ciceronian violence with the Aristotelian bestiality, and the Ciceronian fraud with the Aristotelian malice. Incontinence, being less
guilty, is relegated to the five circles of upper Hell. The sixth
circle, that of the Heretics, occupies an intermediate position—
and may be regarded, like those of the neutrals and virtuous
heathens, as standing outside of the general ethical scheme of the
Inferno. The lower Hell, which Dante is about to enter, is composed of three great circles, each divided into a number of sub-
divisions, and each separated by a chasm from the one above: the
seventh circle of Violence and Bestiality; the eighth circle of

" Are three close circles in gradation placed,
As these which now thou leavest.   Each one is full
Of spirits accurst; but that the sight alone
Hereafter may suffice thee, listen how
And for what cause in durance they abide.

" Of all malicious act abhorr'd in Heaven,
The end is injury; and all such end
Either by force or fraud works other's woe.
But fraud, because of man peculiar evil,
To God is more displeasing; and beneath,
The fraudulent are therefore doom'd to endure
Severer pang.   The violent occupy
All the first circle; and because, to force,
Three persons are obnoxious, in three rounds,
Each within other separate, is it framed.
To God, his neighbour, and himself, by man
Force may be offer'd; to himself I say,
And his possessions, as thou soon shalt hear
At full.   Death, violent death, and painful wounds
Upon his neighbour he inflicts; and wastes,
By devastation, pillage, and the flames,
His substance.   Slayers, and each one that smites
In malice, plunderers, and all robbers, hence
The torment undergo of the first round,
In different herds.   Man can do violence
To himself and his own blessings : and for this,
He, in the second round must aye deplore
With unavailing penitence his crime,
Whoe'er deprives himself of life and light,
In reckless lavishment his talent wastes,
And sorrows there where he should dwell in joy.
To God may force be offer'd, in the heart
Denying and blaspheming His high power,
And Nature with her kindly law contemning.
And thence the inmost round marks with its seal
Sodom, and Cahors,[1] and all such as speak
Contemptuously of the Godhead in their hearts.

" Fraud, that in every conscience leaves a sting,

Malice or Fraud simple; the ninth circle of Malice or Fraud
intensified, or aggravated, as Treachery.   For the whole of this
subject, the reader may be referred to Mr. Wicksteed's Appendix V.
in the English edition of Witte's *Essays on Dante*.
[1] Cahors in Guyenne is synonymous with usury, as Sodom with
unnatural vice.

May be by man employ'd on one, whose trust
He wins, or on another who withholds
Strict confidence. Seems as the latter way
Broke but the bond of love which Nature makes.
Whence in the second circle have their nest,
Dissimulation, witchcraft, flatteries,
Theft, falsehood, simony, all who seduce
To lust, or set their honesty at pawn,[1]
With such vile scum as these. The other way
Forgets both Nature's general love, and that
Which thereto added afterward gives birth
To special faith. Whence in the lesser circle,
Point of the universe, dread seat of Dis,
The traitor is eternally consumed."
     I thus : " Instructor, clearly thy discourse
Proceeds, distinguishing the hideous chasm
And its inhabitants with skill exact.
But tell me this : they of the dull, fat pool,
Whom the rain beats, or whom the tempest drives,
Or who with tongues so fierce conflicting meet,
Wherefore within the city fire-illumed
Are not these punish'd, if God's wrath be on them?
And if it be not, wherefore in such guise
Are they condemn'd?"   He answer thus return'd :
" Wherefore in dotage wanders thus thy mind,
Not so accustom'd? or what other thoughts
Possess it? Dwell not in thy memory
The words, wherein thy ethic page describes
Three dispositions adverse to Heaven's will,
Incontinence, malice, and mad brutishness,
And how incontinence the least offends
God, and least guilt incurs? If well thou note
This judgment, and remember who they are,
Without these walls to vain repentance doom'd,
Thou shalt discern why they apart are placed
From these fell spirits, and less wreakful pours
Justice Divine on them its vengeance down."
     " O sun ! who healest all imperfect sight,
Thou so content'st me, when thou solvest my doubt,
That ignorance not less than knowledge charms.

---

[1] " All who . . . set their honesty at pawn." The Italian word
is *baratti*, " barrators," which is equivalent to the modern
American word " boodlers ": those guilty of corrupt practices in
public life.

Yet somewhat turn thee back," I in these words
Continued, " where thou said'st, that usury
Offends celestial Goodness; and this knot
Perplex'd unravel." He thus made reply:
" Philosophy, to an attentive ear,
Clearly points out, not in one part alone,
How imitative Nature takes her course
From the celestial Mind, and from its art:
And where her laws [1] the Stagirite unfolds,
Not many leaves scann'd o'er, observing well
Thou shalt discover, that your art on her
Obsequious follows, as the learner treads
In his instructor's step; so that your art
Deserves the name of second in descent
From God. These two, if thou recall to mind
Creation's holy book,[2] from the beginning
Were the right source of life and excellence
To human kind. But in another path
The usurer walks; and Nature in herself
And in her follower thus he sets at nought,
Placing elsewhere his hope.[3] But follow now
My steps on forward journey bent; for now
The Pisces play with undulating glance
Along the horizon, and the Wain [4] lies all
O'er the north-west; and onward there a space
Is our steep passage down the rocky height."

1 Aristotle (*Physics*, ii. 2): " Art mimics nature."

2 Genesis ii. 15, iii. 19.

3 " The usurer, trusting in the produce of his wealth lent out on
usury, despises nature directly, because he does not avail himself
of her means for maintaining or enriching himself; and indirectly,
because he does not avail himself of the means which art, the
follower and imitator of nature, would afford him for the same
purpose " (Cary). Usury was regarded as a deadly sin in the
Middle Ages, and even later. In the fifth Lateran Council, held
under Leo X., usury is defined as " the attempt to draw profit and
increment, without labour, without cost, and without risk, out
of the use of a thing that does not fructify." For the modern
Catholic view of the question, *cf.* Rickaby, *Moral Philosophy*,
pp. 255-263.

4 That is, it is about two hours before sunrise on the second
day of Dante's ecstatic journey, *i. e.* Saturday, April 9.

CANTO XII

ARGUMENT

Descending by a very rugged way into the seventh circle, where
the violent are punished, Dante and his leader find it guarded
by the Minotaur; whose fury being pacified by Virgil, they
step downwards from crag to crag; till, drawing near the
bottom, they descry a river of blood, wherein are tormented
such as have committed violence against their neighbour. At
these, when they strive to emerge from the blood, a troop
of Centaurs, running along the side of the river, aim their
arrows; and three of their band opposing our travellers at the
foot of the steep, Virgil prevails so far, that one consents to
carry them both across the stream; and on their passage,
Dante is informed by him of the course of the river, and of
those that are punished therein.

THE place, where to descend the precipice
We came, was rough as Alp; and on its verge
Such object lay, as every eye would shun.

  As is that ruin, which Adice's stream
On this side Trento struck, shouldering the wave,
Or loosed by earthquake or for lack of prop;
For from the mountain's summit, whence it moved
To the low level, so the headlong rock
Is shiver'd, that some passage it might give
To him who from above would pass; e'en such
Into the chasm was that descent : and there
At point of the disparted ridge lay stretch'd
The infamy of Crete,[1] detested brood
Of the feigned heifer : and at sight of us
It gnaw'd itself, as one with rage distract.
To him my guide exclaim'd : " Perchance thou deem'st
The king of Athens here, who, in the world
Above, thy death contrived.   Monster ! avaunt !
He comes not tutor'd by thy sister's art,
But to behold your torments is he come."

  Like to a bull, that with impetuous spring
Darts, at the moment when the fatal blow
Hath struck him, but unable to proceed
Plunges on either side; so saw I plunge

---

[1] The Minotaur, a monster with a man's body and a bull's head,
was the offspring of Pasiphaë (" the feigned heifer "), wife of
Minos of Crete. It was slain by Theseus, King of Athens, with
the aid of Ariadne, the daughter of Pasiphaë by Minos.

The Minotaur; [1] whereat the sage exclaim'd :
" Run to the passage ! while he storms, 'tis well
That thou descend."   Thus down our road we took
Through those dilapidated crags, that oft
Moved underneath my feet, to weight like theirs
Unused.   I pondering went, and thus he spake :
" Perhaps thy thoughts are of this ruin'd steep,
Guarded by the brute violence, which I
Have vanquish'd now.   Know then, that when I erst
Hither descended to the nether Hell,
This rock was not yet fallen.   But past doubt
(If well I mark), not long ere He arrived,
Who carried off from Dis the mighty spoil
Of the highest circle, then through all its bounds
Such trembling seized the deep concave and foul,
I thought the universe was thrill'd with love,
Whereby, there are who deem, the world hath oft
Been into chaos turn'd :[2] and in that point,
Here, and elsewhere, that old rock toppled down.
But fix thine eyes beneath : the river of blood
Approaches, in the which all those are steep'd,
Who have by violence injured."   O blind lust !
O foolish wrath ! who so dost goad us on
In the brief life, and in the eternal then
Thus miserably o'erwhelm us.   I beheld
An ample foss, that in a bow was bent,
As circling all the plain ; for so my guide
Had told.   Between it and the rampart's base,
On trail ran Centaurs, with keen arrows arm'd,
As to the chase they on the earth were wont.[3]

[1] The monster is here the type of violence and bestiality. Mr.
Wicksteed notes, in evidence of the identification of violence with
bestiality or brutishness, that all the guardians and tormentors
of this seventh circle are either beasts or forms of mingled man
and animal.

[2] Virgil's journey into the Giudecca at the bidding of Erichtho
(see notes on Canto ix.) was before the descent of Christ into
Hell—which was preceded by the earthquake recorded in the
Gospel, at the moment of His death upon the Cross, when " the
earth did quake, and the rocks rent " (Matt. xxvii. 51).

[3] The Centaurs are represented in Greek art as monstrous beings
with a man's head, trunk, and arms, and the body and four legs
of a horse. According to the early commentators, they here stand
in the allegorical sense for the mercenary soldiers of the tyrants,
the instruments of their own oppression thus becoming their
chastisement.

At seeing us descend they each one stood;
And issuing from the troop, three sped with bows
And missile weapons chosen first; of whom
One cried from far : " Say, to what pain ye come
Condemn'd, who down this steep have journey'd. Speak
From whence ye stand, or else the bow I draw."

To whom my guide : " Our answer shall be made
To Chiron, there, when nearer him we come.
Ill was thy mind, thus ever quick and rash."
Then me he touch'd, and spake : " Nessus is this,
Who for the fair Deïanira died,
And wrought himself revenge for his own fate.
He in the midst, that on his breast looks down,
Is the great Chiron who Achilles nursed;
That other, Pholus, prone to wrath." [1] Around
The foss these go by thousands, aiming shafts
At whatsoever spirit dares emerge
From out the blood, more than his guilt allows.

We to those beasts, that rapid strode along,
Drew near; when Chiron took an arrow forth,
And with the notch push'd back his shaggy beard
To the cheek-bone, then, his great mouth to view
Exposing, to his fellows thus exclaim'd :
" Are ye aware, that he who comes behind
Moves what he touches? The feet of the dead
Are not so wont." My trusty guide, who now
Stood near his breast, where the two natures join,
Thus made reply : " He is indeed alive,
And solitary so must needs by me
Be shown the gloomy vale, thereto induced

---

[1] Chiron, unlike the other Centaurs, is represented as wise and
just; he was the master of Achilles, Jason, Asclepius, and other
Greek heroes. "We are all monsters, that is, a composition of
Man and Beast, wherein we must endeavour to be as the Poets
fancy that wise man Chiron, that is, to have the Region of Man
above that of Beast, and Sense to sit but at the feet of Reason"
(Sir Thomas Browne, *Religio Medici*). Nessus was the Centaur
who, when mortally wounded by Hercules in his attempt to carry
off Deïanira, gave the latter a garment steeped in his blood, telling her that by its means she would preserve her husband's affections—the result being the death of Hercules, as Nessus had
intended. The Centaur Pholus entertained Hercules, and was
accidentally killed by one of his arrows. Dr. Toynbee suggests
that Dante's description of him as *pien d'ira,* "full of anger,"
is probably a recollection of *Georgics,* ii. 455, 456, where Virgil
speaks of the Centaurs as *furentes.*

By strict necessity, not by delight.
She left her joyful harpings in the sky,
Who this new office to my care consign'd.
He is no robber, no dark spirit I.
But by that virtue, which empowers my step
To tread so wild a path, grant us, I pray,
One of thy band, whom we may trust secure,
Who to the ford may lead us, and convey
Across, him mounted on his back; for he
Is not a spirit that may walk the air."

    Then on his right breast turning, Chiron thus
To Nessus spake : " Return, and be their guide.
And if ye chance to cross another troop,
Command them keep aloof." Onward we moved,
The faithful escort by our side, along
The border of the crimson-seething flood,
Whence, from those steep'd within, loud shrieks arose.

    Some there I mark'd, as high as to their brow
Immersed, of whom the mighty Centaur thus :
" These are the souls of tyrants, who were given
To blood and rapine. Here they wail aloud
Their merciless wrongs. Here Alexander dwells,
And Dionysius fell, who many a year
Of woe wrought for fair Sicily.[1] That brow,
Whereon the hair so jetty clustering hangs,
Is Azzolino; that with flaxen locks
Obizzo of Este, in the world destroy'd
By his foul step-son."[2] To the bard revered

[1] It is disputed whether this Alexander is Alexander the Great
of Macedon (d. B.C. 323), or Alexander of Pheræ (d. B.C. 359), the
Thessalian tyrant who was killed by his own wife. The Dionysius is the elder of that name, tyrant of Syracuse (d. B.C. 367).

[2] Azzolino, or Ezzelino III. da Romano, the most horrible tyrant
of Italian history, whom men called the son of a devil, made
himself lord of Verona, Vicenza, Padua, and other cities in
north-eastern Lombardy, and was imperial vicar under Frederick II. After an appalling career of atrocity, a crusade was
proclaimed against him by Pope Alexander IV., and, in 1259, he
was defeated at Cassano on the Adda, wounded, and taken
prisoner. A few days later, he tore the bandages from his wounds,
and so died. Cf. *Par.* ix. Obizzo II. of Este, fourth Marquis of
Ferrara, was the grandson of Azzo VII., called Azzo Novello, who
had led the Guelf crusaders against Ezzelino. Dying in 1293, he
was said to have been murdered by his son and successor, Azzo
VIII., whom Dante calls his " step-son," to emphasise the unnatural wickedness of his deed—which, for the rest, is highly
doubtful historically. Cf. below, Canto xviii. and *Purg.* v. In

I turn'd me round, and thus he spake : " Let him
Be to thee now first leader, me but next
To him in rank." Then further on a space
The Centaur paused, near some, who at the throat
Were extant from the wave; and, showing us
A spirit by itself apart retired,
Exclaim'd : " He [1] in God's bosom smote the heart,
Which yet is honour'd on the bank of Thames."

A race I next espied who held the head,
And even all the bust, above the stream.
'Midst these I many a face remember'd well.
Thus shallow more and more the blood became,
So that at last it but imbrued the feet;
And there our passage lay athwart the foss.

" As ever on this side the boiling wave
Thou seest diminishing," the Centaur said,
" So on the other, be thou well assured,
It lower still and lower sinks its bed,
Till in that part it re-uniting join,
Where 'tis the lot of tyranny to mourn.
There Heaven's stern justice lays chastising hand
On Attila, who was the scourge of earth,
On Sextus and on Pyrrhus, and extracts
Tears ever by the seething flood unlock'd
From the Rinieri, of Corneto this,
Pazzo the other named, who fill'd the ways
With violence and war." [2] This said, he turn'd,
And quitting us, alone repass'd the ford.

any case, a typical Guelf and a typical Ghibelline tyrant are here
condemned side by side.

[1] Guy de Montfort, in 1271, murdered his cousin Henry, son of
Richard, Earl of Cornwall, and nephew to King Henry III. of
England, in the church of San Silvestro at Viterbo. His intention
was to avenge his father, Simon de Montfort, Earl of Leicester,
who had fallen at the battle of Evesham in 1265. The heart
of the murdered prince was brought to London in a gold casket.

[2] Attila, the famous King of the Huns, known as " the scourge
of God " (d. A.D. 453); Sextus Pompeius (d. B.C. 35), son of
Pompey the Great, who ravaged the coasts of Italy with a pirate
fleet. It is doubtful whether Pyrrhus, the son of Achilles (of
whose cruelty at Troy Dante had read in the Æneid), or Pyrrhus,
King of Epirus (d. B.C. 272), is the person indicated. Rinier da
Corneto and Rinier Pazzo were famous chiefs of highwaymen
in Dante's youth.

CANTO XIII

ARGUMENT

Still in the seventh circle, Dante enters its second compartment,
which contains both those who have done violence on their
own persons and those who have violently consumed their
goods ; the first changed into rough and knotted trees whereon the harpies build their nests, the latter chased and torn
by black female mastiffs. Among the former, Piero delle
Vigne is one who tells him the cause of his having committed
suicide, and moreover in what manner the souls are transformed into those trunks. Of the latter crew, he recognises
Lano, a Sienese, and Giacomo, a Paduan : and lastly, a
Florentine, who had hung himself from his own roof, speaks
to him of the calamities of his countrymen.

ERE Nessus yet had reach'd the other bank,
We enter'd on a forest, where no track
Of steps had worn a way.　　Not verdant there
The foliage, but of dusky hue; not light
The boughs and tapering, but with knares deform'd
And matted thick : fruits there were none, but thorns
Instead, with venom fill'd.　Less sharp than these,
Less intricate the brakes, wherein abide
Those animals, that hate the cultured fields,
Betwixt Corneto and Cecina's stream.[1]

　　Here the brute Harpies make their nest, the same
Who from the Strophades the Trojan band
Drove with dire boding of their future woe.[2]
Broad are their pennons, of the human form
Their neck and countenance, arm'd with talons keen
The feet, and the huge belly fledged with wings.
These sit and wail on the drear mystic wood.

　　The kind instructor in these words began :
" Ere farther thou proceed, know thou art now
I' th' second round, and shalt be, till thou come
Upon the horrid sand : look therefore well
Around thee, and such things thou shalt behold,

---

[1] The district known as the Tuscan Maremma.
[2] Virgil (*Æneid,* iii. 192–267) describes how Æneas and his
companions were driven from the Strophades, islands in the
Ionian Sea, by the Harpies, who polluted their banquet. Celæno,
the chief of these monsters, foretold that the Trojans would be
reduced by starvation to eat their own tables. They, and the
black mastiffs further on, are here to be taken as symbols of
remorse.

As would my speech discredit."   On all sides
I heard sad plainings breathe, and none could see
From whom they might have issued.   In amaze
Fast bound I stood.   He, as it seem'd, believed
That I had thought so many voices came
From some amid those thickets close conceal'd,
And thus his speech resumed : " If thou lop off
A single twig from one of those ill plants,
The thought thou hast conceived shall vanish quite."
    Thereat a little stretching forth my hand,
From a great wilding gather'd I a branch,
And straight the trunk exclaim'd : " Why pluck'st thou
      me ?"
Then, as the dark blood trickled down its side,
These words it added : " Wherefore tear'st me thus?
Is there no touch of mercy in thy breast?
Men once were we, that now are rooted here.
Thy hand might well have spared us, had we been
The souls of serpents."   As a brand yet green,
That burning at one end from the other sends
A groaning sound, and hisses with the wind
That forces out its way, so burst at once
Forth from the broken splinter words and blood.
    I, letting fall the bough, remain'd as one
Assail'd by terror ; and the sage replied :
" If he, O injured spirit ! could have believed
What he hath seen but in my verse described,[1]
He never against thee had stretch'd his hand.
But I, because the thing surpass'd belief,
Prompted him to this deed, which even now
Myself I rue.   But tell him, who thou wast ;
That, for this wrong to do thee some amends,
In the upper world (for thither to return
Is granted him) thy fame he may revive."
" That pleasant word of thine," the trunk replied,
" Hath so inveigled me, that I from speech
Cannot refrain, wherein if I indulge
A little longer, in the snare detain'd,
Count it not grievous.   I it was, who held
Both keys to Frederick's heart, and turn'd the wards,
Opening and shutting, with a skill so sweet,

---

[1] *i.e.* the story of Polydorus at the beginning of the third book
of the *Æneid*, from which this episode is manifestly copied.

That besides me, into his inmost breast
Scarce any other could admittance find.[1]
The faith I bore to my high charge was such,
It cost me the life-blood that warm'd my veins.
The harlot,[2] who ne'er turn'd her gloating eyes
From Cæsar's household, common vice and pest
Of courts, 'gainst me inflamed the minds of all;
And to Augustus they so spread the flame,
That my glad honours changed to bitter woes.
My soul, disdainful and disgusted, sought
Refuge in death from scorn, and I became,
Just as I was, unjust toward myself.
By the new roots, which fix this stem, I swear,
That never faith I broke to my liege lord,
Who merited such honour; and of you,
If any to the world indeed return,
Clear he from wrong my memory, that lies
Yet prostrate under envy's cruel blow."

   First somewhat pausing, till the mournful words
Were ended, then to me the bard began:
"Lose not the time; but speak, and of him ask,
If more thou wish to learn." Whence I replied:
"Question thou him again of whatsoe'er
Will, as thou think'st, content me; for no power
Have I to ask, such pity is at my heart."

   He thus resumed: "So may he do for thee
Freely what thou entreatest, as thou yet
Be pleased, imprison'd spirit! to declare,
How in these gnarled joints the soul is tied;
And whether any ever from such frame
Be loosen'd, if thou canst, that also tell."

   Thereat the trunk breathed hard, and the wind soon
Changed into sounds articulate like these:
"Briefly ye shall be answer'd. When departs
The fierce soul from the body, by itself

---

   [1] This is Piero delle Vigne of Capua, a man of humble birth,
who ultimately became the chief minister and most trusted adviser
of the Emperor Frederick II. He was also a poet, and is said
to have composed the first Italian sonnet. After serving the
Emperor with the utmost fidelity, he was falsely accused of treason
and condemned to lose his eyes; after which, in 1249, he committed
suicide in prison. One of his descendants was the famous Friar
Raymund, the confessor of St. Catherine of Siena and master-
general of the Dominicans at the end of the fourteenth century.
   [2] Envy.

Thence torn asunder, to the seventh gulf
By Minos doom'd, into the wood it falls,
No place assign'd, but wheresoever chance
Hurls it; there sprouting, as a grain of spelt,
It rises to a sapling, growing thence
A savage plant.   The Harpies, on its leaves
Then feeding, cause both pain, and for the pain
A vent to grief.   We, as the rest, shall come
For our own spoils, yet not so that with them
We may again be clad; for what a man
Takes from himself it is not just he have.
Here we perforce shall drag them; and throughout
The dismal glade our bodies shall be hung,
Each on the wild thorn of his wretched shade." [1]
      Attentive yet to listen to the trunk
We stood, expecting further speech, when us
A noise surprised; as when a man perceives
The wild boar and the hunt approach his place
Of station'd watch, who of the beasts and boughs
Loud rustling round him hears.   And lo! there came
Two naked,[2] torn with briers, in headlong flight,
That they before them broke each fan o' th' wood.
" Haste now," the foremost cried, " now haste thee,
death!"
The other, as seem'd, impatient of delay,
Exclaiming, " Lano! not so bent for speed
Thy sinews, in the lists of Toppo's field."
And then, for that perchance no longer breath
Sufficed him, of himself and of a bush
One group he made.   Behind them was the wood
Full of black female mastiffs, gaunt and fleet,
As greyhounds that have newly slipt the leash.
On him, who squatted down, they stuck their fangs,
And having rent him piecemeal bore away

---

[1] These lines concerning the fate of the suicides roused some
controversy, shortly after Dante's death, and were regarded as
heretical as being contrary to the doctrine of the resurrection of
the body.

[2] Lano Maconi, a nobleman of Siena, having squandered all
his patrimony, let himself be killed at the battle of Pieve del
Toppo, where the Sienese were defeated by the Aretines in 1288.
Cf. below, Canto xxix. Jacomo da Sant' Andrea was a wealthy
Paduan noble, who ran through a great fortune in the most insane
pranks.   He is said to have been one of the victims of Ezzelino's
tyranny.

The tortured limbs.   My guide then seized my hand,
And led me to the thicket, which in vain
Mourn'd through its bleeding wounds : " O Giacomo
Of Sant' Andrea ! what avails it thee,"
It cried, " that of me thou hast made thy screen?
For thy ill life, what blame on me recoils?"
     When o'er it he had paused, my master spake :
" Say who wast thou,[1] that at so many points
Breathest out with blood thy lamentable speech?"
     He answer'd : " O ye spirits ! arrived in time
To spy the shameful havoc that from me
My leaves hath sever'd thus, gather them up,
And at the foot of their sad parent-tree
Carefully lay them.   In that city I dwelt,
Who for the Baptist her first patron changed,
Whence he for this shall cease not with his art
To work her woe : and if there still remain'd not
On Arno's passage some faint glimpse of him,
Those citizens, who rear'd once more her walls
Upon the ashes left by Attila,
Had labour'd without profit of their toil.[2]
I slung the fatal noose from my own roof."

[1] This unnamed Florentine suicide is probably either Lotto
degli Agli, a judge who hanged himself after giving a false
sentence for money, or Rocco de' Mozzi, who ended his life in
the same way when bankrupt.

[2] According to tradition, Mars was the patron of the Florentines
in pagan days, and his temple, with a highly venerated statue,
stood on the site of the present Baptistery.   On the advent of
Christianity, Florence took the Baptist for her patron instead,
and the statue was removed from the temple and set upon a
tower by the side of the Arno, the citizens believing that, unless
it were duly reverenced, great misfortunes would fall upon the
State.   The perpetual factions that kept the city divided were
ascribed to its influence (cf. *Par.* xvi.).   When, according to the
legend, Florence was destroyed by the Goths (Dante confuses
Attila with Totila, who sent a force to attack the city, but was
repulsed), the statue fell into the Arno, where it remained all the
time that the city lay in ruins.   It was held that Florence could
not be rebuilt until this image was found again, and accordingly
it was drawn out of the Arno and set upon a pillar at the head
of the Ponte Vecchio, when the city was restored (according to
legend) by Charlemagne.   Thus it became " that maimed stone
which guards the bridge " (*Par.* xvi.), and remained in that
position until the great flood of 1333 carried away bridge and
statue alike.

CANTO XIV

ARGUMENT

They arrive at the beginning of the third of those compartments
into which this seventh circle is divided. It is a plain of dry
and hot sand, where three kinds of violence are punished;
namely, against God, against Nature, and against Art; and
those who have thus sinned, are tormented by flakes of fire,
which are eternally showering down upon them. Among the
violent against God is found Capaneus, whose blasphemies
they hear. Next, turning to the left along the forest of self-
slayers, and having journeyed a little onwards, they meet
with a streamlet of blood that issues from the forest and
traverses the sandy plain. Here Virgil speaks to our Poet
of a huge ancient statue that stands within Mount Ida in
Crete, from a fissure in which statue there is a dripping of
tears, from which the said streamlet, together with the three
other infernal rivers, is formed.

SOON as the charity of native land
Wrought in my bosom, I the scatter'd leaves
Collected, and to him restored, who now
Was hoarse with utterance. To the limit thence
We came, which from the third the second round
Divides, and where of justice is display'd
Contrivance horrible. Things then first seen
Clearlier to manifest, I tell how next
A plain we reach'd, that from its sterile bed
Each plant repell'd. The mournful wood waves round
Its garland on all sides, as round the wood
Spreads the sad foss. There, on the very edge
Our steps we stay'd. It was an area wide
Of arid sand and thick, resembling most
The soil that erst by Cato's foot [1] was trod.

    Vengeance of Heaven! Oh! how shouldst thou be
      fear'd
By all, who read what here mine eyes beheld.

    Of naked spirits many a flock I saw,
All weeping piteously, to different laws
Subjected; for on the earth some lay supine,
Some crouching close were seated, others paced
Incessantly around; the latter tribe
More numerous, those fewer who beneath
The torment lay, but louder in their grief.

[1] Cato of Utica, who marched through the Libyan desert in
B.C. 47, as described by Lucan in Bk. ix. of the *Pharsalia*.

O'er all the sand fell slowly wafting down
Dilated flakes of fire, as flakes of snow
On Alpine summit, when the wind is hush'd.
As, in the torrid Indian clime, the son
Of Ammon [1] saw, upon his warrior band
Descending, solid flames, that to the ground
Came down; whence he bethought him with his troop
To trample on the soil; for easier thus
The vapour was extinguish'd, while alone:
So fell the eternal fiery flood, wherewith
The marle glow'd underneath, as under *steel*
The *tinder*, doubly to augment the pain.
Unceasing was the play of wretched hands,
Now this, now that way glancing, to shake off
The heat, still falling fresh.   I thus began:
" Instructor! thou who all things overcomest,
Except the hardy demons that rush'd forth
To stop our entrance at the gate, say who
Is yon huge spirit, that, as seems, heeds not
The burning, but lies writhen in proud scorn,
As by the sultry tempest immatured?"
   Straight he himself, who was aware I ask'd
My guide of him, exclaim'd: " Such as I was
When living, dead such now I am.   If Jove
Weary his workman out, from whom in ire
He snatch'd the lightnings, that at my last day
Transfix'd me; if the rest he weary out,
At their black smithy labouring by turns,
In Mongibello, [2] while he cries aloud,
' Help, help, good Mulciber!' as erst he cried
In the Phlegræan warfare; [3] and the bolts

---

[1] Dante has simply *Alessandro*, " Alexander." Dr. Oelsner
notes: " These details are taken from an apocryphal letter, very
popular in the Middle Ages, in which Alexander is supposed to
send an account of the marvels of India to Aristotle. The
original narrative says that the soldiers trampled on the snow,
and that they warded off the flames, which subsequently descended
from the sky, by means of their garments. The discrepancy we
note in Dante occurs already in a version of the episode given by
Albertus Magnus in his *De Meteoris*, which must, accordingly,
have been Dante's immediate source."
[2] Mount Ætna, within which Vulcan (Mulciber) and the Cyclopes
forged Jove's thunderbolts.
[3] Phlegra, variously localised, is the scene of the struggle
between the gods and the giants.

Launch he, full aim'd at me, with all his might;
He never should enjoy a sweet revenge."
    Then thus my guide, in accent higher raised
Than I before had heard him : " Capaneus !
Thou art more punish'd, in that this thy pride
Lives yet unquench'd : no torment, save thy rage,
Were to thy fury pain proportion'd full."
    Next turning round to me, with milder lip
He spake : " This of the seven kings was one,[1]
Who girt the Theban walls with siege, and held,
As still he seems to hold, God in disdain,
And sets His high omnipotence at nought.
But, as I told him, his despiteful mood
Is ornament well suits the breast that wears it.
Follow me now ; and look thou set not yet
Thy foot in the hot sand, but to the wood
Keep ever close."   Silently on we pass'd
To where there gushes from the forest's bound
A little brook, whose crimson'd wave yet lifts
My hair with horror.   As the rill, that runs
From Bulicame,[2] to be portion'd out
Among the sinful women ; so ran this
Down through the sand ; its bottom and each bank
Stone-built, and either margin at its side,
Whereon I straight perceived our passage lay.
    " Of all that I have shown thee, since that gate
We enter'd first, whose threshold is to none
Denied, nought else so worthy of regard,
As is this river, has thine eye discern'd,
O'er which the flaming volley all is quench'd."
    So spake my guide ; and I him thence besought,
That having given me appetite to know,
The food he too would give, that hunger craved.
    " In midst of ocean," forthwith he began,
" A desolate country lies, which Crete is named ;
Under whose monarch,[3] in old times, the world
Lived pure and chaste.   A mountain rises there,

---

[1] Capaneus was one of the " seven against Thebes," and boasted
that all the wrath of Jupiter should not protect the city from him ;
for which he was struck by lightning as he scaled the wall.   He
is taken here as the typical blasphemer.
[2] *Il Bulicame* is a warm sulphurous spring, still in use and
frequented, about two miles outside the Porta Faul of Viterbo.
[3] Saturn, under whose sway the world enjoyed the Golden Age.

Call'd Ida, joyous once with leaves and streams,
Deserted now like a forbidden thing.
It was the spot which Rhea, Saturn's spouse,
Chose for the secret cradle of her son;[1]
And better to conceal him, drown'd in shouts
His infant cries.   Within the mount, upright
An ancient form[2] there stands, and huge, that turns
His shoulders towards Damiata; and at Rome,
As in his mirror, looks.   Of finest gold
His head is shaped, pure silver are the breast
And arms, thence to the middle is of brass,
And downward all beneath well-tempered steel,
Save the right foot of potter's clay, on which
Than on the other more erect he stands.
Each part, except the gold, is rent throughout;
And from the fissure tears distil, which join'd
Penetrate to that cave.   They in their course,
Thus far precipitated down the rock,
From Acheron, and Styx, and Phlegethon;
Then by this straiten'd channel passing hence
Beneath, e'en to the lowest depth of all,
Form there Cocytus, of whose lake (thyself
Shalt see it) I here give thee no account."[3]

   Then I to him : " If from our world this sluice
Be thus derived; wherefore to us but now
Appears it at this edge?"   He straight replied :
"The place, thou know'st, is round; and though great
      part

----

[1] Jupiter.

[2] *Un gran veglio*, "a great old man." This image, which
is a combination of Daniel's vision (ii. 31–35) with Ovid's description of the four ages (*Metam.* i.), symbolises the history of the
human race. It has its back to Egypt, as representing the civilisation and monarchies of the past, and looks towards Rome,
which stands for the modern world of thought and action under
the Empire. The four metals represent the Golden, Silver, Bronze,
and Iron Ages. The feet are probably the secular and spiritual
authority, respectively. " Dante differs from Daniel in making
the brass terminate with the trunk, in order no doubt to emphasise his theory of the dual organisation of Church and Empire ;
the right leg with the foot of baked earth, on which the image
rests most, being the symbol of the ecclesiastical power, corrupted
and weakened by the acquisition of the temporal power from
Constantine, but at the same time that to which mankind chiefly
looked for support and guidance " (Toynbee).

[3] The infernal rivers are produced by the tears and sins of all
human generations since the Golden Age, and flow from rock to
rock down the circles of Hell, back to Lucifer at the earth's core.

Thou have already past, still to the left
Descending to the nethermost, not yet
Hast thou the circuit made of the whole orb.
Wherefore, if aught of new to us appear,
It needs not bring up wonder in thy looks."

    Then I again inquired : " Where flow the streams
Of Phlegethon and Lethe? for of one
Thou tell'st not ; and the other, of that shower,
Thou say'st, is form'd." He answer thus return'd :
" Doubtless thy questions all well pleased I hear.
Yet the red seething wave might have resolved
One thou proposest. Lethe thou shalt see,
But not within this hollow, in the place
Whither, to lave themselves, the spirits go,
Whose blame hath been by penitence removed." [1]
He added : " Time is now we quit the wood.
Look thou my steps pursue : the margins give
Safe passage, unimpeded by the flames ;
For over them all vapour is extinct.'

CANTO XV

ARGUMENT

Taking their way upon one of the mounds by which the streamlet, spoken of in the last Canto, was embanked, and having
gone so far that they could no longer have discerned the
forest if they had turned round to look for it, they meet a
troop of spirits that come along the sand by the side of the
pier. These are they who have done violence to Nature ; and
amongst them Dante distinguishes Brunetto Latini, who had
been formerly his master ; with whom, turning a little backward, he holds a discourse which occupies the remainder of
this Canto.

ONE of the solid margins bears us now
Envelop'd in the mist, that, from the stream
Arising, hovers o'er, and saves from fire
Both piers and water. As the Flemings rear
Their mound, 'twixt Ghent and Bruges, to chase back
The ocean, fearing his tumultuous tide
That drives toward them ; or the Paduans theirs
Along the Brenta, to defend their towns

---

[1] This red stream is Phlegethon, but Lethe, which takes away
the memory of sin, he will not see until he has passed through
Purgatory.

And castles, ere the genial warmth be felt
On Chiarentana's [1] top; such were the mounds,
So framed, though not in height or bulk to these
Made equal, by the master, whosoe'er
He was, that raised them here.   We from the wood
Were now so far removed, that turning round
I might not have discern'd it, when we met
A troop of spirits, who came beside the pier.

   They each one eyed us, as at eventide
One eyes another under a new moon;
And toward us sharpen'd their sight, as keen
As an old tailor at his needle's eye.

   Thus narrowly explored by all the tribe,
I was agnized of one, who by the skirt
Caught me, and cried, " What wonder have we here?"

   And I, when he to me outstretch'd his arm,
Intently fix'd my ken on his parch'd looks,
That, although smirch'd with fire, they hinder'd not
But I remember'd him; and towards his face
My hand inclining, answer'd: " Ser Brunetto! [2]
And are ye here?"   He thus to me: " My son!
Oh let it not displease thee, if Brunetto
Latini but a little space with thee
Turn back, and leave his fellows to proceed."

   I thus to him replied: " Much as I can,
I thereto pray thee; and if thou be willing

---

[1] Cary has mistranslated this line, *anzi che Chiarentana il caldo
senta*, which simply means " Before Chiarentana feels the heat."
Chiarentana is the duchy of Carinthia, which included the Val
Sugana where the Brenta rises.   The melting of the snows of
its mountains cause the river to overflow and flood the Paduan
country.

[2] Brunetto Latini, philosopher and politician, was born at
Florence about 1210, and died in 1294.   An ardent Guelf, he took
an active part in Florentine politics, and was influential in the
counsels of the Republic.   He introduced the art of oratory and
the systematic study of political science into Florentine public
life.   His chief works are *Li Livres dou Trésor*, a kind of encyclopedia written in French prose, which " treats of all things that
pertain to mortals," and the *Tesoretto*, an allegorical didactic
poem in Italian, which opens (like the *Divina Commedia*) with
the poet finding himself astray in a wood.   It is noticeable that
in the *Tesoretto* he speaks strongly against the sin for which
he is here condemned to Hell.   Dante doubtless was profoundly
influenced by him in his early life (as this Canto amply shows), but
there is no foundation for the story that Brunetto had been actually
his master.

That I here seat me with thee, I consent;
His leave, with whom I journey, first obtain'd."
    " O son!" said he, " whoever of this throng
One instant stops, lies then a hundred years,
No fan to ventilate him, when the fire
Smites sorest. Pass thou therefore on. I close
Will at thy garments walk, and then rejoin
My troop, who go mourning their endless doom."
    I dared not from the path descend to tread
On equal ground with him, but held my head
Bent down, as one who walks in reverent guise.
    " What chance or destiny," thus he began,
" Ere the last day, conducts thee here below?
And who is this that shows to thee the way?"
    " There up aloft," I answer'd, " in the life
Serene, I wander'd in a valley lost,
Before mine age had to its fulness reach'd.
But yester-morn I left it: then once more
Into that vale returning, him I met;
And by this path homeward he leads me back."
    " If thou," he answer'd, " follow but thy star,
Thou canst not miss at last a glorious haven;
Unless in fairer days my judgment err'd.
And if my fate so early had not chanced,
Seeing the Heavens thus bounteous to thee, I
Had gladly given thee comfort in thy work.
But that ungrateful and malignant race,
Who in old times came down from Fesole,[1]
Ay and still smack of their rough mountain-flint,
Will for thy good deeds show thee enmity.
Nor wonder; for amongst ill-savour'd crabs
It suits not the sweet fig-tree lay her fruit.
Old fame reports them in the world for blind,
Covetous, envious, proud. Look to it well:
Take heed thou cleanse thee of their ways. For thee,
Thy fortune hath such honour in reserve,

---

[1] According to Florentine tradition, the city of Florence was
founded by Cæsar after the destruction of Fiesole, and peopled partly
by Romans, partly by the Fiesolans—whence came the perpetual
factions. " It is not to be wondered," writes Villani, " that the
Florentines are always at war and strife among themselves, being
born and descended from two peoples so contrary and hostile and
different in habits, as were the noble Romans in their virtue and
the rude Fiesolans fierce in war."

That thou by either party [1] shalt be craved
With hunger keen : but be the fresh herb far
From the goat's tooth. The herd of Fesole
May of themselves make litter, not touch the plant,
If any such yet spring on their rank bed,
In which the holy seed revives, transmitted
From those true Romans, who still there remain'd,
When it was made the nest of so much ill."

"Were all my wish fulfill'd," I straight replied,
"Thou from the confines of man's nature yet
Hadst not been driven forth ; for in my mind
Is fix'd, and now strikes full upon my heart,
The dear, benign, paternal image, such
As thine was, when so lately thou didst teach me
The way for man to win eternity :
And how I prized the lesson, it behoves,
That, long as life endures, my tongue should speak.
What of my fate thou tell'st, that write I down ;
And, with another text [2] to comment on,
For her I keep it, the celestial dame,
Who will know all, if I to her arrive.
This only would I have thee clearly note :
That, so my conscience have no plea against me,
Do Fortune as she list, I stand prepared.
Not new or strange such earnest to mine ear.
Speed Fortune then her wheel, as likes her best ;
The clown his mattock ; all things have their course."

Thereat my sapient guide upon his right
Turn'd himself back, then look'd at me, and spake :
"He listens to good purpose who takes note."

I not the less still on my way proceed,
Discoursing with Brunetto, and inquire
Who are most known and chief among his tribe.

"To know of some is well ;" he thus replied,
"But of the rest silence may best beseem.
Time would not serve us for report so long.
In brief I tell thee, that all these were clerks,
Men of great learning and no less renown,
By one same sin polluted in the world.

[1] Both the Neri and the Bianchi. Dante does not mean to
identify one party with the Romans and the other with the
Fiesolans ; both alike smack of "the herd of Fiesole," and it is
for the holy seed of the true Romans to keep clear of both factions.

[2] What Farinata had said to him.

With them is Priscian;[1] and Accorso's son,
Francesco,[2] herds among that wretched throng:
And, if the wish of so impure a blotch
Possess'd thee, him thou also mightst have seen,
Who by the servants' Servant was transferr'd
From Arno's seat to Bacchiglione, where
His ill-strain'd nerves he left.[3] I more would add,
But must from further speech and onward way
Alike desist; for yonder I behold
A mist new-risen on the sandy plain.
A company, with whom I may not sort,
Approaches. I commend my *Treasure* to thee,[4]
Wherein I yet survive; my sole request.''

   This said, he turn'd, and seem'd as one of those
Who o'er Verona's champain try their speed
For the green mantle;[5] and of them he seem'd,
Not he who loses but who gains the prize.

CANTO XVI

ARGUMENT

Journeying along the pier, which crosses the sand, they are now
   so near the end of it as to hear the noise of the stream
   falling into the eighth circle, when they meet the spirits of
   three military men; who judging Dante, from his dress, to
   be a countryman of theirs, entreat him to stop. He complies,
   and speaks with them. The two Poets then reach the place
   where the water descends, being the termination of this third
   compartment in the seventh circle; and here Virgil having
   thrown down into the hollow a cord, wherewith Dante was
   girt, they behold at that signal a monstrous and horrible
   figure come swimming up to them.

Now came I where the water's din was heard,
As down it fell into the other round,

   [1] A famous Latin grammarian of the beginning of the sixth
century A.D.
   [2] Francesco d'Accorso (1225–1293), a famous lawyer and professor of Bologna. His father, Accorso da Bagnolo, a Florentine
by birth, who died at Bologna in 1260, was equally renowned as
a jurist.
   [3] Andrea de' Mozzi, made Bishop of Florence (on the Arno)
in 1287, was in 1295 transferred by Boniface VIII. (*servus servorum*
is one of the papal titles) to the see of Vicenza (on the Bacchiglione), where he died in the following year.
   [4] His *Livres dou Trésor*.
   [5] A green mantle, or *palio*, was the prize given at the annual
foot-race at Verona.

Resounding like the hum of swarming bees :
When forth together issued from a troop,
That pass'd beneath the fierce tormenting storm,
Three spirits, running swift.   They towards us came,
And each one cried aloud, "Oh! do thou stay,
Whom, by the fashion of thy garb, we deem
To be some inmate of our evil land."

Ah me! what wounds I mark'd upon their limbs,
Recent and old, inflicted by the flames.
E'en the remembrance of them grieves me yet.

Attentive to their cry, my teacher paused,
And turn'd to me his visage, and then spake :
"Wait now : our courtesy these merit well :
And were 't not for the nature of the place,
Whence glide the fiery darts, I should have said,
That haste had better suited thee than them."

They, when we stopp'd, resumed their ancient wail,
And, soon as they had reach'd us, all the three
Whirl'd round together in one restless wheel.
As naked champions, smear'd with slippery oil,
Are wont, intent, to watch their place of hold
And vantage, ere in closer strife they meet ;
Thus each one, as he wheel'd, his countenance
At me directed, so that opposite
The neck moved ever to the twinkling feet.

"If woe of this unsound and dreary waste,"
Thus one began, "added to our sad cheer
Thus peel'd with flame, do call forth scorn on us
And our entreaties, let our great renown
Incline thee to inform us who thou art,
That dost imprint, with living feet unharm'd,
The soil of Hell.   He, in whose track thou seest
My steps pursuing, naked though he be
And reft of all, was of more high estate
Than thou believest; grandchild of the chaste
Gualdrada, him they Guidoguerra call'd,
Who in his lifetime many a noble act
Achieved, both by his wisdom and his sword.[1]

1 Gualdrada de' Ravignani, the beautiful and virtuous daughter
of Bellincion Berti (see *Par.* xv. and xvi.), was the ancestress of the
Conti Guidi, the great feudal nobles of the Casentino. This particular Guido Guerra (the name was borne by several members
of his family) was the son of Gualdrada's fourth son, Count
Marcovaldo of Dovadola. Alike in war and in peace, he was a

The other, next to me that beats the sand,
Is Aldobrandi,[1] name deserving well,
In the upper world, of honour; and myself,
Who in this torment do partake with them,
Am Rusticucci,[2] whom, past doubt, my wife,
Of savage temper, more than aught beside
Hath to this evil brought." If from the fire
I had been shelter'd, down amidst them straight
I then had cast me; nor my guide, I deem,
Would have restrain'd my going: but that fear
Of the dire burning vanquish'd the desire,
Which made me eager of their wish'd embrace.

  I then began: " Not scorn, but grief much more,
Such as long time alone can cure, your doom
Fix'd deep within me, soon as this my lord
Spake words, whose tenor taught me to expect
That such a race, as ye are, was at hand.
I am a countryman of yours, who still
Affectionate have utter'd, and have heard
Your deeds and names renown'd.   Leaving the gall,
For the sweet fruit I go, that a sure guide
Hath promised to me.   But behoves that far
As to the centre first I downward tend."

  " So may long space thy spirit guide thy limbs,"
He answer straight return'd; " and so thy fame
Shine bright when thou art gone, as thou shalt tell,
If courtesy and valour, as they wont,
Dwell in our city, or have vanish'd clean:
For one amidst us late condemn'd to wail,
Borsiere,[3] yonder walking with his peers,

leading spirit among the Guelfs of Tuscany from 1250 until his
death in 1272, and played a distinguished part at the battle of
Benevento. Zingarelli has recently shown that he is probably
the person to whom Brunetto Latini dedicated his *Tesoretto*.

  [1] Tegghiaio Aldobrandi, a noble Florentine Guelf, who, together with Guido Guerra, vainly attempted to dissuade his
countrymen from the disastrous enterprise that ended in the defeat
of Montaperti.   He bore himself with much valour at the battle,
and was among the Guelfs who took refuge at Lucca (1260).

  [2] Jacopo Rusticucci, a Florentine burgher of some political
importance among the Guelfs, was driven into immoral practices
by an unhappy marriage.   He was living in 1254.

  [3] Guglielmo Borsiere appears to have been a retired purse-
maker of Florence, who managed to get into aristocratic society.
There is a story about him in the *Decameron* (i. 8).   He seems
to have lived at a somewhat later epoch than his associates in this
Canto, and, as here indicated, died shortly before 1300.

Grieves us no little by the news he brings."
    "An upstart multitude and sudden gains,
Pride and excess, O Florence! have in thee
Engender'd, so that now in tears thou mourn'st!"
    Thus cried I, with my face upraised, and they
All three, who for an answer took my words,
Look'd at each other, as men look when truth
Comes to their ear.   "If at so little cost,"
They all at once rejoin'd, "thou satisfy
Others who question thee, O happy thou!
Gifted with words so apt to speak thy thought.
Wherefore, if thou escape this darksome clime,
Returning to behold the radiant stars,
When thou with pleasure shalt retrace the past,
See that of us thou speak among mankind."
    This said, they broke the circle, and so swift
Fled, that as pinions seem'd their nimble feet.
    Not in so short a time might one have said
"Amen," as they had vanish'd.   Straight my guide
Pursued his track.   I follow'd: and small space
Had we past onward, when the water's sound
Was now so near at hand, that we had scarce
Heard one another's speech for the loud din.
    E'en as the river, that first holds its course
Unmingled, from the Mount of Vesulo,
On the left side of Apennine, toward
The east, which Acquacheta higher up
They call, ere it descend into the vale,
At Forlì, by that name no longer known,[1]
Rebellows o'er Saint Benedict, roll'd on
From the Alpine summit down a precipice,
Where space enough to lodge a thousand spreads;[2]

[1] The Acquacheta, a small river rising in the Apennines above
the monastery of San Benedetto, takes the name of the Montone
at Forlì, whence it flows into the Adriatic.   At the time in which
Dante wrote, it was the first river that, rising between the source
of the Po (Monte Viso, "the Mount of Vesulo," in Piedmont)
and the Apennines, "holds its course unmingled" (more literally,
"has a path of its own"), that is, does not join the Po before
flowing into the sea.

[2] "Either because the abbey was capable of containing more
than those who occupied it, or because (says Landino) the lords
of that territory (the Conti Guidi), as Boccaccio related on the
authority of the abbot, had intended to build a castle near the
waterfall, and to collect within its walls the population of the
neighbouring villages" (Cary).

Thus downward from a craggy steep we found
That this dark wave resounded, roaring loud,
So that the ear its clamour soon had stunn'd.

   I had a cord that braced my girdle round,
Wherewith I erst had thought fast bound to take
The painted leopard.[1]   This when I had all
Unloosen'd from me (so my master bade)
I gather'd up, and stretch'd it forth to him.
Then to the right he turn'd, and from the brink
Standing few paces distant, cast it down
Into the deep abyss.   " And somewhat strange,"
Thus to myself I spake, " signal so strange
Betokens, which my guide with earnest eye
Thus follows."   Ah ! what caution must men use
With those who look not at the deed alone,
But spy into the thoughts with subtle skill.

   " Quickly shall come," he said, " what I expect ;
Thine eye discover quickly that, whereof
Thy thought is dreaming."   Ever to that truth,
Which but the semblance of a falsehood wears,
A man, if possible, should bar his lip ;
Since, although blameless, he incurs reproach.
But silence here were vain ; and by these notes,
Which now I sing, reader, I swear to thee,
So may they favour find to latest times !
That through the gross and murky air I spied
A shape come swimming up, that might have quell'd
The stoutest heart with wonder ; in such guise
As one returns, who hath been down to loose
An anchor grappled fast against some rock,
Or to aught else that in the salt wave lies,
Who, upward springing, close draws in his feet.

---

[1] *Cf.* Isaiah xi. 5. The cord is frequently taken as the well-
known symbol of the Franciscan order, to which Dante is said to
have been associated as a tertiary. " It is thrown down the gulf
to allure Geryon to them with the expectation of carrying down
one who had cloaked his iniquities under the garb of penitence
and self-mortification " (Cary). This interpretation is open to
question, and it may be noted that the wearing of a cord of this
kind, " to take the painted leopard," that is, as an incentive to
purity of heart and body, was not peculiar to the Franciscans.
Whether the Franciscan cord or another, the casting it aside may
simply mean that, after the fearful examples he has just seen, the
Poet no longer needs any such material warning or guard against
temptations of lust.

CANTO XVII

ARGUMENT

The monster Geryon is described; to whom while Virgil is speaking in order that he may carry them both down to the next
circle, Dante, by permission, goes a little further along the
edge of the void, to descry the third species of sinners contained in this compartment, namely, those who have done
violence to Art; and then returning to his master, they both
descend, seated on the back of Geryon.

" Lo ! the fell monster [1] with the deadly sting,
Who passes mountains, breaks through fenced walls
And firm embattled spears, and with his filth
Taints all the world." Thus me my guide address'd,
And beckon'd him, that he should come to shore,
Near to the stony causeway's utmost edge.
	Forthwith that image vile of Fraud appear'd,
His head and upper part exposed on land,
But laid not on the shore his bestial train.
His face the semblance of a just man's wore,
So kind and gracious was its outward cheer;
The rest was serpent all : two shaggy claws
Reach'd to the arm-pits; and the back and breast,
And either side, were painted o'er with nodes
And orbits. Colours variegated more
Nor Turks nor Tartars e'er on cloth of state
With interchangeable embroidery wove,
Nor spread Arachne o'er her curious loom.
As oft-times a light skiff, moor'd to the shore,
Stands part in water, part upon the land;
Or, as where dwells the greedy German boor,
The beaver settles, watching for his prey;
So on the rim, that fenced the sand with rock,
Sat perch'd the fiend of evil. In the void
Glancing, his tail upturn'd its venomous fork,
With sting like scorpion's arm'd. Then thus my guide :
" Now need our way must turn few steps apart,
Far as to that ill beast, who couches there."

1 Geryon, type of fraud or malice, as the Minotaur had been of
violence and bestiality, is here compounded of the mythological
monster killed by Hercules and the angel of the bottomless pit
in the ninth chapter of Revelations. Mediæval writers attributed
to the classical Geryon the practice of treacherously murdering his
guests.

Thereat, toward the right our downward course
We shaped, and, better to escape the flame
And burning marle, ten paces on the verge
Proceeded.   Soon as we to him arrive,
A little farther on mine eye beholds
A tribe of spirits,[1] seated on the sand
Near to the void.   Forthwith my master spake:
" That to the full thy knowledge may extend
Of all this round contains, go now, and mark
The mien these wear: but hold not long discourse.
Till thou returnest, I with him meantime
Will parley, that to us he may vouchsafe
The aid of his strong shoulders."   Thus alone,
Yet forward on the extremity I paced
Of that seventh circle, where the mournful tribe
Were seated.   At the eyes forth gush'd their pangs.
Against the vapours and the torrid soil
Alternately their shifting hands they plied.
Thus use the dogs in summer still to ply
Their jaws and feet by turns, when bitten sore
By gnats, or flies, or gadflies swarming round.

Noting the visages of some, who lay
Beneath the pelting of that dolorous fire,
One of them all I knew not; but perceived
That, pendent from his neck, each bore a pouch
With colours and with emblems various mark'd,
On which it seem'd as if their eye did feed.

And when, amongst them, looking round I came,
A yellow purse I saw with azure wrought,
That wore a lion's countenance and port.[2]
Then, still my sight pursuing its career,
Another I beheld, than blood more red,
A goose display of whiter wing than curd.[3]
And one, who bore a fat and azure swine
Pictured on his white scrip,[4] address'd me thus:

---

[1] The usurers. *Cf.* above, Canto xi. Each is to be identified only by the purse, emblazoned with the armorial bearings that he has degraded by his unlawful gains.   It is noteworthy that Dante's usurers are all Gentiles and nobles.

[2] Lion azure on field or was the arms of the Gianfigliazzi of Florence, who were Black Guelfs.

[3] A goose argent upon field gules was the arms of the Ubbriachi, Florentine Ghibellines.

[4] An azure sow upon an argent field was the arms of the Scrovigni of Padua.   Rinaldo degli Scrovigni is the soul that now

" What dost thou in this deep?   Go now and know,
Since yet thou livest, that my neighbour here
Vitaliano [1] on my left shall sit.
A Paduan with these Florentines am I.
Oft-times they thunder in mine ears, exclaiming,
' Oh ! haste that noble knight, he who the pouch
' With the three goats [2] will bring.' ' " This said, he writhed
The mouth, and loll'd the tongue out, like an ox
That licks his nostrils.   I, lest longer stay
He ill might brook, who bade me stay not long,
Backward my steps from those sad spirits turn'd.

My guide already seated on the haunch
Of the fierce animal I found ; and thus
He me encouraged.   " Be thou stout : be bold.
Down such a steep flight must we now descend.
Mount thou before : for, that no power the tail
May have to harm thee, I will be i' th' midst."

As one, who hath an ague fit so near,
His nails already are turn'd blue, and he
Quivers all o'er, if he but eye the shade ;
Such was my cheer at hearing of his words.
But shame soon interposed her threat,[3] who makes
The servant bold in presence of his lord.

I settled me upon those shoulders huge,
And would have said, but that the words to aid
My purpose came not, " Look thou clasp me firm."

But he whose succour then not first I proved,
Soon as I mounted, in his arms aloft,
Embracing, held me up ; and thus he spake :
" Geryon ! now move thee : be thy wheeling gyres
Of ample circuit, easy thy descent.

addresses Dante. He is said to have been the father of that Enrico
degli Scrovigni who had the Madonna of the Arena built at Padua
(circa 1303), and was painted by Giotto, offering up the model
of the chapel, in the latter's fresco of the Last Judgment.

1 A Paduan usurer still living in 1300 ; it seems doubtful
whether Vitaliano del Dente, as formerly held, or Vitaliano di
Jacopo Vitaliani, as more recently suggested, is the person meant.

2 Cary in a note rightly corrects " goats " to " beaks " (*tre
becchi*). The knight, whose company these shades of usurers
are anticipating in Hell, and who was still living in 1300, is
Giovanni Buiamonte, of the Florentine family of the Bicchi, whose
arms were three eagles' beaks or on field azure.

3 Cary read : *Ma vergogna mi fe le sue minacce*. The right
reading of the line is : *Ma vergogna mi fer le sue minacce ;* " but
his reproofs aroused shame in me."

Think on the unusual burden thou sustain'st."
    As a small vessel, backening out from land,
Her station quits; so thence the monster loosed,
And, when he felt himself at large, turn'd round
There, where the breast had been, his forked tail.
Thus, like an eel, outstretch'd at length he steer'd,
Gathering the air up with retractile claws.
    Not greater was the dread, when Phaëton
The reins let drop at random, whence high heaven,
Whereof signs yet appear, was wrapt in flames;[1]
Nor when ill-fated Icarus perceived,
By liquefaction of the scalded wax,
The trusted pennons loosen'd from his loins,
His sire exclaiming loud, "Ill way thou keep'st;"[2]
Than was my dread, when round me on each part
The air I viewed, and other object none,
Save the fell beast. He, slowly sailing, wheels
His downward motion, unobserved of me,
But that the wind, arising to my face,
Breathes on me from below. Now on our right
I heard the cataract beneath us leap
With hideous crash; whence bending down to explore,
New terror I conceived at the steep plunge;
For flames I saw, and wailings smote mine ear:
So that, all trembling, close I crouch'd my limbs
And then distinguish'd, unperceived before,
By the dread torments that on every side
Drew nearer, how our downward course we wound.
    As falcon, that hath long been on the wing,
But lure nor bird hath seen, while in despair
The falconer cries, "Ah me! thou stoop'st to earth,"
Wearied descends, whence nimbly he arose
In many an airy wheel, and lighting sits

[1] Phaëton, son of Apollo and Clymene, demanded in proof of
his divine parentage to be allowed to drive the chariot of the sun
for one day. The result was that he lost control of the chargers,
scorched a portion of the Heavens (of which the signs were supposed to be still visible in the Milky Way, *Convivio*, ii. 15), and
would have burnt up the earth had not Jupiter struck him dead
with his thunderbolt. Cf. *Par.* xvii.
[2] Dædalus, the typical craftsman of mythology, made wings
for himself and his son Icarus to escape from the labyrinth at
Gnosus, which he himself had originally constructed for the
Minotaur. Icarus flew too near the sun, and, the wax of the wings
melting, fell into the sea and was drowned. Cf. *Par.* viii.

At distance from his lord in angry mood;
So Geryon lighting places us on foot
Low down at base of the deep-furrow'd rock,
And, of his burden there discharged, forthwith
Sprang forward, like an arrow from the string.

CANTO XVIII

Argument

The Poet describes the situation and form of the eighth circle,
divided into ten gulfs, which contain as many different descrip-
tions of fraudulent sinners; but in the present Canto he treats
only of two sorts: the first is of those who, either for their
own pleasure, or for that of another, have seduced any woman
from her duty; and these are scourged of demons in the first
gulf: the other sort is of flatterers, who in the second gulf
are condemned to remain immersed in filth.

THERE is a place within the depths of Hell
Call'd Malebolge, all of rock dark-stain'd
With hue ferruginous, e'en as the steep
That round it circling winds. Right in the midst
Of that abominable region yawns
A spacious gulf profound, whereof the frame
Due time shall tell.[1] The circle, that remains,
Throughout its round, between the gulf and base
Of the high craggy banks, successive forms
Ten bastions, in its hollow bottom raised.

   As where, to guard the walls, full many a foss
Begirds some stately castle, sure defence[2]
Affording to the space within; so here
Were model'd these: and as like fortresses,
E'en from their threshold to the brink without,
Are flank'd with bridges; from the rock's low base
Thus flinty paths advanced, that 'cross the moles
And dikes struck onward far as to the gulf,
That in one bound collected cuts them off.
Such was the place, wherein we found ourselves

---

1 The gulf or gigantic well at the bottom of which is the ninth
circle, the frozen river which holds the traitors.
2 Cary read: *La parte dov' e' son rendon sicura.* The more
generally accepted reading of this line is: *La parte dov' ei son
rende figura.* Carlyle translates: "As is the form that ground
presents, where to defend the walls successive ditches begird a
castle: such image these made here."

From Geryon's back dislodged. The bard to left
Held on his way, and I behind him moved.

  On our right hand new misery I saw,
New pains, new executioners of wrath,
That swarming peopled the first chasm. Below
Were naked sinners. Hitherward they came,
Meeting our faces, from the middle point;
With us beyond,[1] but with a larger stride.
E'en thus the Romans, when the year returns
Of Jubilee, with better speed to rid
The thronging multitudes, their means devise
For such as pass the bridge; that on one side
All front toward the Castle, and approach
Saint Peter's fane, on the other towards the Mount.[2]

  Each diverse way, along the grisly rock,
Horn'd demons I beheld, with lashes huge,
That on their back unmercifully smote.
Ah! how they made them bound at the first stripe!
None for the second waited, nor the third.

  Meantime, as on I pass'd, one met my sight,
Whom soon as view'd, "Of him," cried I, "not yet
Mine eye hath had his fill." I therefore stay'd
My feet to scan him, and the teacher kind
Paused with me, and consented I should walk
Backward a space; and the tormented spirit,
Who thought to hide him, bent his visage down,
But it avail'd him nought; for I exclaim'd:
"Thou who dost cast thine eye upon the ground,
Unless thy features do belie thee much,
Venedico[3] art thou. But what brings thee

---

  [1] " Beyond the middle point they tended the same way with us,
but their pace was quicker than ours " (Cary).
  [2] The first jubilee was instituted by Boniface VIII., to last
from Christmas, 1299, to Christmas, 1300. Because of the great
press of pilgrims passing over the Ponte Sant' Angelo, to and
from St. Peter's, they were compelled to keep to their proper side
of the bridge; those going faced Castello Sant' Angelo, those
returning faced Monte Giordano. Cf. *Purg.* ii.
  [3] Venedico de' Caccianimici, whom Dante had known in life,
was one of the chief Guelfs of Bologna and an adherent of the
Marquis Obizzo II. d' Este of Ferrara (*cf.* above, Canto xii.).
To win the favour of the Marquis, he assisted him in the seduction
of his own sister, Ghisola or Ghisolabella, who afterwards married
Niccolò da Fontana of Ferrara. Venedico was banished from
Bologna in 1289, and it was as an exile (perhaps in Florence) that
Dante met him.

Into this bitter seasoning?"   He replied:
" Unwillingly I answer to thy words.
But thy clear speech, that to my mind recalls
The world I once inhabited, constrains me.
Know then 't was I who led fair Ghisola
To do the Marquis' will, however fame
The shameful tale have bruited.   Nor alone,
Bologna hither sendeth me to mourn;
Rather with us the place is so o'erthrong'd,
That not so many tongues this day are taught,
Betwixt the Reno and Savena's stream,
To answer *Sipa* [1] in their country's phrase.
And if of that securer proof thou need,
Remember but our craving thirst for gold."

    Him speaking thus, a demon with his thong
Struck and exclaim'd, " Away, corrupter! here
Women are none for sale."   Forthwith I join'd
My escort, and few paces thence we came
To where a rock forth issued from the bank.
That easily ascended, to the right
Upon its splinter turning, we depart
From those eternal barriers.   When arrived
Where, underneath, the gaping arch lets pass
The scourged souls: " Pause here," the teacher said,
" And let these others miserable now
Strike on thy ken; faces not yet beheld,
For that together they with us have walk'd."

    From the old bridge we eyed the pack, who came
From the other side toward us, like the rest,
Excoriate from the lash.   My gentle guide,
By me unquestion'd, thus his speech resumed:
" Behold that lofty shade, who this way tends,
And seems too woe-begone to drop a tear.
How yet the regal aspect he retains!
Jason is he, whose skill and prowess won
The ram from Colchis.   To the Lemnian isle
His passage thither led him, when those bold
And pitiless women had slain all their males.
There he with tokens and fair witching words
Hypsipyle beguiled, a virgin young,
Who first had all the rest herself beguiled.
Impregnated, he left her there forlorn:

1 Bologna lies between the Savena and the Reno.   *Sipa* (for *sia*)
is the equivalent to *sì* (yes) in the Bolognese dialect.

Such is the guilt condemns him to this pain;
Here, too, Medea's injuries are avenged.[1]
All bear him company, who like deceit
To his have practised.   And thus much to know
Of the first vale suffice thee, and of those
Whom its keen torments urge."   Now had we come
Where, crossing the next pier, the straiten'd path
Bestrides its shoulders to another arch.

Hence, in the second chasm we heard the ghosts,
Who gibber in low melancholy sounds,
With wide-stretch'd nostrils snort, and on themselves
Smite with their palms.   Upon the banks a scurf,
From the foul steam condensed, encrusting hung,
That held sharp combat with the sight and smell.

So hollow is the depth, that from no part,
Save on the summit of the rocky span,
Could I distinguish aught.   Thus far we came;
And thence I saw, within the foss below,
A crowd immersed in ordure, that appear'd
Draff of the human body.   There beneath
Searching with eye inquisitive, I mark'd
One with his head so grimed, 'twere hard to deem
If he were clerk or layman.   Loud he cried:
" Why greedily thus bendest more on me,
Than on these other filthy ones, thy ken?"

" Because, if true my memory," I replied,
" I heretofore have seen thee with dry locks;
And thou Alessio[2] art, of Lucca sprung.
Therefore than all the rest I scan thee more."

Then beating on his brain, these words he spake:
" Me thus low down my flatteries have sunk,
Wherewith I ne'er enough could glut my tongue."

My leader thus: " A little farther stretch
Thy face, that thou the visage well mayst note
Of that besotted, sluttish courtezan,
Who there doth rend her with defiled nails,
Now crouching down, now risen on her feet.
Thaïs[3] is this, the harlot, whose false lip

---

[1] Jason seduced Hypsipyle, the daughter of Thoas, King of
Lemnos, who had saved her father by deceiving the other Lemnian
women who wished to slay all their menfolk; and he afterwards
treacherously deserted Medea.

[2] Alessio degli Interminelli, a nobleman of Lucca notorious for
his adulation of the great.   He was still living in 1295.

[3] Thaïs, a character in the *Eunuchus* of Terence.   Thraso,

Answer'd her doting paramour that ask'd,
' Thankest me much?'—' Say rather, wondrously.'
And, seeing this, here satiate be our view."

CANTO XIX

ARGUMENT

They come to the third gulf, wherein are punished those who have been guilty of simony. These are fixed with the head downwards in certain apertures, so that no more of them than the legs appears without, and on the soles of their feet are seen burning flames. Dante is taken down by his guide into the bottom of the gulf; and there finds Pope Nicholas the Fifth, whose evil deeds, together with those of other pontiffs, are bitterly reprehended. Virgil then carries him up again to the arch, which affords them a passage over the following gulf.

Woe to thee, Simon Magus ! woe to you,
His wretched followers ! who the things of God,
Which should be wedded unto goodness, them,
Rapacious as ye are, do prostitute
For gold and silver in adultery.[1]
Now must the trumpet sound for you, since yours
Is the third chasm. Upon the following vault
We now had mounted, where the rock impends
Directly o'er the centre of the foss.

　　Wisdom Supreme ! how wonderful the art,
Which Thou dost manifest in Heaven, in earth,
And in the evil world, how just a meed
Allotting by Thy virtue unto all.

　　I saw the livid stone, throughout the sides
And in its bottom full of apertures,
All equal in their width, and circular each.
Nor ample less nor larger they appear'd

having sent a slave-girl as a present to Thaïs by the parasite Gnatho, asks the latter how she received the gift : *Magnas vero agere gratias Thaïs mihi?* ("Did Thaïs really return me great thanks?"); to which Gnatho answers: *Ingentes* ("Wondrous thanks "). Dante, who probably had not read Terence, found the quotation in Cicero's *De Amicitia,* where the substitution of *ingentes* for *magnas* is given as an example of adulatory exaggeration, and jumped to the conclusion that the words were spoken by Thaïs herself.

[1] Simony, the sin of making traffic of sacred things, is derived from the name of Simon the sorcerer (Acts viii.), who " thought that the gift of God may be purchased with money."

Than, in Saint John's fair dome of me beloved,
Those framed to hold the pure baptismal streams,
One of the which I brake, some few years past,
To save a whelming infant : and be this
A seal to undeceive whoever doubts
The motive of my deed.[1]   From out the mouth
Of every one emerged a sinner's feet,
And of the legs high upward as the calf.
The rest beneath was hid.   On either foot
The soles were burning ; whence the flexile joints
Glanced with such violent motion, as had snapt
Asunder cords or twisted withs.   As flame,
Feeding on unctuous matter, glides along
The surface, scarcely touching where it moves ;
So here, from heel to point, glided the flames.

  " Master ! say who is he, than all the rest
Glancing in fiercer agony, on whom
A ruddier flame doth prey ? " I thus inquired.

  " If thou be willing," he replied, " that I
Carry thee down, where least the slope bank falls,
He of himself shall tell thee, and his wrongs."

  I then : " As pleases thee, to me is best.
Thou art my lord ; and know'st that ne'er I quit
Thy will : what silence hides, that knowest thou."

  Thereat on the fourth pier we came, we turn'd,
And on our left descended to the depth,
A narrow strait, and perforated close.
Nor from his side my leader set me down,
Till to his orifice he brought, whose limb
Quivering express'd his pang.   " Whoe'er thou art,
Sad spirit ! thus reversed, and as a stake
Driven in the soil," I in these words began ;
" If thou be able, utter forth thy voice."

  There stood I like the friar, that doth shrive
A wretch for murder doom'd, who, e'en when fix'd,[2]
Calleth him back, whence death awhile delays.

---

1 The ancient font, which stood in the centre of the Baptistery
of Florence, appears to have had round holes or *pozzetti* in its outer
wall, in which the priests stood to baptize. Dante broke one of
these to save a boy (said to have been Antonio, the son of Baldi-
naccio de' Cavicciuoli) who had either tumbled into the font or
climbed head-foremost into one of the *pozzetti*. The Poet implies
that his enemies accused him of sacrilege in consequence.

2 Certain criminals were buried alive, with the head downwards,
the process being known as *propagginazione*.

He shouted : " Ha ! already standest there?
Already standest there, O Boniface ! [1]
By many a year the writing play'd me false.
So early dost thou surfeit with the wealth,
For which thou fearedst not in guile to take
The lovely lady,[2] and then mangle her?"

I felt as those who, piercing not the drift
Of answer made them, stand as if exposed
In mockery, nor know what to reply ;
When Virgil thus admonish'd : " Tell him quick,
' I am not he, not he whom thou believest.' "

And I, as was enjoin'd me, straight replied.
That heard, the spirit all did wrench his feet,
And, sighing, next in woeful accent spake :
" What then of me requirest? If to know
So much imports thee, who I am, that thou
Hast therefore down the bank descended, learn
That in the mighty mantle I was robed,
And of a she-bear was indeed the son,[3]
So eager to advance my whelps, that there
My having in my purse above I stow'd,
And here myself. Under my head are dragg'd
The rest, my predecessors in the guilt
Of simony. Stretch'd at their length, they lie
Along an opening in the rock. 'Midst them
I also low shall fall, soon as he comes,
For whom I took thee, when so hastily
I question'd. But already longer time
Hath past, since my soles kindled, and I thus
Upturn'd have stood, than is his doom to stand
Planted with fiery feet. For after him,
One yet of deeds more ugly shall arrive,
From forth the west, a shepherd without law,[4]

---

[1] The speaker is Nicholas III. (Giovanni Guatani Orsini), who
was Pope from 1277 to 1280. His mistaking Dante for Boniface VIII., the Pope at the epoch of the vision (he died in 1303),
who is coming to take his place, is an intensely dramatic touch.

[2] The Church, which Boniface was supposed to have wrested
by fraud from her lawful spouse, Celestine V. (*Cf.* above,
Canto iii.)

[3] The Bear was the badge of the Orsini.

[4] Clement V. (Bertrand de Goth), who had previously been Archbishop of Bordeaux. Elected Pope in 1305, he removed the Papacy
to Avignon, and made it subservient to the King of France, by
whose favour he was supposed to have obtained the tiara. He

Fated to cover both his form and mine.
He a new Jason shall be call'd, of whom
In Maccabees we read; and favour such
As to that priest his king indulgent show'd,
Shall be of France's monarch shown to him." [1]
      I know not if I here too far presumed,
But in this strain I answer'd : " Tell me now,
What treasures from Saint Peter at the first
Our Lord demanded, when he put the keys
Into his charge?   Surely He ask'd no more
But ' Follow me !'   Nor Peter, nor the rest,
Or gold or silver of Matthias took,
When lots were cast upon the forfeit place
Of the condemned soul. [2]   Abide thou then ;
Thy punishment of right is merited :
And look thou well to that ill-gotten coin,
Which against Charles [3] thy hardihood inspired.
If reverence of the keys restrain'd me not,
Which thou in happier time didst hold, I yet
Severer speech might use.   Your avarice
O'ercasts the world with mourning, under foot
Treading the good, and raising bad men up.
Of shepherds like to you, the Evangelist
Was ware, when her, who sits upon the waves,

died in 1314. Nicholas III., therefore, has to wait twenty-three
years in Hell for Boniface VIII., who in his turn will have to wait
only eleven years for Clement V. Cf. *Purg.* xxxii. and *Par.* xxx.
The Pope who came between Boniface and Clement, Benedict XI.,
a Dominican friar of holy life and enlightened policy, reigned only
a few months (Oct. 22, 1303, to July 7, 1304), and is nowhere
mentioned in the *Divina Commedia*.

[1] " But after the death of Seleucus, when Antiochus, called
Epiphanes, took the kingdom, Jason, the brother of Onias, laboured
underhand to be high priest, promising unto the king, by intercession, three hundred and threescore talents of silver, and of
another revenue eighty talents " (2 Maccabees iv. 7, 8). According
to Giovanni Villani (viii. 80), a somewhat analogous bargain had
been struck between King Philip the Fourth of France (Philip
the Fair) and Pope Clement, previous to the latter's elevation ; but
the story is now rejected by serious historians.

[2] See Acts i. 15–26.

[3] The elder Charles of Anjou, King of Naples and Sicily.
According to Villani (vii. 54), Charles refused to accept one of the
Pope's nieces as wife for a nephew of his, upon which Nicholas
deprived him of the office of Senator of Rome, and accepted money
from the Eastern Emperor, Michael Palæologus, with which he
stirred up the troubles which (after his own death) resulted in the
Sicilian Vespers (1282).

With kings in filthy whoredom he beheld; [1]
She who with seven heads tower'd at her birth,
And from ten horns her proof of glory drew,
Long as her spouse in virtue took delight.
Of gold and silver ye have made your god,
Differing wherein from the idolater,
But that he worships one, a hundred ye?
Ah, Constantine! to how much ill gave birth,
Not thy conversion, but that plenteous dower
Which the first wealthy Father gain'd from thee." [2]

    Meanwhile, as thus I sung, he, whether wrath
Or conscience smote him, violent upsprang
Spinning on either sole. I do believe
My teacher well was pleased, with so composed
A lip he listen'd ever to the sound
Of the true words I utter'd. In both arms
He caught, and, to his bosom lifting me,
Upward retraced the way of his descent.

    Nor weary of his weight, he press'd me close,
Till to the summit of the rock we came,
Our passage from the fourth to the fifth pier.
His cherish'd burden there gently he placed
Upon the rugged rock and steep, a path
Not easy for the clambering goat to mount.

    Thence to my view another vale appear'd.

CANTO XX

ARGUMENT

The Poet relates the punishment of such as presumed, while living,
to predict future events. It is to have their faces reversed and
set the contrary way on their limbs, so that, being deprived
of the power to see before them, they are constrained ever to
walk backwards. Among these Virgil points out to him

---

1 *Cf.* Revelations xvii. 1–3.
2 The Donation of Constantine represented that Emperor as
withdrawing from the west in order to leave the Pope in absolute
possession of Rome. This document, from which the temporal
power of the Papacy was supposed to be derived, was a forgery of
the early Middle Ages. In the *De Monarchia* (iii. 10), Dante urges
that the donation, if really made, was invalid, because Constantine had no power to alienate the imperial dignity, nor the
Church power to receive it. He refers to the matter elsewhere.
Cf. Mon. ii. 13; *Par.* xx.

Amphiaraüs, Tiresias, Aruns, and Manto (from the mention of
whom he takes occasion to speak of the origin of Mantua),
together with several others, who had practised the arts of
divination and astrology.

AND now the verse proceeds to torments new,
Fit argument of this the twentieth strain
Of the first song, whose awful theme records
The spirits whelm'd in woe.   Earnest I look'd
Into the depth, that open'd to my view,
Moisten'd with tears of anguish, and beheld
A tribe, that came along the hollow vale,
In silence weeping : such their step as walk
Quires, chanting solemn litanies, on earth.

As on them more direct mine eye descends,
Each wondrously seem'd to be reversed
At the neck-bone, so that the countenance
Was from the reins averted ; and because
None might before him look, they were compell'd
To advance with backward gait.   Thus one perhaps
Hath been by force of palsy clean transposed,
But I ne'er saw it nor believe it so.

Now, reader ! think within thyself, so God
Fruit of thy reading give thee ! how I long
Could keep my visage dry, when I beheld
Near me our form distorted in such guise,
That on the hinder parts fallen from the face
The tears down-streaming roll'd.   Against a rock
I leant and wept, so that my guide exclaim'd :
" What, and art thou, too, witless as the rest?
Here pity most doth show herself alive,
When she is dead.   What guilt exceedeth his,
Who with Heaven's judgment in his passion strives?
Raise up thy head, raise up, and see the man
Before whose eyes earth gaped in Thebes, when all
Cried out ' Amphiaraüs, whither rushest?
Why leavest thou the war?'[1]   He not the less
Fell ruining far as to Minos down,
Whose grapple none eludes.   Lo ! how he makes
The breast his shoulders ; and who once too far
Before him wish'd to see, now backward looks,

---

[1] Amphiaraüs, prophet and warrior of Argos, was one of the
seven against Thebes, where he was swallowed up by the earth.
See below, *Purg.* xii. and *Par.* iv.

And treads reverse his path.   Tiresias [1] note,
Who semblance changed, when woman he became
Of male, through every limb transform'd; and then
Once more behoved him with his rod to strike
The two entwining serpents, ere the plumes,
That mark'd the better sex, might shoot again.

   " Aruns,[2] with rere his belly facing, comes.
On Luni's mountains 'midst the marbles white,
Where delves Carrara's hind, who wons beneath,
A cavern was his dwelling, whence the stars
And main-sea wide in boundless view he held.

   " The next, whose loosen'd tresses overspread
Her bosom, which thou seest not (for each hair
On that side grows) was Manto,[3] she who search'd
Through many regions, and at length her seat
Fix'd in my native land: whence a short space
My words detain thy audience.   When her sire
From life departed, and in servitude
The city dedicate to Bacchus mourn'd,[4]
Long time she went a wanderer through the world.
Aloft in Italy's delightful land
A lake there lies, at foot of that proud Alp
That o'er the Tyrol locks Germania in,
Its name Benacus, from whose ample breast
A thousand springs, methinks, and more, between
Camonica and Garda, issuing forth,
Water the Apennine.   There is a spot
At midway of that lake, where he who bears
Of Trento's flock the pastoral staff, with him
Of Brescia, and the Veronese, might each
Passing that way his benediction give.[5]

   [1] Tiresias, the blind soothsayer of Thebes. According to Ovid
(*Metam.* iii.), he was changed into a woman because he separated
two serpents with his staff; seven years later, he struck the same
two serpents, and became a man again.
   [2] An Etruscan soothsayer mentioned in Lucan's *Pharsalia* (i. 584–
638).
   [3] Cf. *Purg.* xxii. Manto, the daughter of Tiresias, is here
represented as the founder of Mantua; it is curious that Dante
should thus make Virgil give an account of the origin of his
native city which differs from that given in the *Æneid* (x. 198–
200), where we are told that Mantua was founded by Ocnus, son
of the prophetess Manto and the Tuscan river (the Tiber).
   [4] Thebes, the native city of Bacchus, was subjected to the
tyrannical rule of Creon.
   [5] Mr. Vernon renders this passage : " Up above in beautiful

A garrison of goodly site and strong,
Peschiera stands, to awe with front opposed
The Bergamese and Brescian, whence the shore
More slope each way descends. There, whatsoe'er
Benacus' bosom holds not, tumbling o'er
Down falls, and winds a river flood beneath
Through the green pastures. Soon as in his course
The stream makes head, Benacus then no more
They call the name, but Mincius, till at last
Reaching Governo,[1] into Po he falls.
Not far his course hath run, when a wide flat
It finds, which overstretching as a marsh
It covers, pestilent in summer oft.
Hence journeying, the savage maiden saw
Midst of the fen a territory waste
And naked of inhabitants. To shun
All human converse, here she with her slaves,
Plying her arts, remain'd, and lived, and left
Her body tenantless. Thenceforth the tribes,
Who round were scatter'd, gathering to that place,
Assembled; for its strength was great, enclosed
On all parts by the fen. On those dead bones
They rear'd themselves a city, for her sake
Calling it Mantua, who first chose the spot,
Nor ask'd another omen for the name;
Wherein more numerous the people dwelt,
Ere Casalodi's madness by deceit
Was wrong'd of Pinamonte.[2] If thou hear
Henceforth another origin assign'd
Of that my country, I forewarn thee now,

Italy there is a lake lying at the foot of that Alpine chain which
shuts in Germany above the Tyrol, and it is called Benacus
(*i. e.* the Lake of Garda). Through a thousand springs and more,
I believe, between Garda (the village) and Val Camonica, (Mount)
Apennino is laved by the water which settles in the said lake.
There in the midst of it is a spot where (each one of three Bishops),
the Pastor of Trent, and he of Brescia, and he of Verona, might,
if he travelled that way, make the sign of the Cross (*i. e.* might
give his episcopal benediction in his own diocese)." The Apennine
here is not the chain of the Apennines, but a single mountain called
Apennino, on the western shore of the Lago di Garda.

  [1] Governolo, a small town near where the Mincio flows into
the Po.
  [2] Pinamonte de' Buonaccorsi treacherously drove out Alberto
da Casalodi from Mantua in 1272, and made himself lord of the
city.

That falsehood none beguile thee of the truth."

　　I answer'd, " Teacher, I conclude thy words
So certain, that all else shall be to me
As embers lacking life.　But now of these,
Who here proceed, instruct me, if thou see
Any that merit more especial note.
For thereon is my mind alone intent."

　　He straight replied : " That spirit, from whose cheek
The beard sweeps o'er his shoulders brown, what time
Græcia was emptied of her males, that scarce
The cradles were supplied, the seer was he
In Aulis, who with Calchas gave the sign
When first to cut the cable.　Him they named
Eurypylus : so sings my tragic strain,[1]
In which majestic measure well thou know'st,
Who know'st it all.　That other, round the loins
So slender of his shape, was Michael Scot,[2]
Practised in every slight of magic wile.

　　" Guido Bonatti [3] see : Asdente [4] mark,
Who now were willing he had tended still
The thread and cordwain, and too late repents.

　　" See next the wretches, who the needle left,
The shuttle and the spindle, and became
Diviners : baneful witcheries they wrought
With images and herbs.　But onward now :
For now doth Cain with fork of thorns confine
On either hemisphere, touching the wave
Beneath the towers of Seville.　Yesternight
The moon was round.[5]　Thou mayst remember well :

　　[1] *Æneid*, ii. 114 *et seq*.　The augur Eurypylus, sent by the
Greeks to question the oracle, brought back the reply that, as
they had come to Troy by the sacrifice of Iphigeneia, so they
must obtain their safe return by another human sacrifice.　Such
at least is the story told to the Trojans by the treacherous Sinon.
Cf. below, Canto xxx.

　　[2] Michael Scott of Balwearie, the famous astrologer.

　　[3] Guido Bonatti, an astrologer of Forlì, in the service of Guido
da Montefeltro.　(See below, Canto xxvii.)

　　[4] Asdente (" the toothless "), whose real name was Benvenuto,
was a shoemaker of Parma who attempted to foretell the future.
He died about 1284.　Dante refers to him again in the *Convivio*
(iv. 16).　The testimony of Asdente's contemporary and fellow-
citizen, Fra Salimbene, seems to show that the Poet has treated
the cobbler with somewhat less than his usual justice.

　　[5] Cain with the thorns is equivalent to " the Man in the Moon."
Cf. Par. ii.　" The Pillars of Hercules were regarded by Dante

For she good service did thee in the gloom
Of the deep wood." This said, both onward moved.

CANTO XXI

ARGUMENT

Still in the eighth circle, which bears the name of Malebolge, they
look down from the bridge that passes over its fifth gulf, upon
the barterers or public peculators. These are plunged in a
lake of boiling pitch, and guarded by Demons, to whom
Virgil, leaving Dante apart, presents himself; and license
being obtained to pass onward, both pursue their way.

THUS we from bridge to bridge, with other talk,
The which my drama cares not to rehearse,
Pass'd on; and to the summit reaching, stood
To view another gap, within the round
Of Malebolge, other bootless pangs.
  Marvellous darkness shadow'd o'er the place.
  In the Venetians' arsenal as boils
Through wintry months tenacious pitch, to smear
Their unsound vessels; for the inclement time
Seafaring men restrains, and in that while
His bark one builds anew, another stops
The ribs of his that hath made many a voyage,
One hammers at the prow, one at the poop,
This shapeth oars, that other cables twirls,
The mizen one repairs and mainsail rent;
So, not by force of fire but art divine,
Boil'd here a glutinous thick mass, that round
Limed all the shore beneath. I that beheld,
But therein nought distinguish'd, save the bubbles
Raised by the boiling, and one mighty swell
Heave, and by turns subsiding fall. While there
I fix'd my ken below, "Mark! mark!" my guide
Exclaiming, drew me towards him from the place
Wherein I stood. I turn'd myself, as one

and his contemporaries as the extreme western limit of the world,
and he designates this boundary variously as Spain, Gades, the
Iberus, Morocco, or Seville, as here (see *Par.* xxvii.). During the
night preceding Good Friday, the moon (which guided Dante's
steps in the dark wood, see above, Canto i.) was at full. The Poet
is now describing the setting of the moon (or rising of the sun) on
the Saturday morning " (Oelsner).

Impatient to behold that which beheld
He needs must shun, whom sudden fear unmans,
That he his flight delays not for the view.
Behind me I discern'd a devil black,
That running up advanced along the rock.
Ah! what fierce cruelty his look bespake;
In act how bitter did he seem, with wings
Buoyant outstretch'd and feet of nimblest tread.
His shoulder, proudly eminent and sharp,
Was with a sinner charged; by either haunch
He held him, the foot's sinew griping fast.

" Ye of our bridge!" he cried, " keen-talon'd fiends!
Lo! one of Santa Zita's elders.[1]   Him
Whelm ye beneath, while I return for more.
That land hath store of such.   All men are there,
Except Bonturo, barterers: of ' no '
For lucre there an ' ay ' is quickly made."

Him dashing down, o'er the rough rock he turn'd;
Nor ever after thief a mastiff loosed
Sped with like eager haste.   That other sank,
And forthwith writhing to the surface rose;
But those dark demons, shrouded by the bridge,
Cried, " Here the hallow'd visage saves not: here
Is other swimming than in Serchio's wave:[2]
Wherefore, if thou desire we rend thee not,
Take heed thou mount not o'er the pitch."   This said,

[1] The " elders " or " ancients " (anziani) were the chief magistrates of Lucca, of which city Santa Zita is the patron saint. This particular Lucchese is evidently one who died in April, 1300, and has been conjecturally identified with a certain Martino Bottaio.   The exception of Bonturo Dati, the leader of the democratic party in Lucca (who was still alive at the date of the vision), from the general condemnation is ironical, and meant to imply that he was the worst offender of the lot.   Barattieri, or barterers, are those guilty of corrupt practices and peculation in public offices.   Mr. Vernon notes that the great length of this episode, as told by Dante and illustrated by his early commentators, shows the great importance that they attached to this sin and to its punishment.   It will be remembered that a false accusation of barratry was one of the pretexts for Dante's banishment and the sentence of death passed against him; and it is noteworthy that, although he escapes spotless and scathless, this is the only place in the Inferno in which Dante represents himself as experiencing serious personal danger.
[2] The Serchio is the river that flows by Lucca.   The " hallowed image," santo volto, is a Crucifix, of which the face of Christ is said to have been carved by Nicodemus and finished by Angels, which is still highly venerated in the Cathedral of Lucca.

They grappled him with more than hundred hooks,
And shouted : " Cover'd thou must sport thee here ;
So, if thou canst, in secret mayst thou filch."
E'en thus the cook bestirs him, with his grooms,
To thrust the flesh into the caldron down
With flesh-hooks, that it float not on the top.

   Me then my guide bespake : " Lest they descry
That thou art here, behind a craggy rock
Bend low and screen thee : and whate'er of force
Be offer'd me, or insult, fear thou not ;
For I am well advised, who have been erst
In the like fray." Beyond the bridge's head
Therewith he pass'd ; and reaching the sixth pier,
Behoved him then a forehead terror-proof.

   With storm and fury, as when dogs rush forth
Upon the poor man's back, who suddenly
From whence he standeth makes his suit ; so rush'd
Those from beneath the arch, and against him
Their weapons all they pointed. He, aloud :
" Be none of you outrageous : ere your tine
Dare seize me, come forth from amongst you one,
Who having heard my words, decide he then
If he shall tear these limbs." They shouted loud,
" Go, Malacoda !" Whereat one advanced,
The others standing firm, and as he came,
" What may this turn avail him ?" he exclaim'd.

   " Believest thou, Malacoda ! I had come
Thus far from all your skirmishing secure,"
My teacher answer'd, " without Will Divine
And destiny propitious ? Pass we then ;
For so Heaven's pleasure is, that I should lead
Another through this savage wilderness."

   Forthwith so fell his pride, that he let drop
The instrument of torture at his feet,
And to the rest exclaim'd : " We have no power
To strike him." Then to me my guide : " O thou !
Who on the bridge among the crags dost sit
Low crouching, safely now to me return."
   I rose, and towards him moved with speed ;   the
        fiends
Meantime all forward drew : me terror seized,
Lest they should break the compact they had made.
Thus issuing from Caprona, once I saw
Th' infantry, dreading lest his covenant

The foe should break; [1] so close he hemm'd them round.
  I to my leader's side adhered, mine eyes
With fixt and motionless observance bent
On their unkindly visage.   They their hooks
Protruding, one the other thus bespake :
" Wilt thou I touch him on the hip?"   To whom
Was answer'd : " Even so; nor miss thy aim."
  But he, who was in conference with my guide,
Turn'd rapid round; and thus the demon spake :
" Stay, stay thee, Scarmiglione!"   Then to us
He added :   " Further footing to your step
This rock affords not, shiver'd to the base
Of the sixth arch.   But would ye still proceed,
Up by this cavern go : not distant far,
Another rock will yield you passage safe.
Yesterday, later by five hours than now,
Twelve hundred threescore years and six had fill'd
The circuit of their course, since here the way
Was broken. [2]   Thitherward I straight dispatch
Certain of these my scouts, who shall espy
If any on the surface bask.   With them
Go ye : for ye shall find them nothing fell.
Come, Alichino, forth," with that he cried,
" And Calcabrina, and Cagnazzo thou !
The troop of ten let Barbariccia lead.
With Libicocco, Draghignazzo haste,
Fang'd Ciriatto, Graffiacane fierce,
And Farfarello, and mad Rubicant. [3]
Search ye around the bubbling tar.   For these,
In safety lead them, where the other crag
Uninterrupted traverses the dens."
  I then : " O master ! what a sight is there.
Ah ! without escort, journey we alone,

1 Dante was present, either as a spectator or (as seems more
probable) as a volunteer in the Florentine army, when the Pisan
garrison of Caprona was compelled to capitulate to the Florentines
and Lucchese in August, 1289.

2 " This passage fixes the era of Dante's descent at Good
Friday, in the year 1300 (34 years from our blessed Lord's incarnation being added to 1266), and at the 35th year of our Poet's
age " (Cary).

3 It has been supposed that these *Malebranche*, " evil-claws,"
or " keen-talon'd fiends," with their extraordinary names, represent
Dante's enemies among his fellow-citizens, who had sought to
take his honour and his life, and had succeeded in working his
temporal ruin, by their false accusations of barratry.

Which, if thou know the way, I covet not.
Unless thy prudence fail thee, dost not mark
How they do gnarl upon us, and their scowl
Threatens us present tortures?'' He replied :
'' I charge thee, fear not : let them, as they will,
Gnarl on : 'tis but in token of their spite
Against the souls who mourn in torment steep'd.''

To leftward o'er the pier they turn'd; but each
Had first between his teeth prest close the tongue,
Toward their leader for a signal looking,
Which he with sound obscene triumphant gave.

CANTO XXII

ARGUMENT

Virgil and Dante proceed, accompanied by the Demons, and see
    other sinners of the same description in the same gulf. The
    device of Ciampolo, one of these, to escape from the Demons,
    who had laid hold on him.

It hath been heretofore my chance to see
Horsemen with martial order shifting camp,
To onset sallying, or in muster ranged,
Or in retreat sometimes outstretch'd for flight :
Light-armed squadrons and fleet foragers
Scouring thy plains, Arezzo ! have I seen,
And clashing tournaments, and tilting jousts,
Now with the sound of trumpets, now of bells,
Tabors, or signals made from castled heights,
And with inventions multiform, our own,
Or introduced from foreign land ; but ne'er
To such a strange recorder I beheld
In evolution moving, horse nor foot,
Nor ship, that tack'd by sign from land or star.

With the ten demons on our way we went;
Ah, fearful company ! but in the church
With saints, with gluttons at the tavern's mess.
Still earnest on the pitch I gazed, to mark
All things whate'er the chasm contain'd, and those
Who burn'd within. As dolphins that, in sign
To mariners, heave high their arched backs,
That thence forewarn'd they may advise to save
Their threaten'd vessel; so, at intervals,

To ease the pain, his back some sinner show'd,
Then hid more nimbly than the lightning-glance.
   E'en as the frogs, that of a watery moat
Stand at the brink, with the jaws only out,
Their feet and of the trunk all else conceal'd,
Thus on each part the sinners stood; but soon
As Barbariccia was at hand, so they
Drew back under the wave. I saw, and yet
My heart doth stagger, one, that waited thus,
As it befals that oft one frog remains,
While the next springs away : and Graffiacan,
Who of the fiends was nearest, grappling seized
His clotted locks, and dragg'd him sprawling up,
That he appear'd to me an otter. Each
Already by their names I knew, so well
When they were chosen I observ'd, and mark'd
How one the other call'd. " O Rubicant !
See that his hide thou with thy talons flay,"
Shouted together all the cursed crew.
   Then I : " Inform thee, Master ! if thou may,
What wretched soul is this, on whom their hands
His foes have laid." My leader to his side
Approach'd, and whence he came inquired ; to whom
Was answer'd thus : " Born in Navarre's domain,
My mother placed me in a lord's retinue ;
For she had borne me to a losel vile,
A spendthrift of his substance and himself.
The good king Thibault after that I served : [1]
To peculating here my thoughts were turn'd,
Whereof I give account in this dire heat."
   Straight Ciriatto, from whose mouth a tusk
Issued on either side, as from a boar,
Ripp'd him with one of these. 'Twixt evil claws
The mouse had fallen : but Barbariccia cried,
Seizing him with both arms : " Stand thou apart,
While I do fix him on my prong transpierced."
Then added, turning to my guide his face,
" Inquire of him, if more thou wish to learn,
Ere he again be rent." My leader thus :
" Then tell us of the partners in thy guilt ;

[1] Thibaut II., King of Navarre (1253–1270), son of the poet-
king, Thibaut I., mentioned by Dante in the *De Vulgari Eloquentia*.
Nothing is known of this dishonest servant of his, whose name is
said to have been Ciampolo.

Knowest thou any sprung of Latian land
Under the tar?"—" I parted," he replied,
" But now from one, who sojourn'd not far thence :
So were I under shelter now with him,
Nor hook nor talon then should scare me more."

     " Too long we suffer," Libicocco cried;
Then, darting forth a prong, seized on his arm,
And mangled bore away the sinewy part.
Him Draghignazzo by his thighs beneath
Would next have caught; whence angrily their chief,
Turning on all sides round, with threatening brow
Restrain'd them. When their strife a little ceased,
Of him, who yet was gazing on his wound,
My teacher thus without delay inquired :
" Who was the spirit, from whom by evil hap
Parting, as thou hast told, thou camest to shore?"—

     " It was the friar Gomita," he rejoin'd,
" He of Gallura, vessel of all guile,
Who had his master's enemies in hand,
And used them so that they commend him well.
Money he took, and them at large dismiss'd;
So he reports; and in each other charge
Committed to his keeping play'd the part
Of barterer to the height. With him doth herd
The chief of Logodoro, Michel Zanche;
Sardinia is a theme whereof their tongue
Is never weary.[1] Out! alas! behold
That other, how he grins. More would I say,
But tremble lest he mean to maul me sore."

     Their captain then to Farfarello turning,
Who roll'd his moony eyes in act to strike,
Rebuked him thus : " Off, cursed bird! avaunt!"

     " If ye desire to see or hear," he thus
Quaking with dread resumed, " or Tuscan spirits
Or Lombard, I will cause them to appear.
Meantime let these ill talons bate their fury,

---

[1] Sardinia was divided into four districts or jurisdictions :
Cagliari, Logodoro, Gallura and Arborea, each governed by a
judge. Friar Gomita was the chancellor of Nino Visconti, judge
of Gallura (see *Purg.* viii.), who finally hanged him for conniving
at the escape of prisoners under his charge, by whom he had been
bribed. Michele Zanche, vicar of King Enzio (son of Frederick II.),
carried on similar corrupt practices in the district of Logodoro
until, about 1290, he was murdered by his son-in-law, Branca
d'Oria. (See below, Canto xxxiii.)

So that no vengeance they may fear from them;
And I, remaining in this self-same place,
Will, for myself but one, make seven appear,
When my shrill whistle shall be heard : for so
Our custom is to call each other up."

Cagnazzo at that word deriding grinn'd,
Then wagg'd the head and spake : " Hear his device,
Mischievous as he is, to plunge him down."

Whereto he thus, who fail'd not in rich store
Of nice-wove toils : " Mischief, forsooth, extreme !
Meant only to procure myself more woe." [1]

No longer Alichino then refrain'd,
But thus, the rest gainsaying, him bespake :
" If thou do cast him down, I not on foot
Will chase thee, but above the pitch will beat
My plumes. Quit we the vantage ground, and let
The bank be as a shield; that we may see,
If singly thou prevail against us all."

Now, reader, of new sport expect to hear.

They each one turn'd his eyes to the other shore,
He first, who was the hardest to persuade.
The spirit of Navarre chose well his time,
Planted his feet on land, and at one leap
Escaping, disappointed their resolve.

Them quick resentment stung, but him the most,
Who was the cause of failure : in pursuit
He therefore sped, exclaiming, " Thou art caught."

But little it avail'd; terror outstripp'd
His following flight; the other plunged beneath,
And he with upward pinion raised his breast :
E'en thus the water-fowl, when she perceives
The falcon near, dives instant down, while he
Enraged and spent retires.   That mockery
In Calcabrina fury stirr'd, who flew
After him, with desire of strife inflamed;
And, for the barterer had 'scaped, so turn'd
His talons on his comrade.   O'er the dyke
In grapple close they join'd; but the other proved
A goshawk able to rend well his foe;
And in the boiling lake both fell.   The heat
Was umpire [2] soon between them; but in vain

---

[1] The right reading of this line is : *Quand'io procuro a' miei maggior tristizia;* " when I procure more woe for my companions."
[2] Cary read *schermidor*, but the right reading is *sghermitor*, the-

To lift themselves they strove, so fast were glued
Their pennons.   Barbariccia, as the rest,
That chance lamenting, four in flight dispatch'd
From the other coast, with all their weapons arm'd.
They, to their post on each side speedily
Descending, stretch'd their hooks toward the fiends,
Who flounder'd, inly burning from their scars :
And we departing left them to that broil.

CANTO XXIII

ARGUMENT

The enraged Demons pursue Dante, but he is preserved from them
by Virgil.   On reaching the sixth gulf, he beholds the punishment of the hypocrites ; which is, to pace continually round
the gulf under the pressure of cloaks and hoods, that are gilt
on the outside, but leaden within.   He is addressed by two of
these, Catalano and Loderingo, knights of Saint Mary, otherwise called Joyous Friars, of Bologna.   Caïaphas is seen fixed
to a cross on the ground, and lies so stretched along the way,
that all tread on him in passing.

IN silence and in solitude we went,
One first, the other following his steps,
As minor friars journeying on their road.
    The present fray had turn'd my thoughts to muse
Upon old Æsop's fable,[1] where he told
What fate unto the mouse and frog befel ;
For language hath not sounds more like in sense,
Than are these chances, if the origin
And end of each be heedfully compared.
And as one thought bursts from another forth,
So afterward from that another sprang,
Which added doubly to my former fear.
For thus I reason'd : " These through us have been
So foil'd, with loss and mockery so complete,
As needs must sting them sore.   If anger then
Be to their evil will conjoin'd, more fell

contrary of what grapples : " The heat at once made them
ungrapple."
    [1] A frog offered to carry a mouse across a stream, with the
intention of drowning him, and was himself devoured by a kite.
The fable, in various forms, is found in the mediæval collection of
such stories, but not in the original Æsop.

They shall pursue us, than the savage hound
Snatches the leveret panting 'twixt his jaws."
　　Already I perceived my hair stand all
On end with terror, and look'd eager back.
　　"Teacher," I thus began, " if speedily
Thyself and me thou hide not, much I dread
Those evil talons.　Even now behind
They urge us : quick imagination works
So forcibly, that I already feel them."
　　He answer'd : " Were I form'd of leaded glass,
I should not sooner draw unto myself
Thy outward image, than I now imprint
That from within.　This moment came thy thoughts
Presented before mine, with similar act
And countenance similar, so that from both
I one design have framed.　If the right coast
Incline so much, that we may thence descend
Into the other chasm, we shall escape
Secure from this imagined pursuit."
　　He had not spoke his purpose to the end,
When I from far beheld them with spread wings
Approach to take us.　Suddenly my guide
Caught me, even as a mother that from sleep
Is by the noise aroused, and near her sees
The climbing fires, who snatches up her babe
And flies ne'er pausing, careful more of him
Than of herself, that but a single vest
Clings round her limbs.　Down from the jutting beach
Supine he cast him to that pendent rock,
Which closes on one part the other chasm.
　　Never ran water with such hurrying pace
Adown the tube to turn a land-mill's wheel,
When nearest it approaches to the spokes,
As then along that edge my master ran,
Carrying me in his bosom, as a child,
Not a companion.　Scarcely had his feet
Reach'd to the lowest of the bed beneath,
When over us the steep they reach'd : but fear
In him was none ; for that high Providence,
Which placed them ministers of the fifth foss,
Power of departing thence took from them all.
　　There in the depth we saw a painted tribe,
Who paced with tardy steps around, and wept,
Faint in appearance and o'ercome with toil.

Cloaks had they on, with hoods, that fell low down
Before their eyes, in fashion like to those
Worn by the monks in Cologne.   Their outside
Was overlaid with gold, dazzling to view,
But leaden all within, and of such weight
That Frederick's [1] compared to these were straw.
Oh, everlasting wearisome attire!

We yet once more with them together turn'd
To leftward, on their dismal moan intent.
But, by the weight opprest, so slowly came
The fainting people, that our company
Was changed at every movement of the step.

Whence I my guide address'd : " See that thou find
Some spirit, whose name may by his deeds be known ;
And to that end look round thee as thou go'st."

Then one, who understood the Tuscan voice,
Cried after us aloud : " Hold in your feet,
Ye who so swiftly speed through the dusk air.
Perchance from me thou shalt obtain thy wish."

Whereat my leader, turning, me bespake :
" Pause, and then onward at their pace proceed."

I staid, and saw two spirits in whose look
Impatient eagerness of mind was mark'd
To overtake me ; but the load they bare
And narrow path retarded their approach.

Soon as arrived, they with an eye askance
Perused me, but spake not : then turning, each
To other thus conferring said : " This one
Seems, by the action of his throat, alive ;
And, be they dead, what privilege allows
They walk unmantled by the cumbrous stole?"

Then thus to me : " Tuscan, who visitest
The college of the mourning hypocrites,
Disdain not to instruct us who thou art."

" By Arno's pleasant stream," I thus replied,
" In the great city I was bred and grew,
And wear the body I have ever worn.
But who are ye, from whom such mighty grief,
As now I witness, courseth down your cheeks?
What torment breaks forth in this bitter woe?"

" Our *mantles* gleaming bright with orange hue,"
One of them answer'd, " are so leaden gross,

[1] The Emperor Frederick II. is supposed to have wrapped traitors
in a cloak of lead, which was then melted over a fire.

That with their weight they make the balances
To crack beneath them.   Joyous Friars we were,
Bologna's natives; Catalano I,
He Loderingo named; and by thy land
Together taken, as men used to take
A single and indifferent arbiter,
To reconcile their strifes.   How there we sped,
Gardingo's vicinage can best declare." [1]

    "O friars!" I began, " your miseries—"
But there brake off, for one had caught mine eye,
Fix'd to a cross with three stakes on the ground:
He, when he saw me, writhed himself, throughout
Distorted, ruffling with deep sighs his beard.
And Catalano, who thereof was 'ware,
Thus spake: "That pierced spirit, whom intent
Thou view'st, was he who gave the Pharisees
Counsel, that it were fitting for one man
To suffer for the people.   He doth lie
Transverse; nor any passes, but him first
Behoves make feeling trial how each weighs.
In straits like this along the foss are placed
The father of his consort,[2] and the rest
Partakers in that council, seed of ill
And sorrow to the Jews."   I noted then,
How Virgil gazed with wonder upon him,
Thus abjectly extended on the cross
In banishment eternal.   To the friar
He next his words address'd: "We pray ye tell,
If so be lawful, whether on our right
Lies any opening in the rock, whereby
We both may issue hence, without constraint

---

[1] The *Frati Gaudenti*, or "jovial friars," was the name applied
in derision to a military religious order known as the *Cavalieri di
S. Maria*, which was founded to mediate between rival factions
and to protect the weak.   Their two chief founders, Catalano
de' Catalani, a Guelf, and Loderingo degli Andalò, a Ghibelline,
were summoned from Bologna in 1266, to act together as Podestàs
of Florence and reform the government impartially.   They were
accused of hypocrisy and corruption, and driven from the city—the
district known as the *Gardingo* (the present Piazza di Firenze)
being destroyed in the tumult that arose.   Catalano died in 1285.
They were probably innocent of the charges brought against them,
which, however, Dante and Giovanni Villani seem to have accepted
without hesitation.

[2] Caiaphas and Annas (John xi. and xviii.).   Note the dramatic
touch of Virgil's wonder at the sight.

On the Dark Angels, that compell'd they come
To lead us from this depth." He thus replied:
" Nearer than thou dost hope, there is a rock
From the great circle moving, which o'ersteps
Each vale of horror, save that here his cope
Is shatter'd. By the ruin ye may mount:
For on the side it slants, and most the height
Rises below." With head bent down awhile
My leader stood; then spake: " He warn'd us ill,[1]
Who yonder hangs the sinners on his hook."

   To whom the friar: " At Bologna erst
I many vices of the Devil heard;
Among the rest was said, ' He is a liar,
And the father of lies!' " When he had spoke,
My leader with large strides proceeded on,
Somewhat disturb'd with anger in his look.

   I therefore left the spirits heavy laden,
And, following, his beloved footsteps mark'd.

CANTO XXIV

ARGUMENT

Under the escort of his faithful master, Dante, not without difficulty, makes his way out of the sixth gulf; and, in the
seventh, sees the robbers tormented by venomous and pestilent
serpents. The soul of Vanni Fucci, who had pillaged the
sacristy of Saint James in Pistoia, predicts some calamities
that impended over that city, and over the Florentines.

In the year's early nonage,[2] when the sun
Tempers his tresses in Aquarius' urn,
And now towards equal day the nights recede;
Whenas the rime upon the earth puts on
Her dazzling sister's image, but not long
Her milder sway endures; then riseth up
The village hind, whom fails his wintry store,
And looking out beholds the plain around
All whiten'd; whence impatiently he smites
His thighs, and to his hut returning in,

---

[1] Malacoda had told him that they would find a safe passage.
[2] " At the latter part of January, when the sun enters into
Aquarius, and the equinox is drawing near, when the hoar-frosts
in the morning often wear the appearance of snow, but are melted
by the rising sun " (Cary).

There paces to and fro, wailing his lot,
As a discomfited and helpless man;
Then comes he forth again, and feels new hope
Spring in his bosom, finding e'en thus soon
The world hath changed its countenance, grasps his crook,
And forth to pasture drives his little flock:
So me my guide dishearten'd, when I saw
His troubled forehead; and so speedily
That ill was cured; for at the fallen bridge
Arriving, towards me with a look as sweet,
He turn'd him back, as that I first beheld
At the steep mountain's foot.　Regarding well
The ruin, and some counsel first maintain'd
With his own thought, he open'd wide his arm
And took me up.　As one, who, while he works,
Computes his labour's issue, that he seems
Still to foresee the effect; so lifting me
Up to the summit of one peak, he fix'd
His eye upon another.　"Grapple that,"
Said he, "but first make proof, if it be such
As will sustain thee."　For one *cloak'd* with lead
This were no journey.　Scarcely he, though light,
And I, though onward push'd from crag to crag,
Could mount.　And if the precinct of this coast
Were not less ample than the last, for him
I know not, but my strength had surely fail'd.
But Malebolge all toward the mouth
Inclining of the nethermost abyss,
The site of every valley hence requires
That one side upward slope, the other fall.
　　At length the point from whence the utmost stone
Juts down, we reach'd; soon as to that arrived,
So was the breath exhausted from my lungs,
I could no farther, but did seat me there.
　　"Now needs thy best of man;" so spake my guide:
"For not on downy plumes, nor under shade
Of canopy reposing, fame is won;
Without which whosoe'er consumes his days
Leaveth such vestige of himself on earth,
As smoke in air or foam upon the wave.
Thou therefore rise: vanquish thy weariness
By the mind's effort, in each struggle form'd
To vanquish, if she suffer not the weight
Of her corporeal frame to crush her down.

A longer ladder yet remains to scale :
From these to have escaped sufficeth not;
If well thou note me, profit by my words."

I straightway rose, and show'd myself less spent
Than I in truth did feel me. " On," I cried,
" For I am stout and fearless." Up the rock
Our way we held, more rugged than before,
Narrower, and steeper far to climb. From talk
I ceased not, as we journey'd, so to seem
Least faint; whereat a voice from the other foss
Did issue forth, for utterance suited ill.
Though on the arch that crosses there I stood,
What were the words I knew not, but who spake
Seem'd moved in anger. Down I stoop'd to look;
But my quick eye might reach not to the depth
For shrouding darkness ; wherefore thus I spake :
" To the next circle, teacher, bend thy steps,
And from the wall dismount we; for as hence
I hear and understand not, so I see
Beneath, and nought discern."—" I answer not,"
Said he, " but by the deed. To fair request
Silent performance maketh best return."

We from the bridge's head descended, where
To the eighth mound it joins ; and then, the chasm
Opening to view, I saw a crowd within
Of serpents terrible, so strange of shape
And hideous, that remembrance in my veins
Yet shrinks the vital current. Of her sands
Let Lybia vaunt no more : if Jaculus,
Pareas and Chelyder be her brood,
Cenchris and Amphisbæna, plagues so dire
Or in such numbers swarming ne'er she show'd,
Not with all Ethiopia, and whate'er
Above the Erythræan sea is spawn'd.[1]

Amid this dread exuberance of woe
Ran naked spirits wing'd with horrid fear,
Nor hope had they of crevice where to hide,
Or heliotrope[2] to charm them out of view.
With serpents were their hands behind them bound,

---

[1] As Dr. Moore points out, Dante has borrowed these serpents from Lucan's description of the plagues of Libya, in the ninth book of the *Pharsalia*.

[2] Heliotrope, a kind of chalcedony, was supposed to make its wearer invisible.

Which through their reins infix'd the tail and head,
Twisted in folds before.   And lo ! on one
Near to our side, darted an adder up,
And, where the neck is on the shoulders tied,
Transpierced him.   Far more quickly than e'er pen
Wrote O or I, he kindled, burn'd, and changed
To ashes all, pour'd out upon the earth.
When there dissolved he lay, the dust again
Uproll'd spontaneous, and the self-same form
Instant resumed.   So mighty sages tell,
The Arabian Phœnix, when five hundred years
Have well-nigh circled, dies, and springs forthwith
Renascent : blade nor herb throughout his life
He tastes, but tears of frankincense alone
And odorous amomum : swaths of nard
And myrrh his funeral shroud.   As one that falls,
He knows not how, by force demoniac dragg'd
To earth, or through obstruction fettering up
In chains invisible the powers of man,
Who, risen from his trance, gazeth around,
Bewilder'd with the monstrous agony
He hath endured, and wildly staring sighs ;
So stood aghast the sinner when he rose.
    Oh ! how severe God's judgment, that deals out
Such blows in stormy vengeance.   Who he was,
My teacher next inquired ; and thus in few
He answer'd : " Vanni Fucci [1] am I call'd,
Not long since rained down from Tuscany
To this dire gullet.   Me the bestial life
And not the human pleased, mule that I was,
Who in Pistoia found my worthy den."
    I then to Virgil : " Bid him stir not hence ;
And ask what crime did thrust him hither : once
A man I knew him, choleric and bloody."
    The sinner heard and feign'd not, but towards me
His mind directing and his face, wherein
Was dismal shame depictured, thus he spake :
" It grieves me more to have been caught by thee
In this sad plight, which thou beholdest, than
When I was taken from the other life.

[1] Vanni Fucci, an illegitimate scion of a noble family in Pistoia
and a turbulent Black Guelf, was concerned in the plundering of
the church of San Zeno in Pistoia in 1293, for which crime several
innocent men were put to torture, and one hanged.

I have no power permitted to deny
What thou inquirest. I am doom'd thus low
To dwell, for that the sacristy by me
Was rifled of its goodly ornaments,
And with the guilt another falsely charged.
But that thou mayst not joy to see me thus,
So as thou e'er shalt 'scape this darksome realm,
Open thine ears and hear what I forebode.
Reft of the Neri first Pistoia pines;
Then Florence changeth citizens and laws;
From Valdimagra, drawn by wrathful Mars,
A vapour rises, wrapt in turbid mists,
And sharp and eager driveth on the storm
With arrowy hurtling o'er Piceno's field,
Whence suddenly the cloud shall burst, and strike
Each helpless Bianco prostrate to the ground.[1]
This have I told, that grief may rend thy heart."

CANTO XXV

ARGUMENT

The sacrilegious Fucci vents his fury in blasphemy, is seized by
   serpents, and flying is pursued by Cacus in the form of a
   Centaur, who is described with a swarm of serpents on his
   haunch, and a dragon on his shoulders breathing forth fire.
   Our Poet then meets with the spirits of three of his countrymen, two of whom undergo a marvellous transformation in his
   presence.

WHEN he had spoke, the sinner raised his hands
Pointed in mockery, and cried : "Take them, God!
I level them at thee." From that day forth

[1] Vanni Fucci thus foretells the impending ruin of the White
faction. In May, 1301, the Bianchi, who were then predominant
in Florence, procured the expulsion of the Neri from Pistoia. For
this Dante himself (as the first sentence against him shows) was
one of those held personally responsible. In November, the Neri
entered Florence with the aid of Charles of Valois, and, in April,
1302, made the city " change citizens and laws," by driving out
the Bianchi in their turn. Pistoia now became the last rallying
point of the Bianchi in Tuscany, until their hopes were finally
shattered by the victories of Moroello Malaspina, the lord of the
valley of the Macra (Valdimagra). Campo Piceno, " Piceno's
field," here means the neighbourhood of Pistoia ; but it is doubtful
whether Dante refers to Malaspina's taking of Serravalle in 1302,
or his final reduction of Pistoia in 1306.

The serpents were my friends; for round his neck
One of them rolling twisted, as it said,
" Be silent, tongue!" Another, to his arms
Upgliding, tied them, riveting itself
So close, it took from them the power to move.

    Pistoia! ah, Pistoia! why dost doubt
To turn thee into ashes, cumbering earth
No longer, since in evil act so far
Thou hast outdone thy seed?[1] I did not mark,
Through all the gloomy circles of the abyss,
Spirit, that swell'd so proudly 'gainst his God;
Not him,[2] who headlong fell from Thebes. He fled,
Nor utter'd more; and after him there came
A Centaur full of fury, shouting, " Where,
Where is the caitiff?" On Maremma's marsh
Swarm not the serpent tribe, as on his haunch
They swarm'd, to where the human face begins.
Behind his head, upon the shoulders, lay
With open wings a dragon, breathing fire
On whomsoe'er he met. To me my guide:
" Cacus[3] is this, who underneath the rock
Of Aventine spread oft a lake of blood.
He, from his brethren parted, here must tread
A different journey, for his fraudful theft
Of the great herd that near him stall'd; whence found
His felon deeds their end, beneath the mace
Of stout Alcides, that perchance laid on
A hundred blows, and not the tenth was felt."

    While yet he spake, the Centaur sped away:
And under us three spirits came, of whom
Nor I nor he was ware, till they exclaim'd,
" Say who are ye!"[4] We then brake off discourse,

---

1 Pistoia is said to have been founded by the refugees from the
army of Catiline.

2 Capaneus. *Cf.* above, Canto xiv.

3 A predatory monster who lived on the Aventine, and was slain
by Hercules for stealing the cattle which the latter had taken from
Geryon. Dante (probably misled by Virgil, *Æneid,* viii. 194,
describing him as *semihomo*) makes Cacus a Centaur, separated
in Hell from the other Centaurs because he used fraud while they
employed violence.

4 The extraordinary transformation scene that follows is acted
by the souls of five Florentines of noble birth who lived by thieving:
Agnello Brunelleschi, Buoso degli Abati, and Puccio de' Galigai,
nicknamed Sciancalto (the " lame "); Cianfa de' Donati and
Francesco, or Guercio, de' Cavalcanti. The first three appear in

Intent on these alone. I knew them not:
But, as it chanceth oft, befel that one
Had need to name another. "Where," said he,
"Doth Cianfa lurk?" I, for a sign my guide
Should stand attentive, placed against my lips
The finger lifted. If, O reader! now
Thou be not apt to credit what I tell,
No marvel; for myself do scarce allow
The witness of mine eyes. But as I look'd
Toward them, lo! a serpent with six feet
Springs forth on one, and fastens full upon him:
His midmost grasp'd the belly, a forefoot
Seized on each arm (while deep in either cheek
He flesh'd his fangs); the hinder on the thighs
Were spread, 'twixt which the tail inserted curl'd
Upon the reins behind. Ivy ne'er clasp'd
A dodder'd oak, as round the other's limbs
The hideous monster intertwined his own.
Then, as they both had been of burning wax,
Each melted into other, mingling hues,
That which was either now was seen no more.
Thus up the shrinking paper, ere it burns,
A brown tint glides, not turning yet to black,
And the clean white expires. The other two
Look'd on, exclaiming, "Ah! how dost thou change,
Agnello! See! Thou art nor double now,
Nor only one." The two heads now became
One, and two figures blended in one form
Appear'd, where both were lost. Of the four lengths
Two arms were made: the belly and the chest,
The thighs and legs, into such members changed
As never eye hath seen. Of former shape
All trace was vanish'd. Two, yet neither, seem'd
That image miscreate, and so pass'd on
With tardy steps. As underneath the scourge
Of the fierce dog-star that lays bare the fields,
Shifting from brake to brake the lizard seems

human form; then Cianfa comes as a serpent with six feet, fastens
upon Agnello, and forms one monstrous shape with him; lastly
Cavalcanti, in the form of "an adder all on fire," robs Buoso of
his human shape, while the latter becomes a serpent instead.
Puccio alone remains unchanged. The whole fantastic horror
seems to mean that those who robbed others in the world are now
unable to keep even the bare appearance of humanity for themselves.

A flash of lightning, if he thwart the road;
So toward the entrails of the other two
Approaching seemed an adder all on fire,
As the dark pepper-grain livid and swart.
In that part, whence our life is nourish'd first,
One he transpierced; then down before him fell
Stretch'd out. The pierced spirit look'd on him,
But spake not; yea, stood motionless and yawn'd,
As if by sleep or feverous fit assail'd.
He eyed the serpent, and the serpent him;
One from the wound, the other from the mouth
Breathed a thick smoke, whose vapoury columns join'd.
    Lucan in mute attention now may hear,
Nor thy disastrous fate, Sabellus, tell,
Nor thine, Nasidius.[1] Ovid now be mute.
What if in warbling fiction he record
Cadmus and Arethusa, to a snake
Him changed, and her into a fountain clear,
I envy not; for never face to face
Two natures thus transmuted did he sing,
Wherein both shapes were ready to assume
The other's substance. They in mutual guise
So answer'd that the serpent split his train
Divided to a fork, and the pierced spirit
Drew close his steps together, legs and thighs
Compacted, that no sign of juncture soon
Was visible: the tail, disparted, took
The figure which the spirit lost; its skin
Softening, his indurated to a rind.
The shoulders next I mark'd, that entering join'd
The monster's arm-pits, whose two shorter feet
So lengthen'd, as the others dwindling shrunk.
The feet behind then twisting up became
That part that man conceals, which in the wretch
Was cleft in twain. While both the shadowy smoke
With a new colour veils, and generates
The excrescent pile on one, peeling it off
From the other body, lo! upon his feet
One upright rose, and prone the other fell.

---

[1] In the ninth book of the *Pharsalia*, Lucan describes the appalling effects of serpent's bites upon Sabellus and Nasidius, two of Cato's soldiers, in the Libyan desert. The stories of Cadmus, who was changed into a serpent, and Arethusa, who became a fountain, are told by Ovid, *Metam.* iv. and v.

Nor yet their glaring and malignant lamps
Were shifted, though each feature changed beneath.
Of him who stood erect, the mounting face
Retreated towards the temples, and what there
Superfluous matter came, shot out in ears
From the smooth cheeks; the rest, not backward dragg'd,
Of its excess did shape the nose; and swell'd
Into due size protuberant the lips.
He, on the earth who lay, meanwhile extends
His sharpen'd visage, and draws down the ears
Into the head, as doth the slug his horns.
His tongue, continuous before and apt
For utterance, severs; and the other's fork
Closing unites; that done, the smoke was laid.
The soul, transform'd into the brute, glides off,
Hissing along the vale, and after him
The other talking sputters; but soon turn'd
His new-grown shoulders on him, and in few
Thus to another spake: "Along this path
Crawling, as I have done, speed Buoso now!"

    So saw I fluctuate in successive change
The unsteady ballast of the seventh hold: [1]
And here if aught my pen have swerved, events
So strange may be its warrant. O'er mine eyes
Confusion hung, and on my thoughts amaze.

    Yet scaped they not so covertly, but well
I mark'd Sciancato: he alone it was
Of the three first that came, who changed not: thou
The other's fate, Gaville! still dost rue. [2]

CANTO XXVI

ARGUMENT

Remounting by the steps, down which they had descended to the
    seventh gulf, they go forward to the arch that stretches over
    the eighth, and from thence behold numberless flames wherein
    are punished the evil counsellors, each flame containing a
    sinner—save one, in which were Diomede and Ulysses, the
    latter of whom relates the manner of his death.

FLORENCE, exult! for thou so mightily
Hast thriven, that o'er land and sea thy wings

  [1] The changing inmates of the seventh ring of Malebolge.
  [2] Francesco de' Cavalcanti was killed at Gaville, a village in the
Valdarno, in revenge for which a number of the inhabitants were
murdered by his kinsmen.

Thou beatest, and thy name spreads over Hell.
Among the plunderers, such the three I found,
Thy citizens; whence shame to me thy son,
And no proud honour to thyself redounds.

But if our minds, when dreaming near the dawn,
Are of the truth presageful, thou ere long
Shalt feel what Prato [1] (not to say the rest)
Would fain might come upon thee; and that chance
Were in good time, if it befel thee now.
Would so it were, since it must needs befal!
For as time wears me, I shall grieve the more.

We from the depth departed; and my guide
Remounting scaled the flinty steps, which late
We downward traced, and drew me up the steep.
Pursuing thus our solitary way
Among the crags and splinters of the rock,
Sped not our feet without the help of hands.

Then sorrow seized me, which e'en now revives,
As my thought turns again to what I saw,
And, more than I am wont,[2] I reign and curb
The powers of nature in me, lest they run
Where Virtue guides not; that, if aught of good
My gentle star or something better gave me,
I envy not myself the precious boon.

As in that season, when the sun least veils
His face that lightens all, what time the fly
Gives way to the shrill gnat, the peasant then,
Upon some cliff reclined, beneath him sees
Fire-flies innumerous spangling o'er the vale,

[1] Commentators differ as to whether *Prato* here means the
Tuscan town of that name, which was subject to Florence and had
sometimes been harshly treated by her, or the Cardinal Niccolò da
Prato, legate of Pope Benedict XI., who in June, 1304, being unable
to effect a reconciliation between the factions, laid Florence under
an interdict and excommunicated the citizens. A letter to this
Cardinal is included among Dante's Latin works, but it is very
doubtful if it was really written by him.

[2] " ' When I reflect on the punishment allotted to those who
do not give sincere and upright advice to others, I am more
anxious than ever not to abuse to so bad a purpose those talents,
whatever they may be, which Nature, or rather Providence, has
conferred on me.' It is probable that this declaration was the
result of real feeling in the mind of Dante, whose political
character would have given great weight to any opinion or party
he had espoused, and to whom indigence and exile might have
offered strong temptations to deviate from that line of conduct
which a strict sense of duty prescribed " (Cary).

Vineyard or tilth, where his day-labour lies;
With flames so numberless throughout its space
Shone the eighth chasm, apparent, when the depth
Was to my view exposed. As he, whose wrongs [1]
The bears avenged, at its departure saw
Elijah's chariot, when the steeds erect
Raised their steep flight for heaven; his eyes, meanwhile,
Straining pursued them, till the flame alone,
Upsoaring like a misty speck, he kenn'd:
E'en thus along the gulf moves every flame,
A sinner so enfolded close in each,
That none exhibits token of the theft.

 Upon the bridge I forward bent to look,
And grasp'd a flinty mass, or else had fallen,
Though push'd not from the height. The guide, who mark'd
How I did gaze attentive, thus began:
" Within these ardours are the spirits, each
Swath'd in confining fire."—" Master! thy word,"
I answer'd, " hath assured me; yet I deem'd
Already of the truth, already wish'd
To ask thee who is in yon fire, that comes
So parted at the summit, as it seem'd
Ascending from that funeral pile where lay
The Theban brothers." [2] He replied: " Within,
Ulysses there and Diomede endure
Their penal tortures, thus to vengeance now
Together hasting, as erewhile to wrath.
These in the flame with ceaseless groans deplore
The ambush of the horse, that open'd wide
A portal for that goodly seed to pass,
Which sow'd imperial Rome; nor less the guile
Lament they, whence, of her Achilles 'reft,
Deïdamia yet in death complains.
And there is rued the stratagem that Troy
Of her Palladium spoil'd." [3]—" If they have power

---

[1] Elisha. 2 Kings ii. 24.
[2] Eteocles and Polynices, sons of King Œdipus of Thebes,
the brothers whose quarrel led to the war of the seven against
Thebes. They slew each other, and, when their bodies were being
consumed together on the funeral pile, the flame itself divided in
token of their inextinguishable hatred.
[3] Dante is naturally on the side of the Trojans, whom he regards
as the ancestors of the Roman People. Ulysses and Diomede pre-
vailed upon Achilles to desert Deïdamia and go to Troy; they

Of utterance from within these sparks," said I,
" O Master ! think my prayer a thousand-fold
In repetition urged, that thou vouchsafe
To pause till here the horned flame arrive.
See, how toward it with desire I bend."
    He thus : " Thy prayer is worthy of much praise,
And I accept it therefore ; but do thou
Thy tongue refrain : to question them be mine ;
For I divine thy wish ; and they perchance,
For they were Greeks,[1] might shun discourse with thee."
    When there the flame had come, where time and place
Seem'd fitting to my guide, he thus began :
" O ye, who dwell two spirits in one fire !
If, living, I of you did merit aught,
Whate'er the measure were of that desert,
When in the world my lofty strain I pour'd,
Move ye not on, till one of you unfold
In what clime death o'ertook him self-destroy'd."
    Of the old flame forthwith the greater horn
Began to roll, murmuring, as a fire
That labours with the wind ; then to and fro
Wagging the top, as a tongue uttering sounds,
Threw out its voice, and spake : " When I escaped
From Circe, who beyond a circling year
Had held me near Caieta [2] by her charms,
Ere thus Æneas yet had named the shore ;
Nor fondness for my son, nor reverence
Of my old father, nor return of love,
That should have crown'd Penelope with joy,
Could overcome in me the zeal I had
To explore the world, and search the ways of life,
Man's evil and his virtue. Forth I sail'd
Into the deep illimitable main,
With but one bark, and the small faithful band
That yet cleaved to me. As Iberia far,

stole the Palladium, the image of Pallas, upon which the safety
of Troy depended ; and finally invented the ambush of the wooden
horse, by which Troy was taken, and Æneas compelled to seek
his fortune in Italy, whereby the Roman Empire was founded.
    [1] " There can be no doubt that Dante was ignorant of Greek,
and that his knowledge of everything relating to Greece was
derived from intermediate Latin sources, principally Virgil. Perhaps this is the meaning these verses are intended to convey "
(Oelsner).
    [2] The modern Gaeta.

Far as Marocco, either shore I saw,
And the Sardinian and each isle beside
Which round that ocean bathes.   Tardy with age
Were I and my companions, when we came
To the strait pass, where Hercules ordain'd
The boundaries not to be o'erstepp'd by man.[1]
The walls of Seville to my right I left,
On the other hand already Ceuta past.
'O brothers!' I began, 'who to the west
'Through perils without number now have reach'd;
'To this the short remaining watch, that yet
'Our senses have to wake, refuse not proof
'Of the unpeopled world, following the track
'Of Phœbus.   Call to mind from whence ye sprang:
'Ye were not form'd to live the lives of brutes,
'But virtue to pursue and knowledge high.'
With these few words I sharpen'd for the voyage
The mind of my associates, that I then
Could scarcely have withheld them.   To the dawn
Our poop we turn'd, and for the witless flight
Made our oars wings, still gaining on the left.
Each star of the other pole night now beheld,
And ours so low, that from the ocean floor
It rose not.   Five times re-illumed, as oft
Vanish'd the light from underneath the moon,
Since the deep way we enter'd, when from far
Appear'd a mountain dim,[2] loftiest methought
Of all I e'er beheld.   Joy seized us straight;
But soon to mourning changed.   From the new land
A whirlwind sprung, and at her foremost side
Did strike the vessel.   Thrice it whirl'd her round
With all the waves; the fourth time lifted up
The poop, and sank the prow: so fate decreed:
And over us the booming billow closed.''

[1] The " columns of Hercules," Gibraltar and Mount Abyla, were
held to be the western limit of the inhabited world.

[2] The mountain of Purgatory, to which a pagan soul could not
attain without some ray of divine light. This last voyage of
Ulysses, so finely imitated by Tennyson, seems to be entirely
Dante's own invention.

CANTO XXVII

ARGUMENT

The Poet, treating of the same punishment as in the last Canto, relates that he turned towards a flame in which was the Count Guido da Montefeltro, whose inquiries respecting the state of Romagna he answers; and Guido is thereby induced to declare who he is, and why condemned to that torment.

Now upward rose the flame, and still'd its light
To speak no more, and now pass'd on with leave
From the mild poet gain'd; when following came
Another, from whose top a sound confused,
Forth issuing, drew our eyes that way to look.

　　As the Sicilian bull, that rightfully
His cries first echoed who had shaped its mould,
Did so rebellow, with the voice of him
Tormented, that the brazen monster seem'd
Pierced through with pain; [1] thus, while no way they found,
Nor avenue immediate through the flame,
Into its language turn'd the dismal words:
But soon as they had won their passage forth,
Up from the point, which vibrating obey'd
Their motion at the tongue, these sounds were heard:
" O thou! to whom I now direct my voice,
That lately didst exclaim in Lombard phrase,
' Depart thou; I solicit thee no more;'
Though somewhat tardy I perchance arrive,
Let it not irk thee here to pause awhile,
And with me parley: lo! it irks not me,
And yet I burn. If but e'en now thou fall
Into this blind world, from that pleasant land
Of Latium, whence I draw my sum of guilt,
Tell me if those who in Romagna dwell
Have peace or war. For of the mountains there [2]
Was I, betwixt Urbino and the height
Whence Tiber first unlocks his mighty flood."
　　Leaning I listen'd yet with heedful ear,

[1] Perillus invented a brazen bull for the tyrant Phalaris, in which prisoners were roasted to death, their cries making a sound like the monster's bellowing. The craftsman himself was made the first victim of his device.

[2] Montefeltro lies between Urbino and Monte Coronaro, at the foot of which the Tiber rises.

When, as he touch'd my side, the leader thus :
" Speak thou : he is a Latian."   My reply
Was ready, and I spake without delay :
" O spirit ! who art hidden here below,
Never was thy Romagna without war
In her proud tyrants' bosoms, nor is now :
But open war there left I none.   The state
Ravenna hath maintain'd this many a year,
Is stedfast.   There Polenta's eagle broods ;
And in his broad circumference of plume
O'ershadows Cervia.[1]   The green talons grasp
The land,[2] that stood erewhile the proof so long,
And piled in bloody heap the host of France.
    " The old mastiff of Verrucchio and the young,
That tore Montagna in their wrath, still make,
Where they are wont, an augre of their fangs.[3]
    " Lamone's city, and Santerno's, range
Under the lion of the snowy lair,
Inconstant partisan, that changeth sides,
Or ever summer yields to winter's frost.[4]
And she, whose flank is wash'd of Savio's wave,
As 'twixt the level and the steep she lies,
Lives so 'twixt tyrant power and liberty.[5]
    " Now tell us, I entreat thee, who art thou :
Be not more hard than others.   In the world,
So may thy name still rear its forehead high."
    Then roar'd awhile the fire, its sharpen'd point
On either side waved, and thus breathed at last :
" If I did think my answer were to one
Who ever could return unto the world,

[1] Ravenna and Cervia, in 1300, were ruled by Guido Vecchio da
Polenta, father of Francesca da Rimini and grandfather of Guido
Novello (Dante's friend), whose arms were an eagle, half argent
on an azure field, half gules on field or.
[2] Forlì, which endured a long siege from the French soldiery
of Pope Martin IV., who were finally routed with great slaughter
by Guido da Montefeltro himself, was held in 1300 by Sinibaldo
degli Ordelaffi, whose arms were a lion rampant vert on a field or.
[3] Rimini was still ruled by Malatesta da Verrucchio (" the old
mastiff ") and his son Malatestino, ferocious Guelfs, who had
murdered the Ghibelline Montagna de' Parcitati in 1295.
[4] Faenza and Imola, on the Lamone and Santerno respectively,
were governed by Maghinardo Pagano da Susinana (cf. *Purg.* xiv.),
whose arms were a lion azure on a field argent, and who fought
for Guelf or Ghibelline according to circumstances.
[5] Cesena on the Savio, lying between the plain and the mountain,
alternated between tyranny and freedom.

This flame should rest unshaken.   But since ne'er,
If true be told me, any from this depth
Has found his upward way, I answer thee,
Nor fear lest infamy record the words.

" A man of arms [1] at first, I clothed me then
In good Saint Francis' girdle, hoping so
To have made amends.   And certainly my hope
Had fail'd not, but that he, whom curses light on,
The High Priest, again seduced me into sin.
And how, and wherefore, listen while I tell.
Long as this spirit moved the bones and pulp
My mother gave me, less my deeds bespake
The nature of the lion than the fox.
All ways of winding subtlety I knew,
And with such art conducted, that the sound
Reach'd the world's limit.   Soon as to that part
Of life I found me come, when each behoves
To lower sails [2] and gather in the lines;
That, which before had pleased me, then I rued,
And to repentance and confession turn'd,
Wretch that I was; and well it had bested me.
The chief of the new Pharisees [3] meantime,
Waging his warfare near the Lateran,
Not with the Saracens or Jews (his foes
All Christians were, nor against Acre one
Had fought,[4] nor traffick'd in the Soldan's land),
He his great charge nor sacred ministry

1 Guido da Montefeltro, one of the greatest Ghibelline captains
of the latter half of the thirteenth century and lord of Urbino,
became a Franciscan friar in 1296. According to the story accepted
by Dante, Pope Boniface VIII. summoned him from his convent
to consult him as to the reduction of Palestrina, which was held
by the Colonna who were in arms against the Church. Finding
the place impregnable, Guido, after obtaining the Pope's absolution
in advance, advised him to make large promises and then break
them—by which means Boniface induced the defenders to surrender,
and then razed the fortress to the ground.

2 In the *Convivio* (iv. 28), Dante calls Guido " our most noble
Latin," citing him and Lancelot as two supreme examples of men
who surrendered themselves to God in old age : " In truth, these
noble ones lowered the sails of the activities of the world ; for, in
their advanced age, they gave themselves to religious orders,
putting aside every mundane delight and activity " (Wicksteed's
translation).

3 Boniface VIII.

4 Acre, the last possession of the Christians in the Holy Land
was taken by the Saracens in 1291.

In himself reverenced, nor in me that cord
Which used to mark with leanness whom it girded.
As, in Soracte, Constantine besought,[1]
To cure his leprosy, Sylvester's aid;
So me, to cure the fever of his pride,
This man besought: my counsel to that end
He ask'd; and I was silent; for his words
Seem'd drunken: but forthwith he thus resumed:
' From thy heart banish fear: of all offence
' I hitherto absolve thee. In return,
' Teach me my purpose so to execute,
' That Penestrino [2] cumber earth no more.
' Heaven, as thou knowest, I have power to shut
' And open: and the keys are therefore twain,
' The which my predecessor [3] meanly prized.'

    " Then, yielding to the forceful arguments,
Of silence as more perilous I deem'd,
And answer'd: ' Father! since thou washest me
' Clear of that guilt wherein I now must fall,
' Large promise with performance scant, be sure,
' Shall make thee triumph in thy lofty seat.'

    " When I was number'd with the dead, then came
Saint Francis for me; but a cherub dark
He met, who cried, ' Wrong me not; he is mine,
' And must below to join the wretched crew,
' For the deceitful counsel which he gave.
' E'er since I watch'd him, hovering at his hair.
' No power can the impenitent absolve;
' Nor to repent and will at once consist,
' By contradiction absolute forbid.'
Oh misery! how I shook myself, when he
Seized me, and cried, ' Thou haply thought'st me not
' A disputant in logic so exact!'
To Minos down he bore me; and the judge
Twined eight times round his callous back the tail,
Which biting with excess of rage, he spake:
' This is a guilty soul, that in the fire
' Must vanish.' Hence, perdition-doom'd, I rove
A prey to rankling sorrow, in this garb." [4]

---

[1] According to the legend, Constantine sent for St. Sylvester,
who was in hiding on Mount Soracte, to heal him of leprosy.
[2] Palestrina.
[3] Celestine V. See above, Canto. iii.
[4] Guido died in 1298. There is a designed and tragic contrast

When he had thus fulfill'd his words, the flame
In dolour parted, beating to and fro,
And writhing its sharp horn.   We onward went,
I and my leader, up along the rock,
Far as another arch, that overhangs
The foss, wherein the penalty is paid
Of those who load them with committed sin.

CANTO XXVIII

ARGUMENT

They arrive in the ninth gulf, where the sowers of scandal and
    schismatics 1 are seen with their limbs miserably maimed or
    divided in different ways.   Among these the Poet finds
    Mahomet, Piero da Medicina, Curio, Mosca, and Bertrand
    de Born.

WHO, e'en in words unfetter'd, might at full
Tell of the wounds and blood that now I saw,
Though he repeated oft the tale?   No tongue
So vast a theme could equal, speech and thought
Both impotent alike.   If in one band
Collected, stood the people all, who e'er
Pour'd on Apulia's happy soil 2 their blood,
Slain by the Trojans,3 and in that long war
When of the rings the measured booty made
A pile so high, as Rome's historian writes
Who errs not;4 with the multitude, that felt
The griding force of Guiscard's Norman steel,5

between the account of his death and that of his son, Buonconte da
Montefeltro, in *Purg.* v.
    1 Cary has " schismatics and heretics," of which the latter are
clearly not to be included in this circle.
    2 *La fortunata terra* probably means " fateful," rather than
" happy " land.
    3 The wars of the Romans against the Samnites.   Dante
regards the former as practically one people with the Trojans,
their ancestors.
    4 Livy.   The allusion is to the Punic wars.   Livy records that,
after the battle of Cannæ (B.C. 216), Hannibal showed the
Carthaginian senate three bushels of golden rings taken from
the bodies of the slain Romans.   Dante mentions this again in
the *Convivio*, iv. 5.
    5 Robert Guiscard (*Par.* xviii.), the Norman, carried on san-
guinary wars against the Saracens and Greeks in Southern Italy
and Sicily.   He obtained the title of Duke of Apulia from Pope

And those the rest, whose bones are gather'd yet
At Ceperano, there where treachery
Branded the Apulian name, or where beyond
Thy walls, O Tagliacozzo, without arms
The old Alardo conquer'd ;[1] and his limbs
One were to show transpierced, another his
Clean lopt away ; a spectacle like this
Were but a thing of nought, to the hideous sight
Of the ninth chasm.　A rundlet, that hath lost
Its middle or side stave, gapes not so wide
As one I mark'd torn from the chin throughout
Down to the hinder passage : 'twixt the legs
Dangling his entrails hung, the midriff lay
Open to view, and wretched ventricle,
That turns the englutted aliment to dross.

　　Whilst eagerly I fix on him my gaze,
He eyed me, with his hands laid his breast bare,
And cried, " Now mark how I do rip me : lo !
How is Mohammed mangled :[2] before me
Walks Ali weeping, from the chin his face
Cleft to the forelock ;[3] and the others all,
Whom here thou seest, while they lived, did sow
Scandal and schism, and therefore thus are rent.
A fiend is here behind, who with his sword
Hacks us thus cruelly, slivering again
Each of this ream, when we have compast round
The dismal way ; for first our gashes close
Ere we repass before him.　But, say who
Art thou, that standest musing on the rock,
Haply so lingering to delay the pain
Sentenced upon thy crimes."—" Him death not yet,"
My guide rejoin'd, " hath overta'en, nor sin
Conducts to torment ; but, that he may make
Full trial of your state, I who am dead

Nicholas II. in 1059, and died in 1085, having rescued Gregory
VII. and sacked Rome in the previous year.
　[1] At Ceperano, in 1266, the Apulian barons betrayed the pass
to Charles of Anjou, in consequence of which Manfred was
defeated and slain at Benevento (cf. *Purg.* iii.).　In 1268, Charles,
by means of a stratagem suggested to him by Erard de Valéry
(Alardo), crushed the army of Conradin at the battle of Tagliacozzo.
　[2] Dante regards Mahomet as " a mere Sectarian who had taken
up Christianity and perverted its meaning " (Carlyle).
　[3] Mahomet's son-in-law and fourth successor.

Must through the depths of Hell, from orb to orb,
Conduct him.　Trust my words; for they are true."
　More than a hundred spirits, when that they heard,
Stood in the foss to mark me, through amaze
Forgetful of their pangs.　"Thou, who perchance
Shalt shortly view the sun, this warning thou
Bear to Dolcino:[1] bid him, if he wish not
Here soon to follow me, that with good store
Of food he arm him, lest imprisoning snows
Yield him a victim to Novara's power;
No easy conquest else:" with foot upraised
For stepping, spake Mohammed, on the ground
Then fix'd it to depart.　Another shade,
Pierced in the throat, his nostrils mutilate
E'en from beneath the eyebrows, and one ear
Lopt off, who, with the rest, through wonder stood
Gazing, before the rest advanced, and bared
His wind-pipe, that without was all o'ersmear'd
With crimson stain.　"O thou!" said he, "whom sin
Condemns not, and whom erst (unless too near
Resemblance do deceive me) I aloft
Have seen on Latian ground, call thou to mind
Piero of Medicina,[2] if again
Returning, thou behold'st the pleasant land
That from Vercelli slopes to Marcabò;[3]
And there instruct the twain, whom Fano boasts
Her worthiest sons, Guido and Angelo,
That if 'tis given us here to scan aright
The future, they out of life's tenement
Shall be cast forth, and whelm'd under the waves

1 Fra Dolcino, the head of the sect of the Apostolic Brethren, a native of Novara. A crusade having been proclaimed against him in 1305, he took refuge in the mountains between Novara and Vercelli; but, together with his followers, was reduced by cold and starvation. In 1307 he was burned alive at Vercelli. To what extent he is to be regarded as a reformer, or as a fanatical corruptor of morals, seems still uncertain. Dante evidently accepted the hostile version of his career.

2 Piero de' Biancucci of Medicina, a town between Bologna and Imola, was a nobleman who, when exiled from Bologna in 1287, spent his time in sowing discord among the potentates of Romagna. Dante is said to have met Piero in the house of his family at Medicina.

3 The city of Vercelli in Piedmont, on the Sesia, and the castle of Marcabò near Ravenna, at the mouth of the Po, are here given as the limits of the plain of Lombardy.

Near to Cattolica, through perfidy
Of a fell tyrant. 'Twixt the Cyprian isle
And Balearic, ne'er hath Neptune seen
An injury so foul, by pirates done,
Or Argive crew of old. That one-eyed traitor [1]
(Whose realm, there is a spirit here were fain
His eye had still lack'd sight of) them shall bring
To conference with him, then so shape his end,
That they shall need not 'gainst Focara's [2] wind
Offer up vow nor prayer." I answering thus :
" Declare, as thou dost wish that I above
May carry tidings of thee, who is he,
In whom that sight doth wake such sad remembrance."
    Forthwith he laid his hand on the cheek-bone
Of one, his fellow-spirit, and his jaws
Expanding, cried : " Lo ! this is he I wot of :
He speaks not for himself : the outcast this,
Who overwhelm'd the doubt in Cæsar's mind, [3]
Affirming that delay to men prepared
Was ever harmful." Oh ! how terrified
Methought was Curio, from whose throat was cut
The tongue, which spake that hardy word. Then one,
Maim'd of each hand, uplifted in the gloom
The bleeding stumps, that they with gory spots
Sullied his face, and cried : " Remember thee
Of Mosca too ; I who, alas ! exclaim'd,
' The deed once done, there is an end,' [4] that proved

---

[1] Malatestino Malatesta, the " one-eyed traitor," the " young mastiff " of Canto xxvii., in order to get possession of Fano, invited the two chief nobles of the city, Guido del Cassero and Angelo da Carignano, to meet him at La Cattolica, between Fano and Rimini. At his orders their ship was intercepted off the coast, and they were both flung into the sea and drowned, Fano being annexed to Rimini. This tragedy, here announced in prophetical form, is said to have happened in 1313.

[2] A headland between Fano and La Cattolica, round which a dangerous wind blows. It was here, apparently, that Malatestino's galley met the other ship.

[3] According to Lucan (*Phars.* i.), Curio, with " his venal tongue," advised Cæsar to cross the Rubicon, thus beginning the civil war.

[4] *Capo ha cosa fatta.* When, in 1215, the Amidei were consulting as to what vengeance should be taken upon Buondelmonte de' Buondelmonti, who had broken his engagement with a maiden of their house in order to marry the daughter of Gualdrada Donati, " Mosca de' Lamberti spoke the evil word : *cosa fatta capo ha* (' a thing done has an end ') ; to wit, that he should

A seed of sorrow to the Tuscan race."
    I added : " Ay, and death to thine own tribe."
    Whence, heaping woe on woe, he hurried off,
As one grief-stung to madness. But I there
Still linger'd to behold the troop, and saw
Thing, such as I may fear without more proof
To tell of, but that conscience makes me firm,
The boon companion, who her strong breastplate
Buckles on him, that feels no guilt within,
And bids him on and fear not. Without doubt
I saw, and yet it seems to pass before me,
A headless trunk, that even as the rest
Of the sad flock paced onward. By the hair
It bore the sever'd member, lantern-wise
Pendent in hand, which look'd at us, and said,
" Woe's me !" The spirit lighted thus himself ;
And two there were in one, and one in two.
How that may be, he knows who ordereth so.

    When at the bridge's foot direct he stood,
His arm aloft he rear'd, thrusting the head
Full in our view, that nearer we might hear
The words, which thus it utter'd : " Now behold
This grievous torment, thou, who breathing go'st
To spy the dead : behold, if any else
Be terrible as this. And, that on earth
Thou mayst bear tidings of me, know that I
Am Bertrand, he of Born, who gave king John [1]
The counsel mischievous. Father and son
I set at mutual war. For Absalom

---

be slain ; and so was it done " (Villani, v. 38). This was regarded
as the beginning of the Guelf and Ghibelline factions in Florence.
Cf. above, Canto vi., and below, *Par.* xvi. The Lamberti themselves were practically wiped out of existence by the dissensions
that Mosca had thus originated.

[1] There are two alternative readings : *il Re Giovanni* (" King
John "), here adopted by Cary ; and *il re giovane* (" the Young
King "), which is the one generally accepted at the present day.
The person meant is Prince Henry (whom it is scarcely possible
that Dante could have confused with John), the son of Henry II.
of England, called the " Young King " because twice crowned
in his father's lifetime. Bertran de Born, Lord of Hautefort, is
said to have encouraged Henry to rebel against his father.
Bertran died, about 1215, as a Cistercian monk. He was one
of the most distinguished of the Provençal troubadours, and
composed a striking poem on the death of the " Young English
King " (1183), which is still preserved.

And David more did not Ahitophel,
Spurring them on maliciously to strife.
For parting those so closely knit, my brain
Parted, alas! I carry from its source,
That in this trunk inhabits. Thus the law
Of retribution fiercely works in me."

CANTO XXIX

ARGUMENT

Dante, at the desire of Virgil, proceeds onward to the bridge that
    crosses the tenth gulf, from whence he hears the cries of the
    alchemists and forgers, who are tormented therein; but not
    being able to discern any thing on account of the darkness,
    they descend the rock, that bounds this the last of the com-
    partments in which the eighth circle is divided, and then behold
    the spirits who are afflicted by divers plagues and diseases.
    Two of them, namely, Griffolino of Arezzo and Capocchio of
    Siena, are introduced speaking.

So were mine eyes inebriate with the view
Of the vast multitude, whom various wounds
Disfigured, that they long'd to stay and weep.
    But Virgil roused me : " What yet gazest on?
Wherefore doth fasten yet thy sight below
Among the maim'd and miserable shades?
Thou hast not shown in any chasm beside
This weakness. Know, if thou wouldst number them,
That two-and-twenty miles the valley winds
Its circuit, and already is the moon
Beneath our feet :[1] the time permitted now
Is short; and more, not seen, remains to see."
    " If thou," I straight replied, " hadst weigh'd the
        cause,
For which I look'd, thou hadst perchance excused
The tarrying still." My leader part pursued
His way, the while I follow'd, answering him,
And adding thus : " Within that cave I deem,
Whereon so fixedly I held my ken,
There is a spirit dwells, one of my blood,
Wailing the crime that costs him now so dear."

---

[1] That is, it was about one o'clock in the afternoon of Holy
Saturday.

Then spake my master: " Let thy soul no more
Afflict itself for him.   Direct elsewhere
Its thought, and leave him.   At the bridge's foot
I mark'd how he did point with menacing look
At thee, and heard him by the others named
Geri of Bello.[1]   Thou so wholly then
Wert busied with his spirit, who once ruled
The towers of Hautefort, that thou lookedst not
That way, ere he was gone."—" O guide beloved!
His violent death yet unavenged," said I,
" By any, who are partners in his shame,
Made him contemptuous; therefore, as I think,
He pass'd me speechless by; and, doing so,
Hath made me more compassionate his fate."

So we discoursed to where the rock first show'd
The other valley, had more light been there,
E'en to the lowest depth.   Soon as we came
O'er the last cloister in the dismal rounds
Of Malebolge, and the brotherhood
Were to our view exposed, then many a dart
Of sore lament assail'd me, headed all
With points of thrilling pity, that I closed
Both ears against the volley with mine hands.

As were the torment, if each lazar-house
Of Valdichiana, in the sultry time
'Twixt July and September, with the isle
Sardinia and Maremma's pestilent fen,[2]
Had heap'd their maladies all in one foss
Together; such was here the torment: dire
The stench, as issuing steams from fester'd limbs.

We on the utmost shore of the long rock
Descended still to leftward.   Then my sight
Was livelier to explore the depth, wherein
The minister of the most mighty Lord,
All-searching Justice, dooms to punishment
The forgers noted on her dread record.

---

[1] Geri del Bello Alighieri, a first cousin of Dante's father, was killed by one of the Sacchetti for sowing discord in that family. The date of his death is unknown, but it had not been avenged at the epoch of the vision (1300), though later on (thirty years after the event, according to Benvenuto da Imola) Geri's nephews (sons of Messer Cione del Bello Alighieri) killed one of the Sacchetti in his own house. The Alighieri and Sacchetti were finally reconciled in 1342.

[2] Three regions notoriously unhealthy in the heat.

   More rueful was it not methinks to see
The nation in Ægina droop, what time
Each living thing, e'en to the little worm,
All fell, so full of malice was the air
(And afterward, as bards of yore have told,
The ancient people were restored anew
From seed of emmets),[1] than was here to see
The spirits, that languish'd through the murky vale,
Up-piled on many a stack.   Confused they lay,
One o'er the belly, o'er the shoulders one
Roll'd of another; sideling crawl'd a third
Along the dismal pathway.   Step by step
We journey'd on, in silence looking round,
And listening those diseased, who strove in vain
To lift their forms.   Then two I mark'd, that sat
Propt 'gainst each other, as two brazen pans
Set to retain the heat.   From head to foot,
A tetter bark'd them round.   Nor saw I e'er
Groom currying so fast, for whom his lord
Impatient waited, or himself perchance
Tired with long watching, as of these each one
Plied quickly his keen nails, through furiousness
Of ne'er abated pruriency.   The crust
Came drawn from underneath in flakes, like scales
Scraped from the bream, or fish of broader mail.

   " O thou ! who with thy fingers rendest off
Thy coat of proof," thus spake my guide to one,
" And sometimes makest tearing pincers of them,
Tell me if any born of Latian land
Be among these within : so may thy nails
Serve thee for everlasting to this toil."

   " Both are of Latium," weeping he replied,
" Whom tortured thus thou seest : but who art thou
That hast inquired of us ?"   To whom my guide :
" One that descend with this man, who yet lives,
From rock to rock, and show him hell's abyss."

   Then started they asunder, and each turn'd
Trembling toward us, with the rest, whose ear
Those words redounding struck.   To me my liege
Address'd him : " Speak to them whate'er thou list."
   And I therewith began : " So may no time

   [1] According to Ovid (*Metam.* vii.), when the inhabitants of
Ægina were destroyed by a pestilence, Jupiter restored the population by turning ants into men, who were called the Myrmidons.

Filch your remembrance from the thoughts of men
In the upper world, but after many suns
Survive it, as ye tell me, who ye are,
And of what race ye come.　Your punishment,
Unseemly and disgustful in its kind,
Deter you not from opening thus much to me."

　　"Arezzo was my dwelling,"[1] answer'd one,
"And me Albero of Siena brought,
To die by fire : but that, for which I died,
Leads me not here.　True is, in sport I told him,
That I had learn'd to wing my flight in air ;
And he, admiring much, as he was void
Of wisdom, will'd me to declare to him
The secret of mine art : and only hence,
Because I made him not a Dædalus,
Prevail'd on one supposed his sire to burn me.
But Minos to this chasm, last of the ten,
For that I practised alchemy on earth,
Has doom'd me.　Him no subterfuge eludes."

　　Then to the bard I spake : "Was ever race
Light as Siena's?　Sure not France herself
Can show a tribe so frivolous and vain."

　　The other leprous spirit heard my words,
And thus return'd :[2] "Be Stricca from this charge

---

1 Griffolino of Arezzo, an alchemyst, obtained money from a
Sienese named Albero, on the pretext that he would teach him
to fly.　Albero, finding himself duped, denounced him as a
magician to the Bishop of Siena, who was either his patron or
his father, with the result that Griffolino was burned alive.

2 These exceptions from the general condemnation of the vanity
of the Sienese are, of course, ironical.　The persons mentioned—
Stricca (whose family name is uncertain), Niccolò (either a
Salimbeni or a Buonsignori), who invented a new way of using
cloves in cookery, Caccia de' Cacciaconti of Asciano, and Bartolommeo de' Folcacchieri (whose nickname, Abbagliato, implies the
reverse of wisdom)—were members of the *brigata spendereccia*, or
"spendthrift club," an association of prodigal young Sienese
nobles who ran through their fortunes in an incredibly short
time.　Lano de' Maconi (see above, Canto xiii.) is said also to
have been a member.　It is still a matter of dispute whether this
brigata spendereccia is, or is not, to be identified with the *brigata
nobile e cortese,* "the blithe and lordly fellowship," in honour
of which Folgore da San Gimignano wrote a series of sonnets
(translated by Rossetti, *Early Italian Poets*), and whether the
Niccolò mentioned in this Canto is the Niccolò di Nisi, "whose
praise in Siena springs from lip to lip," to whom Folgore's work
is dedicated.

Exempted, he who knew so temperately
To lay out fortune's gifts; and Niccolò,
Who first the spice's costly luxury
Discover'd in that garden, where such seed
Roots deepest in the soil; and be that troop
Exempted, with whom Caccia of Asciano
Lavish'd his vineyards and wide-spreading woods,
And his rare wisdom Abbagliato show'd
A spectacle for all.   That thou mayst know
Who seconds thee against the Sienese
Thus gladly, bend this way thy sharpen'd sight,
That well my face may answer to thy ken;
So shalt thou see I am Capocchio's ghost,[1]
Who forged transmuted metals by the power
Of alchemy; and if I scan thee right,
Thou needs must well remember how I aped
Creative nature by my subtle art."

CANTO XXX

ARGUMENT

In the same gulf, other kinds of impostors, as those who have
counterfeited the persons of others, or debased the current
coin, or deceived by speech under false pretences, are described
as suffering various diseases. Sinon of Troy and Adamo of
Brescia mutually reproach each other with their several
impostures.

WHAT time resentment burn'd in Juno's breast
For Semele against the Theban blood,
As more than once in dire mischance was rued;
Such fatal frenzy seized on Athamas,[2]
That he his spouse beholding with a babe
Laden on either arm, " Spread out," he cried,
" The meshes, that I take the lioness
And the young lions at the pass :" then forth

1 Capocchio was a Florentine alchemyst, personally known to
Dante, who was burned alive at Siena in 1293.
2 To avenge herself upon Semele and Ino, the daughters of
Cadmus, Juno brought many misfortunes upon the royal family
of Thebes. Among other things, she sent a madness upon
Athamas, the lover of Ino, in which he took the latter and their
little boys, Learchus and Melicertes, for a lioness and her cubs.
The story is told by Ovid, *Metam.* iv.

Stretch'd he his merciless talons, grasping one,
One helpless innocent, Learchus named,
Whom swinging down he dash'd upon a rock;
And with her other burden, self-destroy'd,
The hapless mother plunged.　And when the pride
Of all presuming Troy fell from its height,
By fortune overwhelm'd, and the old king
With his realm perish'd; then did Hecuba,
A wretch forlorn and captive, when she saw
Polyxena first slaughter'd, and her son,
Her Polydorus, on the wild sea-beach
Next met the mourner's view, then reft of sense
Did she run barking even as a dog;[1]
Such mighty power had grief to wrench her soul.
But ne'er the Furies, or of Thebes, or Troy,
With such fell cruelty were seen, their goads
Infixing in the limbs of man or beast,
As now two pale and naked ghosts I saw,
That gnarling wildly scamper'd, like the swine
Excluded from his stye.　One reach'd Capocchio,
And in the neck-joint sticking deep his fangs,
Dragg'd him, that, o'er the solid pavement rubb'd
His belly stretch'd out prone.　The other shape,
He of Arezzo, there left trembling, spake:
"That sprite of air is Schicchi; in like mood
Of random mischief vents he still his spite."
　　To whom I answering: "Oh! as thou dost hope
The other may not flesh its jaws on thee,
Be patient to inform us, who it is,
Ere it speed hence."—"That is the ancient soul
Of wretched Myrrha," he replied, "who burn'd
With most unholy flame for her own sire,
And a false shape assuming, so perform'd
The deed of sin; e'en as the other there,
That onward passes, dared to counterfeit
Donati's features, to feign'd testament
The seal affixing, that himself might gain,
For his own share, the lady of the herd."[2]

[1] Hecuba, Priam's widow, seeing her daughter sacrificed and finding her son murdered, went mad.

[2] Gianni Schicchi de' Cavalcanti, a Florentine famous for his mimicry, at the instigation of Simone Donati, personated the latter's father, Buoso, just deceased, and dictated a will in Simone's favour, in which Gianni himself received a beautiful mare, known as the

When vanish'd the two furious shades, on whom
Mine eye was held, I turn'd it back to view
The other cursed spirits.   One I saw
In fashion like a lute, had but the groin
Been sever'd where it meets the forked part.
Swoln dropsy, disproportioning the limbs
With ill-converted moisture, that the paunch
Suits not the visage, open'd wide his lips,
Gasping as in the hectic man for drought,
One towards the chin, the other upward curl'd.
   " O ye ! who in this world of misery,
Wherefore I know not, are exempt from pain,"
Thus he began, " attentively regard
Adamo's woe.   When living, full supply
Ne'er lack'd me of what most I coveted;
One drop of water now, alas ! I crave.
The rills, that glitter down the grassy slopes
Of Casentino, making fresh and soft
The banks whereby they glide to Arno's stream,
Stand ever in my view; and not in vain;
For more the pictured semblance dries me up,
Much more than the disease, which makes the flesh
Desert these shrivel'd cheeks.   So from the place,
Where I transgress'd, stern justice urging me,
Takes means to quicken more my labouring sighs.
There is Romena, where I falsified
The metal with the Baptist's form imprest,
For which on earth I left my body burnt.
But if I here might see the sorrowing soul
Of Guido, Alessandro, or their brother,
For Branda's limpid spring I would not change
The welcome sight.   One is e'en now within,
If truly the mad spirits tell, that round
Are wandering.   But wherein besteads me that?
My limbs are fetter'd.   Were I but so light,
That I each hundred years might move one inch,
I had set forth already on this path,
Seeking him out amidst the shapeless crew,
Although eleven miles it wind, not less
Than half of one across.   They brought me down
Among this tribe; induced by them, I stamp'd

donna della torma, " the lady of the herd." Myrrha (Ovid,
Metam. x.), daughter of King Cinyras of Cyprus, disguised herself
for a viler motive.

The florens with three carats of alloy." 1
    " Who are that abject pair," I next inquired,
" That closely bounding thee upon thy right
Lie smoking, like a hand in winter steep'd
In the chill stream?"—" When to this gulf I dropp'd,"
He answer'd, " here I found them; since that hour
They have not turn'd, nor ever shall, I ween,
Till time hath run his course.   One is that dame,
The false accuser of the Hebrew youth;
Sinon the other, that false Greek from Troy. 2
Sharp fever drains the reeky moistness out,
In such a cloud upsteam'd."   When that he heard,
One, gall'd perchance to be so darkly named,
With clench'd hand smote him on the braced paunch,
That like a drum resounded : but forthwith
Adamo smote him on the face, the blow
Returning with his arm, that seem'd as hard.
    " Though my o'erweighty limbs have ta'en from me
The power to move," said he, " I have an arm
At liberty for such employ."   To whom
Was answer'd : " When thou wentest to the fire,
Thou hadst it not so ready at command;
Then readier when it coin'd the impostor gold."
    And thus the dropsied : " Ay, now speak'st thou true :
But there thou gavest not such true testimony,
When thou wast question'd of the truth, at Troy."
    " If I spake false, thou falsely stamp'dst the coin,"
Said Sinon; " I am here for but one fault,
And thou for more than any imp beside."
    " Remember," he replied, " O perjured one !
The horse remember, that did teem with death;
And all the world be witness to thy guilt."

1 Maestro Adamo of Brescia, at the instigation of the Conti
Guidi of Romena (Guido, Alessandro, and Aghinolfo), counterfeited the golden florins of Florence. For this, in 1281, he was
burned alive on the Consuma, the pass which leads out of the
Casentino towards Florence, while his aristocratic employers
escaped scot-free. Fonte Branda, " Branda's limpid spring," is
here not the famous fountain of Siena, but a spring of the same
name, near the castle of Romena and in the vicinity of the
spot where Adamo met his doom. The one of the three brothers
who is " e'en now within," that is, already dead, is Count Guido.
The other two were still alive in 1300.
2 Potiphar's wife, who falsely accused Joseph, and the Greek
Sinon, whose treacherous tale induced the Trojans to receive the
wooden horse within their walls.

" To thine," return'd the Greek, " witness the thirst
Whence thy tongue cracks, witness the fluid mound
Rear'd by thy belly up before thine eyes,
A mass corrupt."   To whom the coiner thus :
" Thy mouth gapes wide as ever to let pass
Its evil saying.   Me if thirst assails,
Yet I am stuft with moisture.   Thou art parch'd :
Pains rack thy head : no urging wouldst thou need
To make thee lap Narcissus' mirror up."

  I was all fix'd to listen, when my guide
Admonish'd : " Now beware.   A little more,
And I do quarrel with thee."   I perceived
How angrily he spake, and towards him turn'd
With shame so poignant, as remember'd yet
Confounds me.   As a man that dreams of harm
Befallen him, dreaming wishes it a dream,
And that which is, desires as if it were not;
Such then was I, who, wanting power to speak,
Wish'd to excuse myself, and all the while
Excused me, though unweeting that I did.

  " More grievous fault than thine has been, less
    shame,"
My master cried, " might expiate.   Therefore cast
All sorrow from thy soul; and if again
Chance bring thee, where like conference is held,
Think I am ever at thy side.   To hear
Such wrangling is a joy for vulgar minds."

CANTO XXXI

Argument

The poets, following the sound of a loud horn, are led by it to
    the ninth circle, in which there are four rounds, one enclosed
    within the other, and containing as many sorts of Traitors ;
    but the present Canto shows only that the circle is encompassed
    with Giants, one of whom, Antæus, takes them both in his
    arms and places them at the bottom of the circle.

The very tongue, whose keen reproof before
Had wounded me, that either cheek was stain'd,
Now minister'd my cure.   So have I heard,
Achilles' and his father's javelin caused
Pain first, and then the boon of health restored.

Turning our back upon the vale of woe,
We cross'd the encircled mound in silence.   There
Was less than day and less than night, that far
Mine eye advanced not : but I heard a horn
Sounded so loud, the peal it rang had made
The thunder feeble.   Following its course
The adverse way, my strained eyes were bent
On that one spot.   So terrible a blast
Orlando blew not, when that dismal rout
O'erthrew the host of Charlemain, and quench'd
His saintly warfare.[1]   Thitherward not long
My head was raised, when many a lofty tower
Methought I spied.   " Master," said I, " what land
Is this?"   He answer'd straight : " Too long a space
Of intervening darkness has thine eye
To traverse : thou hast therefore widely err'd
In thy imagining.   Thither arrived
Thou well shalt see, how distance can delude
The sense.   A little therefore urge thee on."
    Then tenderly he caught me by the hand ;
" Yet know," said he, " ere farther we advance,
That it less strange may seem, these are not towers,
But giants.   In the pit they stand immersed,
Each from his navel downward, round the bank."
    As when a fog disperseth gradually,
Our vision traces what the mist involves
Condensed in air ; so piercing through the gross
And gloomy atmosphere, as more and more
We near'd toward the brink, mine error fled
And fear came o'er me.   As with circling round
Of turrets, Montereggion[2] crowns his walls ;
E'en thus the shore, encompassing the abyss,
Was turreted with giants, half their length
Uprearing, horrible, whom Jove from Heaven
Yet threatens, when his muttering thunder rolls.
    Of one already I descried the face,

1 When the rear-guard of Charlemagne's army was attacked
by the Saracens at Roncesvalles, Orlando blew a terrible blast of
his horn to summon the Emperor to his aid ; but Ganellon treacherously persuaded the latter that there was no need for him to turn
back.   The result was that Orlando and all his chivalry were
slain.   *Cf.* below, Canto xxxii., and *Par.* xviii.
2 A castle between Siena and San Gimignano.   The turrets
to which Dante refers can still in part be seen.

Shoulders, and breast, and of the belly huge
Great part, and both arms down along his ribs.[1]
  All-teeming Nature, when her plastic hand
Left framing of these monsters, did display
Past doubt her wisdom, taking from mad War
Such slaves to do his bidding; and if she
Repent her not of the elephant and whale,
Who ponders well confesses her therein
Wiser and more discreet; for when brute force
And evil will are back'd with subtlety,
Resistance none avails.   His visage seem'd
In length and bulk, as doth the pine [2] that tops
Saint Peter's Roman fane; and the other bones
Of like proportion, so that from above
The bank, which girdled him below, such height
Arose his stature, that three Friezelanders
Had striven in vain to reach but to his hair.
Full thirty ample palms was he exposed
Downward from whence a man his garment loops.
" Raphel baï ameth, sabì almì : " [3]
So shouted his fierce lips, which sweeter hymns
Became not; and my guide address'd him thus :
" O senseless spirit ! let thy horn for thee
Interpret : therewith vent thy rage, if rage
Or other passion wring thee.   Search thy neck,
There shalt thou find the belt that binds it on.
Spirit confused ! lo, on thy mighty breast
Where hangs the baldrick ! "   Then to me he spake :
" He doth accuse himself.   Nimrod is this,
Through whose ill counsel in the world no more
One tongue prevails.   But pass we on, nor waste
Our words; for so each language is to him,
As his to others, understood by none."
  Then to the leftward turning sped we forth,
And at a sling's throw found another shade
Far fiercer and more huge.   I cannot say

  [1] Nimrod (Genesis x., xi.), the supposed builder of the Tower
of Babel, is represented by St. Augustine and Orosius as a giant.
Cf. *Purg.* xii.
  [2] The bronze pine-cone, once on the top of the Mausoleum of
Adrian and now in the Vatican gardens, in Dante's time stood in
front of St. Peter's.   It is between seven and eight feet high.
  [3] Words meant to be unintelligible, suggesting the confusion
of languages at the building of the Tower of Babel (Gen. xi.).

What master hand had girt him; but he held
Behind the right arm fetter'd, and before,
The other, with a chain, that fasten'd him
From the neck down; and five times round his form
Apparent met the wreathed links. "This proud one
Would of his strength against almighty Jove
Make trial," said my guide: "whence he is thus
Requited: Ephialtes him they call.
Great was his prowess, when the giants brought
Fear on the gods: those arms, which then he plied,
Now moves he never." Forthwith I return'd:
"Fain would I, if 't were possible, mine eyes,
Of Briareus immeasurable, gain'd
Experience next." [1] He answer'd: "Thou shalt see
Not far from hence Antæus, who both speaks
And is unfetter'd, who shall place us there
Where guilt is at its depth. Far onward stands
Whom thou wouldst fain behold, in chains, and made
Like to this spirit, save that in his looks
More fell he seems." By violent earthquake rock'd
Ne'er shook a tower, so reeling to its base,
As Ephialtes. More than ever then
I dreaded death; nor than the terror more
Had needed, if I had not seen the cords
That held him fast. We, straightway journeying on,
Came to Antæus, who, five ells complete
Without the head, forth issued from the cave. [2]

"O thou, who in the fortunate vale, that made
Great Scipio heir of glory, when his sword
Drove back the troop of Hannibal in flight,
Who thence of old didst carry for thy spoil
An hundred lions; and if thou hadst fought
In the high conflict on thy brethren's side,
Seems as men yet believed, that through thine arm
The sons of earth had conquer'd; now vouchsafe
To place us down beneath, where numbing cold
Locks up Cocytus. Force not that we crave
Or Tityus' help or Typhon's. [3] Here is one

[1] Ephialtes and Briareus were two of the giants who made war upon the gods of Olympus.

[2] Antæus, a giant of Libya, did not join in the war against the gods, and is therefore unfettered. He was ultimately killed by Hercules (Alcides). Dante's account of him, in Virgil's address, is based upon Lucan, *Phars.* iv.

[3] Tityus and Typhon (Typhœus), two giants cast down to

Can give what in this realm ye covet.   Stoop
Therefore, nor scornfully distort thy lip.
He in the upper world can yet bestow
Renown on thee; for he doth live, and looks
For life yet longer, if before the time
Grace call him not unto herself."   Thus spake
The teacher.   He in haste forth stretch'd his hands,
And caught my guide.   Alcides whilom felt
That grapple, straiten'd sore.   Soon as my guide
Had felt it, he bespake me thus :   " This way,
That I may clasp thee ;"   then so caught me up,
That we were both one burden.   As appears
The tower of Carisenda,[1] from beneath
Where it doth lean, if chance a passing cloud
So sail across, that opposite it hangs ;
Such then Antæus seem'd, as at mine ease
I mark'd him stooping.   I were fain at times
To have past another way.   Yet in the abyss,
That Lucifer with Judas low ingulfs,
Lightly he placed us ; nor, there leaning, stay'd ;
But rose, as in a bark the stately mast.

CANTO XXXII

ARGUMENT

This Canto treats of the first, and, in part, of the second of those
    rounds, into which the ninth and last, or frozen circle, is
    divided.   In the former, called Caïna, Dante finds Camiccione
    de' Pazzi, who gives him an account of other sinners who are
    there punished ; and in the next, named Antenora, he hears
    in like manner from Bocca degli Abati who his fellow-sufferers
    are.

COULD I command rough rhymes and hoarse, to suit
That hole of sorrow o'er which every rock
His firm abutment rears, then might the vein
Of fancy rise full springing : but not mine
Such measures, and with faltering awe I touch

Tartarus by Jupiter.   Dr. Toynbee notes that " in coupling these
two, Dante evidently had in mind a passage where Lucan mentions
them together, and implies that Antæus was mightier than they
(*Phars.* iv. 593–597)."
   [1] The Carisenda (or Garisenda) is one of the leaning towers of
Bologna, the other being known as the Torre Asinelli.

The mighty theme; for to describe the depth
Of all the universe, is no emprize
To jest with, and demands a tongue not used
To infant babbling.　But let them assist
My song, the tuneful maidens,[1] by whose aid
Amphion wall'd in Thebes; so with the truth
My speech shall best accord.　Oh ill-starr'd folk,
Beyond all others wretched! who abide
In such a mansion, as scarce thought finds words
To speak of, better had ye here on earth
Been flocks, or mountain goats.　As down we stood
In the dark pit beneath the giants' feet,
But lower far than they, and I did gaze
Still on the lofty battlement, a voice
Bespake me thus: "Look how thou walkest.　Take
Good heed, thy soles do tread not on the heads
Of thy poor brethren."　Thereupon I turn'd,
And saw before and underneath my feet
A lake,[2] whose frozen surface liker seem'd
To glass than water.　Not so thick a veil
In winter e'er hath Austrian Danube spread
O'er his still course, nor Tanais far remote
Under the chilling sky.　Roll'd o'er that mass
Had Tabernich or Pietrapana [3] fallen,
Not e'en its rim had creak'd.　As peeps the frog
Croaking above the wave, what time in dreams
The village gleaner oft pursues her toil,
So, to where modest shame appears, thus low
Blue pinch'd and shrined in ice the spirits stood,
Moving their teeth in shrill note like the stork.
His face each downward held; their mouth the cold,
Their eyes express'd the dolour of their heart.

[1] The Muses.
[2] The infernal river Cocytus is here frozen into a lake of ice,
in which the souls of traitors are embedded. There are four
divisions : (i) *Caïna*, called from Cain, in which are the treacherous
murderers of their own kindred ; (ii) *Antenora,* called from
Antenor, who (without any Homeric or Virgilian warrant) was
supposed to have betrayed Troy to the Greeks, which contains
traitors to their native land ; (iii) *Tolomea,* so named from
Ptolemy, the murderer of Simon Maccabæus, the region of those
who did murder under cover of hospitality ; (iv) *Giudecca,* the
place of Judas, in which are traitors to their lords and benefactors.
[3] Two mountains, one in Slavonia, the other in the district
known as the Garfagnana, between Tuscany and the former duchy
of Modena. The Tanais is the river Don.

A space I look'd around, then at my feet
Saw two so strictly join'd, that of their head
The very hairs were mingled. " Tell me ye,
Whose bosoms thus together press," said I,
" Who are ye?"   At that sound their necks they bent;
And when their looks were lifted up to me,
Straightway their eyes, before all moist within,
Distill'd upon their lips, and the frost bound
The tears betwixt those orbs, and held them there.
Plank unto plank hath never cramp closed up
So stoutly.   Whence, like two enraged goats,
They clash'd together : them such fury seized.

And one, from whom the cold both ears had reft,
Exclaim'd, still looking downward : " Why on us
Dost speculate so long?   If thou wouldst know
Who are these two,[1] the valley, whence his wave
Bisenzio slopes, did for its master own
Their sire Alberto, and next him themselves.
They from one body issued : and throughout
Caïna thou mayst search, nor find a shade
More worthy in congealment to be fix'd;
Not him,[2] whose breast and shadow Arthur's hand
At that one blow dissever'd ; not Focaccia ;[3]
No, not this spirit, whose o'erjutting head
Obstructs my onward view : he bore the name
Of Mascheroni :[4] Tuscan if thou be,
Well knowest who he was.   And to cut short

[1] Alessandro and Napoleone degli Alberti, sons of Count Alberto
degli Alberti of Mangona, whose possessions lay in the valleys of
the Sieve and Bisenzio, quarrelled over the inheritance and killed
each other. The exact date is uncertain, but it was shortly after
1282. They are evidently the *fratei miseri lassi*, alluded to above,
which should be rendered " the weary wretched brothers," and not
" thy poor brethren," as Cary does.

[2] Mordred, nephew and son of King Arthur. In his last battle,
Arthur ran Mordred through with his lance, and, at the same time,
received his own death-wound from his hands. According to the
old French romance, when Arthur drew back his lance, a ray of the
sun passed through the wound.

[3] Focaccia de' Cancellieri of Pistoia, whose treacherous murder
of two of his kinsmen began the disastrous feuds of the Bianchi
and Neri, which spread thence to Florence. Here he is, perhaps,
damned by anticipation, as he was probably still living at the
epoch of the vision.

[4] Sassol Mascheroni, of the Toschi family of Florence, murdered
a child, the only son of his rich uncle, to obtain the latter's
inheritance.

All further question, in my form behold
What once was Camiccione.   I await
Carlino here my kinsman, whose deep guilt
Shall wash out mine."[1]   A thousand visages
Then mark'd I, which the keen and eager cold
Had shaped into a doggish grin ;[2]   whence creeps
A shivering horror o'er me, at the thought
Of those frore shallows.   While we journey'd on
Toward the middle, at whose point unites
All heavy substance, and I trembling went
Through that eternal chilness, I know not
If will it were, or destiny, or chance,
But, passing 'midst the heads, my foot did strike
With violent blow against the face of one.

     "Wherefore dost bruise me?" weeping he exclaim'd ;
"Unless thy errand be some fresh revenge
For Montaperto, wherefore troublest me?"

     I thus : "Instructor, now await me here,
That I through him may rid me of my doubt :
Thenceforth what haste thou wilt." The teacher paused ;
And to that shade I spake, who bitterly
Still cursed me in his wrath.   "What art thou, speak,
That railest thus on others?"   He replied :
"Now who art thou, that smiting others' cheeks,
Through Antenora roamest, with such force
As were past sufferance, wert thou living still?"

     "And I am living, to thy joy perchance,"
Was my reply, "if fame be dear to thee,
That with the rest I may thy name enrol."

     "The contrary of what I covet most,"
Said he, "thou tender'st : hence ! nor vex me more.
Ill knowest thou to flatter in this vale."

     Then seizing on his hinder scalp I cried :
"Name thee, or not a hair shall tarry here."

     "Rend all away," he answer'd, "yet for that
I will not tell, nor show thee, who I am,
Though at my head thou pluck a thousand times."

---

[1] Camiccione de' Pazzi, the speaker, one of the Pazzi of Valdarno, murdered his kinsman, Ubertino. Carlino de' Pazzi, still living, is a deeper traitor, because his treason will be against his country ; in 1302, he surrendered the castle of Piantravigne in Valdarno to the Neri, whereby many Bianchi were slain or taken.

[2] These are the souls in Antenora, Guelf and Ghibelline traitors alike.

Now I had grasp'd his tresses, and stript off
More than one tuft, he barking, with his eyes
Drawn in and downward, when another cried,
" What ails thee, Bocca?[1]   Sound not loud enough
Thy chattering teeth, but thou must bark outright?
What devil wrings thee?"—" Now," said I, " be dumb,
Accursed traitor !   To thy shame, of thee
True tidings will I bear."—" Off !" he replied;
" Tell what thou list : but, as thou scape from hence,
To speak of him whose tongue hath been so glib,
Forget not : here he wails the Frenchman's gold.
' Him of Duera,'[2] thou canst say, ' I mark'd,
' Where the starved sinners pine.'   If thou be ask'd
What other shade was with them, at thy side
Is Beccaria,[3] whose red gorge distain'd
The biting axe of Florence.   Further on,
If I misdeem not, Soldanieri[4] bides,
With Ganellon,[5] and Tribaldello, him
Who oped Faenza when the people slept."[6]
  We now had left him, passing on our way,
When I beheld two spirits by the ice
Pent in one hollow, that the head of one
Was cowl unto the other; and as bread
Is raven'd up through hunger, the uppermost
Did so apply his fangs to the other's brain,

---

[1] Bocca degli Abati, who, though a Ghibelline, was in the ranks
of the Guelfs at the battle of Montaperti (1260), treacherously
struck off the hand of the knight who carried the banner of
the Florentine Republic, and thereby caused the overthrow and
slaughter of his own countrymen.   It is just possible that he was
a kinsman of Dante's mother.

[2] Buoso da Duera, a Ghibelline of Cremona, had been ordered
by Manfred to oppose the advance of Charles of Anjou (1265) ; he
allowed the latter to enter Parma at his will, in consideration,
it was said, of a huge bribe.

[3] Tesauro de' Beccheria, Abbot of Vallombrosa and papal legate,
was beheaded by the Florentine Guelfs in 1258, on a charge of
plotting with the Ghibellines.

[4] Gianni Soldanieri, a Ghibelline noble who apparently went
over to the Guelf democracy with a view to self-aggrandisement
(1266).

[5] Ganellon, the typical traitor of the Carlovingian legend.   Cf.
above, Canto xxxi.

[6] Tebaldello, or Tribaldello de' Zambrasi, in 1280, treacherously
opened the gates of Faenza to the Bolognese Guelfs (the Geremei),
to enable them to slaughter their enemies, the Ghibelline Lambertazzi, who had taken shelter in that city.

Where the spine joins it.   Not more furiously
On Menalippus' temples Tydeus [1] gnaw'd,
Than on that skull and on its garbage he.
    " O thou ! who show'st so beastly sign of hate
'Gainst him thou prey'st on, let me hear," said I,
" The cause, on such condition, that if right
Warrant thy grievance, knowing who ye are,
And what the colour of his sinning was,
I may repay thee in the world above,
If that, wherewith I speak, be moist so long."

CANTO XXXIII

ARGUMENT

The Poet is told by Count Ugolino de' Gherardeschi of the cruel
    manner in which he and his children were famished in the tower
    at Pisa, by command of the Archbishop Ruggieri.   He next
discourses of the third round, called Ptolomea, wherein those
are punished who have betrayed others under the semblance of
kindness; and among these he finds the Friar Alberigo de'
Manfredi, who tells him of one whose soul was already tormented in that place, though his body appeared still to be alive
upon the earth, being yielded up to the governance of a fiend.

His jaws uplifting from their fell repast,
That sinner wiped them on the hairs o' the head,
Which he behind had mangled, then began :
" Thy will obeying, I call up afresh
Sorrow past cure ; which, but to think of, wrings
My heart, or ere I tell on 't.   But if words,
That I may utter, shall prove seed to bear
Fruit of eternal infamy to him,
The traitor whom I gnaw at, thou at once
Shalt see me speak and weep.   Who thou mayst be
I know not, nor how here below art come :
But Florentine thou seemest of a truth,
When I do hear thee.   Know, I was on earth
Count Ugolino,[2] and the Archbishop he

---

[1] Tydeus (the father of Diomede), in the war of the seven against
Thebes, when mortally wounded, gnawed the skull of Menalippus,
who had given him his wound, and whom he himself had
slain.

[2] Giovanni Villani tells us that, in 1288, Pisa was divided into
three factions, each striving for predominance.   The Guelfs had split
into two, one led by Count Ugolino della Gherardesca, the other by

Ruggieri. Why I neighbour him so close,
Now list.   That through effect of his ill thoughts
In him my trust reposing, I was ta'en
And after murder'd, need is not I tell.
What therefore thou canst not have heard, that is,
How cruel was the murder, shalt thou hear,
And know if he have wrong'd me.   A small grate
Within that mew, which for my sake the name
Of famine bears, where others yet must pine,
Already through its opening several moons
Had shown me, when I slept the evil sleep
That from the future tore the curtain off.
This one, methought, as master of the sport,
Rode forth to chase the gaunt wolf, and his whelps,
Unto the mountain which forbids the sight
Of Lucca to the Pisan.   With lean brachs
Inquisitive and keen, before him ranged
Lanfranchi with Sismondi and Gualandi.
After short course the father and the sons
Seem'd tired and lagging, and methought I saw
The sharp tusks gore their sides.   When I awoke,
Before the dawn, amid their sleep I heard
My sons (for they were with me) weep and ask
For bread.   Right cruel art thou, if no pang
Thou feel at thinking what my heart foretold;
And if not now, why use thy tears to flow?

his grandson, Nino Visconti (see *Purg.* viii.) ; while the head of the
Ghibellines was the Archbishop of Pisa, Ruggieri degli Ubaldini
(nephew of the Cardinal, for whom see above, Canto x.), who was
supported by the Lanfranchi, Sismondi, Gualandi, and other
families. Count Ugolino had already acquired a sinister reputation
by his surrender of certain castles to the Florentines and Lucchese
after the defeat of the Pisans by the Genoese at Meloria, in 1284,
as also for his questionable conduct in that naval battle. He now
united with the Archbishop to expel Nino and his party, and thereby
obtained the chief control of the State. Finding the Guelfs thus
weakened and himself used as a mere tool, the Archbishop stirred
up the populace against Ugolino on the grounds of his former
treasons. The Count was seized, with his two sons and two
grandsons (Gaddo, Uguccione, Nino, called Brigata, and Anselm-
uccio, or "Little Anselm"), and imprisoned in the Torre dei
Gualandi. This was in July, 1288. In the following March, 1289,
Guido da Montefeltro having been appointed captain of Pisa, the
keys were thrown into the Arno, and the prisoners left to starve to
death—even the spiritual consolation of a priest being denied them.
The tower was thereafter called the "Torre della Fame," or
"Tower of Famine."

Now had they waken'd; and the hour drew near
When they were wont to bring us food; the mind
Of each misgave him through his dream, and I
Heard, at its outlet underneath, lock'd up
The horrible tower: whence, uttering not a word,
I look'd upon the visage of my sons.
I wept not: so all stone I felt within.
They wept: and one, my little Anselm, cried,
' Thou lookest so! Father, what ails thee?'   Yet
I shed no tear, nor answer'd all that day
Nor the next night, until another sun
Came out upon the world.   When a faint beam
Had to our doleful prison made its way,
And in four countenances I descried
The image of my own, on either hand
Through agony I bit; and they, who thought
I did it through desire of feeding, rose
O' the sudden, and cried, ' Father, we should grieve
' Far less, if thou wouldst eat of us: thou gavest
' These weeds of miserable flesh we wear;
' And do thou strip them off from us again.'
Then, not to make them sadder, I kept down
My spirit in stillness. That day and the next
We all were silent. Ah, obdurate earth!
Why open'dst not upon us? When we came
To the fourth day, then Gaddo at my feet
Outstretch'd did fling him, crying, ' Hast no help
' For me, my father!' There he died; and e'en
Plainly as thou seest me, saw I the three
Fall one by one 'twixt the fifth day and sixth:
Whence I betook me, now grown blind, to grope
Over them all, and for three days aloud
Call'd on them who were dead. Then, fasting got
The mastery of grief.'' [1] Thus having spoke,
Once more upon the wretched skull his teeth
He fasten'd like a mastiff's 'gainst the bone,
Firm and unyielding. Oh, thou Pisa! shame
Of all the people, who their dwelling make
In that fair region, where the Italian voice
Is heard; since that thy neighbours are so slack
To punish, from their deep foundations rise

---

[1] Sorrow for his children could not slay him, but starvation did
the work.

Capraia and Gorgona,[1] and dam up
The mouth of Arno; that each soul in thee
May perish in the waters.   What if fame
Reported that thy castles were betray'd
By Ugolino, yet no right hadst thou
To stretch his children on the rack.   For them,
Brigata, Uguccione, and the pair
Of gentle ones, of whom my song hath told,
Their tender years, thou modern Thebes, did make
Uncapable of guilt.   Onward we pass'd,
Where others, skarf'd in rugged folds of ice,
Not on their feet were turn'd, but each reversed.

    There, very weeping suffers not to weep;
For, at their eyes, grief, seeking passage, finds
Impediment, and rolling inward turns
For increase of sharp anguish : the first tears
Hang cluster'd, and like crystal vizors show,
Under the socket brimming all the cup.

    Now though the cold had from my face dislodged
Each feeling, as 't were callous, yet me seem'd
Some breath of wind I felt.   "Whence cometh this,"
Said I, "my Master?   Is not here below
All vapour quench'd?"   "Thou shalt be speedily,"
He answer'd, "where thine eyes shall tell thee whence,
The cause descrying of this airy shower."

    Then cried out one, in the chill crust who mourn'd :
"O souls ! so cruel, that the farthest post
Hath been assign'd you,[2] from this face remove
The harden'd veil; that I may vent the grief
Impregnate at my heart, some little space,
Ere it congeal again."   I thus replied :
"Say who thou wast, if thou wouldst have mine aid;
And if I extricate thee not, far down
As to the lowest ice may I descend."

    "The friar Alberigo," answer'd he,
"Am I, who from the evil garden pluck'd
Its fruitage, and am here repaid, the date
More luscious for my fig."—"Hah !" I exclaim'd,
"Art thou too dead?"—"How in the world aloft
It fareth with my body," answer'd he,
"I am right ignorant.   Such privilege

1 Islands off the Tuscan coast near Livorno.
2 Not knowing that Dante is a living man, the spirit supposes
that he and his companion are doomed to an even lower place in
Hell than his own.

Hath Ptolomea,[1] that oft-times the soul
Drops hither, ere by Atropos divorced.
And that thou mayst wipe out more willingly
The glazed tear-drops that o'erlay mine eyes,
Know that the soul, that moment she betrays,
As I did, yields her body to a fiend
Who after moves and governs it at will,
Till all its time be rounded : headlong she
Falls to this cistern.   And perchance above
Doth yet appear the body of a ghost,
Who here behind me winters.   Him thou know'st,
If thou but newly art arrived below.
The years are many that have past away,
Since to this fastness Branca Doria came."

" Now," answer'd I, " methinks thou mockest me ;
For Branca Doria never yet hath died,
But doth all natural functions of a man,
Eats, drinks, and sleeps, and putteth raiment on."

He thus : " Not yet unto that upper foss
By th' evil talons guarded, where the pitch
Tenacious boils, had Michel Zanche reach'd,
When this one left a demon in his stead
In his own body, and of one his kin,
Who with him treachery wrought.   But now put forth
Thy hand, and ope mine eyes."   I oped them not.
Ill manners were best courtesy to him.

Ah Genoese ! men perverse in every way,
With every foulness stain'd, why from the earth
Are ye not cancel'd?   Such an one of yours
I with Romagna's darkest spirit [2] found,

1 " Dante assigns to Tolomea the grim ' privilege ' (perhaps
suggested by Psalm lv. 15, ' Let them go down quick into hell,'
and Luke xxii. 3) of receiving damned souls while those to whom
they belong are still alive upon earth, their bodies meanwhile
being tenanted by fiends from hell " (Toynbee).   Alberigo de'
Manfredi of Faenza (of which town his family were rulers), one
of the *frati gaudenti*, or " jovial friars," to avenge a blow received
from his brother Manfred, invited the latter and his son to a
banquet.   His call for the dessert, " Bring the fruit," was the
signal at which his hired murderers rushed in and stabbed his
two guests to death.   The *male frutta*, " evil fruit," of Frate
Alberigo became proverbial.   This was in 1285.   Branca d'Oria
of Genoa, about 1290, invited his father-in-law, Michele Zanche
(see above, Canto xxii.), to a banquet, at which he murdered him
with the aid of a nephew (the kinsman referred to in the text).
Both Alberigo and Branca were still living in 1300, the date of
the vision.
2 Frate Alberigo.

As, for his doings, even now in soul
Is in Cocytus plunged, and yet doth seem
In body still alive upon the earth.

CANTO XXXIV

ARGUMENT

In the fourth and last round of the ninth circle, those who have
betrayed their benefactors are wholly covered with ice. And in
the midst is Lucifer, at whose back Dante and Virgil ascend,
till by a secret path they reach the surface of the other hemisphere of the earth, and once more obtain sight of the stars.

" THE banners of Hell's Monarch do come forth
Toward us ;[1] therefore look," so spake my guide,
" If thou discern him." As, when breathes a cloud
Heavy and dense, or when the shades of night
Fall on our hemisphere, seems view'd from far
A windmill, which the blast stirs briskly round ;
Such was the fabric then methought I saw.
    To shield me from the wind, forthwith I drew
Behind my guide : no covert else was there.
    Now came I (and with fear I bid my strain
Record the marvel) where the souls were all
Whelm'd underneath, transparent, as through glass
Pellucid the frail stem. Some prone were laid ;
Others stood upright, this upon the soles,
That on his head, a third with face to feet
Arch'd like a bow. When to the point we came,
Whereat my guide was pleased that I should see
The creature eminent in beauty once,
He from before me stepp'd and made me pause.
    " Lo !" he exclaim'd, " lo Dis ;[2] and lo the place,
Where thou hast need to arm thy heart with strength."
    How frozen and how faint I then became,
Ask me not, reader ! for I write it not ;
Since words would fail to tell thee of my state.
I was not dead nor living. Think thyself,
If quick conception work in thee at all,
How I did feel. That Emperor, who sways
The realm of sorrow, at mid breast from the ice

[1] *Vexilla regis prodeunt inferni*, a parody of the opening line of
a hymn by Fortunatus which is still sung in procession in Catholic
churches on the morning of Good Friday.
[2] Here identified with Lucifer.

Stood forth; and I in stature am more like
A giant, than the giants are his arms.
Mark now how great that whole must be, which suits
With such a part.   If he were beautiful
As he is hideous now, and yet did dare
To scowl upon his Maker, well from him
May all our misery flow.   Oh what a sight!
How passing strange it seem'd, when I did spy
Upon his head three faces: one in front
Of hue vermilion, the other two with this
Midway each shoulder join'd and at the crest;
The right 'twixt wan and yellow seem'd; the left
To look on, such as come from whence old Nile
Stoops to the lowlands.[1]   Under each shot forth
Two mighty wings, enormous as became
A bird so vast.   Sails never such I saw
Outstretch'd on the wide sea.   No plumes had they,
But were in texture like a bat; and these
He flapp'd i' th' air, that from him issued still
Three winds, wherewith Cocytus to its depth
Was frozen.[2]   At six eyes he wept: the tears
Adown three chins distill'd with bloody foam.
At every mouth his teeth a sinner champ'd,
Bruised as with ponderous engine; so that three
Were in this guise tormented.   But far more
Than from that gnawing, was the foremost pang'd
By the fierce rending, whence oft-times the back
Was stript of all its skin.   "That upper spirit,
Who hath worst punishment," so spake my guide,
"Is Judas, he that hath his head within
And plies the feet without.   Of th' other two,
Whose heads are under, from the murky jaw
Who hangs, is Brutus: lo! how he doth writhe
And speaks not.   The other, Cassius, that appears
So large of limb.[3]   But night now re-ascends;
And it is time for parting.[4]   All is seen."

[1] Lucifer's three faces (yellow, black, and red) are an infernal
antithesis to the attributes of the three Persons of the Blessed
Trinity; impotence, ignorance, and hatred are contrasted with
Power, Wisdom, and Love.
[2] The three winds produced by his wings are lust, pride, and
avarice.
[3] The three arch-traitors: Judas Iscariot, who betrayed the
Divine Founder of the Church; Brutus and Cassius, who murdered the imperial founder of the Empire.
[4] The night of Easter-Eve on earth.

I clipp'd him round the neck; for so he bade :
And noting time and place, he, when the wings
Enough were oped, caught fast the shaggy sides,
And down from pile to pile descending stepp'd
Between the thick fell and the jagged ice.

Soon as he reach'd the point, whereat the thigh
Upon the swelling of the haunches turns,
My leader there, with pain and struggling hard,
Turn'd round his head where his feet stood before,
And grappled at the fell as one who mounts ;
That into Hell methought we turn'd again.

" Expect that by such stairs as these," thus spake
The teacher, panting like a man forespent,
" We must depart from evil so extreme :"
Then at a rocky opening issued forth,
And placed me on the brink to sit, next join'd
With wary step my side.   I raised mine eyes,
Believing that I Lucifer should see
Where he was lately left, but saw him now
With legs held upward.   Let the grosser sort,
Who see not what the point was I had past,
Bethink them if sore toil oppress'd me then.

" Arise," my master cried, " upon thy feet.
The way is long, and much uncouth the road ;
And now within one hour and half of noon
The sun returns."[1]   It was no palace-hall
Lofty and luminous wherein we stood,
But natural dungeon where ill-footing was
And scant supply of light.   " Ere from the abyss
I separate," thus when risen I began :
" My guide ! vouchsafe few words to set me free
From error's thraldom.   Where is now the ice?
How standeth he in posture thus reversed?
And how from eve to morn in space so brief
Hath the sun made his transit?"   He in few
Thus answering spake : " Thou deemest thou art still
On the other side the centre, where I grasp'd
The abhorred worm that boreth through the world.
Thou wast on the other side, so long as I
Descended ; when I turn'd, thou didst o'erpass

[1] The Italian is : *E già il sole a mezza terza riede ;* " And already
the sun returns to middle tierce."   " *Tierce* was the first of the
four canonical divisions of the day, and would, at the equinox,
last from six till nine ; *middle tierce* is therefore equivalent to
half-past seven " (Oelsner).

That point,[1] to which from every part is dragg'd
All heavy substance. Thou art now arrived
Under the hemisphere opposed to that,
Which the great continent doth overspread,
And underneath whose canopy expired
The Man, that was born sinless and so lived.
Thy feet are planted on the smallest sphere,
Whose other aspect is Judecca. Morn
Here rises, when there evening sets : and he,
Whose shaggy pile we scaled, yet standeth fix'd,
As at the first. On this part he fell down
From Heaven ; and th' earth, here prominent before,
Through fear of him did veil her with the sea,
And to our hemisphere retired. Perchance,
To shun him, was the vacant space left here,
By what of firm land on this side appears,
That sprang aloof." [2] There is a place beneath,
From Belzebub as distant, as extends
The vaulted tomb ; discover'd not by sight,
But by the sound of brooklet, that descends
This way along the hollow of a rock,
Which, as it winds with no precipitous course,
The wave hath eaten. By that hidden way
My guide and I did enter, to return
To the fair world : and heedless of repose
We climb'd, he first, I following his steps,
Till on our view the beautiful lights of Heaven
Dawn'd through a circular opening in the cave :
Thence issuing we again beheld the stars.

1 The centre of the universe.
2 Dante has turned completely round (symbolical of his conversion from sin), and now finds himself in a chasm left at
Lucifer's fall, below the southern hemisphere—the hemisphere,
supposed covered with water, opposite to that which man
inhabits. I follow Dr. Moore in taking the morning which Dante
is now to see as the morning of Easter Day in the southern
hemisphere, which is twelve hours behind the time of its antipodes.
The Mountain of Purgatory, the only land in the southern hemisphere, to which Dante now comes, was formed when 'Lucifer fell
by the earth rushing up to escape him. It is the exact antipodes of
Jerusalem and Mount Calvary. The " brooklet " (ruscelletto), which
trickles down from Purgatory into Hell, is Lethe, which takes
away all memory of sin and evil from the purified soul.

THE VISION OF DANTE

Purgatory

CANTO I

ARGUMENT

The Poet describes the delight he experienced at issuing a little
before dawn from the infernal regions, into the pure air that
surrounds the isle of Purgatory; and then relates how, turning
to the right, he beheld four stars never seen before but by
our first parents, and met on his left the shade of Cato of
Utica, who, having warned him and Virgil what is needful
to be done before they proceed on their way through Purgatory, disappears; and the two poets go towards the shore,
where Virgil cleanses Dante's face with the dew, and girds
him with a reed, as Cato had commanded.

O'ER better waves to speed her rapid course
The light bark of my genius lifts the sail,
Well pleased to leave so cruel sea behind;
And of that second region will I sing,
In which the human spirit from sinful blot
Is purged, and for ascent to Heaven prepares.

　　Here, O ye hallow'd Nine! for in your train
I follow, here the deaden'd strain revive;[1]
Nor let Calliope refuse to sound
A somewhat higher song, of that loud tone
Which when the wretched birds of chattering note
Had heard, they of forgiveness lost all hope.[2]

　　Sweet hue of eastern sapphire, that was spread
O'er the serene aspect of the pure air,
High up as the first circle,[3] to mine eyes
Unwonted joy renew'd, soon as I 'scaped

[1] *Risurga*, "rise again." Dante has been a day and a night
in the passage upwards from the centre of the earth, and it is not
yet daybreak on Easter Sunday; "in the end of the Sabbath, as it
began to dawn toward the first day of the week."

[2] The Pierides, nine daughters of King Pierus of Emathia,
challenged the nine Muses to a contest, and were changed into
magpies (Ovid, *Metam.* v.). Calliope is the muse of epic poetry.

[3] Either the moon or the ninth sphere (*primum mobile*).

Forth from the atmosphere of deadly gloom,
That had mine eyes and bosom fill'd with grief.
The radiant planet, that to love invites,
Made all the orient laugh, and veil'd beneath
The Pisces' light, that in [her] escort came.[1]

To the right hand I turn'd, and fix'd my mind
On the other pole attentive, where I saw
Four stars ne'er seen before save by the ken
Of our first parents.[2]   Heaven of their rays
Seem'd joyous.   O thou northern site ! bereft
Indeed, and widow'd, since of these deprived.

As from this view I had desisted, straight
Turning a little towards the other pole,
There from whence now the wain had disappear'd,
I saw an old man standing by my side
Alone, so worthy of reverence in his look,
That ne'er from son to father more was owed.
Low down his beard, and mix'd with hoary white,
Descended, like his locks, which, parting, fell
Upon his breast in double fold.   The beams
Of those four luminaries on his face
So brightly shone, and with such radiance clear
Deck'd it, that I beheld him as the sun.[3]

   " Say who are ye, that stemming the blind stream,
Forth from the eternal prison-house have fled?"

[1] " Venus was not actually in Pisces in the spring of 1300, but Dante is probably following a tradition as to the position of all the planets at the moment of Creation (cf. *Inf.* i.).   In the representation of the Creation in the Collegiate Church at San Gimignano, Venus is depicted as being in Pisces " (Oelsner).

[2] The Southern Cross, of which the four stars here symbolise the Cardinal Virtues : Prudence, Justice, Fortitude, and Temperance.   Since the expulsion of Adam and Eve from the Earthly Paradise, the southern hemisphere has been uninhabited, according to the cosmography adopted by Dante.

[3] Cato of Utica (B.C. 95—B.C. 46).   He is represented playing a similar part in the *Æneid*, viii. 670.   In the allegorical sense, the light of the four mystical stars so shines upon his face that he seems illuminated with the light of the sun of Divine Grace. Cato, " the severest champion of true liberty," " to kindle the love of liberty in the world, gave proof of how dear he held her by preferring to depart from life a free man, rather than remain alive bereft of liberty " (*Mon.* ii. 5).   He was one of those who " saw and believed that this end of human life lies only in rigid virtue " (*Conv.* iv. 6).   He is, therefore, the example man must keep before his eyes in the search for moral liberty that Purgatory symbolises.

He spoke and moved those venerable plumes.
" Who hath conducted, or with lantern sure
Lights you emerging from the depth of night,
That makes the infernal valley ever black?
Are the firm statutes of the dread abyss
Broken, or in high Heaven new laws ordain'd,
That thus, condemn'd, ye to my caves approach?"
    My guide, then laying hold on me, by words
And intimations given with hand and head,
Made my bent knees and eye submissive pay
Due reverence; then thus to him replied :
    " Not of myself I come; a Dame from Heaven
Descending, him besought me in my charge
To bring.   But since thy will implies, that more
Our true condition I unfold at large,
Mine is not to deny thee thy request.
This mortal ne'er hath seen the farthest gloom;[1]
But erring by his folly had approach'd
So near, that little space was left to turn.
Then, as before I told, I was dispatch'd
To work his rescue; and no way remain'd
Save this which I have ta'en.   I have display'd
Before him all the regions of the bad ;
And purpose now those spirits to display,
That under thy command are purged from sin.
How I have brought him would be long to say.
From high descends the virtue, by whose aid
I to thy sight and hearing him have led.
Now may our coming please thee.   In the search
Of liberty he journeys : that how dear,
They know who for her sake have life refused.
Thou knowest, to whom death for her was sweet
In Utica, where thou didst leave those weeds,
That in the last great day will shine so bright.
For us the eternal edicts are unmoved :
He breathes, and I of Minos am not bound,
Abiding in that circle, where the eyes
Of thy chaste Marcia beam, who still in look
Prays thee, O hallow'd spirit ! to own her thine.[2]

[1] *L'ultima sera*, " his last evening "—death in sin and consequent damnation.
[2] Cato's wife Marcia is, like Virgil himself, in Limbo (see above, *Inf.* iv.).   In the *Convivio* (iv. 28), Dante makes the relations of Cato and Marcia an allegory of those between God and the human soul.

Then by her love we implore thee, let us pass
Through thy seven regions; for which, best thanks
I for thy favour will to her return,
If mention there below thou not disdain.''

" Marcia so pleasing in my sight was found,"
He then to him rejoin'd, " while I was there,
That all she ask'd me I was fain to grant.
Now that beyond the accursed stream she dwells,
She may no longer move me, by that law,
Which was ordain'd me, when I issued thence.
Not so, if Dame from Heaven, as thou sayst,
Moves and directs thee; then no flattery needs.
Enough for me that in her name thou ask.
Go therefore now : and with a slender reed
See that thou duly gird him, and his face
Lave, till all sordid stain thou wipe from thence.
For not with eye, by any cloud obscured,
Would it be seemly before him to come,
Who stands the foremost minister in Heaven.
This islet all around, there far beneath,
Where the wave beats it, on the oozy bed
Produces store of reeds. No other plant,
Cover'd with leaves, or harden'd in its stalk,
There lives, not bending to the water's sway.[1]
After, this way return not; but the sun
Will show you, that now rises, where to take
The mountain in its easiest ascent.''

He disappear'd; and I myself upraised
Speechless, and to my guide retiring close,
Toward him turn'd mine eyes. He thus began :
" My son ! observant thou my steps pursue.
We must retreat to rereward; for that way
The champain to its low extreme declines.''

The dawn had chased the matin hour of prime,
Which fled before it, so that from afar
I spied the trembling of the ocean stream.[2]

We traversed the deserted plain, as one
Who, wander'd from his track, thinks every step
Trodden in vain till he regain the path.

When we had come, where yet the tender dew
Strove with the sun, and in a place where fresh

---

1 The rush or reed is a symbol of humility.
2 *Conobbi il tremolar della marina:* Cary hardly renders the beauty of this famous line.

The wind breathed o'er it, while it slowly dried;
Both hands extended on the watery grass
My master placed, in graceful act and kind.
Whence I of his intent before apprized,
Stretch'd out to him my cheeks suffused with tears.
There to my visage he anew restored
That hue which the dun shades of Hell conceal'd.

　　Then on the solitary shore arrived,
That never sailing on its waters saw
Man that could after measure back his course,
He girt me in such manner as had pleased
Him who instructed; and O strange to tell!
As he selected every humble plant,
Wherever one was pluck'd, another there
Resembling, straightway in its place arose.

CANTO II

ARGUMENT

They behold a vessel under conduct of an Angel, coming over the
waves with spirits to Purgatory, among whom, when the
passengers have landed, Dante recognises his friend Casella;
but, while they are entertained by him with a song, they hear
Cato exclaiming against their negligent loitering, and at that
rebuke hasten forwards to the mountain.

Now had the sun to that horizon reach'd,
That covers, with the most exalted point
Of its meridian circle, Salem's walls;
And night, that opposite to him her orb
Rounds, from the stream of Ganges issued forth,
Holding the scales, that from her hands are dropt
When she reigns highest: so that where I was,
Aurora's white and vermeil-tinctured cheek
To orange turn'd as she in age increased.[1]
　　Meanwhile we linger'd by the water's brink,
Like men, who, musing on their road, in thought
Journey, while motionless the body rests.

[1] " It is sunset at Jerusalem; and midnight on the Ganges,
i. e. in India (when the sun is in Aries, the night is in the opposite sign of Libra, or the Scales; and Libra falls from the hand
of night at the time of the autumn equinox, when the sun enters
the constellation, and the nights become longer than the days):
it is therefore sunrise in Purgatory " (T. C. editors).

When lo ! as, near upon the hour of dawn,
Through the thick vapours Mars with fiery beam
Glares down in west, over the ocean floor ;
So seem'd, what once again I hope to view,
A light, so swiftly coming through the sea,
No winged course might equal its career.
From which when for a space I had withdrawn
Mine eyes, to make inquiry of my guide,
Again I look'd, and saw it grown in size
And brightness : then on either side appear'd
Something, but what I knew not, of bright hue,
And by degrees from underneath it came
Another.   My preceptor silent yet
Stood, while the brightness, that we first discern'd,
Open'd the form of wings : then when he knew
The pilot, cried aloud, " Down, down ; bend low
Thy knees ; behold God's Angel : fold thy hands :
Now shalt thou see true ministers indeed.
Lo ! how all human means he sets at nought ;
So that nor oar he needs, nor other sail
Except his wings, between such distant shores.[1]
Lo ! how straight up to Heaven he holds them rear'd,
Winnowing the air with those eternal plumes,
That not like mortal hairs fall off or change."

As more and more toward us came, more bright
Appear'd the bird of God, nor could the eye
Endure his splendour near : I mine bent down.
He drove ashore in a small bark so swift
And light, that in its course no wave it drank.
The heavenly steersman at the prow was seen,
Visibly written Blessed in his looks.
Within, a hundred spirits and more there sat.

" In exitu Israel de Ægypto,"
All with one voice together sang, with what
In the remainder of that hymn is writ.[2]
Then soon as with the sign of holy cross
He bless'd them, they at once leap'd out on land :
He, swiftly as he came, return'd.   The crew,
There left, appear'd astounded with the place,
Gazing around, as one who sees new sights.

[1] The Angel of Faith.

[2] Dante tells us elsewhere (*Epist.* x. 7) that this psalm mystically
signifies the passing of the holy soul from the bondage of this
corruption to the liberty of eternal glory.

From every side the sun darted his beams,
And with his arrowy radiance from mid heaven
Had chased the Capricorn,[1] when that strange tribe,
Lifting their eyes toward us : "If ye know,
Declare what path will lead us to the mount."

  Them Virgil answer'd : "Ye suppose, perchance,
Us well acquainted with this place; but here,
We, as yourselves, are strangers.   Not long erst
We came, before you but a little space,
By other road so rough and hard, that now
The ascent will seem to us as play."   The spirits,
Who from my breathing had perceived I lived,
Grew pale with wonder.   As the multitude
Flock round a herald sent with olive branch,
To hear what news he brings, and in their haste
Tread one another down; e'en so at sight
Of me those happy spirits were fix'd, each one
Forgetful of its errand to depart
Where, cleansed from sin, it might be made all fair.

  Then one I saw darting before the rest
With such fond ardour to embrace me, I
To do the like was moved.   O shadows vain !
Except in outward semblance : thrice my hands
I clasp'd behind it, they as oft return'd
Empty into my breast again.   Surprise
I need must think was painted in my looks,
For that the shadow smiled and backward drew.
To follow it I hasten'd, but with voice
Of sweetness it enjoin'd me to desist.
Then who it was I knew, and pray'd of it,
To talk with me it would a little pause.
It answer'd : "Thee as in my mortal frame
I loved, so loosed from it I love thee still,
And therefore pause : but why walkest thou here?"

  "Not without purpose once more to return,
Thou find'st me, my Casella, where I am,
Journeying this way;" I said : "but how of thee
Hath so much time been lost?"   He answer'd straight :

  "No outrage hath been done to me, if he,
Who when and whom he chooses takes, hath oft
Denied me passage here; since of just will
His will he makes.   These three months past indeed,
He, whoso chose to enter, with free leave
Hath taken; whence I wandering by the shore

[1] The light of the rising sun has quenched that of the Capricorn.

Where Tiber's wave grows salt, of him gain'd kind
Admittance, at that river's mouth, toward which
His wings are pointed; for there always throng
All such as not to Acheron descend."[1]

Then I : " If new law taketh not from thee
Memory or custom of love-tuned song,
That whilom all my cares had power to 'swage;
Please thee therewith a little to console
My spirit, that encumber'd with its frame,
Traveling so far, of pain is overcome."

" Love, that discourses in my thoughts,"[2] he then
Began in such soft accents, that within
The sweetness thrills me yet.   My gentle guide,
And all who came with him, so well were pleased,
That seem'd nought else might in their thoughts have
    room.

Fast fix'd in mute attention to his notes
We stood, when lo ! that old man venerable
Exclaiming, " How is this, ye tardy spirits?
What negligence detains you loitering here?
Run to the mountain to cast off those scales,
That from your eyes the sight of God conceal."

As a wild flock of pigeons, to their food
Collected, blade or tares, without their pride
Accustom'd, and in still and quiet sort,
If aught alarm them, suddenly desert
Their meal, assail'd by more important care;
So I that new-come troop beheld, the song
Deserting, hasten to the mountain's side,
As one who goes, yet, where he tends, knows not.

Nor with less hurried step did we depart.

---

[1] Casella was a Florentine musician and an intimate friend of
Dante's, some of whose lyrics he set to music. He died between
1282 and 1300. Dante's surprise at seeing him only just arrive
implies, perhaps, that he had already been dead for some while
at the latter date. The souls of the redeemed who are to be
detained in Purgatory gather at the mouth of Tiber (Rome being
the " portal of salvation "), as the lost do on the shore of Acheron,
waiting for the Angel to take them in his boat. For three
months, that is, since the proclamation of the papal jubilee (it
began on Christmas Day, 1299, but the bull granting the plenary
indulgence was published on February 22, 1300), he has freely
taken all comers who have died in a " state of grace."

[2] *Amor che nella mente mi ragiona*, the opening line of the
second *canzone* of Dante's *Convivio*, which was probably one of
those set to music by Casella.

CANTO III

ARGUMENT

Our Poet, perceiving no shadow except that cast by his own body,
is fearful that Virgil has deserted him; but he is freed from
that error, and both arrive together at the foot of the mountain: on finding it too steep to climb, they inquire the way
from a troop of spirits that are coming towards them, and are
by them shown which is the easiest ascent. Manfredi, king
of Naples, who is one of these spirits, bids Dante inform his
daughter Costanza, Queen of Aragon, of the manner in which
he had died.

THEM sudden flight had scatter'd o'er the plain,
Turn'd towards the mountain, whither reason's voice
Drives us : I, to my faithful company
Adhering, left it not.   For how, of him
Deprived, might I have sped? or who, beside,
Would o'er the mountainous tract have led my steps?
He, with the bitter pang of self-remorse,
Seem'd smitten.   O clear conscience, and upright!
How doth a little failing wound thee sore.
    Soon as his feet desisted (slackening pace)
From haste, that mars all decency of act,
My mind, that in itself before was wrapt,
Its thought expanded, as with joy restored;
And full against the steep ascent I set
My face, where highest to Heaven its top o'erflows.[1]
    The sun, that flared behind, with ruddy beam
Before my form was broken; for in me
His rays resistance met.   I turn'd aside
With fear of being left, when I beheld
Only before myself the ground obscured.
When thus my solace, turning him around,
Bespake me kindly : " Why distrustest thou?
Believest not I am with thee, thy sure guide?
It now is evening there, where buried lies
The body in which I cast a shade, removed
To Naples [2] from Brundusium's wall.   Nor thou
Marvel, if before me no shadow fall,
More than that in the skyey element

---

[1] Or, as Mr. Okey translates : " which rises highest heaven-
ward from the waters."

[2] Augustus ordered the body of Virgil to be transferred from
Brundusium (Brindisi) to Naples.

One ray obstructs not other.   To endure
Torments of heat and cold extreme, like frames
That virtue hath disposed, which, how it works,
Wills not to us should be reveal'd.   Insane,
Who hopes our reason may that space explore,
Which holds three Persons in one Substance knit.
Seek not the wherefore, race of human kind;
Could ye have seen the whole, no need had been
For Mary to bring forth.   Moreover, ye
Have seen such men desiring fruitlessly;
To whose desires, repose would have been given,
That now but serve them for eternal grief.
I speak of Plato, and the Stagirite,
And others many more." [1]   And then he bent
Downwards his forehead, and in troubled mood
Broke off his speech.   Meanwhile we had arrived
Far as the mountain's foot, and there the rock
Found of so steep ascent, that nimblest steps
To climb it had been vain.   The most remote,
Most wild, untrodden path, in all the tract
'Twixt Lerice and Terbia, were to this
A ladder easy and open of access.

　　" Who knows on which hand now the steep de-
　　　clines?"
My master said, and paused; " so that he may
Ascend, who journeys without aid of wing?"
And while, with looks directed to the ground,
The meaning of the pathway he explored,
And I gazed upward round the stony height;
On the left hand appear'd to us a troop
Of spirits, that toward us moved their steps;
Yet moving seem'd not, they so slow approach'd.

　　I thus my guide address'd : " Upraise thine eyes :
Lo ! that way some, of whom thou mayst obtain
Counsel, if of thyself thou find'st it not."

　　Straightway he look'd, and with free speech replied :
" Let us tend thither : they but softly come.
And thou be firm in hope, my son beloved."

　　Now was that crowd from us distant as far,
(When we some thousand steps, I say, had past),
As at a throw the nervous arm could fling;
When all drew backward on the massy crags

　　1 The souls in Limbo, including the speaker himself.

Of the steep bank, and firmly stood unmoved,
As one, who walks in doubt, might stand to look.
    " O spirits perfect ! O already chosen !"
Virgil to them began :   " by that blest peace,
Which, as I deem, is for you all prepared,
Instruct us where the mountain low declines,
So that attempt to mount it be not vain.
For who knows most, him loss of time most grieves."
    As sheep,[1] that step from forth their fold, by one,
Or pairs, or three at once ; meanwhile the rest
Stand fearfully, bending the eye and nose
To ground, and what the foremost does, that do
The others, gathering round her if she stops,
Simple and quiet, nor the cause discern ;
So saw I moving to advance the first,
Who of that fortunate crew were at the head,
Of modest mien, and graceful in their gait.
When they before me had beheld the light
From my right side fall broken on the ground,
So that the shadow reach'd the cave ; they stopp'd,
And somewhat back retired : the same did all
Who follow'd, though unweeting of the cause.
    " Unask'd of you, yet freely I confess,
This is a human body which ye see.
That the sun's light is broken on the ground,
Marvel not : but believe, that not without
Virtue derived from Heaven, we to climb
Over this wall aspire."   So them bespake
My master ; and that virtuous tribe rejoin'd :
" Turn, and before you there the entrance lies ;"
Making a signal to us with bent hands.
    Then of them one began.   " Whoe'er thou art,
Who journey'st thus this way, thy visage turn ;
Think if me elsewhere thou hast ever seen."
    I towards him turn'd, and with fix'd eye beheld.
Comely and fair, and gentle of aspect
He seem'd, but on one brow a gash was mark'd.
    When humbly I disclaim'd to have beheld
Him ever : " Now behold !" he said, and show'd

[1] These are the souls of those who died excommunicate, under
the ban of the Church, but had time to repent of their sins :
" sheep without a shepherd—for they are the souls of such as
died in contumacy against the Church, and they must dree their
rebellion against the chief Shepherd by thirty times as long a
space of shepherdless wandering" (Wicksteed).

High on his breast a wound : then smiling spake.
" I am Manfredi, grandson to the Queen
Costanza : [1] whence I pray thee, when return'd,
To my fair daughter go, the parent glad
Of Aragonia and Sicilia's pride ;
And of the truth inform her, if of me
Aught else be told.   When by two mortal blows
My frame was shatter'd, I betook myself
Weeping to Him, who of free will forgives.
My sins were horrible : but so wide arms
Hath goodness infinite, that it receives
All who turn to it.   Had this text divine
Been of Cosenza's shepherd better scann'd,
Who then by Clement on my hunt was set,
Yet at the bridge's head my bones had lain,
Near Benevento, by the heavy mole
Protected ; but the rain now drenches them,
And the wind drives, out of the kingdom's bounds,
Far as the stream of Verde, where, with lights
Extinguish'd, he removed them from their bed.
Yet by their curse we are not so destroy'd,
But that the eternal Love may turn, while hope
Retains her verdant blossom.   True it is,
That such one as in contumacy dies
Against the holy Church, though he repent,

---

1 Manfred, grandson of the Empress Constance (*Par.* iii.), because
a natural son of Frederick II. (*Inf.* x.), is described elsewhere by
Dante as *benegenitus*, " well-begotten " (*V. E.* i. 12).   After the
death of the Emperor (1250) and his son Conrad (1254), Manfred
usurped the crown of Sicily from the latter's little son Conradin,
and became the head of the Ghibelline party in Italy.   For a short
while it seemed as though he might have united the whole nation
under one crown.   Excommunicated by three Popes in succession,
he was finally defeated by Charles of Anjou, in February, 1266,
on the plain of Grandella, near Benevento, and fell in the thickest
of the battle.   He was refused Christian burial, as having died
under the Church's ban, but each French soldier laid a stone upon
his body, thus raising the " heavy mole " mentioned by Dante.
It was said that the Bishop of Cosenza, at the bidding of Clement
IV., had the body disinterred, and carried across the Verde (the
river Garigliano), the boundary of the kingdom of Naples, that,
even in death, he might not rest in the realm that he was held to
have usurped from the Church.   Manfred was a prince of charm
and culture, a poet and a patron of letters ; his private life was
immoral and irreligious.   His Guelf contemporaries accuse him
of parricide, fratricide, and incest ; the latter accusation alone
seems to have been true.

Must wander thirty-fold for all the time
In his presumption past; if such decree
Be not by prayers of good men shorter made.
Look therefore if thou canst advance my bliss;
Revealing to my good Costanza,[1] how
Thou hast beheld me, and beside, the terms
Laid on me of that interdict; for here
By means of those below much profit comes."

CANTO IV

ARGUMENT

Dante and Virgil ascend the mountain of Purgatory, by a steep
and narrow path pent in on each side by rock, till they reach
a part of it that opens into a ledge or cornice. There seating
themselves, and turning to the east, Dante wonders at seeing
the sun on their left, the cause of which is explained to him
by Virgil; and while they continue their discourse, a voice
addresses them, at which they turn, and find several spirits
behind the rock, and amongst the rest one named Belacqua,
who had been known to our Poet on earth, and who tells that
he is doomed to linger there on account of his having delayed
his repentance to the last.

WHEN by sensations of delight or pain,
That any of our faculties hath seized,
Entire the soul collects herself, it seems
She is intent upon that power alone;
And thus the error is disproved, which holds
The soul not singly lighted in the breast.
And therefore whenas aught is heard or seen,
That firmly keeps the soul toward it turn'd,
Time passes, and a man perceives it not.
For that, whereby we hearken, is one power;
Another that, which the whole spirit hath:
This is as it were bound, while that is free.[2]

[1] Manfred's daughter Costanza married King Peter III. of
Aragon, who avenged his death by conquering Sicily from Charles
of Anjou in 1282. By him she was the mother of James and
Frederick, who were kings of Aragon and Sicily respectively in
1300, and are described above as "Aragonia and Sicilia's pride."
[2] The doctrine ascribed to Plato that there were diverse souls
with distinct organs in one and the same body had been disproved
by St. Thomas Aquinas. "In the eagerness of his attention to
Manfred's tale, Dante takes no note of the passing time, and

This found I true by proof, hearing that spirit,
And wondering; for full fifty steps aloft
The sun had measured,[1] unobserved of me,
When we arrived where all with one accord
The spirits shouted, " Here is what ye ask."

A larger aperture oft-times is stopt,
With forked stake of thorn by villager,
When the ripe grape imbrowns, than was the path,
By which my guide, and I behind him close,
Ascended solitary, when that troop
Departing left us. On Sanleo's road
Who journeys, or to Noli low descends,
Or mounts Bismantua's [2] height, must use his feet;
But here a man had need to fly, I mean
With the swift wing and plumes of high desire,
Conducted by his aid, who gave me hope,
And with light furnish'd to direct my way.

We through the broken rock ascended, close
Pent on each side, while underneath the ground
Ask'd help of hands and feet. When we arrived
Near on the highest ridge of the steep bank,
Where the plain level open'd, I exclaim'd,
" O Master! say, which way can we proceed."

He answer'd, " Let no step of thine recede.
Behind me gain the mountain, till to us
Some practised guide appear." That eminence
Was lofty, that no eye might reach its point;
And the side proudly rising, more than line [3]
From the mid quadrant to the centre drawn.
I, wearied, thus began: " Parent beloved!
Turn and behold how I remain alone,
If thou stay not."—" My son!" he straight replied,
" Thus far put forth thy strength;" and to a track

thereby furnishes a practical refutation of the Platonic doctrine of
the plurality of souls; for if the soul that presides over hearing
were one, and the soul that notes the passage of time another,
then the completest absorption of the former could not so involve
the latter as to prevent it from exercising its own special function "
(Wicksteed).

[1] That is, it is now three hours and twenty minutes after sunrise,
fifteen degrees being reckoned to the hour.

[2] These are three steep ascents : San Leo near Urbino, Noli on
the Riviera, and Bismantova in the district of Reggio in Emilia.

[3] " It was much nearer to being perpendicular than horizontal "
(Cary).

Pointed, that, on this side projecting, round
Circles the hill.   His words so spurr'd me on,
That I, behind him, clambering, forced myself,
Till my feet press'd the circuit plain beneath.
There both together seated, turn'd we round
To eastward, whence was our ascent : and oft
Many beside have with delight look'd back.

First on the nether shores I turn'd mine eyes,
Then raised them to the sun, and wondering mark'd
That from the left it smote us.   Soon perceived
That poet sage, how at the car of light
Amazed I stood, where 'twixt us and the north
Its course it enter'd.   Whence he thus to me :
" Were Leda's offspring now in company
Of that broad mirror, that high up and low
Imparts his light beneath, thou mightst behold
The ruddy Zodiac nearer to the Bears
Wheel, if its ancient course it not forsook.
How that may be, if thou wouldst think ; within
Pondering, imagine Sion with this mount
Placed on the earth, so that to both be one
Horizon, and two hemispheres apart,
Where lies the path that Phaëton ill knew
To guide his erring chariot : thou wilt see
How of necessity by this, on one,
He passes, while by that on the other side ;[1]
If with clear view thine intellect attend."

" Of truth, kind teacher ! " I exclaim'd, " so clear
Aught saw I never, as I now discern,
Where seem'd my ken to fail, that the mid orb
Of the supernal motion (which in terms
Of art is call'd the Equator, and remains
Still 'twixt the sun and winter) for the cause
Thou hast assign'd, from hence toward the north
Departs, when those, who in the Hebrew land
Were dwellers, saw it towards the warmer part.
But if it please thee, I would gladly know,

---

[1] " Dante is amazed to find that the sun is north of the equator
and strikes on his left shoulder. Virgil explains that this is
because they are in the southern hemisphere, at the antipodes of
Jerusalem.   Were the sun in Gemini instead of Aries, he would be
further to the north yet " (Wicksteed).   The path along which
Phaëton failed to guide his chariot is the ecliptic, the course of
the sun.

How far we have to journey : for the hill
Mounts higher, than this sight of mine can mount."

   He thus to me : " Such is this steep ascent,
That it is ever difficult at first,
But more a man proceeds, less evil grows.
When pleasant it shall seem to thee, so much
That upward going shall be easy to thee
As in a vessel to go down the tide,
Then of this path thou wilt have reach'd the end.
There hope to rest thee from thy toil.   No more
I answer, and thus far for certain know."
As he his words had spoken, near to us
A voice there sounded : " Yet ye first perchance
May to repose you by constraint be led."
At sound thereof each turn'd ; and on the left
A huge stone we beheld, of which nor I
Not he before was ware.   Thither we drew ;
And there were some, who in the shady place
Behind the rock were standing, as a man
Through idleness might stand.[1]   Among them one,
Who seem'd to be much wearied, sat him down,
And with his arms did fold his knees about,
Holding his face between them downward bent.

   " Sweet Sir !" I cried, " behold that man who shows
Himself more idle than if laziness
Were sister to him."   Straight he turn'd to us,
And, o'er the thigh lifting his face, observed,
Then in these accents spake : " Up then, proceed,
Thou valiant one."   Straight who it was I knew ;
Nor could the pain I felt (for want of breath
Still somewhat urged me) hinder my approach.
And when I came to him, he scarce his head
Uplifted, saying, " Well hast thou discern'd,
How from the left the sun his chariot leads?"

   His lazy acts and broken words my lips
To laughter somewhat moved ; when I began :
" Belacqua,[2] now for thee I grieve no more.
But tell, why thou art seated upright there.

---

[1] These are the souls of those who postponed repentance
through indolence, and now, unless aided by the prayers of the
living, have to postpone their purgation for a similar period.

[2] A Florentine maker of musical instruments, described as " an
excellent master of harps and lutes, but a most indolent man in
the affairs of the world as well as in those of the soul."   He was
evidently an intimate friend of Dante's.

Waitest thou escort to conduct thee hence?
Or blame I only thine accustom'd ways?"
Then he: "My brother! of what use to mount,
When, to my suffering, would not let me pass
The bird of God,[1] who at the portal sits?
Behoves so long that Heaven first bear me round
Without its limits, as in life it bore;
Because I, to the end, repentant sighs
Delay'd; if prayer do not aid me first,
That riseth up from heart which lives in grace.
What other kind avails, not heard in Heaven?"
    Before me now the poet, up the mount
Ascending, cried: "Haste thee: for see the sun
Has touch'd the point meridian; and the night
Now covers with her foot Morocco's shore."[2]

CANTO V

ARGUMENT

They meet with others, who had deferred their repentance till they
    were overtaken by a violent death, when sufficient space being
    allowed them, they were then saved; and amongst these,
    Giacopo del Cassero, Buonconte da Montefeltro, and Pia, a
    lady of Siena.

Now had I left those spirits, and pursued
The steps of my conductor; when behind,
Pointing the finger at me, one exclaim'd:
"See, how it seems as if the light not shone
From the left hand of him beneath, and he,
As living, seems to be led on."[3]   Mine eyes
I at that sound reverting, saw them gaze,
Through wonder, first at me; and then at me
And the light broken underneath, by turns.
"Why are thy thoughts thus riveted," my guide
Exclaim'd, "that thou hast slack'd thy pace? or how
Imports it thee, what thing is whisper'd here?
Come after me, and to their babblings leave
The crowd.   Be as a tower, that, firmly set,
Shakes not its top for any blast that blows.

    [1] The Angel at the gate of Purgatory.
    [2] It is sunset at Spain, and therefore noon in Purgatory.
    [3] The souls are astonished at Dante's shadow, which shows he
is a living man.

He, in whose bosom thought on thought shoots out,
Still of his aim is wide, in that the one
Sicklies and wastes to nought the other's strength."
     What other could I answer, save " I come "?
I said it, somewhat with that colour tinged,
Which oft-times pardon meriteth for man.
     Meanwhile traverse along the hill there came,
A little way before us, some who sang
The " Miserere " in responsive strains.
When they perceived that through my body I
Gave way not for the rays to pass, their song
Straight to a long and hoarse exclaim they changed;
And two of them, in guise of messengers,
Ran on to meet us, and inquiring ask'd :
" Of your condition we would gladly learn."
     To them my guide : " Ye may return, and bear
Tidings to them who sent you, that his frame
Is real flesh. If, as I deem, to view
His shade they paused, enough is answer'd them :
Him let them honour : they may prize him well."
     Ne'er saw I fiery vapours [1] with such speed
Cut through the serene air at fall of night,
Nor August's clouds athwart the setting sun,
That upward these did not in shorter space
Return ; and, there arriving, with the rest
Wheel back on us, as with loose rein a troop.
     " Many," exclaim'd the bard, " are these, who throng
Around us : to petition thee, they come.
Go therefore on, and listen as thou go'st."
     " O spirit ! who go'st on to blessedness,
With the same limbs that clad thee at thy birth,"
Shouting they came : " a little rest thy step.
Look if thou any one amongst our tribe
Hast e'er beheld, that tidings of him there [2]
Thou mayst report. Ah, wherefore go'st thou on?
Ah, wherefore tarriest thou not? We all
By violence died, and to our latest hour
Were sinners, but then warn'd by light from Heaven;
So that, repenting and forgiving, we
Did issue out of life at peace with God,
Who, with desire to see Him, fills our heart."

---

[1] Falling stars or summer lightning.
[2] Upon the earth.

Then I : " The visages of all I scan,
Yet none of ye remember.   But if aught
That I can do may please you, gentle spirits !
Speak, and I will perform it ; by that peace,
Which, on the steps of guide so excellent
Following, from world to world, intent I seek."

In answer he began : " None here distrusts
Thy kindness, though not promised with an oath ;
So as the will fail not for want of power.
Whence I, who sole before the others speak,
Entreat thee, if thou ever see that land
Which lies between Romagna and the realm
Of Charles,[1] that of thy courtesy thou pray
Those who inhabit Fano, that for me
Their adorations duly be put up,
By which I may purge off my grievous sins.
From thence I came.   But the deep passages,
Whence issued out the blood wherein I dwelt,
Upon my bosom in Antenor's land
Were made, where to be more secure I thought.
The author of the deed was Este's prince,
Who, more than right could warrant, with his wrath
Pursued me.   Had I towards Mira fled,
When overta'en at Oriaco, still
Might I have breathed.   But to the marsh I sped ;
And in the mire and rushes tangled there
Fell, and beheld my life-blood float the plain."[2]

Then said another : " Ah ! so may the wish,
That takes thee o'er the mountain, be fulfill'd,
As thou shalt graciously give aid to mine.
Of Montefeltro I ; Buonconte I :
Giovanna nor none else have care for me ;
Sorrowing with these I therefore go."[3]   I thus :

1 The March of Ancona, between Romagna and Apulia, the
kingdom of Charles II. of Anjou.
2 The speaker is Jacopo del Cassero, a nobleman of Fano (in
the March of Ancona), who in 1298 was murdered by order of the
Marquis of Ferrara (Azzo VIII. d'Este, cf. Inf. xii. notes) at
Oriaco.   Oriaco is near the river Brenta, in the district of Padua,
which is here called " Antenor's land," because tradition ascribed
its foundation to the Trojan traitor so named.
3 Buonconte da Montefeltro, the son of Guido, commanded the
Ghibelline cavalry at the battle of Campaldino (June 11, 1289),
when Dante was " fighting valiantly on horseback in the front
rank " of the other side.   It is not known to what family his

" From Campaldino's field what force or chance
Drew thee, that ne'er thy sepulture was known?"
    " Oh!" answer'd he, " at Casentino's foot
A stream there courseth, named Archiano, sprung
In Apennine above the hermit's seat.
E'en where its name is cancel'd,[1] there came I,
Pierced in the throat, fleeing away on foot,
And bloodying the plain.   Here sight and speech
Fail'd me; and, finishing with Mary's name,
I fell, and tenantless my flesh remain'd.
I will report the truth; which thou again
Tell to the living.   Me God's Angel took,[2]
Whilst he of Hell exclaim'd : ' O thou from Heaven !
' Say wherefore hast thou robb'd me?   Thou of him
' The eternal portion bear'st with thee away,
' For one poor tear that he deprives me of.
' But of the other, other rule I make.'
    " Thou know'st how in the atmosphere collects
That vapour dank, returning into water
Soon as it mounts where cold condenses it.
That evil will, which in his intellect
Still follows evil, came ;[3] and raised the wind
And smoky mist, by virtue of the power
Given by his nature.   Thence the valley, soon
As day was spent, he cover'd o'er with cloud,
From Pratomagno to the mountain range ;[4]
And stretch'd the sky above ; so that the air
Impregnate changed to water.   Fell the rain ;
And to the fosses came all that the land

wife Giovanna belonged.   Buonconte's body having never been
found, the Poet invents this wonderful and exquisite story of his
death in the rout.

[1] Where it falls into the Arno near Bibbiena.   The Archiano, a
small stream in the Casentino, rises above the hermitage of
Camaldoli, and joins the Arno about an hour's walk from the
battlefield.

[2] Here is a designed and most tragic contrast with the death
of Buonconte's father, Guido da Montefeltro, in *Inf.* xxvii.
Similarly, St. Catherine of Siena writes that " whoso holds Mary
in due reverence, be he a just man or a sinner, shall never be taken
or devoured by the infernal demon."

[3] Mr. Okey translates it better : " He [the demon] united that
evil will, which seeks ill only, with intellect."

[4] He spread a mist over the whole valley of the Casentino, from
the mountain of Pratomagno on the west to the main chain of
the Apennines on the east.   This is a phenomenon that every one
who has stayed in that district will have witnessed.

Contain'd not; and, as mightiest streams are wont,
To the great river, with such headlong sweep,
Rush'd, that nought stay'd its course. My stiffen'd
    frame,
Laid at his mouth, the fell Archiano found,
And dash'd it into Arno; from my breast
Loosening the cross, that of myself I made
When overcome with pain. He hurl'd me on,
Along the banks and bottom of his course;
Then in his muddy spoils encircling wrapt."

"Ah! when thou to the world shalt be return'd,
And rested after thy long road," so spake
Next the third spirit; "then remember me.
I once was Pia. Siena gave me life;
Maremma took it from me. That he knows,
Who me with jewel'd ring had first espoused." [1]

CANTO VI

ARGUMENT

Many besides, who are in like case with those spoken of in the
last Canto, beseech our Poet to obtain for them the prayers
of their friends, when he shall be returned to this world. This
moves him to express a doubt to his guide, how the dead can
be profited by the prayers of the living; for the solution of
which doubt he is referred to Beatrice. Afterwards he meets
with Sordello the Mantuan, whose affection, shown to Virgil
his countryman, leads Dante to break forth into an invective
against the unnatural divisions with which Italy, and more
especially Florence, was distracted.

WHEN from their game of dice men separate,
He who hath lost remains in sadness fix'd,
Revolving in his mind what luckless throws
He cast: but, meanwhile, all the company
Go with the other; one before him runs,
And one behind his mantle twitches, one
Fast by his side bids him remember him.

[1] These lines tell us that Pia was a lady of Siena who was
murdered by her husband in the Maremma. She was probably a
member of the Tolomei family, married to Count Paganello de'
Pannocchieschi, one of the potent feudal lords of the Sienese
contado. There are several alternative readings and interpretations of the last two lines of this Canto; but Cary's translation
adroitly avoids the question—which is not of any vital importance.

He stops not; and each one, to whom his hand
Is stretch'd, well knows he bids him stand aside;
And thus he from the press defends himself.
E'en such was I in that close-crowding throng;
And turning so my face around to all,
And promising, I 'scaped from it with pains.

Here of Arezzo him I saw, who fell
By Ghino's cruel arm;[1] and him beside,
Who in his chase was swallow'd by the stream.[2]
Here Frederic Novello,[3] with his hand
Stretch'd forth, entreated; and of Pisa he,
Who put the good Marzucco to such proof
Of constancy.[4]   Count Orso[5] I beheld;
And from its frame a soul dismiss'd for spite
And envy, as it said, but for no crime;
I speak of Peter de la Brosse: and here,
While she yet lives, that Lady of Brabant,
Let her beware; lest for so false a deed
She herd with worse than these.[6]   When I was freed
From all those spirits, who pray'd for others' prayers
To hasten on their state of blessedness;
Straight I began: "O thou, my luminary!
It seems expressly in thy text denied,
That Heaven's supreme decree can ever bend
To supplication;[7] yet with this design

[1] Benincasa of Arezzo, a judge, was murdered at Rome by
Ghino di Tacco, a notorious bandit whose brother he had sentenced
to death.
[2] Guccio, or Cione, de' Tarlati, an Aretine who was drowned in
the Arno. It is doubtful whether he was chasing his enemies, or
being chased by them.
[3] Federigo Novello, one of the Ghibelline Conti Guidi of Batti-
folle, and grandson of Count Ugolino della Gherardesca, was
murdered in 1289 by the Bostoli, a Guelf family of Arezzo.
[4] Marzucco degli Scornigiani was a Pisan noble who became
a Franciscan friar. When his son Farinata, whom Dante sees
here, was murdered by his personal enemies, or put to death by
Count Ugolino (accounts differ as to the exact details), Marzucco
showed his constancy by forgiving his slayers.
[5] The sons of Counts Napoleone and Alessandro degli Alberti
(*Inf.* xxxii.) continued their fathers' feud, and this Count Orso,
the son of Napoleone, was killed by his cousin Alberto, the son of
Alessandro.
[6] Pierre de la Brosse, chamberlain of King Philip III. of France,
was hanged in 1278 in consequence of a false accusation brought
against him by the queen, Mary of Brabant, whom he had
previously accused of the murder of her step-son.
[7] Virgil, *Æn.* vi. 376, had written: *Desine fata deûm flecti*

Do these entreat.   Can then their hope be vain?
Or is thy saying not to me reveal'd?"
  He thus to me : " Both what I write is plain,
And these deceived not in their hope; if well
Thy mind consider, that the sacred height
Of judgment doth not stoop, because love's flame
In a short moment all fulfils, which he,
Who sojourns here, in right should satisfy.
Besides, when I this point concluded thus,
By praying no defect could be supplied;
Because the prayer had none access to God.
Yet in this deep suspicion rest thou not
Contented, unless she assure thee so,
Who betwixt truth and mind infuses light:
I know not if thou take me right; I mean
Beatrice.[1] Her thou shalt behold above,
Upon this mountain's crown, fair seat of joy."
  Then I : " Sir ! let us mend our speed; for now
I tire not as before : and lo! the hill
Stretches its shadow far."   He answer'd thus :
" Our progress with this day shall be as much
As we may now dispatch; but otherwise
Than thou supposest is the truth.   For there
Thou canst not be, ere thou once more behold
Him back returning, who behind the steep
Is now so hidden, that, as erst, his beam
Thou dost not break.   But lo! a spirit there
Stands solitary, and toward us looks :
It will instruct us in the speediest way."
  We soon approach'd it.   O thou Lombard spirit!
How didst thou stand, in high abstracted mood,
Scarce moving with slow dignity thine eyes.
It spoke not aught, but let us onward pass,
Eyeing us as a lion on his watch.
But Virgil, with entreaty mild, advanced,
Requesting it to show the best ascent.
It answer to his question none return'd;

sparare precando : " Cease to hope that the decrees of the Gods
can yield to prayer."
  [1] " Virgil explains, firstly, that no bending of the divine will is
involved in the granting of prayer; secondly, that his rebuke was
uttered to souls not in grace; and, finally, that the complete
solution of such questions is not for him (Virgil), but for Beatrice "
(Wicksteed).   It is a question for theology, rather than for human
philosophy, to decide.

But of our country and our kind of life
Demanded. When my courteous guide began,
" Mantua," the shadow, in itself absorb'd,
Rose towards us from the place in which it stood,
And cried, " Mantuan ! I am thy countryman,
Sordello." [1] Each the other then embraced.

Ah, slavish Italy ! thou inn of grief !
Vessel without a pilot in loud storm !
Lady no longer of fair provinces,
But brothel-house impure ! this gentle spirit,
Even from the pleasant sound of his dear land
Was prompt to greet a fellow citizen
With such glad cheer : while now thy living ones
In thee abide not without war; and one
Malicious gnaws another; ay, of those
Whom the same wall and the same moat contains.
Seek, wretched one ! around thy sea-coasts wide;
Then homeward to thy bosom turn; and mark,
If any part of thee sweet peace enjoy.
What boots it, that thy reins Justinian's hand [2]
Refitted, if thy saddle be unprest?
Nought doth he now but aggravate thy shame.
[Ah, people ! *that* obedient still shouldst live,
And in the saddle let thy Cæsar sit,
If well thou marked'st that which God commands,

---

[1] Elsewhere (*V. E.* i. 15), Dante writes : " Sordello, he who was
so distinguished by his eloquence, not only in poetry, but in every
other form of utterance, forsook his native dialect." Sordello of
Goito, in the Mantuan district, was born about the year 1200, and
was one of the Italian poets of the thirteenth century who wrote
in Provençal. He carried on an adulterous intrigue with Cunizza
da Romano (*Par.* ix.), the sister of Ezzelino and wife of Count
Ricciardo di San Bonifazio, in consequence of which he was
obliged to seek refuge in Provence in 1229. He returned to Italy
in 1265, as one of the knights in the army of Charles of Anjou, by
whom he was invested with a number of fiefs in the conquered
kingdom of Naples. He apparently died a violent death, some
time after June, 1269. His finest poem (still preserved) is a lament
on the death of Blacatz, a Provençal baron, in which he rebukes
the kings and princes of Europe, and exhorts them to eat the
dead man's heart, and thereby be inspired to valiant deeds. It
was, perhaps, this poem that led Dante to assign to Sordello, in
the following Canto, the part of pointing out and passing judgment
upon these same princes or their successors.

[2] Justinian, the law-giver of the Roman Empire (cf. *Par.* vi.).
In Dante's conception, the Empire is essentially the power divinely
ordained to enforce the observance of Roman Law.

Look how that beast to felness hath relapsed,
From having lost correction of the spur,
Since to the bridle thou hast set thine hand.] [1]
  O German Albert ! who abandon'st her
That is grown savage and unmanageable,
When thou shouldst clasp her flanks with forked heels.
Just judgment from the stars fall on thy blood ;
And be it strange and manifest to all ;
Such as may strike thy successor with dread ;
For that thy sire and thou have suffer'd thus,
Through greediness of yonder realms detain'd,
The garden of the empire to run waste. [2]
Come, see the Capulets and Montagues,
The Filippeschi and Monaldi, [3] man
Who carest for nought ! those sunk in grief, and these
With dire suspicion rack'd. Come, cruel one !
Come, and behold the oppression of the nobles,
And mark their injuries ; and thou mayst see
What safety Santafiore can supply. [4]
Come and behold thy Rome, who calls on thee,
Desolate widow, day and night with moans,
" My Cæsar, why dost thou desert my side ? " [5]

---

[1] I have been compelled to change the punctuation, and in consequence the entire construction of the lines enclosed in brackets, as Cary has misunderstood the Poet's meaning. They are addressed to the clergy, rebuking them for their usurpation of the secular power that pertains only to the Emperor.

[2] Albert of Hapsburg, who is here apostrophized, was King of the Romans and Emperor-elect at the date of the vision, but, like his father Rudolf (see below, Canto vii.), was too much absorbed in his German politics to attend to Italian affairs. The " just judgment " invoked by Dante refers to Albert's murder by his nephew John, on May 1, 1308. Henry of Luxemburg was elected to succeed him in November.

[3] It is doubtful whether the point of this appeal is that these noble families are oppressed by the Guelf democracy, or that they are factious against each other. The Cappelletti were either Ghibellines of Verona (as the countrymen of Shakespeare are bound to maintain) or Guelfs of Cremona (which seems more probable) ; the Montecchi (" Montagues ") were Ghibellines of Verona ; the Monaldi and Filippeschi were Guelf and Ghibelline families of Orvieto.

[4] Santafiore was the chief stronghold of the Aldobrandeschi, a Ghibelline feudal family in the Sienese contado, who held what corresponds to the present province of Grosseto. They were in continual war with the Guelf commune of Siena, which strove to deprive them of their jurisdiction. Cf. below, Canto xi.

[5] Cf. Dante's letter to the Italian Cardinals (Epist. viii. 2, 10).

Come, and behold what love among thy people :
And if no pity touches thee for us,
Come, and blush for thine own report.   For me,
If it be lawful, O Almighty Power !
Who wast on earth for our sakes crucified,
Are Thy just eyes turn'd elsewhere? or is this
A preparation, in the wondrous depth
Of Thy sage counsel made, for some good end,
Entirely from our reach of thought cut off ?
So are the Italian cities all o'erthrong'd
With tyrants, and a great Marcellus [1] made
Of every petty factious villager.

   My Florence ! thou mayst well remain unmoved
At this digression, which affects not thee :
Thanks to thy people, who so wisely speed. [2]
Many have justice in their heart, that long
Waiteth for counsel to direct the bow,
Or ere it dart unto its aim : but thine
Have it on their lip's edge.   Many refuse
To bear the common burdens : readier thine
Answer uncall'd, and cry, " Behold I stoop !"

   Make thyself glad, for thou hast reason now,
Thou wealthy ! thou at peace ! thou wisdom-fraught !
Facts best will witness if I speak the truth.
Athens and Lacedæmon, who of old
Enacted laws, for civil arts renown'd,
Made little progress in improving life
Towards thee, who usest such nice subtlety,
That to the middle of November scarce
Reaches the thread thou in October weavest.
How many times within thy memory,
Customs, and laws, and coins, and offices
Have been by thee renew'd, and people changed.

   If thou remember'st well and canst see clear,
Thou wilt perceive thyself like a sick wretch,
Who finds no rest upon her down, but oft
Shifting her side, short respite seeks from pain.

   [1] M. Claudius Marcellus, Roman consul, who opposed Cæsar,
is here taken as a type of opponents of the Empire.
   [2] " From the reproaches thus launched against the Italians,
Florence is sarcastically excepted, till the sarcasm breaks down in
a wail of reproachful pity " (Wicksteed).

CANTO VII

ARGUMENT

The approach of night hindering further ascent, Sordello conducts
our Poet apart to an eminence, from whence they behold a
pleasant recess, in form of a flowery valley, scooped out of the
mountain; where are many famous spirits, and among them
the Emperor Rodolph, Ottocar king of Bohemia, Philip III.
of France, Henry of Navarre, Peter III. of Aragon, Charles I.
of Naples, Henry III. of England, and William, Marquis of
Montferrat.

AFTER their courteous greetings joyfully
Seven times exchanged, Sordello backward drew,
Exclaiming, " Who are ye?"—" Before this mount
By spirits worthy of ascent to God
Was sought, my bones had by Octavius' care
Been buried. I am Virgil; for no sin
Deprived of Heaven, except for lack of faith."
So answer'd him in few my gentle guide.

As one, who aught before him suddenly
Beholding, whence his wonder riseth, cries,
" It is, yet is not," wavering in belief;
Such he appear'd; then downward bent his eyes,
And, drawing near with reverential step,
Caught him, where of mean estate might clasp
His lord. " Glory of Latium!" he exclaim'd,
" In whom our tongue its utmost power display'd;
Boast of my honour'd birth-place! what desert
Of mine, what favour, rather, undeserved,
Shows thee to me? If I to hear that voice
Am worthy, say if from below thou comest,
And from what cloister's pale."—" Through every orb
Of that sad region," he replied, " thus far
Am I arrived, by heavenly influence led:
And with such aid I come. Not for my doing,
But for not doing, have I lost the sight
Of that high Sun, whom thou desirest, and who
By me too late was known. There is a place
There underneath, not made by torments sad,
But by dun shades alone; where mourning's voice
Sounds not of anguish sharp, but breathes in sighs.
There I with little innocents abide,
Who by death's fangs were bitten, ere exempt

From human taint.   There I with those abide,
Who the three holy virtues [1] put not on,
But understood the rest, and without blame
Follow'd them all.   But, if thou know'st, and canst,
Direct us how we soonest may arrive,
Where Purgatory its true beginning takes."

He answer'd thus : " We have no certain place
Assign'd us : upwards I may go, or round.
Far as I can, I join thee for thy guide.
But thou beholdest now how day declines ;
And upwards to proceed by night, our power
Excels : therefore it may be well to choose
A place of pleasant sojourn.   To the right
Some spirits sit apart retired.   If thou
Consentest, I to these will lead thy steps :
And thou wilt know them, not without delight."

" How chances this?" was answer'd : " whoso wish'd
To ascend by night, would he be thence debarr'd
By other, or through his own weakness fail?"

The good Sordello then, along the ground
Trailing his finger, spoke : " Only this line [2]
Thou shalt not overpass, soon as the sun
Hath disappear'd ; not that aught else impedes
Thy going upwards, save the shades of night.
These, with the want of power, perplex the will.
With them thou haply mightst return beneath,
Or to and fro around the mountain's side
Wander, while day is in the horizon shut."

My master straight, as wondering at his speech,
Exclaim'd : " Then lead us quickly, where thou sayst
That, while we stay, we may enjoy delight."

A little space we were removed from thence,
When I perceived the mountain hollow'd out,
Even as large valleys hollow'd out on earth.

" That way," the escorting spirit cried, " we go,
Where in a bosom the high bank recedes :
And thou await renewal of the day."

Betwixt the steep and plain, a crooked path
Led us traverse into the ridge's side,
Where more than half the sloping edge expires.

---

[1] The three Theological Virtues : Faith, Hope, and Charity.
[2] Cary aptly quotes John xii. 35 : " Walk while ye have the
light, lest darkness come upon you ; for he that walketh in darkness knoweth not whither he goeth."

Refulgent gold, and silver thrice refined,
And scarlet grain and ceruse, Indian wood
Of lucid dye serene, fresh emeralds
But newly broken, by the herbs and flowers
Placed in that fair recess, in colour all
Had been surpass'd, as great surpasses less.
Nor nature only there lavish'd her hues,
But of the sweetness of a thousand smells
A rare and undistinguish'd fragrance made.[1]

    " Salve Regina,"[2] on the grass and flowers,
Here chanting, I beheld those spirits sit,
Who not beyond the valley could be seen.

    " Before the westering sun sink to his bed,"
Began the Mantuan, who our steps had turn'd,
" 'Mid those, desire not that I lead ye on.
For from this eminence ye shall discern
Better the acts and visages of all,
Than, in the nether vale, among them mix'd.
He, who sits high above the rest, and seems
To have neglected that he should have done,
And to the others' song moves not his lip,
The Emperor Rodolph call, who might have heal'd
The wounds whereof fair Italy hath died,
So that by others she revives but slowly.
He, who with kindly visage comforts him,
Sway'd in that country, where the water springs,
That Moldaw's river to the Elbe, and Elbe
Rolls to the ocean : Ottocar his name :
Who in his swaddling clothes was of more worth
Than Winceslaus his son, a bearded man,
Pamper'd with rank luxuriousness and ease.[3]

[1] " In a little lap or dell of the mountain they find the pensive
souls of kings and rulers who had neglected their higher functions
for selfish ease or selfish war. Now they are surrounded by every
soothing beauty of nature ; but relief from the serious cares of
life, which erst they sought unduly, is now an anguish to them,
and their yearning goes forth to the active purgation of the seven
terraces of torment above them " (Wicksteed).

[2] *Salve Regina, mater misericordiæ*, the beginning of one of
the Church's antiphons to the Blessed Virgin.

[3] The deadliest enemies on earth are now comforting each
other, and singing the praises of the Queen of Mercy together.
Rudolf of Hapsburg (nominally Emperor from 1272 till his death
in 1292) found his most strenuous opponent in this Ottocar, King
of Bohemia, whom he finally defeated and killed in the battle of
Marchfield near Vienna in 1278. For Ottocar's son Wenceslaus,

And that one with the nose deprest, who close
In counsel seems with him of gentle look,
Flying expired, withering the lily's flower.
Look there, how he doth knock against his breast.
The other ye behold, who for his cheek
Makes of one hand a couch, with frequent sighs.
They are the father and the father-in-law
Of Gallia's bane : his vicious life they know
And foul; thence comes the grief that rends them thus.[1]
    " He, so robust of limb, who measure keeps
In song with him of feature prominent,
With every virtue bore his girdle braced.
And if that stripling, who behind him sits,
King after him had lived, his virtue then
From vessel to like vessel had been pour'd;
Which may not of the other heirs be said.
By James and Frederick his realms are held;[2]
Neither the better heritage obtains.
Rarely into the branches of the tree
Doth human worth mount up : and so ordains
He who bestows it, that as His free gift
It may be call'd.   To Charles my words apply
No less than to his brother in the song;
Which Pouille and Provence now with grief confess.
So much that plant degenerates from its seed,

whom Rudolf allowed to succeed to the Bohemian crown (annexing
the rest of his dominions), and who was reigning at the epoch of
the vision, see *Par.* xix.

[1] Philip III. of France (1270–1285), the "small-nosed king,"
died at Perpignan, whither he had retreated from Gerona after
the destruction of his fleet by the navy of Peter III. of Aragon.
Henry I. of Navarre, "the Fat" (brother of the king mentioned in
Inf. xxii.), died in 1274. "Gallia's bane," Philip IV. of France,
son of Philip III., married Henry's daughter Joan, whose son,
Louis X., united the two crowns.

[2] Peter III. of Aragon, "so robust of limb," conquered Sicily
(1282) from Charles I. of Anjou, the brother of St. Louis, who
had won the crown of Naples and Sicily by the overthrow of
Manfred (1266) and the judicial murder of Conradin (1268).
Peter's claim to Sicily was due to his being the husband of
Manfred's daughter Costanza (*cf.* above, Canto iii.). Charles is
here indicated by his prominent nose. The two rivals both died
in 1285. Peter was succeeded as King of Aragon by his son,
Alfonso III., the "stripling" who attends him here (died 1291).
At the epoch of the vision, Aragon and Sicily were ruled by Peter's
second and third sons, James and Frederick respectively, whom
Dante here and elsewhere regards as degenerate (*Par.* xix., xx.;
Conv. iv. 6).

As, more than Beatrix and Margaret,
Costanza still boasts of her valorous spouse.[1]

" Behold the king of simple life and plain,
Harry of England, sitting there alone :
He through his branches better issue spreads.[2]

" That one, who, on the ground, beneath the rest,
Sits lowest, yet his gaze directs aloft,
Is William, that brave Marquis,[3] for whose cause,
The deed of Alexandria and his war
Makes Montferrat and Canavese weep."

CANTO VIII

ARGUMENT

Two Angels, with flaming swords broken at the points, descend
to keep watch over the valley, into which Virgil and Dante
entering by desire of Sordello, our Poet meets with joy the
spirit of Nino, the judge of Gallura, one who was well known
to him. Meantime three exceedingly bright stars appear near
the pole, and a serpent creeps subtly into the valley, but flees
at hearing the approach of those angelic guards. Lastly,
Conrad Malaspina predicts to our Poet his future banishment.

Now was the hour that wakens fond desire
In men at sea, and melts their thoughtful heart

[1] Charles II. of Anjou succeeded his father as King of Naples
(Pouille or Apulia) and Count of Provence. This Charles is
as inferior to Charles I. as Costanza's husband Peter is superior
to the latter, who was the husband successively of Beatrice
of Provence and Margaret of Burgundy. Others take Margaret
as Beatrice's sister, the eldest daughter of Count Raymond
Berenger (cf. *Par.* vi.), and wife of Louis IX. of France ; in which
case the passage would mean that Charles II. is as inferior to
Charles I. as Peter is superior to both Charles I. and St. Louis.
[2] Unlike these other kings, Henry III. of England (1216–
1272) is surpassed by his son, Edward I. (1272–1307).
[3] William Longsword, Marquis of Monferrato, was one of the
most powerful nobles and strenuous warriors in northern Italy in
the second half of the thirteenth century. In addition to his
ancestral marquisate, he ruled Tortona, Pavia, and Vercelli. He
was at length taken prisoner by the people of Alessandria, who
had risen against him, and imprisoned in an iron cage till his
death, in 1292. The correct translation is : " William the
Marquis, through whom Alessandria and its war make Monferrato
and the Canavese weep ;" the allusion being to the ensuing war
between the Marquis John of Monferrato, William's son, and
the Alessandrians, in which the territory of the former (which
included the district known as the Canavese) suffered heavily.

Who in the morn have bid sweet friends farewell,
And pilgrim newly on his road with love
Thrills, if he hear the vesper bell from far,
That seems to mourn for the expiring day :
When I, no longer taking heed to hear,
Began, with wonder, from those spirits to mark
One risen from its seat, which with its hand
Audience implored. Both palms it join'd and raised,
Fixing its stedfast gaze toward the east,
As telling God, " I care for nought beside."

  " Te Lucis Ante," [1] so devoutly then
Came from its lip, and in so soft a strain,
That all my sense in ravishment was lost.
And the rest after, softly and devout,
Follow'd through all the hymn, with upward gaze
Directed to the bright supernal wheels.

  Here, reader ! for the truth make thine eyes keen :
For of so subtle texture is this veil,
That thou with ease mayst pass it through unmark'd. [2]

  I saw that gentle band silently next
Look up, as if in expectation held,
Pale and in lowly guise ; and, from on high,
I saw, forth issuing descend beneath,
Two Angels, with two flame-illumined swords,
Broken and mutilated of their points.
Green as the tender leaves but newly born,
Their vesture was, the which, by wings as green
Beaten, they drew behind them, fann'd in air. [3]
A little over us one took his stand ;
The other lighted on the opposing hill ;
So that the troop were in the midst contain'd.

  Well I descried the whiteness on their heads ;

  [1] *Te lucis ante terminum* is the first verse of the Church's
evening hymn, which is sung at Compline.
  [2] Cf. *Inf.* ix. Dante wishes to call the attention of the reader
to the allegorical meaning of the coming of the serpent and its
repulse by the Angels. Souls in Purgatory have not the intrinsic
impossibility of sinning that is possessed by the Blessed of Paradise, but are kept absolutely free from any sin by the Divine
Providence. In the allegorical sense, the meaning is that the
way to moral and intellectual freedom is a hard one, and temptations to fall back in despair are many. The Tempter would draw
man back from regaining the Earthly Paradise, from which he
has once caused his expulsion.
  [3] The Angels of Hope, with the swords of justice tempered
with mercy.

But in their visages the dazzled eye
Was lost, as faculty that by too much
Is overpower'd.   " From Mary's bosom both
Are come," exclaim'd Sordello, " as a guard
Over the vale, 'gainst him who hither tends,
The serpent."   Whence, not knowing by which path
He came, I turn'd me round; and closely press'd,
All frozen, to my leader's trusted side.

     Sordello paused not : " To the valley now
(For it is time) let us descend; and hold
Converse with those great shadows : haply much
Their sight may please ye."   Only three steps down
Methinks I measured, ere I was beneath,
And noted one who look'd as with desire
To know me.   Time was now that air grew dim;
Yet not so dim, that, 'twixt his eyes and mine,
It clear'd not up what was conceal'd before.
Mutually towards each other we advanced.
Nino, thou courteous judge !¹ what joy I felt,
When I perceived thou wert not with the bad.

     No salutation kind on either part
Was left unsaid.   He then inquired : " How long,
Since thou arrived'st at the mountain's foot,
Over the distant waves?"—" Oh !" answer'd I,
" Through the sad seats of woe this morn I came;
And still in my first life, thus journeying on,
The other strive to gain."   Soon as they heard
My words, he and Sordello backward drew,
As suddenly amazed.   To Virgil one,
The other to a spirit turn'd, who near
Was seated, crying : " Conrad !² up with speed :
Come, see what of His grace high God hath will'd."
Then turning round to me : " By that rare mark
Of honour, which thou owest to Him, who hides
So deeply His first cause it hath no ford;
When thou shalt be beyond the vast of waves,
Tell my Giovanna, that for me she call
There, where reply to innocence is made.
Her mother, I believe, loves me no more;

     ¹ Nino Visconti, judge of Gallura in Sardinia, a noble of Pisa
(cf. *Inf.* xxxiii., notes).   He was so ardent a Guelf that at his
death in Sardinia, in 1296, he directed that his heart should be
taken to Lucca in order that it might be buried in Guelf soil.
     ² Corrado Malaspina.

Since she has changed the white and wimpled folds,
Which she is doom'd once more with grief to wish.
By her it easily may be perceived,
How long in woman lasts the flame of love,
If sight and touch do not relume it oft.
For her so fair a burial will not make
The viper, which calls Milan to the field,
As had been made by shrill Gallura's bird." [1]

He spoke, and in his visage took the stamp
Of that right zeal, which with due temperature
Glows in the bosom.   My insatiate eyes
Meanwhile to Heaven had travel'd, even there
Where the bright stars are slowest, as a wheel
Nearest the axle ; when my guide inquired :
" What there aloft, my son, has caught thy gaze?"
I answered : " The three torches, with which here
The pole is all on fire." [2]   He then to me :
" The four resplendent stars, thou saw'st this morn,
Are there beneath ; and these, risen in their stead."

While yet he spoke, Sordello to himself
Drew him, and cried : " Lo there our enemy !"
And with his hand pointed that way to look.

Along the side, where barrier none arose
Around the little vale, a serpent lay,
Such haply as gave Eve the bitter food.
Between the grass and flowers, the evil snake
Came on, reverting oft his lifted head ;
And, as a beast that smooths its polish'd coat,
Licking his back. I saw not, nor can tell,
How those celestial falcons from their seat
Moved, but in motion each one well descried.
Hearing the air cut by their verdant plumes,

[1] Nino married Beatrice d'Este, daughter of the Marquis
Obizzo II. of Ferrara (cf. *Inf.* xii.), by whom he had this daughter,
Giovanna, who afterwards married Riccardo da Cammino of
Treviso. After Nino's death, Beatrice married Galeazzo Visconti
of Milan. The Milanese Visconti were in no way connected with
the Visconti of Pisa ; the arms of one family were a viper, of the
other a cock, as here indicated. The arrangements for Beatrice's
marriage to Galeazzo were in progress at the assumed date of the
vision (April) ; but the wedding actually took place at the end of
June (1300).

[2] These stars symbolise Faith, Hope, and Charity ; but, the
end of the poem being practical, the soul can only continue the
ascent when the other four, that symbolise Prudence, Justice,
Fortitude, and Temperance, are in the sky.

The serpent fled; and, to their stations, back
The Angels up return'd with equal flight.

　　The spirit, (who to Nino, when he call'd,
Had come,) from viewing me with fixed ken,
Through all that conflict, loosen'd not his sight.

　　" So may the lamp,[1] which leads thee up on high,
Find, in thy free resolve, of wax so much,
As may suffice thee to the enamel'd height,"
It thus began : " If any certain news
Of Valdimagra and the neighbour part
Thou know'st, tell me, who once was mighty there.
They call'd me Conrad Malaspina; not
That old one; but from him I sprang.[2]　The love
I bore my people is now here refined."

　　" In your domains," I answer'd, " ne'er was I.
But, through all Europe, where do those men dwell,
To whom their glory is not manifest?
The fame, that honours your illustrious house,
Proclaims the nobles, and proclaims the land;
So that he knows it, who was never there.
I swear to you, so may my upward route
Prosper, your honour'd nation [3] not impairs
The value of her coffer and her sword.
Nature and use give her such privilege,
That while the world is twisted from his course
By a bad head,[4] she only walks aright,
And has the evil way in scorn."　He then :
" Now pass thee on : seven times the tired sun
Revisits not the couch, which with four feet
The forked Aries covers, ere that kind
Opinion shall be nail'd into thy brain
With stronger nails than other's speech can drive;
If the sure course of judgment be not stay'd." [5]

---

[1] The light of Divine Grace.

[2] This Corrado Malaspina, " the Younger," was the grandson of another Corrado, " the Elder," who was married to an illegitimate daughter of the Emperor Frederick II., and died about 1225. The Malaspina were lords of Valdimagra in Lunigiana. Cf. *Inf.* xxiv. The younger Conrad died some five or six years before the date of the vision. He is mentioned in the *Decameron* (ii. 6).

[3] *Vostra gentre onrata,* " your honoured family."

[4] Probably Pope Boniface VIII. is meant.

[5] In less than seven years (the sun being now in Aries), Dante will have personal experience of the noble qualities of the Malaspina. In the autumn of 1306, Dante was the guest of a cousin

CANTO IX

ARGUMENT

Dante is carried up the mountain, asleep and dreaming, by Lucia ;
and, on wakening, finds himself, two hours after sunrise,
with Virgil, near the gate of Purgatory, through which they
are admitted by the Angel deputed by Saint Peter to keep it.

Now the fair consort of Tithonus old,
Arisen from her mate's beloved arms,
Look'd palely o'er the eastern cliff ; her brow,
Lucent with jewels, glitter'd, set in sign
Of that chill animal,[1] who with his train
Smites fearful nations : and where then we were,
Two steps of her ascent the night had past ;
And now the third was closing up its wing,
When I, who had so much of Adam with me,
Sank down upon the grass, o'ercome with sleep,
There where all five [2] were seated.   In that hour,
When near the dawn the swallow her sad lay,
Remembering haply ancient grief,[3] renews ;
And when our minds, more wanderers from the flesh,
And less by thought restrain'd, are, as 't were, full
Of holy divination in their dreams ;
Then, in a vision, did I seem to view
A golden-feather'd eagle [4] in the sky,
With open wings, and hovering for descent ;
And I was in that place, methought, from whence

of Corrado's, the Marquis Franceschino Malaspina, at Sarzana.
A letter ascribed to Dante (*Epist.* iii.) is addressed to another
cousin, Moroello Malaspina (cf. *Inf.* xxiv.), to whom it is said that
the Poet intended to dedicate the *Purgatorio*.

1 The constellation of Scorpio, in which the moon now was.
" Of the six hours in which the night rises, two were gone, and
the third had just passed the summit of its course. The lunar
aurora was therefore on the horizon. By a somewhat odd analogy,
she is called the ' mistress ' of Tithonus, because she is a spurious
aurora, and the genuine Aurora was the ' wife ' of Tithonus "
(Oelsner). *La concubina di Titone antico* should be rendered
" the mistress of old Tithonus," not " fair consort," as Cary
gives it.

2 Virgil, Dante, Sordello, Nino, and Corrado.

3 See below, Canto xvii. notes.

4 The eagle is the symbol alike of Divine Grace and of baptismal regeneration.

Young Ganymede, from his associates 'reft,
Was snatch'd aloft to the high consistory.
" Perhaps," thought I within me, " here alone
He strikes his quarry, and elsewhere disdains
To pounce upon the prey." Therewith, it seem'd
A little wheeling in his aëry tour,
Terrible as the lightning, rush'd he down,
And snatch'd me upward even to the fire.
There both, I thought, the eagle and myself
Did burn; and so intense the imagined flames,
That needs my sleep was broken off. As erst
Achilles shook himself, and round him roll'd
His waken'd eyeballs, wondering where he was,
Whenas his mother had from Chiron fled
To Scyros, with him sleeping in her arms;
There whence the Greeks did after sunder him;[1]
E'en thus I shook me, soon as from my face
The slumber parted, turning deadly pale,
Like one ice-struck with dread. Sole at my side
My comfort stood : and the bright sun was now
More than two hours aloft : and to the sea
My looks were turn'd. " Fear not," my master cried,
" Assured we are at happy point. Thy strength
Shrink not, but rise dilated. Thou art come
To Purgatory now. Lo ! there the cliff
That circling bounds it. Lo ! the entrance there,
Where it doth seem disparted. Ere the dawn
Usher'd the day-light, when thy wearied soul
Slept in thee, o'er the flowery vale beneath
A lady came, and thus bespake me : ' I
' Am Lucia.[2] Suffer me to take this man,
' Who slumbers. Easier so his way shall speed.'
Sordello and the other gentle shapes
Tarrying, she bare thee up : and, as day shone,
This summit reach'd : and I pursued her steps.
Here did she place thee. First, her lovely eyes
That open entrance show'd me; then at once
She vanish'd with thy sleep." Like one, whose doubts
Are chased by certainty, and terror turn'd
To comfort on discovery of the truth,

---

[1] To prevent him going to the Trojan war, Thetis took Achilles from the care of Chiron and concealed him in Scyros, where he was afterwards found by Ulysses.

[2] Illuminating grace. Cf. *Inf.* ii., and *Par.* xxxii.

Such was the change in me : and as my guide
Beheld me fearless, up along the cliff
He moved, and I behind him, towards the height.

   Reader ! thou markest how my theme doth rise ;
Nor wonder therefore, if more artfully
I prop the structure. Nearer now we drew,
Arrived whence, in that part, where first a breach
As of a wall appear'd, I could descry
A portal, and three steps beneath, that led
For inlet there, of different colour each ;
And one who watch'd, but spake not yet a word.
As more and more mine eye did stretch its view,
I mark'd him seated on the highest step,
In visage such, as past my power to bear.
Grasp'd in his hand, a naked sword glanced back
The rays so towards me, that I oft in vain
My sight directed. " Speak, from whence ye stand ; "
He cried : " What would ye? Where is your escort?
Take heed your coming upward harm ye not."

  " A heavenly dame, not skilless of these things,"
Replied the instructor, " told us, even now,
' Pass that way : here the gate is.' "—" And may she,
Befriending, prosper your ascent," resumed
The courteous keeper of the gate : " Come then
Before our steps." We straightway thither came.

  The lowest stair was marble white, so smooth
And polish'd, that therein my mirror'd form
Distinct I saw. The next of hue more dark
Than sablest grain, a rough and singed block,
Crack'd lengthwise and across. The third, that lay
Massy above, seem'd porphyry, that flamed
Red as the life-blood spouting from a vein.
On this God's Angel either foot sustain'd,
Upon the threshold seated, which appear'd
A rock of diamond.[1] Up the trinal steps
My leader cheerly drew me. " Ask," said he,
" With humble heart, that he unbar the bolt."

  Piously at his holy feet devolved

---

[1] The Gate of Purgatory is an allegory of the Sacrament of
Penance. The Angel represents the priestly confessor, while the
three steps are the three essential parts of the Sacrament : Contrition, Confession, and Satisfaction, which derives its efficacy
from the blood of Christ. The rock of diamond signifies the
firm basis of the Church's power to forgive sins.

I cast me, praying him for pity's sake
That he would open to me; but first fell
Thrice on my bosom prostrate. Seven times
The letter, that denotes the inward stain,
He, on my forehead, with the blunted point
Of his drawn sword, inscribed.[1] And " Look," he cried,
" When enter'd, that thou wash these scars away."

　　Ashes, or earth ta'en dry out of the ground,
Were of one colour with the robe he wore.
From underneath that vestment forth he drew
Two keys, of metal twain : the one was gold,
Its fellow silver.　With the pallid first,
And next the burnish'd, he so ply'd the gate,
As to content me well.　" Whenever one
Faileth of these, that in the key-hole straight
It turn not, to this alley then expect
Access in vain." Such were the words he spake.
" One is more precious : but the other needs
Skill and sagacity, large share of each,
Ere its good task to disengage the knot
Be worthily perform'd.[2]　From Peter these
I hold, of him instructed that I err
Rather in opening, than in keeping fast ;
So but the suppliant at my feet implore."

　　Then of that hallow'd gate he thrust the door,
Exclaiming, " Enter, but this warning hear :
He forth again departs who looks behind."

　　As in the hinges of that sacred ward
The swivels turn'd, sonorous metal strong,
Harsh was the grating ; nor so surlily
Roar'd the Tarpeian, when by force bereft
Of good Metellus, thenceforth from his loss
To leanness doom'd.[3]　Attentively I turn'd,
Listening the thunder that first issued forth ;
And " We praise thee, O God," methought I heard,
In accents blended with sweet melody.[4]

---

[1] The seven P's represent the seven capital sins, *peccati capitali*, which are to be purged away in the seven terraces of the mountain.

[2] The silver key is the science and experience by which the confessor judges of the penitent's worthiness and true repentance ; the golden key is the absolution that he pronounces.

[3] The Roman tribune, Metellus, vainly attempted to prevent Cæsar plundering the Roman treasury in the Temple of Saturn on the Tarpeian Hill.

[4] *Te Deum laudamus*, the Ambrosian hymn.

The strains came o'er mine ear, e'en as the sound
Of choral voices, that in solemn chant
With organ mingle, and, now high and clear
Come swelling, now float indistinct away.

CANTO X

ARGUMENT

Being admitted at the gate of Purgatory, our Poets ascend a
    winding path up the rock, till they reach an open and level
    space that extends each way round the mountain. On the side
    that rises, and which is of white marble, are seen artfully
    engraved many stories of humility, which whilst they are con-
    templating, there approach the souls of those who expiate the
    sin of pride, and who are bent down beneath the weight of
    heavy stones.

WHEN we had past the threshold of the gate,
(Which the soul's ill affection doth disuse,
Making the crooked seem the straighter path,)
I heard its closing sound. Had mine eyes turn'd,
For that offence what plea might have avail'd?
    We mounted up the riven rock, that wound
On either side alternate, as the wave
Flies and advances. "Here some little art
Behoves us," said my leader, "that our steps
Observe the varying flexure of the path."
    Thus we so slowly sped, that with cleft orb
The moon once more o'erhangs her watery couch,
Ere we that strait have threaded. But when free,
We came, and open, where the mount above
One solid mass retires; I spent with toil,
And both uncertain of the way, we stood,
Upon a plain more lonesome than the roads
That traverse desert wilds. From whence the brink
Borders upon vacuity, to foot
Of the steep bank that rises still, the space
Had measured thrice the stature of a man:
And, distant as mine eye could wing its flight,
To leftward now and now to right dispatch'd,
That cornice equal in extent appear'd.
    Not yet our feet had on that summit moved,
When I discover'd that the bank, around,
Whose proud uprising all ascent denied,

Was marble white; and so exactly wrought
With quaintest sculpture, that not there alone
Had Polycletus,[1] but e'en nature's self
Been shamed. The Angel (who came down to earth
With tidings of the peace so many years
Wept for in vain, that oped the heavenly gates
From their long interdict) before us seem'd,
In a sweet act, so sculptured to the life,
He look'd no silent image. One had sworn
He had said " Hail !" for she was imaged there,
By whom the key did open to God's love;
And in her act as sensibly imprest
That word, " Behold the handmaid of the Lord,"
As figure seal'd on wax.[2] " Fix not thy mind
On one place only," said the guide beloved,
Who had me near him on that part where lies
The heart of man. My sight forthwith I turn'd,
And mark'd, behind the Virgin Mother's form,
Upon that side where he that moved me stood,
Another story graven on the rock.

I past athwart the bard, and drew me near,
That it might stand more aptly for my view.
There, in the self-same marble, were engraved
The cart and kine, drawing the sacred ark,
That from unbidden office awes mankind.[3]
Before it came much people; and the whole
Parted in seven quires. One sense cried " Nay,"
Another, " Yes, they sing." Like doubt arose
Betwixt the eye and smell, from the curl'd fume
Of incense breathing up the well-wrought toil.
Preceding the blest vessel, onward came
With light dance leaping, girt in humble guise,
Israel's sweet harper : in that hap he seem'd
Less, and yet more, than kingly. Opposite,
At a great palace, from the lattice forth

[1] A famous Greek sculptor in the fifth century before the
Christian era. Dante's " knowledge of Polycletus was probably
derived from Aristotle's references to him " (Toynbee).

[2] On entering each terrace, Dante sees or hears examples of the
virtue contrary to the sin to be expiated in that terrace, and,
before leaving it, similar examples of the punishment or con-
sequences of that sin. In each case, as here, the first example of
virtue is taken from the life of the Blessed Virgin.

[3] Dante refers again to the death of Uzzah (2 Sam. vi.) in his
letter to the Italian Cardinals (*Epist.* viii. 5).

Look'd Michol, like a lady full of scorn
And sorrow.[1] To behold the tablet next,
Which, at the back of Michol, whitely shone,
I moved me. There, was storied on the rock
The exalted glory of the Roman prince,
Whose mighty worth moved Gregory to earn
His mighty conquest, Trajan the Emperor.[2]
A widow at his bridle stood, attired
In tears and mourning. Round about them troop'd
Full throng of knights; and overhead in gold
The eagles floated, struggling with the wind.
The wretch appear'd amid all these to say:
" Grant vengeance, Sire! for, woe beshrew this heart,
My son is murder'd." He replying seem'd:
" Wait now till I return." And she, as one
Made hasty by her grief: " O Sire! if thou
Dost not return?"—" Where I am, who then is,
May right thee."—" What to thee is other's good,
If thou neglect thy own?"—" Now comfort thee;"
At length he answers. " It beseemeth well
My duty be perform'd, ere I move hence:
So justice wills; and pity bids me stay."

He, whose ken nothing new surveys, produced
That visible speaking, new to us and strange,
The like not found on earth. Fondly I gazed
Upon those patterns of meek humbleness,
Shapes yet more precious for their Artist's sake;
When " Lo!" the poet whisper'd, " where this way,
(But slack their pace) a multitude advance.
These to the lofty steps shall guide us on."

Mine eyes, though bent on view of novel sights,
Their loved allurement, were not slow to turn.

Reader! I would not that amazed thou miss
Of thy good purpose, hearing how just God
Decrees our debts be cancel'd. Ponder not
The form of suffering. Think on what succeeds:
Think that, at worst, beyond the mighty doom
It cannot pass. " Instructor!" I began,
" What I see hither tending, bears no trace
Of human semblance, nor of aught beside

---

[1] *Cf.* 2 Sam. vi.
[2] The legend of this act of justice to the poor widow was said
to have inspired St. Gregory the Great to obtain the deliverance of
Trajan from Hell by his prayers. See *Par.* xx.

That my foil'd sight can guess." He answering thus :
" So courb'd to earth, beneath their heavy terms
Of torment stoop they, that mine eye at first
Struggled as thine.   But look intently thither ;
And disentangle with thy labouring view,
What, underneath those stones, approacheth : now,
E'en now, mayst thou discern the pangs of each."

    Christians and proud ! O poor and wretched ones !
That, feeble in the mind's eye, lean your trust
Upon unstaid perverseness : know ye not
That we are worms, yet made at last to form
The winged insect,[1] imp'd with angel plumes,
That to Heaven's justice unobstructed soars ?
Why buoy ye up aloft your unfledged souls ?
Abortive then and shapeless ye remain,
Like the untimely embryon of a worm.

    As, to support incumbent floor or roof,
For corbel, is a figure sometimes seen,
That crumples up its knees unto its breast ;
With the feign'd posture, stirring ruth unfeign'd
In the beholder's fancy ; so I saw
These fashion'd, when I noted well their guise.

    Each, as his back was laden, came indeed
Or more or less contracted ; and it seem'd
As he, who show'd most patience in his look,
Wailing exclaim'd : " I can endure no more."

CANTO XI

ARGUMENT

After a prayer uttered by the spirits, who were spoken of in the
last Canto, Virgil inquires the way upwards, and is answered
by one, who declares himself to have been Omberto, son of
the Count of Santafiore. Next our Poet distinguishes Oderigi,
the illuminator, who discourses on the vanity of worldly fame,
and points out to him the soul of Provenzano Salvani.

" O THOU Almighty Father ! who dost make
The heavens Thy dwelling, not in bounds confined,
But that, with love intenser, there Thou view'st
Thy primal effluence ; hallow'd be Thy name :

    [1] L'angelica farfalla, " the angelic butterfly," the human soul.

Join, each created being, to extol
Thy might; for worthy humblest thanks and praise
Is Thy blest Spirit.   May Thy kingdom's peace
Come unto us; for we, unless it come,
With all our striving, thither tend in vain.
As, of their will, the Angels unto Thee
Tender meet sacrifice, circling Thy throne
With loud hosannas; so of their's be done
By saintly men on earth.   Grant us, this day,
Our daily manna, without which he roams
Through this rough desert retrograde, who most
Toils to advance his steps.   As we to each
Pardon the evil done us, pardon Thou
Benign, and of our merit take no count.
'Gainst the old adversary, prove Thou not
Our virtue, easily subdued; but free
From his incitements, and defeat his wiles.
This last petition, dearest Lord ! is made
Not for ourselves; since that were needless now;
But for their sakes who after us remain.''

    Thus for themselves and us good speed imploring,
Those spirits went beneath a weight like that
We sometimes feel in dreams; all, sore beset,
But with unequal anguish; wearied all;
Round the first circuit; purging as they go
The world's gross darkness off.   In our behoof
If their vows still be offer'd, what can here
For them be vow'd and done by such, whose wills
Have root of goodness in them?   Well beseems
That we should help them wash away the stains
They carried hence; that so, made pure and light,
They may spring upward to the starry spheres.[1]

    "Ah ! so may mercy-temper'd justice rid
Your burdens speedily; that ye have power
To stretch your wing, which e'en to your desire
Shall lift you; as ye show us on which hand
Toward the ladder leads the shortest way.
And if there be more passages than one,
Instruct us of that easiest to ascend :
For this man, who comes with me, and bears yet

---

[1] *Cf.* 2 Maccabees xii. 46 : " It is therefore a holy and whole-
some thought to pray for the dead, that they may be loosed from
sins '' (Vulgate).

The charge of fleshly raiment Adam left him,
Despite his better will, but slowly mounts.''
From whom the answer came unto these words,
Which my guide spake, appear'd not; but 'twas said :
'' Along the bank to rightward come with us ;
And ye shall find a pass that mocks not toil
Of living man to climb : and were it not
That I am hinder'd by the rock, wherewith
This arrogant neck is tamed, whence needs I stoop
My visage to the ground ; him, who yet lives,
Whose name thou speak'st not, him I fain would view ;
To mark if e'er I knew him, and to crave
His pity for the fardel that I bear.
I was of Latium ; of a Tuscan born,
A mighty one : Aldobrandesco's name,
My sire's, I know not if ye e'er have heard.
My old blood and forefathers' gallant deeds
Made me so haughty, that I clean forgot
The common mother ; and to such excess
Wax'd in my scorn of all men, that I fell,
Fell therefore ; by what fate, Siena's sons,
Each child in Campagnatico, can tell.
I am Omberto : not me, only, pride
Hath injured, but my kindred all involved
In mischief with her.[1]   Here my lot ordains
Under this weight to groan, till I appease
God's angry justice, since I did it not
Amongst the living, here amongst the dead.''

  Listening I bent my visage down : and one
(Not he who spake) twisted beneath the weight
That urged him, saw me, knew me straight, and call'd ;
Holding his eyes with difficulty fix'd
Intent upon me, stooping as I went
Companion of their way.   '' O !'' I exclaim'd,
'' Art thou not Oderigi ?[2] art not thou
Agobbio's glory, glory of that art
Which they of Paris call the limner's skill ?''

  [1] Omberto, the son of Guglielmo Aldobrandesco, one of the
Counts of Santafiore (cf. above, Canto vi.), so exasperated the
Sienese by his overbearing conduct, that he was assassinated by
them, in 1259, at Campagnatico near Grosseto.
  [2] Oderisi, or Oderigi, of Gubbio, a famous Umbrian miniature-
painter or illuminator, who worked at Bologna and at Rome,
where he died in 1299.

" Brother !" said he, " with tints, that gayer smile,
Bolognian Franco's pencil lines the leaves.
His all the honour now; my light obscured.[1]
In truth, I had not been thus courteous to him
The whilst I lived, through eagerness of zeal
For that pre-eminence my heart was bent on.
Here, of such pride, the forfeiture is paid.
Nor were I even here, if, able still
To sin, I had not turn'd me unto God.
O powers of man ! how vain your glory, nipt
E'en in its height of verdure, if an age
Less bright succeed not.   Cimabue thought
To lord it over painting's field; and now
The cry is Giotto's, and his name eclipsed.[2]
Thus hath one Guido from the other snatch'd
The letter'd prize : and he, perhaps, is born,
Who shall drive either from their nest.[3]   The noise
Of worldly fame is but a blast of wind,
That blows from diverse points, and shifts its name,
Shifting the point it blows from.   Shalt thou more
Live in the mouths of mankind, if thy flesh
Part shrivel'd from thee, than if thou hadst died
Before the coral and the pap were left;
Or e'er some thousand years have past? and that

---

1 Franco of Bologna, a miniaturist employed by Boniface VIII.,
said to have been Oderisi's pupil.   Cary has missed the full
meaning of the line : *l'onore è tutto or suo, e mio in parte:* " the
honour is now all his, *and mine in part* ": Oderisi shares a little
of Franco's honour, as having been his master.   Franco was still
living in 1300.

2 Giovanni Cimabue (1240–1302), the first great painter of
Florence, was surpassed by his pupil, Giotto di Bondone (1266–
1337), painter, sculptor, and architect, the shepherd-boy who came
from the fields to free Italian painting from Byzantine fetters.
Both artists were personally known to Dante, and Giotto was
probably his intimate friend.

3 " The letter'd prize "; more literally, " the glory of our
language," *la gloria della lingua.* Cf. *De Vulg. El.* i. 13 ; ii. 6 ;
Purg. xxiv. and xxvi.   This is usually taken as meaning that
Guido Cavalcanti has eclipsed Guido Guinicelli, and that both
will be surpassed by Dante himself.   But there is more to be
said for Mr. Wicksteed's interpretation : " The older poetic school
of Guittone, or Guido, of Arezzo and his companions has been
superseded by that of Guido Guinicelli, to which Guido Cavalcanti
and Dante himself belong ; and who knows whether the founder
of yet another school that shall relegate them all to obscurity, may
not already be born !"

H

Is, to eternity compared, a space
Briefer than is the twinkling of an eye
To the heaven's slowest orb. He there, who treads
So leisurely before me, far and wide
Through Tuscany resounded once; and now
Is in Siena scarce with whispers named :
There was he sovereign, when destruction caught
The maddening rage of Florence, in that day
Proud as she now is loathsome. Your renown
Is as the herb, whose hue doth come and go;
And his might withers it, by whom it sprang
Crude from the lap of earth." I thus to him :
"True are thy sayings : to my heart they breathe
The kindly spirit of meekness, and allay
What tumours rankle there. But who is he,
Of whom thou spakest but now?" "This," he replied,
"Is Provenzano. He is here, because
He reach'd, with grasp presumptuous, at the sway
Of all Siena. Thus he still hath gone,
Thus goeth never-resting, since he died.
Such is the acquittance render'd back of him,
Who, in the mortal life, too much hath dared."
I then : "If soul, that to life's verge delays
Repentance, linger in that lower space,
Nor hither mount, (unless good prayers befriend,)
Or ever time, long as it lived, be past;
How chanced admittance was vouchsafed to him?" [1]

   "When at his glory's topmost height," said he,
"Respect of dignity all cast aside,
Freely he fix'd him on Siena's plain,
A suitor to redeem his suffering friend,

---

[1] Provenzano Salvani was the head of the Ghibelline party in Siena, of which city he became virtually ruler after the defeat of the Florentines at the battle of Montaperti in 1260. He it was who, in the council held at Empoli after the battle, proposed that Florence should be razed to the ground. Cf. *Inf*. x. In June, 1269, while leading a mixed force of Tuscan Ghibellines and foreign mercenaries, he was defeated at Colle by a body of French cavalry under Guy de Montfort, taken prisoner, and murdered by an exiled Sienese Guelf of the Tolomei family. Cf. *Purg*. xiii. He has gained admittance to Purgatory by his humility in begging for the means needed to ransom one of his friends who had fallen into the hands of Charles of Anjou. "Siena's plain" is the famous piazza, known as the *Campo*, in front of the great palace of the Commune.

Who languish'd in the prison-house of Charles;
Nor, for his sake, refused through every vein
To tremble. More I will not say; and dark,
I know, my words are; but thy neighbours soon
Shall help thee to a comment on the text.[1]
This is the work, that from these limits freed him."

CANTO XII

ARGUMENT

Dante, being desired by Virgil to look down on the ground which
they are treading, observes that it is wrought over with
imagery exhibiting various instances of pride recorded in
history and fable. They leave the first cornice, and are
ushered to the next by an Angel who points out the way.

WITH equal pace, as oxen in the yoke,
I, with that laden spirit, journey'd on,
Long as the mild instructor suffer'd me;
But, when he bade me quit him, and proceed,
(For " Here," said he, " behoves with sail and oars
Each man, as best he may, push on his bark,")
Upright, as one disposed for speed, I raised
My body, still in thought submissive bow'd.

   I now my leader's track not loth pursued;
And each had shown how light we fared along,
When thus he warned me : " Bend thine eyesight down,
For thou, to ease the way, shalt find it good
To ruminate the bed beneath thy feet."

   As, in memorial of the buried, drawn
Upon earth-level tombs, the sculptured form
Of what was once, appears, (at sight whereof
Tears often stream forth, by remembrance waked,
Whose sacred stings the piteous often feel,)
So saw I there, but with more curious skill
Of portraiture o'erwrought, whate'er of space
From forth the mountain stretches. On one part
Him I beheld, above all creatures erst
Created noblest, lightening fall from Heaven : [2]
On the other side, with bolt celestial pierced,

---

[1] He will soon learn in banishment how bitter a thing it is to
have to crave favours from others.
[2] Lucifer. *Cf.* Luke x. 18.

Briareus; cumbering earth he lay, through dint
Of mortal ice-stroke.[1]   The Thymbræan god,
With Mars, I saw, and Pallas, round their sire,
Arm'd still, and gazing on the giants' limbs
Strewn o'er the ethereal field.[2]   Nimrod I saw:
At foot of the stupendous work he stood,
As if bewilder'd, looking on the crowd
Leagued in his proud attempt on Sennaar's plain.[3]

     O Niobe! in what a trance of woe
Thee I beheld, upon that highway drawn,
Seven sons on either side thee slain.[4]   O Saul!
How ghastly didst thou look, on thine own sword
Expiring, in Gilboa, from that hour
Ne'er visited with rain from heaven, or dew.[5]

     O fond Arachne! thee I also saw,
Half spider now, in anguish, crawling up
The unfinish'd web thou weaved'st to thy bane.[6]

     O Rehoboam! here thy shape doth seem
Louring no more defiance; but fear-smote,
With none to chase him, in his chariot whirl'd.[7]

     Was shown beside upon the solid floor,
How dear Alcmæon forced his mother rate
That ornament, in evil hour received: [8]
How, in the temple, on Sennacherib fell
His sons, and how a corpse they left him there.[9]
Was shown the scath, and cruel mangling made
By Tomyris on Cyrus, when she cried,
" Blood thou didst thirst for : take thy fill of blood." [10]

[1] Cf. *Inf.* xxxi.

[2] The overthrow of the giants who attempted to storm Heaven. Cf. *Inf.* xxxi. The "Thymbræan god" is Apollo.

[3] Cf. *Inf.* xxxi.

[4] Niobe, daughter of Tantalus and Dione, with her sons and daughters, was slain by Apollo and Artemis for exalting herself above their mother, Leto or Latona.

[5] *Cf.* 2 Sam. i. 21.

[6] Arachne was changed to a spider for her pride in challenging Minerva.

[7] *Cf.* 1 Kings xii.

[8] Eriphyle, wife of Amphiaraus (*Inf.* xx.), was bribed by the necklace of Harmonia to reveal the hiding-place of her husband, whereby he was compelled to go to the Theban war, in which he knew that he would be slain. At the latter's bidding, their son Alcmæon killed Eriphyle for her treachery. Cf. *Par.* iv.

[9] *Cf.* 2 Kings xix. 37; Isaiah xxxvii.

[10] When Cyrus, King of the Medes and Persians, was defeated and slain by the Massagetae (B.C. 529), their Queen Tomyris cut

Was shown how routed in the battle fled
The Assyrians, Holofernes slain, and e'en
The relics of the carnage.[1]   Troy I mark'd,
In ashes and in caverns. Oh! how fallen,
How abject, Ilion, was thy semblance there.[2]

    What master of the pencil or the style
Had traced the shades and lines, that might have made
The subtlest workman wonder? Dead, the dead;
The living seem'd alive : with clearer view,
His eye beheld not, who beheld the truth,
Than mine what I did tread on, while I went
Low bending. Now swell out, and with stiff necks
Pass on, ye sons of Eve ! vale not your looks,
Lest they descry the evil of your path.

    I noted not (so busied was my thought)
How much we now had circled of the mount;
And of his course yet more the sun had spent;
When he, who with still wakeful caution went,
Admonish'd : " Raise thou up thy head : for know
Time is not now for slow suspense. Behold,
That way, an Angel hasting towards us. Lo,
Where duly the sixth handmaid[3] doth return
From service on the day. Wear thou, in look
And gesture, seemly grace of reverent awe;
That gladly he may forward us aloft.
Consider that this day ne'er dawns again."

    Time's loss he had so often warn'd me 'gainst,
I could not miss the scope at which he aim'd.

    The goodly shape approach'd us, snowy white
In vesture, and with visage casting streams
Of tremulous lustre like the matin star.
His arms he open'd, then his wings; and spake :
" Onward ! the steps, behold, are near; and now
The ascent is without difficulty gain'd."[4]

    A scanty few are they, who, when they hear

off his head, and threw it into a vessel of blood with the words
that Dante here quotes from Orosius.

  [1] Judith xiii.–xv.
  [2] The pride of Troy was proverbial. This alternation of
historical or scriptural examples with those drawn from mythology
is characteristic of Dante.
  [3] " It is therefore just past noon. The conception of the hours
as handmaidens serving the day is repeated below, in Canto xxii "
(Oelsner).
  [4] This is the Angel of Humility.

Such tidings, hasten.   O, ye race of men!
Though born to soar, why suffer ye a wind
So slight to baffle ye?   He led us on
Where the rock parted; here, against my front,
Did beat his wings; then promised I should fare
In safety on my way.   As to ascend
That steep, upon whose brow the chapel stands,
(O'er Rubaconte, looking lordly down
On the well-guided city,[1]) up the right
The impetuous rise is broken by the steps
Carved in that old and simple age, when still
The registry and label rested safe;[2]
Thus is the acclivity relieved, which here,
Precipitous, from the other circuit falls:
But, on each hand, the tall cliff presses close.

      As, entering, there we turn'd, voices, in strain
Ineffable, sang: "Blessed are the poor
In spirit."   Ah! how far unlike to these
The straits of Hell: here songs to usher us,
There shrieks of woe.   We climb the holy stairs:
And lighter to myself by far I seem'd
Than on the plain before; whence thus I spake:
"Say, master, of what heavy thing have I
Been lighten'd; that scarce aught the sense of toil
Affects me journeying?"   He in few replied:
"When sin's broad characters, that yet remain
Upon thy temples, though well nigh effaced,
Shall be, as one is, all clean razed out;
Then shall thy feet by heartiness of will
Be so o'ercome, they not alone shall feel
No sense of labour, but delight much more
Shall wait them, urged along their upward way."

      Then like to one, upon whose head is placed
Somewhat he deems not of, but from the becks

---

[1] The reference to Florence as "the well-guided city" is, of
course, ironical.   The church of San Miniato may be said to look
down on Florence over the Ponte Rubaconte, the oldest of the
Florentine bridges.

[2] "In 1299 Messer Niccola Acciaiuoli and Messer Baldo d'A-
guglione abstracted from the public records a leaf containing
the evidence of a disreputable transaction, in which they, together
with the Podestà, had been engaged.   At about the same time
Messer Durante de' Chiaramontesi, being officer of the customs
for salt, took away a stave from the standard measure, thus
making it smaller" (Butler).   Cf. *Par.* xvi.

Of others, as they pass him by; his hand
Lends therefore help to assure him, searches, finds,
And well performs such office as the eye
Wants power to execute; so stretching forth
The fingers of my right hand, did I find
Six only of the letters, which his sword,
Who bare the keys, had traced upon my brow.
The leader, as he mark'd mine action, smiled.

CANTO XIII

ARGUMENT

They gain the second cornice, where the sin of envy is purged;
and having proceeded a little to the right, they hear voices
uttered by invisible spirits recounting famous examples of
charity, and next behold the shades, or souls, of the envious
clad in sackcloth, and having their eyes sewed up with an
iron thread. Amongst these Dante finds Sapia, a Sienese
lady, from whom he learns the cause of her being there.

WE reach'd the summit of the scale, and stood
Upon the second buttress of that mount
Which healeth him who climbs. A cornice there,
Like to the former, girdles round the hill;
Save that its arch, with sweep less ample, bends.
   Shadow, nor image there, is seen: all smooth
The rampart and the path, reflecting nought
But the rock's sullen hue. "If here we wait,
For some to question," said the bard, "I fear
Our choice may haply meet too long delay."
   Then fixedly upon the sun his eyes
He fasten'd; made his right the central point
From whence to move; and turn'd the left aside.
"O pleasant light, my confidence and hope!
Conduct us thou," he cried, "on this new way,
Where now I venture; leading to the bourn
We seek. The universal world to thee
Owes warmth and lustre. If no other cause
Forbid, thy beams should ever be our guide."
   Far, as is measured for a mile on earth,
In brief space had we journey'd; such prompt will
Impell'd; and towards us flying, now were heard
Spirits invisible, who courteously
Unto love's table bade the welcome guest.

The voice, that first flew by, call'd forth aloud,
" They have no wine," so on behind us past,
Those sounds reiterating, nor yet lost
In the faint distance, when another came
Crying, " I am Orestes," and alike
Wing'd its fleet way. " O father !" I exclaim'd,
" What tongues are these?" and as I question'd, lo !
A third exclaiming, " Love ye those have wrong'd
     you." [1]

     " This circuit," said my teacher, " knots the scourge
For envy ; and the cords are therefore drawn
By charity's correcting hand. The curb
Is of a harsher sound ; [2] as thou shalt hear
(If I deem rightly) ere thou reach the pass,
Where pardon sets them free. But fix thine eyes
Intently through the air ; and thou shalt see
A multitude before thee seated, each
Along the shelving grot." Then more than erst
I oped mine eyes ; before me view'd ; and saw
Shadows with garments dark as was the rock ;
And when we pass'd a little forth, I heard
A crying, " Blessed Mary ! pray for us,
Michael and Peter ! all ye saintly host !"

     I do not think there walks on earth this day
Man so remorseless, that he had not yearn'd
With pity at the sight that next I saw.
Mine eyes a load of sorrow teem'd, when now
I stood so near them, that their semblances
Came clearly to my view. Of sackcloth vile
Their covering seem'd ; and, on his shoulder, one
Did stay another, leaning ; and all lean'd
Against the cliff. E'en thus the blind and poor,
Near the confessionals, to crave an alms,
Stand, each his head upon his fellow's sunk ;
So most to stir compassion, not by sound
Of words alone, but that which moves not less,
The sight of misery. And as never beam
Of noon-day visiteth the eyeless man,

    [1] These are the examples of charity opposed to envy : the
Blessed Virgin at the marriage in Cana (John ii. 3) ; Pylades
offering himself to death for Orestes ; Christ's admonition to His
disciples (Matt. v. 44).
    [2] The scourge (ferza) is the recital of the examples of the con-
trary virtue, the curb or bit (freno) that of the examples of the
punishment of the sin itself.

E'en so was Heaven a niggard unto these
Of his fair light : for, through the orbs of all,
A thread of wire, impiercing, knits them up,
As for the taming of a haggard hawk.

It were a wrong, methought, to pass and look
On others, yet myself the while unseen.
To my sage counsel therefore did I turn.
He knew the meaning of the mute appeal,
Nor waited for my questioning, but said :
" Speak ; and be brief, be subtile in thy words."

On that part of the cornice, whence no rim
Engarlands its steep fall, did Virgil come ;
On the other side me were the spirits, their cheeks
Bathing devout with penitential tears,
That through the dread impalement forced a way.

I turn'd me to them, and " O shades ! " said I,
" Assured that to your eyes unveil'd shall shine
The lofty light, sole object of your wish,
So may Heaven's grace clear whatsoe'er of foam
Floats turbid on the conscience, that thenceforth
The stream of mind roll limpid from its source ;
As ye declare (for so shall ye impart
A boon I dearly prize) if any soul
Of Latium dwell among ye : and perchance
That soul may profit, if I learn so much."

" My brother ! we are, each one, citizens
Of one true city.[1] Any, thou wouldst say,
Who lived a stranger in Italia's land."

So heard I answering, as appear'd, a voice
That onward came some space from whence I stood.

A spirit I noted, in whose look was mark'd
Expectance. Ask ye how ? The chin was raised
As in one reft of sight. " Spirit," said I,
" Who for thy rise art tutoring, (if thou be
That which didst answer to me,) or by place,
Or name, disclose thyself, that I may know thee."

" I was," it answer'd, " of Siena : here
I cleanse away with these the evil life,
Soliciting with tears that He, who is,
Vouchsafe Him to us. Though Sapia named,
In sapience I excell'd not ; gladder far
Of other's hurt, than of the good befel me.

---

[1] Cary aptly cites Hebrews xiii. 14 : " For here we have no
continuing city, but we seek one to come."

That thou mayst own I now deceive thee not,
Hear, if my folly were not as I speak it.
When now my years sloped waning down the arch,
It so bechanced, my fellow-citizens
Near Colle met their enemies in the field;
And I pray'd God to grant what He had will'd.[1]
There were they vanquish'd, and betook themselves
Unto the bitter passages of flight.
I mark'd the hunt; and waxing out of bounds
In gladness, lifted up my shameless brow,
And, like the merlin cheated by a gleam,
Cried : ' It is over. Heaven ! I fear thee not.'
Upon my verge of life I wish'd for peace
With God; nor yet repentance had supplied
What I did lack of duty, were it not
The hermit Piero,[2] touch'd with charity,
In his devout oraisons thought on me.
But who art thou that question'st of our state,
Who go'st, as I believe, with lids unclosed,
And breathest in thy talk?''—'' Mine eyes,'' said I,
'' May yet be here ta'en from me; but not long;
For they have not offended grievously
With envious glances. But the woe beneath [3]
Urges my soul with more exceeding dread,
That nether load already weighs me down.''
    She thus : '' Who then, amongst us here aloft,
Hath brought thee, if thou weenest to return?''
    '' He,'' answered I, '' who standeth mute beside me.
I live : of me ask therefore, chosen spirit !
If thou desire I yonder yet should move
For thee my mortal feet.''—'' Oh !'' she replied,
'' This is so strange a thing, it is great sign
That God doth love thee. Therefore with thy prayer
Sometime assist me : and, by that I crave,
Which most thou covetest, that if thy feet
E'er tread on Tuscan soil, thou save my fame

---

[1] The defeat of the Sienese. Sapia de' Saracini, a noble lady
of Siena, was one of the Guelf exiles at Colle in Val d' Elsa.
From a tower she watched the rout of her Ghibelline fellow-
countrymen at the battle of Colle (June 11, 1269), when Provenzano
Salvani was slain, and broke out into the expressions of exultation here recorded by the Poet.

[2] Piero Pettignano, a comb-seller and Franciscan tertiary of
Siena, who died in 1289, and was beatified.

[3] Dante's conscience accused him of pride rather than of envy.

Amongst my kindred. Them shalt thou behold
With that vain multitude, who set their hope
On Talamone's haven ; there to fail
Confounded, more than when the fancied stream
They sought, of Dian call'd : but they, who lead
Their navies more than ruin'd hopes shall mourn." [1]

CANTO XIV

ARGUMENT

Our Poet on this second cornice finds also the souls of Guido del
   Duca of Brettinoro, and Rinieri da Calboli of Romagna ; the
   former of whom, hearing that he comes from the banks of the
   Arno, inveighs against the degeneracy of all those who dwell
   in the cities visited by that stream ; and *afterwards*, in like
   manner, against the inhabitants of Romagna. On leaving
   these, our Poets hear voices recording noted instances of envy.

" SAY, who is he around our mountain winds,
Or ever death has pruned his wing for flight ;
That opes his eyes, and covers them at will?"
   " I know not who he is, but know thus much ;
He comes not singly. Do thou ask of him,
For thou art nearer to him ; and take heed,
Accost him gently, so that he may speak."
   Thus on the right two spirits, bending each
Toward the other, talk'd of me ; then both
Addressing me, their faces backward lean'd,
And thus the one [2] began : " O soul, who yet
Pent in the body, tendest towards the sky !
For charity, we pray thee, comfort us ;
Recounting whence thou comest, and who thou art :
For thou dost make us, at the favour shown thee,

---

[1] Cf. *Inf.* xxix. The Sienese, in 1303, purchased the seaport of
Talamone in the Maremma, by means of which they hoped to
become a great maritime power. Vast sums of money were spent
upon it, but with small results, owing to the unhealthiness of the
situation and the impossibility of keeping the harbour clear.
Much money had previously been squandered in the quest of the
Diana, a subterranean stream supposed to exist under Siena, for
which, in 1295, the General Council of the Commune decreed that
the search should be undertaken.

[2] These two spirits are two Romagnole nobles : Guido del
Duca degli Onesti, a Ghibelline of Bertinoro (*d. circa* 1230), and
Rinier da Calboli, a Guelf of Forlì (*d.* 1296). The first speaker is
Guido.

Marvel, as at a thing that ne'er hath been."

  "There stretches through the midst of Tuscany,"
I straight began, " a brooklet, whose well-head
Springs up in Falterona; with his race
Not satisfied, when he some hundred miles
Hath measured.[1]   From his banks bring I this frame.
To tell you who I am were words mis-spent:
For yet my name scarce sounds on rumour's lip."

  " If well I do incorporate with my thought
The meaning of thy speech," said he, who first
Address'd me, " thou dost speak of Arno's wave."

  To whom the other : " Why hath he conceal'd
The title of that river, as a man
Doth of some horrible thing?"   The spirit, who
Thereof was question'd, did acquit him thus :
" I know not : but 'tis fitting well the name
Should perish of that vale; for from the source,[2]
Where teems so plenteously the Alpine steep
Maim'd of Pelorus, (that doth scarcely pass
Beyond that limit,) even to the point
Where unto ocean is restored what heaven
Drains from the exhaustless store for all earth's streams,
Throughout the space is virtue worried down,
As 'twere a snake, by all, for mortal foe ;
Or through disastrous influence on the place,
Or else distortion of misguided wills
That custom goads to evil : whence in those,
The dwellers in that miserable vale,
Nature is so transform'd, it seems as they
Had shared of Circe's feeding.   'Midst brute swine,[3]
Worthier of acorns than of other food
Created for man's use, he shapeth first
His obscure way ; then, sloping onward, finds
Curs,[4] snarlers more in spite than power, from whom
He turns with scorn aside : still journeying down,
By how much more the curst and luckless foss

  [1] The Arno rises in Monte Falterona among the Apennines,
and flows into the Mediterranean near Pisa after a course of a
hundred and fifty miles.
  [2] " From the rise of the Arno in that 'Alpine steep,' the
Apennine, from whence Pelorus in Sicily was torn by a convulsion
of the earth, even to the point where the same river unites its
waters to the ocean, Virtue is persecuted by all " (Cary).
  [3] The inhabitants of the Casentino.
  [4] The Aretines.

Swells out to largeness, e'en so much it finds
Dogs turning into wolves.[1]   Descending still
Through yet more hollow eddies, next he meets
A race of foxes,[2] so replete with craft,
They do not fear that skill can master it.
Nor will I cease because my words are heard
By other ears than thine.   It shall be well
For this man, if he keep in memory
What from no erring spirit I reveal.
Lo! I behold thy grandson, that becomes
A hunter of those wolves, upon the shore
Of the fierce stream; and cows them all with dread.
Their flesh, yet living, sets he up to sale,
Then, like an aged beast, to slaughter dooms.
Many of life he reaves, himself of worth
And goodly estimation.   Smear'd with gore,
Mark how he issues from the rueful wood;
Leaving such havoc, that in thousand years
It spreads not to prime lustihood again." [3]

   As one, who tidings hears of woe to come,
Changes his looks perturb'd, from whate'er part
The peril grasp him; so beheld I change
That spirit, who had turn'd to listen; struck
With sadness, soon as he had caught the word.

   His visage, and the other's speech, did raise
Desire in me to know the names of both;
Whereof, with meek entreaty, I inquired.

   The shade, who late address'd me, thus resumed:
" Thy wish imports, that I vouchsafe to do
For thy sake what thou wilt not do for mine.
But, since God's will is that so largely shine
His grace in thee, I will be liberal too.
Guido of Duca know then that I am.
Envy so parch'd my blood, that had I seen
A fellow man made joyous, thou hadst mark'd
A livid paleness overspread my cheek.
Such harvest reap I of the seed I sow'd.
O man! why place thy heart where there doth need

---

1 The Florentines.
2 The Pisans.
3 Rinier's grandson, Fulcieri da Calboli, was Podestà of
Florence from January to September, 1303, by favour of the Neri,
and committed the most horrible atrocities upon those of the
Bianchi who fell into his hands.

Exclusion of participants in good?
This is Rinieri's spirit; this, the boast
And honour of the house of Calboli;
Where of his worth no heritage remains.
Nor his the only blood, that hath been stript
('Twixt Po, the mount, the Reno, and the shore)[1]
Of all that truth or fancy asks for bliss:
But, in those limits, such a growth has sprung
Of rank and venom'd roots, as long would mock
Slow culture's toil.   Where is good Lizio?[2] where
Mainardi, Traversaro, and Carpigna?[3]
O bastard slips of old Romagna's line!
When in Bologna the low artisan,
And in Faenza yon Bernardin sprouts,
A gentle cyon from ignoble stem.[4]
Wonder not, Tuscan, if thou see me weep,
When I recal to mind those once loved names,
Guido of Prata, and of Azzo him
That dwelt with us; Tignoso and his troop,
With Traversaro's house and Anastagio's,
(Each race disherited;)[5] and beside these,
The ladies and the knights, the toils and ease,
That witch'd us into love and courtesy;
Where now such malice reigns in recreant hearts.
O Brettinoro![6] wherefore tarriest still,

[1] The boundaries of Romagna.
[2] Lizio da Valbona, a Guelf noble of Bertinoro.
[3] Arrigo Mainardi, a Ghibelline of Bertinoro; Pier Traversaro,
a Ghibelline of Ravenna (d. 1225); Guido da Carpigna, member
of an ancient family connected with the Counts of Montefeltro,
renowned for his liberality (d. between 1270 and 1289). Guido
del Duca is contrasting the noble qualities of these past worthies
of Romagna, Guelfs and Ghibellines alike, with the degenerate
character of their successors.
[4] The right rendering of these lines is: " When in Bologna
shall a Fabbro take root again? When in Faenza a Bernardin di
Fosco, noble scion of a lowly plant?" (Okey). Fabbro de'
Lambertazzi, a noble and valiant Ghibelline soldier of Bologna,
died in 1259; Bernardino di Fosco, the son of a field-labourer, and
a Guelf (d. circa 1250), won for himself a place among the nobles
of Faenza.
[5] Guido da Prata of Ravenna, Ugolino d'Azzo Ubaldini of
Faenza (who married a daughter of Provenzano Salvani, and died
in 1293), Federigo Tignoso of Rimini; all deceased Romagnole
worthies. The Traversari and the Anastagi were noble Ghibelline
families of Ravenna, both almost extinct by 1300.
[6] Bertinoro, from which the noble Ghibelline families, famous
for their liberality and hospitality, had been expelled in 1295.

Since forth of thee thy family hath gone,
And many, hating evil, join'd their steps?
Well doeth he, that bids his lineage cease,
Bagnacavallo; Castrocaro ill,
And Conio worse, who care to propagate
A race of Counties from such blood as theirs.[1]
Well shall ye also do, Pagani, then
When from amongst you hies your demon child;[2]
Not so, howe'er, that henceforth there remain
True proof of what ye were. O Hugolin,
Thou sprung of Fantolini's line! thy name
Is safe; since none is look'd for after thee
To cloud its lustre, warping from thy stock.[3]
But, Tuscan! go thy ways; for now I take
Far more delight in weeping, than in words.
Such pity for your sakes hath wrung my heart."[4]
    We knew those gentle spirits, at parting, heard
Our steps.   Their silence therefore, of our way,
Assured us.   Soon as we had quitted them,
Advancing onward, lo! a voice, that seem'd
Like volley'd lightening, when it rives the air,
Met us, and shouted, "Whosoever finds
Will slay me;" then fled from us, as the bolt
Lanced sudden from a downward-rushing cloud.
When it had given short truce unto our hearing,
Behold the other with a crash as loud

1 Cary notes on *Counties:* "I have used this word here for
'Counts,' as it is in Shakespeare." The more correct translation
is : "Well doth Bagnacavallo that begetteth no more offspring,
and ill doth Castrocaro, and Conio worse, that yet troubleth
to beget such counts." The Malavicini, Counts of Bagnacavallo
(a town between Imola and Ravenna), frequently changed sides.
Castrocaro and Conio are small Romagnole towns near Forlì, of
which the latter was ruled by the Barbiano family. A Count
Alberigo da Barbiano of Conio was a famous condottiere in the
next epoch, who won the battle of Marino (1379); to him one of
St. Catherine's most eloquent letters is addressed.

2 *Il demonio loro,* "their demon." The reference is to Maghinardo Pagano da Susinana, for whom see notes on *Inf.* xxvii.

3 Ugolino de' Fantolini of Faenza, a man of noble life and
pacific disposition, died in 1278, leaving two sons, Ottaviano and
Fantolino. The one was killed at Forlì in 1282, fighting for the
Guelfs against Guido da Montefeltro (cf. *Inf.* xxvii.), and the other
died a few years later, thus ending the family.

4 The right reading of this line seems to be : *Sì m'ha nostra
ragion la mente stretta* : " so hath our discourse wrung my spirit "
(Okey).

As the quick-following thunder : " Mark in me
Aglauros, turn'd to rock." [1]   I, at the sound
Retreating, drew more closely to my guide.
    Now in mute stilness rested all the air ;
And thus he spake : " There was the galling bit,
Which should keep man within his boundary.
But your old enemy so baits the hook,
He drags you eager to him.   Hence nor curb
Avails you, nor reclaiming call.   Heaven calls,
And, round about you wheeling, courts your gaze
With everlasting beauties.   Yet your eye
Turns with fond doting still upon the earth.
Therefore he smites you who discerneth all."

CANTO XV

ARGUMENT

An Angel invites them to ascend the next steep. On their way
Dante suggests certain doubts, which are resolved by Virgil ;
and, when they reach the third cornice, where the sin of anger
is purged, our Poet, in a kind of waking dream, beholds
remarkable instances of patience ; and soon after they are
enveloped in a dense fog.

As much as 'twixt the third hour's close and dawn,
Appeareth of Heaven's sphere, that ever whirls
As restless as an infant in his play ;
So much appear'd remaining to the sun
Of his slope journey towards the western goal.
    Evening was there, and here the noon of night ; [2]
And full upon our forehead smote the beams.
For round the mountain, circling, so our path
Had led us, that toward the sunset now

---

[1] Examples of the punishment of envy : Cain (Gen. iv. 14),
and Aglauros, daughter of Cecrops, whom Mercury changed into
stone for her jealousy of her sister Herse.

[2] " It was three hours past noon (*vespero* = from 3 to 6, *sera* =
from 6 to 9 p.m.) in Purgatory, wherefore it must have been three
hours after midnight at Jerusalem, and just midnight at Florence.
Spera is the sphere in which the sun is fixed, which is said to
sport, because its great circle—the ecliptic—is always rising or
falling, to appearance, in the sky " (Butler). Dante always uses
là (" there ") for Purgatory or Paradise, as the case may be, and
qui or *qua* (" here ") for Italy where he is telling the story of his
vision.

Direct we journey'd; when I felt a weight
Of more exceeding splendour, than before,
Press on my front. The cause unknown, amaze
Possess'd me! and both hands against my brows
Lifting, I interposed them, as a screen,
That of its gorgeous superflux of light
Clips the diminish'd orb. As when the ray,
Striking on water or the surface clear
Of mirror, leaps unto the opposite part,
Ascending at a glance, e'en as it fell,
And as much differs from the stone, that falls
Through equal space, (so practic skill hath shown);
Thus, with refracted light, before me seem'd
The ground there smitten; whence, in sudden haste,
My sight recoil'd. "What is this, sire beloved!
'Gainst which I strive to shield the sight in vain?"
Cried I, "and which toward us moving seems?"

     "Marvel not, if the family of Heaven,"
He answer'd, "yet with dazzling radiance dim
Thy sense. It is a messenger who comes,
Inviting man's ascent.[1] Such sights ere long,
Not grievous, shall impart to thee delight,
As thy perception is by nature wrought
Up to their pitch." The blessed Angel, soon
As we had reach'd him, hail'd us with glad voice:
"Here enter on a ladder far less steep
Than ye have yet encounter'd." We forthwith
Ascending, heard behind us chanted sweet,
"Blessed the merciful," and "Happy thou,
That conquer'st." Lonely each, my guide and I,
Pursued our upward way; and as we went,
Some profit from his words I hoped to win,
And thus of him inquiring, framed my speech:
"What meant Romagna's spirit,[2] when he spake
Of bliss exclusive, with no partner shared?"

     He straight replied: "No wonder, since he knows
What sorrow waits on his own worst defect,
If he chide others, that they less may mourn.
Because ye point your wishes at a mark,
Where, by communion of possessors, part
Is lessen'd, envy bloweth up men's sighs.

1 The Angel of Fraternal Love.
2 Guido del Duca.

No fear of that might touch ye, if the love
Of higher sphere exalted your desire.
For there, by how much more they call it 'ours,'
So much propriety of each in good
Encreases more, and heighten'd charity
Wraps that fair cloister in a brighter flame.

  " Now lack I satisfaction more," said I,
" Than if thou hadst been silent at the first;
And doubt more gathers on my labouring thought.
How can it chance, that good distributed,
The many, that possess it, makes more rich,
Than if 'twere shared by few?" He answering thus:
" Thy mind, reverting still to things of earth,
Strikes darkness from true light. The highest Good
Unlimited, ineffable, doth so speed
To love, as beam to lucid body darts,
Giving as much of ardour as it finds.
The sempiternal effluence streams abroad,
Spreading, wherever charity extends;
So that the more aspirants to that bliss
Are multiplied, more good is there to love,
And more is loved; as mirrors, that reflect,
Each unto other, propagated light.
If these my words avail not to allay
Thy thirsting, Beatrice thou shalt see,
Who of this want, and of all else thou hast,
Shall rid thee to the full. Provide but thou,
That from thy temples may be soon erased,
E'en as the two already, those five scars,
That, when they pain thee worst, then kindliest heal.''

  " Thou," I had said, " content'st me;" when I saw
The other round was gain'd, and wondering eyes
Did keep me mute. There suddenly I seem'd
By an extatic vision wrapt away;
And in a temple saw, methought, a crowd
Of many persons; and at the entrance stood
A dame,[1] whose sweet demeanour did express
A mother's love, who said, " Child ! why hast thou
Dealt with us thus? Behold thy sire and I
Sorrowing have sought thee;" and so held her peace;
And straight the vision fled. A female next

  [1] The first example of meekness is the Blessed Virgin. *Cf.*
Luke ii. 48.

Appear'd before me, down whose visage coursed
Those waters, that grief forces out from one
By deep resentment stung, who seem'd to say:
" If thou, Pisistratus, be lord indeed
Over this city, named with such debate
Of adverse gods, and whence each science sparkles,
Avenge thee of those arms, whose bold embrace
Hath clasp'd our daughter;" and to her, meseem'd,
Benign and meek, with visage undisturb'd,
Her sovran spake: " How shall we those requite
Who wish us evil, if we thus condemn
The man that loves us?"[1]   After that I saw
A multitude, in fury burning, slay
With stones a stripling youth,[2] and shout amain
" Destroy, destroy;" and him I saw, who bow'd
Heavy with death unto the ground, yet made
His eyes, unfolded upward, gates to Heaven,
Praying forgiveness of the Almighty Sire,
Amidst that cruel conflict, on his foes,
With looks that win compassion to their aim.

     Soon as my spirit, from her airy flight
Returning, sought again the things whose truth
Depends not on her shaping, I observed
She had not roved to falsehood in her dreams.[3]

     Meanwhile the leader, who might see I moved
As one who struggles to shake off his sleep,
Exclaim'd: " What ails thee, that thou canst not hold
Thy footing firm; but more than half a league
Hast travel'd with closed eyes and tottering gait,
Like to a man by wine or sleep o'ercharged?"

     " Beloved father! so thou deign," said I,
" To listen, I will tell thee what appear'd
Before me, when so fail'd my sinking steps."

     He thus: " Not if thy countenance were mask'd
With hundred vizards, could a thought of thine,
How small soe'er, elude me.   What thou saw'st
Was shown, that freely thou mightst ope thy heart

----

[1] Pisistratus, Lord of Athens, when urged by his wife to put to
death a young man who had kissed their daughter in public, is
said by Valerius Maximus to have given the answer here recorded.

[2] St. Stephen, the first Christian martyr (Acts vii.).

[3] " Dante recognised that the scenes which had passed before
him were merely visions (*errori*), though visions of events that had
actually occurred in times gone by (therefore, *non falsi*)" (Oelsner).

To the waters of peace, that flow diffused
From their eternal fountain.   I not ask'd,
What ails thee? for such cause as he doth, who
Looks only with that eye, which sees no more,
When spiritless the body lies; but ask'd,
To give fresh vigour to thy foot.   Such goads,
The slow and loitering need; that they be found
Not wanting, when their hour of watch returns."
    So on we journey'd, through the evening sky
Gazing intent, far onward as our eyes,
With level view, could stretch against the bright
Vespertine ray: and lo! by slow degrees
Gathering, a fog made towards us, dark as night.
There was no room for 'scaping; and that mist
Bereft us, both of sight and the pure air.

CANTO XVI

ARGUMENT

As they proceed through the mist, they hear the voices of spirits
praying.   Marco Lombardo, one of these, points out to Dante
the error of such as impute our actions to necessity; explains
to him that man is endued with free will; and shows that
much of human depravity results from the undue mixture of
spiritual and temporal authority in rulers.

HELL'S dunnest gloom, or night unlustrous, dark,
Of every planet 'reft, and pall'd in clouds,
Did never spread before the sight a veil
In thickness like that fog, nor to the sense
So palpable and gross.   Entering its shade,
Mine eye endured not with unclosed lids;
Which marking, near me drew the faithful guide,
Offering me his shoulder for a stay.
    As the blind man behind his leader walks,
Lest he should err, or stumble unawares
On what might harm him or perhaps destroy;
I journey'd through that bitter air and foul,
Still listening to my escort's warning voice,
" Look that from me thou part not."   Straight I heard
Voices, and each one seem'd to pray for peace,
And for compassion, to the Lamb of God
That taketh sins away.   Their prelude still
Was " Agnus Dei;" and through all the choir,

One voice, one measure ran, that perfect seem'd
The concord of their song. " Are these I hear
Spirits, O master?" I exclaim'd; and he,
" Thou aim'st aright: these loose the bonds of wrath."
　　" Now who art thou, that through our smoke dost
　　　　cleave,
And speak'st of us, as thou thyself e'en yet
Dividedst time by calends?" [1] So one voice
Bespake me; whence my master said, " Reply;
And ask, if upward hence the passage lead."
　　" O being! who dost make thee pure, to stand
Beautiful once more in thy Maker's sight;
Along with me: and thou shalt hear and wonder."
Thus I, whereto the spirit answering spake:
" Long as 'tis lawful for me, shall my steps
Follow on thine; and since the cloudy smoke
Forbids the seeing, hearing in its stead
Shall keep us join'd."   I then forthwith began:
" Yet in my mortal swathing, I ascend
To higher regions; and am hither come
Thorough the fearful agony of Hell.
And, if so largely God hath doled His grace,
That, clean beside all modern precedent,
He wills me to behold His kingly state;
From me conceal not who thou wast, ere death
Had loosed thee; but instruct me: and instruct
If rightly to the pass I tend; thy words
The way directing, as a safe escort."
　　" I was of Lombardy, and Marco call'd: [2]
Not inexperienced of the world, that worth
I still affected, from which all have turn'd
The nerveless bow aside.   Thy course tends right
Unto the summit:" and, replying thus,
He added, " I beseech thee pray for me,
When thou shalt come aloft."   And I to him:
" Accept my faith for pledge I will perform
What thou requirest.   Yet one doubt remains,
That wrings me sorely, if I solve it not.
Singly before it urged me, doubled now

---

[1] " As though thou wert still alive."
[2] Marco Lombardo, or " the Lombard," was apparently a
Venetian; it is uncertain whether Lombardo was also his family
name.   Villani describes him as " a wise and worthy courtier";
he was famous for his liberality and his pregnant sayings.

By thine opinion, when I couple that
With one elsewhere [1] declared; each strengthening
    other.
The world indeed is even so forlorn
Of all good, as thou speak'st it, and so swarms
With every evil.   Yet, beseech thee, point
The cause out to me, that myself may see,
And unto others show it : for in Heaven
One places it, and one on earth below.''

    Then heaving forth a deep and audible sigh,
'' Brother !'' he thus began, '' the world is blind;
And thou in truth comest from it.   Ye, who live,
Do so each cause refer to Heaven above,
E'en as its motion, of necessity,
Drew with it all that moves.   If this were so,
Free choice in you were none; nor justice would
There should be joy for virtue, woe for ill.
Your movements have their primal bent from Heaven;
Not all : yet said I all; what then ensues?
Light have ye still to follow evil or good,
And of the will free power, which, if it stand
Firm and unwearied in Heaven's first assay,
Conquers at last, so it be cherish'd well,
Triumphant over all.   To mightier force,
To better nature subject, ye abide
Free, not constrain'd by that which forms in you
The reasoning mind uninfluenced of the stars. [2]
If then the present race of mankind err,
Seek in yourselves the cause, and find it there;
Herein thou shalt confess me no false spy.

    '' Forth from His plastic hand, who charm'd beholds
Her image ere she yet exist, the soul
Comes like a babe, that wantons sportively, [3]
Weeping and laughing in its wayward moods;

[1] By Guido del Duca.
[2] The human soul is freely subject to her Creator. Albertus
Magnus holds that there is in man a twofold principle of action,
nature and the will. Nature, indeed, is governed by the stars,
but the will is free. Notwithstanding this freedom, however, the
will will be drawn and inclined by nature, unless it steadfastly
resists ; and, since nature moves with the movements of the stars,
the will then, if it does not resist, begins to be inclined by these
stellar movements.
[3] Cary aptly notes : '' This reminds us of the Emperor Hadrian's
verses to his departing soul : Animula, vagula, blandula, etc.''

As artless, and as ignorant of aught,
Save that her Maker being one who dwells
With gladness ever, willingly she turns
To whate'er yields her joy. Of some slight good
The flavour soon she tastes; and, snared by that,
With fondness she pursues it; if no guide
Recal, no rein direct her wandering course.
Hence it behoved, the law should be a curb;
A sovereign hence behoved, whose piercing view
Might mark at least the fortress and main tower
Of the true city. Laws indeed there are:
But who is he observes them? None; not he,
Who goes before, the shepherd of the flock,
Who chews the cud but doth not cleave the hoof.[1]
Therefore the multitude, who see their guide
Strike at the very good they covet most,
Feed there and look no further. Thus the cause
Is not corrupted nature in yourselves,
But ill-conducting, that hath turn'd the world
To evil. Rome, that turn'd it unto good,
Was wont to boast two suns, whose several beams
Cast light on either way, the world's and God's.[2]
One since hath quench'd the other; and the sword
Is grafted on the crook; and, so conjoin'd,
Each must perforce decline to worse, unawed
By fear of other. If thou doubt me, mark
The blade: each herb is judged of by its seed.
That land,[3] through which Adice and the Po
Their waters roll, was once the residence
Of courtesy and valour, ere the day
That frown'd on Frederick;[4] now secure may pass
Those limits, whosoe'er hath left, for shame,
To talk with good men, or come near their haunts.

---

[1] Cf. Lev. xi. 4. What Dante says is that no man attends to the observance of the laws, *because* the Pope can chew the cud (*i. e.* meditate and understand the Scriptures), but does not divide the hoof (*i. e.* confuses the spiritual with the temporal power).

[2] According to Dante, the Papacy and the Empire alike proceed from God, and are inseparably wedded to Rome, from which as two suns they should shed light upon man's spiritual and temporal paths, as divinely ordained by the infinite goodness of Him from whom the power of Peter and of Cæsar branches as from a point. Cf. *Epist.* v. 5, and *Mon.* iii. 16.

[3] Lombardy.

[4] *Prima che Federico avesse briga*, before Frederick II. was opposed by the Popes.

Three aged ones are still found there, in whom
The old time chides the new : these deem it long
Ere God restore them to a better world :
The good Gherardo ; of Palazzo he,
Conrad ; and Guido of Castello, named
In Gallic phrase more fitly the plain Lombard.[1]
On this at last conclude.   The Church of Rome,
Mixing two governments that ill assort,
Hath miss'd her footing, fallen into the mire,
And there herself and burden much defiled."

   " O Marco !" I replied, " thine arguments
Convince me : and the cause I now discern,
Why of the heritage no portion came
To Levi's offspring.   But resolve me this :
Who that Gherardo is, that as thou say'st
Is left a sample of the perish'd race,
And for rebuke to this untoward age?"

   " Either thy words," said he, " deceive, or else
Are meant to try me ; that thou, speaking Tuscan,
Appear'st not to have heard of good Gherardo ;
The sole addition that, by which I know him ;
Unless I borrow'd from his daughter Gaïa[2]
Another name to grace him.   God be with you.
I bear you company no more.   Behold
The dawn with white ray glimmering through the mist.
I must away—the Angel comes—ere he
Appear."   He said, and would not hear me more.

---

[1] Three old men of Lombardy, still living in 1300, as a standing reproach to the corruption of the new times : Gherardo da Cammino, Lord of Treviso (d. 1306) ; Corrado da Palazzo, a Guelf nobleman of Brescia ; and Guido da Castello, a native of Reggio, highly extolled by Dante in his *Convivio* (iv. 16).

[2] Marco says in effect that Gherardo da Cammino is famous for his own virtues, and for being the father of Gaia (a lady who died in 1311).   It seems uncertain whether Gaia was famous for her beauty and virtue, or notorious for her immoral life.   For her brother, Riccardo da Cammino, the husband of Nino Visconti's daughter Giovanna, see *Par.* ix.

CANTO XVII

ARGUMENT

The Poet issues from that thick vapour; and soon after his fancy
represents to him in lively portraiture some noted examples of
anger. This imagination is dissipated by the appearance of
an Angel, who marshals them onward to the fourth cornice, on
which the sin of gloominess or indifference [1] is purged; and
here Virgil shows him that this vice proceeds from a defect
of love, and that all love can be only of two sorts, either
natural, or of the soul; of which sorts the former is always
right, but the latter may err either in respect of object or of
degree.

CALL to remembrance, reader, if thou e'er
Hast on an Alpine height been ta'en by cloud,
Through which thou saw'st no better than the mole
Doth through opacous membrane; then, whene'er
The watery vapours dense began to melt
Into thin air, how faintly the sun's sphere
Seem'd wading through them: so thy nimble thought
May image, how at first I rebeheld
The sun, that bedward now his couch o'erhung.

   Thus, with my leader's feet still equaling pace,
From forth that cloud I came, when now expired
The parting beams from off the nether shores.

   O quick and forgetive power! [2] that sometimes dost
So rob us of ourselves, we take no mark
Though round about us thousand trumpets clang;
What moves thee, if the senses stir not? Light
Moves thee from Heaven, spontaneous, self-inform'd;
Or, likelier, gliding down with swift illapse
By will divine. Portray'd before me came
The traces of her dire impiety,
Whose form was changed into the bird, that most
Delights itself in song: [3] and here my mind

---

[1] The sin purged away on this terrace is simply *Sloth,* the
fourth of the seven *peccati capitali.*

[2] The fantasy or imagination.

[3] Procne. *Cf.* above, Canto ix. According to the Greek form
of the story (which Dante follows), Procne, who slew her child
Itys, and gave his flesh to his father, Tereus, to eat, was transformed into the nightingale, while her innocent and injured sister
Philomela became the swallow. The Latin poets (and our
English poets, too, as most notably Mr. Swinburne in his *Itylus*)
have generally made Philomela the nightingale, and Procne
the swallow; as Virgil in the *Georgics,* which it is doubtful if

Was inwardly so wrapt, it gave no place
To aught that ask'd admittance from without.
Next shower'd into my fantasy a shape
As of one crucified,[1] whose visage spake
Fell rancour, malice deep, wherein he died;
And round him Ahasuerus the great king;
Esther his bride; and Mordecai the just,
Blameless in word and deed. As of itself
That unsubstantial coinage of the brain
Burst, like a bubble, when the water fails
That fed it; in my vision straight uprose
A damsel weeping loud, and cried, " O queen!
O mother! wherefore has intemperate ire
Driven thee to loathe thy being? Not to lose
Lavinia, desperate thou hast slain thyself.
Now hast thou lost me.[2] I am she, whose tears
Mourn, ere I fall, a mother's timeless end."

E'en as a sleep breaks off, if suddenly
New radiance strike upon the closed lids,
The broken slumber quivering ere it dies;
Thus, from before me, sunk that imagery,
Vanishing, soon as on my face there struck
The light, outshining far our earthly beam.
As round I turn'd me to survey what place
I had arrived at, " Here ye mount:" exclaim'd
A voice, that other purpose left me none
Save will so eager to behold who spake,
I could not chuse but gaze. As 'fore the sun,
That weighs our vision down, and veils his form
In light transcendent, thus my virtue fail'd
Unequal. " This is Spirit from above,
Who marshals us our upward way, unsought;
And in his own light shrouds him.[3] As a man
Doth for himself, so now is done for us.

Dante had read. Dr. Moore suggests that Dante found the
former version of the legend, not in Ovid's *Metamorphoses* (which
does not show which form of the story that poet accepted), but in
a passage in a Latin translation of Aristotle's *Rhetoric*, where
the swallow is called Philomela and a maiden.

[1] Haman. *Cf.* Esther vii.

[2] Lavinia, daughter of Latinus and Amata, was first betrothed
to Turnus, and then promised by her father to Æneas. Amata,
who favoured Turnus, killed herself on a report that the latter had
been slain. *Æn.* xii.

[3] The Angel of Meekness or Peace.

For whoso waits imploring, yet sees need
Of his prompt aidance, sets himself prepared
For blunt denial, ere the suit be made.
Refuse we not to lend a ready foot
At such inviting : haste we to ascend,
Before it darken : for we may not then,
Till morn again return.''   So spake my guide;
And to one ladder both address'd our steps;
And the first stair approaching, I perceived
Near me as 'twere the waving of a wing,
That fann'd my face, and whisper'd : '' Blessed they,
The peace-makers : they know not evil wrath.''

   Now to such height above our heads were raised
The last beams, follow'd close by hooded night,
That many a star on all sides through the gloom
Shone out.   '' Why partest from me, O my strength?''
So with myself I communed; for I felt
My o'ertoil'd sinews slacken.   We had reach'd
The summit, and were fix'd like to a bark
Arrived at land.   And waiting a short space,
If aught should meet mine ear in that new round,
Then to my guide I turn'd, and said : '' Loved Sire !
Declare what guilt is on this circle purged.
If our feet rest, no need thy speech should pause.''

   He thus to me : '' The love of good, whate'er
Wanted of just proportion, here fulfils.
Here plies afresh the oar, that loiter'd ill.
But that thou mayst yet clearlier understand,
Give ear unto my words; and thou shalt cull
Some fruit may please thee well, from this delay.[1]

[1] Virgil now proceeds to expound the whole ethical scheme of
the *Purgatorio,* as he had done that of the *Inferno* in a similar
pause.   '' Not only the Creator, but every creature also, is moved
by love.   Natural love, as that of heavy bodies for the centre, of
fire for the circumference, or of plants for their natural habitat,
is unerring ; but rational love may err by being misdirected ; or
by being disproportionate, by defect or excess.   Love directed to
primal and essential good, or to secondary good in due measure,
cannot lead to sin ; but perverse and disproportionate love is the
seed of all sin, just as much as rightly directed and measured
love is the seed of all virtue.   A human being who has not become
a monster cannot love (that is, cannot be drawn towards and take
delight in) evil to himself, or evil to the God on whom his very
being depends.   All perverse rejoicing, then, must be rejoicing in
the ill of our neighbour, and this may be caused by pride, envy,
or anger, which are purged on the three circles already passed.

" Creator, nor created being, e'er,
My son," he thus began, " was without love,
Or natural, or the free spirit's growth.
Thou hast not that to learn.   The natural still
Is without error : but the other swerves,
If on ill object bent, or through excess
Of vigour, or defect.   While e'er it seeks
The primal blessings, or with measure due
The inferior, no delight, that flows from it,
Partakes of ill.   But let it warp to evil,
Or with more ardour than behoves, or less,
Pursue the good ; the thing created then
Works 'gainst its Maker.   Hence thou must infer,
That love is germin of each virtue in ye,
And of each act no less, that merits pain.
Now since it may not be, but love intend
The welfare mainly of the thing it loves,
All from self-hatred are secure ; and since
No being can be thought to exist apart,
And independent of the first, a bar
Of equal force restrains from hating that.

" Grant the distinction just ; and it remains
The evil must be another's, which is loved.
Three ways such love is gender'd in your clay.
There is who hopes (his neighbour's worth deprest)
Pre-eminence himself ; and covets hence,
For his own greatness, that another fall.[1]
There is who so much fears the loss of power,
Fame, favour, glory, (should his fellow mount
Above him,) and so sickens at the thought,
He loves their opposite :[2] and there is he,
Whom wrong or insult seems to gall and shame,
That he doth thirst for vengeance ; and such needs

Apart from these evil gratifications, everyone has at least some
confused apprehension of a supreme good wherein the soul can
rest, and everyone therefore seeks to gain it. But this supreme
love, which is no other than the love of God, may err by defect,
either speculative or practical ; and the slothful who have thus
erred recover their lost tone in the circle the pilgrims have now
reached.   The innocent or needful enjoyment of which the bodily
frame is the seat, cannot confer true bliss, and may be pursued
with disproportionate keenness, or in neglect of the divinely
imposed restraints.   Such sins are purged in the three uppermost
circles " (Wicksteed).

[1] Pride.   [2] Envy.

Must dote on other's evil.[1] Here beneath,
This threefold love is mourn'd. Of the other sort
Be now instructed; that which follows good,
But with disorder'd and irregular course.

    " All indistinctly apprehend a bliss,
On which the soul may rest; the hearts of all
Yearn after it; and to that wished bourn
All therefore strive to tend. If ye behold,
Or seek it, with a love remiss and lax;[2]
This cornice, after just repenting, lays
Its penal torment on ye. Other good
There is, where man finds not his happiness:
It is not true fruition; not that blest
Essence, of every good the branch and root.
The love too lavishly bestow'd on this,
Along three circles over us, is mourn'd.[3]
Account of that division tripartite
Expect not, fitter for thine own research."

CANTO XVIII

ARGUMENT

Virgil discourses further concerning the nature of love. Then a
    multitude of spirits rush by; two of whom, in van of the
    rest, record instances of zeal and fervent affection, and another,
    who was abbot of San Zeno in Verona, declares himself to
    Virgil and Dante; and lastly follow other spirits, shouting
    forth memorable examples of the sin for which they suffer.
    The Poet, pursuing his meditations, falls into a dreamy
    slumber.

THE teacher ended, and his high discourse
Concluding, earnest in my looks inquired
If I appear'd content; and I, whom still
Unsated thirst to hear him urged, was mute,
Mute outwardly, yet inwardly I said:
" Perchance my too much questioning offends."
But he, true father, mark'd the secret wish
By diffidence restrain'd; and, speaking, gave
Me boldness thus to speak: " Master! my sight
Gathers so lively virtue from thy beams,

----

[1] Anger.   [2] Sloth.
[3] Avarice and Prodigality, Gluttony, Lust.

That all, thy words convey, distinct is seen.
Wherefore I pray thee, father, whom this heart
Holds dearest, thou wouldst deign by proof t' unfold
That love, from which, as from their source, thou
   bring'st
All good deeds and their opposite." He then :
" To what I now disclose be thy clear ken
Directed ; and thou plainly shalt behold
How much those blind have err'd, who make themselves
The guides of men. The soul, created apt
To love, moves versatile which way soe'er
Aught pleasing prompts her, soon as she is waked
By pleasure into act. Of substance true
Your apprehension[1] forms its counterfeit ;
And, in you the ideal shape presenting,
Attracts the soul's regard. If she, thus drawn,
Incline toward it ; love is that inclining,
And a new nature knit by pleasure in ye.
Then, as the fire points up, and mounting seeks
His birthplace and his lasting seat, e'en thus
Enters the captive soul into desire,
Which is a spiritual motion, that ne'er rests
Before enjoyment of the thing it loves.
Enough to show thee, how the truth from those
Is hidden, who aver all love a thing
Praise-worthy in itself ; although perhaps
Its matter seem still good.[2] Yet if the wax
Be good, it follows not the impression must."
  " What love is," I return'd, " thy words, O guide !
And my own docile mind, reveal. Yet thence
New doubts have sprung. For, from without, if love
Be offer'd to us, and the spirit knows
No other footing ; tend she right or wrong,
Is no desert of hers." He answering thus :
" What reason here discovers, I have power
To show thee : that which lies beyond, expect
From Beatrice, faith not reason's task.
Spirit, substantial form, with matter join'd,
Not in confusion mix'd, hath in itself

 [1] " Your apprehensive faculty draws an impression from a real
object, and unfolds it within you, so that it makes the mind turn
thereto " (Okey's translation).
 [2] Love is the material upon which Free Will acts for good or
for evil.

Specific virtue of that union born,
Which is not felt except it work, nor proved
But through effect, as vegetable life
By the green leaf.[1] From whence his intellect
Deduced its primal notices of things,
Man therefore knows not, or his appetites
Their first affections; such in you, as zeal
In bees to gather honey; at the first,
Volition, meriting nor blame nor praise.
But o'er each lower faculty supreme,
That, as she list, are summon'd to her bar,
Ye have that virtue [2] in you, whose just voice
Uttereth counsel, and whose word should keep
The threshold of assent. Here is the source,
Whence cause of merit in you is derived;
E'en as the affections, good or ill, she takes,
Or severs, winnow'd as the chaff. Those men,
Who, reasoning, went to depth profoundest, mark'd
That innate freedom; and were thence induced
To leave their moral teaching to the world.[3]
Grant then, that from necessity arise
All love that glows within you; to dismiss
Or harbour it, the power is in yourselves.
Remember, Beatrice, in her style,
Denominates free choice by eminence
The noble virtue; if in talk with thee
She touch upon that theme." The moon, well nigh
To midnight hour belated, made the stars
Appear to wink and fade; and her broad disk
Seem'd like a crag on fire, as up the vault
That course she journey'd, which the sun then warms
When they of Rome behold him at his set
Betwixt Sardinia and the Corsic isle.
And now the weight, that hung upon my thought,
Was lighten'd by the aid of that clear spirit,
Who raiseth Andes above Mantua's name.[4]

[1] The rational or human soul is a substantial form, separated
from matter and yet abiding in it, which has a specific power by
virtue of which it believes and loves.
[2] Reason.
[3] " The great moral philosophers among the heathens " (Cary).
[4] The literal translation is : " Through whom Pietola is more
famous than any Mantuan village," or, perhaps, " than the town
of Mantua itself." Pietola, near Mantua, Andes, is identified with
the birthplace of Virgil.

I therefore, when my questions had obtain'd
Solution plain and ample, stood as one
Musing in dreamy slumber; but not long
Slumber'd; for suddenly a multitude,
The steep already turning from behind,
Rush'd on.   With fury and like random rout,
As echoing on their shores at midnight heard
Ismenus and Asopus, for his Thebes
If Bacchus' help were needed;[1] so came these
Tumultuous, curving each his rapid step,
By eagerness impell'd of holy love.

   Soon they o'ertook us; with such swiftness moved
The mighty crowd.   Two spirits at their head
Cried, weeping, " Blessed Mary [2] sought with haste
The hilly region.   Cæsar, to subdue
Ilerda, darted in Marseilles his sting,
And flew to Spain." [3]—" Oh, tarry not: away!"
The others shouted; " let not time be lost
Through slackness of affection.   Hearty zeal
To serve reanimates celestial grace."

   " O ye! in whom intenser fervency
Haply supplies, where lukewarm erst ye fail'd,
Slow or neglectful, to absolve your part
Of good and virtuous; this man, who yet lives,
(Credit my tale, though strange,) desires to ascend,
So morning rise to light us.   Therefore say
Which hand leads nearest to the rifted rock."

   So spake my guide; to whom a shade return'd:
" Come after us, and thou shalt find the cleft.
We may not linger: such resistless will
Speeds our unwearied course.   Vouchsafe us then
Thy pardon, if our duty seem to thee
Discourteous rudeness.   In Verona I
Was abbot of San Zeno, when the hand
Of Barbarossa grasp'd Imperial sway,
That name ne'er utter'd without tears in Milan.
And there is he, hath one foot in his grave,
Who for that monastery ere long shall weep,
Ruing his power misused: for that his son,

---

1 Ismenus and Asopus are rivers near Thebes, upon the banks
of which the people invoked the aid of Bacchus for their vineyards.
2 Luke i. 39, 40.
3 Cæsar (B.C. 49) delegated the siege of Marseilles to Brutus,
and hastened to attack Pompey's lieutenants at Lerida.

Of body ill compact, and worse in mind,
And born in evil, he hath set in place
Of its true pastor." [1]   Whether more he spake,
Or here was mute, I know not : he had sped
E'en now so far beyond us.   Yet thus much
I heard, and in remembrance treasured it.

   He then, who never fail'd me at my need,
Cried, " Hither turn.   Lo ! two with sharp remorse
Chiding their sin."   In rear of all the troop
These shouted : " First they died, to whom the sea
Open'd, or ever Jordan saw his heirs :
And they, who with Æneas to the end
Endured not suffering, for their portion chose
Life without glory." [2]   Soon as they had fled
Past reach of sight, new thought within me rose
By others follow'd fast, and each unlike
Its fellow : till led on from thought to thought,
And pleasured with the fleeting train, mine eye
Was closed, and meditation changed to dream.

CANTO XIX

ARGUMENT

The Poet, after describing his dream, relates how, at the summoning of an Angel, he ascends with Virgil to the fifth cornice,
   where the sin of avarice is cleansed, and where he finds Pope
   Adrian the fifth.

IT was the hour, when of diurnal heat
No reliques chafe the cold beams of the moon,
O'erpower'd by earth, or planetary sway

   [1] The speaker is a certain Gherardo, who was Abbot of San
Zeno in the days of the Emperor Frederick I., and died in 1187.
He rebukes Alberto della Scala, Lord of Verona (father of Can
Grande), already an old man in 1300 (he died in the following
year), for having unlawfully made his bastard son Giuseppe abbot
of that monastery.
   [2] Examples of the punishment of sloth, or, at least, of lack
of perseverance : the Israelites, of whom the Lord said, " Surely
there shall not one of these men of this evil generation see that
good land, which I sware to give unto your fathers " (Deut. i. 35) ;
the Trojans, who, " having no desire of high renown," were
left behind in Sicily by Æneas (Æn. v.).   The examples are thus
taken from the history of the chosen people of the old law and of
the imperial race of the new.

I

Of Saturn; and the geomancer sees
His Greater Fortune up the east ascend,
Where grey dawn checkers first the shadowy cone;[1]
When, 'fore me in my dream, a woman's shape
There came, with lips that stammer'd, eyes aslant,
Distorted feet, hands maim'd, and colour pale.

I look'd upon her: and, as sunshine cheers
Limbs numb'd by nightly cold, e'en thus my look
Unloosed her tongue; next, in brief space, her form
Decrepit raised erect, and faded face
With love's own hue illumed. Recovering speech,
She forthwith, warbling, such a strain began,
That I, how loth soe'er, could scarce have held
Attention from the song. " I," thus she sang,
" I am the Syren, whom mariners
On the wide sea are wilder'd when they hear;
Such fulness of delight the listener feels.
I, from his course, Ulysses by my lay
Enchanted drew. Whoe'er frequents me once,
Parts seldom: so I charm him, and his heart
Contented knows no void." [2] Or ere her mouth
Was closed, to shame her, at my side appear'd
A dame of semblance holy.[3] With stern voice
She utter'd: " Say, O Virgil! who is this?"
Which hearing, he approach'd, with eyes still bent
Toward that goodly presence: the other seized her,
And, her robes tearing, open'd her before,
And show'd the belly to me, whence a smell,
Exhaling loathsome, waked me. Round I turn'd
Mine eyes: and thus the teacher: " At the least
Three times my voice hath call'd thee. Rise, begone.
Let us the opening find where thou mayst pass."

I straightway rose. Now day, pour'd down from
    high,
Fill'd all the circuits of the sacred mount;
And, as we journey'd, on our shoulder smote
The early ray. I follow'd, stooping low

---

[1] It is an hour before the dawn, when the last stars in Aquarius
and the first in Pisces together form the figure known as *Fortuna
Major*.
[2] The Siren symbolises concupiscence of the flesh.
[3] She is variously identified with prevenient grace, reason, and
the " wisdom and understanding " of Proverbs vii., which the
whole episode rather suggests.

My forehead, as a man, o'ercharged with thought,
Who bends him to the likeness of an arch
That midway spans the flood; when thus I heard,
" Come, enter here," in tone so soft and mild,
As never met the ear on mortal strand.

    With swan-like wings dispred and pointing up,
Who thus had spoken marshal'd us along,
Where, each side of the solid masonry,
The sloping walls retired; then moved his plumes,
And fanning us, affirm'd that those, who mourn,
Are blessed, for that comfort shall be theirs.[1]

    " What aileth thee, that still thou look'st to earth?"
Began my leader; while the angelic shape
A little over us his station took.

    " New vision," I replied, " hath raised in me
Surmisings strange and anxious doubts, whereon
My soul intent allows no other thought
Or room, or entrance."—" Hast thou seen," said he,
" That old enchantress, her, whose wiles alone
The spirits o'er us weep for? Hast thou seen
How man may free him of her bonds? Enough.
Let thy heels spurn the earth; and thy raised ken
Fix on the lure, which Heaven's eternal King
Whirls in the rolling spheres." As on his feet
The falcon first looks down, then to the sky
Turns, and forth stretches eager for the food,
That wooes him thither; so the call I heard:
So onward, far as the dividing rock
Gave way, I journey'd, till the plain was reach'd.

    On the fifth circle when I stood at large,
A race appear'd before me, on the ground
All downward lying prone and weeping sore.
" My soul [2] hath cleaved to the dust," I heard
With sighs so deep, they well nigh choked the words.

    " O ye elect of God! whose penal woes
Both hope and justice mitigate, direct
Towards the steep rising our uncertain way."

    " If ye approach secure from this our doom,
Prostration, and would urge your course with speed,
See that ye still to rightward keep the brink."

    So them the bard besought; and such the words,
Beyond us some short space, in answer came.

---

[1] The Angel of Zeal.   [2] Psalm cxix.

I noted what remain'd yet hidden from them : [1]
Thence to my liege's eyes mine eyes I bent,
And he, forthwith interpreting their suit,
Beckon'd his glad assent.   Free then to act
As pleased me, I drew near, and took my stand
Over that shade whose words I late had mark'd.
And, " Spirit !" I said, " in whom repentant tears
Mature that blessed hour when thou with God
Shalt find acceptance, for a while suspend
For me that mightier care.   Say who thou wast;
Why thus ye grovel on your bellies prone;
And if, in aught, ye wish my service there,
Whence living I am come."   He answering spake :
" The cause why Heaven our back toward his cope
Reverses, shalt thou know : but me know first,
The successor of Peter, and the name
And title of my lineage, from that stream
That 'twixt Chiaveri and Siestri draws
His limpid waters through the lowly glen. [2]
A month and little more by proof I learnt,
With what a weight that robe of sovereignty
Upon his shoulder rests, who from the mire
Would guard it; that each other fardel seems
But feathers in the balance.   Late, alas !
Was my conversion : but, when I became
Rome's pastor, I discern'd at once the dream
And cozenage of life; saw that the heart
Rested not there, and yet no prouder height
Lured on the climber : wherefore, of that life
No more enamour'd, in my bosom love
Of purer being kindled.   For till then
I was a soul in misery, alienate
From God, and covetous of all earthly things;

[1] The T. C. editors translate : " I noted what else was concealed in the words ;" and interpret : " We take the ' concealed '
or ' implied ' thing, which was involved in the direct answer to the
question, to be a revelation of the fact that souls are purged in as
many circles as may be necessary, but that some may pass free
through certain circles, if they have not been guilty of the sins
purified in them."

[2] Cardinal Ottobuono de' Fieschi, of the family of the Counts of
Lavagna (who took their title from a river of that name between
Chiavari and Sestri on the Gulf of Genoa), was elected Pope on
July 11, 1276, under the title of Adrian V., and died on August 16,
" a month and little more " later.   He had been papal legate to
England, and was a man of noble character.

Now, as thou seest, here punish'd for my doting.
Such cleansing from the taint of avarice,
Do spirits, converted, need. This mount inflicts
No direr penalty. E'en as our eyes
Fasten'd below, nor e'er to loftier clime
Were lifted; thus hath justice level'd us,
Here on the earth. As avarice quench'd our love
Of good, without which is no working; thus
Here justice holds us prison'd, hand and foot
Chain'd down and bound, while Heaven's just Lord
        shall please,
So long to tarry, motionless, outstretch'd.''
  My knees I stoop'd, and would have spoke; but he,
Ere my beginning, by his ear perceived
I did him reverence; and '' What cause,'' said he,
'' Hath bow'd thee thus?''—''Compunction,'' I re-
        join'd,
'' And inward awe of your high dignity.''
  '' Up,'' he exclaim'd, '' brother ! upon thy feet
Arise; err not: thy fellow servant I,
(Thine and all others') of one Sovran Power.
If thou hast ever mark'd those holy sounds
Of gospel truth, ' nor shall be given in marriage,'
Thou mayst discern the reasons of my speech.[1]
Go thy ways now; and linger here no more.
Thy tarrying is a let unto the tears,
With which I hasten that whereof thou spakest.
I have on earth a kinswoman; her name
Alagia,[2] worthy in herself, so ill
Example of our house corrupt her not:
And she is all remaineth of me there.''

CANTO XX

Argument

Among those on the fifth cornice, Hugh Capet records illustrious
    examples of voluntary poverty and of bounty; then tells who
    himself is, and speaks of his descendants on the French
    throne; and, lastly, adds some noted instances of avarice.
    When he has ended, the mountain shakes, and all the spirits
    sing '' Glory to God.''

---

[1] *Cf.* Rev. xix. 10, and Matt. xxii. 30.
[2] Alagia de' Fieschi, the Pope's niece, was the wife of the
Marquis Moroello Malaspina. See above, notes on Canto viii.

ILL strives the will, 'gainst will more wise that strives:
His pleasure therefore to mine own preferr'd,
I drew the sponge yet thirsty from the wave.

Onward I moved: he also onward moved,
Who led me, coasting still, wherever place
Along the rock was vacant; as a man
Walks near the battlements on narrow wall.
For those on the other part, who drop by drop
Wring out their all-infecting malady,
Too closely press the verge.   Accurst be thou,
Inveterate wolf! whose gorge ingluts more prey,
Than every beast beside, yet is not fill'd;
So bottomless thy maw.[1]—Ye spheres of Heaven!
To whom there are, as seems, who attribute
All change in mortal state, when is the day
Of his appearing, for whom fate reserves
To chase her hence?[2]—With wary steps and slow
We pass'd; and I attentive to the shades,
Whom piteously I heard lament and wail;
And, 'midst the wailing, one before us heard
Cry out "O blessed Virgin!" as a dame
In the sharp pangs of childbed; and "How poor
Thou wast," it added, "witness that low roof
Where thou didst lay thy sacred burden down.[3]
O good Fabricius! thou didst virtue chuse
With poverty, before great wealth with vice."[4]

The words so pleased me, that desire to know
The spirit, from whose lip they seem'd to come,
Did draw me onward.   Yet it spake the gift
Of Nicholas, which on the maidens he
Bounteous bestow'd, to save their youthful prime
Unblemish'd.[5]   "Spirit! who dost speak of deeds

---

[1] The *Lupa*, the "she-wolf" of Avarice. Cf. *Inf.* i.

[2] When will the *Veltro*, the "greyhound," the promised deliverer,
come? Cf. *Inf.* i. notes.

[3] *Cf.* Luke ii. 7.

[4] Caius Fabricius, Roman consul and censor (B.C. 282–275),
refused the bribes of the Samnites and the magnificent offers of
Pyrrhus, King of Epirus. Cf. *Conv.* iv. 5; *Mon.* ii. 5.

[5] St. Nicholas of Myra (fourth century), hearing that the chastity
of three maidens was in danger through their poverty, secretly
threw three bags of money into the window of their father's house
to enable them to be married.   He is known as St. Nicholas of
Bari, where his shrine is, and is represented in art (as in Raphael's
great picture in the National Gallery) in his episcopal robes with
some symbol of the three bags of money.

So worthy, tell me who thou wast," I said,
" And why thou dost with single voice renew
Memorial of such praise. That boon vouchsafed
Haply shall meet reward; if I return
To finish the short pilgrimage of life,
Still speeding to its close on restless wing."

" I," answer'd he, " will tell thee; not for help,
Which thence I look for; but that in thyself
Grace so exceeding shines, before thy time
Of mortal dissolution. I was root
Of that ill plant, whose shade such poison sheds
O'er all the Christian land, that seldom thence
Good fruit is gather'd.[1] Vengeance soon should come,
Had Ghent and Douay, Lille and Bruges power,[2]
And vengeance I of Heaven's great Judge implore.
Hugh Capet was I hight: from me descend
The Philips and the Louis, of whom France
Newly is govern'd: born of one, who plied
The slaughterer's trade at Paris. When the race
Of ancient kings had vanish'd (all save one
Wrapt up in sable weeds)[3] within my gripe
I found the reins of empire, and such powers
Of new acquirement, with full store of friends,
That soon the widow'd circlet of the crown
Was girt upon the temples of my son,
He, from whose bones the anointed race begins.
Till the great dower of Provence had removed
The stains, that yet obscured our lowly blood,
Its sway indeed was narrow;[4] but howe'er

---

[1] This is Hugh Capet, founder of the Capetian dynasty and ancestor of the " evil plant," the royal house of France in general, and Philip the Fair in particular. Hugh became King of France in 987, on the death of the last Carlovingian king, Louis V. He died in 996, when he was succeeded by his son Robert, who had previously been crowned king. Dante apparently confuses this Hugh Capet with his father, Hugh the Great, who died in 956, and was supposed by mediæval writers to have been the son of a butcher.

[2] He alludes to the coming defeat of the French by the Flemings, in 1302, at the battle of Courtrai.

[3] On the death of Louis V., the only surviving Carlovingian was his uncle, Duke Charles of Lorraine, whom Hugh Capet captured, and imprisoned till his death in 992. Dante has probably confused him with the last of the Merovingians, Childeric III., who was deposed by Pepin le Bref, in 751, and compelled to become a monk.

[4] Charles I. of Anjou obtained Provence by his marriage, in

It wrought no evil : there, with force and lies,
Began its rapine : after, for amends,
Poitou it seized, Navarre and Gascony.[1]
To Italy came Charles ; and for amends,
Young Conradine, an innocent victim, slew ;
And sent the angelic teacher back to Heaven,
Still for amends.[2]   I see the time at hand,
That forth from France invites another Charles
To make himself and kindred better known.
Unarm'd he issues, saving with that lance,
Which the arch-traitor tilted with ; and that
He carries with so home a thrust, as rives
The bowels of poor Florence.[3]   No increase
Of territory hence, but sin and shame
Shall be his guerdon ; and so much the more
As he more lightly deems of such foul wrong.
I see the other [4] (who a prisoner late
Had stept on shore) exposing to the mart

1246, with Beatrice, daughter of Count Raymond Berenger. Cf.
Par. vi. A more probable interpretation of this line would be :
" Until the great dower of Provence took away the sense of shame
from my race."

[1] Instead of *Navarre*, read " Normandy." The treble repetition
of amends, *per ammenda*, is intense irony.

[2] Cf. *Inf.* xxviii. ; *Purg.* iii. and vii. Charles, in 1268, barbar-
ously had Conradin, the last of the house of Suabia, beheaded after
the battle of Tagliacozzo. There was a tradition, certainly base-
less, that he had St. Thomas Aquinas poisoned in 1274, when the
Angelical Doctor was at the abbey of Fossanuova on his way to the
Council of Lyons.

[3] Charles of Valois, brother of Philip the Fair, entered Florence on
November 1, 1301, nominally as papal peacemaker. By treachery
and perjury, he obtained authority from the Signoria to pacify the
city, which he set about doing by establishing a reign of terror,
recalling the Neri, and persecuting the Bianchi. He left Florence
in April, 1302, covered with disgrace and laden with the plunder
of the city, leaving the Neri absolute masters of the State.

[4] Charles II. of Anjou, eldest son of Charles I., was defeated
and taken prisoner in a naval battle outside Naples, by Ruggiero
di Loria, admiral of Peter of Aragon, in 1284. The Sicilians
wished to make his life pay for that of Conradin ; but he was
spared at the intercession of Manfred's daughter Costanza, and
sent a prisoner to Spain. He was still in captivity when, in the
following year, he succeeded his father as King of Naples. In
1305, he gave his daughter Beatrice as wife to Azzo VIII. d' Este,
the Marquis of Ferrara of evil repute (cf. *Inf.* xii. ; *Purg.* v.),
possibly for pecuniary considerations, or in return for the promised
cession of Reggio and Modena—which cities, however, rose in
insurrection, and succeeded, temporarily, in shaking off the yoke of
the House of Este.

His daughter, whom he bargains for, as do
The Corsairs for their slaves.   O avarice !
What canst thou more, who hast subdued our blood
So wholly to thyself, they feel no care
Of their own flesh?   To hide with direr guilt
Past ill and future, lo ! the flower-de-luce
Enters Alagna ; in his Vicar Christ
Himself a captive, and His mockery
Acted again.   Lo ! to His holy lip
The vinegar and gall once more applied ;
And He 'twixt living robbers doom'd to bleed.[1]
Lo ! the new Pilate, of whose cruelty
Such violence cannot fill the measure up,
With no decree to sanction, pushes on
Into the temple his yet eager sails.[2]

" O sovran Master ! when shall I rejoice
To see the vengeance, which Thy wrath, well-pleased,
In secret silence broods?—While daylight lasts,
So long what thou didst hear of her, sole spouse
Of the Great Spirit, and on which thou turn'dst
To me for comment, is the general theme
Of all our prayers ; but, when it darkens, then
A different strain we utter ; then record
Pygmalion, whom his gluttonous thirst of gold
Made traitor, robber, parricide : the woes
Of Midas, which his greedy wish ensued,
Mark'd for derision to all future times :
And the fond Achan, how he stole the prey,
That yet he seems by Joshua's ire pursued.
Sapphira with her husband next we blame ;
And praise the forefeet, that with furious ramp
Spurn'd Heliodorus.   All the mountain round
Rings with the infamy of Thracia's king,
Who slew his Phrygian charge : and last a shout
Ascends : ' Declare, O Crassus ! for thou know'st,
The flavour of thy gold.'[3]   The voice of each

[1] In September, 1303, Sciarra Colonna and Guillaume de
Nogaret, in the name of Philip the Fair, and with the royal banner
of France displayed, seized Pope Boniface VIII. at Anagni, and
treated the old Pontiff with such barbarity that he died a month
after his release from their hands.

[2] He refers to the persecution of the Order of the Templars by
this " new Pilate," King Philip (1307), in order to possess himself
of their vast wealth.

[3] During the day they rehearse examples of voluntary poverty,

Now high, now low, as each his impulse prompts,
Is led through many a pitch, acute or grave.
Therefore, not singly, I erewhile rehearsed
That blessedness we tell of in the day :
But near me, none, beside, his accent raised.''
    From him we now had parted, and essay'd
With utmost efforts to surmount the way ;
When I did feel, as nodding to its fall,
The mountain tremble ; whence an icy chill
Seized on me, as on one to death convey'd.
So shook not Delos, when Latona there
Couch'd to bring forth the twin-born eyes of Heaven.
    Forthwith from every side a shout arose
So vehement, that suddenly my guide
Drew near, and cried : '' Doubt not, while I conduct
        thee.''
'' Glory !'' all shouted (such the sounds mine ear
Gather'd from those, who near me swell'd the sounds)
'' Glory in the highest be to God.'' We stood
Immoveably suspended, like to those,
The shepherds, who first heard in Bethlehem's field
That song : till ceased the trembling, and the song
Was ended : then our hallow'd path resumed,
Eying the prostrate shadows, who renew'd
Their custom'd mourning. Never in my breast
Did ignorance so struggle with desire
Of knowledge, if my memory do not err,
As in that moment ; nor through haste dared I
To question, nor myself could aught discern.
So on I fared, in thoughtfulness and dread.

beginning with that of the Blessed Virgin, " sole spouse of the
Great Spirit." When night comes, they denounce crimes wrought
for avarice, or its punishment : the murder of Sichæus by Pygmalion (Virgil, *Æn.* i.) ; the greed of Midas, who obtained from
Bacchus that all he touched should turn to gold (Ovid, *Metam.*
xi.) ; the stoning of Achan (Josh. vi., vii.) ; Ananias and Sapphira
(Acts iv., v.) ; the expulsion of Heliodorus from the Temple by the
mounted Angel (2 Macc. iii.) ; the murder of Polydorus, son of
Priam, by King Polymestor of Thrace (*Æn.* iii. ; cf. *Inf.* xxx.) ;
and the fate of Crassus, slain in battle by the Parthians, whose
king, Orodes, poured molten gold down his throat.

CANTO XXI

ARGUMENT

The two Poets are overtaken by the spirit of Statius, who, being
cleansed, is on his way to Paradise, and who explains the cause
of the mountain shaking, and of the hymn; his joy at
beholding Virgil.

THE natural thirst, ne'er quench'd but from the well
Whereof the woman of Samaria craved,[1]
Excited; haste, along the cumber'd path,
After my guide, impell'd; and pity moved
My bosom for the 'vengeful doom though just.
When lo! even as Luke relates, that Christ
Appear'd unto the two upon their way,
New-risen from His vaulted grave;[2] to us
A shade appear'd, and after us approach'd,
Contemplating the crowd beneath its feet.
We were not ware of it; so first it spake,
Saying, "God give you peace, my brethren!" then
Sudden we turn'd: and Virgil such salute,
As fitted that kind greeting, gave; and cried:
"Peace in the blessed council be thy lot,
Awarded by that righteous court which me
To everlasting banishment exiles."

"How!" he exclaim'd, nor from his speed meanwhile
Desisting; "If that ye be spirits whom God
Vouchsafes not room above; who up the height
Has been thus far your guide?" To whom the bard:
"If thou observe the tokens,[3] which this man,
Traced by the finger of the Angel, bears;
'Tis plain that in the kingdom of the just
He needs must share. But sithence she,[4] whose wheel
Spins day and night, for him not yet had drawn
That yarn, which on the fatal distaff piled,
Clotho apportions to each wight that breathes;
His soul, that sister is to mine and thine,
Not of herself could mount; for not like ours
Her ken: whence I, from forth the ample gulf

[1] John iv. 15.
[2] Luke xxiv. 15.
[3] The P's on his forehead.
[4] Lachesis, the one of the three Fates whose office it was to
determine the length of the thread of life.

Of Hell, was ta'en, to lead him, and will lead
Far as my lore avails.   But, if thou know,
Instruct us for what cause, the mount erewhile
Thus shook, and trembled : wherefore all at once
Seem'd shouting, even from his wave-wash'd foot."
    That questioning so tallied with my wish,
The thirst did feel abatement of its edge
E'en from expectance.   He forthwith replied :
" In its devotion, nought irregular
This mount can witness, or by punctual rule
Unsanction'd; here from every change exempt,
Other than that, which Heaven in itself
Doth of itself receive, no influence
Can reach us.   Tempest none, shower, hail, or snow,
Hoar frost, or dewy moistness, higher falls
Than that brief scale of threefold steps : thick clouds,
Nor scudding rack, are ever seen : swift glance
Ne'er lightens ; nor Thaumantian [1] Iris gleams,
That yonder often shifts on each side Heaven.
Vapour adust doth never amount above
The highest of the trinal stairs, whereon
Peter's vicegerent stands.   Lower perchance,
With various motion rock'd, trembles the soil :
But here, through wind in earth's deep hollow pent,
I know not how, yet never trembled : then
Trembles, when any spirit feels itself
So purified, that it may rise, or move
For rising ; and such loud acclaim ensues.
Purification, by the will alone,
Is proved, that free to change society
Seizes the soul rejoicing in her will.
Desire of bliss is present from the first ;
But strong propension hinders, to that wish
By the just ordinance of Heaven opposed ;
Propension now as eager to fulfil
The allotted torment, as erewhile to sin. [2]

[1] Iris, the rainbow, was daughter of Thaumas, and messenger
of the gods, more particularly of Juno.
[2] Mr. Okey translates : " Of the cleansing the will alone gives
proof, which fills the soul, all free to change her cloister, and
avails her to will.   She wills indeed before, but that desire permits
it not which divine justice sets, counter to will, toward the penalty,
even as it was toward the sin."   The pains of Purgatory are
voluntarily endured, since, against the hypothetic or absolute will
(*voglia*) with which they desire the bliss of Paradise, the souls

And I, who in this punishment had lain
Five hundred years and more, but now have felt
Free wish for happier clime. Therefore thou felt'st
The mountain tremble; and the spirits devout
Heard'st, over all his limits, utter praise
To that liege Lord, whom I entreat their joy
To hasten." Thus he spake: and, since the draught
Is grateful ever as the thirst is keen,
No words may speak my fulness of content.

   "Now," said the instructor sage, " I see the net
That takes ye here; and how the toils are loosed;
Why rocks the mountain, and why ye rejoice.
Vouchsafe, that from thy lips I next may learn
Who on the earth thou wast; and wherefore here,
So many an age, wert prostrate."—" In that time,
When the good Titus, with Heaven's King to help,
Avenged those piteous gashes, whence the blood
By Judas sold did issue; with the name [1]
Most lasting and most honour'd, there, was I
Abundantly renown'd," the shade replied,
" Not yet with faith endued. So passing sweet
My vocal spirit; from Tolosa, Rome
To herself drew me, where I merited
A myrtle garland to inwreathe my brow.
Statius they name me still. Of Thebes I sang,
And next of great Achilles; but i' the way
Fell with the second burthen. Of my flame
Those sparkles were the seeds, which I derived
From the bright fountain of celestial fire
That feeds unnumber'd lamps; the song I mean
Which sounds Æneas' wanderings: that the breast
I hung at; that the nurse, from whom my veins
Drank inspiration: whose authority
Was ever sacred with me. To have lived
Coeval with the Mantuan, I would bide
The revolution of another sun
Beyond my stated years in banishment."

   The Mantuan, when he heard him, turn'd to me;
And holding silence, by his countenance
Enjoin'd me silence: but the power, which wills,

---

suffer these purifying pains with the conditional or actual will
(*talento*), which they formerly had to sin. Cf. *Par.* iv. Their
wills alone show them when purification is complete.

1 Of Poet. See note in Index.

Bears not supreme control : laughter and tears
Follow so closely on the passion prompts them,
They wait not for the motions of the will
In natures most sincere.　I did but smile,
As one who winks ; and thereupon the shade
Broke off, and peer'd into mine eyes, where best
Our looks interpret.　" So to good event
Mayst thou conduct such great emprize," he cried,
" Say, why across thy visage beam'd, but now,
The lightning of a smile."　On either part
Now am I straiten'd ; one conjures me speak,
The other to silence binds me : whence a sigh
I utter, and the sigh is heard.　" Speak on,"
The teacher cried :　" and do not fear to speak ;
But tell him what so earnestly he asks."
Whereon I thus :　" Perchance, O ancient spirit !
Thou marvel'st at my smiling.　There is room
For yet more wonder.　He, who guides my ken
On high, he is that Mantuan, led by whom
Thou didst presume of men and gods to sing.
If other cause thou deem'dst for which I smiled,
Leave it as not the true one : and believe
Those words, thou spakest of him, indeed the cause."
　　Now down he bent to embrace my teacher's feet ;
But he forbade him :　" Brother ! do it not :
Thou art a shadow, and behold'st a shade."
He, rising, answer'd thus :　" Now hast thou proved
The force and ardour of the love I bear thee,
When I forget we are but things of air,
And, as a substance, treat an empty shade."

CANTO XXII

Argument

Dante, Virgil, and Statius mount to the sixth cornice, where the
sin of gluttony is cleansed, the two Latin Poets discoursing by
the way.　Turning to the right, they find a tree hung with
sweet-smelling fruit, and watered by a shower that issues
from the rock.　Voices are heard to proceed from among the
leaves, recording examples of temperance.

Now we had left the Angel, who had turn'd
To the sixth circle our ascending step ;
One gash from off my forehead razed ; while they,

Whose wishes tend to justice, shouted forth,
" Blessed !" and ended with " I thirst ;" [1] and I,
More nimble than along the other straits,
So journey'd, that, without the sense of toil,
I follow'd upward the swift-footed shades ;
When Virgil thus began : " Let its pure flame
From virtue flow, and love can never fail
To warm another's bosom, so the light
Shine manifestly forth.   Hence, from that hour,
When, 'mongst us in the purlieus of the deep,
Came down the spirit of Aquinum's bard, [2]
Who told of thine affection, my good will
Hath been for thee of quality as strong
As ever link'd itself to one not seen.
Therefore these stairs will now seem short to me.
But tell me : and, if too secure, I loose
The rein with a friend's licence, as a friend
Forgive me, and speak now as with a friend :
How chanced it covetous desire could find
Place in that bosom, 'midst such ample store
Of wisdom, as thy zeal had treasured there ?"

    First somewhat moved to laughter by his words,
Statius replied : " Each syllable of thine
Is a dear pledge of love.   Things oft appear,
That minister false matter to our doubts,
When their true causes are removed from sight.
Thy question doth assure me, thou believest
I was on earth a covetous man ; perhaps
Because thou found'st me in that circle placed.
Know then I was too wide of avarice :
And e'en for that excess, thousands of moons
Have wax'd and waned upon my sufferings.
And were it not that I with heedful care
Noted, where thou exclaim'st as if in ire
With human nature, ' Why, thou cursed thirst
' Of gold ! dost not with juster measure guide
' The appetite of mortals ?'   I had met

---

1 There are several alternate readings and interpretations of this
passage.   According to the more plausible, the Angel (of Justice)
utters a part of the fifth Beatitude, which in the *Vulgate* has
" justice " instead of " righteousness " : " He had said to us
that those who have their desire set on justice are blessed, and his
words ended with *sitiunt* "—those that *thirst after justice*.

2 Juvenal, *d.* circa 130 A.D.

The fierce encounter of the voluble rock.[1]
Then was I ware that, with too ample wing,
The hands may haste to lavishment; and turn'd,
As from my other evil, so from this,
In penitence.   How many from their grave
Shall with shorn locks arise, who living, ay,
And at life's last extreme, of this offence,
Through ignorance, did not repent!   And know,
The fault, which lies direct from any sin
In level opposition, here, with that,
Wastes its green rankness on one common heap.
Therefore, if I have been with those, who wail
Their avarice, to cleanse me; through reverse
Of their transgression, such hath been my lot."

   To whom the sovran of the pastoral song:
" While thou didst sing that cruel warfare waged
By the twin sorrow of Jocasta's womb,
From thy discourse with Clio there, it seems
As faith had not been thine;[2] without the which,
Good deeds suffice not.   And if so, what sun
Rose on thee, or what candle pierced the dark,
That thou didst after see to hoise the sail,
And follow where the fisherman[3] had led?"

   He answering thus: " By thee conducted first,
I enter'd the Parnassian grots, and quaff'd
Of the clear spring; illumined first by thee,
Open'd mine eyes to God.   Thou didst, as one
Who, journeying through the darkness, bears a light
Behind, that profits not himself, but makes
His followers wise, when thou exclaimed'st, ' Lo!
' A renovated world, Justice return'd,
' Times of primeval innocence restored,
' And a new race descended from above.'[4]
Poet and Christian both to thee I owed.

---

[1] Statius says that he was being punished for prodigality, not
for avarice, and that but for Virgil, Æn. iii. 56, he would never
have seen the wrongfulness of this, and would in consequence have
been among the avaricious and prodigal in Hell, who are butting
each other to all eternity, as shown in Inf. vii.
[2] Statius's handling of his theme (his dealings with Clio, the
Muse of History) in the Thebaid (which tells of the strife of
Jocasta's sons, Eteocles and Polynices) seems to show that he was
a pagan.   How, then, does he come to be in Purgatory?
[3] St. Peter.
[4] Virgil's fourth Eclogue.

That thou mayst mark more clearly what I trace,
My hand shall stretch forth to inform the lines
With livelier colouring. Soon o'er all the world,
By messengers from Heaven, the true belief
Teem'd now prolific; and that word of thine,
Accordant, to the new instructors chimed.
Induced by which agreement, I was wont
Resort to them; and soon their sanctity
So won upon me, that, Domitian's rage
Pursuing them, I mix'd my tears with theirs;
And, while on earth I stay'd, still succour'd them;
And their most righteous customs made me scorn
All sects besides. Before I led the Greeks,
In tuneful fiction, to the streams of Thebes,
I was baptized; but secretly, through fear,
Remain'd a Christian, and conform'd long time
To Pagan rites.[1] Four centuries and more,
I, for that lukewarmness, was fain to pace
Round the fourth circle. Thou then, who hast raised
The covering which did hide such blessing from me,
Whilst much of this ascent is yet to climb,
Say, if thou know, where our old Terence bides,
Cæcilius, Plautus, Varro:[2] if condemn'd
They dwell, and in what province of the deep."
" These," said my guide, " with Persius and myself,
And others many more, are with that Greek,
Of mortals the most cherish'd by the Nine,
In the first ward of darkness.[3] There, oft-times,
We of that mount hold converse, on whose top
For aye our nurses live. We have the bard
Of Pella, and the Teian, Agatho,
Simonides,[4] and many a Grecian else

[1] Statius here says that, before he completed the *Thebaid*, he
had been secretly converted to Christianity by observing how the
teachings of the new religion corresponded with Virgil's fourth
Eclogue, which in the Middle Ages was taken as a prophecy of
the coming of Christ. Dante's conception of the attitude of
Statius towards the Christian religion is probably unhistorical; but
Dr. Verrall has recently suggested that there is a certain psycho-
logical truth underlying it.

[2] Terence (*d.* 159 B.C.), Cæcilius (*d.* 168 B.C.), Plautus (*d.* 184
B.C.), Latin comic poets; Publius Terentius Varro Atacinus (82–
36 B.C.), epic and satiric poet.

[3] These, with Persius Flaccus (Roman satirical poet, 34–62 A.D.),
Virgil himself, and Homer, are in Limbo, where they talk of
Mount Parnassus, the eternal home of the Muses.

[4] Euripides (whom Cary—not Dante—calls " of Pella," in

Ingarlanded with laurel. Of thy train,[1]
Antigone is there, Deïphile,
Argia, and as sorrowful as erst
Ismene, and who show'd Langia's wave :
Deïdamia with her sisters there,
And blind Tiresias' daughter, and the bride
Sea-born of Peleus.'' Either poet now
Was silent ; and no longer by the ascent
Or the steep walls obstructed, round them cast
Inquiring eyes. Four handmaids [2] of the day
Had finish'd now their office, and the fifth
Was at the chariot-beam, directing still
Its flamy point aloof ; when thus my guide :
'' Methinks, it well behoves us to the brink
Bend the right shoulder, circuiting the mount,
As we have ever used.'' So custom there
Was usher to the road ; the which we chose
Less doubtful, as that worthy shade [3] complied.

They on before me went : I sole pursued,
Listening their speech, that to my thoughts convey'd
Mysterious lessons of sweet poesy.
But soon they ceased ; for midway of the road
A tree we found, with goodly fruitage hung,
And pleasant to the smell : and as a fir,
Upward from bough to bough, less ample spreads ;
So downward this less ample spread ; that none,
Methinks, aloft may climb. Upon the side,
That closed our path, a liquid crystal fell

Macedonia, where he died, 405 B.C.) ; Antiphon, extolled by
Aristotle and Plutarch (Cary followed the reading *Anacreonte,*
Anacreon, who was born at Teos) ; Agathon, *d.* circa 402 B.C., all
tragic poets ; Simonides of Ceos, the Greek lyrical poet, *d.* in
Sicily, 468 B.C.

[1] Characters celebrated by Statius in the *Thebaid* and *Achilleid :*
Antigone, sister of Eteocles and Polynices ; Deïphile, the mother
of Diomede ; Argia, wife of Polynices ; Ismene, Antigone's sister ;
Hypsipyle, who showed the fountain Langia to the seven against
Thebes ; Deïdamia, daughter of the King of Scyros, with whom
Thetis, '' the bride sea-born of Peleus,'' had left her son Achilles
(cf. *Inf.* xxvi. ; *Purg.* ix.). The '' daughter of blind Tiresias '' is
apparently that same Manto whom Dante has seen among the
soothsayers in *Inf.* xx., which, Dr. Toynbee observes, '' is an
unique instance of inaccuracy on Dante's part in a matter of this
kind.''

[2] *Cf.* above, Canto xii. It is past ten o'clock in the morning
of Easter Tuesday.

[3] Statius.

From the steep rock, and through the sprays above
Stream'd showering. With associate step the bards
Drew near the plant; and, from amidst the leaves,
A voice was heard : " Ye shall be chary of me;"
And after added : " Mary took more thought
For joy and honour of the nuptial feast,
Than for herself, who answers now for you.[1]
The women of old Rome were satisfied
With water for their beverage. Daniel fed
On pulse, and wisdom gain'd. The primal age
Was beautiful as gold : and hunger then
Made acorns tasteful; thirst, each rivulet
Run nectar. Honey and locusts were the food,
Whereon the Baptist in the wilderness
Fed, and that eminence of glory reach'd
And greatness, which the Evangelist records."

CANTO XXIII

ARGUMENT

They are overtaken by the spirit of Forese, who had been a
friend of our Poet's on earth, and who now inveighs bitterly
against the immodest dress of their countrywomen at Florence.

On the green leaf mine eyes were fix'd, like his
Who throws away his days in idle chase
Of the diminutive birds, when thus I heard
The more than father warn me : " Son ! our time
Asks thriftier using. Linger not : away."
     Thereat my face and steps at once I turn'd
Toward the sages, by whose converse cheer'd
I journey'd on, and felt no toil : and lo !
A sound of weeping, and a song : " My lips,
O Lord !"[2] and these so mingled, it gave birth
To pleasure and to pain. " O Sire beloved !
Say what is this I hear." Thus I inquired.
     " Spirits," said he, " who, as they go, perchance,
Their debt of duty pay." As on their road
The thoughtful pilgrims, overtaking some

[1] Mary is now the intercessor in Paradise for the whole human
race. The first example is that of the Blessed Virgin at the
marriage in Cana.

[2] A verse of the *Miserere* (Ps. l., Vulgate, li., A.V.) : " O Lord,
open Thou my lips ; and my mouth shall show forth Thy praise."

Not known unto them, turn to them, and look,
But stay not; thus, approaching from behind
With speedier motion, eyed us, as they pass'd,
A crowd of spirits, silent and devout.
The eyes of each were dark and hollow; pale
Their visage, and so lean withal, the bones
Stood staring through the skin.   I do not think
Thus dry and meagre Erisicthon show'd,
When pinch'd by sharp-set famine to the quick.[1]
    "Lo!" to myself I mused, "the race, who lost
Jerusalem, when Mary[2] with dire beak
Prey'd on her child."   The sockets seemed as rings,
From which the gems were dropt.   Who reads the
        name
Of man upon his forehead, there the M
Had traced most plainly.[3]   Who would deem, that scent
Of water and an apple could have proved
Powerful to generate such pining want,
Not knowing how it wrought?   While now I stood,
Wondering what thus could waste them, (for the cause
Of their gaunt hollowness and scaly rind
Appear'd not,) lo! a spirit turn'd his eyes
In their deep-sunken cells, and fasten'd them
On me, then cried with vehemence aloud:
"What grace is this vouchsafed me?"   By his looks
I ne'er had recognized him: but the voice
Brought to my knowledge what his cheer conceal'd.
Remembrance of his alter'd lineaments
Was kindled from that spark; and I agnized
The visage of Forese.[4]   "Ah! respect
This wan and leprous-wither'd skin," thus he

1 Erysicthon, who was punished with insatiable hunger for
felling an oak which was sacred to Ceres.
2 A Jewess, recorded by Josephus, who devoured her own child
during the siege of Jerusalem by Titus.
3 "'He who pretends to distinguish the letters which form
OMO in the features of the human face, might easily have traced
out the M on their emaciated countenances.' The temples, nose,
and forehead are supposed to represent this letter; and the eyes
the two O's placed within each side of it " (Cary).
4 Forese di Simone Donati, brother of Corso (cf. below,
Canto xxiv.) and of Piccarda Donati (Par. iii.), was an intimate
associate of Dante's during the years that immediately followed
the death of Beatrice. He was a distant kinsman of Dante's wife,
Gemma Donati, with whose brother, Forese di Manetto Donati,
he has sometimes been confused.

Suppliant implored, " this macerated flesh.
Speak to me truly of thyself.   And who
Are those twain spirits, that escort thee there?
Be it not said thou scorn'st to talk with me."

  " That face of thine," I answer'd him, " which dead
I once bewail'd, disposes me not less
For weeping, when I see it thus transform'd.
Say then, by Heaven, what blasts ye thus?   The whilst
I wonder, ask not speech from me : unapt
Is he to speak, whom other will employs."

  He thus : " The water and the plant, we pass'd,
With power are gifted, by the eternal will
Infused; the which so pines me.   Every spirit,
Whose song bewails his gluttony indulged
Too grossly, here in hunger and in thirst
Is purified.   The odour, which the fruit,
And spray that showers upon the verdure, breathe,
Inflames us with desire to feed and drink.
Nor once alone, encompassing our route,
We come to add fresh fuel to the pain :
Pain, said I? solace rather : for that will,
To the tree, leads us, by which Christ was led
To call on Eli, joyful, when He paid
Our ransom from His vein."   I answering thus :
" Forese ! from that day, in which the world
For better life thou changedst, not five years
Have circled.[1]   If the power of sinning more
Were first concluded in thee, ere thou knew'st
That kindly grief which re-espouses us
To God, how hither art thou come so soon?
I thought to find thee lower,[2] there, where time
Is recompense for time."   He straight replied :
" To drink up the sweet wormwood of affliction
I have been brought thus early, by the tears
Stream'd down my Nella's cheeks.   Her prayers devout,
Her sighs have drawn me from the coast, where oft
Expectance lingers ; and have set me free
From the other circles.   In the sight of God
So much the dearer is my widow prized,
She whom I loved so fondly, as she ranks

---

[1] Forese died in July, 1296.   When on his deathbed, Dante persuaded him to see a priest and receive the last Sacraments.
[2] In the ante-purgatory, like Belacqua.   *Cf.* above, Canto iv.

More singly eminent for virtuous deeds.[1]
The tract, most barbarous of Sardinia's isle,
Hath dames more chaste, and modester by far,
Than that wherein I left her. O sweet brother!
What wouldst thou have me say? A time to come
Stands full within my view, to which this hour
Shall not be counted of an ancient date,
When from the pulpit shall be loudly warn'd
The unblushing dames of Florence, lest they bare
Unkerchief'd bosoms to the common gaze.
What savage women hath the world e'er seen,
What Saracens, for whom there needed scourge
Of spiritual or other discipline,
To force them walk with covering on their limbs?
But did they see, the shameless ones, what Heaven
Wafts on swift wing toward them while I speak,
Their mouths were oped for howling : they shall taste
Of sorrow (unless foresight cheat me here)
Or e'er the cheek of him be clothed with down,
Who is now rock'd with lullaby asleep.
Ah! now, my brother, hide thyself no more :
Thou seest how not I alone, but all,
Gaze, where thou veil'st the intercepted sun."
  Whence I replied : " If thou recal to mind
What we were once together, even yet
Remembrance of those days may grieve thee sore.
That I forsook that life, was due to him
Who there precedes me,[2] some few evenings past,
When she was round, who shines with sister lamp
To his that glisters yonder," and I show'd
The sun. " 'Tis he, who through profoundest night
Of the true dead has brought me, with this flesh
As true, that follows. From that gloom the aid
Of his sure comfort drew me on to climb,
And, climbing, wind along this mountain-steep,
Which rectifies in you whate'er the world

[1] A curious and unpleasant series of six sonnets, interchanged between Dante and Forese, throws light upon what the Poet says presently of the life that the two led together. In one of these sonnets, Dante casts reflections upon the married life of Forese and his relations with his wife Nella. These beautiful and tender lines are his reparation to her memory.
[2] In the allegorical sense, human philosophy first made Dante realise the moral unworthiness of the life he led after the death of Beatrice. Cf. below, Cantos xxx., xxxi.

Made crooked and depraved. I have his word,
That he will bear me company as far
As till I come where Beatrice dwells :
But there must leave me. Virgil is that spirit,
Who thus hath promised," and I pointed to him;
" The other is that shade, for whom so late
Your realm, as he arose, exulting, shook
Through every pendent cliff and rocky bound."

CANTO XXIV

ARGUMENT

Forese points out several others by name who are here, like himself, purifying themselves from the vice of gluttony; and,
amongst the rest, Buonagiunta of Lucca, with whom our
Poet converses. Forese then predicts the violent end of
Dante's political enemy, Corso Donati ; and, when he has
quitted them, the Poet, in company with Statius and Virgil,
arrives at another tree, from whence issue voices that record
ancient examples of gluttony ; and proceeding forwards, they
are directed by an Angel which way to ascend to the next
cornice of the mountain.

Our journey was not slacken'd by our talk,
Nor yet our talk by journeying. Still we spake,
And urged our travel stoutly, like a ship
When the wind sits astern. The shadowy forms,
That seem'd things dead and dead again, drew in
At their deep-delved orbs rare wonder of me,
Perceiving I had life ; and I my words
Continued, and thus spake : " He journeys up
Perhaps more tardily than else he would,
For others' sake.[1] But tell me, if thou know'st,
Where is Piccarda ?[2] Tell me, if I see
Any of mark, among this multitude
Who eye me thus."—" My sister (she for whom,
'Twixt beautiful and good, I cannot say
Which name was fitter) wears e'en now her crown,
And triumphs in Olympus." Saying this,
He added : " Since spare diet hath so worn
Our semblance out, 'tis lawful here to name
Each one. This," and his finger then he raised,

---

[1] *Per l'altrui cagione*, " for another's sake." Statius wishes to
keep as long as possible in Virgil's company.
[2] See *Par.* iii.

" Is Buonagiunta,—Buonagiunta, he
Of Lucca : [1] and that face beyond him, pierced
Unto a leaner fineness than the rest,
Had keeping of the Church; he was of Tours,
And purges by wan abstinence away
Bolsena's eels and cups of muscadel." [2]

He show'd me many others, one by one :
And all, as they were named, seem'd well content ;
For no dark gesture I discern'd in any.
I saw, through hunger, Ubaldino [3] grind
His teeth on emptiness ; and Boniface,
That waved the crozier o'er a numerous flock. [4]
I saw the Marquis, [5] who had time erewhile
To swill at Forlì with less drought ; yet so,
Was one ne'er sated. I howe'er, like him
That, gazing 'midst a crowd, singles out one,
So singled him of Lucca ; for methought
Was none amongst them took such note of me.
Somewhat I heard him whisper of Gentucca :
The sound was indistinct, and murmur'd there,
Where justice, that so strips them, fix'd her sting. [6]

" Spirit !" said I, " it seems as thou wouldst fain
Speak with me. Let me hear thee. Mutual wish
To converse prompts, which let us both indulge."

He, answering, straight began : " Woman is born,
Whose brow no wimple shades yet, that shall make
My city please thee, blame it as they may. [7]

1 Buonagiunta Orbicciani, notary and poet of Lucca, died
between 1296 and 1300. Four of his poems are translated by
Rossetti in the *Early Italian Poets*.
2 Simon de Brie of Tours, who had been papal legate in France,
was elected Pope by the influence of Charles of Anjou in 1281,
under the title of Martin IV. He died in 1285, and is buried at
Viterbo.
3 Ubaldino degli Ubaldini of La Pila, brother of the Cardinal
(*Inf.* x.) and father of the Archbishop Ruggieri (*Inf.* xxxiii.).
4 Bonifazio de' Fieschi, Archbishop of Ravenna, *d.* 1295.
5 Messer Marchese ; *Marchese* (" Marquis ") is not his title,
but his Christian name. He was either one of the Ordelaffi or of
the Argogliosi of Forlì, and died shortly before 1300.
6 The throat and mouth.
7 Buonagiunta tells Dante that a woman then (in 1300) un-
married, and therefore not yet wearing the wimple, will make
the city of Lucca pleasant to him. This lady was probably
Gentucca Morla, wife of Cosciorino Fondora ; Dante's friendship
with her is to be assigned to the year 1315, or thereabouts, when
he seems to have been at Lucca.

Go then with this forewarning.   If aught false
My whisper too implied, the event shall tell.
But say, if of a truth I see the man
Of that new lay the inventor, which begins
With ' Ladies, ye that còn the lore of love.' " [1]

　　To whom I thus :   " Count of me but as one,
Who am the scribe of love; that, when he breathes,
Take up my pen, and, as he dictates, write."

　　" Brother !" said he, " the hindrance, which once
　　　held
The Notary, with Guittone and myself,
Short of that new and sweeter style I hear,
Is now disclosed : I see how ye your plumes
Stretch, as the inditer guides them; which, no question
Ours did not. [2] He that seeks a grace beyond,
Sees not the distance parts one style from other."
And, as contented, here he held his peace.

　　Like as the birds, [3] that winter near the Nile,
In squared regiment direct their course,
Then stretch themselves in file for speedier flight ;
Thus all the tribe of spirits, as they turn'd
Their visage, faster fled, nimble alike
Through leanness and desire.   And as a man,
Tired with the motion of a trotting steed,
Slacks pace, and stays behind his company,
Till his o'erbreathed lungs keep temperate time ;

[1] *Donne ch'avete intelletto d'amore*, the opening line of the
first *canzone* of the *Vita Nuova*. There is much contemporary
evidence as to the immediate and wide success achieved by this
poem, which was accepted at once as a masterpiece revealing a
new poet.

[2] Jacopo da Lentino, " the Notary," was one of the chief poets
of the Sicilian school in the first half of the thirteenth century.
Seven of his pieces are included in Rossetti's *Early Italian Poets*.
An ode of his is quoted anonymously with praise by Dante (*V. E.*
i. 12). Guittone del Viva (1230–1294), known as Fra Guittone
d'Arezzo, was one of the Frati Gaudenti, and the head of a school
of Italian poetry which succeeded to that of the Notary. One of
his sonnets (by no means characteristic of him) is given by Rossetti.
He was also the author of a number of letters in Italian, which
are among the earliest specimens of letters in the vernacular.
These two poets, together with Buonagiunta himself, represent
the older manner of lyrical poetry, which was artificial, and lacked
the genuine inspiration of " the sweet new style," which originated
with Guido Guinicelli of Bologna, was developed by Guido Cavalcanti, and brought to perfection in the earlier poetry of Dante
himself. *Cf.* above, Canto xi., and below, Canto xxvi.

[3] The cranes. Cf. *Par.* xviii., and *Purg.* xxvi.

E'en so Forese let that holy crew
Proceed, behind them lingering at my side,
And saying : " When shall I again behold thee?"

" How long my life may last," said I, " I know not :
This know, how soon soever I return,
My wishes will before me have arrived :
Sithence the place,[1] where I am set to live,
Is, day by day, more scoop'd of all its good;
And dismal ruin seems to threaten it."

" Go now," he cried : " lo ! he, whose guilt is most,
Passes before my vision, dragg'd at heels
Of an infuriate beast. Toward the vale,
Where guilt hath no redemption, on it speeds
Each step increasing swiftness on the last;
Until a blow it strikes, that leaveth him
A corse most vilely shatter'd.[2] No long space
Those wheels have yet to roll," (therewith his eyes
Look'd up to Heaven,) " ere thou shalt plainly see
That which my words may not more plainly tell.
I quit thee : time is precious here : I lose
Too much, thus measuring my pace with thine."

As from a troop of well rank'd chivalry,
One knight, more enterprising than the rest,
Pricks forth at gallop, eager to display
His prowess in the first encounter proved;
So parted he from us, with lengthen'd strides ;
And left me on the way with those twain spirits,
Who were such mighty marshals of the world.

When he beyond us had so fled, mine eyes
No nearer reach'd him, than my thought his words,
The branches of another fruit, thick hung,

---

[1] Florence (Dante speaks from the standpoint of 1300).

[2] Forese here foretells the death of his brother, Corso Donati,
he " whose guilt is most " for the factions that divided Florence.
In 1308, in secret understanding with his father-in-law, Uguccione
della Faggiuola, and the papal legate, Cardinal Napoleone Orsini,
Corso plotted to overthrow the government and make himself lord
of Florence. The plot being discovered, on October 16, he was
condemned as a rebel and a traitor. After a strenuous resistance,
he fled through the Porta Santa Croce, but was overtaken and
murdered by some Catalan mercenaries in the service of the King
of Naples. According to Villani, he threw himself from his horse,
and was run through with a lance while lying on the ground.
Dante's words, if taken literally, imply that he was dragged to
death by his horse, which does not appear in any other contemporary version of the tragedy.

And blooming fresh, appear'd.   E'en as our steps
Turn'd thither; not far off, it rose to view.
Beneath it were a multitude, that raised
Their hands, and shouted forth I know not what
Unto the boughs; like greedy and fond brats,
That beg, and answer none obtain from him,
Of whom they beg; but more to draw them on,
He, at arm's length, the object of their wish
Above them holds aloft, and hides it not.

At length, as undeceived, they went their way:
And we approach the tree, whom vows and tears
Sue to in vain; the mighty tree. " Pass on,
And come not near. Stands higher up the wood,
Whereof Eve tasted: and from it was ta'en
This plant." Such sounds from midst the thickets came
Whence I, with either bard, close to the side
That rose, pass'd forth beyond. " Remember," next
We heard, " those unblest creatures of the clouds,[1]
How they their twyfold bosoms, overgorged,
Opposed in fight to Theseus: call to mind
The Hebrews, how, effeminate, they stoop'd
To ease their thirst; whence Gideon's ranks were
     thinn'd,
As he to Midian march'd adown the hills."[2]

Thus near one border coasting, still we heard
The sins of gluttony, with woe erewhile
Reguerdon'd. Then along the lonely path,
Once more at large, full thousand paces on
We travel'd, each contemplative and mute.

" Why pensive journey so ye three alone?"
Thus suddenly a voice exclaim'd: whereat
I shook, as doth a scared and paltry beast;
Then raised my head, to look from whence it came.

Was ne'er, in furnace, glass, or metal, seen
So bright and glowing red, as was the shape
I now beheld.[3] " If ye desire to mount,"
He cried; " here must ye turn. This way he goes,
Who goes in quest of peace." His countenance
Had dazzled me; and to my guides I faced
Backward, like one who walks as sound directs.

As when, to harbinger the dawn, springs up

---

[1] The Centaurs.   [2] Cf. Judges vii. 4–7.
[3] The Angel of Temperance.

On freshen'd wing the air of May, and breathes
Of fragrance, all impregn'd with herb and flowers;
E'en such a wind I felt upon my front
Blow gently, and the moving of a wing
Perceived, that, moving, shed ambrosial smell;
And then a voice: " Blessed are they, whom grace
Doth so illume, that appetite in them
Exhaleth no inordinate desire,
Still hungering as the rule of temperance wills."

CANTO XXV

ARGUMENT

Virgil and Statius resolve some doubts that have arisen in the mind
of Dante from what he had just seen. They all arrive on the
seventh and last cornice, where the sin of incontinence is
purged in fire; and the spirits of those suffering therein are
heard to record illustrious instances of chastity.

It was an hour, when he who climbs, had need
To walk uncrippled: for the sun had now
To Taurus the meridian circle left,
And to the Scorpion left the night.[1]   As one,
That makes no pause, but presses on his road,
Whate'er betide him, if some urgent need
Impel; so enter'd we upon our way,
One before other; for, but singly, none
That steep and narrow scale admits to climb.

E'en as the young stork lifteth up his wing
Through wish to fly, yet ventures not to quit
The nest, and drops it; so in me desire
Of questioning my guide arose, and fell,
Arriving even to the act that marks
A man prepared for speech.   Him all our haste
Restrain'd not; but thus spake the sire beloved:
" Fear not to speed the shaft, that on thy lip
Stands trembling for its flight."   Encouraged thus,
I straight began: " How there can leanness come,
Where is no want of nourishment to feed?"[2]

1 " In Purgatory it is two o'clock p.m., or later. Aries being on
the Purgatory meridian at noon, the succeeding sign of Taurus
holds that position at 2 p.m.; while at the same time Scorpio (the
sign opposite Taurus) is on the meridian of Jerusalem, where it is
consequently 2 a.m." (Oelsner).

2 "' How can spirits, that need not corporeal nourishment, be

" If thou," he answer'd, " hadst remember'd thee,
How Meleager with the wasting brand [1]
Wasted alike, by equal fires consumed;
This would not trouble thee : and hadst thou thought
How in the mirror your reflected form
With mimic motion vibrates ; [2] what now seems
Hard, had appear'd no harder than the pulp
Of summer-fruit mature. But that thy will
In certainty may find its full repose,
Lo Statius here ! on him I call, and pray
That he would now be healer of thy wound." [3]

" If, in thy presence, I unfold to him
The secrets of Heaven's vengeance, let me plead
Thine own injunction to exculpate me."
So Statius answer'd, and forthwith began :
" Attend my words, O son, and in thy mind
Receive them; so shall they be light to clear
The doubt thou offer'st. Blood, concocted well,
Which by the thirsty veins is ne'er imbibed,
And rests as food superfluous, to be ta'en
From the replenish'd table, in the heart
Derives effectual virtue, that informs
The several human limbs, as being that
Which passes through the veins itself to make them.
Yet more concocted it descends, where shame
Forbids to mention : and from thence distils
In natural vessel on another's blood.
There each unite together; one disposed
To endure, to act the other, through that power
Derived from whence [4] it came; and being met,
It 'gins to work, coagulating first;
Then vivifies what its own substance made

---

subject to leanness?' This question gives rise to the following
explanation of Statius respecting the formation of the human body
from the first, its junction with the soul, and the passage of the
latter to another world " (Cary).

[1] *Cf.* Mr. Swinburne's *Atalanta in Calydon*.

[2] " As the reflection of a form in a mirror is modified in agreement with the modification of the form itself ; so the soul, separated from the earthly body, impresses the image or ghost of that
body with its own affections " (Cary).

[3] Virgil calls upon Statius to expound the matter, because, in
the mysterious origin of the human soul, Christianity has its word
to say as well as natural science.

[4] *Lo perfetto loco*, the heart.

Consist.   With animation now indued,
The active virtue (differing from a plant
No further, than that this is on the way,
And at its limit that) continues yet
To operate, that now it moves, and feels,
As sea-sponge [1] clinging to the rock : and there
Assumes the organic powers its seed convey'd.
This is the moment, son ! at which the virtue,
That from the generating heart proceeds,
Is pliant and expansive; for each limb
Is in the heart by forgeful nature plann'd.
How babe of animal becomes,[2] remains
For thy considering.   At this point, more wise,
Than thou, has err'd, making the soul disjoin'd
From passive intellect, because he saw
No organ for the latter's use assign'd.[3]

   " Open thy bosom to the truth that comes.
Know, soon as in the embryo, to the brain
Articulation is complete, then turns
The primal Mover with a smile of joy
On such great work of nature; and imbreathes
New spirit replete with virtue, that what here
Active it finds, to its own substance draws;
And forms an individual soul, that lives,
And feels, and bends reflective on itself.
And that thou less mayst marvel at the word,
Mark the sun's heat; how that to wine doth change,
Mix'd with the moisture filter'd through the vine.

   " When Lachesis hath spun the thread,[4] the soul
Takes with her both the human and divine,
Memory, intelligence, and will, in act
Far keener than before; the other powers
Inactive all and mute.   No pause allow'd,

---

[1] At this stage in generation the fœtus is in the condition of a zoöphyte, but with the potentiality of further development.

[2] How from an animal it becomes a human creature.

[3] " At the critical point now reached, Averroës himself went wrong, for, finding no organ in the human body appropriated to the immaterial principle of intelligence, he conceived it to be no part of the individual life of man, but a universal all-pervading principle; whereas in truth the human soul or life is inbreathed direct by God into the perfect animal form of the man that is to be; and thereon it draws into itself all the lower vital functions already active there " (Wicksteed).

[4] When man's life on earth is at an end.   Cf. Canto xxi.

In wondrous sort self-moving, to one strand
Of those, where the departed roam, she falls :
Here learns her destined path.   Soon as the place
Receives her, round the plastic virtue beams,
Distinct as in the living limbs before :
And as the air, when saturate with showers,
The casual beam refracting, decks itself
With many a hue ; so here the ambient air
Weareth that form, which influence of the soul
Imprints on it : and like the flame, that where
The fire moves, thither follows ; so, henceforth,
The new form on the spirit follows still :
Hence hath it semblance, and is shadow call'd,
With each sense, even to the sight, endued :
Hence speech is ours, hence laughter, tears, and sighs,
Which thou mayst oft have witness'd on the mount.
The obedient shadow fails not to present
Whatever varying passion moves within us.
And this the cause of what thou marvel'st at."

   Now the last flexure of our way we reach'd ;
And to the right hand turning, other care
Awaits us.   Here the rocky precipice
Hurls forth redundant flames ; and from the rim
A blast up-blown, with forcible rebuff
Driveth them back, sequester'd from its bound.

   Behoved us, one by one, along the side,
That border'd on the void, to pass ; and I
Fear'd on one hand the fire, on the other fear'd
Headlong to fall : when thus the instructor warn'd :
" Strict rein must in this place direct the eyes.
A little swerving and the way is lost."

   Then from the bosom of the burning mass,
" O God of mercy ! " [1] heard I sung, and felt
No less desire to turn.   And when I saw
Spirits along the flame proceeding, I
Between their footsteps and mine own was fain
To share by turns my view.   At the hymn's close
They shouted loud, " I do not know a man ; " [2]
Then in low voice again took up the strain ;

---

[1] The matin hymn, *Summæ Parens clementiæ*, before the revision
of the Breviary in the seventeenth century, began with the words :
Summæ Deus clementiæ.   It contains a prayer for protection
against lust.

[2] Luke i. 34.

Which once more ended, " To the wood," they cried,
" Ran Dian, and drave forth Callisto stung
With Cytherea's poison :" [1] then return'd
Unto their song ; then many a pair extoll'd,
Who lived in virtue chastely and the bands
Of wedded love.   Nor from that task, I ween,
Surcease they ; whilesoe'er the scorching fire
Enclasps them. Of such skill appliance needs,
To medicine the wound that healeth last.

CANTO XXVI

ARGUMENT

The spirits wonder at seeing the shadow cast by the body of Dante
on the flame as he passes it. This moves one of them to
address him. It proves to be Guido Guinicelli, the Italian
poet, who points out to him the spirit of Arnault Daniel, the
Provençal, with whom he also speaks.

WHILE singly thus along the rim we walk'd,
Oft the good master warn'd me : " Look thou well.
Avail it that I caution thee." The sun
Now all the western clime irradiate changed
From azure tinct to white ; and, as I pass'd,
My passing shadow made the umber'd flame
Burn ruddier.   At so strange a sight I mark'd
That many a spirit marvel'd on his way.
    This bred occasion first to speak of me.
" He seems," said they, " no insubstantial frame :"
Then, to obtain what certainty they might,
Stretch'd tow'rds me, careful not to overpass
The burning pale.   " O thou ! who followest
The others, haply not more slow than they,
But moved by reverence ; answer me, who burn
In thirst and fire : nor I alone, but these
All for thine answer do more thirst, than doth
Indian or Æthiop for the cooling stream.
Tell us, how is it that thou makest thyself
A wall against the sun, as thou not yet
Into the inextricable toils of death

---

[1] Callisto was driven away by Diana for having yielded to
carnal love (*Metam.* ii.). This selection of examples of chastity
from the Gospels and Ovid alternately is very characteristic of
Dante.

Hadst enter'd?'' Thus spake one; and I had straight
Declared me, if attention had not turn'd
To new appearance. Meeting these, there came,
Midway the burning path, a crowd, on whom
Earnestly gazing, from each part I view
The shadows all press forward, severally
Each snatch a hasty kiss, and then away.
E'en so the emmets, 'mid their dusky troops,
Peer closely one at other, to spy out
Their mutual road perchance, and how they thrive.

  That friendly greeting parted, ere dispatch
Of the first onward step, from either tribe
Loud clamour rises : those, who newly come,
Shout " Sodom and Gomorrah !" these, '' The cow
Pasiphae enter'd, that the beast she woo'd
Might rush unto her luxury.'' [1] Then as cranes,
That part towards the Riphæan mountains fly,
Part towards the Lybic sands, these to avoid
The ice, and those the sun ; [2] so hasteth off
One crowd, advances the other ; and resume
Their first song, weeping, and their several shout.

  Again drew near my side the very same,
Who had erewhile besought me ; and their looks
Mark'd eagerness to listen. I, who twice
Their will had noted, spake : " O spirits ! secure,
Whene'er the time may be, of peaceful end ;
My limbs, nor crude, nor in mature old age,
Have I left yonder : here they bear me, fed
With blood, and sinew-strung. That I no more
May live in blindness, hence I tend aloft.
There is a Dame on high,[3] who wins for us
This grace, by which my mortal through your realm
I bear.   But may your utmost wish soon meet
Such full fruition, that the orb of Heaven,
Fullest of love, and of most ample space,
Receive you ; as ye tell (upon my page
Henceforth to stand recorded) who ye are ;
And what this multitude, that at your backs
Have past behind us.'' As one, mountain-bred,
Rugged and clownish, if some city's walls

---

[1] Examples of the punishment of lust.
[2] This image is taken from Lucan, *Phars.* vii. *Cf.* above, Canto
xxiv., and below, *Par.* xviii.
[3] The Blessed Virgin.

K

He chance to enter, round him stares agape,
Confounded and struck dumb; e'en such appear'd
Each spirit. But when rid of that amaze,
(Not long the inmate of a noble heart,)
He, who before had question'd, thus resumed:
" O blessed! who, for death preparing, takest
Experience of our limits, in thy bark;
Their crime, who not with us proceed, was that
For which, as he did triumph, Cæsar heard
The shout of 'queen,' to taunt him.[1] Hence their cry
Of 'Sodom,' as they parted; to rebuke
Themselves, and aid the burning by their shame.
Our sinning was hermaphrodite: but we,
Because the law of human kind we broke,
Following like beasts our vile concupiscence,
Hence parting from them, to our own disgrace
Record the name of her, by whom the beast
In bestial tire was acted. Now our deeds
Thou know'st, and how we sinn'd. If thou by name
Wouldst haply know us, time permits not now
To tell so much, nor can I. Of myself
Learn what thou wishest. Guinicelli I;[2]
Who having truly sorrow'd ere my last,
Already cleanse me." With such pious joy,
As the two sons upon their mother gazed
From sad Lycurgus rescued;[3] such my joy
(Save that I more repress'd it) when I heard
From his own lips the name of him pronounced,

---

[1] The Roman soldiers are said to have sung a song to this effect in Cæsar's triumph, with reference to his alleged relations with King Nicomedes of Bithynia.

[2] Guido Guinicelli, or Guinizelli, belonged to the family of the Principi, Ghibellines of Bologna, with whom he was exiled from his native city in 1274. He died a few years afterwards. Guido was the greatest Italian poet before Dante, who here hails him as his father in the poetic art. Cf. *Conv.* iv. 20; *V. N.* § 20; *V. E.* i. 9, i. 15, ii. 5, ii. 6. Six of his poems are translated by Rossetti.

[3] Hypsipyle had left her infant charge, the son of Lycurgus, on a bank, where it was destroyed by a serpent, when she went to show the Argive army the river of Langia; and, on her escaping the effects of Lycurgus's resentment, the joy her own children felt at the sight of her was such as our Poet felt on beholding his predecessor Guinicelli. The incidents are beautifully described in Statius (*Theb.* iv., v.), and seem to have made an impression on Dante, for he before (Canto xxii.) characterises Hypsipyle as her 'who show'd Langia's wave'" (Cary).

Who was a father to me, and to those
My betters, who have ever used the sweet
And pleasant rhymes of love. So nought I heard,
Nor spake; but long time thoughtfully I went,
Gazing on him; and, only for the fire,
Approach'd not nearer.   When my eyes were fed
By looking on him; with such solemn pledge,
As forces credence, I devoted me
Unto his service wholly.   In reply
He thus bespake me: "What from thee I hear
Is graved so deeply on my mind, the waves
Of Lethe shall not wash it off, nor make
A whit less lively.   But as now thy oath
Has seal'd the truth, declare what cause impels
That love, which both thy looks and speech bewray."

"Those dulcet lays," I answer'd; "which, as long
As of our tongue the beauty does not fade,
Shall make us love the very ink that traced them."

"Brother!" he cried, and pointed at the shade
Before him, "there is one, whose mother speech
Doth owe to him a fairer ornament.[1]
He in love ditties, and the tales of prose,
Without a rival stands; and lets the fools
Talk on, who think the songster of Limoges [2]
O'ertops him.   Rumour and the popular voice
They look to, more than truth; and so confirm
Opinion, ere by art or reason taught.
Thus many of the elder time cried up
Guittone,[3] giving him the prize, till truth

[1] This is the Provençal poet, Arnaut Daniel, who wrote at the
end of the twelfth century. Both Dante (cf. *V. E.* ii. 2, 6, 10, 13)
and Petrarch had a profound admiration for him, and certain of
their lyrics show the influence of his peculiar technique. He was
the inventor of the *sestina*. The reference to *versi d'amore e prose
di romanzi* means, "not that Arnaut wrote better love songs and
better prose romances than any one else (for it is practically
certain that he wrote no prose at all), but that he surpassed every
writer in France, not only the troubadours of the South, but also
the authors of the prose romances in the North" (Oelsner).
Modern students by no means share Dante's high esteem of this
curious writer.

[2] Giraut de Borneil, called the "master of the troubadours,"
was a native of Limoges. He died about 1220. Dante quotes
him in the *De Vulgari Eloquentia* (ii. 2, 5, 6), praising him as a
poet of rectitude.

[3] Cf. above, Cantos xi., xxiv.; also *V. E.* i. 13, ii. 6.

By strength of numbers vanquish'd. If thou own
So ample privilege, as to have gain'd
Free entrance to the cloister, whereof Christ
Is Abbot of the college; say to him
One paternoster for me, far as needs [1]
For dwellers in this world, where power to sin
No longer tempts us."   Haply to make way
For one that follow'd next, when that was said,
He vanish'd through the fire, as through the wave
A fish, that glances diving to the deep.

  I, to the spirit he had shown me, drew
A little onward, and besought his name,
For which my heart, I said, kept gracious room.
He frankly thus began : [2] "Thy courtesy
So wins on me, I have nor power nor will
To hide me.   I am Arnault; and with songs,
Sorely waymenting for my folly past,
Thorough this ford of fire I wade, and see
The day, I hope for, smiling in my view.
I pray ye by the worth that guides ye up
Unto the summit of the scale, in time
Remember ye my sufferings."   With such words
He disappear'd in the refining flame.

CANTO XXVII

ARGUMENT

An Angel sends them forward through the fire to the last ascent,
which leads to the Terrestrial Paradise, situated on the summit
of the mountain. They have not proceeded many steps on
their way upward, when the fall of night hinders them from
going further ; and our Poet, who has lain down with Virgil
and Statius to rest, beholds in a dream two females, figuring
the active and contemplative life. With the return of morning, they reach the height ; and here Virgil gives Dante full
liberty to use his own pleasure and judgment in the choice of
his way till he shall meet with Beatrice.

Now was the sun so station'd, as when first
His early radiance quivers on the heights,
Where stream'd his Maker's blood; while Libra hangs

---

  [1] Cf. above, Canto xi.
  [2] The lines that follow are in Provençal, Dante making
Arnaut speak in his own tongue.

Above Hesperian Ebro; and new fires,
Meridian, flash on Ganges' yellow tide.[1]
   So day was sinking, when the Angel of God
Appear'd before us. Joy was in his mien.
Forth of the flame he stood upon the brink;
And with a voice, whose lively clearness far
Surpass'd our human, " Blessed are the pure
In heart," he sang;[2] then near him as we came,
" Go ye not further, holy spirits !" he cried,
" Ere the fire pierce you : enter in; and list
Attentive to the song ye hear from thence."
   I, when I heard his saying, was as one
Laid in the grave. My hands together clasp'd,
And upward stretching, on the fire I look'd;
And busy fancy conjured up the forms
Erewhile beheld alive consumed in flames.
   The escorting spirits turn'd with gentle looks
Toward me; and the Mantuan spake : " My son,
Here torment thou mayst feel, but canst not death.
Remember thee, remember thee, if I
Safe e'en on Geryon brought thee; now I come
More near to God, wilt thou not trust me now?
Of this be sure; though in its womb that flame
A thousand years contain'd thee, from thy head
No hair should perish. If thou doubt my truth,
Approach; and with thy hand thy vesture's hem
Stretch forth, and for thyself confirm belief.
Lay now all fear, oh ! lay all fear aside.
Turn hither, and come onward undismay'd."
   I still, though conscience urged, no step advanced.
   When still he saw me fix'd and obstinate,
Somewhat disturb'd he cried : " Mark now, my son,
From Beatrice thou art by this wall
Divided." As at Thisbe's name the eye
Of Pyramus was open'd, (when life ebb'd
Fast from his veins,) and took one parting glance,
While vermeil dyed the mulberry;[3] thus I turn'd
To my sage guide, relenting, when I heard

---

[1] It was sunrise at Jerusalem, midnight in Spain, noon in
India, and sunset on the mountain of Purgation.
[2] The Angel of Purity.
[3] Ovid, *Metam.* iv. The blood of Thisbe and Pyramus, " slain
of love in Babylon," changed the colour of the mulberry from
white to red.

The name that springs for ever in my breast.

He shook his forehead; and, "How long," he said,
"Linger we now?" then smiled, as one would smile
Upon a child that eyes the fruit and yields.
Into the fire before me then he walk'd;
And Statius, who erewhile no little space
Had parted us, he pray'd to come behind.

I would have cast me into molten glass
To cool me, when I enter'd; so intense
Raged the conflagrant mass. The sire beloved,
To comfort me, as he proceeded, still
Of Beatrice talk'd.   "Her eyes," saith he,
"E'en now I seem to view." From the other side
A voice, that sang, did guide us; and the voice
Following, with heedful ear, we issued forth,
There where the path led upward. "Come,"[1] we heard,
"Come, blessed of my Father." Such the sounds,
That hail'd us from within a light, which shone
So radiant, I could not endure the view.
"The sun," it added, "hastes: and evening comes.
Delay not: ere the western sky is hung
With blackness, strive ye for the pass."   Our way
Upright within the rock arose, and faced
Such part of heaven, that from before my steps
The beams were shrouded of the sinking sun.

Nor many stairs were overpast, when now
By fading of the shadow we perceived
The sun behind us couch'd; and ere one face
Of darkness o'er its measureless expanse
Involved the horizon, and the night her lot
Held individual, each of us had made
A stair his pallet; not that will, but power,
Had fail'd us, by the nature of that mount
Forbidden further travel.   As the goats,
That late have skipt and wanton'd rapidly
Upon the craggy cliffs, ere they had ta'en
Their supper on the herb, now silent lie
And ruminate beneath the umbrage brown,
While noonday rages; and the goatherd leans
Upon his staff, and leaning watches them:
And as the swain, that lodges out all night

[1] Matt. xxv. 34.   The Cherubims with the flaming sword, that
"keep the way of the tree of life," are thus welcoming man's
restoration to the Garden of Eden.

In quiet by his flock, lest beast of prey
Disperse them : even so all three abode,
I as a goat, and as the shepherds they,
Close pent on either side by shelving rock.

A little glimpse of sky was seen above ;
Yet by that little I beheld the stars,
In magnitude and lustre shining forth
With more than wonted glory. As I lay,
Gazing on them, and in that fit of musing,
Sleep overcame me, sleep, that bringeth oft
Tidings of future hap. About the hour,
As I believe, when Venus from the east
First lighten'd on the mountain, she whose orb
Seems alway glowing with the fire of love,
A lady young and beautiful, I dream'd,
Was passing o'er a lea ; and, as she came,
Methought I saw her ever and anon
Bending to cull the flowers ; and thus she sang :
" Know ye, whoever of my name would ask,
That I am Leah : for my brow to weave
A garland, these fair hands unwearied ply.
To please me at the crystal mirror, here
I deck me. But my sister Rachel, she
Before her glass abides the livelong day,
Her radiant eyes beholding, charm'd no less,
Than I with this delightful task. Her joy
In contemplation, as in labour mine." [1]

And now as glimmering dawn appear'd, that breaks
More welcome to the pilgrim still, as he
Sojourns less distant on his homeward way,
Darkness from all sides fled, and with it fled
My slumber ; whence I rose, and saw my guide
Already risen. " That delicious fruit,
Which through so many a branch the zealous care
Of mortals roams in quest of, shall this day
Appease thy hunger." Such the words I heard
From Virgil's lip ; and never greeting heard,
So pleasant as the sounds. Within me straight

[1] Leah and Rachel are types of the active and contemplative
life, respectively. Note that it is only Leah that Dante sees in
this dream. Now that the Earthly Paradise has been reached,
which represents blessedness of this life, which consists in exercise
of man's proper power (*Mon.* iii. 16), the natural powers can be
exercised in action and contemplation ; but it is the active life
alone that can be perfected out of the Celestial Paradise.

Desire so grew upon desire to mount,
Thenceforward at each step I felt the wings
Increasing for my flight. When we had run
O'er all the ladder to its topmost round,
As there we stood, on me the Mantuan fix'd
His eyes, and thus he spake : " Both fires, my son,
The temporal and eternal, thou hast seen ;
And art arrived, where of itself my ken
No further reaches. I, with skill and art,
Thus far have drawn thee. Now thy pleasure take
For guide. Thou hast o'ercome the steeper way,
O'ercome the straiter. Lo ! the sun that darts
His beam upon thy forehead : lo ! the herb,
The arborets and flowers, which of itself
This land pours forth profuse. Till those bright eyes [1]
With gladness come, which, weeping, made me haste
To succour thee, thou mayst or seat thee down,
Or wander where thou wilt. Expect no more
Sanction of warning voice or sign from me,
Free of thy own arbitrement to chuse,
Discreet, judicious. To distrust thy sense
Were henceforth error. I invest thee then
With crown and mitre, sovereign o'er thyself." [2]

CANTO XXVIII

ARGUMENT

Dante wanders through the forest of the Terrestrial Paradise, till
    he is stopped by a stream, on the other side of which he
    beholds a fair lady culling flowers. He speaks to her ; and
    she, in reply, explains to him certain things touching the
    nature of that place, and tells that the water, which flows
    between them, is here called Lethe, and in another place has
    the name of Eunoe.

THROUGH that celestial forest, whose thick shade
With lively greenness the new-springing day
Attemper'd, eager now to roam, and search

[1] Beatrice.
[2] *Io te sopra te corono e mitrio*, " I crown and mitre thee over
thyself." The crown refers to temporal, the mitre to spiritual
authority. " If man had remained in the state of innocence in
which he was made by God, he would have had no need of such
directive regimens," which " are remedial against the infirmity of
sin " (*Mon.* iii. 4). Dante, purified from sin, has now regained
this state of innocence.

Its limits round, forthwith I left the bank;
Along the champain leisurely my way
Pursuing, o'er the ground, that on all sides
Delicious odour breathed. A pleasant air,
That intermitted never, never veer'd,
Smote on my temples, gently, as a wind
Of softest influence: at which the sprays,
Obedient all, lean'd trembling to that part
Where first the holy mountain casts his shade; [1]
Yet were not so disorder'd, but that still
Upon their top the feather'd quiristers
Applied their wonted art, and with full joy
Welcomed those hours of prime, and warbled shrill
Amid the leaves, that to their jocund lays
Kept tenour; even as from branch to branch,
Along the piny forests on the shore
Of Chiassi,[2] rolls the gathering melody,
When Eolus hath from his cavern loosed
The dripping south.[3]　Already had my steps,
Though slow, so far into that ancient wood
Transported me, I could not ken the place
Where I had enter'd; when, behold! my path
Was bounded by a rill, which, to the left,
With little rippling waters bent the grass
That issued from its brink. On earth no wave,
How clean soe'er, that would not seem to have
Some mixture in itself, compared with this,
Transpicuous clear; yet darkly on it roll'd,
Darkly beneath perpetual gloom, which ne'er
Admits or sun or moon-light there to shine.

　　My feet advanced not; but my wondering eyes
Pass'd onward, o'er the streamlet, to survey
The tender may-bloom, flush'd through many a hue,
In prodigal variety: and there,
As object, rising suddenly to view,
That from our bosom every thought beside
With the rare marvel chases, I beheld
A lady [4] all alone, who, singing, went,

---

[1] Towards the west.
[2] The pine-forest of Ravenna.
[3] When Aeolus, the ruler of the winds (*Æn.* i.), sets free the *scirocco*.
[4] This lady is the glorified realisation of the Leah of Dante's dream in the previous Canto.　She represents the active life of the

And culling flower from flower, wherewith her way
Was all o'er painted. "Lady beautiful!
Thou, who (if looks, that use to speak the heart,
Are worthy of our trust) with love's own beam
Dost warm thee," thus to her my speech I framed;
"Ah! please thee hither towards the streamlet bend
Thy steps so near, that I may list thy song.
Beholding thee and this fair place, methinks,
I call to mind where wander'd and how look'd
Proserpine, in that season, when her child
The mother lost, and she the bloomy spring."

　　As when a lady, turning in the dance,
Doth foot it featly, and advances scarce
One step before the other to the ground;
Over the yellow and vermilion flowers
Thus turn'd she at my suit, most maiden-like
Valing her sober eyes; and came so near,
That I distinctly caught the dulcet sound.
Arriving where the limpid waters now
Laved the green swerd, her eyes she deign'd to raise,
That shot such splendour on me, as I ween
Ne'er glanced from Cytherea's, when her son
Had sped his keenest weapon to her heart.
Upon the opposite bank she stood and smiled;
As through her graceful fingers shifted still
The intermingling dyes, which without seed
That lofty land unbosoms. By the stream
Three paces only were we sunder'd: yet,
The Hellespont, where Xerxes pass'd it o'er,
(A curb for ever to the pride of man,)
Was by Leander not more hateful held
For floating, with inhospitable wave,
'Twixt Sestos and Abydos,[1] than by me

new law in the state of Eden, realising in the Church of Christ
what Leah had dimly prefigured in the Old Testament; *innocentia
bonorum operum*, the virtuous use of earthly things, directly
ordered to the love of our neighbour. In Canto xxxiii., her name
is given as Matilda. Dante's earliest commentators, with only one
exception, identify her with the great Countess Matilda of Tuscany
(1046–1115), which still seems the most probable view. In more
recent days, ingenious attempts have been made to prove that she
is one of the ladies of the *Vita Nuova*.

　[1] Leander was drowned in swimming across the Hellespont to
see Hero, "the lamp that Marlowe sang into our skies." Xerxes
crossed the strait from Abydos to Sestos, in B.C. 480, by a bridge

That flood, because it gave no passage thence.
  "Strangers ye come; and haply in this place,
That cradled human nature in its birth,
Wondering, ye not without suspicion view
My smiles : but that sweet strain of psalmody,
'Thou, Lord! hast made me glad,'[1] will give ye light,
Which may uncloud your minds. And thou, who
     stand'st
The foremost, and didst make thy suit to me,
Say if aught else thou wish to hear : for I
Came prompt to answer every doubt of thine."
  She spake; and I replied : "I know not how
To reconcile this wave, and rustling sound
Of forest leaves, with what I late have heard
Of opposite report."[2] She answering thus :
"I will unfold the cause, whence that proceeds,
Which makes thee wonder; and so purge the cloud
That hath enwrapt thee. The First Good, whose joy
Is only in himself, created man,
For happiness; and gave this goodly place,
His pledge and earnest of eternal peace.
Favour'd thus highly, through his own defect
He fell; and here made short sojourn; he fell,
And, for the bitterness of sorrow, changed
Laughter unblamed and ever-new delight.
That vapours none, exhaled from earth beneath,
Or from the waters, (which, wherever heat
Attracts them, follow,) might ascend thus far
To vex man's peaceful state, this mountain rose
So high toward the Heaven, nor fears the rage
Of elements contending; from that part
Exempted, where the gate his limit bars.
Because the circumambient air, throughout,
With its first impulse circles still, unless
Aught interpose to check or thwart its course;
Upon the summit, which on every side
To visitation of the impassive air
Is open, doth that motion strike, and makes
Beneath its sway the umbrageous wood resound :
And in the shaken plant such power resides,
That it impregnates with its efficacy

of boats, with an immense army, and returned, humbled, after the
battle of Salamis, in one small bark. Cf. *Mon.* ii. 9.
  [1] Ps. xcii. (xci. Vulgate).   [2] *Cf.* above, Canto xxi.

The voyaging breeze, upon whose subtle plume
That, wafted, flies abroad; and the other land,[1]
Receiving, (as 'tis worthy in itself,
Or in the clime, that warms it,) doth conceive;
And from its womb produces many a tree
Of various virtue. This when thou hast heard,
The marvel ceases, if in yonder earth
Some plant, without apparent seed, be found
To fix its fibrous stem. And further learn,
That with prolific foison of all seeds
This holy plain is fill'd, and in itself
Bears fruit that ne'er was pluck'd on other soil.

   " The water, thou behold'st, springs not from vein,
Restored by vapour, that the cold converts;
As stream that intermittently repairs
And spends his pulse of life; but issues forth
From fountain, solid, undecaying, sure:
And, by the Will Omnific, full supply
Feeds whatsoe'er on either side it pours;
On this, devolved with power to take away
Remembrance of offence; on that, to bring
Remembrance back of every good deed done.
From whence its name of Lethe on this part;
On the other, Eunoe : both of which must first
Be tasted, ere it work; the last exceeding
All flavours else.[2] Albeit thy thirst may now
Be well contented, if I here break off,
No more revealing; yet a corollary
I freely give beside : nor deem my words
Less grateful to thee, if they somewhat pass
The stretch of promise. They, whose verse of yore

---

[1] " The continent, inhabited by the living, and separated from
Purgatory by the ocean, is affected (and that diversely, according
to the nature of the soil, or the climate) by a virtue, or efficacy,
conveyed to it by the winds from plants growing in the Terrestrial
Paradise, which is situated on the summit of Purgatory; and
this is the cause why some plants are found on earth without any
apparent seed to produce them " (Cary).
[2] Dante is now on one side of Lethe, Matilda on the other. He
will see Eunoe when Lethe is crossed. Eunoe quickens dead virtue,
restoring the memory of every good deed in those who have first
drunk of Lethe, which takes away the recollection of sin. Aquinas
similarly teaches that works done in charity, although in a sense
dead through sin, are brought to life through penance. The
" three paces " that divide Dante from Matilda probably signify
Contrition, Confession, and Satisfaction.

The golden age recorded and its bliss,
On the Parnassian mountain, of this place
Perhaps had dream'd. Here was man guiltless; here
Perpetual spring, and every fruit; and this
The far-famed nectar." Turning to the bards,
When she had ceased, I noted in their looks
A smile at her conclusion;[1] then my face
Again directed to the lovely dame.

CANTO XXIX

ARGUMENT

The lady, who in a following Canto is called Matilda, moves along
the side of the stream in a contrary direction to the current,
and Dante keeps equal pace with her on the opposite bank.
A marvellous sight, preceded by music, appears in view.

SINGING, as if enamour'd, she resumed
And closed the song, with " Blessed they whose sins
Are cover'd."[2]   Like the wood-nymphs then, that
    tripp'd
Singly across the sylvan shadows; one
Eager to view, and one to escape the sun;
So moved she on, against the current, up
The verdant rivage. I, her mincing step
Observing, with as tardy step pursued.
    Between us not an hundred paces trod,
The bank, on each side bending equally,
Gave me to face the orient. Nor our way
Far onward brought us, when to me at once
She turn'd, and cried: " My brother! look, and
    hearken."
And lo! a sudden lustre ran across
Through the great forest on all parts, so bright,
I doubted whether lightning were abroad;
But that, expiring ever in the spleen
That doth unfold it, and this during still,
And waxing still in splendour, made me question
What it might be: and a sweet melody
Ran through the luminous air. Then did I chide,

---

[1] They recognise with delight that the poetic dreams of the
Golden Age find their realisation here.
[2] Ps. xxxii. 1 (Vulgate xxxi.).

With warrantable zeal, the hardihood
Of our first parent; for that there, where earth
Stood in obedience to the Heavens, she only,
Woman, the creature of an hour, endured not
Restraint of any veil, which had she borne
Devoutly, joys, ineffable as these,
Had from the first, and long time since, been mine.[1]

While, through that wilderness of primy sweets
That never fade, suspense I walk'd, and yet
Expectant of beatitude more high;
Before us, like a blazing fire, the air
Under the green boughs glow'd; and, for a song,
Distinct the sound of melody was heard.

O ye thrice holy virgins! for your sakes
If e'er I suffer'd hunger, cold, and watching,
Occasion calls on me to crave your bounty.
Now through my breast let Helicon his stream
Pour copious, and Urania with her choir
Arise to aid me; while the verse unfolds
Things, that do almost mock the grasp of thought.[2]

Onward a space, what seem'd seven trees of gold
The intervening distance to mine eye
Falsely presented; but, when I was come
So near them, that no lineament was lost
Of those, with which a doubtful object, seen
Remotely, plays on the misdeeming sense;
Then did the faculty, that ministers
Discourse to reason, these for tapers of gold
Distinguish;[3] and i' the singing trace the sound
" Hosanna." Above, their beauteous garniture
Flamed with more ample lustre, than the moon
Through cloudless sky at midnight, in her noon.

I turn'd me, full of wonder, to my guide;
And he did answer with a countenance

---

[1] For Dante's curiously harsh judgment of Eve, see also *V. E.* i. 4.

[2] From Helicon, the mountain sacred to the " thrice holy virgins " (the Muses), sprang the streams Aganippe and Hippocrene. Urania is the muse of astronomy, and thence of heavenly things in general. Dante is now invoking her aid to describe the mystical pageant of the Church : " the holy city, new Jerusalem, coming down from God out of heaven, prepared as a bride adorned for her husband " (Rev. xxi. 2).

[3] The seven golden candlesticks (Rev. i. 12, and iv. 5), which represent the seven gifts of the Holy Spirit. Cf. *Conv.* iv. 21.

Charged with no less amazement : whence my view
Reverted to those lofty things, which came
So slowly moving towards us, that the bride
Would have outstript them on her bridal day.

The lady call'd aloud : " Why thus yet burns
Affection in thee for these living lights,
And dost not look on that which follows them?"

I straightway mark'd a tribe behind them walk,
As if attendant on their leaders, clothed
With raiment of such whiteness, as on earth
Was never. On my left, the watery gleam
Borrow'd, and gave me back, when there I look'd
As in a mirror, my left side portray'd.

When I had chosen on the river's edge
Such station, that the distance of the stream
Alone did separate me ; there I stay'd
My steps for clearer prospect, and beheld
The flames go onward, leaving, as they went,
The air behind them painted as with trail
Of liveliest pencils ; so distinct were mark'd
All those seven listed colours, whence the sun
Maketh his bow, and Cynthia her zone.[1]
These streaming gonfalons did flow beyond
My vision ; and ten paces,[2] as I guess,
Parted the outermost. Beneath a sky
So beautiful, came four and twenty elders,
By two and two, with flower-de-luces crown'd.[3]
All sang one song : " Blessed be thou among
The daughters of Adam ! and thy loveliness
Blessed for ever !"[4] After that the flowers,
And the fresh herblets, on the opposite brink,
Were free from that elected race ; as light
In heaven doth second light, came after them
Four animals, each crown'd with verdurous leaf.[5]

[1] The working of " the seven Spirits of God " spreads a
canopy of glory over the whole progress of the Church.
[2] Probably the Ten Commandments.
[3] Cf. Rev. iv. 4. Here the twenty-four elders stand for the
twenty-four books of the Old Testament—the number being obtained by counting the Pentateuch, the historical books, and the
three attributed to Solomon as one each.
[4] Luke i. 42. They are singing the praises of the Blessed
Virgin—to whom the Church of Rome sees mystical allusions
throughout the sacred Scriptures.
[5] The four Gospels, crowned with the green colour of hope in
Christ.

With six wings each was plumed; the plumage full
Of eyes; and the eyes of Argus would be such,
Were they endued with life. Reader! more rhymes
I will not waste in shadowing forth their form:
For other need so straitens, that in this
I may not give my bounty room. But read
Ezekiel; for he paints them, from the north
How he beheld them come by Chebar's flood,
In whirlwind, cloud, and fire; and even such
As thou shalt find them character'd by him,
Here were they; save as to the pennons: there,
From him departing, John accords with me.[1]

The space, surrounded by the four, enclosed
A car triumphal: on two wheels it came,
Drawn at a Gryphon's neck; and he above
Stretch'd either wing uplifted, 'tween the midst
And the three listed hues, on each side, three;
So that the wings did cleave or injure none;
And out of sight they rose. The members, far
As he was bird, were golden; white the rest,
With vermeil intervein'd.[2] So beautiful
A car, in Rome, ne'er graced Augustus' pomp,
Or Africanus': e'en the sun's itself
Were poor to this; that chariot of the sun,
Erroneous, which in blazing ruin fell
At Tellus' prayer devout, by the just doom
Mysterious of all-seeing Jove.[3] Three nymphs,
At the right wheel, came circling in smooth dance:
The one so ruddy, that her form had scarce
Been known within a furnace of clear flame;
The next did look, as if the flesh and bones
Were emerald; snow new-fallen seem'd the third.
Now seem'd the white to lead, the ruddy now;
And from her song who led, the others took
Their measure, swift or slow.[4] At the other wheel,

---

[1] *Cf.* Ezekiel i. 4–24, and Rev. iv. 6–9.

[2] The triumphal chariot is the Church, its two wheels representing either the Old and New Testaments, or the contemplative and
active lives, or the Franciscan and Dominican orders. The
Gryphon, half eagle and half lion, is Christ Himself in His
divine (eagle of gold) and His human (lion of white and red)
Natures.

[3] What Cary calls "Tellus" is simply *terra*, the Earth, in
the original. Dante refers to the fable of Phaëton. *Cf. Inf.* xvii.

[4] The three theological virtues: Charity (red), Hope (green),

A band quaternion, each in purple clad,
Advanced with festal step, as, of them, one
The rest conducted; one, upon whose front
Three eyes were seen.¹ In rear of all this group,
Two old men I beheld, dissimilar
In raiment, but in port and gesture like,
Solid and mainly grave; of whom, the one
Did show himself some favour'd counsellor
Of the great Coan,² him, whom nature made
To serve the costliest creature of her tribe :
His fellow mark'd an opposite intent;
Bearing a sword, whose glitterance and keen edge,
E'en as I view'd it with the flood between,
Appall'd me. Next, four others I beheld,
Of humble seeming : and, behind them all,
One single old man, sleeping as he came,
With a shrewd visage. And these seven,³ each
Like the first troop were habited; but wore
No braid of lilies on their temples wreathed.
Rather, with roses and each vermeil flower,
A sight, but little distant, might have sworn,
That they were all on fire above their brow.⁴

   Whenas the car was o'er against me, straight
Was heard a thundering, at whose voice it seem'd
The chosen multitude were stay'd; for there,
With the first ensigns, made they solemn halt.

Faith (white); which perfect man supernaturally. They take
their step from the song of Charity, which is the greatest of all
virtues, as attaining to God for His own sake. The emerald
maiden never leads, because our motives for hope must arise from
faith or charity, not faith or charity from hope.

¹ The four moral or cardinal virtues : Prudence, Justice, Fortitude, Temperance ; which perfect the intellect and desires of man
according to the capacity of human nature. They follow the
measure of Prudence, which beholds the past, present, and future,
and attains to reason in itself even as Charity does to God.

² Hippocrates, a Greek physician.

³ These seven are usually taken as personifications of the Acts
(regarded as the work of St. Luke, " the beloved physician ") and
the Pauline Epistles (the Apostle of the Gentiles bearing " the sword
of the Spirit, which is the Word of God "), of the canonical
epistles (James, Peter, John, and Jude), and of the Apocalypse
(St. John, the seer of Patmos). Benvenuto da Imola, and other
commentators, take them as St. Peter (who had entrusted to him
the power of healing souls), St. Paul, the four great Latin
doctors (Ambrose, Augustine, Jerome, Gregory), and St. Bernard.

⁴ The glowing red of love of charity.

CANTO XXX

ARGUMENT

Beatrice descends from Heaven, and rebukes the Poet.

SOON as that polar light,[1] fair ornament
Of the first Heaven, which hath never known
Setting nor rising, nor the shadowy veil
Of other cloud than sin, to duty there
Each one convoying, as that lower doth
The steersman to his port, stood firmly fix'd;
Forthwith the saintly tribe, who in the van
Between the Gryphon and its radiance came,
Did turn them to the car, as to their rest:
And one, as if commission'd from above,
In holy chant thrice shouted forth aloud:
" Come, spouse! from Libanus:"[2] and all the rest
Took up the song.—At the last audit, so
The blest shall rise, from forth his cavern each
Uplifting lightly his new-vested flesh;
As, on the sacred litter, at the voice
Authoritative of that elder, sprang
A hundred ministers and messengers
Of life eternal.[3] " Blessed thou, who comest!"
And, " Oh!" they cried, " from full hands scatter ye
Unwithering lilies:"[4] and, so saying, cast
Flowers overhead and round them on all sides.

I have beheld, ere now, at break of day,
The eastern clime all roseate; and the sky
Opposed, one deep and beautiful serene;
And the sun's face so shaded, and with mists
Attemper'd, at his rising, that the eye
Long while endured the sight: thus, in a cloud
Of flowers, that from those hands angelic rose,
And down within and outside of the car
Fell showering, in white veil with olive wreathed,
A virgin in my view appear'd, beneath

---

[1] " The seven candlesticks of gold, which he calls the polar light
of Heaven itself, because they perform the same office for
Christians that the polar star does for mariners, in guiding them
to their port " (Cary).
[2] Song of Solomon, iv. 8.
[3] Angels.
[4] Matt. xxi. 9; Æneid, vi. 883.

Green mantle, robed in hue of living flame : [1]
And o'er my spirit, that so long a time
Had from her presence felt no shuddering dread,
Albeit mine eyes discern'd her not, there moved
A hidden virtue from her, at whose touch
The power of ancient love was strong within me.[2]

No sooner on my vision streaming, smote
The heavenly influence, which, years past, and e'en
In childhood, thrill'd me, than towards Virgil I
Turn'd me to leftward; panting, like a babe,
That flees for refuge to his mother's breast,
If aught have terrified or work'd him woe :
And would have cried, "There is no dram of blood,
That doth not quiver in me.   The old flame
Throws out clear tokens of reviving fire." [3]
But Virgil had bereaved us of himself ;
Virgil, my best-loved father; Virgil, he
To whom I gave me up for safety : nor
All, our prime mother lost, avail'd to save
My undew'd cheeks from blur of soiling tears. [4]

"Dante! weep not, that Virgil leaves thee; nay,
Weep thou not yet : behoves thee feel the edge
Of other sword; and thou shalt weep for that."

As to the prow or stern, some admiral
Paces the deck, inspiriting his crew,
When 'mid the sail-yards all hands ply aloof ;
Thus, on the left side of the car, I saw
(Turning me at the sound of mine own name,
Which here I am compell'd to register)
The virgin station'd, who before appear'd
Veil'd in that festive shower angelical.

Towards me, across the stream, she bent her eyes ;
Though from her brow the veil descending, bound
With foliage of Minerva, suffer'd not

---

[1] Beatrice thus appears in the three mystical colours—robed in charity, mantled with hope, veiled with faith—and crowned with the olive of wisdom.   Here, and further on, where Cary has "virgin," Dante has *donna*, "lady."

[2] The whole of the first part of the *Vita Nuova* is the only adequate commentary upon these lines.

[3] *Conosco i segni dell' antica fiamma.*   A line taken from Virgil, *Æn.* iv. 23 : *Agnosco veteris vestigia flammæ.*

[4] Virgil, his task of leading Dante to the Earthly Paradise fulfilled, has returned to his sad place in Limbo.   Not all the bliss of the Garden of Eden can stay Dante's tears.

That I beheld her clearly : then with act
Full royal, still insulting o'er her thrall,
Added, as one who, speaking, keepeth back
The bitterest saying, to conclude the speech :
" Observe me well.   I am, in sooth, I am
Beatrice.   What ! and hast thou deign'd at last
Approach the mountain ?   Knewest not, O man !
Thy happiness is here ?"   Down fell mine eyes
On the clear fount ; but there, myself espying,
Recoil'd, and sought the greensterd ; such a weight
Of shame was on my forehead.   With a mien
Of that stern majesty, which doth surround
A mother's presence to her awe-struck child,
She look'd ; a flavour of such bitterness
Was mingled in her pity.   There her words
Brake off ; and suddenly the Angels sang,
" In thee, O gracious Lord ! my hope hath been :"
But went no further than, " Thou, Lord ! hast set
My feet in ample room." [1]   As snow, that lies,
Amidst the living rafters on the back
Of Italy, congeal'd, when drifted high
And closely piled by rough Sclavonian blasts ;
Breathe but the land whereon no shadow falls,
And straightway melting it distils away, [2]
Like a fire-wasted taper : thus was I,
Without a sigh or tear, or ever these
Did sing, that, with the chiming of Heaven's sphere,
Still in their warbling chime : but when the strain
Of dulcet symphony express'd for me
Their soft compassion, more than could the words,
" Virgin ! [3] why so consumest him ?" then, the ice,
Congeal'd about my bosom, turn'd itself
To spirit and water ; and with anguish forth
Gush'd, through the lips and eyelids, from the heart.

Upon the chariot's same edge still she stood,
Immoveable ; and thus address'd her words
To those bright semblances with pity touch'd :
" Ye in the eternal day your vigils keep ;

---

[1] Ps. xxxi. 1–8.
[2] " These lines describe the snow on the ridges of the Apennines, first congealed, when the winds blow from the north ; and
then dissolved, at the time of the warm and gentle breezes that
come from Africa " (Oelsner).
[3] In the Italian it is *donna*, " lady."

So that nor night nor slumber, with close stealth,
Conveys from you a single step, in all
The goings on of time : thence, with more heed
I shape mine answer, for his ear intended,
Who there stands weeping ; that the sorrow now
May equal the transgression.   Not alone
Through operation of the mighty orbs,
That mark each seed to some predestined aim,
As with aspect or fortunate or ill
The constellations meet ; but through benign
Largess of heavenly graces, which rain down
From such a height as mocks our vision, this man
Was, in the freshness of his being,[1] such,
So gifted virtually, that in him
All better habits wondrously had thrived.
The more of kindly strength is in the soil,
So much doth evil seed and lack of culture
Mar it the more, and make it run to wildness.
These looks sometime upheld him ; for I show'd
My youthful eyes, and led him by their light
In upright walking.   Soon as I had reach'd
The threshold of my second age, and changed
My mortal for immortal ; then he left me,
And gave himself to others.[2]   When from flesh
To spirit I had risen, and increase
Of beauty and of virtue circled me,
I was less dear to him, and valued less.
His steps were turn'd into deceitful ways,
Following false images of good, that make
No promise perfect.   Nor avail'd me aught
To sue for inspirations, with the which,
I, both in dreams of night, and otherwise,

---

[1] *Questi fu tal nella sua vita nuova,* " this man was such in his new life," by which *new life* is to be understood, not so much " the freshness of his being," as the renovation of that being wrought by his love for Beatrice in the golden days of his youth.

[2] Dante first saw Beatrice in May, 1274, when she was at the beginning of her ninth year ; she died in June, 1290, in her twenty-fifth year. She had thus reached the threshold of her second age, for the first age or period of life, which Dante calls Adolescence, lasts to the twenty-fifth year (*Conv.* iv. 24). She rebukes Dante for the life of moral unworthiness into which he fell after her death—the same to which he had himself alluded in his speech with Forese Donati (Canto xxiii.).

Did call him back; [1] of them, so little reck'd him,
Such depth he fell, that all device was short
Of his preserving, save that he should view
The children of perdition.   To this end
I visited the purlieus of the dead :
And one, who hath conducted him thus high,
Received my supplications urged with weeping.
It were a breaking of God's high decree,
If Lethe should be past, and such food tasted,
Without the cost of some repentant tear.''

CANTO XXXI

ARGUMENT

Beatrice continues her reprehension of Dante, who confesses his
   error, and falls to the ground : coming to himself again, he
   is by Matilda drawn through the waters of Lethe, and presented first to the four virgins who figure the cardinal virtues ;
   these in their turn lead him to the Gryphon, a symbol of our
   Saviour ; and the three virgins, representing the evangelical
   virtues, intercede for him with Beatrice, that she would display
   to him her second beauty.

'' O THOU !'' her words she thus without delay
Resuming, turn'd their point on me, to whom
They, with but lateral edge, seem'd harsh before : [2]
'' Say thou, who stand'st beyond the holy stream,
If this be true.   A charge, so grievous, needs
Thine own avowal.''   On my faculty
Such strange amazement hung, the voice expired
Imperfect, ere its organs gave it birth.
   A little space refraining, then she spake :
'' What dost thou muse on ?   Answer me.   The wave
On thy remembrances of evil yet
Hath done no injury.'' [3]   A mingled sense
Of fear and of confusion, from my lips
Did such a '' Yea '' produce, as needed help
Of vision to interpret.   As when breaks,
In act to be discharged, a cross-bow bent

---

[1] We have the record of one such vision in the *Vita Nuova*
itself, § 40.

[2] '' The words of Beatrice, when not addressed directly to himself, but spoken to the Angels of him, Dante had thought suf-
ficiently harsh '' (Cary).

[3] Thou hast not yet tasted the waters of Lethe.

Beyond its pitch, both nerve and bow o'erstretch'd;
The flagging weapon feebly hits the mark:
Thus, tears and sighs forth gushing, did I burst
Beneath the heavy load: and thus my voice
Was slacken'd on its way.   She straight began:
" When my desire invited thee to love
The good, which sets a bound to our aspirings;
What bar of thwarting foss or linked chain
Did meet thee, that thou so shouldst quit the hope
Of further progress? or what bait of ease,
Or promise of allurement, led thee on
Elsewhere, that thou elsewhere shouldst rather wait?"

    A bitter sigh I drew, then scarce found voice
To answer; hardly to these sounds my lips
Gave utterance, wailing: " Thy fair looks withdrawn,
Things present, with deceitful pleasures, turn'd
My steps aside." She answering spake : " Hadst thou
Been silent, or denied what thou avow'st,
Thou hadst not hid thy sin the more; such eye
Observes it.   But whene'er the sinner's cheek
Breaks forth into precious-streaming tears
Of self-accusing, court the wheel
Of justice doth ter to the edge.[1]
Howe'er, that th profit by thy shame
For errors past, henceforth more strength
May arm thee, wu hear'st the Syren-voice;
Lay thou aside the e to this grief,
And lend attentive while I unfold
How opposite a way my buried flesh
Should have impell'd thee.   Never didst thou spy,
In art or nature, aug so passing sweet,
As were the limbs that in their beauteous frame
Enclosed me, and are scatter'd now in dust.
If sweetest thing th ail'd thee with my death,
What, afterward, rtal, should thy wish
Have tempted?   W thou first hadst felt the dart
Of perishable things n my departing
For better realms, th ing thou shouldst have pruned
To follow me; and r stoop'd again,
To 'bide a second blow, for a slight girl,[2]

[1] " The weapons of Divine Justice are blunted by the confession
and sorrow of the offender " (Cary).

[2] *Pargoletta.   Cf.* Canzone xv.   Most probably, Beatrice is
making a general accusation, without reference to any special

Or other gaud as transient and as vain.
The new and inexperienced bird awaits,
Twice it may be, or thrice, the fowler's aim; [1]
But in the sight of one whose plumes are full,
In vain the net is spread, the arrow wing'd.''

    I stood, as children silent and ashamed
Stand, listening, with their eyes upon the earth,
Acknowledging their fault, and self-condemn'd.
And she resumed : '' If, but to hear, thus pains thee,
Raise thou thy beard, and lo! what sight shall do.''

    With less reluctance yields a sturdy holm,
Rent from its fibres by a blast, that blows
From off the pole, or from Iarbas' land,[2]
Than I at her behest my visage raised :
And thus the face denoting by the beard,
I mark'd the secret sting her words convey'd.[3]

    No sooner lifted I mine aspect up,
Than I perceived those primal creatures [4] cease
Their flowery sprinkling; and mine eyes beheld
(Yet unassured and wavering in their view)
Beatrice; she, who towards the   stic shape,
That joins two natures in one f   had turn'd :
And, even under shadow of he
And parted by the verdant ri   ow'd
Between, in loveliness she se   much
Her former self surpassing, a   arth
All others she surpass'd.   Re   ful goads
Shot sudden through me.   Ea   ing else, the more
Its love had late beguil'd me, no   the more
Was loathsome.   On my heart so keenly smote
The bitter consciousness, that   the ground
O'erpower'd I fell : and what my state was then,
She knows, who was the cause.   When now my
    strength
Flow'd back, returning outwa   om the heart,
The lady,[5] whom alone I first   seen,

offence. This will hold good whether we regard the *pargoletta* as
a real woman, or as a merely allego   figure.
  [1] *Cf.* Proverbs i. 17.
  [2] '' Whether by a native wind [from the north] or by that from
the land of Iarbas ''—from the south. Iarbas was a king of
Libya mentioned by Virgil (*Æn.* iv. 196).
  [3] He is a man, and not a child to be so easily led away.
  [4] The Angels.
  [5] Matilda.

I found above me.   " Loose me not," she cried :
" Loose not thy hold :" and lo ! had dragg'd me high
As to my neck into the stream ; while she,
Still as she drew me after, swept along,
Swift as a shuttle, bounding o'er the wave.

The blessed shore approaching, then was heard
So sweetly, " Tu asperges me," [1] that I
May not remember, much less tell the sound.

The beauteous dame, her arms expanding, clasp'd
My temples, and immerged me where 'twas fit
The wave should drench me : and, thence raising up,
Within the fourfold dance of lovely nymphs
Presented me so laved ; and with their arm
They each did cover me.   " Here are we nymphs,
And in the heaven are stars. [2]   Or ever earth
Was visited of Beatrice, we,
Appointed for her handmaids, tended on her.
We to her eyes will lead thee : but the light
Of gladness, that is in them, well to scan,
Those yonder three, [3] of deeper ken than ours,
Thy sight shall quicken."   Thus began their song :
And then they led me to the Gryphon's breast,
Where, turn'd toward us, Beatrice stood.
" Spare not thy vision.   We have station'd thee
Before the emeralds, [4] whence love, erewhile,
Hath drawn his weapons on thee."   As they spake,
A thousand fervent wishes riveted
Mine eyes upon her beaming eyes, that stood,
Still fix'd toward the Gryphon, motionless.
As the sun strikes a mirror, even thus
Within those orbs the twyfold being shone ;
For ever varying, in one figure now
Reflected, now in other. [5]   Reader ! muse

---

[1] A verse of the *Miserere*, Ps. li. 7 (Vulgate l.), which is sung
during the sprinkling of the people with holy water before High
Mass.
[2] *Cf.* Canto i.
[3] Faith, Hope, and Charity.
[4] The eyes of Beatrice.
[5] " Dante's passionate reminiscences and longings are awed by
the august impersonation of Revelation, whom he has found where
he looked only for the Florentine maiden he had lost on earth.
The divine and human nature of Christ are flashed alternately
from the reflection in her eyes, though ever combined in the
mysterious being himself " (Wicksteed).

How wondrous in my sight it seem'd, to mark
A thing, albeit stedfast in itself,
Yet in its imaged semblance mutable.

　　Full of amaze, and joyous, while my soul
Fed on the viand, whereof still desire
Grows with satiety; the other three,
With gesture that declared a loftier line,
Advanced: to their own carol, on they came
Dancing, in festive ring angelical.

　　" Turn, Beatrice!" was their song: "Oh! turn
Thy saintly sight on this thy faithful one,
Who, to behold thee, many a wearisome pace
Hath measured. Gracious at our prayer, vouchsafe
Unveil to him thy cheeks; that he may mark
Thy second beauty,[1] now conceal'd." O splendour!
O sacred light eternal! who is he,
So pale with musing in Pierian shades,
Or with that fount so lavishly imbued,
Whose spirit should not fail him in the essay
To represent thee such as thou didst seem,
When under cope of the still-chiming Heaven
Thou gavest to open air thy charms reveal'd?

CANTO XXXII

ARGUMENT

Dante is warned not to gaze too fixedly on Beatrice. The procession moves on, accompanied by Matilda, Statius, and Dante,
till they reach an exceeding lofty tree, where divers strange
chances befal.

MINE eyes with such an eager coveting
Were bent to rid them of their ten years' thirst,[2]
No other sense was waking: and e'en they
Were fenced on either side from heed of aught;
So tangled, in its custom'd toils, that smile
Of saintly brightness drew me to itself:
When forcibly, toward the left, my sight
The sacred virgins turn'd; for from their lips
I heard the warning sounds: "Too fix'd a gaze!"

---

[1] Her smile. Cf. *Conv.* iii. 8.
[2] From her death, in June, 1290, until the assumed date of the
vision, April, 1300.

Awhile my vision labour'd; as when late
Upon the o'erstrained eyes the sun hath smote:
But soon, to lesser object, as the view
Was now recover'd, (lesser in respect
To that excess of sensible, whence late
I had perforce been sunder'd,) on their right
I mark'd that glorious army wheel, and turn,
Against the sun and sevenfold lights, their front.
As when, their bucklers for protection raised,
A well-ranged troop, with portly banners curl'd,
Wheel circling, ere the whole can change their ground;
E'en thus the goodly regiment of Heaven,
Proceeding, all did pass us, ere the car
Had sloped his beam. Attendant at the wheels
The damsels turn'd; and on the Gryphon moved
The sacred burden, with a pace so smooth,
No feather on him trembled. The fair dame,
Who through the wave had drawn me, companied
By Statius and myself, pursued the wheel,
Whose orbit, rolling, mark'd a lesser arch.[1]

Through the high wood, now void, (the more her
    blame,
Who by the serpent was beguil'd,) I pass'd,
With step in cadence to the harmony
Angelic. Onward had we moved, as far,
Perchance, as arrow at three several flights
Full wing'd had sped, when from her station down
Descended Beatrice. With one voice
All murmur'd "Adam;" circling next a plant[2]
Despoil'd of flowers and leaf, on every bough.
Its tresses, spreading more as more they rose,
Were such, as 'midst their forest wilds, for height,
The Indians might have gazed at. "Blessed thou,

---

[1] Now that he is purified and illumined, Dante is to see or hear
the past, present, and future of the Church and Empire. The
pageant has shown him the ideal of the Church, as her Divine
Spouse had intended her to be for the guidance of the world; he
is now to behold her history, in conjunction with the Empire, from
the first coming of Christianity to Rome down to the transference
of the papal chair to Avignon; and he is to hear the promise of the
future.

[2] The Tree of knowledge of good and evil, which, since the pro-
hibition to eat of that tree was the beginning of law and of the
duty of obedience, has become the symbol of temporal power, of
the Empire, and of the obedience due to it.

Gryphon! whose beak hath never pluck'd that tree
Pleasant to taste : for hence the appetite
Was warp'd to evil.''   Round the stately trunk
Thus shouted forth the rest, to whom return'd
The animal twice-gender'd : " Yea ! for so
The generation of the just are saved." [1]
And turning to the chariot-pole, to foot
He drew it of the widow'd branch, and bound
There, left unto the stock whereon it grew.[2]

   As when large floods of radiance from above
Stream, with that radiance mingled, which ascends
Next after setting of the scaly sign,[3]
Our plants then burgein, and each wears anew
His wonted colours, ere the sun have yoked
Beneath another star his flamy steeds ;
Thus putting forth a hue more faint than rose,
And deeper than the violet, was renew'd
The plant, erewhile in all its branches bare.[4]
Unearthly was the hymn, which then arose.
I understood it not, nor to the end
Endured the harmony. Had I the skill
To pencil forth how closed the unpitying eyes [5]
Slumbering, when Syrinx warbled, (eyes that paid
So dearly for their watching,) then, like painter,
That with a model paints, I might design
The manner of my falling into sleep.
But feign who will the slumber cunningly,
I pass it by to when I waked ; and tell,
How suddenly a flash of splendour rent
The curtain of my sleep, and one cries out,

   [1] *Cf.* Matt. iii. 15. Justice can be fulfilled only when the
Church follows the example of her Divine Founder, and usurps
none of the temporal sovereignty of the Empire.
   [2] The chariot-pole is the Cross, which, according to legend,
was made from the tree of Eden. It is the binding link between
the Church and the Empire. Cf. *Par.* vi., vii.
   [3] In spring, when the sun enters Aries, the constellation following Pisces.
   [4] The Empire, bare and destitute of virtue until the advent of
Christianity, now breaks out into purple leaves and flowers—the
colour of the four cardinal virtues, which Dante more particularly
associates with the temporal monarchy.
   [5] The many-eyed Argus was lulled to sleep by hearing Mercury
tell the story of Syrinx, and then slain.   Cary has mistranslated
the passage, which should run : " Had I skill to portray how the
pitiless eyes fell asleep in hearing of Syrinx.''

" Arise : what dost thou?"   As the chosen three,
On Tabor's mount, admitted to behold
The blossoming of that fair tree,[1] whose fruit
Is coveted of Angels, and doth make
Perpetual feast in Heaven; to themselves
Returning, at the word whence deeper sleeps [2]
Were broken, they their tribe diminish'd saw;
Both Moses and Elias gone, and changed
The stole their Master wore; thus to myself
Returning, over me beheld I stand
The piteous one,[3] who, cross the stream, had brought
My steps.   " And where," all doubting, I exclaim'd,
" Is Beatrice?"—" See her," she replied,
" Beneath the fresh leaf, seated on its root.
Behold the associate choir, that circles her.
The others, with a melody more sweet
And more profound, journeying to higher realms,
Upon the Gryphon tend." If there her words
Were closed, I know not; but mine eyes had now
Ta'en view of her, by whom all other thoughts
Were barr'd admittance. On the very ground
Alone she sat, as she had there been left
A guard upon the wain, which I beheld
Bound to the twyform beast. The seven nymphs
Did make themselves a cloister round about her;
And, in their hands, upheld those lights secure
From blast septentrion and the gusty south.[4]

    " A little while thou shalt be forester here;
And citizen shalt be, for ever with me,
Of that true Rome, wherein Christ dwells a Roman.[5]
To profit the misguided world, keep now
Thine eyes upon the car; and what thou seest,
Take heed thou write, returning to that place." [6]

    Thus Beatrice : at whose feet inclined
Devout, at her behest, my thought and eyes

---

[1] At the Transfiguration. *Cf.* Song of Solomon, ii. 3.
[2] When, at Christ's word, the ruler's daughter and Lazarus
were restored to life.
[3] Matilda.
[4] Beatrice, Heavenly Wisdom, is left to watch over the Chariot
of the Church, seated beneath the shadow of the Tree of the
Empire, upon its root, which is Rome. She is attended by the
Virtues, who still guard the Seven Gifts of the Holy Spirit.
[5] In the Empyrean Heaven.
[6] To the earth.

I, as she bade, directed.   Never fire,
With so swift motion, forth a stormy cloud
Leap'd downward from the welkin's farthest bound,
As I beheld the bird of Jove descend
Down through the tree; and, as he rush'd, the rind
Disparting crush beneath him; buds much more,
And leaflets.   On the car, with all his might
He struck; [1] whence, staggering, like a ship it reel'd,
At random driven, to starboard now, o'ercome,
And now to larboard, by the vaulting waves.

  Next, springing up into the chariot's womb,
A fox [2] I saw, with hunger seeming pined
Of all good food.   But, for his ugly sins
The saintly maid rebuking him, away
Scampering he turn'd, fast as his hide-bound corpse
Would bear him.   Next, from whence before he came,
I saw the eagle dart into the hull
O' the car, and leave it with his feathers lined : [3]
And then a voice, like that which issues forth
From heart with sorrow rived, did issue forth
From Heaven, and, " O poor bark of mine ! " it cried,
" How badly art thou freighted."   Then it seem'd
That the earth open'd, between either wheel ;
And I beheld a dragon [4] issue thence,
That through the chariot fix'd his forked train ;
And like a wasp, that draggeth back the sting,
So drawing forth his baleful train, he dragg'd
Part of the bottom forth ; and went his way,
Exulting.   What remain'd, as lively turf
With green herb, so did clothe itself with plumes,
Which haply had, with purpose chaste and kind,
Been offer'd ; and therewith were clothed the wheels,
Both one and other, and the beam, so quickly,
A sigh were not breathed sooner.   Thus transform'd,
The holy structure, through its several parts,
Did put forth heads ; three on the beam, and one
On every side : the first like oxen horn'd ;
But with a single horn upon their front,

  [1] This assault signifies the persecution of the Church by the
Roman Emperors figured in the Imperial Eagle.

  [2] The early heresies.

  [3] The donation of Constantine.

  [4] Either schism (and more particularly that of Mahomet) or the
spirit of simony.

The four.[1]   Like monster, sight hath never seen.
O'er it methought there sat, secure as rock
On mountain's lofty top, a shameless whore,[2]
Whose ken roved loosely round her.   At her side,
As 't were that none might bear her off, I saw
A giant stand;[3] and ever and anon
They mingled kisses.   But, her lustful eyes
Chancing on me to wander, that fell minion
Scourged her from head to foot all o'er; then full
Of jealousy, and fierce with rage, unloosed
The monster, and dragg'd on, so far across
The forest, that from me its shades alone
Shielded the harlot and the new-form'd brute.[4]

CANTO XXXIII

ARGUMENT

After a hymn sung, Beatrice leaves the tree, and takes with her
the seven virgins, Matilda, Statius, and Dante. She then
darkly predicts to our Poet some future events. Lastly,
the whole band arrive at the fountain, from whence the two
streams, Lethe and Eunoe, separating, flow different ways;
and Matilda, at the desire of Beatrice, causes our Poet to drink
of the latter stream.

" THE heathen, Lord! are come : "[5] responsive thus,
The trinal now, and now the virgin band
Quaternion, their sweet psalmody began,
Weeping; and Beatrice listen'd, sad
And sighing, to the song, in such a mood,
That Mary, as she stood beside the Cross,
Was scarce more changed.   But when they gave her
     place
To speak, then, risen upright on her feet,
She, with a colour glowing bright as fire,
Did answer : "Yet a little while,[6] and ye

[1] By clothing itself with the plumes of temporal power and
worldly wealth (increased by the Carlovingian Emperors), the
Church becomes transformed into an apocalyptic monster (*Cf.* Rev.
xvii.), adorned with the seven capital sins.

[2] The corrupt Papal Court.

[3] The royal house of France.

[4] This signifies the transference of the Papacy from Rome to
Avignon. Cf. *Inf.* xix.

[5] Ps. lxxix. 1.

[6] *Cf.* John xvi. 16. Heavenly Wisdom, though concealed for

Shall see me not; and, my beloved sisters!
Again a little while, and ye shall see me."
　　Before her then she marshal'd all the seven;
And, beckoning only, motion'd me, the dame,
And that remaining sage,[1] to follow her.
　　So on she pass'd; and had not set, I ween,
Her tenth step to the ground, when, with mine eyes,
Her eyes encounter'd; and, with visage mild,
" So mend thy pace," she cried, " that if my words
Address thee, thou mayst still be aptly placed
To hear them."   Soon as duly to her side
I now had hasten'd: " Brother!" she began,
" Why makest thou no attempt at questioning,
As thus we walk together?"   Like to those
Who, speaking with too reverent an awe
Before their betters, draw not forth the voice
Alive unto their lips, befel me then
That I in sounds imperfect thus began:
" Lady! what I have need of, that thou know'st;
And what will suit my need."   She answering thus:
" Of fearfulness and shame, I will that thou
Henceforth do rid thee; that thou speak no more,
As one who dreams.   Thus far be taught of me:
The vessel which thou saw'st the serpent break,
Was, and is not: let him, who hath the blame,
Hope not to scare God's vengeance with a sop.[2]
Without an heir for ever shall not be
That eagle,[3] he, who left the chariot plumed,
Which monster made it first and next a prey.
Plainly I view, and therefore speak, the stars
E'en now approaching, whose conjunction, free
From all impediment and bar, brings on
A season, in the which, one sent from God,

a while by the corruption of the Papal Court, will never perma-
nently desert the Church of God.
　[1] Statius.
　[2] Corruption and simony have so degraded the Church that she
is no longer recognisable as the Spouse of Christ; but nothing can
save the guilty parties from the vengeance of God. In Dante's
days, a murderer could escape the vengeance of his victim's
family, by eating a sop of bread and wine at his grave within
nine days after the deed.
　[3] The Empire will not remain vacant for ever. Strictly speaking, no Emperor was recognised by the Italians between Frederick
II. (d. 1250) and Henry VII. (elected 1308). Cf. *Conv.* iv. 3.

(Five hundred, five, and ten, do mark him out,)
That foul one, and the accomplice of her guilt,
The giant, both, shall slay.[1]   And if perchance
My saying, dark as Themis or as Sphinx,
Fail to persuade thee, (since like them it foils
The intellect with blindness,) yet ere long
Events shall be the Naïads, that will solve
This knotty riddle; and no damage light
On flock or field.[2]   Take heed; and as these words
By me are utter'd, teach them even so
To those who live that life, which is a race
To death: and when thou writest them, keep in mind
Not to conceal how thou hast seen the plant,
That twice hath now been spoil'd.   This whoso robs,
This whoso plucks, with blasphemy of deed
Sins against God, who for his use alone
Creating hallow'd it.[3]   For taste of this,
In pain and in desire, five thousand years
And upward, the first soul did yearn for him
Who punish'd in himself the fatal gust.[4]

"Thy reason slumbers, if it deem this height,
And summit thus inverted, of the plant,
Without due cause: and were not vainer thoughts,
As Elsa's numbing waters,[5] to thy soul,

---

[1] *Un cinquecento diece e cinque messo da Dio,* "a five hundred ten and five, sent from God." The usual interpretation is that these numbers, slightly transposed, form DVX (*dux*), a leader—who is to be identified with the *Veltro*. Cf. *Inf.* i. Besides Rev. xiii. 18, Dante was probably influenced by Daniel ix. 26, in the Latin version of which the "prince that shall come" is *dux venturus.*

[2] Dante here follows a corruption in the text of Ovid, *Metam.* vii. 759-761, which reads *Naiades* (Naiads), instead of *Laiades* (Œdipus, son of Laius), which is now the universally accepted reading. Themis, in anger at Œdipus having solved the riddle of the Sphinx, sent a wild beast to destroy the flocks and fields of the Thebans.

[3] Dante is to make manifest that the Empire is of divine origin, and to recognise that the precept given by God to our first parents corresponds now with the duty and obedience man owes to the Empire; whoever strives to usurp the imperial prerogatives, sins against God, even as Adam sinned in eating of the fruit of the forbidden tree.

[4] Cf. *Par.* xxvi. "Dante follows the chronology of Eusebius, according to which Adam was on earth for 930 years, and in Limbo for 4302 years, making 5232 years in all" (Oelsner).

[5] The Elsa, a small Tuscan river, has petrifying qualities in part of its course.

And their fond pleasures had not dyed it dark
As Pyramus the mulberry; thou hadst seen,
In such momentous circumstance alone,
God's equal justice morally implied
In the forbidden tree.   But since I mark thee,
In understanding, harden'd into stone,
And, to that hardness, spotted too and stain'd,
So that thine eye is dazzled at my word;
I will, that, if not written, yet at least
Painted thou take it in thee, for the cause,
That one brings home his staff inwreathed with palm." [1]
   I thus : " As wax by seal, that changeth not
Its impress, now is stamp'd my brain by thee.
But wherefore soars thy wish'd-for speech so high
Beyond my sight, that loses it the more,
The more it strains to reach it?"—" To the end
That thou mayst know," she answer'd straight, " the
      school,
That thou hast follow'd; [2] and how far behind,
When following my discourse, its learning halts :
And mayst behold your art, from the divine
As distant, as the disagreement is
'Twixt earth and Heaven's most high and rapturous
      orb."
   " I not remember," I replied, " that e'er
I was estranged from thee; nor for such fault
Doth conscience chide me."   Smiling she return'd :
" If thou canst not remember, call to mind
How lately thou hast drunk of Lethe's wave;
And, sure as smoke doth indicate a flame,
In that forgetfulness itself conclude
Blame from thy alienated will incurr'd.
From henceforth, verily, my words shall be
As naked, as will suit them to appear
In thy unpractised view."   More sparkling now,
And with retarded course, the sun possess'd
The circle of mid-day, that varies still
As the aspect varies of each several clime; [3]

   [1] Pilgrims to the Holy Land brought back their staffs wreathed
with palm (cf. *V. N.* § 41).   Let Dante similarly bring back these
tidings to show where he has been.
   [2] The school of human philosophy, to which there is no dis-
paragement intended in this passage.
   [3] It is noon in Purgatory.

When, as one, sent in vaward of a troop
For escort, pauses, if perchance he spy
Vestige of somewhat strange and rare; so paused
The sevenfold band, arriving at the verge
Of a dun umbrage hoar, such as is seen,
Beneath green leaves and gloomy branches, oft
To overbrow a bleak and alpine cliff.
And, where they stood, before them, as it seem'd,
I, Tigris and Euphrates both, beheld
Forth from one fountain issue; [1] and, like friends,
Linger at parting.   " O enlightening beam !
O glory of our kind ! beseech thee say
What water this, which, from one source derived,
Itself removes to distance from itself?"
    To such entreaty answer thus was made :
" Entreat Matilda, that she teach thee this."
    And here, as one who clears himself of blame
Imputed, the fair dame return'd : " Of me
He this and more hath learnt; and I am safe
That Lethe's water hath not hid it from him."
    And Beatrice : " Some more pressing care,
That oft the memory 'reaves, perchance hath made
His mind's eye dark.   But lo, where Eunoe flows !
Lead thither; and, as thou art wont, revive
His fainting virtue."   As a courteous spirit,
That proffers no excuses, but as soon
As he hath token of another's will,
Makes it his own; when she had ta'en me, thus
The lovely maiden moved her on, and call'd
To Statius, with an air most lady-like :
" Come thou with him."   Were further space allow'd,
Then, Reader ! might I sing, though but in part,
That beverage, with whose sweetness I had ne'er
Been sated.   But, since all the leaves are full,
Appointed for this second strain, mine art
With warning bridle checks me.   I return'd
From the most holy wave, regenerate,
E'en as new plants renew'd with foilage new,
Pure and made apt for mounting to the stars.

---

[1] *Cf.* above, Canto xxviii. The mystical source from which
both Lethe and Eunoe spring is the fountain of the grace of God.

THE VISION OF DANTE

Paradise

CANTO I

ARGUMENT

The Poet ascends with Beatrice towards the first Heaven; and is,
by her, resolved of certain doubts which arise in his mind.

His glory, by whose might all things are moved,
Pierces the universe, and in one part
Sheds more resplendence, elsewhere less.   In Heaven,
That largeliest of his light partakes, was I,[1]
Witness of things, which, to relate again,
Surpasseth power of him who comes from thence;
For that, so near approaching its desire,
Our intellect is to such depth absorb'd,
That memory cannot follow.   Nathless all,
That in my thoughts I of that sacred realm
Could store, shall now be matter of my song.
   Benign Apollo![2] this last labour aid;
And make me such a vessel of thy worth,
As thy own laurel claims, of me beloved.
Thus far hath one of steep Parnassus' brows
Sufficed me; henceforth, there is need of both
For my remaining enterprize.   Do thou
Enter into my bosom, and there breathe
So, as when Marsyas by thy hand was dragg'd
Forth from his limbs, unsheathed.[3]   O power divine!

---

[1] " In that Heaven was I," *i.e.* in the Empyrean: " the
supreme Heaven, containing all the bodies of the universe and
contained by love, within which all bodies move (itself abiding in
eternal rest), receiving its virtue from no corporeal substance.
And it is called the *Empyrean*, which is the same as the heaven
flaming with fire or heat, not because there is any material fire
or heat in it, but spiritual, to wit holy love or charity " (Letter to
Can Grande, *Epist.* x. 24).

[2] Apollo is here a symbol of Christ or of the Divine Grace.

[3] Marsyas challenged Apollo to a musical contest, and was
flayed alive for his presumption.

If thou to me of thine impart so much,
That of that happy realm the shadow'd form
Traced in my thoughts I may set forth to view;
Thou shalt behold me of thy favour'd tree
Come to the foot, and crown myself with leaves :
For to that honour thou, and my high theme
Will fit me.   If but seldom, mighty Sire !
To grace his triumph, gathers thence a wreath
Cæsar, or bard, (more shame for human wills
Depraved,) joy to the Delphic god must spring
From the Peneian foliage,[1] when one breast
Is with such thirst inspired.   From a small spark
Great flame hath risen : after me, perchance,
Others with better voice may pray, and gain,
From the Cyrrhæan city,[2] answer kind.

Through divers passages, the world's bright lamp
Rises to mortals ; but through that which joins
Four circles with the threefold cross, in best
Course, and in happiest constellation set,
He comes ;[3] and, to the worldly wax, best gives
Its temper and impression.   Morning there,
Here eve was well nigh by such passage made;
And whiteness had o'erspread that hemisphere,
Blackness the other part ;[4] when to the left
I saw Beatrice turn'd, and on the sun

[1] Daphne, daughter of Peneus, a nymph beloved by Apollo,
was changed into a laurel.

[2] Dante has simply *Cirra*.   It is doubtful whether he refers to
Cirra, a peak of Parnassus, or Cirrha, a town near Delphi, both
sacred to Apollo.

[3] " Where the four circles, the horizon, the zodiac, the
equator, and the equinoctial colure join ; the last three intersecting
each other so as to form three crosses, as may be seen in the
armillary sphere " (Cary).   In the allegorical sense, the grace of
God shines most upon the soul where the cardinal virtues, which
attain to human reason, are united to the theological virtues,
whose object is God.   The " happiest constellation " is Aries.
Dante is not actually describing sunrise on the mountain, but
merely making a general astronomical statement concerning
sunrise at the spring equinox, the time of his ascent.

[4] " Almost this passage had made (at sunrise) morning there
(in the Earthly Paradise) and evening here (on earth) ; and there
that (southern hemisphere) was all bright, and the other region
(the inhabited world) was dark."   It was now noon in the Earthly
Paradise, the noon of the same day as that upon which Dante
had drunken of the mystical waters, and therefore midnight at
Jerusalem.   There is no interval of time between the end of the
Purgatorio and the beginning of the *Paradiso*.

Gazing, as never eagle fix'd his ken.
As from the first a second beam is wont
To issue, and reflected upwards rise,
Even as a pilgrim bent on his return;
So of her act, that through the eyesight pass'd
Into my fancy, mine was form'd : and straight,
Beyond our mortal wont, I fix'd mine eyes
Upon the sun.   Much is allow'd us there,
That here exceeds our power; thanks to the place
Made for the dwelling of the human kind.[1]

I suffer'd it not long; and yet so long,
That I beheld it bickering sparks around,
As iron that comes boiling from the fire.
And suddenly upon the day appear'd
A day new-risen; as he, who hath the power,
Had with another sun bedeck'd the sky.[2]

Her eyes fast fix'd on the eternal wheels,[3]
Beatrice stood unmoved; and I with ken
Fix'd upon her, from upward gaze removed,
At her aspect, such inwardly became
As Glaucus,[4] when he tasted of the herb
That made him peer among the ocean gods :
Words may not tell of that transhuman change;
And therefore let the example serve, though weak,
For these whom grace hath better proof in store.

If I were only what thou didst create,
Then newly, Love ! by whom the Heaven is ruled;[5]
Thou know'st, who by Thy light didst bear me up.
Whenas the wheel which Thou dost ever guide,
Desired Spirit ! with its harmony,[6]
Temper'd of Thee and measured, charm'd mine ear
Then seem'd to me so much of Heaven to blaze

---

[1] The Earthly Paradise, from which the Poet is about to
ascend.

[2] Because he has already begun to ascend.

[3] " The Heavens, eternal, and always circling " (Cary).

[4] The fisherman Glaucus (Ovid, *Metam.* xiii.), having tasted
certain grass, entered the sea and became a marine god.

[5] Dante, following St. Paul (2 Corinthians xii. 2), cannot tell
whether he was in the body or out of the body. " The Soul is
enbreathed by God when the animal body is perfected (*Purg.*
xxv.), and is therefore that part of a man which is to be regarded
as a new creation by God, not generated by nature " (Wicksteed).

[6] The music of the spheres as they revolve, the ninth Heaven
(*Primum Mobile*) swiftest of all from the fervent longing that each
part has to be united to the Empyrean.

With the sun's flame, that rain or flood ne'er made
A lake so broad.[1]   The newness of the sound,
And that great light, inflamed me with desire,
Keener than e'er was felt, to know their cause.

Whence she, who saw me, clearly as myself,
To calm my troubled mind, before I ask'd,
Open'd her lips, and gracious thus began:
"With false imagination thou thyself
Makest dull; so that thou seest not the thing,
Which thou hadst seen, had that been shaken off.
Thou art not on the earth as thou believest;
For lightning, scaped from its own proper place,
Ne'er ran, as thou hast hither now return'd."

Although divested of my first-raised doubt
By those brief words accompanied with smiles,
Yet in new doubt was I entangled more,
And said: "Already satisfied, I rest
From admiration deep; but now admire
How I above those lighter bodies rise."

Whence, after utterance of a piteous sigh,
She towards me bent her eyes, with such a look,
As on her frenzied child a mother casts;
Then thus began: "Among themselves all things
Have order; and from hence the form, which makes
The universe resemble God.   In this
The higher creatures see the printed steps
Of that eternal worth, which is the end
Whither the line is drawn.[2]   All natures lean,
In this their order, diversly; some more,
Some less approaching to their primal source.
Thus they to different havens are moved on
Through the vast sea of being, and each one
With instinct given, that bears it in its course:
This to the lunar sphere directs the fire;
This moves the hearts of mortal animals;
This the brute earth together knits, and binds.
Nor only creatures, void of intellect,
Are aim'd at by this bow; but even those,
That have intelligence and love, are pierced.[3]

[1] He is passing through the sphere of fire.
[2] All nature is ordained to make up the order and beauty of
the universe, from which intellectual and rational beings gather
the image of the perfection of God, who is the end that all
creatures seek.
[3] God gives to all creatures a principle of inclination, by which

That Providence, who so well orders all,
With her own light makes ever calm the Heaven,[1]
In which the substance, that hath greatest speed,[2]
Is turn'd : and thither now, as to our seat
Predestined, we are carried by the force
Of that strong cord, that never looses dart
But at fair aim and glad.   Yet is it true,
That as, oft-times, but ill accords the form
To the design of art, through sluggishness
Or unreplying matter; so this course
Is sometimes quitted by the creature, who
Hath power, directed thus, to bend elsewhere; [3]
As from a cloud the fire is seen to fall,
From its original impulse warp'd, to earth,
By vitious fondness.   Thou no more admire
Thy soaring, (if I rightly deem,) than lapse
Of torrent downwards from a mountain's height.
There would in thee for wonder be more cause,
If, free of hinderance, thou hadst stay'd below,
As living fire unmoved upon the earth.''
    So said, she turn'd toward the Heaven her face.

CANTO II

ARGUMENT

Dante and his celestial guide enter the moon.   The cause of the
    spots or shadows, which appear in that body, is explained to
    him.

ALL ye, who in small bark have following sail'd,
Eager to listen, on the adventurous track

He draws all things that He has made back to Himself. Inanimate
bodies, like fire and earth, being the furthest removed from God,
seek the end to which they are inclined by virtue of this inherent
principle. Sensitive natures or brutes, "mortal animals," being
a step nearer God, have this natural movement further determined
by sense images, that is, from without. Rational beings, "that
have intelligence and love," have the inclination in their own
power, and freely move themselves.
    [1] The motionless Empyrean.
    [2] The *Primum Mobile*.
    [3] Man, the rational creature, being endowed with free will,
although necessarily impelled by his nature to universal good,
can turn aside to a particular seeming good, which in reality may
be false and contrary to the Divine will. "A ship is moved
towards the west by the wind, but the pilot, by turning the helm,
can freely direct it to this or that port of the west " (Cornoldi).

Of my proud keel, that singing cuts her way,
Backward return with speed, and your own shores
Revisit; nor put out to open sea,
Where losing me, perchance ye may remain
Bewilder'd in deep maze.   The way I pass,
Ne'er yet was run : Minerva breathes the gale;
Apollo guides me; and another Nine,
To my rapt sight, the arctic beams reveal.
Ye other few who have outstretch'd the neck
Timely for food of angels, on which here
They live, yet never know satiety;
Through the deep brine ye fearless may put out
Your vessel; marking well the furrow broad
Before you in the wave, that on both sides
Equal returns.   Those, glorious, who pass'd o'er
To Colchis, wonder'd not as ye will do,
When they saw Jason following the plough.

    The increate perpetual thirst,[1] that draws
Toward the realm of God's own form, bore us
Swift almost as the Heaven ye behold.

    Beatrice upward gazed, and I on her;
And in such space as on the notch a dart
Is placed, then loosen'd flies, I saw myself
Arrived, where wonderous thing engaged my sight.
Whence she, to whom no care of mine was hid,
Turning to me, with aspect glad as fair,
Bespake me : " Gratefully direct thy mind
To God, through whom to this first star [2] we come."

    Meseem'd as if a cloud had cover'd us,
Translucent, solid, firm, and polish'd bright,
Like adamant, which the sun's beam had smit.
Within itself the ever-during pearl
Received us; as the wave a ray of light
Receives, and rests unbroken.   If I then
Was of corporeal frame, and it transcend
Our weaker thought, how one dimension thus
Another could endure, which needs must be
If body enter body; how much more
Must the desire inflame us to behold
That Essence, which discovers by what means
God and our nature join'd !   There will be seen
That, which we hold through faith; not shown by proof,

---

[1] The desire of God.   [2] The moon.

But in itself intelligibly plain,
E'en as the truth that man at first believes.[1]

I answer'd : " Lady ! I with thoughts devout,
Such as I best can frame, give thanks to Him,
Who hath removed me from the mortal world.
But tell, I pray thee, whence the gloomy spots
Upon this body, which below on earth
Give rise to talk of Cain [2] in fabling quaint?"

She somewhat smiled, then spake : " If mortals err
In their opinion, when the key of sense
Unlocks not, surely wonder's weapon keen
Ought not to pierce thee : since thou find'st the wings
Of reason to pursue the senses' flight
Are short. But what thy own thought is, declare."

Then I : " What various here above appears,
Is caused, I deem, by bodies dense or rare." [3]

She then resumed : " Thou certainly wilt see
In falsehood thy belief o'erwhelm'd, if well
Thou listen to the arguments which I
Shall bring to face it. The eighth sphere displays
Numberless lights, the which, in kind and size,
May be remark'd of different aspects :
If rare or dense of that were cause alone,
One single virtue then would be in all ;
Alike distributed, or more, or less.
Different virtues needs must be the fruits
Of formal principles ; and these, save one,
Will by thy reasoning be destroy'd. Beside,
If rarity were of that dusk the cause,
Which thou inquirest, either in some part
That planet must throughout be void, nor fed
With its own matter ; or, as bodies share
Their fat and leanness, in like manner this
Must in its volume change the leaves.[4] The first,

---

[1] They reach the moon and inconceivably penetrate into her substance without cleaving it, even as deity penetrated into humanity in Christ ; which mystery shall in Heaven be seen as axiomatic truth " (Wicksteed)—a truth, that is, which is self-evident and needs no demonstration.

[2] Cf. *Inf.* xx.

[3] This is the view already expressed by Dante in the *Convivio* (ii. 14), that these spots in the moon are due to relative rarity and density of its substance.

[4] Starting from the eighth sphere, or Stellar Heaven, where the stars are seen to differ in size and in light, and found (according

If it were true, had through the sun's eclipse
Been manifested, by transparency
Of light, as through aught rare beside effused.
But this is not. Therefore remains to see
The other cause : and, if the other fall,
Erroneous so must prove what seem'd to thee.
If not from side to side this rarity
Pass through, there needs must be a limit, whence
Its contrary no further lets it pass.
And hence the beam, that from without proceeds,
Must be pour'd back ; as colour comes, through glass
Reflected, which behind it lead conceals.
Now wilt thou say, that there of murkier hue,
Than, in the other part, the ray is shown,
By being thence refracted farther back.
From this perplexity will free thee soon
Experience, if thereof thou trial make,
The fountain whence your arts derive their streams.
Three mirrors shalt thou take, and two remove
From thee alike ; and more remote the third,
Betwixt the former pair, shall meet thine eyes :
Then turn'd toward them, cause behind thy back
A light to stand, that on the three shall shine,
And thus reflected come to thee from all.
Though that, beheld most distant, do not stretch
A space so ample, yet in brightness thou
Wilt own it equaling the rest. But now,
As under snow the ground, if the warm ray
Smites it, remains dismantled of the hue
And cold, that cover'd it before ; so thee,
Dismantled in thy mind, I will inform
With light so lively, that the tremulous beam
Shall quiver where it falls. Within the Heaven,
Where peace divine inhabits,[1] circles round
A body, in whose virtue lies the being

to the science of Dante's day) to have effects which differ not in
degree but in kind, and assuming that the same thing applies to
the diversity of the luminous substance of the moon, Beatrice first
shows from this general law—that different effects must proceed
from different formal principles—that Dante's explanation is
wrong, and then points out that, on his own ground, reasoning
based upon common experience and a simple experiment proves
that his theory will not work. He must seek the real cause in
the government of the universe by the celestial intelligences.

[1] The Empyrean Heaven.

Of all that it contains.[1]   The following Heaven,
That hath so many lights, this being divides,
Through different essences, from it distinct,
And yet contain'd within it.[2]   The other orbs
Their separate distinctions variously
Dispose, for their own seed and produce apt.[3]
Thus do these organs of the world proceed,
As thou beholdest now, from step to step;
Their influences from above deriving,
And thence transmitting downwards.   Mark me well;
How through this passage to the truth I ford,
The truth thou lovest; that thou henceforth, alone,
Mayst know to keep the shallows, safe, untold.
    " The virtue and motion of the sacred orbs,
As mallet by the workman's hand, must needs
By blessed movers [4] be inspired.   This Heaven,
Made beauteous by so many luminaries,
From the deep spirit, that moves its circling sphere,[5]
Its image takes and impress as a seal:
And as the soul, that dwells within your dust,
Through members different, yet together form'd,
In different powers resolves itself; e'en so
The intellectual efficacy unfolds
Its goodness multiplied throughout the stars;
On its own unity revolving still.
Different virtue compact different
Makes with the precious body it enlivens,
With which it knits, as life in you is knit.
From its original nature full of joy,
The virtue mingled through the body shines,
As joy through pupil of the living eye.[6]

    [1] The ninth Heaven, the *Primum Mobile*.
    [2] The Stellar Heaven.   [3] The seven lower Heavens.
    [4] The Angels.
    [5] The Stellar Heaven, which is guided by the Cherubim.
    [6] In the virtue of the *Primum Mobile* lies the existence of all
that is contained within it; that is, of all nature.   It communicates
its divinely received influence to the Stellar Heaven, which this in
turn divides among the stars, " the diverse essences distinct from
it and contained by it," and each of the seven lower Heavens
similarly receives the influence from the one above it, disposing it
differently in its different parts, " receiving from above and
working downward."   All the virtue and motion of the Heavens
comes from the spirits who move them—the spheres are as hammers in the hands of the Angels to stamp the Divine ideas upon
the universe.   The Stellar Heaven is animated by the deep spirit

From hence proceeds that which from light to light
Seems different, and not from dense or rare.
This is the formal cause, that generates,
Proportion'd to its power, the dusk or clear."

CANTO III

ARGUMENT

In the moon Dante meets with Piccarda, the sister of Forese, who
tells him that this planet is allotted to those, who, after having
made profession of chastity and a religious life, had been
compelled to violate their vows; and she then points out to
him the spirit of the Empress Costanza.

THAT sun,[1] which erst with love my bosom warmed,
Had of fair truth unveil'd the sweet aspect,
By proof of right, and of the false reproof;
And I, to own myself convinced and free
Of doubt, as much as needed, raised my head
Erect for speech.   But soon a sight appear'd,
Which, so intent to mark it, held me fix'd
That of confession I no longer thought.

  As through translucent and smooth glass, or wave
Clear and unmoved, and flowing not so deep
As that its bed is dark, the shape returns
So faint of our impictured lineaments,
That, on white forehead set, a pearl as strong
Comes to the eye; such saw I many a face,
All stretch'd to speak; from whence I straight conceived,
Delusion opposite to that, which raised,
Between the man and fountain, amorous flame.[2]

  Sudden, as I perceived them, deeming these
Reflected semblances, to see of whom
They were, I turn'd mine eyes, and nothing saw;
Then turn'd them back, directed on the light
Of my sweet guide, who, smiling, shot forth beams

of the Cherubim, as the soul within the body.   Flowing thus
direct from God, the mingled virtue of Angel and planet shines
through the sphere, manifesting itself diversely in the various
stars and in the various parts of each Heaven.
  [1] Beatrice.
  [2] "An error the contrary to that of Narcissus; because he
mistook a shadow for a substance; I, a substance for a shadow"
(Cary).

From her celestial eyes. "Wonder not thou,"
She cried, "at this my smiling, when I see
Thy childish judgment; since not yet on truth
It rests the foot, but, as it still is wont,
Makes thee fall back in unsound vacancy.
True substances are these, which thou behold'st,
Hither through failure of their vow exiled.
But speak thou with them; listen, and believe,
That the true light, which fills them with desire,
Permits not from its beams their feet to stray."

Straight to the shadow, which for converse seem'd
Most earnest, I address'd me; and began
As one by over-eagerness perplex'd:
"O spirit, born for joy! who in the rays
Of life eternal, of that sweetness know'st
The flavour, which, not tasted, passes far
All apprehension; me it well would please,
If thou wouldst tell me of thy name, and this
Your station here." Whence she with kindness prompt,
And eyes glist'ring with smiles: "Our charity,
To any wish by justice introduced,
Bars not the door; no more than She above,
Who would have all her court be like herself.
I was a virgin sister in the earth;
And if thy mind observe me well, this form,
With such addition graced of loveliness,
Will not conceal me long; but thou wilt know
Piccarda,[1] in the tardiest sphere thus placed,
Here 'mid these other blessed also blest.
Our hearts, whose high affections burn alone
With pleasure from the Holy Spirit conceived,
Admitted to His order, dwell in joy.
And this condition, which appears so low,
Is for this cause assign'd us, that our vows
Were, in some part, neglected and made void."

Whence I to her replied: "Something divine
Beams in your countenances wondrous fair;
From former knowledge quite transmuting you.
Therefore to recollect was I so slow.
But what thou sayst hath to my memory
Given now such aid, that to retrace your forms
Is easier. Yet inform me, ye, who here

[1] Piccarda Donati, daughter of Simone, and sister of Corso and
Forese Donati. Cf. *Purg.* xxiv.

Are happy; long ye for a higher place,
More to behold, and more in love to dwell?"
　　She with those other spirits gently smiled;
Then answer'd with such gladness, that she seem'd
With love's first flame to glow: " Brother! our will
Is, in composure, settled by the power
Of charity, who makes us will alone
What we possess, and nought beyond desire:
If we should wish to be exalted more,
Then must our wishes jar with the high will
Of Him, who sets us here; which in these orbs
Thou wilt confess not possible, if here
To be in charity must needs befal,
And if her nature well thou contemplate.
Rather it is inherent in this state
Of blessedness, to keep ourselves within
The Divine Will, by which our wills with His
Are one. So that as we, from step to step,
Are placed throughout this kingdom, pleases all,
Even as our King, who in us plants His will;
And in His will is our tranquillity:
It is the mighty ocean, whither tends
Whatever it creates and nature makes."
　　Then saw I clearly how each spot in Heaven
Is Paradise, though with like gracious dew
The supreme virtue shower not over all.[1]
　　But as it chances, if one sort of food
Hath satiated, and of another still
The appetite remains, that this is ask'd,
And thanks for that return'd; e'en so did I,
In word and motion, bent from her to learn
What web it was, through which she had not drawn
The shuttle to its point. She thus began:
" Exalted worth and perfectness of life
The Lady higher up inshrine in Heaven,

---

[1] Piccarda's words enable him to comprehend the mystery of the Mansions of Beatitude. There are degrees in glory, though the vision that gives that glory is the same in all, and each soul is perfectly blessed, for each is perfectly full according to her capacity of the supreme grace of knowledge and love. " The house is one, that is, the penny is one [cf. the parable of the labourers in the vineyard, Matt. xx.]; but there is a diversity of mansions there, that is, difference in brightness; for the supreme good, beatitude, and life of all, God Himself, is also one " (Peter the Lombard).

By whose pure laws upon your nether earth
The robe and veil they wear; [1] to that intent,
That e'en till death they may keep watch, or sleep,
With their great Bridegroom, who accepts each vow,
Which to His gracious pleasure love conforms.
I from the world, to follow her, when young
Escaped; and, in her vesture mantling me,
Made promise of the way her sect enjoins.
Thereafter men, for ill than good more apt,
Forth snatch'd me from the pleasant cloister's pale.
God knows how, after that, my life was framed. [2]
This other splendid shape, which thou behold'st
At my right side, burning with all the light
Of this our orb, what of myself I tell
May to herself apply.   From her, like me
A sister, with like violence were torn
The saintly folds, that shaded her fair brows.
E'en when she to the world again was brought
In spite of her own will and better wont,
Yet not for that the bosom's inward veil
Did she renounce. This is the luminary
Of mighty Constance, who from that loud blast,
Which blew the second over Suabia's realm,
That power produced, which was the third and last." [3]
     She ceased from further talk, and then began
"Ave Maria" singing; and with that song
Vanish'd, as heavy substance through deep wave.
     Mine eye, that, far as it was capable,
Pursued her, when in dimness she was lost,
Turn'd to the mark where greater want impell'd,

[1] Chiara Scifi of Assisi, now known as St. Clare (1194–1253),
the friend and disciple of St. Francis, who founded the order of
Franciscan nuns called "the Poor Clares."

[2] Piccarda, when still a young girl, took the Franciscan habit
in the convent of the Poor Clares at Florence, from which she
was forcibly abducted by her brother Corso, probably in 1288,
and compelled to marry Rossellino della Tosa, a turbulent noble
of the Black faction. She died shortly afterwards.

[3] Constance, daughter of King Roger and heiress of the Norman
sovereigns of Sicily and Naples, was married in 1185 to Henry,
son of Frederick Barbarossa, afterwards the Emperor Henry VI.
("the second blast of Suabia"), to whom she bore Frederick II.
("the third and last blast"). Cf. *Purg.* iii. She died in 1198.
Dante follows the tradition that she had been a nun, and that she
had been taken from her convent, against her will, to make this
political marriage for reasons of state.

And bent on Beatrice all its gaze.
But she, as lightning, beam'd upon my looks;
So that the sight sustain'd it not at first.
Whence I to question her became less prompt.

CANTO IV

ARGUMENT

While they still continue in the moon, Beatrice removes certain
doubts which Dante had conceived respecting the place
assigned to the blessed, and respecting the will absolute or
conditional. He inquires whether it is possible to make satisfaction for a vow broken.

BETWEEN two kinds of food, both equally
Remote and tempting, first a man might die
Of hunger, ere he one could freely chuse.
E'en so would stand a lamb between the maw
Of two fierce wolves, in dread of both alike:
E'en so between two deer a dog would stand.
Wherefore, if I was silent, fault nor praise
I to myself impute; by equal doubts
Held in suspense; since of necessity
It happen'd. Silent was I, yet desire
Was painted in my looks; and thus I spake
My wish more earnestly than language could.

As Daniel,[1] when the haughty king he freed
From ire, that spurr'd him on to deeds unjust
And violent; so did Beatrice then.

" Well I discern," she thus her words address'd,
" How thou art drawn by each of these desires; [2]
So that thy anxious thought is in itself
Bound up and stifled, nor breathes freely forth.
Thou arguest: if the good intent remain;
What reason that another's violence
Should stint the measure of my fair desert?

" Cause too thou find'st for doubt, in that it seems,
That spirits to the stars, as Plato [3] deem'd,

---

[1] *Cf.* Daniel ii.
[2] His desire to have each of his two difficulties solved. The
word *dubbio*, which Cary translates " doubt," means simply a
" question " or a " difficulty."
[3] " In the *Timæus*, which was accessible to Dante in the Latin
paraphrase of Chalcidius. Dante's direct knowledge of Plato

Return.   These are the questions which thy will
Urge equally; and therefore I, the first,
Of that will treat which hath the more of gall.[1]
Of Seraphim he who is most enskied,
Moses and Samuel, and either John,
Chuse which thou wilt, nor even Mary's self,
Have not in any other Heaven their seats,
Than have those spirits which so late thou saw'st;
Nor more or fewer years exist; but all
Make the first circle beauteous, diversely
Partaking of sweet life, as more or less
Afflation of eternal bliss pervades them.[2]
Here were they shown thee, not that fate assigns
This for their sphere, but for a sign to thee
Of that celestial furthest from the height.
Thus needs, that ye may apprehend, we speak:
Since from things sensible alone ye learn
That, which, digested rightly, after turns
To intellectual.   For no other cause
The Scripture, condescending graciously
To your perception, hands and feet to God
Attributes, nor so means: and holy Church
Doth represent with human countenance
Gabriel, and Michäel, and him who made
Tobias whole.   Unlike what here thou seest,
The judgment of Timæus, who affirms
Each soul restored to its particular star;
Believing it to have been taken thence,
When nature gave it to inform her mold:
Yet to appearance his intention is
Not what his words declare: and so to shun
Derision, haply thus he hath disguised

was doubtless confined to this one dialogue. The doctrine ascribed
to Plato, implicitly here and explicitly in *Conv.* ii. 14, iv. 21
(compare *Eclogue* ii. 16, 17), goes somewhat beyond the warrant of
the text either in the Greek or Latin " (Wicksteed).

[1] More dangerous because opposed to the doctrine of free will.

[2] These spirits enjoy the Beatific Vision for all eternity in the
Empyrean Heaven ("the first circle") together with the divinest
order of the Angels and the greatest of the Saints, even the
Blessed Virgin herself.   They only appear in this lowest sphere to
give Dante a visible sign that the grade of their blessedness in the
Empyrean is the lowest, albeit it is full and perfect according to
their capacity of love and knowledge. The same, in its degree,
applies to all the spirits who thus temporarily appear to Dante in
the lower Heavens.

His true opinion.[1]　If his meaning be,
That to the influencing of these orbs revert
The honour and the blame in human acts,
Perchance he doth not wholly miss the truth.
This principle, not understood aright,
Erewhile perverted well nigh all the world;
So that it fell to fabled names of Jove,
And Mercury, and Mars.　That other doubt,
Which moves thee, is less harmful; for it brings
No peril of removing thee from me.

　" That, to the eye of man, our justice seems
Unjust, is argument for faith, and not
For heretic declension.[2]　But, to the end
This truth may stand more clearly in your view,
I will content thee even to thy wish.

　" If violence be, when that which suffers, nought
Consents to that which forceth, not for this
These spirits stood exculpate.　For the will,
That wills not, still survives unquench'd, and doth,
As nature doth in fire, though violence
Wrest it a thousand times; for, if it yield
Or more or less, so far it follows force.
And thus did these, when they had power to seek
The hallow'd place again.　In them, had will
Been perfect, such as once upon the bars
Held Laurence firm, or wrought in Scævola
To his own hand remorseless; to the path,
Whence they were drawn, their steps had hasten'd
　　back,
When liberty return'd: but in too few,
Resolve, so stedfast, dwells.[3]　And by these words,
If duly weigh'd, that argument is void,

　[1] From the days of Aristotle downwards, it was disputed as to
how far these views expressed by Plato in the *Timæus* should be
taken literally.
　[2] " That the ways of Divine Justice are often inscrutable to
man, ought rather to be a motive to faith than an inducement to
heresy " (Cary).　There are several other interpretations of this
passage.
　[3] Aristotle defines a compulsory action as one of which the
origination is from without, the agent's will contributing nothing.
As regards the proper act of the will itself, no violence can be
done to the will.　Dante's examples of such firm resolution are
drawn, as usual, impartially from religious and secular history;
St. Laurence in his fiery martyrdom on the gridiron, and Mucius
Scævola burning his own hand before Porsenna.

Which oft might have perplex'd thee still.　But now
Another question thwarts thee, which, to solve,
Might try thy patience without better aid.
I have, no doubt, instill'd into thy mind,
That blessed spirit may not lie; since near
The source of primal truth it dwells for aye:
And thou mightst after of Piccarda learn
That Constance held affection to the veil;
So that she seems to contradict me here.
Not seldom, brother, it hath chanced for men
To do what they had gladly left undone;
Yet, to shun peril, they have done amiss:
E'en as Alcmæon, at his father's suit
Slew his own mother; [1] so made pitiless
Not to lose pity.　On this point bethink thee,
That force and will are blended in such wise
As not to make the offence excusable.
Absolute will agrees not to the wrong;
But inasmuch as there is fear of woe
From non-compliance, it agrees.　Of will
Thus absolute, Piccarda spake, and I
Of the other; [2] so that both have truly said."

　　Such was the flow of that pure rill, that well'd
From forth the fountain of all truth; and such
The rest, that to my wandering thoughts I found.

　　"O thou, of primal love the prime delight,
Goddess!" I straight replied, "whose lively words
Still shed new heat and vigour through my soul;
Affection fails me to requite thy grace
With equal sum of gratitude: be His
To recompense, who sees and can reward thee.
Well I discern, that by that Truth [3] alone
Enlighten'd, beyond which no truth may roam,
Our mind can satisfy her thirst to know:
Therein she resteth, e'en as in his lair

----

[1] Cf. *Inf.* xx. and *Purg.* xii.

[2] The distinction is between the absolute (or hypothetical) will,
which does not consent to what is bad, and the respective (or actual)
will, which chooses what under the circumstances seems the lesser
evil.　The absolute will of Piccarda and Constance kept firm to their
vows, but their respective or actual wills yielded to violence; and,
in this sense, they fell voluntarily from the state of perfection to
which they had been called.

[3] God, the First Cause, who as universal truth is the object of
the intellect.

The wild beast, soon as she hath reach'd that bound.
And she hath power to reach it; else desire
Were given to no end. And thence doth doubt
Spring, like a shoot, around the stock of truth;
And it is nature which, from height to height,
On to the summit prompts us. This invites
This doth assure me, Lady! reverently
To ask thee of another truth, that yet
Is dark to me. I fain would know, if man
By other works well done may so supply
The failure of his vows, that in your scale
They lack not weight." I spake; and on me straight
Beatrice look'd, with eyes that shot forth sparks
Of love celestial, in such copious stream,
That, virtue sinking in me overpower'd,
I turn'd; and downward bent, confused, my sight.

CANTO V

ARGUMENT

The question proposed in the last Canto is answered. Dante
    ascends with Beatrice to the planet Mercury, which is the
    second Heaven; and here he finds a multitude of spirits, one
    of whom offers to satisfy him of any thing he may desire to
    know from them.

" IF beyond earthly wont, the flame of love
Illume me, so that I o'ercome thy power
Of vision, marvel not: but learn the cause
In that perfection of the sight, which, soon
As apprehending, hasteneth on to reach
The good it apprehends. I well discern,
How in thine intellect already shines
The light eternal, which to view alone
Ne'er fails to kindle love; and if aught else
Your love seduces, 'tis but that it shows
Some ill-mark'd vestige of that primal beam.

" This wouldst thou know: if failure of the vow
By other service may be so supplied,
As from self-question to assure the soul."

Thus she her words, not heedless of my wish,
Began; and thus, as one who breaks not off
Discourse, continued in her saintly strain.
" Supreme of gifts, which God, creating, gave

Of His free bounty, sign most evident
Of goodness, and in His account most prized,
Was liberty of will; the boon, wherewith
All intellectual creatures, and them sole,
He hath endow'd.[1]   Hence now thou mayst infer
Of what high worth the vow, which so is framed,
That when man offers, God well-pleased accepts:
For in the compact between God and him,
This treasure, such as I describe it to thee,
He makes the victim; and of his own act.
What compensation therefore may he find?
If that, whereof thou hast oblation made,
By using well thou think'st to consecrate,
Thou wouldst of theft do charitable deed.
Thus I resolve thee of the greater point.

   " But forasmuch as holy Church, herein
Dispensing, seems to contradict the truth
I have discover'd to thee, yet behoves
Thou rest a little longer at the board,
Ere the crude aliment which thou hast ta'en,
Digested fitly, to nutrition turn;
Open thy mind to what I now unfold;
And give it inward keeping. Knowledge comes
Of learning well retain'd, unfruitful else.

   " This sacrifice, in essence, of two things
Consisteth: one is that, whereof 'tis made;
The covenant, the other. For the last,
It ne'er is cancel'd, if not kept: and hence
I spake, erewhile, so strictly of its force.
For this it was enjoin'd the Israelites,
Though leave were given them, as thou know'st, to change
The offering, still to offer.[2] The other part,
The matter and the substance of the vow,
May well be such, as that, without offence,
It may for other substance be exchanged.
But, at his own discretion, none may shift
The burden on his shoulders; unreleased
By either key, the yellow and the white.

[1] " Nothing in man is more sublime, nothing more worthy than free will. In it man was created to the image of God. Liberty of the will is impressed with the image of changeless eternity and the likeness of the Divine Majesty " (Richard of St. Victor).
[2] Cf. Leviticus xxvii.

Nor deem of any change, as less than vain,
If the last bond be not within the new
Included, as the quatre in the six.
No satisfaction therefore can be paid
For what so precious in the balance weighs,
That all in counterpoise must kick the beam.[1]
Take then no vow at random : ta'en, with faith
Preserve it ; yet not bent, as Jephthah once,
Blindly to execute a rash resolve,
Whom better it had suited to exclaim,
' I have done ill,' than to redeem his pledge
By doing worse : or, not unlike to him
In folly, that great leader of the Greeks ;
Whence, on the altar, Iphigenia mourn'd
Her virgin beauty, and hath since made mourn
Both wise and simple, even all, who hear
Of so fell sacrifice.[2]   Be ye more staid,
O Christians ! not, like feather, by each wind
Removeable ; nor think to cleanse yourselves
In every water.   Either testament,
The old and new, is yours : and for your guide,
The shepherd of the Church.   Let this suffice
To save you.   When by evil lust enticed,
Remember ye be men, not senseless beasts ;
Nor let the Jew, who dwelleth in your streets,
Hold you in mockery.   Be not, as the lamb,
That, fickle wanton, leaves its mother's milk,
To dally with itself in idle play.''

[1] The essence of a vow comprises two things : the matter that
is vowed and the sacrifice of the will.   The latter can never be
cancelled ; the former may be commuted to another matter of
greater value, not on the individual's own responsibility, but by
the authority of the Church with the keys of judgment and absolution (cf. *Purg.* ix.).   But there are some vows for which compensation is impossible, such as the solemn vow of perpetual
chastity—a doctrine that mediæval theologians mainly based
upon Ecclesiasticus xxvi. 20, which in the Vulgate reads : *Omnis
ponderatio non est digna continentis animæ:* "There is no
price worthy of a continent soul."

[2] The examples of rash vows from Scripture and mythology :
Jephthah the Gileadite who sacrificed his daughter, in fulfilment
of his vow to offer up whatever should come forth of the doors
of his house to meet him, when he returned from subduing the
children of Ammon ; Agamemnon who, having vowed to sacrifice
to Artemis the fairest thing that the year brought forth, was compelled to give his daughter Iphigenia as victim (she was, however, saved by the intervention of the goddess).

Such were the words that Beatrice spake :
These ended, to that region,[1] where the world
Is liveliest, full of fond desire she turn'd.

   Though mainly prompt new question to propose,
Her silence and changed look did keep me dumb.
And as the arrow, ere the cord is still,
Leapeth unto its mark ; so on we sped
Into the second realm. There I beheld
The dame, so joyous, enter, that the orb
Grew brighter at her smiles ; and, if the star
Were moved to gladness, what then was my cheer,
Whom nature hath made apt for every change !

   As in a quiet and clear lake the fish,
If aught approach them from without, do draw
Towards it, deeming it their food ; so drew
Full more than thousand splendours towards us ;
And in each one was heard : " Lo ! one arrived
To multiply our loves !" and as each came,
The shadow, streaming forth effulgence new,
Witness'd augmented joy.[2] Here, Reader ! think,
If thou didst miss the sequel of my tale,
To know the rest how sorely thou wouldst crave ;
And thou shalt see what vehement desire
Possess'd me, soon as these had met my view,
To know their state. " O born in happy hour !
Thou, to whom grace vouchsafes, or e'er thy close
Of fleshly warfare, to behold the thrones
Of that eternal triumph ; know, to us
The light communicated, which through Heaven
Expatiates without bound. Therefore, if aught
Thou of our beams wouldst borrow for thine aid,
Spare not ; and, of our radiance, take thy fill."

   Thus of those piteous spirits one bespake me ;
And Beatrice next : " Say on ; and trust
As unto gods."—" How in the light supreme
Thou harbour'st, and from thence the virtue bring'st,

[1] " The equator is the swiftest part of the heaven (*Conv.* ii. 4).
The equinoctial point is the germinal point of the universe (*Par.* x.
1–21). The sun is the source of all mortal life (*Par.* xxii. 116).
Dante's words may apply to any of the three ; but since, at the
date of the Vision, the sun is at the equinoctial point, they all
coincide " (Wicksteed).

[2] The accidental joy of the Saints (as distinguished from their
essential joy, which consists in the possession of the Beatific
Vision) is increased with every soul that enters Paradise.

That, sparkling in thine eyes, denotes thy joy,
I mark : but, who thou art, am still to seek;
Or wherefore, worthy spirit ! for thy lot
This sphere assign'd, that oft from mortal ken
Is veil'd by other's beams." [1]　I said; and turn'd
Toward the lustre, that with greeting kind
Erewhile had hail'd me.　Forthwith, brighter far
Than erst, it wax'd : and, as himself the sun
Hides through excess of light, when his warm gaze
Hath on the mantle of thick vapours prey'd;
Within its proper ray the saintly shape
Was, through increase of gladness, thus conceal'd;
And, shrouded so in splendour, answer'd me,
E'en as the tenour of my song declares.

CANTO VI

ARGUMENT

The spirit, who had offered to satisfy the inquiries of Dante,
declares himself to be the Emperor Justinian; and after
speaking of his own actions, recounts the victories, before
him, obtained under the Roman Eagle.　He then informs our
Poet that the soul of Romeo the pilgrim is in the same star.

" AFTER that Constantine the eagle turn'd
Against the motions of the Heaven, that roll'd
Consenting with its course, when he of yore,
Lavinia's spouse, was leader of the flight; [2]
A hundred years twice told and more, his seat
At Europe's extreme point, the bird of Jove
Held, near the mountains, whence he issued first; [3]
There under shadow of his sacred plumes
Swaying the world, till through successive hands

[1] The planet Mercury, being nearest the sun, is constantly
hidden by it.　The second part of Dante's question, why this spirit
appears in this sphere, is answered at the end of the following
Canto.

[2] " Constantine, in transferring the seat of empire from Rome
to Byzantium, carried the eagle, the imperial ensign, from the west
to the east.　Æneas, on the contrary, had, with better augury,
moved along with the sun's course, when he passed from Troy
to Italy " (Cary).

[3] " Constantinople being situated at the extreme of Europe, and
on the borders of Asia, near those mountains in the neighbourhood
of Troy, from whence the first founders of Rome had emigrated "
(Cary).

To mine he came devolved. Cæsar I was;
And am Justinian; destined by the will
Of that Prime Love, whose influence I feel,
From vain excess to clear the incumber'd laws.[1]
Or e'er that work engaged me, I did hold
In Christ one nature only; with such faith
Contented. But the blessed Agapete,
Who was chief shepherd, he with warning voice
To the true faith recall'd me.[2] I believed
His words: and what he taught, now plainly see,
As thou in every contradiction seest
The true and false opposed. Soon as my feet
Were to the Church reclaim'd, to my great task,
By inspiration of God's grace impell'd,
I gave me wholly; and consign'd mine arms
To Belisarius, with whom Heaven's right hand
Was link'd in such conjointment, 'twas a sign
That I should rest. To thy first question thus
I shape mine answer, which were ended here,
But that its tendency doth prompt perforce
To some addition; that thou well mayst mark,
What reason on each side they have to plead,
By whom that holiest banner is withstood,
Both who pretend its power and who oppose.[3]

" Beginning from that hour, when Pallas died [4]

1 Justinian the Great became Emperor in 527, " a hundred years
twice told and more " since Constantine in 324 had transferred
the seat of empire to Byzantium. Justinian codified Roman Law,
and, by means of his generals, Belisarius and Narses, overthrew
the Goths in Italy, and (temporarily) won back Rome for the
Empire. According to Dante's reading of Roman history, in
Mr. Wicksteed's words, " the Roman Empire existed for the
elaboration and promulgation of Roman Law, as the chosen people
for the preparation of the Gospel." The discourse, which the Poet
puts into the mouth of the imperial legislator, is intended to show
the sanctity of the Empire as a thing immeasurably above the
turmoil of party politics.

2 Justinian does not seem ever to have adhered to the sect of
the Monophysites, who held that in Christ there was the Divine
nature alone. He protected them for a while, through the
influence of his wife Theodora, but was persuaded by Pope
Agapetus (536) to take measures against them.

3 The Ghibellines and Guelfs alike, whether they profess to
support or to oppose the Empire, are foes to its true mission.

4 Pallas, son of Evander, an Arcadian prince who ruled a city
on the site of Rome, formed an alliance with Æneas, and was
slain by Turnus (Æneid, viii.–x.). The summary of Roman history
that follows points the moral, inculcated in Book II. of the De

To give it rule, behold the valorous deeds
Have made it worthy reverence.   Not unknown
To thee, how for three hundred years and more
It dwelt in Alba, up to those fell lists
Where, for its sake, were met the rival three ; [1]
Nor aught unknown to thee, which it achieved
Down from the Sabines' wrong to Lucrece' woe,
With its seven kings conquering the nations round ; [2]
Nor all it wrought, by Roman worthies borne
'Gainst Brennus and the Epirot prince, and hosts
Of single chiefs, or states in league combined
Of social warfare : hence, Torquatus stern,
And Quintius named of his neglected locks,
The Decii, and the Fabii hence acquired
Their fame, which I with duteous zeal embalm. [3]
By it the pride of Arab hordes was quell'd,
When they, led on by Hannibal, o'erpass'd
The Alpine rocks, whence glide thy currents, Po ![4]
Beneath its guidance, in their prime of days
Scipio and Pompey triumph'd ; [5] and that hill

Monarchia, and more slightly in the *Convivio* (iv. 4, 5), that the
Roman People conquered the world not by force of arms, but by
right : " not force but right, and divine right, too, was the beginning of the Roman Empire." The Empire is personified throughout the Canto by the Eagle.

[1] The contention between Alba Longa, where Æneas's son
Ascanius had founded his kingdom, and Rome, which had been
founded by Romulus, an exile from Alba, was decided by the ordeal
of combat between the three Horatii and the three Curiatii :
" Then it was that, the three Alban champions and two of the
Romans being slain, the palm of victory went over to the Romans
under King Hostilius " (*Mon.* ii. 11).

[2] Rome was ruled by seven kings, from the rape of the Sabine
women under Romulus to the violation of Lucretia by Sextus
Tarquinius, which led to the overthrow of the monarchy in
B.C. 510.

[3] Brennus, chief of the Senonian Gauls, who sacked Rome,
B.C. 390 ; Pyrrhus, King of Epirus, defeated by Curius Dentatus at
Beneventum, B.C. 275 ; Titus Manlius Torquatus, dictator and
consul, B.C. 353–340 ; Lucius Quintius Cincinnatus, dictator, B.C.
458, 439.   Three Decii, Publius Decius Mus, died for the common-
wealth " in unbroken family succession," B.C. 340, 295, 279 (cf.
Mon. ii. 5) ; of the numerous Roman heroes of the Fabian family,
the most famous was Quintus Fabius Maximus, who acquired the
surname of *Cunctator* from his prudent policy of delay when
appointed dictator after Hannibal's victory at Lake Trasimene,
B.C. 217.

[4] By an anachronism, Dante identifies the Carthaginians with
the Arabs, the inhabitants of Northern Africa in his own days.

[5] Scipio Africanus the elder distinguished himself against

Under whose summit thou didst see the light,
Rued its stern bearing.[1]   After, near the hour,
When Heaven was minded that o'er all the world
His own deep calm should brood, to Cæsar's hand
Did Rome consign it; [2] and what then it wrought
From Var unto the Rhine, saw Isere's flood,
Saw Loire and Seine, and every vale, that fills
The torrent Rhone.   What after that it wrought,
When from Ravenna it came forth, and leap'd
The Rubicon, was of so bold a flight,
That tongue nor pen may follow it.   Towards Spain
It wheel'd its bands, then toward Dyrrachium smote,
And on Pharsalia, with so fierce a plunge,
E'en the warm Nile was conscious to the pang;
Its native shores Antandros, and the streams
Of Simois revisited, and there
Where Hector lies; then ill for Ptolemy
His pennons shook again; lightening thence fell
On Juba; and the next, upon your west,
At sound of the Pompeian trump, return'd.[3]
  " What following, and in its next bearer's gripe,
It wrought, is now by Cassius and Brutus
Bark'd of in Hell; and by Perugia's sons,
And Modena's, was mourn'd.[4]   Hence weepeth still
Sad Cleopatra, who, pursued by it,

Hannibal at the battle of Ticinus, B.C. 218, when seventeen years
old; Pompey (Cneius Pompeius Magnus) obtained the title of " the
Great " and was awarded a triumph, after his victory over the
Numidian Hiarbas, B.C. 81, in his twenty-fifth year.
  [1] Fiesole, at the foot of which Florence is situated, was destroyed by the Roman Eagle after the defeat of Catiline, B.C. 62.
  [2] The foundation of the Empire by Julius Cæsar was to prepare
the way for that season of universal peace, the earth being
united under one monarch, when the Redeemer should be born.
  [3] In the hands of Cæsar, the Eagle conquered Gaul (B.C. 58–
50), crossed the Rubicon, and carried on war against Pompey's
adherents in Spain (B.C. 49), fought unsuccessfully at Durazzo
(Dyrrachium) and won the decisive victory of Pharsalia (B.C. 48),
after which Pompey fled to Egypt.   In pursuit of Pompey, it
visited the Troad (indicated by the river Simois, that " Hector
once loved," and Antandros, where Æneas started), whence it
had originally come, and in succession overthrew Ptolemy XII.
of Egypt (B.C. 47), compelled King Juba of Numidia to commit
suicide (B.C. 46), and defeated the sons of Pompey at Munda in
Spain (B.C. 45).
  [4] In the hands of Augustus, the Eagle overthrew Brutus and
Cassius at Philippi (B.C. 42), and destroyed Perugia (B.C. 40).   It
had previously (B.C. 43) defeated Mark Antony at Mutina (Modena).

Took from the adder black and sudden death.[1]
With him it ran e'en to the Red Sea coast;
With him composed the world to such a peace,
That of his temple Janus barr'd the door.[2]

" But all the mighty standard yet had wrought,
And was appointed to perform thereafter,
Throughout the mortal kingdom which it sway'd,
Falls in appearance dwindled and obscured,
If one with steady eye and perfect thought
On the third Cæsar [3] look; for to his hands,
The living Justice, in whose breath I move,
Committed glory, e'en into his hands,
To execute the vengeance of its wrath.

" Hear now, and wonder at, what next I tell.
After with Titus it was sent to wreak
Vengeance for vengeance [4] of the ancient sin.
And, when the Lombard tooth, with fang impure,
Did gore the bosom of the holy Church,
Under its wings, victorious Charlemagne
Sped to her rescue.[5]   Judge then for thyself
Of those, whom I erewhile accused to thee,
What they are, and how grievous their offending,
Who are the cause of all your ills.   The one
Against the universal ensign rears
The yellow lilies; and with partial aim,
That, to himself, the other arrogates :
So that 'tis hard to see who most offends.[6]

---

[1] After the battle of Actium and suicide of Antony, B.C. 30,
Cleopatra killed herself by the bite of an asp.

[2] Egypt being now annexed to the Roman Empire, the temple
of Janus was closed in sign of universal peace.

[3] " The eagle in the hand of Tiberius, the third of the Cæsars,
outdid all its achievements, both past and future, by becoming
the instrument of that mighty and mysterious act of satisfaction
made to the Divine Justice in the Crucifixion of Our Lord "
(Cary).

[4] The destruction of Jerusalem, A.D. 70.   Cf. next Canto.

[5] Charlemagne, in 774, at the summons of Pope Adrian I.,
overthrew Desiderius, King of the Lombards, who was assailing
the papal dominions.   " Dante could not be ignorant that the
reign of Justinian was long prior to that of Charlemagne; but
the spirit of the former emperor is represented, both in this instance and in what follows, as conscious of the events that had
taken place after his own time " (Cary).

[6] The Guelfs oppose the golden lilies of the royal house of
France to the imperial Eagle, the Ghibellines degrade the Eagle
by making it the badge of a party.

Be yours, ye Ghibellines, to veil your arts [1]
Beneath another standard : ill is this
Follow'd of him, who severs it and justice :
And let not with his Guelphs the new-crown'd Charles [2]
Assail it ; but those talons hold in dread,
Which from a lion of more lofty port
Have rent the casing.   Many a time ere now
The sons have for the sire's transgression wail'd :
Nor let him trust the fond belief, that Heaven
Will truck its armour for his lilied shield.

     " This little star is furnish'd with good spirits,
Whose mortal lives were busied to that end,
That honour and renown might wait on them :
And, when desires thus err in their intention,
True love must needs ascend with slacker beam. [3]
But it is part of our delight, to measure
Our wages with the merit ; and admire
The close proportion.   Hence doth heavenly justice
Temper so evenly affection in us,
It ne'er can warp to any wrongfulness.
Of diverse voices is sweet music made :
So in our life the different degrees
Render sweet harmony among these wheels.

     " Within the pearl, that now encloseth us,
Shines Romeo's light, [4] whose goodly deed and fair

---

[1] *Faccian lor arte,* " let them ply their art," carry on their
petty politics.

[2] *Esto Carlo novello,* " this new Charles " (as contrasted with
the *Carlo Magno* mentioned above) : Charles II. of Naples, the
head of the Guelfs in Italy in 1300.

[3] These are the souls of those who in life wrought great deeds
from mixed motives : " those souls whose virtuous deeds had in
them some taint of worldly ambition or anxiety for good repute "
(Wicksteed).

[4] Romeo of Villeneuve (1170–1250) was the chamberlain, or
seneschal, of Count Raymond Berenger IV. of Provence, who died
in 1245, leaving his dominions to his youngest daughter Beatrice,
whom he had made his heiress, under Romeo's guardianship.
According to the legend (told by Villani, vi. 90), a certain *Romeo*
(which means simply " a pilgrim ") came to Raymond's court and
was made his chief minister. He managed the Count's affairs
with fidelity and prudence, and procured royal marriages for his
four daughters. Moved by envy, the Provençal barons persuaded
Raymond to call upon the Romeo to give an account of his
stewardship, upon which the latter demanded his mule, his staff,
and his scrip, and departed as mysteriously as he had come.
The fact that Raymond's chief minister was named Romeo
appears to be the sole foundation for this romantic story.

Met ill acceptance.   But the Provençals,
That were his foes, have little cause for mirth.
Ill shapes that man his course, who makes his wrong
Of other's worth.   Four daughters were there born
To Raymond Berenger; and every one
Became a queen :[1] and this for him did Romeo,
Though of mean state and from a foreign land.
Yet envious tongues incited him to ask
A reckoning of that just one, who return'd
Twelve fold to him for ten.   Aged and poor
He parted thence : and if the world did know
The heart he had, begging his life by morsels,
'Twould deem the praise, it yields him, scantly dealt.''

CANTO VII

ARGUMENT

In consequence of what had been said by Justinian, who together
    with the other spirits has now disappeared, some doubts
    arise in the mind of Dante respecting the human redemption.
    These difficulties are fully explained by Beatrice.

'' *Hosanna Sanctus Deus Sabaoth,*
Superillustrans claritate tuâ
Felices ignes horum malachoth.'' [2]
Thus chanting saw I turn that substance bright,
With fourfold lustre to its orb again,
Revolving; [3] and the rest, unto their dance,
With it, moved also; and, like swiftest sparks,
In sudden distance from my sight were veil'd.

  Me doubt possess'd; and '' Speak,'' it whisper'd me,

[1] Raymond's eldest daughter, Margaret, married St. Louis IX.
of France; the second, Eleanor, married Henry III. of England;
the third, Sancha, married Henry's brother, Richard of Cornwall,
titular King of the Romans; Beatrice, the youngest, inherited
Provence from her father, and, after his death, married Charles
the elder of Anjou, who later became King of Naples and Sicily.
Provence thus became subject to the house of Anjou, under whose
sway the Provençals had '' little cause for mirth.'' Cf. *Purg.* vii.
and xx.

[2] '' Hosanna, holy God of Sabaoth, that with Thy brightness
from on high dost illumine the blessed fires of these kingdoms.''

[3] More accurately : '' Thus, revolving to its own note, I saw
that spirit [Justinian] singing, upon whom the double lustre
[of Legislator and of Emperor] is combined.''

" Speak, speak unto thy lady ; that she quench
Thy thirst with drops of sweetness." Yet blank awe,
Which lords it o'er me, even at the sound
Of Beatrice's name, did bow me down
As one in slumber held.   Not long that mood
Beatrice suffer'd : she, with such a smile,
As might have made one blest amid the flames,
Beaming upon me, thus her words began :
" Thou in thy thought art pondering (as I deem,
And what I deem is truth) how just revenge
Could be with justice punish'd : [1] from which doubt
I soon will free thee ; so thou mark my words ;
For they of weighty matter shall possess thee.
Through suffering not a curb upon the power
That will'd in him, to his own profiting,
That man, who was unborn,[2] condemn'd himself ;
And, in himself, all, who since him have lived,
His offspring : whence, below, the human kind
Lay sick in grievous error many an age ;
Until it pleased the Word of God to come
Amongst them down, to His own person joining
The nature from its Maker far estranged,
By the mere act of His eternal love.
Contemplate here the wonder I unfold :
The nature with its Maker thus conjoin'd,
Created first was blameless, pure and good ;
But, through itself alone, was driven forth
From Paradise, because it had eschew'd
The way of truth and life, to evil turn'd.
Ne'er then was penalty so just as that
Inflicted by the Cross, if thou regard
The nature in assumption doom'd ; ne'er wrong
So great, in reference to Him, who took
Such nature on Him, and endured the doom.
So different effects flow'd from one act :
For by one death God and the Jews were pleased ;

[1] The connection of the Roman Empire with the Atonement is
regarded by Dante as a sovereign argument that its power is
derived from the Divine Will. Even as Christ by His birth,
under the edict of Augustus, confirmed the imperial jurisdiction
from which that edict proceeded, so, by His death under the
vicar of Tiberius, He confirmed the universal penal jurisdiction
of the Emperor over all the human race which was to be
punished in His flesh (*Mon.* ii. 12, 13).

[2] Adam.

And Heaven was open'd, though the earth did quake.
Count it not hard henceforth, when thou dost hear
That a just vengeance was, by righteous court,
Justly revenged.[1] But yet I see thy mind,
By thought on thought arising, sore perplex'd;
And, with how vehement desire, it asks
Solution of the maze.   What I have heard,
Is plain, thou sayst : but wherefore God this way
For our redemption chose, eludes my search.

    " Brother ! no eye of man not perfected,
Nor fully ripen'd in the flame of love,
May fathom this decree.   It is a mark,
In sooth, much aim'd at, and but little kenn'd :
And I will therefore show thee why such way
Was worthiest.   The celestial Love, that spurns
All envying in its bounty, in itself
With such effulgence blazeth, as sends forth
All beauteous things eternal.   What distils
Immediate thence, no end of being knows;
Bearing its seal immutably imprest.
Whatever thence immediate falls, is free,
Free wholly, uncontrollable by power
Of each thing new : by such conformity
More grateful to its Author, whose bright beams,
Though all partake their shining, yet in those
Are liveliest, which resemble Him the most.[2]
These tokens of pre-eminence on man
Largely bestow'd, if any of them fail,
He needs must forfeit his nobility,
No longer stainless.   Sin alone is that,
Which doth disfranchise him, and make unlike
To the Chief Good ; for that its light in him
Is darken'd.   And to dignity thus lost

---

[1] The " righteous court " possibly means the imperial jurisdiction, Dante regarding the Crucifixion as a judicial penalty inflicted
upon the whole of human nature, by the sentence of a regular
judge who had lawfully jurisdiction over the whole world.   It
was only as the work of the Jews, shedding innocent blood for
envy, and wrought upon Christ alone, that it was rightfully
avenged by Titus in the destruction of Jerusalem.

[2] Creation is the work of Divine Love.   What God creates immediately, without the intervention of secondary causes, is
immortal, utterly free, most like to its Creator, and therefore
most beloved by Him.   With these three high prerogatives was
the human soul endowed.   Man lost them when, by Adam's sin, he
was cast out of the Earthly Paradise.

Is no return; unless, where guilt makes void,
He for ill pleasure pay with equal pain.
Your nature, which entirely in its seed
Transgress'd, from these distinctions fell, no less
Than from its state in Paradise; nor means
Found of recovery (search all methods out
As strictly as thou may) save one of these,
The only fords were left through which to wade:
Either, that God had of His courtesy
Released him merely: or else, man himself
For his own folly by himself atoned.

" Fix now thine eye, intently as thou canst,
On the everlasting counsel; and explore,
Instructed by my words, the dread abyss.

" Man in himself had ever lack'd the means
Of satisfaction, for he could not stoop
Obeying, in humility so low,
As high, he, disobeying, thought to soar:
And, for this reason, he had vainly tried,
Out of his own sufficiency, to pay
The rigid satisfaction. Then behoved
That God should by His own ways lead him back
Unto the life, from whence he fell, restored;
By both His ways, I mean, or one alone.
But since the deed is ever prized the more,
The more the doer's good intent appears;
Goodness celestial, whose broad signature
Is on the universe, of all its ways
To raise ye up, was fain to leave out none.
Nor aught so vast or so magnificent,
Either for Him who gave or who received,
Between the last night and the primal day,
Was or can be. For God more bounty show'd,
Giving Himself to make man capable
Of his return to life, than had the terms
Been mere and unconditional release.
And for His justice, every method else
Were all too scant, had not the Son of God
Humbled Himself to put on mortal flesh.[1]

---

[1] The lost prerogatives of the human race could only be recovered
by God freely pardoning, or by man making satisfaction. The
latter course is impossible; a creature's disobedience to an infinite
Creator must be expiated by an act of infinite humility, and man's
satisfaction is finite. It remained, therefore, for God to restore

" Now, to content thee fully, I revert;
And further in some part unfold my speech,
That thou mayst see it clearly as myself.

" I see, thou sayst, the air, the fire I see,
The earth and water, and all things of them
Compounded, to corruption turn, and soon
Dissolve.   Yet these were also things create.
Because, if what were told me, had been true,
They from corruption had been therefore free.

" The Angels, O my brother! and this clime
Wherein thou art, impassible and pure,
I call created, even as they are
In their whole being.   But the elements,
Which thou hast named, and what of them is made,
Are by created virtue inform'd : create,
Their substance; and create, the informing virtue
In these bright stars, that round them circling move.
The soul of every brute and of each plant,
The ray and motion of the sacred lights,
Draw from complexion with meet power endued.[1]
But this our life the Eternal Good inspires
Immediate, and enamours of itself;
So that our wishes rest for ever here.

" And hence thou mayst by inference conclude
Our resurrection certain, if thy mind
Consider how the human flesh was framed,
When both our parents at the first were made." [2]

man by the way of mercy, or by the way of justice, or by both;
and the last course (mercy and justice combined) was most in
accordance with the Divine Goodness—God giving Himself to
man that the Divine Justice might be satisfied by the infinite
humiliation of the Word made Flesh.

[1] The Angels and the Heavens, being created immediately by
God, are immortal and incorruptible, as also is the primal matter,
which is the same in all bodies and still remains through all
changes.   But the substantial forms, which give actual being to
matter, are produced by secondary causes, by the " informing
virtue " which God has created in the stars.   By the influence of
these " sacred lights," the vital principles of plants and animals
(" vegetative " and " sensitive " souls) are similarly drawn out
of their stage of mere potentiality in this primal matter, and given
actual being.   All corporeal substances, thus brought into being by
secondary causes, are subject to corruption and decay.   But the
soul of man is created immediately by God, who has made it
immortal and restless till it rests in Him.

[2] Since the flesh of Adam and Eve was created immediately
by God, and man is to be restored to the prerogatives which were
lost by their fall, the human body also should be immortal.

CANTO VIII

ARGUMENT

The Poet ascends with Beatrice to the third Heaven, which is the
planet Venus; and here finds the soul of Charles Martel, King
of Hungary, who had been Dante's friend on earth, and who
now, after speaking of the realms to which he was heir,
unfolds the cause why children differ in disposition from their
parents.

THE world was, in its day of peril dark,
Wont to believe the dotage of fond love,
From the fair Cyprian deity, who rolls
In her third epicycle,[1] shed on men
By stream of potent radiance: therefore they
Of elder time, in their old error blind,
Not her alone with sacrifice adored
And invocation, but like honours paid
To Cupid and Dione, deem'd of them
Her mother, and her son, him whom they feign'd
To sit in Dido's bosom:[2] and from her,
Whom I have sung preluding, borrow'd they
The appellation of that star, which views
Now obvious, and now averse, the sun.[3]

  I was not ware that I was wafted up
Into its orb; but the new loveliness,
That graced my lady, gave me ample proof
That we had enter'd there.   And as in flame
A sparkle is distinct, or voice in voice
Discern'd, when one its even tenour keeps,
The other comes and goes; so in that light
I other luminaries saw, that coursed
In circling motion, rapid more or less,
As their eternal vision each impels.[4]

   Never was blast from vapour charged with cold,
Whether invisible to eye or no,[5]
Descended with such speed, it had not seem'd

---

[1] The third epicycle is the smaller sphere upon which the planet
of Venus revolves in the third Heaven. Cf. *Conv.* ii. 4.

[2] *Æneid*, i. 718.

[3] Venus appears as a morning star at one part of the year, and
as an evening star at another.

[4] " As each, according to their several deserts, partakes more
or less of the Beatific Vision " (Cary).

[5] Wind or lightning.

To linger in dull tardiness, compared
To those celestial lights, that towards us came,
Leaving the circuit of their joyous ring,
Conducted by the lofty Seraphim.
And after them, who in the van appear'd,
Such an Hosanna sounded as hath left
Desire, ne'er since extinct in me, to hear
Renew'd the strain.   Then, parting from the rest,
One near us drew, and sole began : " We all
Are ready at thy pleasure, well disposed
To do thee gentle service.   We are they
To whom thou in the world erewhile didst sing ;
' O ye ! whose intellectual ministry
' Moves the third Heaven :' [1] and in one orb we roll,
One motion, one impulse, with those who rule
Princedoms in Heaven ; [2] yet are of love so full,
That to please thee 'twill be as sweet to rest."
    After mine eyes had with meek reverence
Sought the celestial guide, and were by her
Assured, they turn'd again unto the light,
Who had so largely promised ; and with voice
That bare the lively pressure of my zeal,
" Tell who ye are," I cried.   Forthwith it grew
In size and splendour, through augmented joy ;
And thus it answer'd : " A short date, below,
The world possess'd me.   Had the time been more,
Much evil, that will come, had never chanced.
My gladness hides thee from me, which doth shine
Around, and shroud me, as an animal
In its own silk enswathed.   Thou lovedst me well,
And hadst good cause ; [3] for had my sojourning

---

[1] *Voi che intendendo il terzo ciel movete:* " Ye who, by understanding, move the third Heaven ;" the opening line of the first
canzone of the *Convivio.*

[2] In the *Convivio* (ii. 6), Dante supposed that it was the Angelic
order of the Thrones that ruled the third Heaven ; he now learns
that it is the Princedoms, or Principalities.

[3] The speaker is Charles Martel (1271–1295), eldest son of
Charles II. of Naples and Mary of Hungary, daughter of Stephen
IV.   Dante probably made his acquaintance in March, 1295,
when he came in great state to Florence, and made himself
exceedingly popular.   His death in the following August, in the
flower of his youth, dispelled the hopes that had been raised by
his amiable character and gallant bearing.   The allusion below,
to " a race of monarchs, sprung through me from Charles and
Rodolph," perhaps indicates the work that Dante expected his

Been longer on the earth, the love I bare thee
Had put forth more than blossoms.   The left bank,
That Rhone, when he hath mixed with Sorga, laves,[1]
In me its lord expected, and that horn
Of fair Ausonia, with its boroughs old,
Bari, and Croton, and Gaeta piled,
From where the Trento disembogues his waves,
With Verde mingled, to the salt-sea flood.[2]
Already on my temples beam'd the crown,
Which gave me sovereignty over the land
By Danube wash'd whenas he strays beyond
The limits of his German shores.[3]   The realm,
Where, on the gulf by stormy Eurus lash'd,
Betwixt Pelorus and Pachynian heights,
The beautiful Trinacria lies in gloom,
(Not through Typhœus, but the vapoury cloud
Bituminous upsteam'd), that too did look
To have its sceptre wielded by a race
Of monarchs, sprung through me from Charles and
        Rodolph ;[4]
Had not ill-lording, which doth desperate make
The people ever, in Palermo raised
The shout of ' death,' re-echoed loud and long.
Had but my brother's foresight kenn'd as much,
He had been warier, that the greedy want
Of Catalonia might not work his bale.[5]

friend to do for Italy.   Married through the influence of Gregory
X., the peacemaking Pope, to Clemenza, or Clementina, the
daughter of the Emperor Rudolf of Hapsburg, his issue might
have reconciled the claims of Guelf and Ghibelline. *Cf.* Villani,
viii. 13, and *Purg.* vii.   He now describes the regions over which
he would have ruled, had he lived.

    [1] Provence, of which the Angevin sovereigns of Naples were
Counts in succession to the elder Charles.

    [2] The kingdom of Naples.

    [3] Hungary, of which he had already (1290) been crowned king
at Naples in his mother's right.

    [4] Sicily, too, would have expected his issue as her kings, had
not the misgovernment of his house led to the Sicilian Vespers
in Palermo (1282), the general rising against the French which
resulted in the island accepting the rule of the house of Aragon.

    [5] Let the speaker's brother Robert, Duke of Calabria, take
warning from the Sicilian Vespers.   While Robert and his
brothers, Louis and John, were hostages in Spain after the
release of their father Charles in 1288 [cf. *Purg.* xx.], until 1295,
the former made the acquaintance of a number of needy Catalan adventurers who accompanied him to Italy, and were given

And truly need there is that he forecast,
Or other for him, lest more freight be laid
On his already over-laden bark.
Nature in him, from bounty fallen to thrift,
Would ask the guard of braver arms, than such
As only care to have their coffers fill'd."

　" My liege ! it doth enhance the joy thy words
Infuse into me, mighty as it is,
To think my gladness manifest to thee,
As to myself, who own it, when thou look'st
Into the source and limit of all good,
There, where thou markest that which thou dost speak,
Thence prized of me the more.　Glad thou hast made
　　me :
Now make intelligent, clearing the doubt
Thy speech hath raised in me ; for much I muse,
How bitter can spring up,[1] when sweet is sown."

　I thus inquiring ; he forthwith replied :
" If I have power to show one truth, soon that
Shall face thee, which thy questioning declares
Behind thee now conceal'd.　The Good, that guides
And blessed makes this realm which thou dost mount,
Ordains its providence to be the virtue
In these great bodies : nor the natures only
The all-perfect Mind provides for, but with them
That which preserves them too ; for nought, that lies
Within the range of that unerring bow,
But is as level with the destined aim,
As ever mark to arrow's point opposed.[2]

office and employment by him when he succeeded to the throne of
Naples.　Their grasping conduct made both them and their master
detested.　The lines that follow are supposed to allude to Robert's
shipwreck in 1301.

[1] How is it that, in spite of what we read in the Gospels about
a good tree bringing forth good fruit, the contrary is actually
found among mankind?

[2] " The Supreme Being uses these spheres as the intelligent instruments of His providence in the conduct of terrestrial natures ;
so that these natures cannot but be conducted aright, unless
these heavenly bodies should themselves fail from not having been
made perfect at first, or the Creator of them should fail.　To this
Dante replies, that nature, he is satisfied, thus directed must do
her part.　Charles Martel then reminds him, that he had learned
from Aristotle, that human society requires a variety of conditions,
and consequently a variety of qualifications in its members.　Accordingly, men, he concludes, are born with different powers and

Were it not thus, these Heavens, thou dost visit,
Would their effect so work, it would not be
Art, but destruction; and this may not chance,
If th' intellectual powers, that move these stars,
Fail not, and who, first faulty made them, fail.
Wilt thou this truth more clearly evidenced?"

To whom I thus: " It is enough: no fear,
I see, lest nature in her part should tire."

He straight rejoin'd: " Say, were it worse for man,
If he lived not in fellowship on earth?"

" Yea," answer'd I; " nor here a reason needs."

" And may that be, if different estates
Grow not of different duties in your life?
Consult your teacher,[1] and he tells you ' no.' "

Thus did he come, deducing to this point,
And then concluded: " For this cause behoves,
The roots, from whence your operations come,
Must differ. Therefore one is Solon born;
Another, Xerxes; and Melchisedec
A third; and he a fourth, whose airy voyage
Cost him his son. In her circuitous course,
Nature, that is the seal to mortal wax,
Doth well her art, but no distinction owns
'Twixt one or other household.[2] Hence befals
That Esau is so wide of Jacob: hence
Quirinus[3] of so base a father springs,

capacities, caused by the influence of the heavenly bodies at the
time of their nativity; on which influence, and not on their parents,
those powers and capacities depend. Having thus resolved the
question proposed, Charles Martel adds, by way of corollary, that
the want of observing their natural bent in the destination of men
to their several offices in life, is the occasion of much of the
disorder that prevails in the world " (Cary).

[1] Aristotle, in the *Politics*, shows that the individual, when
isolated, is not self-sufficing, but like a mere part in relation to
the whole. A State is a body of citizens sufficing for the purposes
of life. In order that a State should be sulf-sufficing, there must
be distribution of functions and of duties. Cf. *Conv.* iv. 4.

[2] This diversity in offices and professions being necessary, it
must proceed from the diversity of different dispositions in man—
there must be different dispositions, that is, to produce this result.
The legislator (Solon), the leader of armies (Xerxes), the priest
(Melchisedec), and the craftsman (Dædalus) are all needed, and
the revolving Heavens stamp men with these qualities without
regard to the origin of the individual.

[3] " Romulus, born of so obscure a father that his parentage was
attributed to Mars " (Cary).

He dates from Mars his lineage.   Were it not
That Providence celestial overruled,
Nature, in generation, must the path
Traced by the generator still pursue
Unswervingly.   Thus place I in thy sight
That, which was late behind thee.   But, in sign
Of more affection for thee, 'tis my will
Thou wear this corollary.   Nature ever,
Finding discordant fortune, like all seed
Out of its proper climate, thrives but ill.
And were the world below content to mark
And work on the foundation nature lays,
It would not lack supply of excellence.
But ye perversely to religion strain
Him, who was born to gird on him the sword,
And of the fluent phraseman make your king :
Therefore your steps have wander'd from the path." [1]

CANTO IX

ARGUMENT

The next spirit, who converses with our Poet in the planet Venus,
is the amorous Cunizza. To her succeeds Folco, or Folques,
the Provençal bard, who declares that the soul of Rahab the
harlot is there also ; and then, blaming the Pope for his
neglect of the Holy Land, prognosticates some reverse to the
papal power.

AFTER solution of my doubt, thy Charles,
O fair Clemenza, of the treachery spake,
That must befal his seed : but, " Tell it not,"
Said he, " and let the destined years come round."
Nor may I tell thee more, save that the meed
Of sorrow well-deserved shall quit your wrongs. [2]

---

[1] "The Wisdom of God hath divided the Genius of men according to the different affairs of the World ; and varied their inclination according to the variety of Actions to be performed therein.
Which they who consider not, rudely rushing upon professions and
ways of life unequal to their natures, dishonour not only themselves and their Functions, but pervert the harmony of the whole
World " (Sir Thomas Browne, *Vulgar and Common Errors*).   The
" fluent phraseman " is Robert of Calabria, who as king was sur-
named " the wise," and highly extolled by Petrarch.

[2] The Clemenza here addressed, as one living while Dante is
relating his vision, is the daughter of Charles Martel and wife of
Louis X. of France.   Her mother, the elder Clemenza, died in

And now the visage of that saintly light
Was to the sun, that fills it, turn'd again,
As to the good, whose plenitude of bliss
Sufficeth all. O ye misguided souls!
Infatuate, who from such a good estrange
Your hearts, and bend your gaze on vanity,
Alas for you!—And lo! toward me, next,
Another of those splendent forms approach'd,
That, by its outward bright'ning, testified
The will it had to pleasure me. The eyes
Of Beatrice, resting, as before,
Firmly upon me, manifested forth
Approval of my wish. "And O," I cried,
"Blest spirit! quickly be my will perform'd;
And prove thou to me, that my inmost thoughts
I can reflect on thee." [1] Thereat the light,
That yet was new to me, from the recess,
Where it before was singing, thus began,
As one who joys in kindness: "In that part
Of the depraved Italian land, which lies
Between Rialto and the fountain-springs
Of Brenta and of Piava, there doth rise,
But to no lofty eminence, a hill,
From whence erewhile a firebrand did descend,
That sorely shent the region. [2] From one root
I and it sprang; my name on earth Cunizza:
And here I glitter, for that by its light
This star o'ercame me. Yet I nought repine,
Nor grudge myself the cause of this my lot:

1296. On the death of Charles II., in 1309, Robert usurped the crown of Naples, to the exclusion of Carobert, the son of Charles Martel, who had become King of Hungary in 1308.

[1] In the Beatific Vision the spirits see all that it concerns them to see, even thoughts that have not found utterance. Let this soul prove this by answering Dante's unspoken questions.

[2] In the castle of Romano, between Venice and the sources of the Brenta and Piave, was born the horrible tyrant Ezzelino (cf. *Inf.* xii.). The speaker is his sister, Cunizza da Romano, famous for her amorous intrigues. She was successively the wife of four husbands and the mistress of various lovers, of whom the poet Sordello (*Purg.* vi.–viii.) was one; but she had also a reputation for deeds of charity. In 1265, in the house of Cavalcante de' Cavalcanti, she executed a deed liberating the serfs of her father's family (of which she was the sole survivor). She died, probably in Florence, in 1279 or 1280. Dante places her here as the type of a penitent.

Which haply vulgar hearts can scarce conceive.[1]
  " This jewel, that is next me in our Heaven,
Lustrous and costly, great renown hath left,
And not to perish, ere these hundred years
Five times absolve their round. Consider thou,
If to excel be worthy man's endeavour,
When such life may attend the first.[2] Yet they
Care not for this, the crowd that now are girt
By Adice and Tagliamento, still
Impenitent, though scourged.[3] The hour is near
When for their stubbornness, at Padua's marsh
The water shall be changed, that laves Vicenza.[4]
And where Cagnano meets with Sile, one
Lords it, and bears his head aloft, for whom
The web is now a-warping.[5] Feltro too
Shall sorrow for its godless shepherd's fault,
Of so deep stain, that never, for the like,
Was Malta's bar unclosed. Too large should be
The skillet that would hold Ferrara's blood,
And wearied he, who ounce by ounce would weigh it,
The which this priest, in show of party-zeal,
Courteous will give;[6] nor will the gift ill suit
The country's custom. We descry above
Mirrors, ye call them Thrones, from which to us
Reflected shine the judgments of our God:[7]
Whence these our sayings we avouch for good."

[1] She no longer remembers the sins of her past, nor desires a
higher place in Paradise.

[2] " When the mortal life of man may be attended by so lasting
and glorious a memory, which is a kind of second life " (Cary).
This " jewel " is Folco, of whom more below.

[3] The inhabitants of the March of Treviso (the scene of her own
sinful life), bounded by the Adige and the Tagliamento.

[4] The Bacchiglione shall be dyed red with blood of the Paduans
defeated by Can Grande in 1314.

[5] Riccardo da Cammino, brother of Gaia (*Purg.* xvi.) and husband of Giovanna Visconti (*Purg.* viii.), was treacherously murdered at Treviso, where the rivers Sile and Cagnano meet, in 1312.

[6] In 1314, the Bishop of Feltre, Alessandro Novello, surrendered
certain Ferrarese gentlemen who had sought his protection to
Pino della Tosa, who then governed Ferrara as vicar of King
Robert, by whom they were put to death. Malta was either a
tower near Padua where Ezzelino incarcerated his victims, or a
papal prison for criminal priests either at Viterbo or on the Lake
of Bolsena.

[7] The Angelic order of the Thrones are the mirrors of God's
judgments, which He executes by them.

She ended; and appear'd on other thoughts
Intent, re-entering on the wheel she late
Had left. That other joyance [1] meanwhile wax'd
A thing to marvel at, in splendour glowing,
Like choicest ruby stricken by the sun.
For, in that upper clime, effulgence comes
Of gladness, as here laughter : and below,
As the mind saddens, murkier grows the shade. [2]
    " God seeth all : and in Him is thy sight,"
Said I, " blest spirit ! Therefore will of His
Cannot to thee be dark. Why then delays
Thy voice to satisfy my wish untold ;
That voice, which joins the inexpressive song,
Pastime of Heaven, the which those Ardours sing,
That cowl them with six shadowing wings outspread ? [3]
I would not wait thy asking, wert thou known
To me, as throughly I to thee am known."
    He, forthwith answering, thus his words began :
" The valley of waters, widest next to that
Which doth the earth engarland, shapes its course,
Between discordant shores, against the sun
Inward so far, it makes meridian there,
Where was before the horizon. [4] Of that vale
Dwelt I upon the shore, 'twixt Ebro's stream
And Macra's, that divides with passage brief
Genoan bounds from Tuscan. East and west
Are nearly one to Begga and my land
Whose haven erst was with its own blood warm. [5]

---

[1] Folco.

[2] " As joy is expressed by laughter on earth, so is it by an
increase of splendour in Paradise ; and, on the contrary, grief is
betokened in Hell by augmented darkness " (Cary).

[3] *Cf.* Isaiah vi. 2. The Seraphim, the Angels that represent
the Divine Love, set the measure to the mystical music of Paradise.

[4] " At Gibraltar, where the Mediterranean [' the valley of
waters '] flows out of the ocean, the sun (according to Dante's
geography) is on the horizon when it is noon-day on the Levant.
Thus the stretch of the sea makes zenith at its end of what is
horizon at its beginning ; *i. e.* it extends over a quadrant "
(Wicksteed).

[5] He describes Marseilles, which is on nearly the same meridian
as Bougia in Algeria. The bloodshed referred to was on the
occasion of Cæsar's victory in B.C. 49. The troubadour Folquet,
whom the Italians call Folco, or Folchetto, a Genoese by origin,
was born at Marseilles shortly before 1160. A famous lover in
early manhood, he became a Cistercian monk, and in 1205 was
made Bishop of Toulouse, in which capacity he befriended St.

Who knew my name, were wont to call me Folco;
And I did bear impression of this Heaven,
That now bears mine : for not with fiercer flame
Glow'd Belus' daughter, injuring alike
Sichæus and Creusa,[1] than did I,
Long as it suited the unripen'd down
That fledged my cheek; nor she of Rhodope,
That was beguiled of Demophoon;[2]
Nor Jove's son, when the charms of Iole
Were shrined within his heart.[3]   And yet there bides
No sorrowful repentance here, but mirth,
Not for the fault, (that doth not come to mind,)
But for the virtue, whose o'erruling sway
And providence have wrought thus quaintly.[4]   Here
The skill is look'd into, that fashioneth
With such effectual working, and the good
Discern'd, accruing to the lower world
From this above.[5]   But fully to content
Thy wishes all that in this sphere have birth,
Demands my further parle.   Inquire thou wouldst,
Who of this light is denizen, that here
Beside me sparkles, as the sunbeam doth
On the clear wave.   Know then, the soul of Rahab [6]
Is in that gladsome harbour; to our tribe
United, and the foremost rank assign'd.
She to this Heaven, at which the shadow ends

Dominic, and carried on a sanguinary persecution of the Albigenses until his death in 1231.

[1] By her intrigue with Æneas, Dido wronged the memory of the latter's wife Creusa and of her own husband Sychæus.

[2] The Thracian (" Rhodopeian ") Phyllis slew herself for love of Demophoon, the son of Theseus.

[3] Dante has not " Jove's son," but *Alcide*, Hercules, whose love for Iole caused his death.

[4] *Ma del valor ch'ordinò e provide*, " but for the Power which ordained and provided."

[5] *Il bene per che al mondo di su quel di giù torna:* " the good whereby the world below is brought back unto the world above." Mr. Wicksteed explains : " In Heaven there is no repentance, because the sin is only seen or remembered as the occasion of the act of God by which the fallen one was uplifted again into his true element : and it is on this divine power and grace that the soul's whole thought and love are centred."

[6] Rahab, the harlot of Jericho, was regarded by the Fathers as a type of the Church, the scarlet cord being a symbol of the blood of Christ, and the two spies she received from Joshua being the two Testaments.

Of your sublunar world,[1] was taken up,
First, in Christ's triumph, of all souls redeem'd:
For well behoved, that, in some part of Heaven,
She should remain a trophy, to declare
The mighty conquest won with either palm;[2]
For that she favour'd first the high exploit
Of Joshua on the Holy Land, whereof
The Pope recks little now. Thy city, plant
Of him, that on his Maker turn'd the back,
And of whose envying so much woe hath sprung,
Engenders and expands the cursed flower,
That hath made wander both the sheep and lambs,
Turning the shepherd to a wolf.[3] For this,
The Gospel and great teachers laid aside,
The decretals, as their stuft margins show,
Are the sole study.[4] Pope and Cardinals,
Intent on these, ne'er journey but in thought
To Nazareth, where Gabriel oped his wings.
Yet it may chance, ere long, the Vatican,
And other most selected parts of Rome,
That were the grave of Peter's soldiery,
Shall be deliver'd from the adulterous bond."[5]

CANTO X

ARGUMENT

Their next ascent carries them into the sun, which is the fourth
    Heaven. Here they are encompassed with a wreath of blessed
    spirits, twelve in number. Thomas Aquinas, who is one of
    these, declares the names and endowments of the rest.

LOOKING into His First-Born with the Love,
Which breathes from both eternal, the first Might

[1] The third Heaven is the last of the three spheres which, according to the astronomy of Dante's day, lie within reach of the
conical shadow cast by the earth through space. In the allegory,
it signifies the earthly taint in the lives of the three classes of
blessed spirits that appear to Dante in these three lower spheres.

[2] When His hands were nailed to the Cross.

[3] Florence, founded by Mars (who is here identified with Satan),
coins the lily-stamped florin which is seducing Pope and people alike.

[4] The Scriptures and the writings of the great Doctors are
neglected for the study of the books of canon and ecclesiastical
law, in which lies the way to preferment. Cf. *Epist.* viii. 7, and
Mon. iii. 3.

[5] He refers most probably to the general reformation and renovation of the Church that is to follow the coming of the *Veltro.*

Ineffable, wherever eye or mind
Can roam, hath in such order all disposed,
As none may see and fail to enjoy. Raise, then,
O reader ! to the lofty wheels, with me,
Thy ken directed to the point, whereat
One motion strikes on the other.[1] There begin
Thy wonder of the mighty Architect,
Who loves His work so inwardly, His eye
Doth ever watch it. See, how thence oblique
Brancheth the circle, where the planets roll [2]
To pour their wished influence on the world ;
Whose path not bending thus, in Heaven above
Much virtue would be lost, and here on earth
All power well nigh extinct : or, from direct
Were its departure distant more or less,
I' the universal order, great defect
Must, both in Heaven and here beneath, ensue.[3]

Now rest thee, reader ! on thy bench, and muse
Anticipative of the feast to come ;
So shall delight make thee not feel thy toil.
Lo ! I have set before thee ; for thyself
Feed now : the matter I indite, henceforth
Demands entire my thought. Join'd with the part,
Which late we told of, the great minister
Of nature, that upon the world imprints
The virtue of the Heaven, and doles out
Time for us with his beam, went circling on
Along the spires, where each hour sooner comes ;[4]
And I was with him, weetless of ascent,
But as a man, that weets his thought, ere thinking.[5]

For Beatrice, she who passeth on

---

[1] The equinoctial point where the equator and the zodiac inter-
sect, and the daily and the annual movements of the sun may
therefore be said to strike one upon the other.

[2] The zodiac.

[3] " Let him reflect how the influences of the sun and planets—
the seasons and other alternations—would be effective over a
smaller part of the earth if the inclination of the ecliptic were less,
and would be too violent in their contrasts if it were greater "
(Wicksteed).

[4] The sun, which moves along a spiral up or down, had reached
the spring equinoctial point in his upward spiral, during which
he rises earlier every day.

[5] " But of the ascent I was not conscious, otherwise than a
man is conscious, before the beginning of a thought, of its
coming " (Vernon).

So suddenly from good to better, time
Counts not the act, oh then how great must needs
Have been her brightness! What there was i' th'
    sun,
(Where I had enter'd,) not through change of hue,
But light transparent—did I summon up
Genius, art, practice—I might not so speak,
It should be e'er imagined: yet believed
It may be, and the sight be justly craved.
And if our fantasy fail of such height,
What marvel, since no eye above the sun
Hath ever travel'd? Such are they dwell here,
Fourth family of the Omnipotent Sire,
Who of His Spirit and of His Offspring shows;
And holds them still enraptured with the view.[1]
And thus to me Beatrice: " Thank, oh thank
The Sun of Angels, Him, who by His grace
To this perceptible hath lifted thee.''

    Never was heart in such devotion bound,
And with complacency so absolute
Disposed to render up itself to God,
As mine was at those words: and so entire
The love for Him, that held me, it eclipsed
Beatrice in oblivion. Nought displeased
Was she, but smiled thereat so joyously,
That of her laughing eyes the radiance brake
And scatter'd my collected mind abroad.

    Then saw I a bright band, in liveliness
Surpassing, who themselves did make the crown,
And us their centre: yet more sweet in voice,
Than, in their visage, beaming. Cinctured thus,
Sometime Latona's daughter we behold,
When the impregnate air retains the thread
That weaves her zone. In the celestial court,
Whence I return, are many jewels found,
So dear and beautiful, they cannot brook
Transporting from that realm: and of these lights
Such was the song. Who doth not prune his wing
To soar up thither, let him look from thence

----

[1] " Such was here the fourth family of the high Father (the fourth group of Saints, the Doctors and great Teachers), who ever satiates it by showing how He breathes and how He begets ''—by revealing to them the generation of the Son and the procession of the Holy Ghost.

For tidings from the dumb.[1]   When, singing thus,
Those burning suns had circled round us thrice,
As nearest stars around the fixed pole;
Then seem'd they like to ladies, from the dance
Not ceasing, but suspense, in silent pause,
Listening, till they have caught the strain anew:
Suspended so they stood: and, from within,
Thus heard I one, who spake: " Since with its beam
The Grace, whence true love lighteth first his flame,
That after doth increase by loving, shines
So multiplied in thee, it leads thee up
Along this ladder, down whose hallow'd steps
None e'er descend, and mount them not again;
Who from his phial should refuse thee wine
To slake thy thirst, no less constrained were,
Than water flowing not unto the sea.[2]
Thou fain wouldst hear, what plants are these, that
     bloom
In the bright garland, which, admiring, girds
This fair dame round, who strengthens thee for Heaven.
I, then, was of the lambs, that Dominic
Leads, for his saintly flock, along the way
Where well they thrive, not swoln with vanity.
He, nearest on my right hand, brother was,
And master to me: Albert of Cologne
Is this; and, of Aquinum, Thomas I.[3]
If thou of all the rest wouldst be assured,
Let thine eye, waiting on the words I speak,
In circuit journey round the blessed wreath.
That next resplendence issues from the smile

[1] The song cannot be translated into mortal speech, but will be comprehended by those who win their way to Paradise.

[2] " The rivers might as easily cease to flow towards the sea, as we could deny thee thy request " (Cary).

[3] Albertus Magnus (1193–1280) of Cologne, " the Universal Doctor," and Thomas Aquinas (1225–1274), of the Counts of Aquino in the kingdom of Naples, " the Angelical Doctor," master and pupil, are the great theological lights of the Dominican order. Albertus began what is known as " christianising " Aristotle, adopting his wisdom and philosophical method to give a new shape to the truths of revelation. Aquinas completed this work in his Aristotelian treatises, in his *Summa contra Gentiles*, and his *Summa Theologica*—by all of which Dante was profoundly influenced. A man of extraordinary sweetness and holiness, he was canonized in 1323, two years after Dante's death. His *Summa Theologica* is still regarded as of supreme authority in the Church of Rome.

Of Gratian, who to either forum lent
Such help, as favour wins in Paradise.[1]
The other, nearest, who adorns our quire,
Was Peter, he that with the widow gave
To holy Church his treasure.[2] The fifth light,
Goodliest of all, is by such love inspired,
That all your world craves tidings of his doom:
Within, there is a lofty light, endow'd
With sapience so profound, if truth be truth,
That with a ken of such wide amplitude
No second hath arisen.[3] Next behold
That taper's radiance, to whose view was shown,
Clearliest, the nature and the ministry
Angelical, while yet in flesh it dwelt.[4]
In the other little light serenely smiles
That pleader for the christian temples, he,
Who did provide Augustin of his lore.[5]
Now, if thy mind's eye pass from light to light,
Upon my praises following, of the eighth
Thy thirst is next. The saintly soul, that shows
The world's deceitfulness, to all who hear him,
Is, with the sight of all the good that is,
Blest there. The limbs, whence it was driven, lie
Down in Cieldauro;[6] and from martyrdom

---

[1] Franciscus Gratianus, an Italian Benedictine monk of the twelfth century, strove to bring civil and ecclesiastical law into harmony.

[2] Peter the Lombard (d. circa 1160), an Augustinian, known as the "Master of the Sentences," wrote the four books of *Sentences*, the chief summary of mediæval theology before the advent of St. Thomas Aquinas, who composed a commentary upon it. In the prologue, Peter speaks of himself as "desiring with the poor widow (Luke xxi. 1–4) to cast something out of our poverty into the treasury of the Lord."

[3] Solomon, concerning whose salvation men disputed in the Middle Ages.

[4] Dionysius the Areopagite (Acts xvii.), to whom were ascribed certain mystical writings, especially one on the *Celestial Hierarchy*, which were probably composed in the fifth or sixth century. Cf. *Par.* xxviii.

[5] Paolus Orosius, whose *Historiæ adversum Paganos* was written at the suggestion of St. Augustine, to show by the evidence of history that Christianity had not ruined the world as the Pagans asserted. For "christian temples," read "christian times."

[6] This "saintly soul" is Boëthius (Anicius Manlius Torquatus Severinus Boëthius), Roman consul and philosopher, who was tortured to death at Pavia by order of Theodoric in 525. While in prison awaiting his end, he wrote his great book, *De Consolatione*

And exile came it here.　Lo! further on,
Where flames the ardurous spirit of Isidore; [1]
Of Bede; [2] and Richard, more than man, erewhile,
In deep discernment.[3]　Lastly this, from whom
Thy look on me reverteth, was the beam
Of one, whose spirit, on high musings bent,
Rebuked the lingering tardiness of death.
It is the eternal light of Sigebert
Who 'scaped not envy, when of truth he argued,
Reading in the straw-litter'd street." [4]　Forthwith,
As clock, that calleth up the spouse of God [5]
To win her Bridegroom's love at matin's hour,
Each part of other fitly drawn and urged,
Sends out a tinkling sound, of note so sweet,
Affection springs in well-disposed breast;
Thus saw I move the glorious wheel; thus heard
Voice answering voice, so musical and soft,
It can be known but where day endless shines.

Philosophiæ, " a book of noble pagan morality and religion, maintaining that even in this world, and as judged by human reason, the life of the virtuous man is to be preferred before that of the vicious, and the ways of God to man may be justified " (Wicksteed).　Cf. *Conv.* ii. 13.　He was buried in S. Piero Cieldauro at Pavia.　His persecutors being Arians, the Church has claimed him as a Catholic martyr.　His influence upon Dante is very marked throughout the *Convivio* and the *Divina Commedia*.

1 Isidore of Seville, *d.* 636, the writer of the chief mediæval encyclopedia.

2 Venerable Bede, the English ecclesiastical historian, died at Jarrow in 735.

3 Richard of St. Victor, the great Augustinian mystic and friend of St. Bernard (*d.* 1173).　In the letter to Can Grande (*Epist.* x. 28), Dante appeals to Richard's chief treatise on Contemplation (known as *Benjamin major*).

4 Sigier of Brabant, a professor in the University of Paris in the latter part of the thirteenth century, opposed the mendicant orders and was driven from his chair.　He was either murdered by a fanatical friar, or executed by the papal authorities at Orvieto, probably in 1283.　The " straw-litter'd street " is the Rue du Fouarre in Paris, where he delivered his lectures.

5 The Church.

CANTO XI

ARGUMENT

Thomas Aquinas enters at large into the life and character of
St. Francis; and then solves one of two difficulties, which
he perceived to have risen in Dante's mind from what he had
heard in the last Canto.

O FOND anxiety of mortal men!
How vain and inconclusive arguments
Are those, which make thee beat thy wings below.
For statutes one, and one for aphorisms
Was hunting; [1] this the priesthood follow'd; that,
By force or sophistry, aspired to rule;
To rob, another; and another sought,
By civil business, wealth; one, moiling, lay
Tangled in net of sensual delight;
And one to wistless indolence resign'd;
What time from all these empty things escaped,
With Beatrice, I thus gloriously
Was raised aloft, and made the guest of Heaven.
  They of the circle to that point, each one,
Where erst it was, had turn'd; and steady glow'd,
As candle in his socket.   Then within
The lustre,[2] that erewhile bespake me, smiling
With merer gladness, heard I thus begin:
  " E'en as His beam illumes me, so I look
Into the Eternal Light, and clearly mark
Thy thoughts, from whence they rise.   Thou art in
      doubt,
And wouldst, that I should bolt my words afresh
In such plain open phrase, as may be smooth
To thy perception, where I told thee late
That ' well they thrive;' and that ' no second such
Hath risen,' which no small distinction needs.
  " The Providence, that governeth the world,
In depth of counsel by created ken
Unfathomable, to the end that she,[3]
Who with loud cries was 'spoused in precious blood,
Might keep her footing towards her well-beloved,[4]
Safe in herself and constant unto Him,

---

[1] One was studying law, another medicine.
[2] The spirit of St. Thomas Aquinas.   [3] The Church.
[4] Christ.

Hath two ordain'd, who should on either hand
In chief escort her : one, seraphic all
In fervency ; for wisdom upon earth,
The other, splendour of cherubic light.
I but of one will tell : he tells of both,
Who one commendeth, which of them soe'er
Be taken : for their deeds were to one end.[1]

     " Between Tupino, and the wave that falls
From blest Ubaldo's chosen hill, there hangs
Rich slope of mountain high, whence heat and cold
Are wafted through Perugia's eastern gate :
And Nocera with Gualdo, in its rear,
Mourn for their heavy yoke.[2]   Upon that side,
Where it doth break its steepness most, arose
A sun upon the world, as duly this
From Ganges doth : therefore let none, who speak
Of that place, say Ascesi ; for its name
Were lamely so deliver'd ; but the East,
To call things rightly, be it henceforth styled.[3]
He was not yet much distant from his rising,
When his good influence 'gan to bless the earth.
A dame,[4] to whom none openeth pleasure's gate
More than to death, was, 'gainst his father's will,
His stripling choice : and he did make her his,
Before the spiritual court, by nuptial bonds,
And in his father's sight : [5] from day to day,
Then loved her more devoutly.   She, bereaved

[1] St. Francis, the seraphical saint of love, and St. Dominic, the cherubical saint of wisdom, gave new life to the Church. Aquinas, as a Dominican, utters the panegyric of St. Francis, and bewails the degeneration of his own order.

[2] Aquinas describes Assisi (where St. Francis was born in 1182), between the Tupino and the Chiascio, which rises in a mountain near Gubbio, where St. Ubaldo (d. 1160) chose out a hermitage. Nocera and Gualdo, small towns in central Italy, were subjected to the heavy yoke of the house of Anjou.

[3] " Ascesi, an old form of Assisi, may be translated ' I have ascended.' A play upon the word, in connection with Oriente, is found by some commentators. The comparison of Francis to the rising Sun is ancient and widespread. ' Glowing as the light-bearer and as the morning star, yea, even as the rising Sun, illuminating, cleansing and fertilising the world like some new luminary, was Francis seen to arise,' says the Prologue of one of the earliest Lives " (Wicksteed).

[4] Holy Poverty.

[5] Francis renounced his possessions before the Bishop of Assisi, in the presence of his father, Pietro Bernardone.

Of her first husband,[1] slighted and obscure,
Thousand and hundred years and more, remain'd
Without a single suitor, till he came.
Nor aught avail'd, that, with Amyclas,[2] she
Was found unmoved at rumour of his voice,
Who shook the world : nor aught her constant boldness,
Whereby with Christ she mounted on the Cross,
When Mary stay'd beneath.   But not to deal
Thus closely with thee longer, take at large
The lovers' titles—Poverty and Francis.
Their concord and glad looks, wonder and love,
And sweet regard gave birth to holy thoughts,
So much, that venerable Bernard[3] first
Did bare his feet, and, in pursuit of peace
So heavenly, ran, yet deem'd his footing slow.
O hidden riches !   O prolific good !
Egidius bares him next, and next Sylvester,[4]
And follow, both, the bridegroom : so the bride
Can please them.   Thenceforth goes he on his way,
The father and the master, with his spouse,
And with that family, whom now the cord
Girt humbly : nor did abjectness of heart
Weigh down his eyelids, for that he was son
Of Pietro Bernardone, and by men
In wonderous sort despised.   But royally
His hard intention he to Innocent
Set forth ; and, from him, first received the seal
On his religion.[5]   Then, when numerous flock'd
The tribe of lowly ones, that traced his steps,
Whose marvelous life deservedly were sung
In heights empyreal ; through Honorius' hand
A second crown, to deck their Guardian's virtues,

[1] Christ.

[2] The fisherman Amyclas, secure in his poverty, was unawed at
Cæsar's summons and untouched by the tumults of the times. *Cf.*
Lucan, *Phars.* v. 520–531.

[3] Bernard of Quintavalle, a wealthy citizen of Assisi, gave up
all his possessions and became the first follower of St. Francis.

[4] Egidio (Giles) was the third companion of St. Francis (Dante
does not mention Peter of Catania, the second) ; his sayings,
Verba Aurea, are still read. He died in 1261. Silvestro was a
priest of Assisi, the only ecclesiastic among the first Franciscans ;
he was a kinsman of St. Clare.

[5] The Franciscan rule was approved by Pope Innocent III. in
1210.

Was by the eternal Spirit inwreath'd : [1] and when
He had, through thirst of martyrdom, stood up
In the proud Soldan's presence, and there preach'd
Christ and His followers,[2] but found the race
Unripen'd for conversion; back once more
He hasted, (not to intermit his toil,)
And reap'd Ausonian lands.   On the hard rock,
'Twixt Arno and the Tiber, he from Christ
Took the last signet, which his limbs two years
Did carry.[3]   Then, the season come that He,
Who to such good had destined him, was pleased
To advance him to the meed, which he had earn'd
By his self-humbling; to his brotherhood,
As their just heritage, he gave in charge
His dearest lady : and enjoin'd their love
And faith to her; and, from her bosom, will'd
His goodly spirit should move forth, returning
To its appointed kingdom; nor would have
His body laid upon another bier.[4]

   " Think now of one, who were a fit colleague
To keep the bark of Peter, in deep sea,
Helm'd to right point; and such our Patriarch [5] was.
Therefore who follow him as he enjoins,
Thou mayst be certain, take good lading in.
But hunger of new viands tempts his flock; [6]
So that they needs into strange pastures wide
Must spread them : and the more remote from him
The stragglers wander, so much more they come
Home, to the sheep-fold, destitute of milk.
There are of them, in truth, who fear their harm,
And to the shepherd cleave; but these so few,
A little stuff may furnish out their cloaks.

   [1] The papal approbation was confirmed by Honorius III. in
1223.
   [2] In 1219, Francis went to the East and attempted to convert
the Soldan of Egypt.
   [3] The third and final confirmation of his work was given to
Francis by Christ Himself, when in 1224, on " the hard rock " of
La Verna, he received the *stigmata*, the imprint of the five wounds
of the Lord's Passion.
   [4] He died at Assisi, October 4, 1226—stretched naked on the
ground, according to his wish, in the arms of Poverty, " his
dearest lady."
   [5] St. Dominic.
   [6] The Dominicans, who have deserted their founder's sheep-fold
in the quest of ecclesiastical honours and preferment.

" Now, if my words be clear; if thou have ta'en
Good heed; if that, which I have told, recal
To mind; thy wish may be in part fulfill'd :
For thou wilt see the plant from whence they split; [1]
And he shall see, who girds him, what that means,[2]
' That well they thrive, not swoln with vanity.' "

CANTO XII

ARGUMENT

A second circle of glorified souls encompasses the first. Buonaven-
tura, who is one of them, celebrates the praises of Saint
Dominic, and informs Dante who the other eleven are, that
are in this second circle or garland.

SOON as its final word the blessed flame
Had raised for utterance, straight the holy mill [3]
Began to wheel; nor yet had once revolved,
Or e'er another, circling, compass'd it,
Motion to motion, song to song, conjoining;
Song, that as much our muses doth excel,
Our Syrens with their tuneful pipes, as ray
Of primal splendour doth its faint reflex.

As when, if Juno bid her handmaid forth,
Two arches parallel, and trick'd alike,
Span the thin cloud, the outer taking birth
From that within (in manner of that voice
Whom love did melt away, as sun the mist),[4]

[1] The rule ordained by St. Dominic.

[2] There are two alternative readings : *vedrai il coregger che
argomenta*, " thou shalt see the rebuke that is intended;" and
vedrai il coreggier che argomenta, " thou shalt see the leather-girt
friar (the ideal Dominican) what he means," when he thus rebukes
his degenerate order. The Dominicans wear a leather girdle
instead of the Franciscan cord.

[3] As soon as Aquinas has ended, the circle of blessed spirits
moves round the Poet.

[4] " One rainbow giving back the image of the other, as sound
is reflected by Echo, that nymph who was melted away by her
fondness for Narcissus, as vapour is melted by the sun. The
reader will observe in the text not only a second and third simile
within the first, but two mythological and one sacred allusion
bound up together with the whole. Even after this accumulation
of imagery, the two circles of spirits, by whom Dante and Beatrice
were encompassed, are by a bold figure termed two garlands of
never-fading roses. Indeed there is a fulness of splendour, even
to prodigality, throughout the beginning of this Canto " (Cary).

And they who gaze, presageful call to mind
The compact, made with Noah, of the world
No more to be o'erflow'd; about us thus,
Of sempiternal roses, bending, wreathed
Those garlands twain; and to the innermost
E'en thus the external answer'd. When the footing,
And other great festivity, of song,
And radiance, light with light accordant, each
Jocund and blythe, had at their pleasure still'd,
(E'en as the eyes, by quick volition moved,
Are shut and raised together,) from the heart
Of one amongst the new lights moved a voice,
That made me seem like needle to the star,
In turning to its whereabout; [1] and thus
Began : " The love, that makes me beautiful,
Prompts me to tell of the other guide, for whom
Such good of mine is spoken.   Where one is,
The other worthily should also be;
That as their warfare was alike, alike
Should be their glory.   Slow, and full of doubt,
And with thin ranks, after its banner moved
The army of Christ, (which it so dearly cost
To reappoint,) when its imperial Head,
Who reigneth ever, for the drooping host
Did make provision, thorough grace alone,
And not through its deserving.   As thou heard'st,
Two champions to the succour of His spouse
He sent, who by their deeds and words might join
Again His scatter'd people.   In that clime
Where springs the pleasant west-wind to unfold
The fresh leaves, with which Europe sees herself
New-garmented; nor from those billows far,
Beyond whose chiding, after weary course,
The sun doth sometimes hide him; safe abides

[1] This spirit out of the second circle, who makes Dante turn
to him as the magnetic needle to the pole, is the Franciscan
" Seraphic Doctor," St. Bonaventura (1221–1274), whose name in
the world was Giovanni Fidanza. In life he was an intimate
friend and colleague of Thomas Aquinas. As minister-general of
the Franciscans, he wrote the official life of St. Francis, which
Dante has closely followed in the previous Canto. Shortly before
his death, he was made Cardinal and Bishop of Albano by
Gregory X. He was a voluminous writer on mystical and
scholastic theology. Following the example of Aquinas, he now
proceeds to extol St. Dominic, and to rebuke the corruption of his
own Franciscan order.

The happy Callaroga,[1] under guard
Of the great shield, wherein the lion lies
Subjected and supreme. And there was born
The loving minion of the Christian faith,
The hallow'd wrestler, gentle to his own,
And to his enemies terrible.[2] So replete
His soul with lively virtue, that when first
Created, even in the mother's womb,
It prophesied. When, at the sacred font,
The spousals were complete 'twixt faith and him,
Where pledge of mutual safety was exchanged,
The dame, who was his surety, in her sleep
Beheld the wondrous fruit, that was from him
And from his heirs to issue.[3] And that such
He might be construed, as indeed he was,
She was inspired to name him of his owner,
Whose he was wholly; and so call'd him Dominic.[4]
And I speak of him, as the labourer,
Whom Christ in His own garden chose to be
His help-mate. Messenger he seem'd, and friend
Fast-knit to Christ; and the first love he show'd,
Was after the first counsel [5] that Christ gave.
Many a time his nurse, at entering, found
That he had risen in silence, and was prostrate,
As who should say, ' My errand was for this.'
O happy father ! Felix rightly named.
O favour'd mother ! rightly named Joanna;
If that do mean, as men interpret it.[6]
Not for the world's sake, for which now they toil
Upon Ostiense and Taddeo's lore;[7]

1 Calahorra, near the Gulf of Gascony, under the rule of the
kings of Castile, in whose arms the lion is now above, now below
the castle.

2 St. Dominic (Guzman) was born at Calahorra in 1170, and
died at Bologna in 1221.

3 Before his birth, Dominic's mother dreamed that she was
going to bring forth a dog with a burning torch in his mouth
that would set the world aflame. His godmother had a vision, in
which she saw a star upon his brow that illumined all the earth.

4 *Dominicus* = belonging to the Lord.

5 Evangelical Poverty. Matt. xix. 21.

6 Felix, " favoured by fortune ;" Joanna, " grace of the Lord."

7 Henry of Susa, Cardinal Bishop of Ostia (*d.* 1271), a famous
Decretalist ; Taddeo Alderotti (*d.* 1303), a writer on medicine who
made a bad translation into Italian of Aristotle's *Ethics* (cf. *Conv.*
i. 10).

But for the real manna, soon he grew
Mighty in learning; and did set himself
To go about the vineyard, that soon turns
To wan and wither'd, if not tended well:
And from the see,[1] (whose bounty to the just
And needy is gone by, not through its fault,
But his who fills it basely,) he besought,
No dispensation for commuted wrong,
Nor the first vacant fortune, nor the tenths
That to God's paupers rightly appertain,
But, 'gainst an erring and degenerate world,
Licence to fight, in favour of that seed
From which the twice twelve cions gird thee round.[2]
Then, with sage doctrine and good will to help,
Forth on his great apostleship he fared,
Like torrent bursting from a lofty vein;
And, dashing 'gainst the stocks of heresy,[3]
Smote fiercest, where resistance was most stout.
Thence many rivulets have since been turn'd,
Over the garden catholic to lead
Their living waters, and have fed its plants.

" If such, one wheel [4] of that two-yoked car,
Wherein the holy Church defended her,
And rode triumphant through the civil broil;
Thou canst not doubt its fellow's excellence,[5]
Which Thomas, ere my coming, hath declared
So courteously unto thee. But the track,
Which its smooth fellies made, is now deserted:
That, mouldy mother is, where late were lees.[6]
His family, that wont to trace his path,

1 " The apostolic see, which no longer continues its wonted
liberality towards the indigent and deserving; not indeed through
its own fault, as its doctrines are still the same, but through the
fault of the pontiff, who is seated in it " (Cary).

2 When Dominic went to Rome (in 1202), he did not ask leave
to make unjust gains on condition of devoting a part to pious
purposes, nor for the next fat benefice vacant, nor to apply tithes
to his own advantage, but leave to fight against the heretics in
behalf of Catholic truth, the seed from which these twenty-four
blessed spirits have sprung. He founded his order of Dominicans,
or Friars Preachers, at Toulouse in 1215.

3 The Albigenses.

4 St. Dominic.

5 The excellence of St. Francis.

6 " But the rule of St. Francis is already deserted; and the lees
of the wine are turned into mouldiness " (Cary).

Turn backward, and invert their steps; erelong
To rue the gathering in of their ill crop,
When the rejected tares in vain shall ask
Admittance to the barn. I question not
But he, who search'd our volume, leaf by leaf,
Might still find page with this inscription on't,
'I am as I was wont.' Yet such were not
From Acquasparta nor Casale, whence,
Of those who come to meddle with the text,
One stretches and another cramps its rule.[1]
Bonaventura's life in me behold,
From Bagnoregio; one, who, in discharge
Of my great offices, still laid aside
All sinister aim.[2] Illuminato here,
And Agostino join me :[3] two they were,
Among the first of those barefooted meek ones,
Who sought God's friendship in the cord : with them
Hugues of Saint Victor; Pietro Mangiadore;
And he of Spain in his twelve volumes shining;
Nathan the prophet; Metropolitan
Chrysostom; and Anselmo; and, who deign'd
To put his hand to the first art, Donatus.
Raban is here;[4] and at my side there shines

[1] There are some faithful followers of St. Francis still; but
such will not be found among the adherents of Matteo d'Acquasparta, the minister-general of the order at the epoch of the
vision, who relaxed the rule, nor those of Ubertino da Casale, who
was leading the "spirituals," or party of the strict observance,
who wished to make the said rule impossibly severe. Matteo,
one of the Cardinals of Boniface VIII., interfered as papal legate in
the Florentine factions, in 1300 and 1301, with disastrous results;
Ubertino, to avoid making a fresh schism among the Franciscans,
left the order in 1317.

[2] Sempre posposi la sinistra cura, "always placed the care of
temporal affairs behind." Bonaventura was born at Bagnoregio,
or Bagnorea, near Bolsena. As minister-general of the Franciscans, he attempted at once to put a check upon the relaxations
of one party and to restrain the spiritual vagaries of the other.

[3] Illuminato accompanied St. Francis in his mission to the
Soldan, and was still living, as Bishop of Assisi, in 1282; Agostino
died on the same day as St. Francis, after a wonderful vision of
the latter's going up into Paradise.

[4] Hugh of St. Victor (d. 1141), the master of Peter the Lombard
and Richard of St. Victor, was the first of the Augustinian school
of mystics that flourished at the abbey of St. Victor's at Paris;
to which also belonged Pietro Mangiadore (Petrus Comestor,
"Peter the Eater of Books," d. 1179), who wrote the Historia
Scholastica, a history of the Church from Genesis to the Acts of

Calabria's abbot, Joachim, endow'd
With soul prophetic.[1] The bright courtesy
Of friar Thomas and his goodly lore,
Have moved me to the blazon of a peer
So worthy;[2] and with me have moved this throng.''

CANTO XIII

ARGUMENT

Thomas Aquinas resumes his speech. He solves the other of those
doubts which he discerned in the mind of Dante, and warns
him earnestly against assenting to any proposition without
having duly examined it.

LET him, who would conceive what now I saw,
Imagine, (and retain the image firm
As mountain rock, the whilst he hears me speak,)
Of stars, fifteen, from midst the ethereal host
Selected, that, with lively ray serene,
O'ercome the massiest air : thereto imagine
The wain, that, in the bosom of our sky,

the Apostles. Peter of Spain wrote a much-used treatise on
Logic in twelve books ; he was Pope for a few months as John
XXI., in succession to Adrian V. (*Purg.* xix.), and was killed in
1277 by the fall of the papal palace at Viterbo. Nathan the prophet
(2 Sam. xii.) and John Chrysostom (*d.* 407), Archbishop of Constantinople, alike, under the old law and the new, rebuked wickedness in high places. St. Anselm (1033–1109), Archbishop of Can-
terbury, who wrote profound treatises on the Blessed Trinity and
the Incarnation, is side by side with Ælius Donatus, who wrote
an elementary Latin grammar in the fourth century. Rabanus
Maurus, Archbishop of Mayence (*d.* 856), a Benedictine who had
been a pupil of Alcuin, may be said in his voluminous writings
to sum up the learning of the ninth century.

1 Joachim, called of Flora, or Fiore, in Calabria, where he
founded a monastery, was a Cistercian monk who died in 1202.
He claimed to have a peculiar gift from God of interpreting the
prophetical books of the Scriptures with special reference to the
history of the Church. He taught that a new dispensation was
at hand, the third epoch, which would be one of perfect love and
spiritual freedom. This was known as the " Eternal Gospel "
(*cf.* Rev. xiv. 6), and was greedily seized upon by the spiritual
party among the Franciscans, one of whom, Fra Gherardo da
Borgo San Donnino, wrote a book entitled *Introduction to the
Eternal Gospel*, which in 1256 was condemned as heretical. Bonaventura himself was, probably against his own will, largely concerned in the persecution of the friars who held these views and
were known as Joachists.

2 *Cotanto paladino*, St. Dominic.

Spins ever on its axle night and day,
With the bright summit of that horn, which swells
Due from the pole, round which the first wheel rolls,
To have ranged themselves in fashion of two signs
In Heaven, such as Ariadne made,
When death's chill seized her; and that one of them
Did compass in the other's beam; and both
In such sort whirl around, that each should tend
With opposite motion; [1] and, conceiving thus,
Of that true constellation, and the dance
Twofold, that circled me, he shall attain
As 'twere the shadow; for things there as much
Surpass our usage, as the swiftest Heaven
Is swifter than the Chiana. [2]   There was sung
No Bacchus, and no Io Pæan, but
Three Persons in the Godhead, and in one
Person that nature and the human join'd.

The song and round were measured : and to us
Those saintly lights attended, happier made
At each new ministering. Then silence brake
Amid the accordant sons of Deity,
That luminary, [3] in which the wondrous life
Of the meek man of God was told to me;
And thus it spake : " One ear o' the harvest thresh'd,
And its grain safely stored, sweet charity
Invites me with the other to like toil. [4]

" Thou know'st, that in the bosom, whence the rib
Was ta'en to fashion that fair cheek, whose taste
All the world pays for; and in that, which pierced
By the keen lance, both after and before
Such satisfaction offer'd as outweighs
Each evil in the scale; whate'er of light

[1] " Whoever would conceive the sight that now presented itself
to me, must imagine to himself fifteen of the brightest stars in
Heaven, together with seven stars of Arcturus Major and two of
Arcturus Minor, ranged in two circles, one within the other,
each resembling the crown of Ariadne, and moving round in
opposite directions " (Cary).

[2] A river in Tuscany, noted in Dante's time for its slow
motion, flowing through the pestilential Valdichiana into the
Tiber. Its course was completely altered in the nineteenth
century.

[3] Thomas Aquinas, who had related the life of St. Francis.

[4] He has answered Dante's first difficulty, touching the ideals
of the mendicant orders, and will now solve the second, concerning
the wisdom of Solomon.

To human nature is allow'd, must all
Have by His virtue been infused, who form'd
Both one and other: and thou thence admirest
In that I told thee, of beatitudes,
A second there is none to him enclosed
In the fifth radiance.[1]   Open now thine eyes
To what I answer thee; and thou shalt see
Thy deeming and my saying meet in truth,
As centre in the round. That which dies not,
And that which can die, are but each the beam
Of that idea, which our Sovereign Sire
Engendereth loving;[2] for that lively light,
Which passeth from His splendour,[3] not disjoin'd
From Him, nor from His love triune with them,[4]
Doth, through His bounty, congregate itself,
Mirror'd, as 'twere, in new existences;[5]
Itself unalterable, and ever one.

"Descending hence unto the lowest powers,[6]
Its energy so sinks, at last it makes
But brief contingencies; for so I name
Things generated, which the heavenly orbs
Moving, with seed or without seed, produce.
Their wax, and that which molds it, differ much:
And thence with lustre, more or less, it shows
The ideal stamp imprest:[7] so that one tree,
According to his kind, hath better fruit,
And worse: and, at your birth, ye, mortal men,
Are in your talents various. Were the wax

[1] Adam and Christ must have had all the perfection of human
nature. How then could the wisdom of Solomon, the spirit in
the fifth light of the first circle, have been peerless?
[2] All created things, immortal or mortal, are reflections of the
Divine Idea, the Word of God.
[3] *Quella viva luce che sì mea dal suo lucente*, "that living
Light [the Word] that emanates from its Source of Light;" the
lumen de lumine of the Nicene Creed.
[4] The Holy Spirit.
[5] The right reading is *nove sussistenze*, "nine existences,"
either the nine moving Heavens or the nine orders of Angels.
[6] Lowest potentialities, the lowest vegetative and sensitive life.
[7] The substantial form, that which gives a thing its being,
is the likeness of a Divine idea stamped upon matter. But the
primal matter ("their wax"), and the influence of the heavenly
spheres ("that which molds it") which give form to what is not
created immediately by God, are not uniformly correspondent
("molded with nice exactness") and in their best disposition;
and, therefore, the idea is more or less imperfectly expressed.

Molded with nice exactness, and the Heaven
In its disposing influence supreme,
The brightness of the seal should be complete :
But nature [1] renders it imperfect ever ;
Resembling thus the artist, in her work,
Whose faltering hand is faithless to his skill.
Therefore, if fervent Love dispose, and mark
The lustrous Image of the primal Virtue,
There all perfection is vouchsafed ; and such
The clay was made, accomplish'd with each gift,
That life can teem with ; such the burden fill'd
The virgin's bosom : [2] so that I commend
Thy judgment, that the human nature ne'er
Was, or can be, such as in them it was.

" Did I advance no further than this point ;
' How then had he no peer ?' thou might'st reply.
But, that what now appears not, may appear
Right plainly, ponder, who he was, and what
(When he was bidden ' Ask ') the motive, sway'd
To his requesting. I have spoken thus,
That thou mayst see, he was a king, who ask'd
For wisdom, to the end he might be king
Sufficient : not, the number to search out
Of the celestial movers ; or to know,
If necessary with contingent e'er
Have made necessity ; or whether that
Be granted, that first motion is ; or if,
Of the mid circle, can by art be made
Triangle, with its corner blunt or sharp. [3]

" Whence, noting that, which I have said, and this,
Thou kingly prudence and that ken mayst learn,
At which the dart of my intention aims.
And, marking clearly, that I told thee, ' Risen,'
Thou shalt discern it only hath respect
To kings, of whom are many, and the good

---

[1] God's instrument when He employs secondary causes.

[2] When the Blessed Trinity (the primal Virtue or Power of the
Father, the clear Vision—i. e. Wisdom, hardly " lustrous image "—
of the Son, the fervent Love of the Holy Spirit) creates immediately,
all perfection is acquired. Therefore, in Adam and in the humanity of Christ, human nature was at its highest perfection.

[3] Solomon did not ask for the wisdom that would enable him
to comprehend all theological, metaphysical, or scientific problems,
but simply the wisdom that would fit him to be a king ; " an
understanding heart to judge the people." Cf. 1 Kings iii.

Are rare. With this distinction take my words;
And they may well consist with that which thou
Of the first human father dost believe,
And of our well-beloved.[1]   And let this
Henceforth be lead unto thy feet, to make
Thee slow in motion, as a weary man,
Both to the ' yea ' and to the ' nay ' thou seest not.
For he among the fools is down full low,
Whose affirmation, or denial,[2] is
Without distinction, in each case alike.
Since it befals, that in most instances
Current opinion leans to false : and then
Affection bends the judgment to her ply.

   " Much more than vainly doth he loose from shore,
Since he returns not such as he set forth,
Who fishes for the truth and wanteth skill.
And open proofs of this unto the world
Have been afforded in Parmenides,
Melissus, Bryso,[3] and the crowd beside,
Who journey'd on, and knew not whither : so did
Sabellius, Arius,[4] and the other fools,
Who, like to scymitars, reflected back
The scripture-image by distortion marr'd.

   " Let not the people be too swift to judge;
As one who reckons on the blades in field,
Or e'er the crop be ripe.   For I have seen
The thorn frown rudely all the winter long,
And after bear the rose upon its top;
And bark, that all her way across the sea
Ran straight and speedy, perish at the last
E'en in the haven's mouth. Seeing one steal,
Another bring his offering to the priest,
Let not Dame Birtha and Sir Martin thence
Into Heaven's counsels deem that they can pry;[5]
For one of these may rise, the other fall."

---

[1] Adam and Christ.

[2] Cary quotes Plato, *Theætetus:* " For any one might make
yet absurder concessions than these, not paying strict attention to
terms, according to the way in which we are for the most part
accustomed both to affirm and to deny."

[3] These three Greek philosophers are held up by Aristotle as
examples of false reasoning; Dante refers to the Stagirite's con-
futation of the two former in *Mon.* iii. 4.

[4] The famous heretics of the third and fourth centuries.

[5] "'Let not short-sighted mortals presume to decide on the

CANTO XIV

ARGUMENT

Solomon, who is one of the spirits in the inner circle, declares what the appearance of the blest will be after the resurrection of the body. Beatrice and Dante are translated into the fifth Heaven, which is that of Mars; and here behold the souls of those, who had died fighting for the true faith, ranged in the sign of a cross, athwart which the spirits move to the sound of a melodious hymn.

FROM centre to the circle, and so back
From circle to the centre, water moves
In the round chalice, even as the blow
Impels it, inwardly, or from without.
Such was the image [1] glanced into my mind,
As the great spirit of Aquinum ceased;
And Beatrice, after him, her words
Resumed alternate : " Need there is (though yet
He tells it to you not in words, nor e'en
In thought) that he should fathom to its depth
Another mystery. Tell him, if the light,
Wherewith your substance blooms, shall stay with you
Eternally, as now; and, if it doth,
How, when ye shall regain your visible forms, [2]
The sight may without harm endure the change,
That also tell." As those, who in a ring
Tread the light measure, in their fitful mirth
Raise loud the voice, and spring with gladder bound;
Thus, at the hearing of that pious suit,
The saintly circles, in their tourneying
And wondrous note, attested new delight.

Whoso laments, that we must doff this garb
Of frail mortality, thenceforth to live
Immortally above; he hath not seen
The sweet refreshing of that heavenly shower.

future doom of any man, from a consideration of his present character and actions.' This is meant as an answer to the doubts entertained respecting the salvation of Solomon " (Cary). *Donna Berta* and *Ser Martino,* proverbial names for a gossip, or " the man in the street."

[1] " The voice of Thomas Aquinas proceeding from the circle to the centre; and that of Beatrice, from the centre to the circle " (Cary).

[2] At the resurrection of the body.

Him, who lives ever, and for ever reigns
In mystic union of the Three in One,
Unbounded, bounding all, each spirit thrice
Sang, with such melody, as, but to hear,
For highest merit were an ample meed.
And from the lesser orb the goodliest light,[1]
With gentle voice and mild, such as perhaps
The Angel's once to Mary, thus replied :
" Long as the joy of Paradise shall last,
Our love shall shine around that raiment, bright
As fervent ; fervent as, in vision, blest ;
And that as far, in blessedness, exceeding,
As it hath grace, beyond its virtue, great.
Our shape, regarmented with glorious weeds
Of saintly flesh, must, being thus entire,
Show yet more gracious.   Therefore shall increase
Whate'er, of light, gratuitous imparts
The Supreme Good ; light, ministering aid,
The better to disclose His glory : whence,
The vision needs increasing, must increase
The fervour, which it kindles ; and that too
The ray, that comes from it.   But as the gleed
Which gives out flame, yet in its whiteness shines
More livelily than that, and so preserves
Its proper semblance ; thus this circling sphere
Of splendour shall to view less radiant seem,
Than shall our fleshly robe, which yonder earth
Now covers.   Nor will such excess of light
O'erpower us, in corporeal organs made
Firm, and susceptible of all delight."
    So ready and so cordial an " Amen "
Follow'd from either choir, as plainly spoke
Desire of their dead bodies ; yet perchance
Not for themselves, but for their kindred dear,
Mothers and sires, and those whom best they loved,
Ere they were made imperishable flame.
    And lo ! forthwith there rose up round about
A lustre, over that already there ;
Of equal clearness, like the brightening up
Of the horizon.   As at evening hour
Of twilight, new appearances through Heaven
Peer with faint glimmer, doubtfully descried ;

[1] Solomon, speaking from the brightest light of the inner circle.

So, there, new substances,[1] methought, began
To rise in view beyond the other twain,
And wheeling, sweep their ampler circuit wide.
   O genuine glitter of eternal Beam !
With what a sudden whiteness did it flow,
O'erpowering vision in me. But so fair,
So passing lovely, Beatrice show'd,
Mind cannot follow it, nor words express
Her infinite sweetness.   Thence mine eyes regain'd
Power to look up ; and I beheld myself,
Sole with my lady, to more lofty bliss
Translated : [2] for the star, with warmer smile
Impurpled, well denoted our ascent.
   With all the heart, and with that tongue which speaks
The same in all, an holocaust I made
To God, befitting the new grace vouchsafed.
And from my bosom had not yet upsteam'd
The fuming of that incense, when I knew
The rite accepted. With such mighty sheen
And mantling crimson, in two listed rays
The splendours shot before me, that I cried,
" God of Sabaoth ! that dost prank them thus ! "
   As leads the galaxy from pole to pole,
Distinguish'd into greater lights and less,
Its pathway, which the wisest fail to spell ; [3]
So thickly studded, in the depth of Mars,
Those rays described the venerable sign,
That quadrants in the round conjoining frame.[4]
   Here memory mocks the toil of genius. Christ
Beam'd on that cross ; and pattern fails me now.
But whoso takes his cross, and follows Christ,
Will pardon me for that I leave untold,
When in the flecker'd dawning he shall spy

   [1] A third circle of spirits, dimly at first and then with dazzling
vividness, appears beyond the two circles that already surround
Dante and Beatrice. A mysterious passage of which various
allegorical explanations have been offered. It has been plausibly
connected with the Joachist doctrine of the third epoch, the kingdom or dispensation of the Holy Spirit.
   [2] To the fifth Heaven, the sphere of Mars.
   [3] In the Convivio (ii. 15), Dante discusses the various opinions
held by philosophers concerning the origin of the galaxy, or
milky way.
   [4] Not simply a Cross, but a blood-red figure of the Crucified
Lord Himself : " And then shall appear the sign of the Son of
Man in Heaven " (Matt. xxiv. 30).

The glitterance of Christ. From horn to horn,
And 'tween the summit and the base, did move
Lights, scintillating, as they met and pass'd.[1]
Thus oft are seen with ever-changeful glance,
Straight or athwart, now rapid and now slow,
The atomies of bodies, long or short,
To move along the sunbeam, whose slant line
Checkers the shadow interposed by art
Against the noontide heat. And as the chime
Of minstrel music, dulcimer, and harp
With many strings, a pleasant dinning makes
To him, who heareth not distinct the note;
So from the lights, which there appear'd to me,
Gather'd along the cross a melody,
That, indistinctly heard, with ravishment
Possess'd me. Yet I mark'd it was a hymn
Of lofty praises; for there came to me
"Arise," and "Conquer," as to one who hears
And comprehends not. Me such ecstasy
O'ercame, that never, till that hour, was thing
That held me in so sweet imprisonment.

Perhaps my saying overbold appears,
Accounting less the pleasure of those eyes,
Whereon to look fulfilleth all desire.
But he,[2] who is aware those living seals
Of every beauty work with quicker force,
The higher they are risen; and that there
I had not turn'd me to them; he may well
Excuse me that, whereof in my excuse
I do accuse me, and may own my truth;
That holy pleasure here not yet reveal'd,[3]
Which grows in transport as we mount aloof.

---

[1] These are the souls of those who fought for the chosen people of the old law, or for Christ's Church in the new.

[2] "He, who considers that the eyes of Beatrice became more radiant the higher we ascended, must not wonder that I do not except even them, as I had not yet beheld them since our entrance into this planet" (Cary).

[3] The alternative explanation given by Cary in a note, "that holy pleasure not excluded here," is the one more usually adopted.

CANTO XV

ARGUMENT

The spirit of Cacciaguida, our Poet's ancestor, glides rapidly to
the foot of the cross; tells who he is; and speaks of the
simplicity of the Florentines in his days, since then much
corrupted.

TRUE love, that ever shows itself as clear
In kindness, as loose appetite in wrong,
Silenced that lyre harmonious, and still'd
The sacred cords, that are by Heaven's right hand
Unwound and tighten'd.   How to righteous prayers
Should they not hearken, who, to give me will
For praying, in accordance thus were mute?
He hath in sooth good cause for endless grief,
Who, for the love of thing that lasteth not,
Despoils himself for ever of that love.

As oft along the still and pure serene,
At nightfall, glides a sudden trail of fire,
Attracting with involuntary heed
The eye to follow it, erewhile at rest;
And seems some star that shifted place in Heaven,
Only that, whence it kindles, none is lost,
And it is soon extinct : thus from the horn,
That on the dexter of the cross extends,
Down to its foot, one luminary ran
From mid the cluster shone there; yet no gem
Dropp'd from its foil : and through the beamy list,
Like flame in alabaster, glow'd its course.

So forward stretch'd him (if of credence aught
Our greater muse [1] may claim) the pious ghost
Of old Anchises, in the Elysian bower,
When he perceived his son.   " O thou, my blood !
O most exceeding grace divine ! to whom,
As now to thee, hath twice the heavenly gate
Been e'er unclosed?"   So spake the light : whence I
Turn'd me toward him; then unto my dame
My sight directed : and on either side
Amazement waited me; for in her eyes
Was lighted such a smile, I thought that mine

[1] He refers to Virgil's account of the meeting of Anchises and
Æneas in Elysium.   *Æn.* vi. 679–694.

Had dived unto the bottom of my grace
And of my bliss in Paradise. Forthwith,
To hearing and to sight grateful alike,
The spirit to his proem added things
I understood not, so profound he spake :
Yet not of choice, but through necessity,
Mysterious ; for his high conception soar'd
Beyond the mark of mortals. When the flight
Of holy transport had so spent its rage,
That nearer to the level of our thought
The speech descended ; the first sounds I heard
Were, " Blest be Thou, Triunal Deity !
That hast such favour in my seed vouchsafed."
Then follow'd : " No unpleasant thirst, though long,[1]
Which took me reading in the sacred book,
Whose leaves or white or dusky never change,
Thou hast allay'd, my son ! within this light,
From whence my voice thou hear'st : more thanks to
     her,
Who, for such lofty mounting, has with plumes
Begirt thee. Thou dost deem thy thoughts to me
From Him transmitted, who is first of all,
E'en as all numbers ray from unity ;[2]
And therefore dost not ask me who I am,
Or why to thee more joyous I appear,
Than any other in this gladsome throng.
The truth is as thou deem'st ; for in this life
Both less and greater in that Mirror look,
In which thy thoughts, or e'er thou think'st, are shown.
But, that the love, which keeps me wakeful ever,
Urging with sacred thirst of sweet desire,
May be contented fully ; let thy voice,
Fearless, and frank, and jocund, utter forth
Thy will distinctly, utter forth the wish,
Whereto my ready answer stands decreed."
     I turn'd me to Beatrice ; and she heard
Ere I had spoken, smiling an assent,
That to my will gave wings ; and I began :

[1] Reading in the Divine Mirror, wherein all times are present,
Cacciaguida had learned that this ecstatic pilgrimage of Dante to
the world beyond the grave was decreed by God, and would
inevitably come to pass.
[2] The Saints see in God all that it concerns them to know, even
as all numbers are known in the clear conception of the
mathematical unit.

" To each among your tribe,[1] what time ye kenn'd
The nature, in whom nought unequal dwells,
Wisdom and love were in one measure dealt;
For that they are so equal in the Sun,
From whence ye drew your radiance and your heat,
As makes all likeness scant.   But will and means,
In mortals, for the cause ye well discern,
With unlike wings are fledged.   A mortal, I
Experience inequality like this;
And therefore give no thanks, but in the heart,
For thy paternal greeting.   This howe'er
I pray thee, living topaz! that ingemm'st
This precious jewel; let me hear thy name."

    " I am thy root, O leaf! whom to expect
Even, hath pleased me."   Thus the prompt reply
Prefacing, next it added : " He, of whom
Thy kindred appellation comes, and who,
These hundred years and more, on its first ledge
Hath circuited the mountain, was my son,
And thy great-grandsire.[2]   Well befits, his long
Endurance should be shorten'd by thy deeds.

    " Florence, within her ancient limit-mark,
Which calls her still to matin prayers and noon,[3]
Was chaste and sober, and abode in peace.
She had no armlets and no head-tires then;
No purfled dames; no zone, that caught the eye
More than the person did.   Time was not yet,
When [4] at his daughter's birth the sire grew pale,
For fear the age and dowry should exceed,
On each side, just proportion.   House was none

[1] " God who is the supreme ' equality,' i. e. in whom all things
realise their absolute proportion and perfection, fills the blessed
spirits with love and insight in equal measure, so that their
utterance is the perfect expression of their emotion, but we mortals
find our wills out-flying our power of utterance " (Wicksteed).

[2] Alighiero I., Cacciaguida's son and Dante's great-grandfather,
is here said to have been more than a hundred years in the first
terrace of Purgatory; but there is documentary evidence that he
was alive in 1201.

[3] The Badia, from which the canonical hours sounded, is close
to the site of the ancient circle of walls, within which, in Cacciaguida's days, Florence was still enclosed.   The second circle of
walls was built in 1173 ; the third circle, which in part still stands,
at the beginning of the fourteenth century.

[4] " When the women were not married at too early an age,
and did not expect too large a portion " (Cary).

Void [1] of its family : nor yet had come
Sardanapalus, to exhibit feats
Of chamber prowess. [2] Montemalo yet
O'er our suburban turret rose; as much
To be surpast in fall, as in its rising. [3]
I saw Bellincion Berti walk abroad
In leathern girdle, and a clasp of bone;
And, with no artful colouring on her cheeks,
His lady leave the glass. The sons I saw
Of Nerli, and of Vecchio, well content
With unrobed jerkin; and their good dames handling
The spindle and the flax : [4] O happy they !
Each sure of burial in her native land,
And none left desolate a-bed for France. [5]
One waked to tend the cradle, hushing it
With sounds that lull'd the parent's infancy :
Another, with her maidens, drawing off
The tresses from the distaff, lectured them
Old tales of Troy, and Fesole, and Rome.
A Salterello and Cianghella we
Had held as strange a marvel, as ye would
A Cincinnatus or Cornelia now. [6]
　　" In such composed and seemly fellowship,
Such faithful and such fair equality,
In so sweet household, Mary [7] at my birth

[1] Through exile, as Guelfs or Ghibellines alternately got the
upper hand.

[2] Sardanapalus, King of Assyria, is here taken as a type of
luxury.

[3] " Montemalo was not yet surpassed by your Uccellatoio."
Montemario is the first point at which Rome is seen by one coming
from Viterbo, Uccellatoio the first where Florence is visible on the
old road from Bologna. Florence had not yet attempted to rival
Rome in her magnificence.

[4] In Cacciaguida's days, the Florentine nobles and their wives
were merely members of a society of unpretentious citizens.
Bellincion Berti de' Ravignani, whom Villani calls " the greatest
and most honoured knight of Florence," was the father of the
good Gualdrada (cf. notes on Inf. xvi.) ; the Nerli and the Vecchi-
etti were old Guelf families of the city.

[5] " None fearful either of dying in banishment, or of being
deserted by her husband on a scheme of traffic in France " (Cary).

[6] Such degenerate women and corrupt political lawyers of
Dante's own day as Cianghella della Tosa and Lapo Salterello (one
of the White exiles of 1302) would have seemed as strange then as
a Cornelia or a Cincinnatus in the Florence that the Poet knew.

[7] The name of the Blessed Virgin was invoked in child-birth
(Madonna del parto). Cf. Purg. xx.

N 2

Bestow'd me, call'd on with loud cries; and there,
In your old baptistery, I was made
Christian at once and Cacciaguida; as were
My brethren, Eliseo and Moronto.

    " From Valdipado [1] came to me my spouse;
And hence thy surname grew. I follow'd then
The Emperor Conrad: and his knighthood he
Did gird on me; in such good part he took
My valiant service. After him I went
To testify against that evil law,
Whose people, by the Shepherd's fault, possess
Your right usurp'd. There I by that foul crew
Was disentangled from the treacherous world
Whose base affection many a spirit soils;
And from the martyrdom came to this peace." [2]

CANTO XVI

ARGUMENT

Cacciaguida relates the time of his birth; and, describing the
extent of Florence when he lived there, recounts the names
of the chief families who then inhabited it. Its degeneracy,
and subsequent disgrace, he attributes to the introduction of
families from the neighbouring country and villages, and to
their mixture with the primitive citizens.

O SLIGHT respect of man's nobility!
I never shall account it marvellous,
That our infirm affection here below
Thou movest to boasting; when I could not chuse,
E'en in that region of unwarp'd desire,
In Heaven itself, but make my vaunt in thee.
Yet cloak thou art soon shorten'd; for that Time,
Unless thou be eked out from day to day,
Goes round thee with his shears. Resuming then,
With greeting [3] such as Rome was first to bear,

    [1] From the Valley of the Po. Cacciaguida's wife is (rather
questionably) said to have been Alighiera of the Aldighieri family
of Ferrara.
    [2] Cacciaguida took part in the Crusade of 1147, under the
Emperor Conrad III., and was slain. For the papal neglect of
the Holy Land, cf. Par. ix.
    [3] To show his reverence, Dante addresses Cacciaguida as voi
(instead of tu)—the plural form supposed to have been first given
by Rome to Julius Cæsar.

But since hath disaccustom'd, I began:
And Beatrice, that a little space
Was sever'd, smiled;[1] reminding me of her,
Whose cough embolden'd (as the story holds)
To first offence the doubting Guenever.[2]

  "You are my sire," said I: "you give me heart
Freely to speak my thought: above myself
You raise me.   Through so many streams with joy
My soul is fill'd, that gladness wells from it;
So that it bears the mighty tide, and bursts not.
Say then, my honour'd stem! what ancestors
Were those you sprang from, and what years were
        mark'd
In your first childhood?   Tell me of the fold,[3]
That hath Saint John for guardian, what was then
Its state, and who in it were highest seated!"

  As embers, at the breathing of the wind,
Their flame enliven; so that light I saw
Shine at my blandishments; and, as it grew
More fair to look on, so with voice more sweet,
Yet not in this our modern phrase, forthwith
It answer'd: "From the day,[4] when it was said
'Hail Virgin!' to the throes by which my mother,
Who now is sainted, lighten'd her of me
Whom she was heavy with, this fire had come
Five hundred times and fourscore, to relume
Its radiance underneath the burning foot
Of its own lion.   They, of whom I sprang,
And I, had there our birth-place, where the last
Partition of our city first is reach'd
By him that runs her annual game.[5]   Thus much

---

[1] Beatrice stands apart, because this conversation has little to
do with Divine Philosophy, but smiles indulgently at Dante's
keenness in such matters.

[2] "She who coughed at the first fault recorded of Guenever."
The Lady of Malehaut coughed during the first interview of
Lancelot with the Queen.   *Cf.* notes on *Inf.* v. Cary has mistranslated the passage; the lovers were by no means "embold-
ened" by her conduct.   [3] Florence.

[4] From the Incarnation of Christ to the birth of Cacciaguida,
the planet Mars had returned to the constellation of Leo five
hundred and eighty times (according to the reading, probably
rightly, here adopted).   Taking the period of the revolution of
Mars as 687 days, this gives us 1091 as the year in which Cacciaguida was born.

[5] Florence was divided into six sections, *sesti*.   In the annual

Suffice of my forefathers : who they were,
And whence they hither came, more honourable
It is to pass in silence than to tell.
All those, who at that time were there, betwixt
Mars and the Baptist, fit to carry arms,
Were but the fifth of them this day alive.
But then the citizen's blood, that now is mix'd
From Campi and Certaldo and Fighine,
Ran purely through the last mechanic's veins.[1]
O how much better were it, that these people
Were neighbours to you; and that at Galluzzo
And at Trespiano ye should have your boundary ;
Than to have them within, and bear the stench
Of Aguglione's hind, and Signa's, him,
That hath his eye already keen for bartering.[2]
Had not the people, which of all the world
Degenerates most, been stepdame unto Cæsar,[3]
But, as a mother to her son, been kind,
Such one, as hath become a Florentine,
And trades and traffics, hath been turn'd adrift
To Simifonte,[4] where his grandsire plied
The beggar's craft : the Conti were possest
Of Montemurlo[5] still : the Cerchi still
Were in Acone's parish : nor had haply

race the *Sesto di San Piero* was the last to be entered ; the Elisei,
with whom the Alighieri were connected, had their house at the
beginning of this *sesto*, near the Mercato Vecchio.
[1] The Baptistery and the statue of Mars at the Ponte Vecchio
are here taken as the northern and southern boundaries of the
city. The population in Cacciaguida's time was a fifth of that at
the epoch of the vision, but pure Florentine, not yet contaminated
by the immigration of new families from the towns of the
Contado.
[2] In the eleventh century, Galuzzo and Trespiano were the
southern and northern limits of Florentine territory—which, therefore, did not include Aguglione and Signa, from which were to
come Baldo and Bonifazio, respectively, two unscrupulous lawyers
and corrupt Guelf politicians of Dante's own day. There is an
allusion to Baldo d'Aguglione in *Purg.* xii. ; it was he who, in
1311, drew up the " reform " by which Dante was included among
the exiles for ever to be excepted from amnesty.
[3] If the clergy had not caused the Guelf and Ghibelline factions
by their hostility to the Emperors.
[4] Simifonti, a fortress in the Valdelsa destroyed by the Florentines in 1202. The person meant is doubtfully identified with
Lippo del Velluto, an opponent of Giano della Bella (see below).
[5] The Conti Guidi, being unable to defend their castle of Montemurlo from the Pistoians, sold it to Florence in 1254.

From Valdigreve past the Buondelmonti.[1]
The city's malady hath ever source
In the confusion of its persons, as
The body's, in variety of food:
And the blind bull falls with a steeper plunge,
Than the blind lamb: and oftentimes one sword
Doth more and better execution,
Than five. Mark Luni; Urbisaglia mark;
How they are gone; and after them how go
Chiusi and Sinigaglia![2] and 'twill seem
No longer new, or strange to thee, to hear
That families fail, when cities have their end.
All things that appertain to ye, like yourselves,
Are mortal: but mortality in some
Ye mark not; they endure so long, and you
Pass by so suddenly. And as the moon
Doth, by the rolling of her heavenly sphere,
Hide and reveal the strand unceasingly;
So fortune deals with Florence. Hence admire not
At what of them I tell thee, whose renown
Time covers, the first Florentines. I saw
The Ughi, Catilini, and Filippi,
The Alberichi, Greci, and Ormanni,
Now in their wane, illustrious citizens;
And great as ancient, of Sannella him,
With him of Arca saw, and Soldanieri,
And Ardinghi, and Bostichi.[3] At the poop
That now is laden with new felony
So cumbrous it may speedily sink the bark,
The Ravignani sat, of whom is sprung
The County Guido, and whoso hath since
His title from the famed Bellincion ta'en.[4]

[1] But for the quarrel between the Church and the Empire, the Cerchi and the Buondelmonti (who played a leading part in the factions of 1300 and 1215, respectively) would still be in their former homes in the country, and not have come to cause dissensions in the city.
[2] Four decayed or decaying Italian cities. Chiusi and Sinigaglia, however, still survive.
[3] Ancient families of Cacciaguida's day. The Bostichi were still powerful at the date of the vision.
[4] For " at the poop," read " over the gate " (sopra la porta). Shortly before 1300, the Cerchi had purchased the houses over the Porta San Piero, which had been those of the Ravignani, from whom (through Bellincion Berti's daughter Gualdrada) the Conti Guidi were descended.

Fair governance was yet an art well prized
By him of Pressa : Galigaio show'd
The gilded hilt and pommel,[1] in his house :
The column, clothed with verrey,[2] still was seen
Unshaken ; the Sacchetti still were great,
Giuochi, Fifanti, Galli, and Barucci,
With them [3] who blush to hear the bushel named.
Of the Calfucci still the branchy trunk
Was in its strength : and, to the curule chairs,
Sizii and Arrigucci yet were drawn.
How mighty them [4] I saw, whom, since, their pride
Hath undone ! And in all their goodly deeds
Florence was, by the bullets of bright gold,[5]
O'erflourish'd. Such the sires of those, who now,
As surely as your church is vacant, flock
Into her consistory, and at leisure
There stall them and grow fat.[6] The o'erweening
          brood,
That plays the dragon after him that flees,
But unto such as turn and show the tooth,
Ay or the purse, is gentle as a lamb,
Was on its rise, but yet so slight esteem'd,
That Ubertino of Donati grudged
His father-in-law should yoke him to its tribe.[7]
Already Caponsacco [8] had descended
Into the mart from Fesole : and Giuda

<hr>

[1] The insignia of knighthood.

[2] The arms of the Pigli.

[3] The Chiaramontesi, one of which family had committed the fraud referred to in *Purg.* xii.

[4] The Uberti. Cf. *Inf.* x.

[5] The Lamberti. Cf. *Inf.* xxviii.

[6] The ancestors of the Visdomini and the della Tosa, families which, having the revenues of the bishopric of Florence in their hands, were accused of perverting them to their own uses whenever the see was vacant.

[7] The Adimari, to one branch of which family Filippo Argenti (*Inf.* viii.) belonged. Ubertino Donati, the ancestor of Dante's wife, had married one of the daughters of Bellincion Berti (a sister, therefore, of Gualdrada), and strongly objected to his father-in-law giving a third daughter in marriage to one of the Adimari. It has recently been shown (by Zingarelli) that Dante's son Pietro asserts that a fourth daughter of Bellincion was the wife of the poet's great-grandfather, Alighiero I.

[8] The Caponsacchi had come down from Fiesole to live in the Mercato Vecchio.

And Infangato [1] were good citizens.
A thing incredible I tell, though true:
The gateway, named from those of Pera, led
Into the narrow circuit of your walls. [2]
Each one, who bears the sightly quarterings
Of the great Baron, [3] (he whose name and worth
The festival of Thomas still revives,)
His knighthood and his privilege retain'd;
Albeit one, [4] who borders them with gold,
This day is mingled with the common herd.
In Borgo yet the Gualterotti dwelt,
And Importuni: well for its repose,
Had it still lack'd of newer neighbourhood. [5]
The house, [6] from whence your tears have had their
      spring,
Through the just anger, that hath murder'd ye
And put a period to your gladsome days,
Was honour'd; it, and those consorted with it.
O Buondelmonte! what ill counseling
Prevail'd on thee to break the plighted bond?
Many, who now are weeping, would rejoice,
Had God to Ema given thee, the first time
Thou near our city camest. But so was doom'd:
Florence! on that maim'd stone which guards the
      bridge,
The victim, when thy peace departed, fell. [7]

[1] The Giudi and Infangati were Ghibelline families who shared
the ruin of their faction.
[2] This probably means, it seems incredible that the della Pera
were ever of such importance as to have a gate of the city named
after them.
[3] Ugo, Marquis of Tuscany and imperial vicar of Otho III.,
ennobled several Florentine families, and gave them the right to
bear his arms. Dying on the feast of St. Thomas, December 21,
1101, he was buried in the Badia which had been founded by his
mother, where he is still annually commemorated on that day.
[4] Giano della Bella, who bore the arms of the Marquis, barry
red and white, bordered with gold, identified himself with the
popular cause in Florence, and was instrumental in establishing
the Ordinances of Justice in 1293, whereby the nobles were excluded from office and subjected to severe penalties for offences
against the people. It is doubtful whether he, or his family in
general, is indicated.
[5] Well had it been for the peace of Florence, if the Buondelmonti
had never left the Valdigreve (cf. above) and settled in the Borgo
Santi Apostoli, near the old families of Gualterotti and Importuni!
[6] The Amidei.
[7] The refusal of Buondelmonte de' Buondelmonti, at the instigation

" With these and others like to them, I saw
Florence in such assured tranquillity,
She had no cause at which to grieve : with these
Saw her so glorious and so just, that ne'er
The lily from the lance had hung reverse,
Or through division been with vermeil dyed." [1]

CANTO XVII

ARGUMENT

Cacciaguida predicts to our Poet his exile and the calamities he
had to suffer ; and, lastly, exhorts him to write the present
poem.

SUCH as the youth,[2] who came to Clymene,
To certify himself of that reproach
Which had been fasten'd on him, (he whose end,
Still makes the fathers chary to their sons,)
E'en such was I ; nor unobserved was such
Of Beatrice, and that saintly lamp,[3]
Who had erewhile for me his station moved ;
When thus my lady : " Give thy wish free vent,
That it may issue, bearing true report
Of the mind's impress : not that aught thy words
May to our knowledge add, but to the end
That thou mayst use thyself to own thy thirst,
And men may mingle for thee when they hear."

" O plant, from whence I spring ! revered and loved !
Who soar'st so high a pitch, that thou as clear,
As earthly thought determines two obtuse
In one triangle not contain'd, so clear

of Gualdrada Donati, to keep his plighted troth to a maiden
of the Amidei, led to his murder, in 1215, at the foot of the statue
of Mars, " the maimed stone which guards the bridge," and the
division of the whole city into Guelfs and Ghibellines. Cf. *Inf.*
xiii. and xxviii. The Ema is the small stream over which the
Buondelmonti would have to pass in coming from the Valdigreve
to Florence.

[1] The lily on the Florentine standard was never reversed in
derision by victorious foes, nor changed from white to red, as it
was by the Guelfs in 1251 (the idea of its being stained red by
the blood of citizens slain in civil war is likewise to be understood).

[2] Phaëton came to his mother Clymene to know if he were
really Apollo's son. Cf. *Inf.* xvii.

[3] Cacciaguida.

Dost see contingencies, ere in themselves
Existent, looking at the point whereto
All times are present;[1] I, the whilst I scaled
With Virgil the soul-purifying mount
And visited the nether world of woe,
Touching my future destiny have heard
Words grievous,[2] though I feel me on all sides
Well squared to fortune's blows.   Therefore my will
Were satisfied to know the lot awaits me;
The arrow, seen beforehand, slacks his flight."
    So said I to the brightness, which erewhile
To me had spoken; and my will declared,
As Beatrice will'd, explicitly.
Nor with oracular response obscure,
Such as, or e'er the Lamb of God was slain,
Beguiled the credulous nations : but, in terms
Precise, and unambiguous lore, replied
The spirit of paternal love, enshrined,
Yet in his smile apparent; and thus spake :
" Contingency, whose verge extendeth not
Beyond the tablet of your mortal mold,
Is all depictured in the eternal sight;
But hence deriveth not necessity,
More than the tall ship, hurried down the flood,
Is driven by the eye that looks on it.[3]
From thence,[4] as to the ear sweet harmony
From organ comes, so comes before mine eye
The time prepared for thee.   Such as driven out
From Athens, by his cruel stepdame's wiles,

[1] As clearly as we see that a triangle cannot contain two obtuse angles, so do the blessed behold contingent things (things which depend upon the free action of the human will) in their vision of God, to whom all things and all times are present.

[2] Cf. *Inf.* x., xv., xxv., and *Purg.* xi.

[3] Contingency, as opposed to necessity, includes all that happens but might not have done so ; all things that depend upon the acts freely determined by the human will. It has no place beyond man's material limitations, and, though all beheld by the Divine Vision, does not become necessary because of this, any more than a ship's course down a stream from the eye of one who is gazing at her.   Boëthius (*De Cons. Philos.* v.) shows that God's prescience is not foreknowledge as of something future, but knowledge of a never-passing moment : " If we may, without unfitness, compare God's present and man's, just as ye see certain things in this your temporary present, so does He see all things in His eternal present " (H. R. James's translation).

[4] From the vision of God.

Hippolytus departed; [1] such must thou
Depart from Florence.   This they wish, and this
Contrive, and will ere long effectuate, there, [2]
Where gainful merchandize is made of Christ
Throughout the live-long day.   The common cry,
Will, as 'tis ever wont, affix the blame
Unto the party injured : but the truth
Shall, in the vengeance it dispenseth, find
A faithful witness.   Thou shalt leave each thing
Beloved most dearly : this is the first shaft
Shot from the bow of exile.   Thou shalt prove
How salt the savour is of other's bread ;
How hard the passage, to descend and climb
By other's stairs.   But that shall gall thee most,
Will be the worthless and vile company,
With whom thou must be thrown into these straits.
For all ungrateful, impious all, and mad,
Shall turn 'gainst thee : but in a little while,
Theirs, and not thine, shall be the crimson'd brow.
Their course shall so evince their brutishness,
To have ta'en thy stand apart shall well become thee. [3]
   "First refuge thou must find, first place of rest,
In the great Lombard's [4] courtesy, who bears,
Upon the ladder perch'd, the sacred bird.
He shall behold thee with such kind regard,
That 'twixt ye two, the contrary to that
Which 'fals 'twixt other men, the granting shall
Forerun the asking.   With him shalt thou see
That mortal, [5] who was at his birth imprest
So strongly from this star, that of his deeds

---

[1] Phædra wrongfully accused Hippolytus of her own unchaste
desires ; so will the corrupt citizens of Florence accuse Dante of
malversation and treason.

[2] In the Court of Pope Boniface at Rome.

[3] Documentary evidence shows that Dante broke away from
his fellow-exiles between June 8, 1302, and June 18, 1303 ; that is,
before the worst of the misfortunes here foretold fell upon them.

[4] Bartolommeo della Scala, Lord of Verona, the arms of whose
family were a ladder surmounted by the imperial eagle. Dante
took refuge with him sometime between the summer of 1302 and
his death in March, 1304.

[5] Bartolommeo's younger brother, Can Grande della Scala
(1291–1329), destined to be the greatest Italian soldier of his age,
and the chief upholder of the imperial cause in northern Italy.
At the epoch of the vision (April, 1300), he was nine years and a
month old.

The nations shall take note.   His unripe age
Yet holds him from observance; for these wheels
Only nine years have compast him about.
But, ere the Gascon practise on great Harry,[1]
Sparkles of virtue shall shoot forth in him,
In equal scorn of labours and of gold.
His bounty shall be spread abroad so widely,
As not to let the tongues, e'en of his foes,
Be idle in its praise.   Look thou to him,
And his beneficence : for he shall cause
Reversal of their lot to many people ;
Rich men and beggars interchanging fortunes.
And thou shalt bear this written in thy soul,
Of him, but tell it not :" and things he told
Incredible to those who witness them ;[2]
Then added : " So interpret thou, my son,
What hath been told thee.—Lo ! the ambushment
That a few circling seasons hide for thee.
Yet envy not thy neighbours : time extends
Thy span beyond their treason's chastisement."

Soon as the saintly spirit, by silence, mark'd
Completion of that web, which I had stretch'd
Before it, warp'd for weaving ; I began,
As one, who in perplexity desires
Counsel of other, wise, benign and friendly :
" My father ! well I mark how time spurs on
Toward me, ready to inflict the blow,
Which falls most heavily on him who most
Abandoneth himself.   Therefore 'tis good
I should forecast, that, driven from the place
Most dear to me, I may not lose myself[3]
All other by my song.   Down through the world
Of infinite mourning ; and along the mount,
From whose fair height my lady's eyes did lift me ;
And, after, through this Heaven, from light to light ;

[1] Pope Clement V., by origin a Gascon, at first seemed to
favour the Emperor Henry VII. (1308–1313), but afterwards
secretly opposed him. Cf. *Inf.* xix. and *Par.* xxx. Before the
latter date, Can Grande showed his mettle by recovering Brescia
and taking Vicenza in 1311.

[2] "Incredible even to those who shall witness them." Cf. *Inf.* i.
and *Purg.* xxxiii.

[3] "That being driven out of my country, I may not deprive
myself of every other place by the boldness with which I expose
in my writings the vices of mankind " (Cary).

Have I learnt that, which if I tell again,
It may with many wofully disrelish :
And, if I am a timid friend to truth,
I fear my life may perish among those,
To whom these days shall be of ancient date."

The brightness, where enclosed the treasure [1] smiled,
Which I had found there, first shone glisteringly,
Like to a golden mirror in the sun ;
Next answer'd : " Conscience, dimm'd or by its own
Or other's shame, will feel thy saying sharp.
Thou, notwithstanding, all deceit removed,
See the whole vision be made manifest ;
And let them wince, who have their withers wrung.
What though, when tasted first, thy voice shall prove
Unwelcome : on digestion, it will turn
To vital nourishment.   The cry thou raisest,
Shall, as the wind doth, smite the proudest summits
Which is of honour no light argument. [2]
For this, there only have been shown to thee,
Throughout these orbs, the mountain, and the deep,
Spirits, whom fame hath note of.   For the mind
Of him, who hears, is loth to acquiesce
And fix its faith, unless the instance brought
Be palpable, and proof apparent urge."

CANTO XVIII

ARGUMENT

Dante sees the souls of many renowned warriors and crusaders in
     the planet Mars ; and then ascends with Beatrice to Jupiter,
     the sixth Heaven, in which he finds the souls of those who had
     administered justice rightly in the world, so disposed, as to
     form the figure of an eagle. The Canto concludes with an
     invective against the avarice of the clergy, and especially of
     the Pope.

Now in his word, sole, ruminating, joy'd
That blessed spirit : and I fed on mine,
Tempering the sweet with bitter. [3]   She meanwhile,

[1] The soul of Cacciaguida.
[2] Let him fearlessly assail wickedness in the highest places ;
for this very purpose has the vision been vouchsafed to him. *Cf.*
the opening of the third book of the *De Monarchia.*
[3] *Verbo,* " word," is here taken as meaning " thought," or
" conception."

Who led me unto God, admonish'd : " Muse
On other thoughts : bethink thee, that near Him
I dwell, who recompenseth every wrong."

   At the sweet sounds of comfort straight I turn'd;
And, in the saintly eyes what love was seen,
I leave in silence here, nor through distrust
Of my words only, but that to such bliss
The mind remounts not without aid. Thus much
Yet may I speak ; that, as I gazed on her,
Affection found no room for other wish.
While the everlasting pleasure, that did full
On Beatrice shine, with second view
From her fair countenance my gladden'd soul
Contented ; vanquishing me with a beam
Of her soft smile, she spake : " Turn thee, and list.
These eyes are not thy only Paradise." [1]

   As here, we sometimes in the looks may see
The affection mark'd, when that its sway hath ta'en
The spirit wholly ; thus the hallow'd light, [2]
To whom I turn'd, flashing, bewray'd its will
To talk yet further with me, and began :
" On this fifth lodgment of the tree, [3] whose life
Is from its top, whose fruit is ever fair
And leaf unwithering, blessed spirits abide,
That were below, ere they arrived in Heaven,
So mighty in renown, as every muse
Might grace her triumph with them. On the horns
Look, therefore, of the cross : he whom I name,
Shall there enact, as doth in summer cloud
Its nimble fire." Along the cross I saw,
At the repeated name of Joshua,
A splendour gliding ; nor, the word was said,
Ere it was done : then, at the naming, saw,
Of the great Maccabee, [4] another move
With whirling speed ; and gladness was the scourge
Unto that top. The next for Charlemagne

[1] In the allegorical sense, blessedness must be sought after,
not only in the contemplation of revealed truth, but also by following the examples set by those who have done great deeds for
the Kingdom of Heaven.
[2] The soul of Cacciaguida.
[3] The fifth sphere of Paradise.
[4] Joshua, the original conqueror of the Holy Land, and Judas
Maccabæus, the champion of the chosen people against their
oppressors.

And for the peer Orlando,[1] two my gaze
Pursued, intently, as the eye pursues
A falcon flying. Last, along the cross,
William, and Renard,[2] and Duke Godfrey drew
My ken, and Robert Guiscard.[3] And the soul
Who spake with me, among the other lights
Did move away, and mix; and with the quire
Of heavenly songsters proved his tuneful skill.

To Beatrice on my right I bent,
Looking for intimation, or by word
Or act, what next behoved; and did descry
Such mere effulgence in her eyes, such joy,
It pass'd all former wont. And, as by sense
Of new delight, the man, who perseveres
In good deeds, doth perceive, from day to day,
His virtue growing; I e'en thus perceived,
Of my ascent, together with the Heaven,
The circuit widen'd; noting the increase
Of beauty in that wonder. Like the change
In a brief moment on some maiden's cheek,
Which, from its fairness, doth discharge the weight
Of pudency, that stain'd it; such in her,
And to mine eyes so sudden was the change,
Through silvery whiteness of that temperate star,[4]

[1] Charlemagne (742–814), the historical restorer of the Western
Empire and legendary rebuilder of Florence, is placed in Paradise
as the warrior of the Church, not as the righteous ruler. Cf.
Par. vi. and *Mon.* iii. 11. Orlando, or Roland, Charlemagne's
nephew, the chief hero of the Carlovingian cycle of romances, was
slain at Roncesvalles in 778. Cf. *Inf.* xxxi.

[2] William of Orange, a hero of French romance, was historically one of Charlemagne's knights, who, after a strenuous career
of warfare against the Saracens, died a monk in 812 ; Renard,
or Renouard, his brother-in-law, a converted Saracen who became
his companion on the field and in the cloister, is a purely mythical
personage.

[3] Godfrey of Bouillon, a descendant of Charlemagne in the
female line, led the first Crusade which captured Jerusalem in
1099, and ruled as king until his death in the following year,
refusing the royal crown and title. Robert Guiscard, son of
Tancred de Hauteville, founded the Norman dynasty in southern
Italy and Sicily (*d.* 1085) ; he is presumably here for his services
against the Greeks and Saracens, rather than his defence of Pope
Gregory VII., in which he perpetrated the fearful sack of Rome,
of which the traces may still be seen on the Cælian Hill. Cf.
Inf. xxviii.

[4] According to Ptolemaic astronomy, Jupiter is a star of temperate composition, between the cold of Saturn and the heat of

Whose sixth orb now enfolded us. I saw,
Within that Jovial cresset, the clear sparks
Of love, that reign'd there, fashion to my view
Our language. And as birds, from river banks
Arisen,[1] now in round, now lengthen'd troop,
Array them in their flight, greeting, as seems,
Their new-found pastures; so, within the lights,
The saintly creatures flying, sang; and made
Now D, now I, now L, figured i' the air.
First singing to their notes they moved; then, one
Becoming of these signs, a little while
Did rest them, and were mute. O nymph divine,
Of Pegasean race![2] who souls, which thou
Inspirest, makest glorious and long-lived, as they.
Cities and realms by thee; thou with thyself
Inform me; that I may set forth the shapes,
As fancy doth present them : be thy power
Display'd in this brief song. The characters,
Vocal and consonant, were five-fold seven.
In order, each, as they appear'd, I mark'd.
Diligite Justitiam, the first,
Both verb and noun all blazon'd; and the extreme,
Qui judicatis terram. In the M
Of the fifth word they held their station;
Making the star seem silver streak'd with gold.[3]
And on the summit of the M, I saw
Descending other lights, that rested there,
Singing, methinks, their bliss and primal good.
Then, as at shaking of a lighted brand,
Sparkles innumerable on all sides
Rise scatter'd, source of augury to the unwise ;[4]
Thus more than thousand twinkling lustres hence
Seem'd reascending; and a higher pitch

Mars. Also, it appears white among the stars, as though of silver (*Conv.* ii. 14).

[1] Cranes on the banks of the Nile. The image is from Lucan, *Phars.* v. 711–716.

[2] The Muse to whom Hippocrene, the fountain struck out by the hoof of Pegasus, is sacred.

[3] The spirits form successively the letters of the opening text of the Book of Wisdom in the Vulgate : *Diligite justitiam qui judicatis terram:* " Love righteousness, ye that be judges of the earth ;" until they rest in the *M* of *terram*, the initial letter of " Monarchia," which for Dante is synonymous with the Empire.

[4] Who prognosticate their luck according to the number of sparks which rise.

Some mounting, and some less, e'en as the Sun,
Which kindleth them, decreed.   And when each one
Had settled in his place; the head and neck
Then saw I of an eagle, livelily
Graved in that streaky fire.   Who painteth there,
Hath none to guide Him: of Himself He guides:
And every line and texture of the nest
Doth own from Him the virtue fashions it.
The other bright beatitude,[1] that seem'd
Erewhile, with lilied crowning, well content
To over-canopy the M, moved forth,
Following gently the impress of the bird.

Sweet star! what glorious and thick-studded gems
Declared to me our justice on the earth
To be the effluence of that Heaven, which thou,
Thyself a costly jewel, dost inlay.
Therefore I pray the Sovran Mind, from whom
Thy motion and thy virtue be begun,
That He would look from whence the fog doth rise,
To vitiate thy beam; so that once more [2]
He may put forth His hand 'gainst such, as drive
Their traffic in that sanctuary, whose walls
With miracles and martyrdoms were built.

Ye host of Heaven, whose glory I survey!
O beg ye grace for those, that are, on earth,
All after ill example gone astray.
War once had for his instrument the sword:
But now 'tis made, taking the bread away,[3]
Which the good Father locks from none.—And thou,
That writest but to cancel,[4] think, that they,

---

[1] The other band of spirits. By a series of transformations—
in the course of which the lily is temporarily combined with the
M, perhaps in allusion to the brief period during which the
Monarchy belonged to the Franks (whom Dante did not discrimi-
nate from French)—the M becomes transformed into an heraldic
Eagle, the symbol of the Roman People, which with Dane represents Law and Justice. The meaning is that this sign of the
Roman Empire is the idea of dominion within the mind of God,
and its power therefore comes direct from Him.

[2] Matt. xxi. 12, 13; Luke xix. 45, 46; John ii. 14–17. Cf.
Epist. viii. 4.

[3] Excommunication, by which men are deprived of the Blessed
Sacrament, is used as a weapon of political warfare.

[4] This is addressed to John XXII. (1316–1334), the reigning
Pontiff while Dante was actually writing. The suggestion is that
he excommunicates in order to cancel the sentence for money.

Who for the vineyard, which thou wastest, died,
Peter and Paul, live yet, and mark thy doings.
Thou hast good cause to cry, "My heart so cleaves
To him, that lived in solitude remote,
And for a dance was dragg'd to martyrdom,
I wist not of the Fisherman nor Paul." [1]

CANTO XIX

ARGUMENT

The eagle speaks as with one voice proceeding from a multitude
of spirits, that compose it; and declares the cause for which
it is exalted to that state of glory. It then solves a doubt,
which our Poet had entertained, respecting the possibility of
salvation without belief in Christ; exposes the inefficacy of a
mere profession of such belief; and prophesies the evil appearance that many Christian potentates will make at the day of
judgment.

BEFORE my sight appear'd, with open wings,
The beauteous image; in fruition sweet,
Gladdening the thronged spirits.　Each did seem
A little ruby, whereon so intense
The sun-beam glow'd, that to mine eyes it came
In clear refraction.　And that, which next
Befals me to pourtray, voice hath not utter'd,
Nor hath ink written, nor in fantasy
Was e'er conceived.　For I beheld and heard
The beak discourse; and, what intention form'd
Of many, singly as of one express,
Beginning: "For that I was just and piteous,
I am exalted to this height of glory,
The which no wish exceeds: and there on earth
Have I my memory left, e'en by the bad
Commended, while they leave its course untrod." [2]
　　Thus is one heat from many embers felt;
As in that image many were the loves,

[1] The Pope is so much absorbed in worshipping the Baptist
on the golden florins of Florence (which bore the impression of
the Saint as well as that of the Lily), that he has forgotten St.
Peter and St. Paul.

[2] "The just Kings, who compose the eagle of Jupiter, speak
as one person, just as many brands give out one warmth, so
indicating that the work of all righteous governors is one and the
same, the voice of all of them being the one voice of justice"
(Wicksteed).

And one the voice, that issued from them all :
Whence I address'd them : " O perennial flowers
Of gladness everlasting ! that exhale
In single breath your odours manifold ;
Breathe now : and let the hunger be appeased,
That with great craving long hath held my soul,
Finding no food on earth. This well I know ;
That if there be in Heaven a realm, that shows
In faithful mirror the celestial Justice,
Yours without veil reflects it.   Ye discern
The heed, wherewith I do prepare myself
To hearken ; ye, the doubt, that urges me
With such inveterate craving." [1]   Straight I saw,
Like to a falcon issuing from the hood,
That rears his head, and claps him with his wings,
His beauty and his eagerness bewraying ;
So saw I move that stately sign, with praise
Of grace divine inwoven, and high song
Of inexpressive joy. " He," it began,
" Who turn'd His compass [2] on the world's extreme,
And in that space so variously hath wrought,
Both openly and in secret ; in such wise
Could not, through all the universe, display
Impression of His glory, that the Word [3]
Of His omniscience should not still remain
In infinite excess. In proof whereof,
He first through pride supplanted, who was sum
Of each created being, [4] waited not
For light celestial ; and abortive fell.
Whence needs each lesser nature is but scant
Receptacle unto that Good, which knows
No limit, measured by itself alone.

[1] The question of the justice of the exclusion of the righteous
heathen from eternal blessedness. Cf. *Mon.* ii. 8 : " There are
certain judgments of God to which human reason, albeit unable
to attain of its proper strength, is nevertheless raised by dint of
faith in what is said to us in the sacred writings ; as, for instance,
this : That no one, however perfect in the moral and intellectual
virtues, both as to disposition and practice, may be saved without
faith, if he have never heard aught of Christ. For human reason
of itself cannot see that this is just, but helped by faith it may."

[2] *Cf.* Proverbs viii. 27.

[3] The Divine Wisdom, which is in infinite excess of what a finite
intellect can apprehend. All God's perfections, including His
Justice, are identified in His Divine Essence.

[4] Lucifer. Cf. *V. E.* i. 2.

Therefore your sight, of the omnipresent Mind
A single beam, its origin must own
Surpassing far its utmost potency.
The ken, your world is gifted with, descends
In the everlasting Justice as low down,
As eye doth in the sea; which, though it mark
The bottom from the shore, in the wide main
Discerns it not; and ne'ertheless it is;
But hidden through its deepness. Light is none,
Save that which cometh from the pure serene
Of ne'er disturbed ether: for the rest,
'Tis darkness all; or shadow of the flesh,
Or else its poison. Here confess reveal'd
That covert, which hath hidden from thy search
The living justice, of the which thou madest
Such frequent question; for thou said'st—'A man
Is born on Indus' banks, and none is there
Who speaks of Christ, nor who doth read nor write;
And all his inclinations and his acts,
As far as human reason sees, are good;
And he offendeth not in word or deed:
But unbaptized he dies, and void of faith.
Where is the justice that condemns him? where
His blame, if he believeth not?'—What then,
And who art thou, that on the stool wouldst sit
To judge at distance of a thousand miles
With the short-sighted vision of a span?
To him,[1] who subtilizes thus with me,
There would assuredly be room for doubt
Even to wonder, did not the safe word
Of Scripture hold supreme authority.

   "O animals of clay! O spirits gross!
The Primal Will, that in itself is good,
Hath from itself, the chief Good, ne'er been moved.
Justice consists in consonance with it,
Derivable by no created good,
Whose very cause depends upon its beam."[2]

---

[1] "He, who should argue, on the words I have just used,
respecting the fate of those who have wanted means of knowing
the Gospel, would certainly have cause enough to doubt, if he did
not defer to the authority of Scripture, which pronounces God to
be thoroughly just" (Cary).

[2] Justice is the Primal Will, the will of God, neither more nor
less, and the will of God is Justice. Cf. *Mon.* ii. 2.

As on her nest the stork, that turns about
Unto her young, whom lately she hath fed,
Whiles they with upward eyes do look on her;
So lifted I my gaze; and, bending so,
The ever-blessed image waved its wings,
Labouring with such deep counsel.   Wheeling round
It warbled, and did say : "As are my notes
To thee, who understand'st them not; such is
The eternal judgment unto mortal ken."

   Then still abiding in that ensign ranged,
Wherewith the Romans overawed the world,
Those burning splendours of the Holy Spirit
Took up the strain; and thus it spake again :
"None ever hath ascended to this realm,
Who hath not a believer been in Christ,
Either before or after the blest limbs
Were nail'd upon the wood.   But lo ! of those
Who call ' Christ, Christ,' [1] there shall be many found,
In judgment, further off from him by far,
Than such to whom His name was never known.
Christians like these the Æthiop [2] shall condemn :
When that the two assemblages shall part;
One rich eternally, the other poor.

   "What may the Persians say unto your kings,
When they shall see that volume,[3] in the which
All their dispraise is written, spread to view?
There amidst Albert's works shall that be read,
Which will give speedy motion to the pen,
When Prague shall mourn her desolated realm.[4]
There shall be read the woe, that he doth work
With his adulterate money on the Seine,
Who by the tusk will perish ; [5] there be read
The thirsting pride, that maketh fool alike

---

[1] Cf. Matt. vii. 21.   [2] Cf. Matt. xii. 41.
[3] Cf. Rev. xx. 12.

[4] The Eagle passes over the map of Europe, whose princes
" join no philosophical authority to their government " (Conv. iv.
6), and in every land finds the temporal rulers (no less than Dante
had found the spiritual) obscuring the light of justice.   The first
offender is the Emperor himself, Albert of Hapsburg (cf. Purg. vi.),
who is about to plunge into an unjust war of aggression against
Bohemia (1304).

[5] Philip the Fair of France, who debased the coinage, was killed
in 1314, through his horse being overthrown by the attack of a
wild boar.

The English and Scot, impatient of their bound.[1]
There shall be seen the Spaniard's luxury;[2]
The delicate living there of the Bohemian,[3]
Who still to worth has been a willing stranger.
The halter of Jerusalem[4] shall see
A unit for his virtue; for his vices,
No less a mark than million.   He,[5] who guards
The isle of fire by old Anchises honour'd,
Shall find his avarice there and cowardice;
And better to denote his littleness,
The writing must be letters maim'd, that speak
Much in a narrow space.   All there shall know
His uncle and his brother's filthy doings,
Who so renown'd a nation and two crowns
Have bastardized.[6]   And they, of Portugal
And Norway, there shall be exposed, with him
Of Ratza, who hath counterfeited ill
The coin of Venice.[7]   O blest Hungary!
If thou no longer patiently abidest
Thy ill-entreating:[8] and, O blest Navarre!
If with thy mountainous girdle thou wouldst arm thee.
In earnest of that day, e'en now are heard
Wailings and groans in Famagosta's streets
And Nicosia's, grudging at their beast,
Who keepeth even footing with the rest."[9]

[1] He refers to the Scotch wars of Edward I., who was reigning in England in 1300.

[2] Ferdinand IV., King of Castile and Leon (1295-1312).

[3] Wenceslaus IV. of Bohemia (1278-1305). Cf. *Purg.* vii.

[4] Charles II. of Naples (1285-1309), titular King of Jerusalem. He was called *il Ciotto*, " the cripple," because slightly lame. Cf. *Purg.* vii. and xx.

[5] Frederick II., King of Sicily (1296-1337). Cf. *Purg.* iii. and vii.

[6] James, King of the Balearic Islands (1276-1311), brother of Peter III. of Aragon, and therefore uncle of Frederick; James II., King of Aragon (1291-1327), son of Peter, and elder brother of Frederick. Cf. *Purg.* vii.

[7] Dionysius, King of Portugal (1279-1325); Hakon V. of Norway (1299-1319); Stephen Ouros II. of Servia, called *Rascia* from its capital (1275-1321).

[8] Hungary in 1300 was ruled by Andrew III., who had usurped the crown that belonged by right to Carobert, the son of Charles Martel.

[9] Happy would Navarre be, if the Pyrenees could preserve her independence from France, to which she was destined to be annexed in 1314! As a warning to her (*per arra di questo*, " as a pledge of this," which Cary wrongly translates " in earnest of that

CANTO XX

ARGUMENT

The eagle celebrates the praise of certain kings, whose glorified
    spirits form the eye of the bird. In the pupil is David; and,
    in the circle round it, Trajan, Hezekiah, Constantine, William
    II. of Sicily, and Ripheus. It explains to our Poet, how the
    souls of those whom he supposed to have had no means of
    believing in Christ, came to be in Heaven; and concludes
    with an admonition against presuming to fathom the counsels
    of God.

WHEN, disappearing from our hemisphere,
The world's enlightener vanishes, and day
On all sides wasteth; suddenly the sky,
Erewhile irradiate only with his beam,
Is yet again unfolded, putting forth
Innumerable lights wherein one shines.[1]
Of such vicissitude in Heaven I thought;
As the great sign, that marshaleth the world
And the world's leaders, in the blessed beak
Was silent: for that all those living lights,
Waxing in splendour, burst forth into songs,
Such as from memory glide and fall away.

    Sweet Love, that dost apparel thee in smiles!
How lustrous was thy semblance in those sparkles,
Which merely are from holy thoughts inspired.

    After the precious and bright beaming stones,
That did ingem the sixth light, ceased the chiming
Of their angelic bells; methought I heard
The murmuring of a river, that doth fall
From rock to rock transpicuous, making known
The richness of his spring-head:[2] and as sound
Of cittern, at the fret-board, or of pipe,
Is, at the wind-hole, modulate and tuned;
Thus up the neck, as it were hollow, rose
That murmuring of the eagle; and forthwith

day," and refers to "the last doom"), the cities of Cyprus are
bewailing the evil government of their French King, Henry II. of
Lusignan (d. 1324).

[1] As the stars in Dante's astronomy reflect the light of the sun,
so does the power of minor kings and princes proceed from that of
the Emperor. The "great sign" is, of course, the imperial
Eagle.

[2] After the spirits in this sixth Heaven have ceased their song,
the Eagle, speaking for all, sets forth the glory of their six leaders.

Voice there assumed; and thence along the beak
Issued in form of words, such as my heart
Did look for, on whose tables I inscribed them.

"The part [1] in me, that sees and bears the sun
In mortal eagles," it began, "must now
Be noted stedfastly: for, of the fires
That figure me, those, glittering in mine eye,
Are chief of all the greatest. This, that shines
Midmost for pupil, was the same who [2] sang
The Holy Spirit's song, and bare about
The ark from town to town: now doth he know
The merit of his soul-impassion'd strains
By their well-fitted guerdon. Of the five,
That make the circle of the vision, he,[3]
Who to the beak is nearest, comforted
The widow for her son: now doth he know,
How dear it costeth not to follow Christ;
Both from experience of this pleasant life,
And of its opposite. He next,[4] who follows
In the circumference, for the over-arch,
By true repenting slack'd the pace of death:
Now knoweth he, that the decrees of Heaven
Alter not, when, through pious prayer below,
To-day is made to-morrow's destiny.[5]
The other following, with the laws and me,
To yield the Shepherd room, pass'd o'er to Greece;[6]
From good intent, producing evil fruit:
Now knoweth he, how all the ill, derived
From his well doing, doth not harm him aught;
Though it have brought destruction on the world.

---

[1] The eye. The head of the Eagle is seen in profile.

[2] David, the ancestor of Christ according to the flesh, the King who was born at the time when Æneas came to Italy, thus making manifest the Divine election of the Roman Empire (*Conv.* iv. 5).

[3] The Emperor Trajan (98–117). Cf. *Purg.* x.

[4] Hezekiah, King of Judah. *Cf.* 2 Kings xx.

[5] Aquinas teaches that the immutability of God's decrees is consistent with the efficacy of prayer, because prayer does not alter the Divine plan, but simply fulfils what God has ordained to be fulfilled by prayer.

[6] Constantine the Great (*d.* 337) transferred the seat of empire from Rome to Byzantium, in order (according to ecclesiastical tradition supported by the famous forged "Donation") to make over Rome to the Pope. Cf. *Inf.* xix., *Purg.* xxxii., and *Mon.* ii. 12, 13, iii. 10, 13.

That, which thou seest in the under bow,
Was William,[1] whom that land bewails, which weeps
For Charles and Frederick living : now he knows,
How well is loved in Heaven the righteous king ;
Which he betokens by his radiant seeming.
Who, in the erring world beneath, would deem
That Trojan Ripheus,[2] in this round, was set,
Fifth of the saintly splendours ? now he knows
Enough of that, which the world cannot see ;
The grace divine : albeit e'en his sight
Reach not its utmost depth.'' Like to the lark,
That warbling in the air expatiates long,
Then, trilling out his last sweet melody,
Drops, satiate with the sweetness ; such appear'd
That image, stampt by the everlasting pleasure,
Which fashions, as they are, all things that be.

I, though my doubting were as manifest,
As is through glass the hue that mantles it,
In silence waited not ; for to my lips
'' What things are these ?'' involuntary rush'd,
And forced a passage out : whereat I mark'd
A sudden lightening and new revelry.
The eye was kindled ; and the blessed sign,
No more to keep me wondering and suspense,
Replied : '' I see that thou believest these things,
Because I tell them, but discern'st not how ;
So that thy knowledge waits not on thy faith :
As one, who knows the name of thing by rote,
But is a stranger to its properties,
Till other's tongue reveal them. Fervent love,
And lively hope, with violence assail
The Kingdom of the Heavens, and overcome
The will of the Most High ; not in such sort
As man prevails o'er man ; but conquers it,

---

[1] William II., called the Good, Norman King of Sicily and
Naples (1166–1189), the realms ruled in 1300 by the Aragonese
Frederick II. and the Angevin Charles II., respectively. Cf. *Conv.*
iv. 6, and *V. E.* i. 12. He was the nephew of the Empress Constance (*Par.* iii.).

[2] Ripheus the Trojan, described by Virgil (*Æn.* ii. 426) as
'' above all others the most just among the Trojans, and the
strictest observer of right.'' Dante connects this with Acts x. 34,
35 : '' God is no respecter of persons ; but in every nation he that
feareth Him, and worketh righteousness, is accepted with Him.''
The Vulgate has *justitia*, where the English version reads
'' righteousness.''

Because 'tis willing to be conquer'd; still,
Though conquer'd, by its mercy, conquering.

" Those, in the eye who live the first and fifth,
Cause thee to marvel, in that thou behold'st
The region of the Angels deck'd with them.
They quitted not their bodies, as thou deem'st,
Gentiles, but Christians; in firm rooted faith,
This, of the feet in future to be pierced,
That, of feet nail'd already to the Cross.[1]
One from the barrier of the dark abyss,
Where never any with good will returns,[2]
Came back unto his bones.   Of lively hope
Such was the meed; of lively hope, that wing'd
The prayers sent up to God for his release,
And put power into them to bend his will.[3]
The glorious Spirit, of whom I speak to thee,
A little while returning to the flesh,
Believed in Him, who had the means to help;
And, in believing, nourish'd such a flame
Of holy love, that at the second death
He was made sharer in our gamesome mirth.
The other,[4] through the riches of that grace,
Which from so deep a fountain doth distil,
As never eye created saw its rising,
Placed all his love below on just and right:
Wherefore, of grace, God oped in him the eye
To the redemption of mankind to come;
Wherein believing, he endured no more
The filth of Paganism, and for their ways
Rebuked the stubborn nations.   The three nymphs,[5]

[1] By the power of Love and Hope, respectively, Ripheus and
Trajan died with faith in the Redeemer, who was to suffer, or had
suffered, for man.

[2] Cary has mistranslated this passage.   By his prayers, St.
Gregory the Great (cf. *Purg.* x.) was said to have obtained from
God that Trajan should be brought back to life from Hell—*u' non
si riede giammai a buon voler*, " where no soul ever returns *to
good will* "—free will in the damned being for ever fixed upon evil.

[3] *Sì che potesse sua voglia esser mossa*, " so that his [Trajan's]
will could be moved to good."

[4] Ripheus.   "A man may prepare himself for the reception of
faith through what is contained in natural reason.   Wherefore it
is said that, if any one who is born in barbarous nations does what
lieth in him, God will reveal to him what is necessary for salvation,
either by inspiration or by sending a teacher " (Aquinas).

[5] The theological virtues, Faith, Hope, and Charity.   Cf. *Purg.*
xxix.

O

Whom at the right wheel thou beheld'st advancing,
Were sponsors for him, more than thousand years
Before baptizing. O how far removed,
Predestination ! is thy root from such
As see not the First Cause entire : and ye,
O mortal men ! be wary how ye judge :
For we, who see our Maker, know not yet
The number of the chosen ; and esteem
Such scantiness of knowledge our delight :
For all our good is, in that primal good,
Concentrate ; and God's will and ours are one."

So, by that form divine, was given to me
Sweet medicine to clear and strengthen sight.
And, as one handling skilfully the harp,
Attendant on some skilful songster's voice
Bids the chord vibrate ; and therein the song
Acquires more pleasure : so the whilst it spake,
It doth remember me, that I beheld
The pair [1] of blessed luminaries move,
Like the accordant twinkling of two eyes,
Their beamy circlets, dancing to the sounds.

CANTO XXI

ARGUMENT

Dante ascends with Beatrice to the seventh Heaven, which is the
planet Saturn ; wherein is placed a ladder, so lofty, that the
top of it is out of his sight. Here are the souls of those who
had passed their life in holy retirement and contemplation.
Piero Damiano comes near them, and answers questions put
to him by Dante ; then declares who he was on earth ; and
ends by declaiming against the luxury of pastors and prelates
in those times.

AGAIN mine eyes were fix'd on Beatrice ;
And, with mine eyes, my soul that in her looks
Found all contentment. Yet no smile she wore :
And, " Did I smile," quoth she, " thou wouldst be
    straight
Like Semele when into ashes turn'd : [2]
For, mounting these eternal palace-stairs,

---

[1] Trajan and Ripheus.
[2] Semele, daughter of Cadmus and mother of Bacchus, was
destroyed by the splendour of Jupiter's divine aspect. Cf. *Inf.* xxx.

My beauty, which the loftier it climbs,
As thou hast noted, still doth kindle more,
So shines, that, were no tempering interposed,
Thy mortal puissance would from its rays
Shrink, as the leaf doth from the thunderbolt.
Into the seventh splendour are we wafted,
That, underneath the burning lion's breast,
Beams, in this hour, commingled with his might.[1]
Thy mind be with thine eyes; and, in them, mirror'd
The shape, which in this mirror shall be shown." [2]

    Whoso can deem, how fondly I had fed
My sight upon her blissful countenance,
May know, when to new thoughts I changed, what joy
To do the bidding of my heavenly guide;
In equal balance, poising either weight.[3]

    Within the crystal, which records the name
(As its remoter circle girds the world)
Of that loved monarch, in whose happy reign
No ill had power to harm,[4] I saw rear'd up,
In colour like to sun-illumined gold,
A ladder, which my ken pursued in vain,
So lofty was the summit; down whose steps
I saw the splendours in such multitude
Descending, every light in Heaven, methought,
Was shed thence. As the rooks, at dawn of day,
Bestirring them to dry their feathers chill,
Some speed their way a-field; and homeward some,
Returning, cross their flight; while some abide,
And wheel around their airy lodge: so seem'd
That glitterance,[5] wafted on alternate wing,
As upon certain stair it came, and clash'd
Its shining. And one, lingering near us, wax'd
So bright, that in my thought I said: " The love,
Which this betokens me, admits no doubt."

    Unwillingly from question I refrain;
To her, by whom my silence and my speech

---

[1] Saturn was then in the constellation of Leo.

[2] Let him look upon the sign that will appear to him in this sphere.

[3] " The joy of contemplation against that of obedience " (Wicksteed).

[4] Saturn. Cf. *Inf.* xiv.

[5] " *Quello sfavillar.* That multitude of shining spirits, who, coming to a certain point of the ladder, made those different movements, which he has described as made by the birds " (Cary).

Are order'd, looking for a sign : whence she,
Who in the sight of Him, that seeth all,
Saw wherefore I was silent, prompted me
To indulge the fervent wish ; and I began :
" I am not worthy, of my own desert,
That thou shouldst answer me : but for her sake,
Who hath vouchsafed my asking, spirit blest,
That in thy joy art shrouded ! say the cause,
Which bringeth thee so near : and wherefore, say,
Doth the sweet symphony of Paradise
Keep silence here, pervading with such sounds
Of rapt devotion every lower sphere ?"
" Mortal art thou in hearing, as in sight ;"
Was the reply : " and what forbade the smile
Of Beatrice interrupts our song.[1]
Only to yield thee gladness of my voice,
And of the light that vests me, I thus far
Descend these hallow'd steps : not that more love
Invites me ; for, lo ! there aloft,[2] as much
Or more of love is witness'd in those flames :
But such my lot by charity assign'd,
That makes us ready servants, as thou seest,
To execute the counsel of the Highest."
　　" That in this court," said I, " O sacred lamp !
Love no compulsion needs, but follows free
The eternal Providence, I well discern :
This harder find to deem : why, of thy peers,
Thou only, to this office wert foredoom'd."
　　I had not ended, when, like rapid mill,
Upon its centre whirl'd the light ; and then
The love that did inhabit there, replied :
" Splendour eternal, piercing through these folds,
Its virtue to my vision knits ; and thus
Supported, lifts me so above myself,
That on the sovran Essence, which it wells from,
I have the power to gaze : and hence the joy,
Wherewith I sparkle, equaling with my blaze
The keenness of my sight.　But not the soul,
That is in Heaven most lustrous, nor the Seraph,
That hath his eyes most fix'd on God, shall solve

---

[1] Consideration for Dante's mortal powers, that cannot yet sustain such glory.

[2] He disclaims any excess of charity over the other spirits of this sphere.

What thou hast ask'd : [1] for in the abyss it lies
Of th' everlasting statute sunk so low,
That no created ken may fathom it.
And, to the mortal world when thou return'st,
Be this reported : that none henceforth dare
Direct his footsteps to so dread a bourn.
The mind, that here is radiant, on the earth
Is wrapt in mist.　Look then if she may do
Below, what passeth her ability
When she is ta'en to Heaven."　By words like these
Admonish'd, I the question urged no more ;
And of the spirit humbly sued alone
To instruct me of its state.　" 'Twixt either shore
Of Italy, nor distant from thy land,
A stony ridge ariseth ; in such sort,
The thunder doth not lift his voice so high.
They call it Catria : [2] at whose foot, a cell
Is sacred to the lonely Eremite ;
For worship set apart and holy rites."
A third time thus it spake ; then added : " There
So firmly to God's service I adhered,
That with no costlier viands than the juice
Of olives, easily I pass'd the heats
Of summer and the winter frosts ; content
In heaven-ward musings.　Rich were the returns
And fertile, which that cloister once was used
To render to these Heavens : now 'tis fallen
Into a waste so empty, that ere long
Detection must lay bare its vanity.
Pietro Damiano [3] there was I y-clept :
Pietro the sinner, when before I dwelt,
Beside the Adriatic, in the house
Of our blest Lady. [4]　Near upon my close

[1] Not the most glorious of the Saints, nor the most love-illumined
of the Angels, can penetrate the mysteries of predestination.

[2] Monte Catria in the Apennines, near Gubbio.　Beneath it is
the monastery of Santa Croce di Fonte Avellana, of which Peter
Damian was some time abbot.　Here Dante is said to have found
refuge after the death of Henry VII.

[3] St. Peter Damian of Ravenna was an ardent reformer of
Church discipline, and one of the chief ecclesiastical writers of the
eleventh century.　He was a friend and ally of Hildebrand, afterwards St. Gregory VII.　He died at Faenza in 1072.

[4] The monastery in question, " the house of our blest Lady,"
is now believed to be that of Pomposa near Comacchio.　St. Peter
Damian frequently signs his letters *Petrus peccator*, " Peter the

Of mortal life, through much importuning
I was constrain'd to wear the hat,[1] that still
From bad to worse is shifted.—Cephas came;
He came, who was the Holy Spirit's vessel;[2]
Barefoot and lean; eating their bread, as chanced,
At the first table.   Modern Shepherds need
Those who on either hand may prop and lead them,
So burly are they grown; and from behind,
Others to hoist them.   Down the palfrey's sides
Spread their broad mantles, so as both the beasts
Are cover'd with one skin.   O patience ! thou
That look'st on this, and dost endure so long.''

I at those accents saw the splendours down
From step to step alight, and wheel, and wax,
Each circuiting, more beautiful.   Round this[3]
They came, and stay'd them; utter'd then a shout
So loud, it hath no likeness here : nor I
Wist what it spake, so deafening was the thunder.

CANTO XXII

ARGUMENT

He beholds many other spirits of the devout and contemplative ;
and amongst these is addressed by Saint Benedict, who, after
disclosing his own name and the names of certain of his
companions in bliss, replies to the request made by our Poet
that he might look on the form of the saint, without that
covering of splendour, which then invested it ; and then proceeds, lastly, to inveigh against the corruption of the monks.
Next Dante mounts with his heavenly conductress to the
eighth Heaven, or that of the fixed stars, which he enters at
the constellation of the Twins ; and thence looking back,
reviews all the space he has past between his present station
and the earth.

ASTOUNDED, to the guardian of my steps
I turn'd me, like the child, who always runs
Thither for succour, where he trusteth most :
And she was like the mother, who her son

Sinner.''   There are several alternative readings and interpretations of these lines.
[1] The cardinal's hat.   Peter Damian, against his will, was made
Cardinal and Bishop of Ostia by Pope Stephen IX. in 1058.
[2] St. Peter and St. Paul.
[3] Round Peter Damian to confirm his testimony against the
modern pastors of the Church.

Beholding pale and breathless, with her voice
Soothes him, and he is cheer'd; for thus she spake,
Soothing me: " Know'st not thou, thou art in Heaven?
And know'st not thou, whatever is in Heaven,
Is holy; and that nothing there is done,
But is done zealously and well? Deem now,
What change in thee the song, and what my smile
Had wrought, since thus the shout had power to move
    thee;
In which, couldst thou have understood their prayers,
The vengeance [1] were already known to thee,
Which thou must witness ere thy mortal hour.
The sword of Heaven is not in haste to smite,
Nor yet doth linger; save unto his seeming,
Who, in desire or fear, doth look for it.
But elsewhere now I bid thee turn thy view;
So shalt thou many a famous spirit behold."

    Mine eyes directing, as she will'd, I saw
A hundred little spheres, that fairer grew
By interchange of splendour. I remain'd,
As one, who fearful of o'er-much presuming,
Abates in him the keenness of desire,
Nor dares to question; when, amid those pearls,
One largest and most lustrous [2] onward drew,
That it might yield contentment to my wish;
And, from within it, these the sounds I heard.

    " If thou, like me, beheld'st the charity
That burns amongst us; what thy mind conceives
Were utter'd. But that, ere the lofty bound
Thou reach, expectance may not weary thee;
I will make answer even to the thought,
Which thou hast such respect of. In old days,
That mountain, at whose side Cassino rests,
Was, on its height, frequented by a race
Deceived and ill-disposed: and I it was,
Who thither carried first the name of Him,
Who brought the soul-subliming truth to man.[3]

[1] Dante is probably not alluding to events that had already
happened while he was writing (such as the death of Boniface
VIII.), but to such future contingencies as the coming of the
Veltro.

[2] St. Benedict.

[3] These lines are the literal translation of a passage in the
account of the Life and Miracles of St. Benedict, which forms the
second book of the *Dialogues* of Gregory the Great. In 528,

And such a speeding grace shone over me,
That from their impious worship I reclaim'd
The dwellers round about, who with the world
Were in delusion lost.   These other flames,
The spirits of men contemplative, were all
Enliven'd by that warmth, whose kindly force
Gives birth to flowers and fruits of holiness.
Here is Macarius;[1] Romoaldo[2] here;
And here my brethren, who their steps refrain'd
Within the cloisters, and held firm their heart.''

     I answering thus : " Thy gentle words and kind,
And this the cheerful semblance I behold,
Not unobservant, beaming in ye all,
Have raised assurance in me; wakening it
Full-blossom'd in my bosom, as a rose
Before the sun, when the consummate flower
Has spread to utmost amplitude.   Of thee
Therefore intreat I, father, to declare
If I may gain such favour, as to gaze
Upon thine image by no covering veil'd.''

     " Brother !'' he thus rejoin'd, " in the last sphere[3]
Expect completion of thy lofty aim :
For there on each desire completion waits,
And there on mine; where every aim is found
Perfect, entire, and for fulfilment ripe.
There all things are as they have ever been :
For space is none to bound; nor pole divides.

Benedict founded the famous abbey of Monte Cassino, on a
mountain in Campania between Rome and Naples, where a temple
of Apollo then stood.   Here he converted the people round to
Christianity, and instituted the great Benedictine order, and here,
too, he died in 543, " and was buried in the oratory of St. John
Baptist, which himself built, when he overthrew the altar of
Apollo.''

[1] Either St. Macarius the Egyptian (d. 391), the disciple of
St. Anthony, or St. Macarius the Alexandrian (d. 405), the friend of
Palladius (who wrote the famous histories of the fathers of the
desert called the *Paradise*).

[2] St. Romualdus (d. 1027), a nobleman of the Onesti family of
Ravenna, who " saw in a vision a ladder stretching from earth to
Heaven, whereby men in white raiment ascended and descended,''
and was thereby inspired to found the order of the Camaldolese,
white-robed monks who formed a stricter branch of the Benedictine
rule.

[3] The Empyrean Heaven, where all the Saints possess the
Beatific Vision, and are seen by Dante in the glorified semblance
of the forms they bore on earth.

Our ladder reaches even to that clime;
And so, at giddy distance, mocks thy view.
Thither the patriarch Jacob [1] saw it stretch
Its topmost round; when it appear'd to him
With Angels laden.　But to mount it now
None lifts his foot from earth : and hence my rule
Is left a profitless stain upon the leaves;
The walls, for abbey rear'd, turn'd into dens;
The cowls, to sacks choak'd up with musty meal.
Foul usury doth not more lift itself
Against God's pleasure, than that fruit, which makes,
The hearts of monks so wanton : for whate'er
Is in the Church's keeping, all pertains
To such, as sue for Heaven's sweet sake; and not
To those, who in respect of kindred claim,
Or on more vile allowance.　Mortal flesh
Is grown so dainty, good beginnings last not
From the oak's birth unto the acorn's setting.
His convent Peter founded without gold
Or silver; I, with prayers and fasting, mine;
And Francis, his in meek humility.
And if thou note the point, whence each proceeds,
Then look what it hath err'd to; thou shalt find
The white grown murky.　Jordan was turn'd back :
And a less wonder, than the refluent sea,
May, at God's pleasure, work amendment here.''

　So saying, to his assembly back he drew :
And they together cluster'd into one;
Then all roll'd upward, like an eddying wind.

　The sweet dame beckon'd me to follow them :
And, by that influence only, so prevail'd
Over my nature, that no natural motion,
Ascending or descending here below,
Had, as I mounted, with my pennon vied.

　So, reader, as my hope is to return
Unto the holy triumph, for the which
I oft-times wail my sins, and smite my breast;
Thou hadst been longer drawing out and thrusting
Thy finger in the fire, than I was, ere
The sign,[2] that followeth Taurus, I beheld,

---

[1] Gen. xxviii. 12.　The ladder here symbolises Contemplation,
which mystics call " the science of love."

[2] The constellation of the Gemini, in which the sun was when
Dante was born.　"This fixes Dante's birthday as somewhere

And enter'd its precinct.   O glorious stars !
O light impregnate with exceeding virtue !
To whom whate'er of genius lifteth me
Above the vulgar, grateful I refer;
With ye the parent of all mortal life
Arose and set, when I did first inhale
The Tuscan air; and afterward, when grace
Vouchsafed me entrance to the lofty wheel [1]
That in its orb impels ye, fate decreed
My passage at your clime.   To you my soul
Devoutly sighs, for virtue, even now,
To meet the hard emprize that draws me on.

" Thou art so near the sum of blessedness,"
Said Beatrice, " that behoves thy ken
Be vigilant and clear.   And, to this end,
Or ever thou advance thee further, hence
Look downward, and contemplate, what a world
Already stretch'd under our feet there lies :
So as thy heart may, in its blithest mood,
Present itself to the triumphal throng,
Which, through the ethereal concave, comes rejoicing."

   I straight obey'd; and with mine eye return'd
Through all the seven spheres; and saw this globe
So pitiful of semblance, that perforce
It moved my smiles : [2] and him in truth I hold
For wisest, who esteems it least; whose thoughts
Elsewhere are fix'd, him worthiest call and best.
I saw the daughter of Latona [3] shine
Without the shadow, whereof late I deem'd
That dense and rare were cause.   Here I sustain'd
The visage, Hyperion, of thy son ; [4]
And mark'd, how near him with their circles, round

between May 18 and June 17 (both inclusive), the time during
which the sun was in Gemini " (Wicksteed).

   [1] The eighth or Stellar Heaven.
   [2] Boëthius similarly argues the pettiness of human glory from
the narrow limits within which it is necessarily circumscribed :
" The whole of the earth's globe, as thou hast learned from the
demonstration of astronomy, compared with the expanse of
Heaven, is found no bigger than a point : that is to say, if
measured by the vastness of Heaven's sphere, it is held to occupy
absolutely no space at all " (H. R. James's translation).
   [3] The moon, whose upper surface is free from the spots of the
lower. Cf. *Par.* ii.
   [4] Ovid describes the sun as the offspring of Hyperion.

Move Maia and Dione; [1] here discern'd
Jove's tempering 'twixt his sire and son; [2] and hence,
Their changes and their various aspects,
Distinctly scann'd. Nor might I not descry
Of all the seven, how bulky each, how swift;
Nor, of their several distances, not learn.
This petty area, (o'er the which we stride
So fiercely,) as along the eternal Twins
I wound my way, appear'd before me all,
Forth from the havens stretch'd unto the hills. [3]
Then, to the beauteous eyes, mine eyes return'd.

CANTO XXIII

ARGUMENT

He sees Christ triumphing with his Church. The Saviour
ascends, followed by his Virgin Mother. The others remain
with Saint Peter.

E'en as the bird, who midst the leafy bower
Has, in her nest, sat darkling through the night,
With her sweet brood; impatient to descry
Their wished looks, and to bring home their food,
In the fond quest unconscious of her toil:
She, of the time prevenient, on the spray,
That overhangs their couch, with wakeful gaze
Expects the sun; nor ever, till the dawn,
Removeth from the east her eager ken:
So stood the dame erect, and bent her glance
Wistfully on that region, [4] where the sun
Abateth most his speed; that, seeing her
Suspense and wondering, I became as one,
In whom desire is waken'd, and the hope
Of somewhat new to come fills with delight.
    Short space ensued; I was not held, I say,

---

[1] Mercury, the son of Maia; Venus, the daughter of Dione.
[2] Between the cold of Saturn and the heat of Mars.
[3] The close of this Canto is somewhat like a vision ascribed by
St. Gregory to St. Benedict, in which "the whole world, gathered
as it were together under one beam of the sun, was presented before
his eyes" (Dialogues, ii. 35). Mr. Wicksteed, however, urges that it
does not mean that the whole inhabited area of the earth was then
visible to the Poet.
[4] "Towards the south, where the course of the sun appears less
rapid, than when he is in the east or the west" (Cary).

Long in expectance, when I saw the Heaven
Wax more and more resplendent; and, " Behold,"
Cried Beatrice, " the triumphal hosts
Of Christ, and all the harvest gather'd in,
Made ripe by these revolving spheres." [1]   Meseem'd,
That, while she spake, her image all did burn;
And in her eyes such fulness was of joy,
As I am fain to pass unconstrued by.

     As in the calm full moon, when Trivia smiles,
In peerless beauty, 'mid the eternal nymphs, [2]
That paint through all its gulfs the blue profound;
In bright pre-eminence so saw I there
O'er million lamps a Sun, from whom all drew
Their radiance, as from ours the starry train:
And, through the living light, so lustrous glow'd
The substance, that my ken endured it not.

     O Beatrice ! sweet and precious guide,
Who cheer'd me with her comfortable words :
" Against the virtue, that o'erpowereth thee,
Avails not to resist.   Here is the Might,
And here the Wisdom, [3] which did open lay
The path, that had been yearned for so long,
Betwixt the Heaven and earth."   Like to the fire,
That, in a cloud imprison'd, doth break out
Expansive, so that from its womb enlarged,
It falleth against nature to the ground;
Thus, in that heavenly banqueting, my soul
Outgrew herself; and, in the transport lost,
Holds now remembrance none of what she was.

     " Ope thou thine eyes, and mark me : thou hast seen
Things, that empower thee to sustain my smile."

     I was as one, when a forgotten dream
Doth come across him, and he strives in vain
To shape it in his fantasy again :
Whenas that gracious boon was proffer'd me,

---

[1] " Dante has seen in the seven planetary spheres the different classes and grades of blessedness representing the ' many mansions.'   Now, in the heaven of the stars, he sees in varied groups the whole fruit of creation and history gathered together, as typifying the ' one home.'   The ' circling of these spheres ' signifies the whole cosmic evolution, and the working of the spirit of God upon man " (Wicksteed).

[2] The moon (Trivia = Diana) among the stars.

[3] The might and wisdom of the Saviour, who is the Sun from which all the Saints draw their light.

Which never may be cancel'd from the book
Wherein the past is written.   Now were all
Those tongues to sound, that have, on sweetest milk
Of Polyhymnia [1] and her sisters, fed
And fatten'd; not with all their help to boot,
Unto the thousandth parcel of the truth,
My song might shadow forth that saintly smile,
How merely, in her saintly looks, it wrought.
And, with such figuring of Paradise,
The sacred strain must leap, like one that meets
A sudden interruption to his road.
But he, who thinks how ponderous the theme,
And that 'tis laid upon a mortal shoulder,
May pardon, if it tremble with the burden.
The track, our venturous keel must furrow, brooks
No unribb'd pinnace, no self-sparing pilot.

  " Why doth my face," said Beatrice, " thus
Enamour thee, as that thou dost not turn
Unto the beautiful garden, blossoming
Beneath the rays of Christ?   Here is the Rose,[2]
Wherein the Word Divine was made incarnate;
And here the lilies,[3] by whose odour known
The way of life was follow'd."   Prompt I heard
Her bidding, and encounter'd once again
The strife of aching vision.   As, erewhile,
Through glance of sun-light, stream'd through broken
    cloud,
Mine eyes a flower-besprinkled mead have seen;
Though veil'd themselves in shade : so saw I there
Legions of splendours, on whom burning rays
Shed lightnings from above; yet saw I not
The fountain whence they flow'd.   O gracious Virtue
Thou, whose broad stamp is on them, higher up
Thou didst exalt Thy glory,[4] to give room
To my o'erlabour'd sight; when at the name
Of that fair flower,[5] whom duly I invoke
Both morn and eve, my soul with all her might

[1] The Muse of sacred poetry.
[2] The Blessed Virgin Mary, *Rosa Mystica*.
[3] The Apostles of Christ.   *Cf.* Ecclesiasticus xxxix. 19.
[4] A symbolical representation of the Ascension of Christ, after
the work of Redemption had been accomplished.
[5] Mary, on the feast of whose Assumption the Church sings :
" And about her it was as the flower of roses in the spring of the
year and as lilies of the valleys."

Collected, on the goodliest ardour fix'd.
And, as the bright dimensions of the star
In Heaven excelling, as once here on earth,
Were, in my eye-balls livelily pourtray'd;
Lo! from within the sky a cresset [1] fell,
Circling in fashion of a diadem;
And girt the star; and, hovering, round it wheel'd.

Whatever melody sounds sweetest here,
And draws the spirit most unto itself,
Might seem a rent cloud, when it grates the thunder;
Compared unto the sounding of that lyre,
Wherewith the goodliest sapphire, that inlays
The floor of Heaven, was crown'd. "Angelic love
I am, who thus with hovering flight enwheel
The lofty rapture from that womb inspired,
Where our desire did dwell: and round thee so,
Lady of Heaven! will hover; long as thou
Thy Son shalt follow, and diviner joy
Shall from thy presence gild the highest sphere."

Such close was to the circling melody:
And, as it ended, all the other lights
Took up the strain, and echoed Mary's name.

The robe,[2] that with its regal folds enwraps
The world, and with the nearer breath of God
Doth burn and quiver, held so far retired
Its inner hem and skirting over us,
That yet no glimmer of its majesty
Had stream'd unto me: therefore were mine eyes
Unequal to pursue the crowned flame,[3]
That towering rose, and sought the seed it bore.
And like to babe, that stretches forth its arms
For very eagerness toward the breast,
After the milk is taken; so outstretch'd

[1] Gabriel the Archangel, who with ineffable music ("the sounding of that lyre") descends to crown Mary ("the goodliest sapphire").

[2] "The ninth Heaven, the *primum mobile*, that enfolds and moves the eight lower Heavens" (Cary).

[3] The Blessed Virgin following her "seed," her Divine Son, in her Assumption. "This day the holy and animated Ark of the living God, which had held within it its own Maker, is borne to rest in that Temple of the Lord which is not made with hands. The stainless Virgin returned not to dust, but, being herself a living Heaven, took her place among the Heavenly Mansions" (John of Damascus).

Their wavy summits all the fervent band,
Through zealous love to Mary : then, in view,
There halted ; and " Regina Cœli "[1] sang
So sweetly, the delight hath left me never.

    Oh ! what o'erflowing plenty is up-piled
In those rich-laden coffers,[2] which below
Sow'd the good seed, whose harvest now they keep.
Here are the treasures tasted, that with tears
Were in the Babylonian exile[3] won,
When gold had fail'd them. Here, in synod high
Of ancient council with the new convened,
Under the Son of Mary and of God,
Victorious he[4] his mighty triumph holds,
To whom the keys of glory were assign'd.

CANTO XXIV

ARGUMENT

Saint Peter examines Dante touching Faith, and is contented with his answers.

" O YE ! in chosen fellowship advanced
To the great supper of the blessed Lamb,
Whereon who feeds hath every wish fulfill'd ;
If to this man through God's grace be vouchsafed
Foretaste of that, which from your table falls,
Or ever death his fated term prescribe ;
Be ye not heedless of his urgent will :
But may some influence of your sacred dews
Sprinkle him. Of the fount ye alway drink,
Whence flows what most he craves." Beatrice spake ;
And the rejoicing spirits, like to spheres
On firm-set poles revolving, trail'd a blaze
Of comet splendour : and as wheels, that wind
Their circles in the horologe so work
The stated rounds, that to the observant eye
The first seems still, and as it flew, the last ;
E'en thus their carols[5] weaving variously,

---

1 *Regina Cœli lætare*, the Easter antiphon of the Blessed Virgin.
2 The Apostles and other Saints of God.
3 In their earthly pilgrimage.   4 St. Peter.
5 " *Carol*, in old English as in Italian, signifies a group of dancers " (Wicksteed).

They, by the measure paced, or swift, or slow,
Made me to rate the riches of their joy.

From that, which I did note in beauty most
Excelling, saw I issue forth a flame [1]
So bright, as none was left more goodly there.
Round Beatrice thrice it wheel'd about,
With so divine a song, that fancy's ear
Records it not; and the pen passeth on,
And leaves a blank: for that our mortal speech,
Nor e'en the inward shaping of the brain,
Hath colours fine enough to trace such folds.

"O saintly sister mine! thy prayer devout
Is with so vehement affection urged,
Thou dost unbind me from that beauteous sphere."

Such were the accents towards my lady breathed
From that blest ardour, soon as it was stay'd;
To whom she thus: "O everlasting light
Of him, within whose mighty grasp our Lord
Did leave the keys, which of this wondrous bliss
He bare below! tent [2] this man as thou wilt,
With lighter probe or deep, touching the faith,
By the which thou didst on the billows walk.
If he in love, in hope, and in belief,
Be stedfast, [3] is not hid from thee: for thou
Hast there thy ken, where all things are beheld
In liveliest portraiture. But since true faith
Has peopled this fair realm with citizens;
Meet is, that to exalt its glory more,
Thou, in his audience, shouldst thereof discourse."

Like to the bachelor, who arms himself,
And speaks not, till the master have proposed
The question, to approve, and not to end it; [4]
So I, in silence, arm'd me, while she spake,
Summoning up each argument to aid;

[1] From the most glorious group of Saints issues the flaming
spirit of St. Peter.

[2] "*Tenta.* The word 'tent,' *try*, is used by our old writers"
(Cary).

[3] Cf. *Conv.* iii. 14. According to Aquinas, Faith, Hope, and
Charity are the principles added by the gift of God to human
nature, to lead man to supernatural happiness, and they correspond
to the three essential constituents of that happiness: Vision, Com-
prehension, Fruition.

[4] "Even as the Bachelor arms himself—and speaks not, until
the Master has propounded the question—to argue it with proofs,
not to decide it" (Vernon).

As was behoveful for such questioner,
And such profession : " As good Christian ought,
Declare thee, what is faith?"   Whereat I raised
My forehead to the light, whence this had breathed ;
Then turn'd to Beatrice ; and in her looks
Approval met, that from their inmost fount
I should unlock the waters.   " May the grace,
That giveth me the captain of the Church
For confessor," said I, " vouchsafe to me
Apt utterance for my thoughts ;" then added : " Sire !
E'en as set down by the unerring style
Of thy dear brother, who with thee conspired
To bring Rome in unto the way of life,
Faith of things hoped is substance, and the proof
Of things not seen ;[1] and herein doth consist
Methinks its essence."—" Rightly hast thou deem'd,"
Was answer'd ; " if thou well discern, why first
He hath defined it substance, and then proof."

   " The deep things," I replied, " which here I scan
Distinctly, are below from mortal eye
So hidden, they have in belief alone
Their being ; on which credence, hope sublime
Is built : and, therefore substance, it intends.
And inasmuch as we must needs infer
From such belief our reasoning, all respect
To other view excluded ; hence of proof
The intention is derived."   Forthwith I heard :
" If thus, whate'er by learning men attain,
Were understood ; the sophist would want room
To exercise his wit."   So breathed the flame
Of love ; then added : " Current [2] is the coin
Thou utter'st, both in weight and in alloy.
But tell me, if thou hast it in thy purse."

   " Even so glittering and so round," said I,
" I not a whit misdoubt of its assay."

   Next issued from the deep-imbosom'd splendour :
" Say, whence the costly jewel, on the which
Is founded every virtue, came to thee."

   " The flood," I answer'd, " from the Spirit of God

---

[1] The definition is taken from Hebrews xi. 1, which Dante
accepts as written by St. Paul : " Faith is the substance of things
hoped for, the evidence of things not seen."
[2] " The answer thou hast made, is right : but let me know if thy
inward persuasion be conformable to thy profession " (Cary).

Rain'd down upon the ancient bond and new,[1]—
Here is the reasoning, that convinceth me
So feelingly, each argument beside
Seems blunt, and forceless, in comparison."
Then heard I : " Wherefore holdest thou that each,
The elder proposition and the new,
Which so persuade thee, are the voice of Heaven?"

" The works, that follow'd, evidence their truth,"
I answer'd : " Nature did not make for these
The iron hot, or on her anvil mold them."

" Who voucheth to thee of the works themselves,"
Was the reply, " that they in very deed
Are that they purport? None hath sworn so to thee."

" That all the world,"[2] said I, " should have been
     turn'd
To Christian, and no miracle been wrought,
Would in itself be such a miracle,
The rest were not an hundredth part so great.
E'en thou went'st forth in poverty and hunger
To set the goodly plant, that, from the vine
It once was, now is grown unsightly bramble."

That ended, through the high celestial court
Resounded all the spheres, " Praise we one God!"
In song of most unearthly melody.
And when that Worthy[3] thus, from branch to branch,
Examining, had led me, that we now
Approach'd the topmost bough; he straight resumed :
" The grace, that holds sweet dalliance with thy soul,
So far discreetly hath thy lips unclosed;
That, whatsoe'er has past them, I commend.
Behoves thee to express, what thou believest,
The next ; and, whereon, thy belief hath grown."

" O saintly sire and spirit !" I began,
" Who seest that, which thou didst so believe,
As to outstrip[4] feet younger than thine own,

---

[1] The revelation of the Holy Spirit in the Old and New Testaments.

[2] That the doctrines thus contained in the Scriptures were revealed by God is shown by the miracles that followed and confirmed them. As to the truth of these miracles, the Poet answers, with St. Augustine, that the conversion of the world to Christianity without miracles would have been a greater miracle than any of those recorded.

[3] *Quel baron :* St. Peter.

[4] *Cf.* John xx. 3-6. " John also says that he (Peter) went

Toward the sepulchre; thy will is here,
That I the tenour of my creed unfold;
And thou, the cause of it, hast likewise ask'd.
And I reply: I in one God believe;
One sole eternal Godhead, of whose love
All Heaven is moved, Himself unmoved the while.[1]
Nor demonstration physical alone,
Or more intelligential and abstruse,
Persuades me to this faith: but from that truth
It cometh to me rather, which is shed
Through Moses; the rapt Prophets; and the Psalms;
The Gospel; and what ye yourselves did write,
When ye were gifted of the Holy Ghost.
In three eternal Persons I believe;
Essence threefold and one; mysterious league
Of union absolute, which, many a time,
The word of gospel lore upon my mind
Imprints: and from this germ, this firstling spark
The lively flame dilates; and, like Heaven's star,
Doth glitter in me." As the master hears,
Well pleased, and then enfoldeth in his arms
The servant, who hath joyful tidings brought,
And having told the errand keeps his peace;
Thus benediction uttering with song,
Soon as my peace I held, compass'd me thrice
The apostolic radiance, whose behest
Had oped my lips: so well their answer pleased.

straight in when he came to the tomb, seeing the other disciple
lingering at the entrance " (*Mon.* iii. 9).
　[1] " I believe in one God, sole and eternal, who moveth all the
Heaven with love and with desire, Himself unmoved." In a
passage in the *Metaphysics*, Aristotle shows that the Prime Movent, which causes motion without itself being moved, must be
eternal, must be a substance (so in the Latin translation, which
for Dante means " spirit "), and actuality; it must be the prime
object of desire and the prime object of intellectual apprehension.
Upon this Aquinas bases his five philosophical proofs of the existence of God.

CANTO XXV

ARGUMENT

Saint James questions our Poet concerning Hope. Next Saint
John appears; and, on perceiving that Dante looks intently on
him, informs him that he, Saint John, had left his body
resolved into earth, upon the earth; and that Christ and the
Virgin alone had come with their bodies into Heaven.

IF e'er the sacred poem, that hath made
Both Heaven and earth copartners in its toil,
And with lean abstinence, through many a year,
Faded my brow, be destined to prevail
Over the cruelty, which bars me forth
Of the fair sheep-fold,[1] where, a sleeping lamb,
The wolves set on and fain had worried me;
With other voice, and fleece of other grain,
I shall forthwith return; and, standing up
At my baptismal font, shall claim the wreath
Due to the poet's temples:[2] for I there
First enter'd on the faith, which maketh souls
Acceptable to God: and, for its sake,
Peter had then circled my forehead thus.

Next from the squadron, whence had issued forth
The first fruit of Christ's vicars on the earth,
Toward us moved a light, at view whereof
My Lady, full of gladness, spake to me:
" Lo! lo! behold the peer of mickle might,
That makes Galicia throng'd with visitants."[3]

As when the ring-dove by his mate alights;
In circles, each about the other wheels,
And, murmuring, cooes his fondness: thus saw I
One, of the other great and glorious prince,[4]
With kindly greeting, hail'd; extolling, both,

[1] " The fair sheep-fold (Florence), where I slept, a lamb, foe to
the wolves who are making war upon it." Cary has quaintly
mistranslated these two lines.

[2] In 1318, Dante declined to take the laurel crown at Bologna,
to which Giovanni del Virgilio had invited him: " Were it not
better to crown my locks, and hide my grey hair, that once was
golden, under the twined leaves, when, if it happen, I return to my
native Arno?" (*Eclogue* I.)

[3] St. James " the Greater," the son of Zebedee, whose shrine at
Compostela in Galicia was (and still is) much frequented by pilgrims. Cf. *Vita Nuova*, § 41.

[4] St. Peter and St. James.

Their heavenly banqueting : but when an end
Was to their gratulation, silent, each,
Before me sat they down, so burning bright,
I could not look upon them. Smiling then,
Beatrice spake : " O life in glory shrined !
Who didst the largess of our kingly court
Set down with faithful pen,[1] let now thy voice,
Of hope the praises, in this height resound.
For well thou know'st, who figurest it as oft,
As Jesus, to ye three, more brightly shone." [2]

   " Lift up thy head ; and be thou strong in trust :
For that, which hither from the mortal world
Arriveth, must be ripen'd in our beam."

   Such cheering accents from the second flame
Assured me ; and mine eyes I lifted up [3]
Unto the mountains, that had bow'd them late
With over-heavy burden. " Sith our Liege
Wills of His grace, that thou, or e'er thy death,
In the most secret council with His lords
Shouldst be confronted, so that having view'd
The glories of our court, thou mayest therewith
Thyself, and all who hear, invigorate
With hope, that leads to blissful end ; declare,
What is that hope ? how it doth flourish in thee ?
And whence thou hadst it ?" Thus, proceeding still,
The second light : and she, whose gentle love
My soaring pennons in that lofty flight
Escorted, thus preventing me, rejoin'd :
" Among her sons, not one more full of hope,
Hath the Church Militant : so 'tis of him
Recorded in the Sun, whose liberal orb
Enlightened all our tribe : and ere his term
Of warfare, hence permitted he is come,
From Egypt to Jerusalem,[4] to see.
The other points, both which thou hast inquired,

---

1 Dante here attributes to this St. James the Epistle more
usually ascribed to the other Apostle of that name, " James the
brother of the Lord." The reference is to James i. 5, 12, 17.

2 Peter and James and John were taken as signifying the three
theological virtues, when Christ made to them the clearest mani-
festation of His divine nature in the Transfiguration and His
human nature on the Mount of Olives.

3 Cf. Psalm cxxi. 1.

4 " From the slavery of this corruption to the liberty of eternal
glory " (Epist. x. 7).

Not for more knowledge, but that he may tell
How dear thou hold'st the virtue; these to him
Leave I: for he may answer thee with ease,
And without boasting, so God give him grace."
　　Like to the scholar, practised in his task,
Who, willing to give proof of diligence,
Seconds his teacher gladly; "Hope,"[1] said I,
"Is of the joy to come a sure expectance,
The effect of grace divine and merit preceding.
This light from many a star, visits my heart;
But flow'd to me, the first, from him who sang
The songs of the Supreme; himself supreme
Among his tuneful brethren. 'Let all hope
In thee,' so spake his anthem,[2] 'who have known
Thy name;' and, with my faith, who know not that?
From thee, the next, distilling from his spring,
In thine epistle,[3] fell on me the drops
So plenteously, that I on others shower
The influence of their dew." Whileas I spake,
A lamping, as of quick and volley'd lightning,
Within the bosom of that mighty sheen[4]
Play'd tremulous; then forth these accents breathed:
"Love for the virtue, which attended me
E'en to the palm, and issuing from the field,
Glows vigorous yet within me; and inspires
To ask of thee, whom also it delights,
What promise thou from hope, in chief, dost win."
　　"Both scriptures, new and ancient," I replied,
"Propose the mark (which even now I view)
For souls beloved of God. Isaias saith,
'That, in their own land, each one must be clad
In two-fold vesture;' and their proper land
Is this delicious life. In terms more full,
And clearer far, thy brother hath set forth
This revelation to us, where he tells

---

[1] Dante gives the definition of Peter the Lombard: "Hope is
the certain expectation of future beatitude, coming from the grace
of God and from precedent merits;" that is, from the grace of God
and man's correspondence with that grace by good works; "for
to hope for anything without merits should not be called hope, but
presumption."

[2] Psalm ix. 10: "They that know Thy name will put their trust
in Thee."

[3] James i. 12.　　　　　　　[4] Quello incendio, St. James.

Of the white raiment destined to the saints." [1]
And, as the words were ending, from above,
"They hope in Thee!" first heard we cried: whereto
Answer'd the carols all. Amidst them next,
A light of so clear amplitude emerged,
That winter's month [2] were but a single day,
Were such a crystal in the Cancer's sign.

Like as a virgin riseth up, and goes,
And enters on the mazes of the dance;
Though gay, yet innocent of worse intent,
Than to do fitting honour to the bride:
So I beheld the new effulgence come
Unto the other two, who in a ring
Wheel'd, as became their rapture. In the dance,
And in the song, it mingled. And the dame
Held on them fix'd her looks; e'en as the spouse,
Silent, and moveless. "This [3] is he, who lay
Upon the bosom of our Pelican:
This he, into whose keeping, from the Cross,
The mighty charge was given." Thus she spake:
Yet therefore nought the more removed her sight
From marking them: or e'er her words began,
Or when they closed. As he, who looks intent,
And strives with searching ken, how he may see
The sun in his eclipse, and, through desire
Of seeing, loseth power of sight; so I [4]
Peer'd on that last resplendence, while I heard:
"Why dazzlest thou thine eyes in seeking that,
Which here abides not? Earth my body is,
In earth; and shall be, with the rest, so long,
As till our number equal the decree

[1] The object of Hope is eternal beatitude, the immortality of the soul and the resurrection of the body to share in that immortality, as shown by Isaiah (lxi. 7, 10) and St. John (Rev. vii. 9).

[2] "If a luminary, like that which now appeared, were to shine throughout the month following the winter solstice, during which the constellation Cancer appears in the east at the setting of the sun, there would be no interruption to the light, but the whole month would be as a single day" (Cary).

[3] St. John, who at the Last Supper "was leaning on Jesus' bosom" (John xiii. 23), and to whose charge Mary was committed from the Cross (John xix. 26, 27).

[4] There was a legend, based upon John xxi. 22, 23, and frequently represented in Italian art, that the beloved disciple had not died as other men, but had been taken up into Heaven, body and soul. Dante wishes to see if this is true.

Of the Most High. The two [1] that have ascended,
In this our blessed cloister, shine alone
With the two garments. So report below."
    As when, for ease of labour, or to shun
Suspected peril, at a whistle's breath,
The oars, erewhile dash'd frequent in the wave,
All rest : the flamy circle at that voice
So rested; and the mingling sound was still,
Which from the trinal band, soft-breathing, rose.
I turn'd, but ah! how trembled in my thought,
When, looking at my side again to see
Beatrice, I descried her not; although,
Not distant, on the happy coast she stood.

CANTO XXVI

ARGUMENT

Saint John examines our Poet touching Charity. Afterwards
    Adam tells when he was created, and placed in the Terrestrial
    Paradise; how long he remained in that state; what was the
    occasion of his fall; when he was admitted into Heaven; and
    what language he spake.

WITH dazzled eyes, whilst wondering I remain'd;
Forth of the beamy flame,[2] which dazzled me,
Issued a breath, that in attention mute
Detain'd me; and these words it spake : " 'Twere well
That, long as till thy vision, on my form
O'erspent, regain its virtue, with discourse
Thou compensate the brief delay. Say then,
Beginning, to what point thy soul aspires :
And meanwhile rest assured, that sight in thee
Is but o'erpower'd a space, not wholly quench'd;
Since thy fair guide and lovely, in her look
Hath potency, the like to that, which dwelt
In Ananias' hand." [3]   I answering thus :
" Be to mine eyes the remedy, or late
Or early, at her pleasure; for they were
The gates, at which she enter'd, and did light
Her never-dying fire. My wishes here

---

[1] **Christ and Mary alone** have body and soul already united in
glory. He refers to the Ascension and Assumption, which Dante
has seen mystically represented in Canto xxiii.
[2] St. John.   [3] *Cf.* Acts ix. 17.

Are centred : in this palace is the weal,
That Alpha and Omega is, to all
The lessons love can read me." Yet again
The voice, which had dispersed my fear when dazed
With that excess, to converse urged, and spake :
" Behoves thee sift more narrowly thy terms ;
And say, who level'd at this scope thy bow."

" Philosophy," said I, " hath arguments,
And this place hath authority enough,
To imprint in me such love : for, of constraint,
Good, inasmuch as we perceive the good,
Kindles our love ; and in degree the more,
As it comprises more of goodness in 't.[1]
The Essence then, where such advantage is,
That each good, found without it, is nought else
But of His light the beam, must needs attract
The soul of each one, loving, who the truth
Discerns, on which this proof is built. Such truth
Learn I from him,[2] who shows me the first love
Of all intelligential substances
Eternal : from His voice I learn, whose word
Is truth ; that of Himself to Moses saith,
' I will make all My good before thee pass :'[3]
Lastly, from thee I learn, who chief proclaim'st,
E'en at the outset of thy heralding,
In mortal ears the mystery of Heaven."[4]

" Through human wisdom, and the authority
Therewith agreeing," heard I answer'd, " keep
The choicest of thy love for God. But say,
If thou yet other cords within thee feel'st,
That draw thee towards Him ; so that thou report
How many are the fangs, with which this love
Is grappled to thy soul." I did not miss,
To what intent the eagle of our Lord[5]

[1] Love is the natural tendency of the will to anything apprehended by the intellect as good ; and the greater the good apprehended, the stronger the tendency, the more ardent the love.

[2] Aristotle, the reference being to the passage in the *Metaphysics* where the Philosopher shows that the Prime Movent is " the
primary object of love in which desire and reason fall into unity "
(Wallace). *Cf.* notes on Canto xxiv.

[3] Exodus xxxiii. 19.

[4] Rev. i. 8 : " I am Alpha and Omega, the beginning and the
ending."

[5] The emblem of St. John in art is the Eagle.

Had pointed his demand; yea, noted well
The avowal which he led to; and resumed:
"All grappling bonds, that knit the heart to God,
Confederate to make fast our charity.
The being of the world; and mine own being;
The death which He endured, that I should live;
And that, which all the faithful hope, as I do;
To the foremention'd lively knowledge join'd;
Have from the sea of ill love saved my bark,
And on the coast secured it of the right.
As for the leaves,[1] that in the garden bloom,
My love for them is great, as is the good
Dealt by the eternal hand, that tends them all."

I ended: and therewith a song most sweet
Rang through the spheres; and "Holy, holy, holy,"
Accordant with the rest, my lady sang.
And as a sleep is broken and dispersed
Through sharp encounter of the nimble light,
With the eye's spirit running forth to meet
The ray, from membrane on to membrane urged;
And the upstartled wight loathes that he sees;
So, at his sudden waking, he misdeems
Of all around him, till assurance waits
On better judgment: thus the saintly dame
Drove from before mine eyes the motes away,
With the resplendence of her own, that cast
Their brightness downward, thousand miles below.
Whence I my vision, clearer than before,
Recover'd; and well nigh astounded, ask'd
Of a fourth light, that now with us I saw.

And Beatrice: "The first living soul,[2]
That ever the first Virtue framed, admires
Within these rays his Maker." Like the leaf,
That bows its lithe top till the blast is blown;
By its own virtue rear'd, then stands aloof:
So I, the whilst she said, awe-stricken bow'd.
Then eagerness to speak embolden'd me;
And I began: "O fruit! that wast alone

[1] Creatures. This refers to what is called the order of Charity:
"The love of charity tends to God, as to the principle of blessedness in the communication of which the friendship of charity is
founded; it is therefore necessary that, in those things which are
loved in charity, there should be some order kept in relation to the
first principle of this love, which is God" (Aquinas).
[2] Adam.

Mature, when first engender'd; ancient father!
That doubly seest in every wedded bride
Thy daughter, by affinity and blood;
Devoutly as I may, I pray thee hold
Converse with me: my will thou seest: and I,
More speedily to hear thee, tell it not."
  It chanceth oft some animal bewrays,
Through the sleek covering [1] of his furry coat,
The fondness, that stirs in him, and conforms
His outside seeming to the cheer within:
And in like guise was Adam's spirit moved
To joyous mood, that through the covering shone,
Transparent, when to pleasure me it spake:
" No need thy will be told, which I untold
Better discern, than thou whatever thing
Thou hold'st most certain: for that will I see
In Him, who is truth's mirror; and Himself,
Parhelion [2] unto all things, and nought else,
To Him. This wouldst thou hear: how long since, God
Placed me in that high garden, from whose bounds
She [3] led thee up this ladder, steep and long;
What space endured my season of delight;
Whence truly sprang the wrath that banish'd me;
And what the language, which I spake and framed.
Not that I tasted of the tree, my son,
Was in itself the cause of that exile,
But only my transgressing of the mark
Assign'd me. [4] There, whence at thy lady's hest
The Mantuan moved him, still was I debarr'd
This council, till the sun had made complete,
Four thousand and three hundred rounds and twice,
His annual journey; and, through every light
In his broad pathway, saw I him return,

---

[1] *Tal volta un animal coperto broglia;* the image is more usually taken as that of an animal struggling under some covering.

[2] *Pareglio.* A much disputed passage. Mr. Wicksteed translates: " Because I see it in the veracious Mirror which doth make himself reflector of all other things, and nought doth make itself reflector unto him." He takes it as meaning: " Everything is perfectly reflected in God, and therefore he who looks on God sees everything perfectly. But no single thing and no single truth (nor even the sum of them all) is a complete and perfect reflection of God."

[3] Beatrice.

[4] Aquinas shows that Adam's sin was pride, in that he desired a certain spiritual good beyond his measure.

Thousand save seventy times, the whilst I dwelt
Upon the earth.[1]   The language I did use
Was worn away, or ever Nimrod's race
Their unaccomplishable work began.
For nought, that man inclines to, e'er was lasting ;
Left by his reason free, and variable
As is the sky that sways him.[2]   That he speaks,
Is nature's prompting : whether thus, or thus,
She leaves to you, as ye do most affect it.
Ere I descended into Hell's abyss,
El was the name on earth of the Chief Good,
Whose joy enfolds me : Eli then 'twas call'd.
And so beseemeth :[3] for, in mortals, use
Is as the leaf upon the bough : that goes,
And other comes instead.   Upon the mount
Most high above the waters, all my life,
Both innocent and guilty, did but reach
From the first hour, to that which cometh next
(As the sun changes quarter) to the sixth."[4]

[1] Adam lived 930 years on the earth, and was then 4,302 years in Limbo, whence Virgil, at Beatrice's prayer, moved to succour Dante.

[2] Here Adam states that the language which he spoke was entirely extinct before the confusion of Babel ; but, in the *De Vulgari Eloquentia* (i. 6), Dante says that the language of the first speaker was Hebrew, which remained with the sons of Heber in order that Christ might use the language, not of confusion, but of grace.   For his view of the changes that man's speech undergoes, cf. *V. E.* i. 9.

[3] The change in man's speech is illustrated by the name which he gives to God.   Cf. *V. E.* i. 4.   For *El* and *Eli*, we should read *J* and *El*.

[4] " ' I remained in the Terrestrial Paradise only to the seventh hour.'   In the *Historia Scholastica* of Petrus Comestor, it is said of our first parents : ' Quidam tradunt eos fuisse in Paradiso septem horas ' " (Cary).

CANTO XXVII

ARGUMENT

Saint Peter bitterly rebukes the covetousness of his successors in
the apostolic see, while all the heavenly host sympathize in
his indignation: they then vanish upwards. Beatrice bids
Dante again cast his view below. Afterwards they are borne
into the ninth Heaven, of which she shows him the nature and
properties; blaming the perverseness of man, who places his
will on low and perishable things.

THEN " Glory to the Father, to the Son,
And to the Holy Spirit," rang aloud
Throughout all Paradise; that with the song
My spirit reel'd, so passing sweet the strain.
And what I saw was equal ecstasy:
One universal smile it seem'd of all things;
Joy past compare; gladness unutterable;
Imperishable life of peace and love;
Exhaustless riches, and unmeasured bliss.
　　Before mine eyes stood the four torches [1] lit:
And that, which first had come, began to wax
In brightness; and, in semblance, such became,
As Jove might be, if he and Mars were birds,
And interchanged their plumes. [2]　Silence ensued,
Through the blest quire; by Him, who here appoints
Vicissitude of ministry, enjoin'd;
When thus I heard: " Wonder not, if my hue
Be changed; for, while I speak, these shalt thou see
All in like manner change with me.　My place
He [3] who usurps on earth, (my place, ay, mine,
Which in the presence of the Son of God
Is void,) the same hath made my cemetery
A common sewer of puddle and of blood:
The more below his triumph, who from hence
Malignant fell." [4]　Such colour, as the sun,
At eve or morning, paints an adverse cloud,
Then saw I sprinkled over all the sky.

　[1] The three Apostles and Adam.
　[2] St. Peter, glowing with celestial anger, changes from silver
white to sanguine red.
　[3] Pope Boniface VIII.　Cf. Jeremiah vii. 4.
　[4] More literally: " has made my cemetery (Rome) a sewer for
the blood and the filth whereby the Evil One (Satan), who fell
from here above, is delighted there below."

And as the unblemish'd dame, who, in herself
Secure of censure, yet at bare report
Of other's failing, shrinks with maiden fear;
So Beatrice, in her semblance, changed:
And such eclipse in Heaven, methinks, was seen,
When the Most Holy suffer'd.   Then the words
Proceeded, with voice, alter'd from itself
So clean, the semblance did not alter more.
" Not to this end was Christ's spouse with my blood,
With that of Linus, and of Cletus, fed;
That she might serve for purchase of base gold :
But for the purchase of this happy life,
Did Sextus, Pius, and Callixtus bleed,
And Urban; [1] they, whose doom was not without
Much weeping seal'd.   No purpose was of ours,
That on the right hand of our successors,
Part of the Christian people should be set,
And part upon their left; [2] nor that the keys,
Which were vouchsafed me, should for ensign serve
Unto the banners, that do levy war
On the baptized; nor I, for sigil-mark,
Set upon sold and lying privileges :
Which makes me oft to bicker and turn red.
In shepherd's clothing, greedy wolves [3] below
Range wide o'er all the pastures.   Arm of God !
Why longer sleep'st thou?   Cahorsines and Gascons [4]
Prepare to quaff our blood.   O good beginning !
To what a vile conclusion must thou stoop.
But the high Providence, which did defend,
Through Scipio, the world's empery for Rome,
Will not delay its succour : and thou, son, [5]
Who through thy mortal weight shalt yet again
Return below, open thy lips, nor hide

[1] Early Popes who, according to Roman tradition, died for the
faith : St. Linus (66–76), St. Cletus (76–88), St. Sextus, or Sixtus I.
(115–125), St. Pius I. (140–155), St. Callixtus I. (217–222), St.
Urban I. (222–230).

[2] It was not St. Peter's intention that his successors should
favour one Christian faction and persecute another, that the mystical keys should appear on a battle-standard, or that his figure
should be stamped as a seal upon the corrupt transactions of the
Papal Court.   [3] Cf. Jeremiah xxiii. 1.

[4] Clement V. (1305–1314), a Gascon, and John XXII. (1316–
1334), a native of Cahors. Cf. Inf. xix., Par. xvii., xviii., and
xxx.

[5] Cf. Cacciaguida's injunction, Par. xvii. ad finem.

What is by me not hidden." As a flood
Of frozen vapours streams adown the air,
What time the she-goat with her skiey horn
Touches the sun; [1] so saw I there stream wide
The vapours, who with us had linger'd late,
And with glad triumph deck the ethereal cope.
Onward my sight their semblances pursued;
So far pursued, as till the space between
From its reach sever'd them : whereat the guide
Celestial, marking me no more intent
On upward gazing, said, " Look down, and see
What circuit thou hast compast." From the hour [2]
When I before had cast my view beneath,
All the first region overpast I saw,
Which from the midmost to the boundary winds;
That onward, thence, from Gades, I beheld
The unwise passage of Laertes' son; [3]
And hitherward the shore, [4] where thou, Europa,
Madest thee a joyful burden; and yet more
Of this dim spot had seen, but that the sun,
A constellation off and more, had ta'en
His progress in the zodiac underneath. [5]

Then by the spirit, that doth never leave
Its amorous dalliance with my lady's looks,
Back with redoubled ardour were mine eyes
Led unto her : and from her radiant smiles,
Whenas I turn'd me, pleasure so divine
Did lighten on me, that whatever bait
Or art or nature in the human flesh,
Or in its limn'd resemblance, can combine
Through greedy eyes to take the soul withal,
Were, to her beauty, nothing. Its boon influence
From the fair nest of Leda [6] rapt me forth,

[1] The sun is in Capricorn in mid-winter.

[2] Since Dante last looked down (in Canto xxii.), he has " moved
through all the arc which the first clima (latitudinal division)
makes from the middle to the end." Mr. Wicksteed takes it as
meaning : " I had revolved, with the first clima, through a whole
quadrant."   [3] Ulysses. Cf. *Inf*. xxvi.

[4] " Phœnicia, where Europa, the daughter of Agenor, mounted
on the back of Jupiter, in his shape of a bull " (Cary).

[5] " Dante was in the constellation of Gemini, and the sun in
Aries. There was, therefore, part of those two constellations, and
the whole of Taurus, between them " (Cary).

[6] The Gemini ; Castor and Pollux were the twin sons of Leda
and Jupiter.

And wafted on into the swiftest Heaven.[1]
    What place for entrance Beatrice chose,
I may not say; so uniform was all,
Liveliest and loftiest. She my secret wish
Divined; and, with such gladness, that God's love
Seem'd from her visage shining, thus began:
" Here is the goal, whence motion on his race
Starts: motionless the centre, and the rest
All moved around. Except the soul divine,
Place in this Heaven is none; the soul divine,
Wherein the love, which ruleth o'er its orb,
Is kindled, and the virtue, that it sheds:
One circle, light and love, enclasping it,
As this doth clasp the others; and to Him,
Who draws the bound, its limit only known.
Measured itself by none, it doth divide
Motion to all, counted unto them forth,
As by the fifth or half ye count forth ten.
The vase, wherein time's roots[2] are plunged, thou
      seest:
Look elsewhere for the leaves. O mortal lust![3]
That canst not lift thy head above the waves
Which whelm and sink thee down. The will in man
Bears goodly blossoms; but its ruddy promise
Is, by the dripping of perpetual rain,
Made mere abortion: faith and innocence
Are met with but in babes; each taking leave,
Ere cheeks with down are sprinkled: he, that fasts
While yet a stammerer, with his tongue let loose

[1] " By reason of the most fervent longing that each part of
this ninth Heaven hath to be united with each part of the tenth
most divine Heaven of quiet, it revolves within it with such great
desire that its velocity is, as it were, incomprehensible " (*Conv.* ii.
4). Cf. *Par.* xxiii.

[2] Nature, the first principle of motion and of rest, which in the
Ptolemaic system makes the earth motionless in the centre and the
Heavens revolving round it, has its starting-point in this ninth
sphere, the *Primum Mobile*, which itself is bounded only by the
light and love of the Empyrean, where God directly rules. In the
Divine Mind is enkindled the love (of the Seraphim) which turns
it, and the virtue that it rains down upon the universe. All motion
is caused and measured by its motion, and therefore in this sphere
is the first measure of time. Time has its roots in the invisible
motion of this Heaven, while its leaves are manifest in the lower
spheres, whose motion is our visible measure of time.

[3] *Cupidigia*, covetousness, or avarice.

Gluts every food alike in every moon :
One, yet a babbler, loves and listens to
His mother ; but no sooner hath free use
Of speech, than he doth wish her in her grave.
So suddenly doth the fair child of him,[1]
Whose welcome is the morn and eve his parting,
To negro blackness change her virgin white.

" Thou, to abate thy wonder, note, that none [2]
Bears rule in earth ; and its frail family
Are therefore wanderers.   Yet before the date,[3]
When, through the hundredth in his reckoning dropt,
Pale January must be shoved aside
From winter's calendar, these heavenly spheres
Shall roar so loud, that fortune shall be fain [4]
To turn the poop, where she hath now the prow ;
So that the fleet run onward : and true fruit,
Expected long, shall crown at last the bloom."

CANTO XXVIII

ARGUMENT

Still in the ninth Heaven, our Poet is permitted to behold the
Divine Essence ; and then sees, in three hierarchies, the nine
choirs of Angels. Beatrice clears some difficulties which occur
to him on this occasion.

So she, who doth imparadise my soul,
Had drawn the veil from off our present life,
And bared the truth of poor mortality :
When lo ! as one who, in a mirror, spies
The shining of a flambeau at his back,

[1] The human race, which is the son of Heaven, for, according
to the Philosopher, " man is begotten by man and the sun."
Cf. *Mon.* i. 9, and *Par.* xxii., where the sun is " the parent of all
mortal life."

[2] *Cf.* Marco Lombardo's discourse, in *Purg.* xvi.

[3] " The Julian calendar (which we rectified in 1752) makes the
year 11 m. 14 sec. (very roughly one-hundredth of a day) too long.
In Dante's time, therefore, January began, by calendar, a little
later in the real year every season ; and thus, in the course of
ages, it would begin so late that winter would really be over
before we came to New Year's Day by calendar. The substitution
of an immense period for a short one is parallel to our ' not a
thousand miles hence ' " (Wicksteed).

[4] *Cf.* Jeremiah xxv. 30. Dante probably alludes once more to
the coming of the *Veltro.*

P

Lit sudden ere he deem of its approach,
And turneth to resolve him, if the glass
Have told him true, and sees the record faithful
As note is to its metre; even thus,
I well remember, did befal to me,
Looking upon the beauteous eyes, whence love
Had made the leash to take me. As I turn'd:
And that which none, who in that volume looks,
Can miss of, in itself apparent, struck
My view;[1] a point I saw, that darted light
So sharp, no lid, unclosing, may bear up
Against its keenness. The least star we ken
From hence, had seem'd a moon; set by its side,
As star by side of star. And so far off,
Perchance, as is the halo from the light
Which paints it, when most dense the vapour spreads;
There wheel'd about the point a circle of fire,
More rapid than the motion which surrounds,
Speediest, the world. Another this enring'd;
And that a third; the third a fourth, and that
A fifth encompass'd; which a sixth next bound;
And over this, a seventh, following, reach'd
Circumference so ample, that its bow,
Within the span of Juno's messenger,
Had scarce been held entire. Beyond the seventh,
Ensued yet other two. And every one,
As more in number distant from the first,
Was tardier in motion: and that glow'd
With flame most pure, that to the sparkle of truth,
Was nearest; as partaking most, methinks,
Of its reality. The guide beloved
Saw me in anxious thought suspense, and spake:
"Heaven, and all nature, hangs upon that point.[2]
The circle thereto most conjoin'd observe;
And know, that by intenser love its course
Is, to this swiftness, wing'd." To whom I thus:
"It were enough; nor should I further seek,

[1] "When I turned, and my eyes were struck by what appears
in that volume when one gazes rightly upon its circling." He
who studies the Heavens rightly perceives that they "declare the
glory of God" (Psalm xix. 1). So Mr. Wicksteed interprets the
passage.

[2] Dante quotes the famous passage in Aristotle's *Metaphysics*,
xxx. (referred to in notes on Cantos xxiv. and xxvi.): "From that
principle (the Prime Movent) depend Heaven and all Nature."

Had I but witness'd order, in the world
Appointed, such as in these wheels is seen.
But in the sensible world such difference is,
That in each round shows more divinity,
As each is wider from the centre.[1]   Hence,
If in this wondrous and angelic temple,
That hath, for confine, only light and love,
My wish may have completion, I must know
Wherefore such disagreement is between
The exemplar and its copy : for myself,
Contemplating, I fail to pierce the cause."

  " It is no marvel, if thy fingers foil'd
Do leave the knot untied : so hard 'tis grown
For want of tenting."   Thus she said : " But take,"
She added, " if thou wish thy cure, my words,
And entertain them subtly.   Every orb,
Corporeal, doth proportion its extent
Unto the virtue through its parts diffused.
The greater blessedness preserves the more ;
The greater is the body (if all parts
Share equally) the more is to preserve.
Therefore the circle, whose swift course enwheels
The universal frame, answers to that
Which is supreme in knowledge and in love.
Thus by the virtue, not the seeming breadth
Of substance, measuring, thou shalt see the Heavens,
Each to the intelligence that ruleth it,
Greater to more, and smaller unto less,
Suited in strict and wondrous harmony."

  As when the north blows from his milder cheek
A blast, that scours the sky, forthwith our air,

---

[1] " The material world and the intelligential (the copy and the pattern) appear to Dante to differ in this respect, that the orbits of the latter are more swift, the nearer they are to the centre, whereas the contrary is the case with the orbits of the former. The seeming contradiction is thus accounted for by Beatrice. In the material world, the more ample the body is, the greater is the good of which it is capable ; supposing all the parts to be equally perfect. But in the intelligential world, the circles are more excellent and powerful, the more they approximate to the central point, which is God. Thus the first circle, that of the Seraphim, corresponds to the ninth sphere, or *primum mobile ;* the second, that of the Cherubim, to the eighth sphere, or heaven of fixed stars ; the third, or circle of Thrones, to the seventh sphere, or planet of Saturn ; and in like manner throughout the two other trines of circles and spheres " (Cary).

Clear'd of the rack that hung on it before,
Glitters; and, with his beauties all unveil'd,
The firmament looks forth serene, and smiles:
Such was my cheer, when Beatrice drove
With clear reply the shadows back, and truth
Was manifested, as a star in Heaven.
And when the words were ended, not unlike
To iron in the furnace, every cirque,
Ebullient, shot forth scintillating fires:
And every sparkle shivering to new blaze,
In number [1] did outmillion the account
Reduplicate upon the chequer'd board.
Then heard I echoing on, from choir to choir,
"Hosanna," to the fixed point, that holds,
And shall for ever hold them to their place,
From everlasting, irremovable.

  Musing awhile I stood: and she, who saw
My inward meditations, thus began:
" In the first circles, they, whom thou beheld'st,
Are Seraphim and Cherubim. Thus swift
Follow their hoops, in likeness to the point,
Near as they can, approaching; and they can
The more, the loftier their vision.[2] Those
That round them fleet, gazing the Godhead next,
Are Thrones;[3] in whom the first trine ends. And all
Are blessed, even as their sight descends
Deeper into the Truth, wherein rest is
For every mind. Thus happiness hath root
In seeing, not in loving, which of sight
Is aftergrowth. And of the seeing such
The meed, as unto each, in due degree,
Grace and good-will their measure have assign'd.
The other trine, that with still opening buds
In this eternal springtide blossom fair,
Fearless of bruising from the nightly ram,[4]

  [1] " The sparkles exceeded the number which would be produced
by the sixty-four squares of a chess-board, if for the first we
reckoned one; for the next, two; for the third, four; and so went
on doubling to the end of the account " (Cary).

  [2] The division of the Angels into three Hierarchies, each composed of three orders, is based upon the diversity of their par-
ticipation in the Divine Perfection. The Seraphim are named from
excess of love, the Cherubim from plenitude of knowledge.

  [3] The Thrones are the mirrors of God's judgments, and represent
especially His steadfastness.

  [4] " From the autumn equinox all through the winter till the

Breathe up in warbled melodies threefold
Hosannas, blending ever; from the three,
Transmitted, hierarchy of gods, for aye
Rejoicing; Dominations first; next them,
Virtues; and Powers the third; [1] the next to whom
Are Princedoms and Archangels, with glad round
To tread their festal ring; and last, the band
Angelical, disporting in their sphere. [2]
All, as they circle in their orders, look
Aloft; and, downward, with such sway prevail,
That all with mutual impulse tend to God.
These once a mortal view beheld. Desire,
In Dionysius, so intensely wrought,
That he, as I have done, ranged them; and named
Their orders, marshal'd in his thought. From him,
Dissentient, one refused his sacred read;
But soon as in this Heaven his doubting eyes
Were open'd, Gregory at his error smiled.
Nor marvel, that a denizen of earth
Should scan such secret truth; for he had learnt
Both this and much beside of these our orbs,
From an eye-witness to Heaven's mysteries." [3]

spring equinox, the sign of Aries is visible in the sky at nightfall.
The line, therefore, means 'where there is no autumn nor winter'"
(Wicksteed).

[1] The second Hierarchy is composed of Dominations, Virtues,
and Powers, those orders whose names designate a certain common
government or disposition. The Dominations are "an express
image of the true and archetypal dominion in God;" the Virtues
imitate the Divine strength and fortitude; the Powers represent
the Divine power and majesty.

[2] The third Hierarchy includes Principalities or Princedoms,
Archangels, and Angels, those orders which are more particularly
concerned with the things of the world, contemplating the love of
the Holy Spirit, and communicating the gifts of God to man.
The last name is also applied to all these celestial intelligences;
for Angels signify "messengers," and in this respect the higher
Angels can execute the functions of the lower, while they have in
addition the special qualities from which they derive their own
names. Thus Christ Himself is called the Angel of the Great
Counsel.

[3] The mystical writings of the pseudo-Dionysius first appeared
in the early part of the sixth century, and were ascribed to the
Areopagite, St. Paul's convert on Mars' hill. One of them, the
Celestial Hierarchy, became the great text-book for all that concerns "the angelic nature and its ministry" (cf. Par. x.); Dionysius being supposed to have learned these and other celestial
mysteries from St. Paul himself, who had beheld them when rapt
up to the third Heaven. St. Gregory the Great (590–604), in a

CANTO XXIX

Argument

Beatrice beholds, in the mirror of divine truth, some doubts which
had entered the mind of Dante. These she resolves; and
then digresses into a vehement reprehension of certain theologians and preachers in those days, whose ignorance or
avarice induced them to substitute their own inventions for
the pure word of the Gospel.

No longer, than what time Latona's twins
Cover'd of Libra and the fleecy star,
Together both, girding the horizon hang;
In even balance, from the zenith poised;[1]
Till from that verge, each, changing hemisphere,
Part the nice level; e'en so brief a space
Did Beatrice's silence hold. A smile
Sat painted on her cheek; and her fix'd gaze
Bent on the point, at which my vision fail'd:
When thus, her words resuming, she began:
"I speak, nor what thou wouldst inquire, demand;
For I have mark'd it, where all time and place
Are present. Not for increase to Himself
Of good, which may not be increased, but forth
To manifest His glory by its beams;[2]
Inhabiting His own eternity,
Beyond time's limit or what bound soe'er
To circumscribe His being; as He will'd,
Into new natures, like unto Himself,
Eternal Love unfolded. Nor before,
As if in dull inaction, torpid, lay;

sermon on Luke xv. 1, adopted a slightly different arrangement
from that of Dionysius, whose work he only knew by vague
report. In the *Convivio* (ii. 6), Dante had followed a third
classification, differing considerably from the Dionysian, which he
here accepts—but one which was regarded in his day as hardly less
orthodox.

[1] "As short a space as the sun and moon are in changing
hemispheres, when they are opposite to one another, the one under
the sign of Aries, and the other under that of Libra, and both
hang, for a moment, poised as it were in the hand of the zenith"
(Cary).

[2] *Ma perchè suo splendore potesse, risplendendo, dir:* SUBSISTO;
"but that His splendour (His creatures who reflect His glory)
might, by glowing, say: I exist;" may resemble Himself, that is,
in the joy of conscious existence. God thus created for His infinite
love alone.

For, not in process of before or aft,[1]
Upon these waters moved the Spirit of God.
Simple and mix'd, both form and substance,[2] forth
To perfect being started, like three darts
Shot from a bow three-corded.   And as ray
In crystal, glass, and amber, shines entire,
E'en at the moment of its issuing ; thus
Did, from the eternal Sovran, beam entire
His threefold operation, at one act
Produced coeval.[3]   Yet, in order, each
Created his due station knew : those highest,
Who pure intelligence were made ; mere power,
The lowest ; in the midst, bound with strict league,
Intelligence and power, unsever'd bond.
Long tract of ages by the Angels past,
Ere the creating of another world,
Described on Jerome's pages, thou hast seen.
But that what I disclose to thee is true,
Those penmen, whom the Holy Spirit moved,
In many a passage of their sacred book,
Attest ;[4] as thou by diligent search shalt find :
And reason, in some sort, discerns the same,
Who scarce would grant the heavenly ministers,
Of their perfection void, so long a space.[5]
Thus when and where these spirits of love were made,
Thou know'st, and how : and, knowing, hast allay'd
Thy thirst, which from the triple question[6] rose.
Ere one had reckon'd twenty, e'en so soon,
Part of the Angels fell : and, in their fall,
Confusion to your elements ensued.

[1] Time began when the Spirit of God moved over the waters,
imprinting upon the formless primal matter the substantial forms,
or Divine ideas, whereby created things are brought into being.

[2] For " substance " read " matter " (*materia*).

[3] " Pure form or act (the Angels), pure matter or potentiality
(the *materia prima*), and inseparably united act and potentiality
(the material Heavens), issued into simultaneous being " (Wicksteed).

[4] " St. Jerome had described the Angels as created long before
the rest of the universe : an opinion which Thomas Aquinas con-
troverted ; and the latter, as Dante thinks, had Scripture on his
side " (Cary).   *Cf.* Gen. i. 1, and Ecclesiasticus xviii. 1.

[5] Had they existed before the moving Heavens which it is their
office to sway.

[6] Where, when, and how the celestial intelligences had been
created.

The others kept their station : and this task,
Whereon thou look'st, began, with such delight,
That they surcease not ever, day nor night,
Their circling. Of that fatal lapse the cause
Was the curst pride of him,[1] whom thou hast seen
Pent with the world's incumbrance. Those, whom here
Thou seest, were lowly to confess themselves
Of His free bounty, who had made them apt
For ministries so high : therefore their views
Were, by enlightening grace and their own merit,
Exalted ; so that in their will confirm'd
They stand, nor fear to fall. For do not doubt,
But to receive the grace, which Heaven vouchsafes,
Is meritorious, even as the soul
With prompt affection welcometh the guest.
Now, without further help, if with good heed
My words thy mind have treasured, thou henceforth
This consistory round about mayst scan,
And gaze thy fill. But, since thou hast on earth
Heard vain disputers, reasoners in the schools,
Canvass the angelic nature, and dispute
Its powers of apprehension, memory, choice ;
Therefore, 'tis well thou take from me the truth,
Pure and without disguise ; which they below,
Equivocating, darken and perplex.

" Know thou, that, from the first, these substances,
Rejoicing in the countenance of God,
Have held unceasingly their view, intent
Upon the glorious vision, from the which
Nought absent is nor hid : where then no change
Of newness, with succession, interrupts,
Remembrance, there, needs none to gather up
Divided thought and images remote.[2]

" So that men, thus at variance with the truth,
Dream, though their eyes be open ; reckless some
Of error ; others well aware they err,
To whom more guilt and shame are justly due.
Each the known track of sage philosophy
Deserts, and has a bye-way of his own :

[1] Lucifer, whom Dante has seen embedded at the very bottom
and centre of the universe. Cf. *Inf.* xxxiv.

[2] The Angels need no memory, for nothing has ever severed
their gaze from that Divine Essence wherein all things are
depicted.

So much the restless eagerness to shine,
And love of singularity, prevail.
Yet this, offensive as it is, provokes
Heaven's anger less, than when the book of God
Is forced to yield to man's authority,
Or from its straightness warp'd : no reckoning made
What blood the sowing of it in the world
Has cost ; what favour for himself he wins,
Who meekly clings to it.   The aim of all
Is how to shine : e'en they, whose office is
To preach the Gospel, let the Gospel sleep,
And pass their own inventions off instead.
One tells, how at Christ's suffering the wan moon
Bent back her steps, and shadow'd o'er the sun
With intervenient disk, as she withdrew :
Another, how the light shrouded itself
Within its tabernacle, and left dark
The Spaniard, and the Indian, with the Jew.
Such fables Florence in her pulpit hears,
Bandied about more frequent, than the names
Of Bindi and of Lapi [1] in her streets.
The sheep, meanwhile, poor witless ones, return
From pasture, fed with wind : and what avails
For their excuse, they do not see their harm?
Christ said not to His first conventicle,
' Go forth and preach impostures to the world,'
But gave them truth [2] to build on ; and the sound
Was mighty on their lips : nor needed they,
Beside the Gospel, other spear or shield,
To aid them in their warfare for the faith.
The preacher now provides himself with store
Of jests and gibes ; and, so there be no lack
Of laughter, while he vents them, his big cowl
Distends, and he has won the meed he sought.
Could but the vulgar catch a glimpse the while
Of that dark bird [3] which nestles in his hood,
They scarce would wait to hear the blessing said,
Which now the dotards hold in such esteem,
That every counterfeit, who spreads abroad
The hands of holy promise, finds a throng
Of credulous fools beneath.   Saint Anthony

---

[1] The commonest Florentine names.   [2] Cf. Mark xvi. 15.
[3] A waiting devil.   Cf. Inf. xxvii. ad finem.

Fattens with this his swine, and others worse
Than swine, who diet at his lazy board,
Paying with unstampt metal for their fare.[1]
    " But (for we far have wander'd) let us seek
The forward path again; so as the way
Be shorten'd with the time.   No mortal tongue,
Nor thought of man, hath ever reach'd so far,
That of these natures he might count the tribes.
What Daniel of their thousands hath reveal'd,
With finite number, infinite conceals.[2]
The fountain, at whose source these drink their beams,
With light supplies them in as many modes,
As there are splendours that it shines on: each
According to the virtue it conceives,
Differing in love and sweet affection.
Look then how lofty and how huge in breadth
The eternal Might, which, broken and dispersed
Over such countless mirrors, yet remains
Whole in itself and one, as at the first.''

CANTO XXX

ARGUMENT

Dante is taken up with Beatrice into the Empyrean; and there
having his sight strengthened by her aid, and by the virtue
derived from looking on the river of light, he sees the
triumph of the Angels and of the souls of the blessed.

NOON's fervid hour perchance six thousand miles [3]
From hence is distant; and the shadowy cone
Almost to level on our earth declines;
When, from the midmost of this blue abyss,

[1] By selling these spurious and unauthorised indulgences, the
monks of St. Anthony's congregation feed their pigs, and worse.
[2] Daniel vii. 10. The number of the Angels surpasses human
computation, and each differs from the other in its reception of
the Divine light, and in its consequent enkindling with the sweetness of Divine love. In things incorruptible, there is only one
individual of each single species: " Each of these beings is an
intellectual species, and their being is no other than the act of
continuous understanding " (Mon. i. 3).
[3] " He compares the vanishing of the vision to the fading away
of the stars at dawn, when it is noonday six thousand miles off,
and the shadow, formed by the earth over the part of it inhabited
by the Poet, is about to disappear " (Cary).

By turns some star is to our vision lost.
And straightway as the handmaid of the sun
Puts forth her radiant brow, all, light by light,
Fade; and the spangled firmament shuts in,
E'en to the loveliest of the glittering throng.
Thus vanish'd gradually from my sight
The triumph, which plays ever round the point,
That overcame me, seeming (for it did)
Engirt [1] by that it girdeth.   Wherefore love,
With loss of other object, forced me bend
Mine eyes on Beatrice once again.

   If all, that hitherto is told of her,
Were in one praise concluded, 'twere too weak
To furnish out this turn.   Mine eyes did look
On beauty, such, as I believe in sooth,
Not merely to exceed our human; but,
That save its Maker, none can to the full
Enjoy it.   At this point o'erpower'd I fail;
Unequal to my theme; as never bard
Of buskin or of sock [2] hath fail'd before.
For as the sun doth to the feeblest sight,
E'en so remembrance of that witching smile
Hath dispossest my spirit of itself.
Not from that day, when on this earth I first
Beheld her charms, up to that view of them,
Have I with song applausive ever ceased
To follow; but now follow them no more;
My course here bounded, as each artist's is,
When it doth touch the limit of his skill.

   She, (such as I bequeath her to the bruit
Of louder trump than mine, which hasteneth on,
Urging its arduous matter to the close,)
Her words resumed, in gesture and in voice
Resembling one accustom'd to command:
" Forth from the last corporeal are we come
Into the Heaven, that is unbodied light; [3]
Light intellectual, replete with love;
Love of true happiness, replete with joy;

---

[1] " Appearing to be encompassed by these angelic bands, which
are in reality encompassed by it " (Cary).
[2] Dante has simply *comico o tragedo*, " comic or tragic poet."
[3] They have issued from the last material sphere, the last stage
of intellectual preparation, into the true Paradise, the Empyrean
of light, love, and joy.

Joy, that transcends all sweetness of delight.
Here shalt thou look on either mighty host [1]
Of Paradise; and one in that array,
Which in the final judgment thou shalt see."

As when the lightning, in a sudden spleen
Unfolded, dashes from the blinding eyes
The visive spirits, dazzled and bedimm'd;
So, round about me, fulminating streams
Of living radiance play'd, and left me swathed
And veil'd in dense impenetrable blaze.
Such weal is in the love, that stills this Heaven;
For its own flame [2] the torch thus fitting ever.

No sooner to my listening ear had come
The brief assurance, than I understood
New virtue into me infused, and sight
Kindled afresh, with vigour to sustain
Excess of light however pure.   I look'd;
And, in the likeness of a river, saw
Light flowing,[3] from whose amber-seeming waves
Flash'd up effulgence, as they glided on
'Twixt banks, on either side, painted with spring,
Incredible how fair: and, from the tide,
There ever and anon, outstarting, flew
Sparkles instinct with life; and in the flowers
Did set them, like to rubies chased in gold:
Then, as if drunk with odours, plunged again
Into the wondrous flood; from which, as one
Re-enter'd, still another rose.   "The thirst
Of knowledge high, whereby thou art inflamed,
To search the meaning of what here thou seest,
The more it warms thee, pleases me the more.
But first behoves thee of this water drink,
Or e'er that longing be allay'd."   So spake
The day-star of mine eyes: then thus subjoin'd:
"This stream; and these, forth issuing from its gulf,
And diving back, a living topaz each;

[1] The Angels and redeemed souls, the latter of whom he will see
in their true forms, no longer concealed in dazzling light, but as
they will appear at the last day, in glorified resemblances of what
they were on earth.

[2] "Thus disposing the spirits to receive its own beatific light"
(Cary).

[3] The "river of water of life." *Cf.* Rev. xxii. 1; Psalm
xlvi. 4. It symbolises the effusion of the Divine Grace upon all
creatures, flowing down from the Source of Light.

With all this laughter on its bloomy shores;
Are but a preface, shadowy of the truth [1]
They emblem: not that, in themselves, the things
Are crude; but on thy part is the defect,
For that thy views not yet aspire so high."
    Never did babe, that had outslept his wont,
Rush, with such eager straining, to the milk,
As I toward the water; bending me,
To make the better mirrors of mine eyes
In the refining wave: and as the eaves
Of mine eye-lids did drink of it, forthwith
Seem'd it unto me turn'd from length to round. [2]
Then as a troop of maskers, when they put
Their vizors off, look other than before;
The counterfeited semblance thrown aside:
So into greater jubilee were changed
Those flowers and sparkles; and distinct I saw,
Before me, either court of Heaven display'd. [3]
    O prime enlightener! Thou who gavest me strength
On the high triumph of Thy realm to gaze;
Grant virtue now to utter what I kenn'd.
    There is in Heaven a light, whose goodly shine
Makes the Creator visible to all
Created, [4] that in seeing Him alone
Have peace; and in a circle spreads so far,
That the circumference were too loose a zone
To girdle in the sun.   All is one beam,
Reflected from the summit of the first
That moves, which being hence and vigour takes.
And as some cliff, that from the bottom eyes
His image mirror'd in the crystal flood,
As if to admire his brave appareling
Of verdure and of flowers; so, round about,
Eying the light, on more than million thrones,
Stood, eminent, whatever from our earth
Has to the skies return'd.   How wide the leaves,

    [1] It is still a mere foreshadowing preface to the truth, although
a much nearer approximation to it than any of his former visions
have been.
    [2] Symbolising the passing of Time into Eternity.
    [3] The flowers and sparkles are revealed as the Saints and
Angels, respectively.
    [4] The *lumen gloriæ*, or light of glory, by which the rational
creature is made like to God, and rendered capable of seeing Him
in His essence.

Extended to their utmost, of this rose,
Whose lowest step embosoms such a space
Of ample radiance! Yet, nor amplitude
Nor height impeded, but my view with ease
Took in the full dimensions of that joy.
Near or remote, what there avails, where God
Immediate rules, and Nature, awed, suspends
Her sway?[1] Into the yellow of the rose
Perennial, which, in bright expansiveness,
Lays forth its gradual blooming, redolent
Of praises to the never-wintering sun,
As one, who fain would speak yet holds his peace,
Beatrice led me; and, "Behold," she said,
"This fair assemblage; stoles of snowy white,
How numberless. The city, where we dwell,
Behold how vast; and these our seats so throng'd,
Few now are wanting here. In that proud stall,
On which, the crown, already o'er its state
Suspended, holds thine eyes—or e'er thyself
Mayst at the wedding sup,—shall rest the soul
Of the great Harry,[2] he who, by the world
Augustus hail'd, to Italy must come,
Before her day be ripe. But ye are sick,
And in your tetchy wantonness as blind,
As is the bantling, that of hunger dies,
And drives away the nurse. Nor may it be,
That he,[3] who in the sacred forum sways,
Openly or in secret, shall with him
Accordant walk: whom God will not endure
I' the holy office long; but thrust him down
To Simon Magus, where Alagna's priest[4]
Will sink beneath him: such will be his meed."

[1] "It had been maintained by Democritus, but was denied by Aristotle, that, were it not for the medium, even the smallest things could be seen at any distance whatsoever. This is one of the many instances in which Dante gives a spiritual turn to the physical speculations of the Greeks" (Wicksteed).

[2] Henry of Luxemburg, the Emperor Henry VII., died in 1313. *Cf.* Dante's Letters v., vi. and vii.

[3] Pope Clement V., who died in 1314. Cf. *Inf.* xix., and *Par.* xvii.

[4] Pope Boniface VIII. Cf. *Inf.* xix.

CANTO XXXI

ARGUMENT

The Poet expatiates further on the glorious vision described in the last Canto. On looking round for Beatrice, he finds that she has left him, and that an old man is at his side. This proves to be Saint Bernard, who shows him that Beatrice has returned to her throne, and then points out to him the blessedness of the Virgin Mother.

In fashion, as a snow white rose, lay then
Before my view the saintly multitude,[1]
Which in His own blood Christ espoused.   Meanwhile,
That other host, that soar aloft to gaze
And celebrate His glory, whom they love,
Hover'd around; [2] and, like a troop of bees,
Amid the vernal sweets alighting now,
Now, clustering, where their fragrant labour glows,
Flew downward to the mighty flower, or rose
From the redundant petals, streaming back
Unto the stedfast dwelling of their joy.
Faces had they of flame, and wings of gold;
The rest was whiter than the driven snow; [3]
And, as they flitted down into the flower,
From range to range, fanning their plumy loins,
Whisper'd the peace and ardour, which they won
From that soft winnowing.   Shadow none, the vast
Interposition of such numerous flight
Cast, from above, upon the flower, or view
Obstructed aught.   For, through the universe,
Wherever merited, celestial light
Glides freely, and no obstacle prevents.
    All there, who reign in safety and in bliss,
Ages long past or new, on one sole mark
Their love and vision fix'd.   O trinal beam
Of individual star, that charm'st them thus!
Vouchsafe one glance to gild our storm below. [4]
    If the grim brood, from Arctic shores that roam'd,

---

1 The souls of the Blessed redeemed by the Blood of Christ.
2 The Angels, whom St. Anselm likens to busy bees in God's service, flying between the flowers of earth and the hives of Heaven.
3 The three colours symbolise Love, Knowledge, and Purity.
4 Dante has simply *guarda quaggiù alla nostra procella,* "look down upon our storm."

(Where Helice for ever, as she wheels,
Sparkles a mother's fondness on her son,)
Stood in mute wonder 'mid the works of Rome,
When to their view the Lateran arose
In greatness more than earthly ; [1] I, who then
From human to divine had past, from time
Unto eternity, and out of Florence
To justice and to truth, how might I chuse
But marvel too?   'Twixt gladness and amaze,
In sooth no will had I to utter aught,
Or hear.   And, as a pilgrim, when he rests
Within the temple of his vow, looks round
In breathless awe, and hopes some time to tell
Of all its goodly state; e'en so mine eyes
Coursed up and down along the living light,
Now low, and now aloft, and now around,
Visiting every step.   Looks I beheld,
Where charity in soft persuasion sat ;
Smiles from within, and radiance from above ;
And, in each gesture, grace and honour high.

    So roved my ken, and in its general form
All Paradise survey'd : when round I turn'd
With purpose of my lady to inquire
Once more of things, that held my thought suspense.
But answer found from other than I ween'd ;
For, Beatrice when I thought to see,
I saw instead a senior, at my side,
Robed, as the rest, in glory.   Joy benign
Glow'd in his eye, and o'er his cheek diffused,
With gestures such as spake a father's love.
And, " Whither is she vanish'd?" straight I ask'd.

    " By Beatrice summon'd," he replied,
" I come to aid thy wish.   Looking aloft
To the third circle from the highest, there
Behold her on the throne, wherein her merit
Hath placed her."   Answering not, mine eyes I raised,
And saw her, where aloof she sat, her brow
A wreath reflecting of eternal beams.[2]

    [1] Lateran here stands for Rome in general, at the splendour
of which the barbarians from the north were amazed. Helice, or
Callisto (cf. *Purg.* xxv.), was changed into the Great Bear, and
her son Arcas into Boötes.
    [2] Dante now beholds Beatrice no longer under her symbolical
disguise, but in all the transfigured beauty of her human
personality.

Not from the centre of the sea so far
Unto the region of the highest thunder,
As was my ken from hers ; and yet the form
Came through that medium down, unmix'd and pure.

"O Lady! thou in whom my hopes have rest ;
Who, for my safety, hast not scorn'd, in Hell
To leave the traces of thy footsteps mark'd ;
For all mine eyes have seen, I to thy power
And goodness, virtue owe and grace.   Of slave
Thou hast to freedom brought me : and no means,
For my deliverance apt, hast left untried.
Thy liberal bounty still toward me keep :
That, when my spirit, which thou madest whole,
Is loosen'd from this body, it may find
Favour with thee."   So I my suit preferr'd :
And she, so distant, as appear'd, look'd down,
And smiled ; then towards the eternal fountain turn'd.

And thus the senior, holy and revered :
"That thou at length mayst happily conclude
Thy voyage, (to which end I was dispatch'd,
By supplication moved and holy love,)
Let thy upsoaring vision range, at large,
This garden through : for so, by ray divine
Kindled, thy ken a higher flight shall mount ;
And from Heaven's Queen, whom fervent I adore,
All gracious aid befriend us ; for that I
Am her own faithful Bernard."[1]   Like a wight,
Who haply from Croatia wends to see
Our Veronica ; and, the while 'tis shown,
Hangs over it with never-sated gaze,
And, all that he hath heard revolving, saith
Unto himself in thought : "And didst Thou look
E'en thus, O Jesus, my true Lord and God ?
And was this semblance Thine ?"[2]   So gazed I then

---

[1] St. Bernard (1091–1153), the famous Abbot of Clairvaux and
the greatest Churchman of the twelfth century. It was he who
preached the disastrous second Crusade, for which his impassioned
apologia may still be read in his *De Consideratione*—a work which
profoundly influenced Dante (cf. *Epist.* x. 28). His intense devotion to the Blessed Virgin finds eloquent expression in his sermons,
from which Dante has borrowed several passages in these cantos.
He here represents the loving contemplation of God, in which the
eternal life of the human soul consists.

[2] The *Veronica* is the representation of the countenance of
Christ, still solemnly venerated in St. Peter's at Rome, said to

Adoring; for the charity of him,
Who musing, in this world that peace enjoy'd,[1]
Stood livelily before me. "Child of grace!"
Thus he began: "thou shalt not knowledge gain
Of this glad being, if thine eyes are held
Still in this depth below. But search around
The circles, to the furthest, till thou spy
Seated in state, the Queen,[2] that of this realm
Is sovran." Straight mine eyes I raised; and bright,
As, at the birth of morn, the eastern clime
Above the horizon, where the sun declines;
So to mine eyes, that upward, as from vale
To mountain sped, at the extreme bound, a part
Excell'd in lustre all the front opposed.
And as the glow burns ruddiest o'er the wave,
That waits the ascending team, which Phaëton
Ill knew to guide, and on each part the light
Diminish'd fades, intensest in the midst;
So burn'd the peaceful oriflame,[3] and slack'd
On every side the living flame decay'd.
And in that midst their sportive pennons waved
Thousands of Angels; in resplendence each
Distinct, and quaint adornment. At their glee
And carol, smiled the Lovely One of Heaven,
That joy was in the eyes of all the blest.
     Had I a tongue in eloquence as rich,
As is the colouring in fancy's loom,
'Twere all too poor to utter the least part
Of that enchantment. When he saw mine eyes
Intent on her, that charm'd him; Bernard gazed
With so exceeding fondness, as infused
Ardour into my breast, unfelt before.

---

have been miraculously imprinted upon the handkerchief of a holy
woman who wiped Christ's face on the way to Calvary. Cf. *Vita
Nuova*, § 41.

[1] Bernard, while still living, anticipated the peace of heavenly
contemplation.

[2] The Blessed Virgin.

[3] "The Oriflame (*aurea flamma*) was the standard given by the
Angel Gabriel to the ancient kings of France, representing a
flame on a golden ground. No one who fought under it could be
conquered. The golden glow of Heaven is the invincible ensign
not of war, but peace" (Wicksteed). Cf. *Vita Nuova*, § 29.

CANTO XXXII

ARGUMENT

Saint Bernard shows him, on their several thrones, the other
blessed souls, both of the old and new Testament; explains to
him that their places are assigned them by grace, and not
according to merit; and lastly, tells him that if he would
obtain power to descry what remained of the heavenly vision,
he must unite with him in supplication to Mary.

FREELY the sage, though wrapt in musings high,
Assumed the teacher's part, and mild began:
"The wound, that Mary closed, she [1] open'd first,
Who sits so beautiful at Mary's feet.
The third in order, underneath her, lo!
Rachel with Beatrice: Sarah next;
Judith; Rebecca; and the gleaner-maid,
Meek ancestress [2] of him, who sang the songs
Of sore repentance in his sorrowful mood.
All, as I name them, down from leaf to leaf,
Are, in gradation, throned on the rose.
And from the seventh step, successively,
Adown the breathing tresses of the flower,
Still doth the file of Hebrew dames proceed;
For these are a partition wall, whereby
The sacred stairs are sever'd, as the faith
In Christ divides them.[3]   On this part, where blooms
Each leaf in full maturity, are set
Such as in Christ, or e'er He came, believed.
On the other, where an intersected space
Yet shows the semicircle void, abide
All they, who look'd to Christ already come.
And as our Lady on her glorious stool,
And they who on their stools beneath her sit,
This way distinction make; e'en so on his,
The mighty Baptist that way marks the line,
(He who endured the desert, and the pains

---

[1] Eve.   [2] Ruth, the ancestress of David.
[3] Two descending lines throughout the Rose divide the blessed
of the Old Law from the blessed of the New: the one, passing
down from Mary's throne, is composed of the Hebrew women,
ancestresses of Christ and types of His Church; the other, passing
down from the seat of St. John the Baptist, is similarly composed
of men who continued the work of Christ's Precursor in preparing
" a perfect people."

Of martyrdom, and, for two years,[1] of Hell,
Yet still continued holy,) and beneath,
Augustin; [2] Francis; Benedict; and the rest,
Thus far from round to round.   So Heaven's decree
Forecasts, this garden equally to fill,
With faith in either view, past or to come.
Learn too, that downward from the step, which cleaves,
Midway, the twain compartments, none there are
Who place obtain for merit of their own,
But have through others' merit been advanced,
On set conditions; spirits all released,
Ere for themselves they had the power to chuse.
And, if thou mark and listen to them well,
Their childish looks and voice declare as much.

   " Here, silent as thou art, I know thy doubt;
And gladly will I loose the knot, wherein
Thy subtil thoughts have bound thee.   From this realm
Excluded, chance no entrance here may find;
No more than hunger, thirst, or sorrow can.
A law immutable hath stablish'd all;
Nor is there aught thou seest, that doth not fit,
Exactly, as the finger to the ring.
It is not, therefore, without cause, that these,
O'erspeedy comers to immortal life,
Are different in their shares of excellence.
Our Sovran Lord, that settleth this estate
In love and in delight so absolute,
That wish can dare no further, every soul,
Created in His joyous sight to dwell,
With grace, at pleasure, variously endows;
And for a proof the effect may well suffice.
And 'tis moreover most expressly mark'd
In holy Scripture, where the twins are said
To have struggled in the womb.[3]   Therefore, as grace
Inweaves the coronet, so every brow

   [1] He was for two years in Limbo after his death, until the
Crucifixion.
   [2] Cary has altered the order, which in Dante is significant:
Francis, Benedict, and Augustine.   Francis comes first, as being
Christ's most perfect imitator, in whose body the marks of the
Passion were renewed; while Benedict, the great contemplative,
is in the place opposite to Rachel, the type of Contemplation.
   [3] *Cf.* Gen. xxv. 22; Rom. ix. 10-14.   " The children are ranked
in accordance with the abysmal but just and orderly judgments of
God in the assignment of primal endowment " (Wicksteed).

Weareth its proper hue of orient light.
And merely in respect to his prime gift,
Not in reward of meritorious deed,
Hath each his several degree assign'd.
In early times with their own innocence
More was not wanting, than the parents' faith,
To save them : those first ages past, behoved
That circumcision in the males should imp
The flight of innocent wings : but since the day
Of grace hath come, without baptismal rites
In Christ accomplish'd, innocence herself
Must linger yet below.   Now raise thy view
Unto the visage most resembling Christ :
For, in her splendour only, shalt thou win
The power to look on Him.''   Forthwith I saw
Such floods of gladness on her visage shower'd,
From holy spirits, winging that profound ;
That, whatsoever I had yet beheld,
Had not so much suspended me with wonder,
Or shown me such similitude of God.
And he, who had to her descended, once,
On earth, now hail'd in Heaven ; and on poised wing,
'' Ave, Maria, Gratia Plena,'' sang :
To whose sweet anthem all the blissful court,
From all parts answering, rang : that holier joy
Brooded the deep serene.   '' Father revered !
Who deign'st, for me, to quit the pleasant place
Wherein thou sittest, by eternal lot ;
Say, who that Angel is, that with such glee
Beholds our Queen, and so enamour'd glows
Of her high beauty, that all fire he seems.''
    So I again resorted to the lore
Of my wise teacher, he, whom Mary's charms
Embellish'd, as the sun the morning star ;
Who thus in answer spake :   '' In him are summ'd,
Whate'er of buxomness and free delight [1]
May be in spirit, or in Angel, met :
And so beseems : for that he bare the palm
Down unto Mary, when the Son of God
Vouchsafed to clothe Him in terrestrial weeds.
Now let thine eyes wait heedful on my words ;
And note thou of this just and pious realm

---

[1] *Baldezza e leggiadria*, '' exultancy and celestial chivalry.''

The chiefest nobles. Those, highest in bliss,
The twain, on each hand next our Empress throned,
Are as it were two roots unto this rose :
He to the left, the parent, whose rash taste
Proves bitter to his seed ; and, on the right,
That ancient father of the holy Church,
Into whose keeping Christ did give the keys
Of this sweet flower ; [1] near whom behold the seer,
That, ere he died, saw all the grievous times
Of the fair bride, who with the lance and nails
Was won. [2] And, near unto the other, rests
The leader, under whom, on manna, fed
The ungrateful nation, fickle and perverse. [3]
On the other part, facing to Peter, lo !
Where Anna sits, so well content to look
On her loved daughter, that with moveless eye
She chants the loud hosanna : while, opposed
To the first father of your mortal kind,
Is Lucia, at whose hest thy lady sped,
When on the edge of ruin closed thine eye. [4]
      " But (for the vision hasteneth to an end)
Here break we off, as the good workman doth,
That shapes the cloak according to the cloth ;
And to the Primal Love our ken shall rise ;
That thou mayst penetrate the brightness, far
As sight can bear thee. Yet, alas ! in sooth
Beating thy pennons, thinking to advance,
Thou backward fall'st. Grace then must first be gain'd ;
Her grace, whose might can help thee. Thou in prayer
Seek her : and, with affection, whilst I sue,
Attend, and yield me all thy heart." He said ;
And thus the saintly orison began.

---

[1] Adam and St. Peter.   [2] St. John the Evangelist.
[3] Moses.   [4] Cf. *Inf.* ii. ; *Purg.* ix.

CANTO XXXIII

ARGUMENT

Saint Bernard supplicates the Virgin Mary that Dante may have
grace given him to contemplate the brightness of the Divine
Majesty, which is accordingly granted; and Dante then himself prays to God for ability to show forth some part of the
celestial glory in his writings. Lastly, he is admitted to a
glimpse of the great mystery; the Trinity, and the Union of
Man with God.

"O VIRGIN Mother,[1] daughter of thy Son!
Created beings all in lowliness
Surpassing, as in height above them all;
Term by the eternal counsel pre-ordain'd;
Ennobler of thy nature, so advanced
In thee, that its great Maker did not scorn,
To make Himself his own creation;
For in thy womb rekindling shone the love
Reveal'd, whose genial influence makes now
This flower to germin in eternal peace:
Here thou to us, of charity and love,
Art, as the noon-day torch; and art, beneath,
To mortal men, of hope a living spring.
So mighty art thou, Lady, and so great,
That he, who grace desireth, and comes not
To thee for aidance, fain would have desire
Fly without wings.[2]   Not only him, who asks,
Thy bounty succours; but doth freely oft
Forerun the asking.   Whatsoe'er may be
Of excellence in creature, pity mild,
Relenting mercy, large munificence,
Are all combined in thee.   Here kneeleth one,
Who of all spirits hath review'd the state,
From the world's lowest gap unto this height.
Suppliant to thee he kneels, imploring grace
For virtue yet more high, to lift his ken
Toward the bliss supreme.   And I, who ne'er
Coveted sight, more fondly, for myself,
Than now for him, my prayers to thee prefer,

---

[1] This prayer to the Blessed Virgin is translated by Chaucer as
the *Prologe of the Seconde Nonnes Tale.*

[2] *Sua disianza vuol volar senz'ali,* "his longing would fain
fly without wings."

(And pray they be not scant,) that thou wouldst drive
Each cloud of his mortality away,
Through thine own prayers, that on the sovran joy
Unveil'd he gaze. This yet, I pray thee, Queen,
Who canst do what thou wilt; that in him thou
Wouldst, after all he hath beheld, preserve
Affection sound, and human passions quell.[1]
Lo! where, with Beatrice, many a saint
Stretch their clasp'd hands, in furtherance of my suit."

    The eyes, that Heaven with love and awe regards,
Fix'd on the suitor, witness'd, how benign
She looks on pious prayers: then fasten'd they
On the everlasting light, wherein no eye
Of creature, as may well be thought, so far
Can travel inward. I, meanwhile, who drew
Near to the limit, where all wishes end,
The ardour of my wish (for so behoved)
Ended within me. Beckoning smiled the sage,
That I should look aloft: but, ere he bade,
Already of myself aloft I look'd;
For visual strength, refining more and more,
Bare me into the ray authentical
Of sovran light. Thenceforward, what I saw,
Was not for words to speak, nor memory's self
To stand against such outrage on her skill.

    As one, who from a dream awaken'd, straight,
All he hath seen forgets; yet still retains
Impression of the feeling in his dream;
E'en such am I: for all the vision dies,
As 'twere, away; and yet the sense of sweet,
That sprang from it, still trickles in my heart.
Thus in the sun-thaw is the snow unseal'd;
Thus in the winds on flitting leaves was lost
The Sibyl's sentence.[2]   O eternal beam!
(Whose height what reach of mortal thought may soar?)
Yield me again some little particle
Of what Thou then appearedst; give my tongue
Power, but to leave one sparkle of Thy glory,
Unto the race to come, that shall not lose

---

[1] He prays that Mary may obtain for Dante the grace of final perseverance.

[2] The Cumæan Sibyl wrote her prophecies upon leaves, which she arranged in order and then suffered to be scattered by the wind. Virgil, Æn. iii. 441-452.

Thy triumph wholly, if Thou waken aught
Of memory in me, and endure to hear
The record sound in this unequal strain.

　　Such keenness from the living ray I met,
That, if mine eyes had turn'd away, methinks,
I had been lost; but, so embolden'd, on
I pass'd, as I remember, till my view
Hover'd the brink of dread infinitude.[1]

　　O grace, unenvying of Thy boon! that gavest
Boldness to fix so earnestly my ken
On the everlasting splendour, that I look'd,
While sight was unconsumed,[2] and, in that depth,
Saw in one volume clasp'd of love, whate'er
The universe unfolds; all properties
Of substance and of accident,[3] beheld,
Compounded, yet one individual light
The whole.　And of such bond methinks I saw
The universal form; for that whene'er
I do but speak of it, my soul dilates
Beyond her proper self; and, till I speak,
One moment seems a longer lethargy,
Than five-and-twenty ages had appear'd
To that emprize, that first made Neptune wonder
At Argo's shadow darkening on his flood.[4]

　　With fixed heed, suspense and motionless,
Wondering I gazed; and admiration still
Was kindled as I gazed.　It may not be,

[1] *Io giunsi l'aspetto mio col valor infinito*, " I united my gaze with the infinite Worth." According to Aquinas, in the Beatific Vision the Divine Essence itself becomes " the intelligible form " of the understanding.

[2] *Tanto che la veduta vi consunsi*, " so long that I consumed my sight therein," that is, actualised all possibilities of spiritual vision.

[3] *Sustanzia ed accidenti e lor costume*, everything conceivable by thought as capable of existence in itself (substanca), or only in something else as a mode of being (accidents), and all their relations (*costume*).

[4] " When the vision broke, a single moment plunged the actual thing he saw into a deeper oblivion than five and twenty centuries had wrought over the voyage of the Argonauts. The memory of an intent gaze, of deepening vision, of absorbed volition, of a final flash of insight—the assured possession of a will and affections laid to rest by the sweetness of what came to him—the uncertain impression of the images and symbols amid which it came—all these remain : but the vision itself is utterly past recall " (Wicksteed).

That one, who looks upon that light, can turn
To other object, willingly, his view.
For all the good, that will may covet, there
Is summ'd; and all, elsewhere defective found,
Complete. My tongue shall utter now, no more
E'en what remembrance keeps, than could the babe's,
That yet is moisten'd at his mother's breast.
Not that the semblance of the living light
Was changed, (that ever as at first remain'd,)
But that my vision quickening, in that sole
Appearance, still new miracles descried,
And toil'd me with the change.[1] In that abyss
Of radiance, clear and lofty, seem'd, methought,
Three orbs of triple hue, clipt in one bound:[2]
And, from another, one reflected seem'd,
As rainbow is from rainbow: and the third
Seem'd fire, breathed equally from both. O speech!
How feeble and how faint art thou, to give
Conception birth. Yet this to what I saw
Is less than little. O eternal Light!
Sole in Thyself that dwell'st; and of Thyself
Sole understood, past, present, or to come;
Thou smiledst, on that circling, which in Thee
Seem'd as reflected splendour, while I mused;
For I therein, methought, in its own hue
Beheld our image painted:[3] stedfastly
I therefore pored upon the view. As one,
Who versed in geometric lore, would fain
Measure the circle; and, though pondering long
And deeply, that beginning, which he needs,

[1] Unchanging in itself, it seemed ever to change to me, as my spiritual intuition became more perfect.

[2] The Blessed Trinity; unity in essence, distinction in persons, equality in majesty.

[3] "O Light Eternal, who abidest only in Thyself, only understandest Thyself, and, understood by Thyself and understanding, to Thyself dost love and smile! That circling, which appeared in Thee conceived as a reflected light, after being contemplated for a while by my eyes, in itself, of its own very colour, appeared to me painted with our likeness." In the invocation to the Light Eternal, the three Persons of the Blessed Trinity are indicated: the Father who, understanding Himself, begets the Son; the Holy Spirit, the eternal Love, which proceeds from both. The second circling reveals the union of the Divine Nature ("its own very colour") with the Human Nature ("our likeness") in the Person of the Word.

Finds not : e'en such was I, intent to scan
The novel wonder, and trace out the form,
How to the circle fitted, and therein
How placed : but the flight was not for my wing ;
Had not a flash darted athwart my mind,
And, in the spleen, unfolded what it sought.
   Here vigour fail'd the towering fantasy :
But yet the will roll'd onward, like a wheel
In even motion, by the Love impell'd,
That moves the sun in Heaven and all the stars.

Finds not: e'en such was I, intent to scan
The novel wonder, and trace out the form,
How to the circle fitted, and therein
How placed: but the flight was not for my wing;
Had not a flash darted athwart my mind,
And, in the spleen, unfolded what it sought.
Here vigour fail'd the towering fantasy:
But yet the will roll'd onward, like a wheel
In even motion, by the Love impell'd,
That moves the sun in Heaven and all the stars.

INDEX OF PERSONS

INTRODUCED OR REFERRED TO IN THE *DIVINE COMEDY*

445

---

[1] Publius Papinius Statius was born, not at Toulouse, but at Naples, where he died in A.D. 96 or thereabouts. Most of his life was passed at Rome, in the reign of Domitian, to whom he dedicated his *Thebaid*, an epic on the war of the Seven against Thebes. His *Achilleid*, dealing with the Trojan war (which Dante calls his "second burden"), was left unfinished. His shorter poems, the *Silvæ*, were unknown in Dante's age (Note on *Purg.* xxi, p. 237).

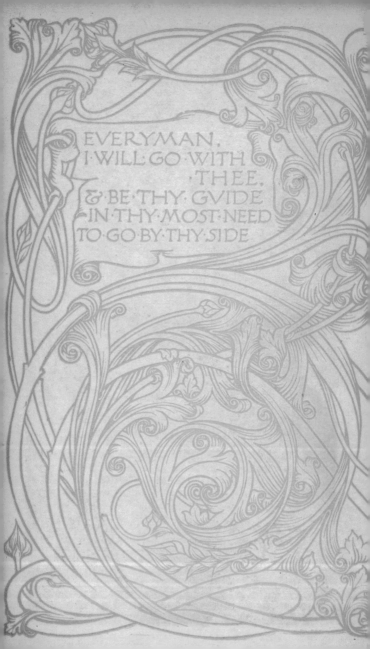

EVERYMAN,
I WILL GO WITH
THEE,
& BE THY GVIDE
IN THY MOST NEED
TO GO BY THY SIDE